International
Accounting

International Accounting

Frederick D. S. Choi
New York University

Gerhard G. Mueller
University of Washington

Prentice-Hall, Inc., Englewood Cliffs, New Jersey 07632

Library of Congress Cataloging in Publication Data

CHOI, FREDERICK D. S.
    International accounting.
    Rev. ed. of: An introduction to multinational
accounting. c1978.

    Includes bibliographies and index.
    1. International business enterprises—Accounting.
I. Mueller, Gerhard G.   II. Choi, Frederick D. S.,
Introduction to multinational accounting.
III. Title.
HF5686.I56C53 1984   657'.95   83-20192
ISBN 0-13-470931-4

Editorial/production supervision and interior design: Eve Mossman
Cover design: Wanda Lubelska Design
Manufacturing buyer: Ray Keating

Previous edition published under the title of *Introduction to Multinational Accounting.*

Printed in the United States of America

10 9 8 7 6 5 4 3

ISBN 0-13-470931-4

Prentice-Hall International, Inc., *London*
Prentice-Hall of Australia Pty. Limited, *Sydney*
Editora Prentice-Hall do Brasil, Ltda., *Rio de Janeiro*
Prentice-Hall Canada Inc., *Toronto*
Prentice-Hall of India Private Limited, *New Delhi*
Prentice-Hall of Japan, Inc., *Tokyo*
Prentice-Hall of Southeast Asia Pte. Ltd., *Singapore*
Whitehall Books Limited, *Wellington, New Zealand*

To Lois and Coralie . . . with fond aloha.

Contents

Preface

International accounting has not remained immune from the so-called information explosion that has inundated civilized societies. Bits and pieces of information are often outdated before they are printed or stored. We have made an effort to update the 1978 predecessor book, in terms of both data and subject matter. More than 90 percent of the material in the present edition is new.

Six years ago we asserted that international accounting had come of age. Now the field is shifting from adolescence to young adulthood. Some of the early impetuousness has given way to serious scholarship. Highly emotional issues, like setting international standards of accounting and auditing or recognizing foreign exchange translation gains or losses in the operating results of the current period, are now recognized as important but nevertheless modest components of the much larger international accounting field. Such issues are receiving research attention and are subject to matter-of-fact ongoing business and governmental decision making. Early maturity has set in.

This book has accounting roots. It is written from an accounting perspective rather than a legal, socioeconomic, or multinational business perspective. The book was written, and the end-of-chapter discussion questions, exercises, and cases assembled, with students in mind. We made a deliberate effort to keep our writing style simple and to use illustrations and numeric examples to enhance learning efficiency. Upper-division undergraduate and masters students are our target audience along with practicing professional accountants and financial managers of multinational enterprises and international institutions. In an undergraduate setting, this book will either stand on its own or benefit from supplementation through a readings collection. At the graduate level, research-based current literature will serve useful supplementation purposes. This type of literature is identified in the selected references cited at the end of each chapter.

Mainline international subject matter comprises the scope of this book. There are a number of issues and/or topical areas that might have been treated more comprehensively had additional space been available. Examples of such topics are international balance of payments accounting, accounting and control in centrally controlled economies like those of Eastern Europe, the special accounting problems of the developing nations, and internationally comparative accounting education and experience patterns. These speciality issues within the international accounting field are best pursued through current periodical literature or the occasional special-purpose book they have spawned.

Textbooks assimilate many different sources and wide ranges of ideas as well as practices. In this respect, our effort is no exception. A growing number of academics are specializing in international accounting and their writings have benefited our work. The same holds for the output from all of the institutions and organizations identified in Chapter 12. Many of our students have brought fresh ideas to classroom sessions and triggered new thought patterns in term papers submitted. To all of these, we express our collective thanks.

Several individuals warrant special credit. Professors Maureen H. Berry at University of Illinois at Urbana-Champaign, Frank D. Ewing at California State Polytechnic University–Pomona, and Mary J. Phelan at College of Holy Cross reviewed the predecessor book and made many useful suggestions that found their way into this new book. Professor R. S. Gupta of Chicago State University reviewed our manuscript and provided a full measure of helpful hints and suggestions. We have a better product as a consequence of the contributions received from these individuals and we wish to acknowledge their assistance with a personal note of thanks.

Many individuals furnished able assistance in producing the manuscript—especially Ms. Norma Cancellieri at New York University and Ms. Gracie Robledo at the University of Washington. The publisher's personnel encouraged us during the writing period, were patient with us when deadlines could not be met, and provided much help and good advice throughout the production period. Our sincere "Mahalo" to the entire production crew!

However hard one tries to avoid them, a number of errors are certain to occur in a project of this type. As authors we accept full responsibilities for any failures in judgment, communication, or physical production of the manuscript. We would much like to have the opportunity of receiving comments from all those who have occasion to use this book.

Frederick D. S. Choi
New York, New York
Gerhard G. Mueller
Seattle, Washington

1

International
Dimensions
of Accounting

The first name of this book is *International.* This term screams at us from newspaper headlines and the six o'clock news. It has become a common feature of lead articles in magazines and the mainstay of the travel industry. Politicians use it to support or castigate, as the case may be, almost any political issue of the day. To some it triggers fear, helplessness, or even despair. Others see in it much of the hope for tomorrow. The literature on international topics has become so enormously voluminous that any attempt to summarize it would be doomed from the start. Thus, we have picked four short quotes at random to set the scene for this book.

Economic Interdependence

Under the title of "The Changing World of Corporate Finance," Deloitte Haskins & Sells recently offered its views on some international dimensions of today's business:

> Global competitiveness has been dubbed the "new game" or the "next economics." As nations attempt to speed their economic progress, enlightened corporate managements are increasingly viewing domestic and overseas markets as integral parts of a single market. Innovative companies are moving quickly to improve their ability to manage strategically on a global scale, as chief executives and chief financial officers adopt multinational strategies and financial policies that foresee changing competitive and regulatory environments.

1

With the emergence of an expanding interdependent global economy in place of distinct national economies, nations and individual firms no longer enjoy insular prosperity or self-sufficiency. Over the next 20 years, they will become even more closely linked within a global web of resources, markets, financing, production, capabilities, economics and politics. Governments will be participating directly and indirectly to help their own businesses and industries compete.

Developed and developing nations will become more interdependent. In the developed countries, the trend is already away from heavy manufacturing toward high technology and knowledge-intensive industries.

Developing nations are seeking to benefit by "adding value" to raw materials *before* they are exported. They are increasing the rate of technological transfer from industrial nations into their economies to capitalize on their resources and lower labor costs. Developing nations are aligning themselves with trading partners that will provide reciprocal access to markets. They reject industries being "discarded" by developed nations, and instead are encouraging their own growth industries.[1]

How worthwhile is this new worldwide economic interdependence? Professor Paul W. McCracken, the noted economist now teaching at the University of Michigan, recently commented in the *Wall Street Journal* on the benefits of international trade. Here is an excerpt from his observations:

On the whole the liberal and open postwar trading and financial system has acquitted itself well. During the last three decades the proportion of world output finding a market across national boundaries rose steadily. Indeed, for much of this period the rate of increase in the volume of international trade was almost double that for world output. Economic well-being was doubly served. Real incomes rose more rapidly as nations could move away from costly self-sufficiency and toward areas in which they had a comparative advantage. And some discipline was imposed on inflationary tendencies, since markets where costs are getting out of line or product development is allowed to lag are markets that attract imports.

This liberal order worked well for the U.S. too. The proportion of our output of products (GNP less services) exported reached about 20% as the 1980s opened, compared with about 10% a decade earlier. And these U.S. products that found their markets in other countries are more than grains. The ratio of exports of manufacturing products to "Goods GNP" during the last decade also doubled. Thus the U.S. is much more influenced by and dependent upon the world economy than only a few years ago. The growth of this interdependence has outpaced our thinking about these matters.[2]

Since multinational companies (MNCs)—also referred to as multinational enterprises (MNEs) or transnational corporations (TNCs)—are a dominant group of standard-bearers in today's world of economic outreach, they are often praised and condemned in the same breath. A view from the Third World is provided by Y. G. Chouksey:

The MNCs, like the curate's egg, have proved to be good in parts. They have offered many gains to the developed countries. They could have done much more

---

[1] Reprinted with the special permission of *Dun's Business Month* (formerly *Dun's Review*), June, 1982, copyright 1982, Dun & Bradstreet Publications Corporation, p. 92.

[2] Reprinted with the author's permission from the *Wall Street Journal*, June 25, 1982.

for the third world. However, their errors of omission and commission in pursuing their economic goals are not so exasperating as to ask them to pack off lock, stock and barrel. Multinationals can play an effective role in overcoming the drudgery and economic stagnation of the poor countries. They can win the acceptance and confidence of the poor countries by practising more intently what they have been professing. Their R & D brilliance needs finding a wider expression and implementation. A more effective and more frequent give-and-take in this respect is very necessary.[3]

And what does it all mean to individual entities? There are stories of bank failures because foreign loans became uncollectable. Unemployed industrial workers are angry because their jobs were "exported" to other countries. In contrast, here is a news item about a local CPA practice office:

> In many ways, Geller and Geller is what the public accounting profession calls a local practice office. Its 20 employees, including four partners, operate in unpretentious offices in midtown Manhattan, literally in the shadow of some of the largest CPA firms' national headquarters.
>
> But there the resemblance to other small firms ends, for nearly 40 percent of Geller and Geller's work is done for international clients. The firm is 1 of 18 members of Jeffreys Henry International (JHI), a partnership of small and medium-sized firms in 13 countries with administrative offices in London. And while such international federations of smaller firms generally are considered new phenomena, JHI began, in an informal way, nearly two decades ago.[4]

Thus, we have a glimpse of international business during the 1980s. Convention has it that elaborate statistics on volumes of world trade and direct foreign investments should be presented to underscore the point. International balances of payments data could be used as further evidence, as could lists of percentages of international activities by the world's largest corporations.[5] The ready availability of such data suggests that we forego the temptation to reiterate them once again here.

Accounting Specialization

Accounting is the surname of our title. As the field of accounting and the practicing accounting profession mature, they are experiencing many parallels to other professional fields like law and medicine. Of particular interest is the seemingly unavoidable need to specialize. Law and medicine already have well-entrenched specializations (i.e., civil, criminal, and international law, and "colleges" of gynecologists, surgeons, and urologists). Recognized specializations in accounting have developed in recent years and are coming fully into their own as the twentieth century draws to a close.

[3] Y. G. Chouksey, "Multinational Corporations: An Evaluation," *Lok Udyog* (India), July 1978, p. 30.

[4] "A Local Practitioner's Global Outlook," *Journal of Accountancy*, November 1980, p. 58. Report of an interview of Morton Geller by *Journal* news editor Tom Bisky.

[5] James Cook, "A Game Any Number Can Play," *Forbes*, June 25, 1979, pp. 49–62.

The year 1975 is probably a good benchmark for the full recognition of subareas in accounting. Until then everything in accounting was asserted to be "general purposes"—from higher education programs in colleges and universities to professional examinations (i.e., the *Uniform* Certified Public Accountants Examination) and the preparation of published financial statements. "Generally accepted accounting principles" were deemed to have utility for all users of financial information (e.g., banks, government regulators and policy makers, business management, stockholders, and unions). Taxation and management consultancy services provided by professional CPA firms were deemed "in-house" specialties *not* requiring much special outside training or, least of all, separate certification.

Today, specialization in accounting is an accomplished fact. In the United States, separate professional examinations now recognize Certified Public Accountants, Certified Internal Auditors, Certified Management Accountants, and Chartered Financial Analysts. In Germany, the Public Auditor Certificate must be surrendered if the holder earns less than one-half of his or her professional income from public auditing services. In some Commonwealth countries, management consultancy practices are relegated to separate professional services companies established by (but operating separately from) firms of Chartered Accountants.

In the United Kingdom, annual accounts are often published separately from directors' reports as well as reports to a company's employees. In the United States, the American Institute of Certified Public Accountants (AICPA) now has membership divisions for firms serving clients with Securities and Exchange Commission (SEC) filing and reporting requirements and others with closely held clients. The Financial Accounting Standards Board (FASB) has exempted closely held companies from certain of its financial accounting requirements (e.g., segmental reporting). Multinational enterprises face a number of reporting requirements not applicable to domestic enterprises.

International (or multinational or transnational) accounting is one of several recognized specialties in the accounting field. It takes its place alongside governmental accounting, tax accounting, auditing, management accounting, behavioral accounting, and financial information systems.

INTERNATIONALIZATION
OF ACCOUNTING

The internationalization of accounting is induced by four critical factors:

1. Multinational enterprise operations
2. Internationalization of money capital markets
3. International nature of some technical accounting problems
4. Historical antecedents

Multinational Enterprise (MNE) Operations

The organizational phenomenon of the multinational enterprise is here to stay. Depending on how one measures, there are probably 1,000 corporations in the world that can be classified as multinational and whose total annual sales volume each exceeds $250 million. Again, depending on the measuring rod applied, the MNEs produce approximately one-fourth of the world's total economic output. To repeat an earlier point, some persons hold the MNEs in contempt for their asserted rise beyond most national laws, international economic exploitation, and power-play strategies. Others see them as highly efficient economic engines, transferers of knowledge and skills to multitudes of countries, and as significant economic and social development agents. Whatever one's view, the economic power of the MNEs as a group is substantial and unquestioned. Careful scholarly study, like that undertaken by Professor Raymond Vernon of Harvard University, supports the thought that the MNEs are here to stay. Their relative growth rates may have been largest during the 1950s and 1960s, but their collective strength is unlikely to diminish.

Parenthetically, we note that MNEs headquartered outside the United States have grown relatively faster than those domiciled in the United States. Table 1.1 portrays this trend.

Multinational enterprises are highly adaptable organizations. They constantly shift resources on a worldwide scale. These shifts cannot be accomplished in an effective and efficient manner unless highly reliable financial information permits careful analysis of investment opportunities and continuous control of the deployment of available resources.

Aside from analyzing economic opportunities and controlling multinational operations, the MNEs must somehow reconcile the plethora of existing

TABLE 1.1   The World's 500 Largest Industrial Corporations: Number of Companies by Sales

	1963		1971		1979	
SALES ($ MILLION)	U.S.	NON-U.S.	U.S.	NON-U.S.	U.S.	NON-U.S.
Over $10,000	2	0	3	1	20	27
$5,000–$9,999	1	1	9	3	38	43
$3,000–$4,999	5	1	14	14	53	53
$1,000–$2,999	41	13	101	66	108	158
$ 800–$ 999	16	16	29	19	—	—
$ 600–$ 799	25	20	51	48	—	—
$ 400–$ 599	51	43	73	69	—	—
$ 200–$ 399	127	87	—	—	—	—
Less than $200	32	19	—	—	—	—
Total	300	200	280	220	219	281

Source: Conference Board (US), *The World's Multinationals: A Global Challenge*, 1981. Table adapted from "The 'Migration' of Multinational Corporations," *Chronicle* (Arthur Andersen & Co.), Vol. 40, No. 1, 1981, p. 8.

national accounting rules and regulations. For example, a sociological view of accounting would hold that different national, socioeconomic environments require different types of managerial decision making and therefore different accounting systems and procedures. Thus the accounting needs of a centrally controlled economy like that of the People's Republic of China are quite different from those found in free or administered market economies.

Similarly, accounting in developing country situations functions differently from accounting in highly developed nations. The MNEs must somehow bridge existing national accounting differences if real benefits are to be gained from worldwide optimal resource allocation patterns. Aside from the conflicts and difficulties induced by different national accounting standards and practices, the MNEs are faced with an organizational paradox. On the one hand, their goal of efficient worldwide economic resource allocations literally dictates highly centralized management decision-making systems. Decision centralization implies that harmonized or worldwide accounting procedures be employed. Yet at the same time, multinational enterprises are very eager to lose their strict national identities in favor of cross-country or multinational acceptance in the many host countries in which they operate. Multinationality, in this sense, suggests acceptance of *national* accounting standards and practices. One form of solution to this paradox is found in so-called multiple financial reporting—that is, the simultaneous preparation of several differently based financial reports according to possibly (1) some sets of international standards and recommendations, (2) some regulatory or tax requirements, and (3) a selected few national accounting rules and dictates. Whether the multiple financial reporting approach is desirable for the MNEs remains to be demonstrated. Significant experimentation in this respect is occurring in Japan, the Netherlands, and Switzerland, among others (see Chapter 7 for details).

Internationalization of Money Capital Markets

There was a time in the economic history of nations that most money capital needs were supplied domestically. The United States is an important example of a country whose large-scale and very broad money capital markets were fueled primarily by domestic capital sources. In addition, the United States has probably the strongest and deepest secondary markets for financial securities.

Post–World War II international monetary developments abidingly changed several conventional patterns of financial investment. The conduct of World War II and subsequent major international economic assistance programs brought about, in the first instance, a so-called "dollar gap" abroad. Among other things, this dollar gap fostered large-scale multinational investments by U.S. enterprises.

Twenty-five years later, the "dollar gap" turned into a dollar "glut." Increased U.S. spending abroad, combined with significant domestic budget deficits, reduced the international exchange value of the U.S. dollar and eventually triggered a realignment of the entire world monetary system.

Two additional factors are important. One is the recent development of an acute worldwide shortage of new investment funds. In the main, this shortage has three basic causes:

1. As more and more countries operate more and more far-flung domestic income security programs, their savings rates are receding.
2. As domestic social programs in many countries of the world continue their expansion, they require more and more public borrowing in money capital markets, which increases the competition for available investment funds.
3. As major economic developments (e.g., the evolution of the OPEC cartel) shift investable funds between countries without any net changes in total world economic output, there is an increasing separation between capital supplying nations and capital absorbing nations.

In various combinations, the foregoing events and developments have triggered new and important international money capital market developments. This is the other key internationalization factor. There are now highly active Eurodollar, Asia-dollar, and Eurocurrency money markets in addition to the conventional national markets. Important externalities exist in these new markets. For example, Japan, even though a major generator of internationally investable money capital, still insists on tight domestic control of all of its money market affairs and thus prevents the internationalization of these markets.

Of special concern at the time of writing is the recent significant growth of foreign debt by the non-oil-producing countries of the Third World.

> On the eve of the first oil price shock in 1973, the total foreign debt—public and private, long-term and short-term—of non-OPEC developing countries was slightly less than $100 billion. By the end of 1982, this total had grown to roughly $530 billion.
>
> A very large proportion of this increase in debt is accounted for by commercial bank lending and, somewhat unnoticed, the number of banks involved in this lending has grown appreciably. At the end of 1973, the international banking system held 36% of the foreign debt of the non-oil LDCs. By the end of 1981, this proportion had grown to 53%—or $250 billion.[6]

Overall, the internationalization of world money capital markets is likely to continue. In turn, this means an increasing role for comparable and reliable financial information supporting the transactions and operations of these markets. Multinational accounting is an important facilitator of international capital markets. Parenthetically, it should be underscored that MNEs are not the only participants in international money capital markets. Strictly domestic organizations have been forced into international market participation as well. In

---

[6] William S. Ogden, "A Banker's View of the Foreign Debt Issue," *Wall Street Journal*, November 8, 1982, p. 22. Reprinted by permission of the *Wall Street Journal*, © Dow Jones & Company, Inc., 1982. All rights reserved.

the United States, for instance, a major domestic retailer and a large California savings and loan institution have, in recent years, tapped the Eurodollar market for additional sources of investable funds.

International Nature of Some Technical Accounting Problems

International commerce, multinational business operations, foreign investments, and international money capital market transactions all involve the use of foreign currencies. Underlying transactions occur in terms of two or more national currencies and hence create foreign exchange translation problems for accounting. Thus we are faced with a unique technical problem brought about by the internationalization of accounting (see Chapter 4 for full elaboration).

Consolidation of the financial statements of foreign subsidiaries or affiliates is another accounting problem unique to the multinational setting. For example, the proposed accounting rules of the European Economic Community (EEC) for consolidations contemplate partial consolidations according to geographic criteria. This notion is completely alien to Anglo-American accounting thought. German Companies Law requires the consolidation of controlled domestic subsidiaries only—controlled foreign subsidiaries have merely the option of consolidation. In many other countries of the world—for example, Switzerland—financial statement consolidation is still optional altogether. This topic is treated more fully in Chapter 6.

Related to the consolidation problem are general purchasing power adjustments of financial statements. On a consolidated basis, should the price index of the home country be used (parent company viewpoint) or the price index of the subsidiary's country (multinational viewpoint) for the restatement of a subsidiary company's financial statement? There is also the "restate and then translate" versus "translate and then restate" controversy. Given different national accounting standards and practices and different national rates of inflation, differential accounting results are produced if one first restates the financial statements from one set of accounting standards to another and then translates them to common units of purchasing power, as opposed to doing the two operations in reverse order. These and related issues are discussed in Chapter 5.

Finally, the entire technology for recasting financial statements from one set of underlying accounting standards and practices to another is a technical problem unique to the internationalization of accounting. For one thing, procedural restatements may or may not convey the same intrinsic relationships and meanings as the original statements had. For another, enterprise management decision making typically occurs in reference to a particular set of national accounting standards. If different accounting rules had been enforced, management might have arrived at different business decisions. Does this mean that financial statements really should not be restated from one set of accounting standards to another, once they have been prepared? If the answer is no, then single-domicile financial reporting is called for in all situations, and the acceptability of multiple financial reports drawn into question.

Historical Antecedents

The history of accounting is an international history. Double-entry bookkeeping, often thought of as the genesis of today's accounting, emanated from the Italian city-states of the fourteenth and fifteenth centuries. In due course, "Italian bookkeeping" migrated to Germany, France, and the Lowlands. From there, it reached Britain, whose dominating world economic position during the seventeenth and eighteenth centuries made her an ideal missionary on behalf of accounting. British influence spread accounting and auditing techniques not only to North America but throughout the then-existing British Commonwealth.

Parallel developments occurred when Dutch accounting was carried to Indonesia and South Africa. The French made sure that Polynesia and French-administered territories in Africa would come to rely on French accounting systems, and the Germans extended their accounting influence to, among others, Japan, Sweden, and Czarist Russia.

As the economic influence of the United States grew during the first half of the present century, U.S. accounting thought and practice was transmitted not only to Germany and Japan but also to developing countries like Brazil, Israel, Mexico, and the Philippines.

The heritage of accounting, therefore, is international. While intense nationalistic developments have taken place in accounting during different periods and in different countries, there is clearly an international tradition that should help to facilitate today's internationalization of the discipline.

INTERNATIONALIZATION OF THE ACCOUNTING PROFESSION

Accountants follow business investments. This was the case when commerce moved from the Italian city-states to the Hanseatic city-states. It was also the case when British investments first helped to finance North American railroads and insurance companies. Of late, it applies to the worldwide investments and operations of the MNEs.

For reasons not germane to the present discussion, the accounting profession has internationalized itself more slowly than the field of accounting. Tight national regulation and licensing of the profession may be one explanation thereof. Barriers to the international movement of human resources might be another. Outright protectionism of a developing industry may be yet a third. In the Philippines, for example, the practice of public accounting is restricted to nationals. At the same time, the international specialties of the field are not only well known but are projected from the Philippines to other Asian and Pacific countries.

William S. Kanaga, Chairman of Arthur Young & Company and 1980–1981 Chairman of the AICPA, observed that "Today, nationalistic initiatives are leading to what appears to be a worldwide epidemic of restrictive legislation, strict new licensing requirements and sudden enforcement of rules largely ignored previously."[7] He cited the French restrictions on foreign accountants, the proposed Eighth Directive of the EEC (see Chapter 12), and, of course, the restrictive practices in the United States. Still, his conclusion is that today's international investment community will require corresponding international cooperation among professional accountants and that international accounting organizations already in place will be able to bring about greater professional harmony worldwide. His final assessment of international professional developments "on the horizon" is worded thus:

> Even if nationalistic regulation prohibits partnership interests across national borders or otherwise limits the participation of foreigners in national practices, international firms will still be able to deliver high-quality, consistent services to clients worldwide. One indication is an emerging trend toward "federalism," whereby national firms may affiliate with each other and with international firms on the basis of mutual agreements to meet specified standards of auditing, reporting, professional education, independence and ethics. These organizations each establish a central office to provide administrative and technical services to firms in the group and to act as an overall coordinating body. The format provides national firms of all sizes with a vehicle that both satisfies the legal and professional requirements of the various countries in which they practice and allays fears of national firms concerning the possible domination of international practice by any other firm in the group.[8]

International Professional Practice

The international practice of professional accounting occurs in three tiers, somewhat parallel to the structure observable in industrial sectors of the economy or general organizational patterns of professional services delivery systems.

The most integrated tier is that of the "Big Eight" British-American domiciled firms operating under single names throughout the world. The international organizational mode of these firms is typically one of an international "partnership of partnerships." In other words, six to ten regional partnerships (e.g., in Europe, South America, North America, the Near East and Africa, the Far East and South Pacific) are integrated into an administrative international partnership. The world headquarters location for Price Waterhouse & Co. is in London; for Arthur Andersen & Co. it is split between Chicago and Geneva; and for Touche Ross & Co. it is in New York (further detail is provided in Chapter 9).

While there are some operational differences between these eight firms,

---

[7] William S. Kanaga, "International Accounting: The Challenge and the Changes," *Journal of Accountancy,* November 1980, p. 56.

[8] Ibid., p. 60.

they are by and large highly similar to each other. There is profit sharing among the partners worldwide. Technical accounting, auditing, and consultancy services are harmonized globally through elaborate internal control procedures and integrated training programs. Business development activities and public relations with clients are conducted under a single name and with uniform thrust. Technical backup for almost any conceivable problem is available from highly specialized staffs. The majority of these firms now publish periodic reports about themselves which are a good source of information about the size, scope, and international philosophy of each respective firm.

In the next tier are another eight to ten firms that operate worldwide under single names but on the basis of federation among selected national firms. Examples are the KMG Group domiciled on the European Continent, the SGV Group domiciled in the Philippines, and Panell, Kerr, and Foster of British-American origins.

These federations combine the advantage of international name identification and internationally agreed standards of professional work with national firm identity and business development efforts in individual countries. Financial arrangements between member firms are typically on a referral fee basis. There is typically an international secretariat to facilitate liaison, education, and technical work, plus a fairly democratic, nationally autonomous governing structure. Occasionally these federations have geographic representation and/or structural problems. There is typically no great cost to an individual national firm to joining (or for that matter leaving again) an international federation of firms. Still, it appears that the federated approach to the provision of international accounting services is gaining momentum—as was noted by Kanaga—possibly because it parallels the dominant organizational pattern of the multinational clients of the professional accounting service firms.

The arrangements prevailing in the third tier are quite informal and often limited to an "as needed" basis. These arrangements apply to regional professional accounting firms and to small firms and individual practitioners who participate in cooperative CPA firm associations. On a cost-sharing basis, associations of CPA firms provide various educational, practice development, staff, and technical services to their members.

Internationally, these smaller organizations typically align themselves with practitioners in other countries through various forms of correspondence agreements. Correspondent firms seldom have direct organizational affiliations but agree to do work for each other respecting each other's quality standards and reporting requirements.

Since there is normally no international secretariat to guide transnational work, local firms bill their work directly to local clients and allow some type of referral fee to a foreign correspondent for a limited period of time. In turn, clients have the satisfaction of knowing that the work of a foreign auditor is acceptable to their home country auditor by prearrangement.

Aside from occasional personal visits, professional correspondence arrangements are fostered and furthered by international professional meetings. Quite often, partners' or administrative meetings of international professional firms or correspondents of national firms meet in conjunction with International Congresses of Accountants or regional meetings of accounting associations. To lend some institutional support, most national institutes or societies of professional accountants maintain active international liaison committees.

Research and Development

To borrow a thought from Ross M. Skinner, "No other profession has attempted to do what we are attempting."[9] Skinner refers to a common conceptual framework and principles useful in practice. Fields such as economics, law, and sociology, do not have common principles agreed to by all in their respective professions. Yet accountants, for some decades, have attempted to reach such an agreement. Underlying efforts have occurred mostly on the national level, but there is also some activity internationally (for elaboration, see Chapter 2). Research has become the cornerstone of "narrowing existing areas of differences" in financial accounting.

Of course, accounting research and development should not be confused with accounting policy making and standard setting. The latter is a socioeconomic and/or political process that utilizes the former but depends on many other factors as well (e.g., prevailing types of economic systems, forms of business organization, strength and influence of financial statement user groups, and all the other pressures found in public policy formulation processes).

There is also a question about who should do needed research. In accounting four groups participate most actively:

1. National associations, institutes, or policy-making bodies
2. Academic researchers
3. Professional accounting firms
4. Business enterprises

The four groups, quite naturally, focus their research efforts differently. While technical, applied, proprietary research characterizes the corresponding activities of professional accounting firms, normative and empirical work is the rule for academic endeavors. Accounting research in business enterprises often has an industry or a specific technical focus. The Accounting Research Studies published by the Financial Executives Research Foundation in the United States are a good example.

A great deal of published research is available in the area of international accounting—most of it descriptive and comparative in nature. In more limited quantities there is also empirical research related to securities prices, economic effects, and behavioral effects. There is some nonquantitative normative research as well as a fair amount of biographical-historical analysis (see Chapter 2).

The additional source references provided at the end of this chapter con-

---

[9] Ross M. Skinner, *Accounting Principles* (Toronto: The Canadian Institute of Chartered Accountants, 1972).

stitute a concise guide to this literature in general. When checking for available research materials or results, one might cover the following publications:

Accountants Index

Accounting Articles (CCH Looseleaf Service)

Proceedings of International Congresses of Accountants and other international meetings and conferences (see Chapter 12)

International accounting *bibliographies* (e.g., the one published by the International Accounting Section of the American Accounting Association)

Pamphlets, brochures, and monographs published by the *international CPA firms* and dealing with international accounting issues

Periodic issues of the *house journals* of major professional accounting firms

Journals of the member bodies of the International Accounting Standards Committee (IASC) and the International Federation of Accountants (IFAC) (e.g., *Journal of Accountancy* in the United States, *Accountant's Magazine* in Scotland, *Accountants Journal* in New Zealand, *Die Wirtschaftsprüfung* in West Germany, *Maandblad voor Accountancy en Bedrijfshuishoudkunde* in the Netherlands, and *Schweizer Treuhänder* in Switzerland)

Periodic *journals* devoted specifically to international accounting (e.g., *International Journal of Accounting Education and Research* published by the University of Illinois)

Periodicals devoted specifically to multinational business and finance (e.g., *Journal of International Business Studies, Columbia Journal of World Business, Management International, Business International,* and *Euro-Money*)

Research studies on international accounting topics from professional accountancy bodies like the Research Committee of the Institute of Chartered Accountants in England and Wales, the Nederlands Instituut van Registeraccountants (NIvRA) in the Netherlands, the Financial Executives Institute (FEI) and the FASB in the United States, and similar other bodies throughout the world)

Special studies and documents published by governmental organizations like the United Nations, the Organization for Economic Cooperation and Development (OECD), the International Finance Corporation, the Brookings Institution, the Conference Board, and generally national ministries of justice and/or finance

Relevant *Ph.D. dissertations* (list obtainable from International Accounting Section, American Accounting Association, 5717 Bessie Drive, Sarasota, Florida, 33583)

International accounting *newsletters* (e.g., *International Accounting Bulletin, World Accounting Report,* and *International Accounting & Financial Report*—all published monthly in London, U.K.)

Licensing and Reciprocity

Licensing of professional accountants is a prerogative of individual legal jurisdictions and is consequently highly diverse internationally. For present purposes, it is important to recognize that the rather wide range of prerequisites for professional licensing has made international licensing reciprocity all but impossible. The IFAC (see Chapter 12) operates committees whose specific goal it is to harmonize professional education for accountants around the world and to advocate greater standardization in professional licensing. However, these efforts are still at very early stages and have not yet produced any tangible results.

When it comes to educational backgrounds as professional licensing pre-requisites, baccalaureate degrees (either in accounting or generally from an accredited college or university) are required in nearly all 53 jurisdictions in the United States. An advanced graduate degree from a university is a necessity in Germany. In the Netherlands and the United Kingdom, entry routes to the profession are twofold: either through (1) university training or (2) on-the-job training with evening school and other educational requirements to be satisfied through courses offered by national professional institutes or societies. In still other countries, high school graduation combined with rigorous professional training and part-time course work through local institutes and societies is the only available educational route to professional certification. The existing international diversity in the educational backgrounds of professional accountants is pronounced and pervasive.

When it comes to continuing education as a condition for professional relicensing, differences range from specified minimum numbers of formal education hours per year, sometimes specifically directed to accounting and auditing subjects, to no continuing education at all. In fact, there are situations in which professional accounting licenses are granted for life without any periodical renewal obligations.

Many jurisdictions license several different types of accountants (and bookkeepers) so that it becomes unclear whether a certain "licensed tax return preparer" could or should be considered a licensed professional accountant. There are other jurisdictions that sublicense professional specialties (e.g., auditing, taxation, and management consultancy). Differential concurrent licensing also contributes to difficulties with international reciprocity.

In addition to educational requirements and specialty recognition, professional licensing typically involves passing of a uniform professional examination, commitment to a publicly promulgated professional code of ethics, and, at times, ancillary conditions like minimum age, nationality, and length of professional experience under the supervision of other licensees. Of the foregoing factors, the professional examination is probably the most harmonious internationally. While professional examinations are structured differently from country to country (e.g., single sittings in some instances and interim and final examinations in others), their nature and scope are fairly similar. The final examination in Switzerland stresses a lengthy audit and financial analysis case. Relatively speaking, accounting theory is weighted more heavily in United States examinations. The examination in Germany stresses applicable laws and regulations.

Availability of professional accountancy examinations probably depends most on the number of persons interested in taking it. In the United States the examination is given in every jurisdiction twice every year, during May and November. In Switzerland, on the other hand, the final examination is offered only once every other year.

Until there is significantly greater international harmony in professional licensing prerequisites, reciprocity will remain a difficult factor for internationally active professional accountants. Some national institutes of professional accountants have commenced to grant associate membership status to licensed professionals from other countries. While such a first step is professionally very desirable, it still does not resolve licensing reciprocity. Reciprocity for public license to practice is, in most instances, different from passing a professional examination or becoming a member or associate member of a professional accounting institute.

Educational Support

Teaching and sensitizing students and practicing professionals to the nature and scope of international accounting issues and opportunities has become a major linkage in the internationalization of the accounting profession. The organizational aspects of this endeavor are sketched in Chapter 12. Some underlying processes are mentioned in the paragraphs which follow.

A primary thrust of educational activities aimed at international accounting are courses and seminars offered at institutions of higher learning. Probably 100 such courses now exist in the United States in a mixture of undergraduate and graduate offerings. Outside the United States one finds at least an equal number of such courses. Considering the fact that 20 years ago there were none, one must conclude that an important internationalization force is at work. Another dimension of this same phenomenon is the steadily rising number of Ph.D. dissertations devoted to international accounting topics. Also, there exists now at least one introductory financial accounting textbook that explicitly devotes a section to international considerations.

A major catalyst in the growth of the internationalization of collegiate programs of accounting education has been the American Assembly of Collegiate Schools of Business (AACSB). This organization changed its business curriculum accreditation standards in 1974 to require a reflection of "worldwide" as well as domestic aspects of business. Then, in 1976 the International Affairs Committee of the AACSB undertook a major international curriculum-planning seminar attended by 41 business school deans, associate deans, department chairpersons, and some professors. Beginning in 1977, the AACSB has offered a variety of workshops and seminars aimed at implementing the desired internationalization of the business school curriculum. A most useful reference in this respect is the 1979 AACSB publication entitled *The Internationalization of The Business School Curriculum*. The field of accounting has been a part of the AACSB workshops and seminars from the start. More recently, accounting curriculum internationalization workshops have also been held at the annual meetings of the American Accounting Association and various of its regional groups.

Aside from collegiate educational offerings, professional-level workshops and seminars are now regularly available. For example, the American Management Association offers appropriate seminars throughout North America and the World Trade Institute at New York's World Trade Center lists in its catalog of courses and seminars offerings like "Introduction to International Accounting" and "Essentials of International Finance and Accounting." Other private professional education institutes do likewise.

Finally, the broad educational effects of media attention, relevant committee structures of professional organizations, and general attention to international accounting during international conferences, annual convention programs, and other professional gatherings are developing a dynamic of their own. Federal tax collection departments, most securities regulatory agencies, and governmental audit offices (e.g., the GAO in the United States) all have international divisions and therefore in-house educational programs like professional accounting firms and industrial and service-sector firms. Among many other outward manifestations, international accounting expertise increasingly is mentioned on professional personal resumes, during introductions of speakers, and in biographical notes appearing in the literature. All of this aggregates to a rather widespread educational thrust—for business in general and for accounting in particular.

THE IDEA OF INTERNATIONAL ACCOUNTING

International accounting is placed most advantageously within the context of the accounting discipline as a whole. It does not seek to supersede or replace existing accounting thought and practices; rather, it strives to "stretch" the existing field as a whole by giving it more conceptual precision as well as more practical usefulness. Not every accountant needs to be a multinational accounting expert. But a well-informed accountant should know what the core problems of international accounting are and in which direction appropriate solutions are being developed.

Since we cannot improve on the profile of the international accountant developed by Arun K. Deva, partner of Touche Ross & Co., in *Tempo* magazine (1981), we reproduce it in Exhibit 1.1 for the benefit of our readers.

EXHIBIT 1.1   A Profile of the International Accountant

Considering the business environment as it exists, is there such a person as an international accountant? If so, what is his profile, and what special services does he provide?

The accountant's role has been primarily an evolving one; it has paralleled the growth of the profession. But the new accountant with a global perspective and expertise finds himself in a unique position in an interdependent world in which he must provide not only services but leadership as well. This leadership reflects his increasingly important role not only in reporting but in interpreting and defining business needs and translating them in ways that have useful applications in different countries.

With the world in a state of flux politically and economically, the accountant must have greater flexibility and adaptability to pluralistic conditions. Events may render long-range assumptions invalid, and services must be provided under greater uncertainty. Also, international audits may well be performed by task

EXHIBIT 1.1   (*continued*)

forces, due to the increased regulatory environment, surges of nationalism, and the demands for social responsibility and accountability.

With the internationalization of business, a greater need will be felt for continuing professional education and training seminars. The accountant will need an overall understanding of differing accounting systems, requirements, and terminology. For example, the relevance to international accounting of the Companies Act, which virtually defines business practices in the United Kingdom and in some Commonwealth countries, must be understood by those using American or other accounting systems and having operations in those countries.

No longer is the understanding confined to reporting applications and consolidations. The world capital markets, investment flows, and funding organizations require the preparation of financial statements that must deal with the intricacies of valuations and exchange rates. This includes accounting for varying inflation rates in different countries and the accounting provisions made for these. Care must be taken when comparison ratios are developed, since distortions can be caused by transfer pricing. International tax planning and strategy also require new approaches.

In a broad sense, every practicing accountant is an international accountant whether he perceives himself in that light or not. The scope of services provided by an auditor to a transnational corporation, regardless of size, impinges on internationalism even if only *domestic* services are being provided. A conglomerate may need diversified accounting services that are international in scope, but so may an individually owned enterprise or business partnership if it is operated in two or more countries.

The international accountant, by the very nature of his profession, cannot take the back seat. He has the challenging responsibility of defining harmonized financial data for a global economic community held together by transnational business, investments, and capital market interests.

Source: Arun K. Deva, partner, Touche Ross & Co. A Profile of the ''International'' Accountant, *Tempo* (New York: 1981), p. 32.

Definitions

There now remains the task of providing a definition of *international accounting*. In 1971, Professors Thomas R. Weirich, Clarence G. Avery, and Henry R. Anderson distinguished among three approaches: (1) a universal system, (2) a descriptive and informative approach covering all the methods and standards of all countries, and (3) accounting practices of foreign subsidiaries and parent companies. They named and defined these definitional approaches, respectively, as follows:

World Accounting. In the framework of this concept, international accounting is considered to be a universal system that could be adopted in all countries. A worldwide set of generally accepted accounting principles (GAAP), such as the set maintained in the United States, would be established. Practices and principles would be developed which were applicable to all countries. This concept would be the ultimate goal of an international accounting system.

International Accounting. A second major concept of the term international accounting involves a descriptive and informative approach. Under this concept, international accounting includes *all* varieties of principles, methods and stan-

dards of accounting of *all* countries. This concept includes a set of generally accepted accounting principles established for each country, thereby requiring the
accountant to be multiple principle conscious when studying international accounting. . . . No universal or perfect set of principles would be expected to be
established. A collection of all principles, methods and standards of all countries
would be considered as the international accounting system. These variations result because of differing geographic, social, economic, political and legal influences.

Accounting for Foreign Subsidiaries. The third major concept that may be applied
to "international accounting" refers to the accounting practices of a parent company and a foreign subsidiary. A reference to a particular country or domicile is
needed under the concept for effective international financial reporting. The accountant is concerned mainly with the translation and adjustment of the subsidiary's financial statement. Different accounting problems arise and different
accounting principles are to be followed depending upon which country is used
as a reference for translation and adjustment purposes.[10]

The definitions advanced by Weirich, Avery, and Anderson have with-
stood the test of time. Your authors have built upon them—only to make four
rather than three basic distinctions. We utilize these categories throughout the
book:

1. *Comparative International Accounting*—in the spirit of the approach utilized
   by Professors C. W. Nobes and R. H. Parker.[11]
2. *Standardized International Accounting*—as primarily reflected in the work of
   IASC (see Chapter 12).
3. *Operational International Accounting*—encompassing the specific requirements of accounting for the operations of MNCs
4. *Politicized International Accounting*—as emanating from world political institutions like the United Nations and the OECD

Our definition of *international accounting* is this:

International accounting extends general-purpose, nationally oriented accounting in its broadest sense to: (1) international comparative analysis, (2) accounting
measurement and reporting issues unique to multinational business transactions
and the business form of the multinational enterprise, (3) accounting needs of international financial markets, and (4) harmonization of worldwide accounting
and financial reporting diversity via political, organizational, professional, and
standard-setting activities.

SELECTED REFERENCES

ALHASHIM, DHIA D., and JAMES W. ROBERTSON, eds., *Accounting for Multinational Enterprises*, Indianapolis: Bobbs-Merrill Educational Publishing, 1978, 307
pp.
AMERICAN ACCOUNTING ASSOCIATION, *Accounting Education for the Third*

---

[10] Thomas R. Weirich, Clarence G. Avery, and Henry R. Anderson, "International
Accounting: Varying Definitions," *International Journal of Accounting*, Fall 1971, pp. 80–81.

[11] C. W. Nobes and R. H. Parker, eds., *Comparative International Accounting* (Homewood, Ill.: Richard D. Irwin, Inc., 1981).

World (Report of the Committee on International Accounting Operations and Education, 1976–1978), Sarasota, Fla.: AAA 1978, 109 pp.

AMERICAN ACCOUNTING ASSOCIATION, INTERNATIONAL ACCOUNTING SECTION, *Notable Contributions to the Periodical International Accounting Literature—1975–1978*, Sarasota, Fla.: AAA 1979, 168 pp.

ARPAN, JEFFREY, and LEE H. RADEBAUGH, *International Accounting and Multinational Enterprises*, Boston: Warren, Gorham & Lamont, 1981, 400 pp.

BRENNAN, W. JOHN, ed., *The Internationalization of the Accountancy Profession*, Toronto: The Canadian Institute of Chartered Accountants, 1979, 172 pp.

BURTON, JOHN C., ed., *The International World of Accounting* (1980 Proceedings of the Arthur Young Professors' Round Table), Reston, Va.: The Council of Arthur Young Professors, 1981, 218 pp.

CHOI, FREDERICK D. S., and GERHARD G. MUELLER, *An Introduction to Multinational Accounting*, Englewood Cliffs, N.J.: Prentice-Hall, Inc., 1978, 365 pp.

CHOI, FREDERICK D. S. and GERHARD G. MUELLER, *Essentials of Multinational Accounting: An Anthology*, Ann Arbor, Mich.: University Microfilms International, 1979, 469 pp.

CHOUKSEY, Y. G., "Multinational Corporations: An Evaluation," *Lok Udyog* (Monthly Journal of the Bureau of Public Enterprises and the Public Sector of India), July 1978, pp. 27–30.

COSTOUROS, GEORGE J., and A. VAN SEVENTER, *Contemporary Accounting Issues*, Palo Alto, Calif.: Bay Books, 1979, 231 pp. (especially Chapter 15, "Problems of International Accounting").

DELOITTE HASKINS & SELLS, "The Changing World of Corporate Finance" (Special Report), *Dun's Business Month*, June 1982, pp. 92–93, 97, 99, 101–106, 110.

EITEMAN, DAVID K., and ARTHUR I. STONEHILL, *Multinational Business Finance* (3rd ed.), Reading, Mass.: Addison-Wesley Publishing Co., 1982, 721 pp.

ENTHOVEN, ADOLF J. H., *Accounting Education in Economic Development Management*, Amsterdam: North-Holland Publishing Co., 1981, 448 pp. (also see *Accountancy and Economic Development*, same publisher, 1970).

KANAGA, WILLIAM S., "International Accounting: The Challenge and the Changes," *Journal of Accountancy*, November 1980, pp. 55–60.

MUELLER, GERHARD G., *International Accounting*, New York: Macmillan Company, 1967, 225 pp.

NOBES, C. W., and R. H. PARKER, eds., *Comparative International Accounting*, Homewood, Ill.: Richard D. Irwin, Inc., 1981, 379 pp.

QURESHI, MAHMOOD A., "Pragmatic and Academic Bases of International Accounting," *Management International Review*, Vol. 19, No. 2, 1979, pp. 61–67.

SCHOENFELD, HANNS-MARTIN W., "International Accounting: Development, Issues and Future Directions," *Journal of International Business Studies*, Fall 1981, pp. 83–100.

SEIDLER, LEE, "International Accounting—The Ultimate Theory Course," *Accounting Review*, October 1967, pp. 775–781.

WATT, GEORGE C., RICHARD H. HAMMER, and MARIANNE BURGE, *Accounting for the Multinational Corporation*, New York: Research Foundation of the Financial Executives Institute, 1977, 526 pp.

DISCUSSION QUESTIONS

1. International law and international accounting are specializations within their respective disciplines. Identify five similarities and five dissimilarities between these two specializations.

2.   Some observers suggest that multinational enterprises are fairly tightly controlled by a great number of (and often conflicting) national laws. Others contend that there is no effective international law governing the multinationals, which allows them too many freedoms and privileges. What are the implications of these two positions for future developments in multinational accounting? Provide your answer in the form of two concise paragraphs.

3.   What is the organizational paradox of multinational enterprises? What solution has been suggested for this paradox? Can you think of other possible solutions?

4.   North American accounting was imported from Great Britain in the late nineteenth and early twentieth centuries. Would you expect British and U.S. accounting to be quite similar today? Why or why not?

5.   Despite its thoroughly international heritage, international professional practice in accounting is subjected increasingly to nationalistic initiatives and restrictions. A way of overcoming nationalistic professional practice tendencies is international accounting firm ''federalism.'' How does this federalism work? What is its antithesis? Do large practice firms have the same international operations problems as do second- and third-tier firms?

6.   Four groups of participants in international accounting research are identified in the chapter. For each group identify a likely international accounting research project.

7.   In the text of the chapter it is asserted that ''the accounting profession has internationalized itself more slowly than the field of accounting.'' If you have a basis of evaluating this statement, do so. In the absence thereof, use your best judgment to marshall some arguments both in support of and counter to the assertion.

8.   Define, in your own terms, the notions of (a) world accounting, (b) international accounting, and (c) accounting for foreign subsidiaries. Do these definitions imply that subareas are already developing within the multinational accounting field?

9.   What evidence is there that the international dimension is beginning to impact the accounting curriculum in higher education?

10.   With reference to economic development, sociologists have posited the so-called *convergence hypothesis*. This hypothesis suggests that economic and social systems become more and more alike as different countries reach similar stages of economic development. Is there any evidence of convergence in the multinational accounting field?

EXERCISES

1.   Table 1.2 reports non-U.S. revenue, operating profit, and assets in relation to company totals for the ten largest U.S. multinationals according to a ranking by *Forbes*.

TABLE 1.2 The Ten Largest U.S. Multinationals

RANK	COMPANY	FOREIGN REVENUE (MILLIONS)	TOTAL REVENUE (MILLIONS)	FOREIGN OPERATING PROFIT[a] (MILLIONS)	TOTAL OPERATING PROFIT[a] (MILLIONS)	FOREIGN ASSETS (MILLIONS)	TOTAL ASSETS (MILLIONS)
1	Exxon	$44,333	$60,335	$1,947	$3,434	$22,645	$41,531
2	Mobil	20,481	34,736	639[b]	1,126[b]	11,827	22,611
3	Texaco	18,927	28,608	436[b]	853[b]	10,840	20,249
4	Ford	14,985	42,784	780[b]	1,589[b]	10,730	22,085
5	General Motors	14,172	63,221	453[b]	3,508[b]	7,217	30,417
6	Standard Oil of Calif	14,150	23,232	563[b]	1,106[b]	8,321	16,754
7	Intl Business Machines	11,040	21,076	1,584[b]	3,111[b]	11,021	20,771
8	International Tel & Tel	10,023	19,399	799	1,461	10,394	23,342
9	Gulf Oil	9,229	18,069	277[b]	791[b]	5,861	15,036
10	Citicorp	5,157[c]	7,556	645[d]	827[d]	50,931[e]	78,952[e]

[a] Unless otherwise indicated.
[b] Net income.
[c] Estimated.
[d] Pretax income.
[e] Average assets.

Source: *Forbes*, June 25, 1979, p. 56.

TABLE 1.3   The Nine Largest Public Accounting Firms Worldwide

FIRMS	TOTAL STAFF 1980	WORLDWIDE REVENUES (MILLIONS) FOR THE YEAR ENDING IN:		YEAR-END
		1982	1980	
Arthur Andersen & Co.	19,900	$1,123	$805	8/31
Arthur Young & Company	18,000	955	750[a]	12/31
Coopers & Lybrand	25,100	1,066	846	9/30
Deloitte Haskins & Sells	20,700	852	690[a]	4/30
Ernst & Whinney	19,000	887	706[a]	9/30
Klynveld Main Goerdeler & Co.	25,000	970	800[a]	9/30
Peat, Marwick, Mitchell & Co.	21,600	1,150	816	6/30
Price Waterhouse	22,300	946	752	6/30
Touche Ross & Co.	19,500	800	611	8/31

[a] These firms do not publish financial information. Their revenues were estimated by *Public Accounting Report*, May 1981, p. 4, and March 1983, p. 8. Source of other data was the firms' annual reports and directories.

Required: Prepare a table ranking the ten companies in terms of their degree of international involvement. Which criterion—revenues, profits, or assets—do you think is the best indicator of the degree of a company's "multinationality"?

2. The chapter text presents a profile of the international accountant. *Required:* Prepare a similar profile of a "domestic" (i.e., uninational) accountant. What similarities and what differences emerge between the two profiles?

3. Table 1.3 reports total staff and worldwide revenues for the nine largest international public accounting firms. A size test of firms in terms of total staff produces one ranking scheme. Similar procedures using worldwide revenues as a size criterion yields another. *Required:* Using the data provided, propose a ranking scheme that overcomes this inconsistency. On the basis of your ranking, which firm appears to exhibit the greatest degree of international involvement?

4. Table 1.1 provides some time series data on the world's largest industrial corporations. *Required:* Analyze the pattern of development of the world's largest corporations in terms of size and geographical location (i.e., U.S. vs. non-U.S.). Discuss the implications of your observations for the development of international accounting standards.

5. A number of international accounting reference leads are provided in the chapter. *Required:* Identify ten recent articles dealing with international accounting issues or concerns. For each piece, note the title, author(s), and citation. Also in a sentence or two, identify the main conclusion reached in each respective piece.

CASE

Crossing The Atlantic

A company's domicile may be its country of incorporation or major business operations, sources of long-term financing, or residence or nationality of the majority of owners, and so forth. The following news item illustrates the point:

> In an unusual move, International Signals and Control, the fast-growing Pennsylvania electronics systems company, acquired a listing on the London Stock Exchange in preference to Wall Street, thus formally changing its domicile from the United States to the United Kingdom.
>
> According to ISC Chairman James Guerin, the chief reason for the move is to avoid complying with Securities and Exchange Commission rules that oblige the company to disclose confidential information about its clients. "Customers prefer us to be U.K.-based because of confidentiality," he claims. "They trust the British more than the Americans in this regard."
>
> London is also better placed as a marketing center, Guerin explains, since ISC, which has an established presence in defense and communications equipment, gets 80% of its revenues outside the U.S., predominantly in Africa and the Middle East.

Founded by Guerin in 1971, ISC has been represented abroad for the past three years by a 52.2%-owned London-based but Luxembourg-listed subsidiary, Electronic Systems International. In making the changeover, the minority share in ESI—held by British institutions—were exchanged for stock in the parent company and ISC was set up as a holding company, International Signals and Control Group.[12]

Required

1. Should a company like ISC be allowed to "have its cake and eat it too" by gaining access to a major stock exchange listing and yet avoiding SEC disclosure requirements?
2. ISC is a U.S. company gaining 80 percent of its revenues in Africa and the Middle East and raising its public equity capital through the London financial market. Does such an arrangement conflict with any one country's national public interest? Why don't more U.S.-based companies do likewise? (Canada and several South American countries host a number of similar "transnational" companies.)
3. In preparing annual financial reports, should ISC henceforth use U.S. or U.K. financial accounting standards, or should it prepare two separate annual reports—one for each of the two sets of requirements?

[12] Reprinted with the special permission of *Dun's Business Month* (formerly *Dun's Review*) November 1982. Copyright 1982, Dun & Bradstreet Publications Corporation, p. 14.

2

Conceptual Development

In society, accounting performs a service function. This function is put in jeopardy unless accounting remains above all technically and socially useful. Thus, it must respond to ever-changing needs of society and must reflect the cultural, economic, legal, social, and political conditions within which it operates. Its technical and social usefulness depends on its ability to mirror these conditions.

The history of accounting and accountants reveals continuing change— a process that accounting seems to undergo fairly consistently. At one time, accounting was little more than a recording system for certain banking services and tax collection schemes. Later it responded with double-entry bookkeeping systems to meet the needs of trading ventures. Industrialization and division of labor made possible cost behavior analysis and managerial accounting. The advent of the modern corporation stimulated periodic financial reporting and auditing. More recently, accounting has revealed a capacity for public interest responses in such forms as human asset accounting and measuring, reporting, and auditing the social responsibility of various organizations. At present, accounting operates in the behavioral, public sector and international spheres, among others. It provides decision information for huge public securities markets—both domestic and international. It has even extended into the management consulting area. It is clearly concerned with its environment.

Periods of Development

The various stimuli and events that have affected the ever-changing characteristics of accounting have long intrigued scholars, historians, and practitioners. Since international accounting is still in a developmental process, it is instructive to reflect briefly upon the development of accounting as a whole. Many schemes have been devised to accommodate classification and analysis. One such classification was put forth by Dean Athol S. Carrington.[1] He proposed "Seven Ages of Development" for accounting standards and the profession.

The age of innocence.   The age of innocence was one of no standards. "Accountants knew what they were doing."[2] So long as the bookkeeping was correct and balance sheets balanced, there was nothing to argue about.

The age of improvisation.   The age of improvisation dawned when the world began to question accountants and to point out problems like grossly divergent practices and lack of realism. A few standards were improvised to rule out some of the more misleading or invalid practices. Accounting "principles" were thought to be the business of accountants. Problems were met as they arose and resolved on technical accounting grounds. The attitude prevailed that even if accounting was not perfect or even very useful, it was the user's task to adapt.

The age of uniformity.   The age of uniformity began as "users of accounting reports came to realize that most of the figures were so hedged around with technicalities as to be incomprehensible."[3] The accounting profession developed a sense of mission. An answer seemed to be imposing uniform accounting standards. New issues like pooling of interest, investment tax credits, and comprehensive income tax allocation "did not involve outlawing something explicitly wrong but, in the interest of uniformity, opting for one or two or more potentially valid solutions."[4] Professional pronouncements were no longer received with passive acceptance. They were met with protest, noncompliance, and political lobbying. There were real confrontations. Corporations with millions at stake were unimpressed with arguments about "improved matching" or "consistency."

The age of inflation.   Inflation destroyed many of the hallowed premises and traditions of accounting. The financial problems of business were caught in a cost-tax-dividend squeeze and intensified dissatisfaction with exist-

---

[1] Athol S. Carrington, "Accounting Standards and the Profession—Seven Ages of Development," seminar address reprinted in *The Multinational Corporation: Accounting and Social Implications*, V. K. Zimmerman, ed. (Urbana, Ill.: University of Illinois, Center for International Education and Research in Accounting, 1977), pp. 41–46.

[2] Ibid., p. 42.

[3] Ibid.

[4] Ibid., p. 43.

ing accounting methods. Had effective inflation accounting methods been in place, the United States might never have subjected its petroleum companies to an excess profits tax in the late 1970s. Another interesting feature of this age of accounting development is the fact that it brought a return to intense accounting nationalism. Each country proposing inflation-related accounting responses came up with different technical approaches. This issue and its multifaceted ramifications are discussed in greater detail in Chapter 5.

The age of intervention. The age of intervention brought a shift of accounting standard setting and development away from the profession to regulatory or quasi-regulatory bodies. "The reaction of the profession to the actual intervention and to threats of more has been one of predictable concern and outrage."[5] In general, professional accountants "see governmental agencies as potentially bureaucratic, rigid, unresponsive to needs, and subject to self-interested lobbying."[6]

> Unfortunately, the track record of accountants to date does not prove very helpful in this age of intervention. The profession has been very slow to recognize or research the broad economic impact of its proposed standards. It seldom seems to have recognized ahead of time the unavoidably political nature of its decisions when there are conflict of interest situations involving contending groups. It seems to have been obsessed by the impossible dream of finding a set of accounting standards that will please everybody, meet all user requirements, and be objective, fair, relevant, and not too inconvenient for management or auditors.[7]

The age of integration. The age of integration is dawning at present. It is premised on a working relationship between the accounting profession and government to "enable accountants to play a more effective and unchallenged role as professional advisors and researchers, without usurping the political or judicial roles of government."[8] Integration in the sense used by Dean Carrington means high recognition of the public interest. During this developmental stage the profession would become the prime and most influential accounting advisor to government and to the public, but would not assume the role of imposing mandatory requirements in its own right. Parallels are drawn to the Institute of Automotive Engineers *not* imposing rules of permissible air pollution standards or enforcing gasoline rationing. "Even the American Medical Association would presumably stop short of seeking to impose a final verdict on the legitimacy of 'pot' or abortion on demand."[9]

The age of innovation. The age of innovation is a future period, after a substantial degree of integration has been achieved. Now accounting has been

[5] Ibid., p. 44.
[6] Ibid.
[7] Ibid., p. 45.
[8] Ibid.
[9] Ibid., p. 46.

freed from the burden of imposing requirements on reluctant parties. It can "devote its whole research potential and professional expertise to developing and evaluating new and improved methods of information generation and communication."[10]

In terms of these seven categories, financial accounting in general probably straddles the intervention-integration periods at present. At the same time, international accounting is probably still somewhere in the uniformity-inflation phases. Accounting within the European Economic Community (EEC) has recently moved to the intervention level, albeit cautiously.

Need for Conceptual Development

Living, as we do, in an age of high technology, widespread scientific reasoning, and a general belief in logic and analysis, it is understandable that over the years and decades significant resources have been devoted to theoretical accounting endeavors. Many books carry the term *accounting theory* in their respective titles. Many dissertations have been written on the subject and no issue has received more attention from the American Accounting Association than theory construction and verification. For reasons still unclear to even the most knowledgable observers of the phenomena involved, traditional accounting theory development has been unsuccessful by and large. Some observations on this topic follow later in the chapter.

Since accounting theory development has left the field wanting, a change of direction from "theorizing" to "conceptualizing" has evolved. Using composite definitions from several dictionaries,[11] we assert that *theory* is:

1. An integrated group of the fundamental principles underlying a science or its practical applications
2. Abstract knowledge of any art as opposed to the practice of it
3. A closely reasoned set of propositions derived from and supported by established evidence and intended to serve as an explanation for a group of phenomena
4. An arrangement of results or a body of theorems presenting a systematic view of some subject

On the other hand, a *concept* is a "mental image—especially a generalized idea formed by combining the elements of a class into the notion of one object." The activity involved in conceptualization is *conceptualism.* It is defined as:

The doctrine, intermediate between the extremes of nominalism and realism, that universals, or abstract characteristics, have no independent reality and exist only as ideas in the mind, or as traits embodied in particular things.[12]

[10] Ibid.

[11] Especially Funk and Wagnall's *Standard College Dictionary*, 1975 ed., s. v. "theory."

[12] Ibid., s. v. "conceptualism."

From a philosophy of science perspective then, conceptual development is less ambitious than theoretical development. Concepts are less abstract than theories. Conceptualism exists somewhere between stark realism on the one hand and remote nominalism on the other. For purposes of an endeavor like accounting, a conceptual approach to its development may be more useful than a theoretical approach.

In the United States the Financial Accounting Standards Board (FASB) considers forging *Statements of Financial Accounting Concepts* one of its highest priorities. The Organization for Economic Cooperation and Development (OECD) and other internationally concerned agencies lament the fact that an internationally usable conceptual framework of financial accounting is unavailable. They also express the view, time and time again, that such a framework would be highly desirable. Accounting academics in West Germany and Japan, for example, devote significantly more teaching resources to conceptual issues than to indoctrination of technical standards. Accounting research, when lacking firm conceptual grounds, becomes spurious, emotional, and often a disservice to society.

There is, presently, a great need for conceptualization efforts in international accounting. The nature of existing efforts, in terms of both approaches and methodologies, is sketched later on in this chapter.

Before proceeding, a few caveats are in order. First, a workable conceptual framework must extend beyond the establishment of broad international financial accounting standards. At best, international standardization or harmonization are small subareas within the field of international accounting. At worst, international harmonization is a complete pipedream. Professor Lee J. Seidler, of New York University and Bear Stearns & Co., observes that "Fortunately for the peripatetic savants of the international harmonization movement, there is little chance of achieving worldwide accounting uniformity. To the contrary, current trends seem to indicate that international accountants are doing little more than piddling into the wind."[13]

International accounting conceptualization also has little to offer those who want to build a worldwide control system to circumscribe the activities of multinational enterprises. The operations of multinational enterprises and their information and control needs are a conceptual issue in international accounting—the political economy elements of macro-level control are not.

Finally, we wish to establish at the outset that we know of no person, group, or organization seriously advocating or pursuing a theory of international accounting. Theory construction and verification has proven most elusive for accounting as a whole and therefore, at this time, is not an appropriate goal for a special field of the discipline. Conceptual work in international accounting is not aimed at somehow establishing a "new" accounting, an "umbrella" for the discipline, or a "redirection" of its basic thrust. International accounting conceptual premises are unlikely to change anything of a basic na-

---

[13] Lee J. Seidler, "Technical Issues in International Accounting," in *Multinational Accounting: A Research Framework for the Eighties*, Frederick D. S. Choi, ed. (Ann Arbor, MI: UMI Research Press, 1981), p. 40.

ture within the discipline. They are best seen as expansions of subject matter and extensions of traditional boundaries.

Status of Traditional Approaches

We intimated earlier in this chapter that financial accounting "theory" development is in the midst of significant change. Many a critical observer has become convinced that each individual academician and each individual practitioner has his or her own individually formulated accounting theory to work with. Professor Ahmed Belkaoui observes that the traditional approach to the formulation of accounting theory has used either a normative or a descriptive methodology, a theoretical or a nontheoretical approach, a deductive or an inductive line of reasoning, and has focused on a concept of "fairness," "social welfare," or "economic welfare." He concludes that "The traditional approach has evolved into an eclectic and political approach."[14]

Distillation of related factors.   Professor S. A. Zeff first demonstrated that *accounting principles development* does not come from specific scientific theory but from interactions among theory, practice, and various social, economic, and political influences.[15] Corollary to this major conclusion is Zeff's proposition (based on a substantial amount of research in the five countries concerned—Canada, England, Mexico, Scotland, and the United States) that the formulation of accounting principles cannot be achieved by an accounting profession alone but necessarily depends on the tacit or expressed support of the real "power centers" in an economy—for example, governmental agencies, industry associations, and investor groups and their representatives.

Zeff's book was published in 1971 and turned out to be as prophetic as it is penetrating. Literally all serious financial accounting conceptual development since that time has taken the interactive approach between theory, practice, and socioeconomic-political "power centers." A good example of this is the strategy adopted by the FASB in the United States. First, the FASB is forging financial accounting policies through a shared power system involving the Securities and Exchange Commission (SEC), the practicing profession, various groups of users of financial statements, and researchers. Second, the FASB sees itself as a participative, consensus-developing force rather than an authoritarian and/or disciplinarian unit. Third, the FASB has opted for conceptual development rather than strict theory construction. It has accorded this effort a high priority on its work schedules. Finally, the FASB has stayed clear of any single ideology in approaching its tasks. It has accommodated accrual concepts along with cash concepts, historical cost measurements along with current cost measurements, and so forth.

Developments in countries other than the United States are following

[14] Ahmed Belkaoui, *Accounting Theory* (New York: Harcourt Brace Jovanovich, Inc., 1981), p. 27.

[15] Stephen A. Zeff, *Forging Accounting Principles in Five Countries: A History and an Analysis of Trends* (Champaign, Ill.: Stipes Publishing Company, 1971).

somewhat similar patterns. Code law countries (e.g., West Germany, Japan, and the Netherlands) are increasingly involving practicing accountants and representatives of financial statements user groups in their financial accounting policy-making processes. On the other hand, case law countries (e.g., Australia, Canada, and the United Kingdom) are giving considerable recognition to political forces and the public interest in general.

Thus the traditional goal of constructing unequivocal and universal accounting theory and then directly deriving usable accounting standards and practices from such theory has been abandoned. Broad and often fuzzy conceptualization efforts are now the order of the day. Consensus making is now the watchword for those engaged in forging financial accounting standards on both national and international levels.

Research really has not helped much either. At the 1982 annual meeting of the American Accounting Association, Professor Robert E. Jensen explained some of the reasons why:

> Academic research tends to be highly rigorous in the realm of fantasy land. Economic theorists, for example, are experts at rigorous argument constructed upon assumptions of complete markets, costless and timeless communication, and equilibrium assumptions that exist only in the realm of fantasy. Behavioral experiments can be rigorous in terms of carefully controlled conditions far removed from real-world complexity and circumstance. The findings, accordingly, may have dubious validity and veracity in the real world.[16]

In attempts to overcome these shortcomings, more recent approaches to the formulation of accounting theory have, as Belkaoui has pointed out, utilized predictive approaches, behavioral approaches, and events approaches. Here is Belkaoui's conclusion regarding these efforts:

> The new approaches to the formulation of an accounting theory differ from the traditional approaches in terms of their novelty, their less general acceptance, and their reliance on verification. They present innovative and more empirically oriented methods of resolving accounting issues. The influence of the new approaches is manifested in the accounting literature of the last decade.
>
> Both the new and the traditional approaches to the formulation of an accounting theory may be perceived as emanating from different accounting paradigms competing in a period of crisis for the domination of accounting thought. It may be assumed that some of the approaches to the formulation of an accounting theory and their respective paradigms will likely be replaced in the future by other paradigms. The attempts for theoretical closure may lead to an "infinite regress" caused by continuous reappraisal of the nature and scope of the field of accounting.[17]

Notwithstanding the new approaches to the construction of financial accounting theory, breakthroughs or effective closure of the issue are unlikely at the present state of the art. Belkaoui's negative assessment is shared widely.

[16] Robert E. Jensen, "On the Validity and Veracity of International Accounting Research," paper presented at Annual Meeting of the American Accounting Association, San Diego, Calif., 1982, p. 3.

[17] Belkaoui, *Accounting Theory*, p. 56.

APPROACHES
TO CONCEPTUALIZATION

So far in this chapter we have looked at historical periods of accounting development and established that the present worldwide financial accounting environment can be characterized as one of "intervention." Standard setters everywhere are at work bending and twisting the technology of accounting toward a vast array of economic, legal, political, social, and other public or special interests.

We have also stated our view that accounting conceptualization is more important today than ever before. To reinforce this premise, the third lead-in to the topic of this chapter is a brief excursion through recent efforts to (1) synthesize existing accounting practices, (2) construct *usable* accounting theory or theories, and (3) develop theoretical frameworks for corporate direct foreign investments and/or the socioeconomic phenomenon of the multinational enterprise.

As observed in Chapter 1, international accounting has garnered a significant amount of attention from practitioners and public officials. Since its developmental needs are urgent and significant, there have been various efforts aimed at creating a conceptual framework for this new field. These efforts have not been categorized before, and only a few pieces of literature analyze and describe them. We have chosen to group the discernible approaches to international accounting conceptualization under five separate headings. This is a choice of convenience rather than rigorous definition.

Classification According
to Existing Practices

If we knew how existing accounting systems develop, why some systems dominate at one stage in history and later on others, and what the broad social and economic costs and benefits of a given system might be, we could begin to model desirable characteristics of theoretically defensible accounting systems. This would shed light on issues like convergence versus divergence of systems between comparable countries, selection of an appropriate accounting system for a developing country, or even international standard setting. But first existing practices must be analyzed and classified so that some descriptive hierarchies and morphologies can be constructed as an initial step toward later modeling and concept formulation.

The initial work on classifying existing accounting practices is traceable to Professor G. G. Mueller.[18] In a completely subjective and nonhierarchical manner, he asserted that ten different "sets" of accounting practices can be discerned. He related the ten groupings to the respectively different business environments in which they operate. Each set was reportedly different from all others in at least one important respect. The ten are as follows:

[18] Gerhard G. Mueller, "Accounting Principles Generally Accepted in the United States versus Those Generally Accepted Elsewhere," *International Journal of Accounting*, Spring 1968, pp. 91–103.

ever, it is closer to any of these than to French accounting, which is in a different "class" entirely. U.K. and Irish accounting are so similar that these individual systems could be said to be twins.[21]

The thoughtful work produced by Professor Nobes seems likely to have considerable influence on future conceptual developments in international accounting.

Another significant extension of this work occurred at the hands of Professors R. C. Da Costa, J. C. Bourgeois, and W. M. Lawson on the one hand and Professors W. G. Frank and R. D. Nair on the other. They, as well as other researchers, have applied factor analysis to arrive at statistically based "clusters" of existing accounting practices. The clustering studies utilize qualitative survey data on accounting principles and reporting practices prepared and published by Price Waterhouse International. At the time of this writing the PWI survey data are available in three editions—1973, 1975, and 1979.[22] The

TABLE 2.1   DaCosta-Bourgeois-Lawson Accounting Groups

GROUP I	GROUP II	UNCLASSIFIABLE
Japan	United Kingdom	Netherlands
Philippines	Eire	Canada
Mexico	Rhodesia	
Argentina	Singapore	
West Germany	South Africa	
Chile	Australia	
Bolivia	Jamaica	
Panama	Kenya	
Italy	New Zealand	
Peru	Fiji	
Venezuela		
Colombia		
Paraguay		
United States		
Pakistan		
Spain		
Switzerland		
Brazil		
France		
Uruguay		
Sweden		
India		
Ethiopia		
Belgium		
Trinidad		
Bahamas		

Source: DaCosta, Bourgeois, and Lawson, "Linkages," p. 79.

[21] Christopher Nobes and Robert Parker, eds., *Comparative International Accounting* (Homewood, Ill.: Richard D. Irwin, Inc., 1981), p. 212.

[22] Price Waterhouse International, *Accounting Principles and Reporting Practices—A Survey in 46 Countries* (London: PWI, 1973, 1975, 1979).

TABLE 2.2   Frank Accounting Groups

GROUP I	GROUP II	GROUP III	GROUP IV
Australia	Argentina	Belgium	Canada
Bahamas	Bolivia	Colombia	West Germany
Ethiopia	Brazil	France	Japan
Eire	Chile	Italy	Mexico
Fiji	India	Spain	Netherlands
Jamaica	Pakistan	Sweden	Panama
Kenya	Paraguay	Switzerland	Philippines
New Zealand	Peru	Venezuela	United States
Rhodesia	Uruguay		
Singapore			
South Africa			
Trinidad & Tobago			
United Kingdom			

Source: Frank, ''An Empirical Analysis,'' p. 596.

TABLE 2.3   Nair-Frank 1973 Measurement Groups

GROUP I	GROUP II	GROUP III	GROUP IV
Australia	Argentina	Belgium	Canada
Bahamas	Bolivia	France	Japan
Eire	Brazil	West Ger-	Mexico
Fiji	Chile	many	Panama
Jamaica	Columbia	Italy	Philippines
Kenya	Ethiopia	Spain	United States
Netherlands	India	Sweden	
New Zealand	Paraguay	Switzerland	
Pakistan	Peru	Venezuela	
Rhodesia	Uruguay		
Singapore			
South Africa			
Trinidad & Tobago			
United Kingdom			

Source: Nair and Frank, ''The Impact of Disclosure,'' p. 429.

effort by Da Costa, Bourgeois, and Lawson used the 1973 PWI data and came up with two distinct groupings of accounting practices, influenced by the United Kingdom and the United States as respective group leaders.[23] These accounting groups are shown in Table 2.1.

Professor W. G. Frank structured his analysis differently and derived four groups, as indicated in Table 2.2.[24]

[23] R. C. Da Costa, J. C. Bourgeois, and W. M. Lawson, "Linkages in the International Business Community: Accounting Evidence," *International Journal of Accounting*, Spring 1978, pp. 92–102.

[24] Werner G. Frank, "An Empirical Analysis of International Accounting Principles," *Journal of Accounting Research*, Autumn 1979, pp. 593–605.

TABLE 2.4   Nair-Frank 1973 Disclosure Groups

I	II	III	IV	V	VI	VII
Australia	Bolivia	Belgium	Canada	Argentina	Sweden	Switzer-
Bahamas	West Ger-	Brazil	Mexico	Chile		land
Fiji	many	Colombia	Netherlands	Ethiopia		
Jamaica	India	France	Panama	Uruguay		
Kenya	Japan	Italy	Philippines			
New Zea-	Pakistan	Paraguay	United			
land	Peru	Spain	States			
Eire		Venezuela				
Rhodesia						
Singapore						
South Africa						
Trinidad						
United						
Kingdom						

Source: Nair and Frank, "The Impact of Disclosure," p. 431.

TABLE 2.5   Nair-Frank 1975 Measurement Groups

GROUP I	GROUP II	GROUP III	GROUP IV	GROUP V
Australia	Argentina	Belgium	Bermuda	Chile
Bahamas	Bolivia	Denmark	Canada	
Fiji	Brazil	France	Japan	
Iran	Colombia	West Germany	Mexico	
Jamaica	Ethiopia	Norway	Philippines	
Malaysia	Greece	Sweden	United States	
Netherlands	India	Switzerland	Venezuela	
New Zealand	Italy	Zaire		
Nicaragua	Pakistan			
Eire	Panama			
Rhodesia	Paraguay			
Singapore	Peru			
South Africa	Spain			
Trinidad	Uruguay			
United				
Kingdom				

Source: Nair and Frank, "The Impact of Disclosure," p. 433.

Adding Professor R. D. Nair to the research team, Frank extended the study of the 1973 data base by breaking it into measurement groups and disclosure groups.[25] Quite understandably, different clustering was observed—not only between the respective measurement and disclosure patterns but also between the aggregate grouping and a segmented approach. Tables 2.3 and 2.4, respectively, report the measurement and the disclosure-based results.

[25] R. D. Nair and Werner G. Frank, "The Impact of Disclosure and Measurement Practices on International Accounting Classifications," *Accounting Review*, July 1980, pp. 426–50.

TABLE 2.6   Nair-Frank 1975 Disclosure Groups

I	II	III	IV	V	VI	VII
Belgium	Australia	Bahamas	Bermuda	Argentina	Denmark	Italy
Bolivia	Ethiopia	West Ger-	Canada	India	Norway	Switzer-
Brazil	Fiji	many	Jamaica	Iran	Sweden	land
Chile	Kenya	Japan	Netherlands	Pakistan		
Colombia	Malaysia	Mexico	Eire	Peru		
France	New Zea-	Panama	Rhodesia			
Greece	land	Philippines	United			
Paraguay	Nigeria	United	Kingdom			
Spain	Singapore	States				
Uruguay	South Africa	Venezuela				
Zaire	Trinidad					

Source: Nair and Frank, "The Impact of Disclosure," p. 436.

In the same article, the PWI survey data for 1975 is analyzed similarly and groupings established in terms of the factor analysis performed. Results for the 1975 data are shown in Tables 2.5 and 2.6.

The most recent published effort of the Nair and Frank team uses the cluster analysis methodology to examine whether there exists a discernible trend toward international harmonization among the 131 accounting practices common to the 1973, 1975 and 1979 PWI surveys of accounting and reporting practices around the world.[26] It found (1) a clear trend, between 1973 and 1979, of harmonization among accounting practices reported by the PWI survey; (2) "many of the topics on which the International Standards Committee has issued pronouncements are those on which the authors observe harmonization,"[27] and (3) "the accounting practices in the United States seem to serve as a model for this [international] harmonization process."[28] Thus we have an example of applied follow-up research to conceptually clustering, grouping or otherwise classifying existing accounting practices.

Empirical research, springing from the world of everyday, ongoing professional practice, is becoming a major avenue of international accounting conceptual development. Its limits are at once apparent when one weighs the results of earlier comparable efforts like *A Statement of Accounting Principles*[29] and *Inventory of Generally Accepted Accounting Principles for Business Enterprises.*[30] At the same time, these two U.S. studies were important precursors to the current FASB conceptual framework project which, in turn, is a definite

[26] R. D. Nair and Werner G. Frank, "The Harmonization of International Accounting Standards, 1973–1979," *International Journal of Accounting*, Fall 1981, pp. 61–77.

[27] Ibid., p. 77.

[28] Ibid.

[29] Thomas H. Sanders, Henry Rand Hatfield, and Underhill Moore, *A Statement of Accounting Principles* (New York: American Institute of Certified Public Accountants, 1938).

[30] Paul Grady, *Inventory of Generally Accepted Accounting Principles for Business Enterprises*, AICPA Accounting Research Study No. 7 (New York: American Institute of Certified Public Accountants, 1965).

link in the evolutionary chain of accounting concepts. Whatever the outcome in the international accounting field, critical study of its present practices is an important step toward conceptualization.

Linkages with Nonaccounting (External) Factors

Many observers have long proclaimed that accounting is influenced by its environment and, in turn, reciprocates that influence. In essence, this thesis holds that accounting innovation and development are triggered by nonaccounting factors. Auditing standards surfaced after major lawsuits against accountants, LIFO was spawned by inflationary conditions, and broad financial disclosures appear to be a consequence of broad public securities markets. It seems reasonable to assume that conceptual advances might be derived from different evaluations of various systems, conditions, or other factors that are thought to impinge international accounting. One line of inquiry in this respect was pioneered by Professor F. D. S. Choi, who postulated and then empirically tested this competitive disclosure hypothesis.[31] The hypothesis addressed the relationship between entry to nonregulated public securities markets and amount and quality of financial disclosure. Empirical findings suggested that disclosure increases appreciably up to the point of initial issue of a corporate equity or bond security in a large public securities market, and stabilizes thereafter. This type of analysis facilitates disclosure predictions, strategies regarding corporate earnings announcements at home and abroad, and possible new issue pricing.

The most elaborate, albeit somewhat disjointed, exposition and analysis of external effects upon international accounting development was undertaken by the 1975–1976 Committee on International Accounting Operations and Education of the American Accounting Association.[32] Over 68 pages of closely printed report text, the committee addressed its aim "to outline a methodology for the comparative study of accounting systems in an international context."[33] Many systems and subsystems were considered, and in the end a "morphology for comparative accounting systems" emerged. This morphology is reproduced in Table 2.7 to convey a flavor of not only the range of factors considered by that committee but also the structures postulated. (Note that *morphology* is "the study of the form and structure of plants and animals considered apart from function; also a particular theory or work dealing with this subject.")

The AAA Committee report has not spawned any follow-up because it is not an integrated single-logic and unity-of-methods type of report. Quite apparently, individual committee members wrote individual report sections with-

---

[31] Frederick D. S. Choi, "European Disclosure: The Competitive Disclosure Hypothesis," *Journal of International Business Studies*, Fall 1974, pp. 15–23.

[32] American Accounting Association, "Report of 1975–76 Committee on International Accounting."

[33] Ibid., p. 105.

TABLE 2.7 Morphology for Comparative Accounting Systems

STATES OF NATURE

PARAMETERS	1	2	3	4	5
P_1 — Political System	Traditional Oligarchy	Totalitarian Oligarchy	Modernizing Oligarchy	Tutelary Democracy	Political Democracy
P_2 — Economic System	Traditional	Market	Planned Market	Plan	
P_3 — Stages of Economic Development	Traditional Society	Pre-Take-off	Take-off	Drive to Maturity	Mass Consumption
P_4 — Objectives of Financial Reporting	Investment Decisions	Management Performance	Social Measurement	Sector Planning & Control	National Policy Objectives
	——————Micro——————			————Macro————	
P_5 — Source of, or Authority for, Standards	Executive Decree	Legislative Action	Government Administrative Unit	Public-Private Consortium	Private
P_6 — Education, Training, & Licensing	Informal	Formal	Informal	Formal	
	————Public————			————Private————	
P_7 — Enforcement of Ethics & Standards	Executive	Government Administrative	Judicial	Private	Private
P_8 — Client	Government	Public	Public	Enterprises	Private
	————Public————			————Private————	

Source: American Accounting Association, "Report of Committee on International Accounting Operations and Education 1975–1976," *The Accounting Review*, Vol. 52 (Supplement), 1977, p. 99.

out much integration between sections. Moreover, the report is heavily slanted toward the Third World (i.e., circumstances pertaining uniquely to developing countries). Still the report contains a wealth of ideas. It is *must* reading for anyone concerned with abstract research addressing conceptualization of international accounting.

The work of Dr. P. S. Goodrich fits the present category and is noteworthy.[34] His starting point is an effort similar to that of the "classification of existing practices" researchers. He employs a different statistical methodology and thus reaches slightly varied results. Five different groups of accounting practices are used, with the United States and the United Kingdom groupings being numerically the largest.

However, Goodrich does not stop here. He investigates political science groupings of countries developed by the same analytical methodology. He further draws on national groupings based on similarity of political attitudes and membership and voting records in international organizations. Then accounting groups are compared with the various political science groups.

> There would appear to be little significance between the derived accounting groups and socio-economic factors. . . . Furthermore, political attitudes as measured by United Nations voting do not seem to coincide with the accounting groups. However, political factors, like political system types and international organizational membership, are significantly linked to the accounting groups.[35]

Table 2.8 reports the Goodrich linkages in summary form.

Notwithstanding the appeal of the more quantitative scenarios just identified, we would like to conclude with a list of environmental factors that we believe to have direct effects upon accounting development.

1. *Legal System.* Codification of accounting standards and procedures appears natural and appropriate in Roman or code law countries. By contrast, the nonlegalistic establishment of accounting policies by professional organizations working in the private sector of an economy is more in keeping with the system prevailing in common law countries. Under martial law or other na-

TABLE 2.8   Goodrich's Linkages between Accounting Groups and Political Systems

GROUPS	CHI-SQUARE	SIGNIFICANCE	CRAMER'S V
Political systems	30.2	.02	.37
Socioeconomic factors	10.0	.26	.32
Political attitudes	16.2	.18	.34
International organizations	37.0	.01	.43

Source: Goodrich, "Accounting and Political Systems," p. 24.

[34] Peter S. Goodrich, "Accounting and Political Systems," Discussion Paper No. 109 (School of Economic Studies, University of Leeds, U.K., 1982, mimeographed).

[35] Ibid., pp. 24–25.

tional emergency situations, all aspects of the accounting function may be regulated by some central governmental court or agency. This was the case, for instance, in Nazi Germany when intensive war preparations and later World War II itself required a highly uniform national accounting system for purposes of total control of all national economic activities.

2. *Political System.* It seems almost self-evident that an accounting system that is useful to a centrally controlled economy must be different from an accounting system that is optimal for a market-oriented economy. In the former, the state owns all fixed assets and land; there is very little or no private ownership of business equities; "outside" auditors are simply government employees from another government agency; and the concept of periodic profit determination makes no sense.

Of course, political systems also export and import accounting standards and practices. For instance, British accounting, as it existed at the turn of the twentieth century, was exported in large measure to other Commonwealth countries. As mentioned in Chapter 1, the Dutch did the same with the Philippines and the French with their possessions in Africa and Asia. The Germans used political sympathy to influence accounting in Japan and Sweden, among others. Modern-day political systems have even larger impacts upon accounting.

3. *Nature of Business Ownership.* Widespread public ownership of corporate securities suggests financial reporting and disclosure principles different from those applicable to predominantly family- or bank-owned corporate interests. For instance, the huge public interest in corporate securities in the United States has produced many so-called "sunshine" accounting standards of wide open disclosure, whereas the virtual absence of public participation in corporate equities ownership in France has limited effective financial communications there largely to "insider" communication channels. Heavy bank ownership of corporate equities in West Germany produces still different accounting responses. In the United States, the American Institute of Certified Public Accountants (AICPA) made special recommendations for particular financial accounting standards and practices to be used by smaller, closely held enterprises.

4. *Differences in Size and Complexity of Business Firms.* Self-insurance may be acceptable for a very large firm but not for a small firm. Similarly, a large firm mounting an extensive advertising campaign directed at a specific market or season may be justified in deferring part of the resultant expenditure, whereas smaller programs in smaller firms may need to be expensed directly. This dichotomy extends over the entire range of parent company–subsidiary company accounting and specific technical problems like research and development expenditures or restructuring of long-term debt.

The complexity argument is equally applicable. Large conglomerate enterprises operating in significantly different lines of business need financial reporting techniques different from those for a small firm producing a single product. Similarly, multinational enterprises need accounting systems different from those for strictly domestic firms. Product testing (and accounting for it) is a different matter for a worldwide pharmaceutical firm than it is for a local firm producing only oil additives in a provincial capital in Mexico.

5. *Social Climate.* Developments in the United States point toward public reporting and examination by independent auditors of efforts to discharge corporate social responsibility by individual enterprises. There is also public reporting of both foreign and domestic corporate (possibly illegal) payoffs. "Consumerism," as it is called, is beginning to produce accounting changes.

In contrast, the social climate in Switzerland is still much more conservative and therefore demands considerably less financial disclosure by large Swiss companies. Italians still play tax games and hence are suspicious of anything and everything having to do with accounting. In some Eastern and South American countries, accounting is equated with bookkeeping and regarded as socially disagreeable—remaining underdeveloped and largely ineffective.

6. *Level of Sophistication of Business Management and the Financial Community.* Highly refined accounting standards and practices have no place in an environment where they are misunderstood and misused. A complex technical report on cost behavior variances is meaningless unless the reader understands cost accounting well. Statements of changes in financial position are useless unless they can be read competently. Capitalization of leases, consolidation of foreign subsidiaries, separate parent company financial statements, or financial forecasts are all counterproductive accounting techniques in the hands of the unsophisticated.

7. *Degree of Legislative Business Interference.* Tax legislation may require the application of certain accounting principles. This is the case in Sweden where certain tax allowances must be entered into the accounts before they can be claimed for tax purposes; this is also the situation for LIFO inventory valuations in the United States (which the U.S. Treasury Department attempted to extend to all foreign subsidiaries of domestic parent companies). Varying social security laws also affect accounting standards. Severance pay requirements in several South American countries are one illustration of this effect. Pension accounting in the United States is another.

8. *Presence of Specific Accounting Legislation.* In some instances there are specific legislative provisions for certain accounting rules and techniques. In the United States, the SEC prescribes accounting and disclosure standards for larger companies, but it does so by relying heavily on the authoritative and private sector Financial Accounting Standards Board (see SEC Accounting Series Release No. 150).

In most other countries of the Western world, local companies acts contain accounting provisions that are binding upon the accounting profession and business firms. So-called royal commissions propose changes to companies acts in the United Kingdom. Hence new accounting provisions emanating from successive British companies acts come essentially from the private sector. In West Germany, on the other hand, companies legislation is predominantly a political process and therefore any accounting changes promulgated through such legislation are determined largely in the political arena. These different *systems* naturally have different consequences for accounting development.

9.   *Speed of Business Innovations.* Business combinations became popular in Europe only a few years ago. Before that, European countries had little need for accounting standards and practices relating to mergers and acquisitions of going concerns. Very small stock distributions (so-called "stock dividends") occur most generally in the United States. Again, this is a business innovation that has directly affected U.S. accounting. Examples of this type abound. For instance, equipment leasing is not practiced at all in a number of countries, and consequently there is simply no need for lease accounting standards in those situations.

10.   *Stage of Economic Development.* A one-crop agricultural economy needs accounting principles different from those of a sophisticated, industrialized country. In the former, for example, there is probably relatively little dependence on credit and long-term business contracts. Thus sophisticated accrual accounting is out of place, and basic cash accounting is needed.

11.   *Growth Pattern of an Economy.* Companies and industries seem to grow, stabilize, or decline. The same applies to national economies and other organized forms of human endeavor. If growth and expansion are typical, the capitalization of certain deferred charges is more feasible than in stable or declining conditions. Stable conditions intensify competition for existing markets and thus require more restrictive credit and inventory methods. Declining conditions may dictate write-offs and adjustments not warranted in other situations. Protracted civil war (as in Ireland or Lebanon) may dictate accounting patterns quite different from those prevailing in politically stable environments.

12.   *Status of Professional Education and Organization.* In the absence of organized accounting professionalism and native sources of accounting authority, standards from other areas or countries are likely to be utilized in filling existing voids. Adaptation of accounting factors from Great Britain was a significant environmental influence in accounting the world over until about the end of World War II. Since that time international adaptive processes have relied more on U.S. sources. Native or adapted, accounting development is unlikely to succeed unless environmental circumstances such as those enumerated in the present list are fully considered.

Many have speculated that the external linkages of accounting are the key to effective concept building. As just one example, consider the following observation of Professor Natwar M. Gandhi:

> Even in a postindustrial society the basic accounting functions of measurement and communication do not change. What does change, and change radically, is the content of those functions and the environment in which they are to be performed. The new content—the information to be measured and communicated—and the new environment are no longer responsive to the traditional ac-

counting tools of measurement and communication. In sum, this is the heart of the accounting crisis.[36]

To an important extent, many concepts in the social sciences are premised on or derived from environmental analysis. It stands to reason that international accounting will not become a glaring exception.

COMPARATIVE DEVELOPMENT PATTERNS

Developmental concepts are found in most fields of study. Among many others, we broadly recognize economic development, organizational development, early childhood development, and human emotional development. Accounting is no exception. There are at least four distinct approaches to accounting development that can be observed among Western nations with market-oriented economic systems. These four approaches, or patterns, of accounting development are:

1. The macroeconomic pattern
2. The microeconomic pattern
3. The independent discipline approach
4. The uniform accounting approach

The concepts underlying these developmental patterns were first put into an internationally comparative context by Professor G. G. Mueller.[37] We offer them here as still another approach to international accounting conceptualization.

Macroeconomic Pattern

If the mass of research and writing in business and economics were reduced to two central propositions, we would probably find that (1) individual firms establish formal and informal goals and then gear their operations toward optimizing these goals and (2) nations establish formal and informal national policies and then adopt administrative procedures toward optimal implementation of these policies. Firm goals and national policies are not always clearly defined, and they are often perceived differently by different individuals or groups. Yet that does not invalidate the assertion that such goals and policies exist and that they become guides to actions for the organization concerned.

Business firm goals are necessarily narrower than national economic policy. A firm has more specific purposes to accomplish, often operates in more

[36] Natwar M. Gandhi, "The Emergence of the Postindustrial Society and the Future of the Accounting Function," *International Journal of Accounting*, Spring 1976, p. 48.

[37] Gerhard G. Mueller, *International Accounting* (New York: Macmillan Company, 1967).

circumscribed space and time dimensions, and is accountable to more identifiable interest groups. As a consequence, firm goals normally follow rather than lead national economic policies. This is not an absolute condition since business firms are a part of the public interest that influences and directs national policies; hence, reciprocal cause-and-effect relationships exist.

If the foregoing views of a developed economic environment are accepted, the following three propositions might be postulated:

1. The business enterprise is the essential unit in the economic fabric of a nation.
2. The business enterprise accomplishes its goals best through close coordination of its activities with the national economic policies of its environment.
3. Public interest is served best if business enterprise accounting interrelates closely with national economic policies.

What are the accounting implications of such a formulation? Let us postulate, for example, a policy of relatively full employment. This implies, above all, sustained efforts toward economic and business stability. It also means administrative efforts to minimize effects of business cycles or, better yet, avoidance of pronounced swings in business cycles altogether. Accounting could be adapted to such a policy through, for example, requiring some averaging of reported business income for the firm over the length of the typical business cycle.

Another national policy might be the achievement of a predetermined rate of economic growth. Here accounting might adjust its depreciation and amortization procedures with regard to firms or industries that are most likely to be significant contributors to the rate of economic growth in a given period. Moreover, accounting might incorporate the measurements on a firm's contributions to gross national product or on changes in rates of productivity. For example, an accounting system could readily encompass information on percentages of utilization of resources. Expressed differently, accounting could measure the waste of resources.

Many of our newer accounting concerns appear to fit into the macroeconomic pattern of accounting development. Accounting for corporate social responsibilities and reporting and auditing the "social conscience" of a firm clearly fits the picture. So does accounting for human resources. Even the public interest, that is, "consumerism," concerned with corporate payoffs for illegal purposes, contributions of corporate funds to charitable organizations, and disclosure responsibilities to the public at large rather than to existing and prospective shareholders only are manifestations of macroeconomically oriented developments.

Periodic income smoothing, as found in Europe and South America, is one application of the macroeconomic pattern. West German income statements, which report as revenues amounts realized from the sale of goods and services plus amounts of value created by a firm's construction or development of assets intended for its own use plus amounts of value added to inventories of goods and materials, are another.

Macroeconomically oriented financial accounting might formally recognize discovery values of mineral or oil deposits, might compute depreciation charges on productive equipment on a unit of production basis wherever possible, and might permit fast write-off of certain costs when this would be in the interest of regional or national economic development. In the past, such write-offs have aided the Scandinavian shipbuilding industry, construction of employer-owned dwellings for employees in West Germany and France, and capital expenditures for defense purposes in the United States during World War II under certificates of necessity. The country in which the macroeconomic development pattern of accounting has found the relatively most comprehensive acceptance is Sweden. In this connection, the accounting procedures surrounding Swedish capital investment reserves are of special interest.

The Microeconomic Approach

Market-oriented economies, including those with some degree of central government administrative interference, entrust much of their economic well-being to the business activities of individuals and of individual business firms. Therefore, in these economies, a fundamental orientation exists to the individual cells of economic activity. This is so deeply ingrained in Western economic organizations that it is simply assumed for many business, judicial, legislative, and social processes.

The intellectual part of economics reflects this orientation as well. The tradition of Western economic thought is overwhelmingly a tradition of microeconomic thought. To be sure, more recent decades have seen a broadening of economics into areas such as social economics, national income models, econometrics, and economic forecasting. These specialty areas are not, however, the foundation of the economics discipline in Western culture. They are an outgrowth of it. The traditional elements of Western economic thinking come from the band of great political economists and economic philosophers among whom we find Hume, Locke, Marshall, Mill, Ricardo, and Smith. Their oratory and writings have shaped much of what remains fundamental in economics to this day.

With private and business activities at the core of the economic affairs in a market-oriented economy and with accounting oriented to a service function for business and business enterprises, it seems natural enough that accounting would seek to orient itself to the same micro considerations that are so strongly represented in its environment. In fact, in many European universities, accounting is typically considered as a tool area of microeconomics.

Several propositions can again be postulated using a microeconomic framework for accounting:

1. Individual firms provide focal points for business activities.
2. The main policy of the business firm is to ensure its continued existence.
3. Optimization in an economic sense is a firm's best policy for survival.
4. Accounting, as a branch of business economics, derives its concepts and applications from economic analysis.

The central accounting concept in a development pattern based on microeconomics is that the accounting process must hold constant in real terms the amount of monetary capital invested in the firm. This is essential on three counts: (1) The continued survival of the firm is impossible if its real capital base is eroded away by tax or dividend payments that fully or in part invade the real investment capital base; (2) the permanently invested capital is the economic root of the firm and, therefore, the capital investment in the firm must receive key considerations as long as the firm itself is the focal point of business activities; and (3) an effective separation of capital and income is prerequisite to evaluating and controlling the firm's business activities.

Most advocates of the microeconomic approach to accounting conclude that an accounting measurement system based on replacement costs fits microeconomic concepts best. A brief illustration of the replacement cost measurement idea is provided in Chapter 5. Under this approach, monetary amounts needed to maintain invested capital in real terms are not considered a part of periodic accounting income. Vice versa, changes in replacement costs are a part of accounting income to the extent that they are not needed for required capital investment adjustments. A full set of operational accounting standards and principles has been developed along this line—for instance, by several multinational enterprises based in Holland.

When microeconomics plays a heavy role in accounting considerations, a general managerial emphasis prevails in *all* accounting reports, including those issued to shareholders annually *and* quarterly. Segmented reporting (by product lines, market areas, or international sectors) for revenues, gross business assets, and other important financial indicators is one logical consequence. Others would be accounting reports detailing compositions of wages and other production costs, giving a fair airing to internal enterprise affairs in categories like pension schemes, listings of firms' securities on different stock exchanges, long-term commitments not yet accountable, and so forth. Accounting, as advocated and practiced in the Netherlands, represents the most comprehensive example of the microeconomic pattern of accounting development.

Independent Discipline

History has not accorded much glamour to business people. Scholars have scorned business studies as void of theoretical complexity and as too commonplace for intellectual pursuits. The moneychangers of the Bible were little more than outcasts of society. While artisans and craftsmen (often through their respective guilds) flourished during the Middle Ages, merchants were seldom able to improve their lowly social status. Even in the early decades of the present century, businessmen found relatively little sympathy for their skills and abilities. Today they are implicated as wasters of social resources, polluters of the environment, and unethical payers of bribes and kickbacks. The chronicles of business are filled with Scrooges and slave traders—people of great greed and little social distinction. The perpetration of spectacular financial swindles only added coals to smouldering fires of public wrath.

Reflecting upon this historical background, there is little wonder that business has become introspective. It has turned primarily to itself for analysis and innovation. Good business practices have become identified with those practices that are profitable and effective in generating more business. A deep-seated respect for pragmatism developed.

Factors of judgment and estimate cannot be eliminated from business processes. Business deals significantly with human want satisfactions whose origins and patterns are forever changing. From the inception of producing a product or a service to its final sale to an actual user, a very complex fabric of human emotions and reactions must be accommodated. Add to this the ever-present condition of uncertainty, and the significance of business judgment becomes all too apparent.

Thus business people have learned to use intuition. They find and use signs of changes that are not evident to the inexperienced. The trial and error method is often the only avenue open to them, and they manage to use it with facility and expediency. The ability to make sound business judgments often is the most important attribute of a successful business person.

Earlier discussions in this chapter suggested a direct interrelationship between accounting and its environment. If business is the main interest served by accounting and if accounting provides primarily an efficient and effective service to business, the inevitable question is, Should not accounting and business practices have the same basis and follow the same pattern of development? If the answer to this question is affirmative, a case is made for regarding accounting as an independent discipline. If business can produce its own concepts and methods from experience and practice, the argument follows that accounting can (or should) do the same. If business can develop itself from within, why should accounting not be capable of doing the same?

Viewing accounting as a service function of business provides ample room for concluding that accounting can construct for itself a meaningful framework derived essentially from the business processes it serves. When this is held possible, conceptual support from a discipline like economics is not needed. Accounting, in other words, relies on itself—it becomes an independent discipline.

Regarding accounting as an independent discipline with roots in the practical affairs of everyday business implies, first of all, that a cohesive and complete conceptual structure of accounting is difficult to erect. In the United States, for example, we have struggled through the 1938 Sanders, Hatfield, and Moore study and the long and arduous efforts of both the AICPA's Committee on Accounting Procedure and Accounting Principles Board without much success in this respect. At present, the Financial Accounting Standards Board is trying its luck with its conceptual framework project.

A second point is that the piecemeal approach to evolving and establishing accounting standards is the only possible avenue of approach in the absence of a comprehensive conceptual framework for the discipline. Under the independent discipline philosophy, each individual accounting standard or principle has to meet the conditions of practical business usefulness and therefore has to reach back to related and proved business practices. Interrelationships and consistency among various accounting standards and principles are of only secondary importance under this approach because the general business community does not seem greatly concerned about the intellectual niceties of a single conceptual structure.

A strictly conventional definition of business income is yet another hallmark of this particular approach to accounting development. *Income* here is simply a defined quantity that seems useful in practice. Even though "constructed" pragmatically, this income notion enjoys wide acceptance and has found its way into business literature, accounting textbooks and handbooks, and even legal cases and positions. It is a significant illustration of a pragmatic response to the practical needs of the business communities affected.

Full and fair disclosure in published financial reports has developed over the years into one of the more important standards of accounting within an independent discipline development pattern. One might go so far as to say that the full and fair disclosure tenet might be seen as a substitute for a comprehensive conceptual framework under this approach.

The United Kingdom and the United States are comprehensive examples of countries in which accounting has developed as an independent discipline.

Uniform Accounting

Accounting development based on a pattern of uniformity in accounting has long intrigued scholars and others concerned with accounting information. Most important in this regard is probably the long quest to make accounting more scientific. At a time when society broadly seems to rely more and more upon the application of the scientific method for many of its undertakings, it is not difficult to find supporters for the proposition that accounting should conform to this trend and also become more scientific. In the views of many, more uniform accounting means more scientific accounting.

A second reason why the uniformity pattern of accounting development holds much appeal is the *cameralistic* aspect of accounting—as the phrase is used in Europe. *Cameralistic* can be translated roughly to mean that something is an ideal administrative device. Thus, when used in the accounting sense, it can be employed to control a small, one-person business as well as a giant government apparatus. In government, in particular, it can become the central tool of administration. Accounting procedures can allocate funds to functions, measure performance by assuming proportionality between administrative effectiveness and fund changes, classify functions in terms of monetary rewards and vice versa, and perform other similar functions.

Beyond administrative convenience, however, accounting also presents itself as a tool for economic and business control by government. This was suggested earlier in the chapter and is clearly demonstrated in totalitarian regimes like Nazi Germany or several present-day communist countries. As mentioned previously, centrally directed economies plan, administer, control, and reward many facets of their societies on the basis of accounting information. But they can do this only if accounting is as uniform as their systems are absolute.

A third major appeal of accounting uniformity lies in the simplicity it affords. Uniformity is a pattern that is very simple on most counts—recording and classifying financial data, manipulating the data toward financial reports, and finally understanding and interpreting financial reports. For example, the French plan of accounts provides instruction for the recording of the simplest of all transactions as well as a completely detailed prenumbered chart of accounts. *Alternative* financial accounting principles is something such a system does not know!

Most tax accounting systems are uniform accounting systems. Thus a uniform system for financial accounting often holds advantages for the corresponding tax accounting system.

Three practical approaches to the uniform accounting development pattern can be distinguished. Each is identified in the paragraphs immediately following.

Business approach.   In the business approach accounting uniformity is oriented specifically to particular users of accounting data. This approach takes full account of the business characteristics and the business environment under which the data are collected, processed, and communicated. It is a pragmatic approach that relies heavily on convention and is employed most frequently in the design of sectional uniform charts of accounts, that is, for a branch of industry or trade. Railroad or utilities companies' accounting in the United States falls into this category by reason of the governmental regulations to which it is subject. The Swedish "M-Chart" is another example. It is a blueprint for a comprehensive accounting system for Swedish companies in the metalworking industries prepared by the industry association in question.

Economic approach.   The economic approach to accounting uniformity is in essence a macro approach. It links accounting to public policy. Public laws and regulatory agencies are used to enforce the system established within such a pattern of development. Technical accounting considerations are secondary, and national economic policy considerations uppermost. H. W. Singer sketches this approach as it was utilized in Nazi Germany between 1937 and 1945.

> The new aims of the German economy call for increased output and efficiency from business undertakings. The fulfillment of this great task requires a thorough knowledge and close control of all business transactions. Thus a well-developed accounting system is a primary factor in the reorganization of industries. The public interest, and in particular the aims of the four-year plan, demand that the accounting system of all firms should be arranged on uniform principles. Systematic mutual exchange of experience, especially in the form of comparative analysis of companies, will help toward this end (from the 1937 Nazi regime decree which made uniform accounting mandatory in Germany.)[38]

[38] Hans W. Singer, *Standardized Accountancy in Germany* (Cambridge: Cambridge University Press, 1944), p. 15. Parenthesis added.

Technical approach.   The technical accounting approach to uniformity development is by and large the work of academics. This approach is *analytical* in that it attempts to derive uniformity schemes from the basic tenets of
double entry bookkeeping. It is also a *general* approach because direct attention is paid to specific business characteristics of accounting transactions or accounting processes. Finally, the broad orientation of this approach is *theoretical*
in nature. For example, it seeks to establish linkages between accounts of the
same type so that they can be treated consistently within the overall framework
of a particular scheme (i.e., to group accounts by functions or by substance but
not indiscriminately). European professors identified with generalizing accounting processes from comprehensive flow charts of accounts include K.
Käfer (Switzerland), L. L. Illetschko (Austria), E. Schmalenbach (West Germany), and A. ter Vehn (Sweden). France, without doubt, is the country most
identified with the uniformity pattern of accounting development.

The appeal of the comparative developmental approach lies in its *deductive* nature. Classification of practices is *inductive*. Factor analysis (i.e., the
study of linkages) usually combines the two approaches and seeks verification
by way of empiricism. To date, all three approaches have contributed substantially to conceptual developments in international accounting. None can be
said to be superior to the others. They are likely to continue side by side for
some time to come.

For the sake of completeness, we now sketch briefly two additional
modes of international accounting conceptualization. They are less developed
and in some ways speculative. Nonetheless they appear to hold promise and
are thus worthy of attention.

Intrinsic Premises and Variables
of Accounting

Born of the pressures already alluded to, the FASB in the United States
has been embarked on a major effort to construct a conceptual framework for
financial accounting since the organization's very beginning in 1973. In terms
of linkages, the project seeks to relate financial accounting standard-setting to
environmental forces. Mr. Donald J. Kirk, Chairman of the FASB, commented
early in 1982, "We live in an uncertain world—an economic world that has
changed faster than the concepts of accounting that attempt to reflect that
world. It is that changing world that has regularly required standard setters to
relook at recurring issues such as leasing, business combinations, foreign currency translation, and pension accounting."[39]

The conceptual framework project also utilizes the specific premise of accounting as an independent discipline. Internal or intrinsic (i.e., "belonging to
or arising from the true or fundamental nature of a thing; essential; inherent")
factors of accounting are ordered in hierarchical and horizontally related fash-

---

[39] Donald J. Kirk, "The FASB's Role in a Changing World," speech quoted in *The
Week in Review* (Deloitte Haskins & Sells), May 14, 1982, p. 2.

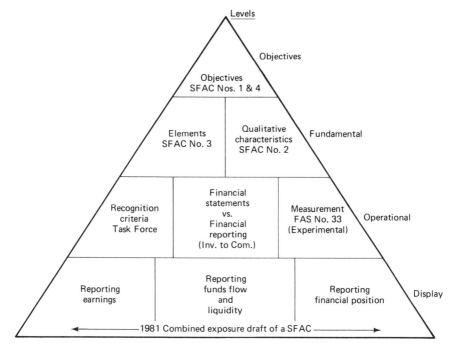

FIGURE 2.2   Norby's Model of the FASB's Conceptual Framework for Financial Accounting and Reporting

Source: William C. Norby, ''Accounting for Financial Analysis,'' *Financial Analysts Journal,* March–April 1982, p. 22.

ion in an attempt to evolve an internally consistent and comprehensive structure for all aspects of the financial accounting discipline. William C. Norby modeled the entire framework project into a pyramid of interrelationships. Since it provides a useful and concise overview, his model is reproduced in Figure 2.2.

There are two key dimensions to any endeavor aimed at concept construction from within—the qualitative characteristics of the variables identified and an enumeration of these variables. This is the second tier labeled "Fundamental" in Figure 2.2. Respectively, the FASB has addressed these two dimensions in its Statements of Financial Accounting Concepts (SFAC) Nos. 2 and 3, both published in 1980. Figure 2.3 shows the FASB's hierarchy of accounting qualities.

A list of the internal accounting variables to be encompassed by the conceptual framework is developed and discussed in SFAC No. 3. The FASB identifies these items as "Elements of Financial Statements." The ten interrelated elements identified are as follows:

Assets are probable future economic benefits obtained or controlled by a particular entity as a result of past transactions or events.

Liabilities are probable future sacrifices of economic benefits arising from present

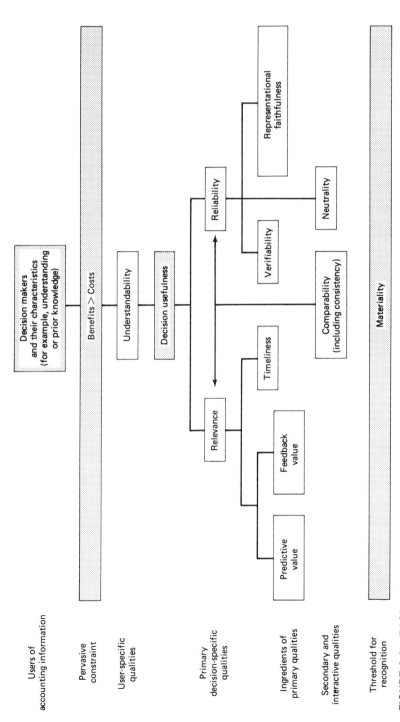

FIGURE 2.3   FASB's Hierarchy of Accounting Qualities

Source: Financial Accounting Standards Board, *Statement of Financial Accounting Concepts No. 2* (Stamford, Conn.: FASB, 1980), p. 15.

obligations of a particular entity to transfer assets or provide services to other entities in the future as a result of past transactions or events.

Equity is the residual interest in the assets of an entity that remains after deducting its liabilities. In a business enterprise, the equity is the ownership interest.

Investments by owners are increases in net assets of a particular enterprise resulting from transfers to it from other entities of something of value to obtain or increase ownership interests (or equity) in it. Assets are most commonly received as investments by owners, but that which is received may also include services or satisfaction or conversion of liabilities of the enterprise.

Distributions to owners are decreases in net assets of a particular enterprise resulting from transfering assets, rendering services, or incurring liabilities by the enterprise to owners. Distributions to owners decrease ownership interests (or equity) in an enterprise.

Comprehensive income is the change in equity (net assets) of an entity during a period from transactions and other events and circumstances from nonowner sources. It includes all changes in equity during a period except those resulting from investments by owners and distributions to owners.

Revenues are inflows or other enhancements of assets of an entity or settlements of its liabilities (or a combination of both) during a period from delivering or producing goods, rendering services, or other activities that constitute the entity's ongoing major or central operations.

Expenses are outflows or other using up of assets or incurrences of liabilities (or a combination of both) during a period from delivering or producing goods, rendering services, or carrying out other activities that constitute the entity's ongoing major or central operations.

Gains are increases in equity (net assets) from peripheral or incidental transactions of an entity and from all other transactions and other events and circumstances affecting the entity during a period except those that result from revenues or investments by owners.

Losses are decreases in equity (net assets) from peripheral or incidental transactions of an entity and from all other transactions and other events and circumstances affecting the entity during a period except those that result from expenses or distributions to owners.[40]

It is fair to say that the FASB's conceptual framework project has made considerable progress over the last ten years and appears destined to continue this progress. This suggests, in turn, that the international accounting subarea of the discipline might benefit from similar conceptual development by extending the boundaries of the framework from the domestic U.S. environment to the international environment. Alternatively, international accounting characteristics and variables might eventually be built into the FASB's framework directly.

On the latter point a caveat is in order. In 1980 Professor Edward Stamp produced a research study for the Canadian Institute of Chartered Accountants entitled *Corporate Reporting: Its Future Evolution.* In an article describing his own study, Stamp makes the following observation:

[40] Copyright by Financial Accounting Standards Board, High Ridge Park, Stamford, Connecticut, 06905, U.S.A. Reprinted with permission. Copies of the complete document are available from the FASB.

The research study presents a strong argument, however, that, although the FASB approach may be appropriate for the needs of the United States, it is not suitable for Canada. The American approach depends too much on normative, axiomatic and even authoritarian prescriptions, and it is also too narrow in its scope, since it is confined largely to the needs of investors. In fact, the FASB's stated primary concern is with the needs of investors, whereas in Canada . . . it would seem appropriate to acknowledge the interest of a much wider group of users.[41]

Professor Stamp leaves little doubt that he is of the opinion that the Canadians need a different financial accounting conceptual framework from that being developed in the United States. This may or may not be the case. For international accounting purposes, though, it is quite clear that the FASB's framework will not serve financial accounting in all other nations unless it is significantly adapted to local objectives and circumstances. In summary, the FASB's *approach* to conceptualization might prove useful to international accounting. The direct use of the FASB's conceptual product in other countries or regions is likely to turn into failure and frustration.

Another "model" is suggested by Professor Klaus Macharzina in his description of financial reporting in West Germany. In order to understand the West German financial reporting system, he urges consideration of "the variables connected with the goals, means, context and efficiency of accounting:

Goal variables include reporting objectives.

Means variables represent the variety of accounting methods and the reporting instruments.

Contextual variables describe the accounting environment, including the rule-making bodies.

Efficiency variables measure the quality of accounting information and the level of disclosure in terms of the objectives.[42]

The variables identified by Professor Macharzina are internal or intrinsic accounting factors similar to those used within the FASB's conceptual framework. Since the former are deemed to be useful in understanding the structure of West German financial reporting, they should also hold promise for a corresponding conceptual framework. While such a framework may end up with hierarchies and horizontal interrelationships that differ in number, sensitivity, and definition, the overall result should be comparable to the U.S. effort. If several country-specific conceptual frameworks could be developed and applied to ongoing accounting practices, comparative conceptual studies would emerge. In turn, the cause of international accounting conceptualization would benefit, since the intrinsic accounting variables triggering international conceptual differences would be highlighted.

---

[41] Edward Stamp, "Accounting Standard Setting . . . A New Beginning: Evolution, Not Revolution," CA *Magazine*, September 1980, p. 41.

[42] Klaus Macharzina, "Financial Reporting in West Germany," in *Comparative International Accounting*, Nobes and Parker, eds., 1981, p. 124.

Innovation through Multinational Corporations (MNCs)

In Chapter 12 the question of international accounting standard setting is discussed in terms of the growing number of international agencies and organizations presently engaged in this endeavor. Most observers feel that, for the time being, comprehensive international harmonization of accounting measurements and financial disclosure is highly remote. Nonetheless, the desirability of greater worldwide accounting harmonization is widely acknowledged. The International Accounting Standards Committee (IASC) has embarked upon a course that seeks to harmonize accounting among all countries and all companies. It has adopted a global village philosophy for all of accounting.

Other opinion, including that of the authors, favors the less ambitious goal of seeking accounting standardization for MNCs as a first step. Professors S. J. Gray and J. C. Shaw along with L. B. McSweeney reached the following conclusion: "Perhaps there is a case for standards applicable to MNCs only, as opposed to all large companies worldwide, at least in the short term."[43]

George C. Watt, R. M. Hammer, and M. Burge reached a similar conclusion.[44] They support the idea that MNCs should prepare primary financial statements, expressed in terms of the accounting and reporting standards and the currency of the country in which the MNC is domiciled. Concurrently, though, secondary financial statements should be prepared for use in another country or countries. Secondary financial statements may well be based on international accounting standards specifically developed for MNC use. Professors G. G. Mueller and L. M. Walker commented that "We foresee a period during the building of a set of international accounting standards when primary/secondary financial statements recommended by the Accountants International Study Group might be the best solution available."[45]

If, indeed, a body of financial accounting standards were to evolve for specific MNC purposes, these enterprises would be thrust into an accounting innovation role of major proportions. Since their very existence depends upon organizational, economic, political, and other innovation, such a role would be familiar territory to them. Put differently, we see no reason why MNCs as a group might not prove to be successful accounting innovators.

Pursuing this line of reasoning one step further, it seems plausible that an international accounting conceptual framework could be forged along with the development of financial accounting standards specifically aimed at MNCs. Justification for one is, by definition, justification for the other. Aside from sporadic observations and judgments such as those quoted immediately above, no

---

[43] S. J. Gray, J. C. Shaw, and L. B. McSweeney, "Accounting Standards and Multinational Corporations," *Journal of International Business Studies*, Spring-Summer 1981, p. 127.

[44] George C. Watt, R. M. Hammer, and M. Burge, *Accounting for the Multinational Corporation* (New York: Research Foundation of the Financial Executives Institute, 1977).

[45] G. G. Mueller and L. M. Walker, "The Coming of Age of Transnational Financial Reporting," *Journal of Accountancy*, July 1976, p. 74.

clear research or policy-making thrusts are discernible at this time toward a strictly MNC-based international accounting conceptual development. The U.N. effort described in Chapter 12 comes closest, but its emotion-charged political nature does not augur well for short-term success.

So long as the IASC retains its global village perspective, MNC-oriented approaches will have little or no professional support. Yet the MNCs may choose to take accounting innovation into their own hands if more realistic responses to their own unique accounting problems are not forthcoming soon. Again, this issue is discussed at greater length in Chapter 12.

Professor H. B. Thorelli, in his 1977 address to the University of Illinois International Seminar on Accounting, commented:

> But when all has been said and done at the local level, it is the mission of accounting to retain and extend the global perspective of the MNC. Never should we lose sight of the fact that it represents a more successful instance of international cooperation and a closer approach to global thinking than we have thus far encountered among governments. The MNC is the torchbearer of One World, and here in the end lies its lasting service to humanity.[46]

Professor Thorelli may have overstated his case. Yet few dispute the facts that the MNC (1) is here to stay, (2) is unique among existing organizations, and (3) faces a unique set of financial accounting and reporting problems. Why would it not be worthwhile to pursue an approach to international accounting conceptualization by taking these unique factors as the starting point?

POSTSCRIPT ON METHODOLOGY

The body of this chapter is devoted to the many analysis and evaluation processes leading to the construction and eventual use of international accounting concepts. Much of this endeavor involves research, which we broadly define as contribution to knowledge. There are many ways of classifying types of research, one of which is to segment it simply between a priori and empirical efforts. A priori research makes assumptions or generalizations about the world and then logically deducts either testable hypotheses or axiomatic conclusions from these generalizations. The initial assumptions may or may not be derived from real-world observations. Stipulated hypotheses may be tested in rigorous scientific fashion. Models or theories that allow predictions typically result. Moreover, this work may allow normative (i.e., "ought to") prescriptions for desirable accounting and financial accounting and reporting practices.

Empirical research classifies and analyzes real-world behavior and events. Its methodologies include laboratory and field studies, questionnaire surveys, interviews, historical analysis, tests of association between related

---

[46] H. B. Thorelli, seminar address reprinted in *The Multinational Corporation: Accounting and Social Implications*, V. K. Zimmerman, ed., 1977, p. 19.

events, and so on. Empirical research may either test hypotheses derived from a priori logic formulations or develop descriptive generalizations from its observations. As one would expect, there exists a substantial body of literature on the procedures, types, efficiency, and effectiveness of accounting research.

With regard to international accounting research, there has been concern in recent years "that the widely acknowledged importance of the international accounting and auditing fields is at present not adequately reflected in . . . the quantity and quality of research applied to these fields."[47]

This same concern prompted the publication of *Multinational Accounting: A Research Framework for the Eighties* by Professor F. D. S. Choi.[48] This compendium is *must* reading for anyone interested in or doing conceptual work in international accounting. For example, its Chapter 2 is devoted to methodological considerations, and Chapter 6 addresses behavioral dimensions. A major review of the book singled out the latter by observing that it "poses a significant challenge to future researchers. The interrelationship of cultural and economic 'values' has been ignored in most 'traditional' accounting research. If international accounting researchers can incorporate cultural analysis in their studies, it will be a significant breakthrough in the dimensions of accounting research."[49]

Other significant references on appropriate methodology for international accounting conceptualization (i.e., research) include the various publications of the Research Committee of the International Accounting Section of the American Accounting Association. Among other items, this group published a monograph by Professors G. M. Scott and P. Troberg entitled *Eight-eight International Accounting Problems in Rank Order of Importance.*[50] Similarly, the European Accounting Association, at its annual meetings in 1981 and 1982, conducted major working sessions on the international accounting research topic. The 1982 session was specifically devoted to state-of-the-art assessments of international accounting research in Japan, the United Kingdom, and West Germany.

At the 1982 annual meeting of the American Accounting Association, there was a panel discussion, "On the Validity and Veracity of International Accounting Research." The papers prepared for this discussion are incorporated in the "Report of the 1981–1982 American Accounting Association International Accounting and Auditing Committee."[51]

The gist of the discussion about international accounting research and its methodology is (1) such research is receiving major attention at present, (2) it is occurring in a number of countries throughout the world, and (3) its methodologies are the same as those utilized in accounting in general. Serious students of

---

[47] American Accounting Association, *Report of the 1980-81 International Accounting and Auditing Standards Committee* (Sarasota, Fla.: AAA, 1981, mimeographed), pp. 1–2.

[48] Frederick D. S. Choi, ed., *Multinational Accounting: A Research Framework for the Eighties* (Ann Arbor, Mich.: UMI Research Press, 1981).

[49] *Journal of Accountancy*, September 1982, p. 112.

[50] Sarasota, Fla.: AAA, 1980.

[51] Sarasota, Fla.: AAA, 1981 (mimeographed).

the field should know where and how to find references for this work, which is not always easy to do due to its international setting.

SELECTED REFERENCES

AMERICAN ACCOUNTING ASSOCIATION, *"Report of the 1980–81 International Accounting and Auditing Standards Committee,"* Sarasota, Fla.: AAA, 1981, 76 pp. (mimeographed).

BELKAOUI, AHMED, *Accounting Theory*, New York: Harcourt Brace Jovanovich, Inc., 1981, 318 pp.

CHOI, FREDERICK D. S., *Multinational Accounting: A Research Framework for the Eighties*, Ann Arbor, Mich.: UMI Research Press, 1981, 248 pp.

CHOI, FREDERICK D. S., "European Disclosure: The Competitive Disclosure Hypothesis," *Journal of International Business Studies*, Fall 1974, pp. 15–23.

DA COSTA, RICHARD C., JAMES FISHER, and WILLIAM M. LAWSON, "Linkages in the International Business Community: Accounting Evidence," *Journal of International Business Studies*, Fall 1980, pp. 92–102.

FINANCIAL ACCOUNTING STANDARDS BOARD, *Statements of Financial Accounting Concepts Nos. 1–3*, Stamford, Conn.: FASB, 1978, 1980, 1981, 31 pp., 73 pp., 80 pp.

FRANK, WERNER G., "An Empirical Analysis of International Accounting Principles," *Journal of Accounting Research*, Autumn 1979, pp. 593–605.

GANDHI, NATWAR M., "The Emergence of the Postindustrial Society and the Future of the Accounting Function," *International Journal of Accounting*, Spring 1976, pp. 33–49.

GOODRICH, PETER S., "Accounting and Political Systems," Discussion Paper No. 109 (School of Economic Studies, University of Leeds, U.K., 1982, mimeographed), 29 pp.

GRAY, SIDNEY J., J. C. SHAW, and L. B. McSWEENEY, "Accounting Standards and Multinational Corporations," *Journal of International Business Studies*, Spring-Summer 1981, pp. 121–136.

HENDRIKSEN, ELDON S., *Accounting Theory* (4th ed.), Homewood, Ill.: Richard D. Irwin, Inc., 1982, 589 pp.

HORNGREN, CHARLES T., "Uses and Limitations of a Conceptual Framework," *Journal of Accountancy*, April 1981, pp. 86, 88, 90, 92, 94–95.

KIRK, DONALD J., "Concepts, Consensus, Compromise and Consequences: Their Roles in Standard Setting," *Journal of Accountancy*, April 1981, pp. 83–86.

MUELLER, GERHARD G., "Accounting Principles Generally Accepted in the United States versus Those Generally Accepted Elsewhere," *International Journal of Accounting*, Spring 1968, pp. 91–103.

MUELLER, GERHARD G., *International Accounting*, New York: Macmillan Company, 1967, 255 pp.

NAIR, R. D., and WERNER G. FRANK, "The Impact of Disclosure and Measurement Practices on International Accounting Classifications," *Accounting Review*, July 1980, pp. 426–450.

NOBES, CHRISTOPHER, and ROBERT PARKER, eds., *Comparative International Accounting*, Homewood, Ill.: Richard D. Irwin, Inc., 1981, 379 pp.

STAMP, EDWARD, "Accounting Standard Setting . . . A New Beginning: Evolution, Not Revolution," *CA Magazine*, September 1980, pp. 38–43.

WATTS, ROSS L., and JEROLD L. ZIMMERMAN, "Towards a Positive Theory of the Determination of Accounting Standards," *Accounting Review*, January 1978, pp. 112–134.

ZEFF, STEPHEN A., *Forging Accounting Principles in Five Countries: A History and an Analysis of Trends*, Champaign, Ill.: Stipes Publishing Company, 1971, 332 pp.

DISCUSSION QUESTIONS

1. What are the key differences between theory development and conceptual development in accounting? Why has traditional accounting theory building been unsuccessful? What are some implications of this lack of success for conceptual development in international accounting?

2. In 1965, Paul Grady published the AICPA's Accounting Research Study No. 7 entitled *Inventory of Generally Accepted Accounting Principles for Business Enterprises.* On pages 23 to 24 of this study, Mr. Grady lists ten basic concepts to which accepted accounting principles are oriented. What items might be included on a list of basic concepts for accounting appropriate to (a) developing economies and (b) centrally controlled economies?

3. Suppose that financial accounting and reporting the world over can indeed be grouped into 10 to 12 distinct clusters. What conditions or circumstances might cause a particular country to shift from one such cluster to another? Which variables might be appropriate in distinguishing one cluster from another?

4. Five possible approaches to the conceptualization of international accounting are put forth in this chapter. Identify these different approaches in terms of their most significant distinguishing features and assess their likely respective impacts on national accounting standards and practices in your own country.

5. The chapter lists 12 environmental circumstances that are said to have a direct effect on accounting development. From your own personal vantage point, rank order these 12 items from most to least important as far as accounting development is concerned. Then justify both the top and bottom items in your ranking.

6. Authoritative and sophisticated observers seem to agree that financial accounting policy making is increasingly becoming a political process. Do you agree with this assertion? What evidence is available on the politicization of financial accounting?

7. The chapter text identifies the FASB's ten interrelated "Elements of Financial Statements of Business Enterprises." Considering these elements one by one, assess their suitability for international accounting purposes.

8. Assume that the Netherlands is a good representative of the microeconomic pattern of accounting development and that the United States best represents the independent discipline approach. Has one of these two development patterns been more successful than the other? How might one go about measuring the success of these two different patterns?

9. During the 1960s the "uniformity versus flexibility" issue was ardently debated in the United States but has since lost momentum and appeal. On the other hand, the French not only like uniform accounting but are actively proposing its acceptance throughout the European Economic Community (EEC). The uniformity issue is alive, well, and gaining in France. Why this difference between the United

States and France? Is one wrong and the other right? What future developments do you foresee with regard to uniformity in France on the one hand and the United States on the other?

10. What accounting research methodology is particularly germane to international accounting research? Why has "the interrelationship of cultural and economic values been ignored in most traditional accounting research"?

EXERCISES

1. *Changes in national accounting systems.* Compare the information contained in Table 2.3 with that in Table 2.5, as well as the content of Table 2.4 with that of Table 2.6.
   Required:
   A. Prepare lists of countries that are differently classified between 1973 and 1975 base data. Indicate the groups from and to which each shift took place.
   B. What factors might explain the shifts you just identified?
   C. What explains the different clustering between accounting measurements and financial disclosure for data years 1973 and 1975? Extending the data to 1979, the researchers found that the attempts at harmonization of accounting practices have met considerable success.[52] Write two short paragraphs of assessment with respect to the conclusion just stated.

2. *Consideration of international accounting aspects in national standard setting.* Keeping in mind the entirety of the materials discussed in Chapter 2, write an executive memorandum to the members of the FASB outlining to what extent, if any, they should consider "international accounting factors" as input to their work. Be as specific as you can. Use short examples or illustrations to underscore major points. Remember that FASB Discussion Memoranda are issue-oriented. Your memorandum should be likewise.

3. *Assessment of comparative approaches to international accounting conceptualization.* Prepare an assessment table (in matrix form) by listing the five approaches to international accounting concept-building identified in the text across the horizontal axis. Vertically list the following factors:

   Is a usable research base now available?
   Major research methodologies employed
   Are research results consistent with one another?
   Major advantage of approach
   Major disadvantage of approach
   Probable impact on international financial accounting standard
        setting (e.g. high, moderate, low, none)
   Rank order of significance for future research

[52] Nair and Frank, "The Harmonization of International Accounting Standards," p. 62.

Required: Fill in each matrix cell (with appropriate footnote explanations where needed).

4. *Examples of different approaches to accounting development.* The chapter text distinguishes among four basic accounting development patterns. Naturally, these four patterns overlap and hence are not found in completely pure forms. Thinking of generally accepted accounting principles in the United States, LIFO inventory pricing methods are available for financial purposes only if they are also applied in parallel fashion for tax accounting purposes. This is a good example of the uniform approach to accounting development. *Required:* For each of the other three basic accounting development patterns cited in the text, identify three specific U.S. financial accounting standards, principles, or practices that illustrate the respective patterns.

5. *Countries representing different accounting development stages.* Let us arbitrarily divide accounting development stages into a spectrum of five categories: (a) highly developed and complex; (b) well developed and mature; (c) reasonably developed, with a character of its own; (d) beginning development, mostly under outside influences; and (e) little or no measurable development. *Required:* Place five different countries in each of the five accounting development categories identified. Do enough reference work to make sure that you can justify each individual country selection.

CASE

Götterdämmerung of Accounting Theory

In 1922, Professor W. A. Paton published his *Accounting Theory.* Here are some statements from its Preface:

> As commonly presented in current textbooks and other writings, the theory of accounting is saturated with the "proprietorship" concept.... Indeed, the prevailing accounting theory might well be described as "proprietary accounting" ... These doctrines of proprietorship ... are not an entirely adequate statement of the theory of accounts under the conditions of modern business organization ... As an explanation of the accounting system of the *corporation* [proprietary accounting] is seriously defective.
>
> In this book, accordingly, an attempt has been made to present a restatement of the theory of accounting consistent with the conditions and needs of the business enterprise *par excellence,* the large corporation, as well as applicable to the simpler, more primitive forms of organization. The conception of the business enterprise as in all cases a distinct entity or personality is adopted.... In other words, the view that the balance sheet is composed of *three* distinct categories, *assets, liabilities,* and *proprietorship,* and that the first two of these classes are of importance primarily in that their difference discloses the last, is abandoned, and the theory of the accounting system is presented in terms of the two fundamental dimensions, *properties* and *equities.*

The relations between certain accounting concepts and fundamental classes of economic theory are noted in this study. . . . The use of the terms "debit" and "credit" is avoided entirely in the early chapters. This procedure implies that the theory of accounting consists in a body of doctrine which can best be developed without reference to any system of clerical routine . . . No attempt has been made to discuss the problems of valuation except in so far as the explanation of the structure of the accounts here developed has a bearing upon these matters.[53]

Sixty years later, Professor Eldon S. Hendriksen published the fourth edition of his *Accounting Theory*. Here are some excerpts from his Chapter 1:

Accounting theory may be defined as logical reasoning in the form of a set of broad principles that (1) provide a general frame of reference by which accounting practice can be evaluated and (2) guide the development of new practices and procedures. Accounting theory may also be used to explain existing practices to obtain a better understanding of them. But the most important goal of accounting theory should be to provide a coherent set of logical principles that form the general frame of reference for the evaluation and development of sound accounting practices.

A single general theory of accounting may be desirable, but accounting as a logical and empirical science is still in too primitive a stage for such a development. The best that can be accomplished in this developmental stage is a set of theories (models) and subtheories that may be complementary or competing.

Although there are several ways of classifying accounting theories, a useful frame of reference is to classify theories according to prediction levels. Three major levels of theory are as follows:

1.   Theories which attempt to explain current accounting practices and predict how accountants would react to certain situations or how they would report specific events. These theories relate to the *structure* of the data collection process and financial reporting (syntactical theories).

2.   Theories which concentrate on the relationship between a phenomenon (object or event) and the term or symbol representing it. These can be referred to as *interpretational* (semantical) theories.

3.   Theories that emphasize the behavioral or decision-oriented effects of accounting reports and statements. These are referred to as *behavioral* (pragmatic) theories.[54]

Professor Ahmed Belkaoui's 1981 book also has the title *Accounting Theory*. His work is referred to in the text of the chapter. Specifically, here are some relevant excerpts:

. . . accounting is a multiple paradigmatic science, with each of its paradigms competing for hegemony within the discipline. . . . Each of the currently compet-

[53] W. A. Patton, *Accounting Theory* (Chicago: Accounting Studies Press, 1922), pp. iii, iv, v, vi, vii (excerpts only).

[54] Eldon S. Hendriksen, *Accounting Theory*, 4th ed. (Homewood, Ill.: Richard D. Irwin, Inc., 1982), pp. 1–2.

ing accounting paradigms tends to specify a different empirical domain over which an accounting theory ought to apply.

An examination of the existing accounting literature allows us to identify the following basic accounting paradigms:

1. *The anthropological paradigm*, which specifies accounting practices as the domain of accounting.
2. *The behavior of the markets paradigm*, which specifies the capital market reaction as the domain of accounting.
3. *The economic event paradigm*, which specifies the prediction of economic events as the domain of accounting.
4. *The decision process paradigm*, which specifies the decision theories and the decision processes of individuals as the domain of accounting.
5. *The ideal income paradigm*, which specifies the measurement of performance as the domain of accounting.
6. *The information economics paradigm*, which specifies the evaluation of information as the domain of accounting.
7. *The users' behavior paradigm*, which specifies the information recipients' behavior as the domain of accounting.[55]

Required

1. The three books referred to have the identical title, *Accounting Theory*. Are all three addressing the same subject matter? Is it the first or the second word in this title that seems to have changed over time?
2. Identify and briefly describe what you consider to be substantive changes in accounting theory formulations as represented by the three excerpts quoted.
3. Construct an international accounting paradigm and write an explanatory paragraph in its defense.
4. On the basis of the chapter text and the quotes in the case, evaluate accounting theory progress since 1922. Has it been progressive or regressive? Has it improved or worsened the social utility of the accounting discipline? Has it made accounting more scientific or more of an art form?

[55] Belkaoui, *Accounting Theory*, p. 55.

3

Comparative
Practices

This chapter compares accounting and reporting practices among ten developed nations, each with substantial financial markets. Short descriptions of the financial accounting systems prevailing in these ten countries are provided in an effort to highlight differences.

WORLD SCENE
OF ACCOUNTING PRACTICES

Accounting practices change. Prior to World War II, British accounting influence was dominant throughout the English-speaking world and a Franco-German influence permeated code law countries like Belgium, Japan, Sweden, and Switzerland. The latter, for instance, produced a great deal of emphasis on national charts of accounts and uniform accounting in general.

Today the United States is the signal force in accounting worldwide. It leads other countries in such matters as expenditures for accounting research, numbers of accounting publications, and college and university graduates with degree concentrations in accounting. At the same time, and properly so, other nations are not eager to adopt U.S.–developed accounting standards and principles. In fact, substantial diversity still characterizes the world scene of accounting.

What are some of the points that evolve from a review of world accounting practices?

Asset and liability measurement.   It is abundantly clear that accountants still measure most of the world's business assets in terms of original transaction costs. This measurement concept is not applied in pure form anywhere, however. To greater or lesser degree, original transaction cost applications are mixed with some forms of appraisals or current market valuation techniques, some specific and general price level change adjustment techniques, some imputed interest calculations, and estimates of future transaction levels—especially in the areas of foreign exchange and future collections of receivables. At the conclusion of Chapter 5 we speculate that current cost measurement applications might soon make additional inroads into the historical cost bulwark of present accounting practices.

The term *asset* does not have a well-established meaning in terms of which resources are included or excluded. Comparatively, it covers various interpretations of intangibles such as goodwill and research and development. In South America the definition of an asset includes foreign exchange losses arising from liabilities payable in foreign currencies. In Continental European countries assets may or may not include various types of leases, tax loss carry-forwards, or economic interests in affiliated companies.

Similarly, different liability concepts are applied from country to country. Accounting for income taxes provides a specific example. In Argentina, for instance, income tax liabilities are not accrued and are recognized on a cash basis only. In Switzerland, periodic accruals take place without the recognition of deferred income tax liabilities. Deferral may require one of several different methods of tax allocation. In the Netherlands the amount of deferred income taxes is sometimes a discounted amount.

Other examples of differential definitions of a liability can be discovered readily. In some European and South American countries, provisions are not made for all known liabilities or losses. This may include items like severance pay obligations to workers, pension agreements or death benefits like burial costs, and estimated losses on purchase commitments or other forward contracts. Conversely, the definition of a liability is sometimes stretched to allow for the creation of "secret" reserves. German and Swiss practices, for example, often deliberately overestimate contingent liabilities and the effects of uncertain future events.

Owners' equity and periodic income determination.   The greatest comparative variation in the owners' equity area concerns the question of whether certain enterprise resources or obligations may be written off directly to retained earnings—the well-known "clean versus adjusted surplus" concept. Because of the difficulty in separating normal business operations from unusual events and the problems of periodicity in past period adjustments, the United States requires that all transactions except stockholder investments, capital donations, or capital accretion flow through the income statement. Yet all non-English-speaking countries still permit direct owners' equity adjustments for unusual gains or losses.

Another major variation is the concept of periodicity in measuring the results of operations. Generally accepted accounting principles in the United States require sharp annual cutoffs. But in many European and South American countries applicable accounting principles insist that a calendar year is too short a period for reasonable determination of business results. Therefore they allow some smoothing between report periods. In Sweden the length of the business cycle is sometimes considered to be the most appropriate time period over which business results should be measured and reported.

Legal requirements clearly interfere with accounting for investment capital transactions. For instance, some countries have uniform par values for a given class of shares, others have different par value denominations for specific classes of shares, and still others permit no par value shares. Also, many variations exist in the principles that guide accounting for share distributions (in United States–North American terminology, stock dividends and stock splits), stock option plans, and treasury stock transactions. Earnings per share is a nonsensical notion in West Germany because most par value common stocks have different German mark denominations per share. The charging of retained earnings with a market value equivalent of small share distributions is a practice unique to the United States. Undoubtedly, this practice evolved from a concern over potential abuse of the stock dividend mechanism since market value charges to retained earnings limit the share distribution possibilities, especially where there are miniscule legal par values in relation to current market values.

Financial statement consolidation practices also vary widely. There is no comparable agreement on the meaning of an accounting entity. Consequently a "full range" of multinational consolidation practices is observable. Foreign subsidiaries are normally consolidated in the United States but not in West Germany. In countries such as Japan, separate parent company statements are considered more important than consolidated financial statements. In other countries, joint ventures are accounted for at cost, in some on the equity basis, and in still others on arithmetic percentages of ownership (see Chapter 6 for further details). Minority interests and the amounts of positive or negative goodwill arising from business combinations are also sources of practice variations. These differences relating to consolidation practices are usually considered important enough to warrant the first (and presumably most important) footnote to published financial statements.

The interrelationship of asset and liability measurements with periodic income determination naturally causes reciprocal effects. Usually, over- or understatements of assets or liabilities are accomplished through corresponding income statement inclusions or exclusions. This we have already pointed out. It should also be noted, however, that a great many smaller procedural variations exist as well. For instance, purchased goodwill may be amortized in the United States over a period of 40 years, whereas in West Germany the maximum allowable amortization period is 5 years. In Australia, Ireland, New Zealand, Peru, and the United Kingdom, goodwill is generally not amortized at all. Similar procedural accounting variations apply to research and development, oil and mineral exploration costs, sales promotions, education and staff training, and many other accountable transactions or events. A representative number of these variations is explored more fully throughout Chapters 4 to 7.

EFFECTS ON BUSINESS DECISIONS

It is now appropriate to ask what difference, if any, does it make to have a variety rather than uniformity of financial accounting practices from country to country? Your authors submit that it does make a difference indeed! The available evidence suggests that enterprise management decisions as well as investor decisions are affected by the diversity of worldwide accounting practices. The aggregate cost-benefit dimension of this diversity has not yet been assessed, but we believe it to be substantial. To illustrate, some selected problem situations are briefly described in the following paragraphs.

Issuance of Corporate Financial Securities

In recent years, the competition for new investable funds has become intense and international financial markets are increasingly utilized to supply new or additional money funds unavailable at home. For instance, the amount of corporate bonds sold by companies outside their home countries grew from less than $5 billion per year in 1970 to over $40 billion per year by 1979.[1]

Aside from market conditions and respective issue costs, do different accounting and financial reporting practices affect the location choice of issuance of a new corporate security? Some evidence suggests this to be the case. For example, Professor Norman J. Bartczak investigated this question using samples drawn from the U.S. bond market and the Eurobond market.[2] His empirical results indicate that in making their corporate bond investment decisions, investors appear to attach more weight to firm-specific information relative to market-related information in a government-regulated disclosure environment (e.g., the United States) as compared to a self-regulated disclosure environment (e.g., the Eurobond Market). In the same vein, Bartczak observes that investors exhibit relatively the same amount of uncertainty in their estimates of corporate bond risk premiums in a government-regulated disclosure environment as compared to a self-regulated disclosure environment. In explaining his find-

---

[1] Stan Crock, "Differences in Rules Tangle Trading in Growing World Securities Market," *Wall Street Journal*, November 10, 1981, p. 25.

[2] Norman J. Bartczak, "Effects of Financial Disclosure on Corporate Bond Risk Premiums," Ph.D. diss., University of Washington, 1978.

ings, Professor Bartczak declares, "A government-regulated disclosure environment may foster *too much* disclosure, in the sense that beyond a certain point there are negative marginal returns to disclosure, e.g. in the form of confusion, resulting in increased marginal uncertainty."[3] In other words, there may be "information overload" in the U.S. financial reporting system relating to issuance of new corporate securities. Investors do not use the "overload" portion of information provided and issuing companies deliberately seem to avoid countries where costly financial reporting and disclosure requirements are in effect.

Foreign Exchange–Related Decisions

The imposition of Financial Accounting Standard (FAS) No. 8 in October 1975 triggered a great deal of criticism among the U.S. corporate community. The nature and extent of this criticism are fully discussed in Chapter 4.

One major concern about the economic consequences of applying alternative foreign exchange translation accounting rules was their impact on management practices of American multinationals. Thus in June of 1977 the Financial Accounting Standards Board (FASB) agreed to sponsor a relevant survey research study which was published the following year.[4] With respect to Foreign Exchange Risk Management (FERM), here are some of the conclusions:

1. There is clear evidence that firms, whose accounting practices did not conform closely to Statement No. 8 when it was issued, are pursuing more aggressive FERM programs and can be seen as still adjusting to Statement No. 8. Since differences in firms' behavior were discovered and related to their past selection of accounting principles, it is evident that the particular accounting standard in use did have an impact on the way that firms manage foreign exchange.

2. Our results show definitely that firms are now more sophisticated in various aspects of FERM and spend more time and money on this function.

3. Statement No. 8 has had an impact on investment policies. Some firms reported that they have refrained from making investments that were otherwise acceptable. Others have adjusted their investment "hurdle rate" due to exchange risk. The quarterly reporting of exchange gains and losses has led a number of firms to accelerate their dividend payments from subsidiaries in weak currency countries to reduce exposure.[5]

It goes almost without saying that these conclusions support the contention that enterprise management decisions are differentially affected by different accounting standards and practices.

[3] Ibid., p. 280.

[4] T. G. Evans, W. R. Folks, Jr., and M. Jilling, *The Impact of Statement of Financial Accounting Standards No. 8 on the Foreign Exchange Risk Management Practices of American Multinationals: An Economic Impact Study* (Stamford, Conn.: Financial Accounting Standards Board, 1978).

[5] Ibid., p. 20.

Additional Empirical Evidence

While the studies cited and others of like nature support our claim that comparatively different national accounting practices tend to produce differential effects on business decisions, a few additional situations are described below to round out the discussion.

Straightjacket of short-term reporting.   In the United States, managers must formally report the results of their operations every three months. This is an incredibly short period when compared with the average lengths of a product life cycle or a general business cycle. It is also short in comparison to the economic life of average business assets. The quarterly profit thinking, it is alleged, has led to suboptimal short-term management decisions in the United States. For example, in comparisons drawn to Japanese management styles it has been pointed out that the "tyranny of the three-months profit report" is absent in Japan and thus lets Japanese enterprises take a much longer-term approach to product and market development. While there are many other factors at work in the contrast between U.S. and Japanese management, accounting effects appear to be one of them.

Merger mania.   International business often expands through merger activities. During the early 1960s, many U.S.-based companies invested very heavily in Continental Europe. Twenty years later, many European and Japanese companies are making direct investments in North America. This activity appears to be accelerating.

There is, however, a key economic effect emanating from comparative merger accounting requirements (see Chapter 6 for additional discussion on this point). If, for instance, an American company purchases a company in another country, the U.S. buyer must amortize the excess of the purchase price over fair market asset values as goodwill. Such annual write-offs are not deductible expenses for U.S. income taxation purposes. These accounting rules do not apply to most non-U.S. firms. They typically may write off any purchased goodwill directly to owners' equity. Hence their future earnings are unaffected, which in turn may allow them to outbid a U.S. firm in a potential merger negotiation.   How! why! better for taxes

non-tax deductible.

Dirtying up reported earnings.   In many code law countries, various asset, liability, and owners' equity reserves may be created or dissolved, as the case may be, to smooth the stream of earnings reported in successive income statements. This discretion does not exist in the United States where companies are subject to the "all-inclusive" format of reporting net earnings for successive accounting periods. Therefore, U.S. managements have to add or forego *actual* business transactions if they wish to influence their periodic operating statements. Some non-U.S. companies can undertake the transactions in question and later decide for which period they wish to have the accounting effect reported. Both approaches make the income statement available as a repository for gains and losses or reserve movements aside from strict operating income. But the U.S. approach is more restrictive on management actions. To reiterate, if a U.S. company wishes to report a predetermined level of operating results, it must undertake or refrain from *actual* transactions to achieve an accounting goal. Many other countries permit prerecognition or deferral of certain accounting effects. So as to leave a given income statement "untouched" when this occurs, a direct effect on business decision making is produced.

Growing attention to accounting information.   Any reader of international business newspapers and periodicals is aware of the fact that national economies are growing more interdependent and that the multinational business enterprise seems here to stay. In turn, this has brought a wave of new interest in accounting information—from bankers to public officials, from groups of employees to international agencies, and from television audiences to investors. Corporate annual report surveys, like the one conducted by the *Financial Times* (London), have garnered keen interest from business executives. More and more financial data is published in daily newspapers, and the public at large is taking more than a passing interest in massive business failures. All of this suggests that comparative accounting standards and practices (1) are now a matter of considerable public interest, and (2) appear to increase their stake in actual business decision making. Business is not indifferent as to how their decisions are reported. And since accounting is a major medium of business communications, the medium itself has become a likely business decision factor.

SYNTHESIS OF EXISTING DIVERSITY

Looking at the same meteorological charts, one weather forecaster might announce the next day's weather as "partly sunny," whereas another might label it "partly cloudy." So it is with the worldwide diversity of accounting practices. There can be no question that considerable diversity exists. At the same time, common practices (e.g., use of the accrual method and preparation of periodic financial statements) are readily observable from country to country. Therefore, is worldwide accounting practice "partly common" or "partly diverse"? Your authors tend toward the latter view because the existing diversity typically relates to significant accounting measurement rules as well as important reporting practices (e.g., publication of statements of changes in financial position).

Many surveys and compilations have appeared in the literature with the object of documenting and explaining worldwide accounting practice diversity (refer to relevant portions of Chapter 2). Probably the most useful of the existing compilations is the one prepared by Professors Frederick D. S. Choi and Vinod B. Bavishi in August 1982.[6] These two researchers assembled corporate

---

[6] Frederick D. S. Choi and Vinod B. Bavishi, "Diversity in Multinational Accounting," *Financial Executive*, August 1982, pp. 45–49.

TABLE 3.1   Sample Composition for Choi–Bavishi Study

COUNTRY	NUMBER OF COMPANIES INCLUDED
Australia	17
Canada	36
France	49
Germany	66
Japan	111
The Netherlands	21
Sweden	31
Switzerland	18
United Kingdom	107
United States	413
Total	869

annual reports for 1979 and 1980 on a total of 869 companies. The two selection criteria employed were (1) inclusion of only industrial firms with 1980 consolidated sales in excess of $500 million, and (2) home country location in one of the ten countries having the largest domestic equity securities markets. The number of companies included in the sample and their respective domicile countries are shown in Table 3.1.

Thirty-two different accounting principles are synthesized in Table 3.2. To quote the authors:

1. Items chosen for inclusion were accounting principles that appeared'in a representative sample of foreign annual reports, as well as those obtained from a survey of existing literature. An item was selected if it was deemed to have material asset value or income determination implications for accounting-based ratio analysis.

2. To minimize the number of cross-country comparisons (total possible combinations were 9 × 9 = 81), the reporting practices of all ten countries chosen for the analysis were compared with a single norm. In the absence of a definitive set of international accounting standards, U.S. practices were used as a proxy norm.

3. To simplify cross-country analysis, matrix cells of the checklist contain discreet yes/no responses to signify adherence or nonadherence to a given accounting principle.

4. "Mixed" designations indicate those instances where alternative practices were found with no predominant practice being apparent (e.g. straight line or accelerated in the case of depreciation, FIFO, LIFO or average cost in the case of inventories, etc.).[7]

Going through Table 3.2 one quickly observes that all ten countries value marketable securities at the lower of cost or market, value inventories at the lower of cost or market, consolidate financial statements regularly, provide for company pension fund contributions, expense research and development expenditures, and eliminate intercompany sales/profits upon consolidation.

[7] Ibid., p. 46.

TABLE 3.2 Choi-Bavishi Synthesis of World Diversity in Financial Accounting Practices

ACCOUNTING PRINCIPLES	AUSTRALIA	CANADA	FRANCE	GERMANY	JAPAN	NETH.	SWEDEN	SWITZ.	U.K.	U.S.
1. Marketable securities recorded at the lower cost or market?	Yes	Yes	Yes	Yes	Yes	Yes	Yes	Yes	Yes	Yes
2. Provision for uncollectible accounts made?	Yes	Yes	No	Yes	Yes	Yes	Yes	Yes	Yes	Yes
3. Inventory costed using FIFO?	Yes	Mixed	Mixed	Yes	Mixed	Mixed	Yes	Yes	Yes	Mixed
4. Manufacturing overhead allocated to year-end inventory?	Yes	Yes	Yes	Yes	Yes	Yes	Yes	No	Yes	Yes
5. Inventory valued at the lower of cost or market?	Yes	Yes	Yes	Yes	Yes	Yes	Yes	Yes	Yes	Yes
6. Accounting for long-term investments: less than 20 percent ownership: cost method.	Yes	Yes	Yes*	Yes	Yes	No(K)	Yes	Yes	Yes	Yes
7. Accounting for long-term investments: 21-50 percent ownership: equity method	No(G)	Yes	Yes*	No(B)	No(B)	Yes	No(B)	No(B)	Yes	Yes
8. Accounting for long-term investments more than 50 percent ownership: full consolidation	Yes	Yes	Yes*	Yes	Yes	Yes	Yes	Yes	Yes	Yes
9. Both domestic and foreign subsidiaries consolidated?	Yes	Yes	Yes	No**	Yes	Yes.	Yes	Yes	Yes	Yes
10. Acquisitions accounted for under the pooling of interest method?	No(C)	No(C)	No(C)	No(C)	No(C)	No(C)	No(C)	No(C)	No(C)	Yes
11. Intangible assets: goodwill amortized?	Yes	Yes	Yes	No	Yes	Mixed	Yes	No**	No**	Yes

	C1	C2	C3	C4	C5	C6	C7	C8
12. Intangible assets: other than goodwill amortized?	Yes	Yes	Yes	Yes	Yes	No**	No*	No**
13. Long-term debt includes maturities longer than one year?	Yes	Yes	No(D)	Yes	Yes	Yes	Yes	Yes
14. Discount/premium on long-term debt amortized?	Yes	No	No	Yes	Yes	No	No	No
15. Deferred taxes recorded when accounting income is not equal to taxable income?	Yes	Yes	Yes	Yes	Yes	No	No	Yes
16. Financial leases (long-term) capitalized?	No	No	No	No	No	No	No	No
17. Company pension fund contribution provided regularly?	Yes	Yes	Yes	Yes	Yes	Yes	Yes	Yes
18. Total pension fund assets and liabilities excluded from company's financial statement?	Yes	Yes	No	Yes	Yes	Yes	Yes	Yes
19. Research & development expensed?	Yes	Yes	Yes	Yes	Yes	Yes	Yes	Yes
20. Treasury stock deducted from owner's equity?	NF	Yes	No	Yes	Yes	Mixed	NF	NF
21. Gains or losses on treasury stock taken to owner's equity?	NF	Yes	No	Yes	No**	Mixed	NF	NF
22. No general purpose (purely discretionary) reserves allowed?	Yes	No	No	No	No	No	No	Yes
23. Dismissal indemnities accounted for on a pay-as-you-go basis?	Yes	Yes	Yes	Yes	Yes	NF	NF	Yes
24. Minority interest excluded from consolidated income?	Yes	Yes	No	Yes	Yes	Yes	Yes	Yes

(continued)

TABLE 3.2 Choi-Bavishi Synthesis of World Diversity in Financial Accounting Practices (continued)

ACCOUNTING PRINCIPLES	AUSTRALIA	CANADA	FRANCE	GERMANY	JAPAN	NETH.	SWEDEN	SWITZ.	U.K.	U.S.
25. Minority interest excluded from consolidated owner's equity?	Yes	Yes	Yes	No	Yes	Yes	Yes	Yes	Yes	Yes
26. Are intercompany sales/profits eliminated upon consolidation?	Yes	Yes	Yes	Yes	Yes	Yes	Yes	Yes	Yes	Yes
27. Basic financial statements reflect a historical cost valuation (no price level adjustment)?	No	Yes	No	Yes	Yes	No**	No	No	No	Yes
28. Supplementary inflation-adjusted financial statements provided?	No**	No**	No	No	No	No**	No	No**	Yes	Yes
29. Straight-line depreciation adhered to?	Yes	Yes	Mixed	Mixed	Mixed	Yes	Yes	Yes	Yes	Yes
30. No excess depreciation permitted?	No	Yes	No	Yes	Yes	No	No	No	No	Yes
31. Temporal method of foreign currency translation employed?	Mixed	Yes	No(E)	No(E)	Mixed	No(E)	No(L)	No(E)	No(E)	Yes
32. Currency translation gains or losses reflected in current income?	Mixed	Yes	Mixed	Mixed	Mixed	No(J)	Mixed	No(H)	No	Yes

Yes— Predominant practice.
Yes*— Minor modifications, but still predominant practice.
No**— Minority practice
No— Accounting principle in question not adhered to.
NF— Not found
Mixed— Alternative practices followed with no majority.
B— Cost method is used.
C— Purchase method is used.

D— Long-term debt includes maturities longer than four years.
E— Current rate method of foreign currency translation.
F— Weighted average is used.
G— Cost or equity.
H— Translation gains and losses are deferred.
I— Market is used.
J— Owners' equity.
K— Equity.
L— Monetary/Nonmonetary.

Source: Frederick D. S. Choi and Vinod B. Bavishi, "Diversity in Multinational Accounting," *Financial Executive*, August 1982, pp. 46–49.

In some instances, U.S. practice constitutes minority practice. For instance, among the ten countries, only the United States capitalizes long-term financial leases and permits the pooling of interest method in accounting for business combinations. For the majority of the accounting principles identified, comparative practices among the ten countries are mixed. Diversity is a fact of life in international accounting practice, and readers of financial statements are well advised never to lose sight of this condition.

SYNOPSES OF SELECTED
NATIONAL PRACTICE SYSTEMS

The remainder of this chapter is devoted to highly condensed descriptions of national accounting practice systems in the ten countries covered in Table 3.2. Australia, Canada, the United Kingdom, and the United States are common law countries, whereas the other six are code law countries. This is one fundamental difference among them. Another relates to the relative number of qualified accountants in practice. When compared to a norm like Gross National Product, the United Kingdom has the largest number of practicing professional accountants, and Switzerland the smallest. Each of the ten countries now has its own national financial accounting standard-setting body. Each country is the domicile of a very active group of multinational enterprises. All ten countries are developed nations. The special accounting problems of Third World countries (i.e., developing nations) are referenced in Chapter 12.

Australia

British traditions and practices characterize Australia to a significant extent. Companies law governs business affairs. The Companies Acts of the States and Commonwealth territories comprise the "Uniform" Act of 1961, which, with subsequent amendments, constitutes the underlying legislation presently in effect. At the time of this writing, the Australian Federal Government and the States have agreed that each state will adopt the companies laws presently applicable to the Australian Capital Territory. This would create national companies legislation similar to that existing in Britain.

As far as accounting is concerned, companies laws, among various other provisions, address (1) the accountability of directors to the shareholders, particularly through the presentation of the annual accounts, and the directors' report thereon, and (2) audit of the annual accounts.

Companies laws in Australia require financial statements to give a "true and fair view." However, these terms are not defined. Moreover, the legislation does not refer to any authoritative accounting standards nor generally accepted accounting principles. Finally, the legislation does not refer to any statements of accounting standards issued by the accounting profession. Thus, in the end, courts determine what constitutes "true and fair." Most Australian accounting measurement rules are derived from professional recommendations, as are the majority of disclosure rules.

The two principal professional accounting organizations are the Institute of Chartered Accountants in Australia (approximately 10,000 members) and the Australian Society of Accountants (approximately 45,000 members). Amalgamation of the two bodies is periodically proposed but typically defeated by membership votes. Both bodies sponsor the Australian Accounting Research Foundation which, through appropriate committee structures, recommends accounting and auditing standards. After due approvals, the Councils of the two professional organizations, respectively, issue joint statements containing the standards to be observed by members in their professional capacities.

Several major features of Australian financial accounting standards are reflected in Table 3.2. For example, generally accepted accounting practices in Australia do not require the capitalization of financial leases, do not allow LIFO methods of inventory valuation, tolerate the "pooling of interest" method of accounting for business combinations in only the most exceptional circumstances, and at times permit the capitalization of R & D expenditures. The terms "provisions" and "reserves" are sharply distinguished in Australia. The former refer to known liabilities or diminutions in asset values when the amounts involved cannot be determined with reasonable accuracy.

Reserves are divided between "capital reserves" and "revenue reserves." The former may arise from premiums received upon the issue of capital stock, revaluations of fixed assets, or other capital transactions. These reserves are generally unavailable for distribution to shareholders. Revenue reserves, on the other hand, are typically unappropriated net income. They are available for general company purposes and not created in accordance with any statutory requirements.

Some real property and machinery and equipment may be written up after a "director's" or "independent" valuation. Such write-ups trigger depreciation charges in excess of cost in the income statement and capital reserves in the balance sheet.

Negative goodwill may be recognized in Australia and labeled "Reserve Arising on Consolidation." Such negative goodwill is rarely amortized. Positive goodwill (i.e., the excess of the purchase price over the fair value of the assets acquired in a business combination) may be amortized, but typically not until it is apparent that it has diminished in value.

University-level accounting education flourishes in Australia. Most new entry-level professionals hold a university degree, often with a major in accounting.

Professional auditing in Australia is very similar to comparable practices in the United Kingdom and the United States. Statements of Auditing Standards as well as Statements of Auditing Practice are issued by the Australian Accounting Research Foundation and widely observed. A significant body of case law provides guidance on basic principles and objectives for independent audits. The tenor of this case law is directly reflected in the auditing standards and practice guidelines promulgated. Typically auditors' reports refer to the specific companies act upon which financial statements are based, state that the named financial statements "give a true and fair view," and indicate that required records have been "properly kept."

In response to heightened awareness of corporate social responsibilities, leading Australian companies publish annual reports to employees along with their annual financial statements. For example, the 1982 *Report to Employees* of Australian Consolidated Industries Limited is 15 pages in length. Among other things, the message it contains from the managing director is made available not only in English but also in Italian, Greek, Serbo-Croatian, Turkish, and Arabic.

Canada

In some ways, the Canadian accounting scene is highly similar to that of the United States and in others it is significantly different. Some major differences are as follows:

1. Administrative laws (i.e., securities laws) provide the legal basis of financial reporting for public and large private companies in the United States. The Canada Business Corporations Act and the Corporations Acts of some provinces (i.e., corporation laws) effuse the comparable legal substance in Canada.
2. U.S. financial accounting standards are established by an independent board of experts. Comparable Canadian standards are formulated strictly within the accounting profession through the Accounting Research Committee of the Canadian Institute of Chartered Accountants (CICA).
3. The public accounting profession is unified in the United States through the American Institute of Certified Public Accountants (AICPA) as exemplified, for instance, by the Uniform Public Accountancy Examination. Public accountants in Canada attain membership in one of ten provincial Institutes of Chartered Accountants after passing a series of examinations set in each of the provinces. Each provincial institute is a self-governing body. Members in good standing of any of the provincial institutes are automatically members of the CICA. The board of governors of the CICA is chosen by the provincial institutes.
4. Professional fragmentation in Canada reaches even further. In addition to the CICA, there are two other major professional accounting groups in Canada, namely the Society of Management Accountants and the Canadian Certified General Accountants' Association. At the time of this writing, the latter is locked in a bitter jurisdictional dispute with the CICA over the right to do public accounting work—particularly corporate audits.
5. Canada is probably a world leader in the area of public sector accounting. In 1981, the CICA established a formal Public Sector Accounting and Auditing Committee with a mandate to produce or support financial reporting and auditing rules on the same basis as the authoritative pronouncements in the CICA Handbook for the corporate sector. As early as 1977, the Auditor General of Canada received an expanded mandate to assess the efficiency, effectiveness, and economy of government operations as well as the traditional reporting accuracy. In concert with provincial and federal auditors in Canada, the CICA founded the Canadian Comprehensive Auditing Foundation. The latter conducts research on public sector financial controls.

6. In the United States, corporate financial reporting has a strong equity investor orientation (as evidenced significantly in the FASB's Statements of Financial Accounting Concepts). Professor Edward Stamp, in his 1980 CICA-sponsored research study entitled *Corporate Reporting: Its Future Evolution* asserts that the Canadian focus is significantly broader and more concerned with the public interest at large.

7. In each of the ten provinces with a local Institute of Chartered Accountants, a university degree is a necessary prerequisite to qualify as a chartered accountant. Yet the Canadian university system is too limited and Canadian university-level accounting faculty are too few to handle the corresponding captive demand. By any relative measure, significantly larger amounts of resources are devoted to accounting education and research in the United States.

Close economic links between the United States and Canada have fostered a tendency toward similar financial accounting principles and practices in the two countries. Existing differences are relatively minor. For example, the LIFO inventory measurement method is not considered acceptable for Canadian income tax purposes and hence is seldom used in Canada. Foreign currency translation differs with regard to the treatment of translation "gains and losses" even though current rate translations were acceptable in Canada from the start (see Chapter 4 for additional details).

Accounting for the effects of changing prices is an issue only recently resolved in Canada. Consideration of this complex problem started in 1976 with a CICA discussion paper. There was an exposure draft of an authoritative recommendation in 1979, and a reexposure draft in 1981. A final standard was adopted in 1982 (see Chapter 5 for details).

The majority of companies in Canada issue no par value shares. Stock dividends are rare. In provinces where the acquisition of a company's own shares is permitted, such shares are carried at cost and shown as a deduction from shareholders' equity until canceled or resold. Accounting for intercompany investments is the same in Canada and the United States. Canadian disclosure in published financial statements is substantial (see additional discussion in Chapter 7).

Readers interested in greater detail on financial accounting and reporting practices in Canada are referred to the accounting recommendations contained in the *CICA Handbook* (Canadian source) and the Organization for Economic Cooperation and Development's (OECD) 1980 publication entitled *Accounting Practices in OECD Member Countries* (non-Canadian source).[8] The latter contains informative descriptions of financial accounting practices in 20 of the OECD's 24 member countries.

Audited financial statements must be prepared and published annually by all corporations incorporated under the Canada Business Corporations Act, and/or those whose securities are publicly traded or whose gross annual revenues exceed $10 million or whose assets exceed $5 million for the most recent financial year. Auditing standards and procedures are based on official

---

[8] See Selected References for this chapter.

pronouncements by the Auditing Standards Committee of the CICA. These pronouncements are included in the auditing section of the *CICA Handbook*. Again, it is fair to say that auditing standards and procedures are highly similar between Canada and the United States, even though the latter has codified auditing standards and procedures to a much greater extent.

France

The French Republic is the world's leading advocate of national uniform accounting. The first formal Plan Comptable was approved by the Ministry of National Economy in September 1947. A revised Plan came into effect in 1957. Under the influence of the Fourth Directive of the European Economic Community (EEC) (see Chapter 12), yet another revision of the Plan was worked out to ensure full compliance with EEC statutes. The latest Plan must be utilized by French companies as from February 1, 1982. While the new Plan is silent on the recognition of inflation effects, it devotes considerable attention to foreign currency translation issues. In general, the Plan provides:

1. A national uniform chart of accounts
2. Definitions and explanations of terminology
3. Explanations, where necessary, of the form of entries and which accounts to debit and/or credit in the recording of special events and transactions
4. Principles of accounting measurements (valuation)
5. Standard forms for financial statements
6. Acceptable cost accounting methods

The most significant element of the new Plan is its requirement for substantial disclosures in footnotes to "generally accepted" financial statements. These disclosures extend to a wide variety of items, for example:

Departures from generally applied accounting principles
Explanation of valuation rules employed
Accounting treatment of foreign currency items
Statement of changes in fixed assets and depreciation
Details of provisions
Details of any revaluation
Contingent liabilities related to leases
Breakdown of liabilities by maturity
Analysis of deferred charges, deferred items arising from currency translation and unusual items
Details of the impact of tax on the financial statement
Disclosure of liabilities secured by collaterals
Statement showing how the profit or loss has been appropriated
The average number of employed listed by category
A list of marketable securities held
Analysis of turnover by activity and geographically

The mandatory use of the National Uniform Chart of Accounts is not really burdensome to French enterprises since the Plan Comptable has found wide acceptance in practice and since all academic training in France is based on it. Moreover, various schedules required for income tax returns are also based on the official National Chart of Accounts.

The French Professional Institute (L'Ordre National des Experts Comptables) and the National Council of Accountancy (Conseil National de la Comptabilité), composed of high public officials and prominent members of the accounting profession, industry, commerce, labor unions, and others chosen for competence in accounting matters, issue opinions and recommendations on accounting principles needed to implement and expand the Plan Comptable. These opinions and recommendations, however, are *not* mandatory. They cover issues such as

1. Sources and uses of funds statements
2. Accounting for research and development costs
3. Treatment of value-added tax
4. Income and expenditure allocations
5. Off–balance sheet agreements
6. Investment tax credit treatment
7. EEC agricultural transactions
8. Leasing
9. Profit-sharing plans
10. Accounting for welfare benefits granted to employees

A noteworthy development is the 1968 advent of the Commission des Opérations de Bourse (COB). Among other things, COB requires initial opinion audits of companies seeking to list their securities on a French stock exchange. The COB's aim is to play a significant role in the improvement of French financial reporting. It has taken a most aggressive stance in calling attention to "dubious" accounting practices—referring flagrant breaches of existing rules to the French Public Prosecutor. One example of a COB challenge is the following:

> Other practices deplored by the COB include the timely writing-back of provisions, and the alteration of the book values of investments. The COB gives the example of one company which added to its holding in a subsidiary at a time when the subsidiary was loss-making, purchasing shares at a considerable discount to the book value of the original stake. It then adjusted the increased holding at a weighted average of the original book value and the new purchase price—"totally unjustified: the averaging of two mutually contradictory valuations," according to the COB.[9]

Accounting education in France is underdeveloped by international standards. There exists a wide range of professional background and expertise among practicing accountants.

---

[9] Martin Taylor, "COB Attacks Dubious Accounting Techniques," *World Accounting Report*, January 1980, p. 13.

Statutory auditors (Commissaires aux Comptes) must be appointed for all French companies with capital in excess of F 300,000. The Commissaires have their own institute and, since April 1, 1975, only listed members may be appointed as statutory auditors. The more highly qualified Experts Comptables (numbering about 9,000 in all) may act as Commissaires but work primarily on opinion audits like those required by the COB or larger French enterprises seeking capital in the international capital markets. If the present French government is indeed able to expand equity markets in France and make Paris into more of an international financial center, significant growth of the Expert Comptables' profession may be expected.

Germany

West German financial accounting is marked by three critical dimensions: (1) principles of proper bookkeeping (ordnungsmässige Buchführung) are basically determined by tax laws and regulations, (2) the German Commercial Code sets up requirements for procedures such as the physical count of inventories and other assets and the annual preparation of financial statements, and (3) the Stock Corporation Law of 1965 governs basic accounting principles (e.g., valuation) for incorporated business entities.

Unless kept in accordance with very specific tax accounting principles, accounting records can be rejected by tax authorities as a basis for taxation. The authorities are then entitled to estimate in whole or in part any taxable income to the best of their ability. This is a powerful incentive to keep *all* accounting records on a basis acceptable to tax authorities.

The Commercial Code provisions are too general to be of much use in a modern economic system. Their influence on present-day accounting standards and principles is nil.

The regulations embodied in the 1965 Stock Corporation Law are pervasive, however. Among its requirements are the following:

1. Fixed assets are to be stated at cost less appropriate depreciation.
2. Current assets are to be priced at the lowest of cost, net realizable value, or replacement price.
3. Intangible assets may be capitalized only if acquired from third parties.
4. All liabilities including unrealized losses must be provided for fully.
5. Unrealized profits may not be recognized.

A major controversy is currently embroiling the West German accounting scene over the adoption of the EEC's Fourth Directive into the German statutory framework. Among other things, it is estimated that an additional 30,000 limited liability companies would be required to be audited if the EEC Directive were implemented fully.[10] Seventeen thousand of these would be first-time audits. Also, the Certified Tax Advisors are seeking authority to act

---

[10] Arlene G. Wenig and Godehard H. Puckler, "Public Accounting in West Germany: An Overview," *Journal of Accountancy*, April 1982, pp. 83–84, 86.

as outside auditors, largely because they have prepared the (so far nonaudited) financial statements of the companies affected for tax authorities. Overall, West German financial accounting is almost totally tax-based, inflexible, and highly conservative.

The German Institute (about 4,000 members) makes recommendations (interpretations?) on accounting standards and principles anchored in the corresponding provisions of the Stock Corporation Law. For example, the following apply:

1. Consolidation requirements exclude foreign subsidiaries.
2. Minimum amortization of purchased goodwill is at 20 percent per year.
3. Pension liabilities are not always fully recognized.
4. Some deferred charges must be fully written off against income in the year in which they are incurred.
5. Income tax allocation is not recognized since tax basis amounts are typically reported in published financial statements.
6. Retained earnings are typically carried in some form of disclosed reserve accounts.

Published German financial statements are comparable in scope and disclosure to Anglo-American statements. However, most financial statements of German companies carry only one or two perfunctory "notes." The essence of disclosure occurs in the Management Report that accompanies each set of financial statements and is covered by the auditor's opinion insofar as it elaborates the financial statements. Much of the contents of the Management Report, as well as the requirement for examinations of financial statements by independent public accountants, is anchored in the August 15, 1969, Corporate Publicity Law. This law covers companies falling under at least two of the following conditions:

1. A German statutory balance sheet total exceeding DM 125 million.
2. Annual sales exceeding DM 250 million.
3. Average monthly number of employees during the year exceeding 5,000.

In Germany all statutory auditor appointments must go to Certified Public Accountants (Wirtschaftsprüfer). Some larger closely held companies also employ independent auditors. Educational requirements to become a CPA in Germany are probably the highest worldwide. Needless to say, entry to the profession is very restricted in Germany. Further details on auditing and professional auditors in West Germany are provided in Chapter 9.

Japan

Japanese accounting practices operate on a dual track. All joint stock corporations (more than one million) are subject to the accounting and financial reporting requirements of the Japanese Commercial Code, which is administered by the Justice Ministry. Fairly simple nonconsolidated statements must be prepared and are attested to by a statutory auditor who typically is a member of the reporting company's organization and not usually a CPA. Very large joint stock corporations (effective from 1984, those with capital stock of 500 million yen or more, or total liabilities of 20,000 million yen or more) have some special reporting requirements and must have their statements audited by CPAs.

The second track is covered by the Securities and Exchange Law (SEL), as administered by the Ministry of Finance. Approximately 3,000 public corporations are affected. Exposure under the SEL is significantly greater than under the Commercial Code. Securities and Exchange Law registration statements and annual reports must be audited by CPAs. As of mid-1982, the total number of CPAs in Japan was approximately 7,000.

The Japanese Institute of Certified Public Accountants is organized and operates much along the lines of the American Institute of Certified Public Accountants.

Corporate accounting principles and auditing standards are generally established by the Business Accounting Deliberating Council (BADC), which is an advisory body to the Ministry of France. Members are appointed by the Ministry of Finance and represent academics, government, business circles, and the accounting profession. Some of its more important pronouncements are the following:

1949	*Financial Accounting Standards for Business Enterprises*
1950	*Auditing Standards and Working Rules of Field Work*
1956	*Working Rules of Reporting*
1962	*Cost Accounting Standards*
1975	*Financial Accounting Standard on Consolidated Financial Statements*
1977	*Opinion on Interim Financial Statements Included in Semi-Annual Reports*
1979	*Accounting Standards for Foreign Currency Transactions*

It follows that the Council has played a leading role in determining the course of the Japanese corporate accounting after the war. These standards have always been published in a "codified" style.

The tax laws have a relatively heavy influence on accounting practices in Japan. The Corporation Tax Law and its related regulations specify the methods to be used in recording various allowances in order for them to be tax deductible. For example, a company is permitted, for tax purposes, to provide an allowance for depreciation computed under an accelerated method or an allowance in an amount equal to the gain realized from an exchange of properties, if it is appropriately recorded in the books of account. The company, however, cannot record an allowance under one method (e.g., straight-line method of depreciation) in the books and report differently for tax purposes (e.g., declining balance method). Since the effect of recording these allowances permitted under tax laws and regulations is a deferral of otherwise currently payable income taxes, most Japanese companies follow tax accounting, when applicable, in preparing their financial statements.

In this regard, the Audit Certificate Administration Rule of the Ministry of Finance permits a CPA to express an "unqualified opinion" for SEL purposes with respect to financial statements that conform to tax laws and regulations even though they may not be in conformity with generally accepted accounting principles as promulgated by the BADC.

Most Japanese companies have a lump-sum severance indemnity plan, although annuity-type pensions are becoming more popular. Benefits under the lump-sum severance plan are usually determined based on the type of severance (voluntary or involuntary separation), length of service and current rate of pay. The benefits under an involuntary severance are more than those under a voluntary severance. Some companies provide for the liability under the plan at 100 percent of the amount that would be required if the employees voluntarily separated at the end of a fiscal year. However, the usual accounting practice is to accrue in accordance with tax regulations that limit the account of accrual to 40 percent of the liability computed on a voluntary separation basis.

The equity method of accounting for investments in the common stock of unconsolidated subsidiaries and 20–50 percent owned affiliated companies is not required in the individual financial statements in Japan. However, in the preparation of consolidated financial statements, the equity method of accounting may be applied but will be required for the year beginning on or after April 1, 1983 (see also the discussion in Chapter 6 concerning this issue).

Other special features of Japanese accounting practices are that statements of changes in financial positions are not required, and that most Japanese companies have fiscal years ending March 31, which coincides with the Japanese government's fiscal year.

Stock dividends are accounted for at par values as are free share distributions from paid-in surplus or legal reserve accounts. Bonuses paid to directors are charged directly to retained earnings, whereas regular directors' fees are charged to current income. The Commercial Code generally prohibits the acquisition of treasury stock, except in a few defined instances like cancelation of shares or in connection with a business combination. When treasury stock is retained, it should be shown as an asset at cost.

The concepts of "fair presentation" in all financial statements covered and "conformity with generally accepted accounting principles consistently applied" underlie independent auditors' reports. Deviations from an "unqualified" opinion are required if the professional auditor is unable to satisfy himself or herself as to any of the statements made in the typical short-form report. Auditing in Japan is discussed further in Chapter 9.

The Netherlands

The Dutch Commercial Code requires the keeping of records that must show a company's financial position and give comprehensive information about its business transactions. In very summary terms, it also specifies the contents of financial statements to be published. Since the statutory provisions of the Commercial Code are very general, the Dutch Institute has played an active role in developing recommendations on accounting and auditing standards to supplement Code provisions over the years.

A major change came with the 1970 Act on Annual Accounts, which became effective for financial years ending on or after May 1, 1971. It contains detailed provisions for financial reporting by Dutch companies but left the development of specific accounting standards and principles to those concerned with them—that is, companies, professional accountants, labor union representatives, and government officials. The interested parties have combined into an official study group known as the Netherlands Tripartite Accounting Standards Committee. This committee published *Draft Netherlands Accounting Guidelines* in October 1981. These draft guidelines are a compiled version of all earlier opinions and recommendations and will, in due course, become the foundation of Dutch financial accounting and reporting.

Among the provisions of the Act on Annual Accounts are the following:

1. Annual financial statements shall show a fair picture of the financial position and results for the year, and all items therein must be appropriately grouped and described.
2. Financial statements must be drawn up in accordance with "sound business practice" (i.e., accounting principles acceptable to the business community).
3. The bases of stating assets and liabilities and determining results of operations must be disclosed.
4. Financial statements shall be prepared on a consistent basis and material effects of changes in accounting principles properly disclosed.
5. Comparative financial information for the preceding period shall be disclosed in the financial statements and accompanying footnotes.

The Netherlands Accounting Guidelines are broadly consistent with International Accounting Standards Committee (IASC) Standards, generally in harmony with British-American practices, and supportive of current cost accounting measurements. In over 152 pages of text, the Guidelines cover:

1. Objectives and Basic Principles
2. Pricing (i.e., valuation) Policies
3. The Relationship between the Various Parts of the Accounts
4. Criteria for the Inclusion and Disclosure of Information
5. Changes in System and Accounting for the Effects of Such Changes
6. Fixed Assets and Depreciation
7. Participating Interests and Income from Participating Interests
8. Long-term Investments and Investment Income
9. Other Durable Assets
10. Stocks and Costs of Consumption of Goods
11. Receivables
12. Liquid Assets Temporarily Invested and Freely Available
13. Other Assets
14. Shareholders' Equity

The foregoing enumerations suggest that financial accounting and reporting standards and principles in the Netherlands are highly developed. They take their place with the most sophisticated in the world. The Dutch separate strictly financial accounting from tax accounting. Differences between the two are typically linked through tax allocation procedures.

Consolidated financial statements are the rule, and the equity method of accounting for intercorporate investments is widely applied.

A rather novel feature of generally accepted accounting principles in the Netherlands is the inclusion therein of current replacement value measurements. Especially, larger Dutch companies carry certain inventory and depreciable fixed asset items at their current replacement values, with corresponding replacement value-based depreciation expenses in income statements and replacement valuation "reserves" in the owners' equity sections of balance sheets. The large and well-known Philips Company has used replacement value measurements in its published financial statements since 1951.

The Dutch Institute of "Register Accountants" has approximately 4,000 members, half of whom are in public practice. Close to 6,000 individuals are student members of the Dutch Institute. Qualification as a public accountant in the Netherlands occurs predominantly through extension study with the Institute of Register Accountants. The necessary study period is reduced for university graduates with appropriate degree concentrations. Practical experience is necessary in all cases prior to certification.

Statutory audits became obligatory for the first time in 1970 during the introduction of the Act on Annual Accounts. Only Register Accountants or other experts (usually professional auditors with foreign qualifications) may act as statutory auditors. The professional and ethical rules governing independent auditors in the Netherlands are as strict as any in the world. Further discussion of the auditing environment in Holland is offered in Chapter 9.

Finally, the Netherlands is the only country that explicitly provides for legal review of the administration of the Act of Annual Accounts. Any interested party who is of the opinion that the annual accounts of an enterprise do not meet the relevant requirements as laid down in the Act may take legal action to force the enterprise to prepare its annual accounts in accordance with directions to be given by order of the Court. Such legal actions are exclusively within the jurisdiction of the Enterprise Chamber of the Court of Justice of Amsterdam. Two Register Accountants have been appointed to this Court to serve as experts. Appeals of the Chamber's judgments may only be lodged with the Supreme Court in The Hague and are restricted to points of law.

Sweden

Swedish financial accounting and reporting practices differ from internationally accepted norms in several important respects. The main reason for this difference is that Swedish accounting practices reflect the availability of significant governmental incentives and subsidies to the business sector. As explained in Chapter 2, accounting and reporting practices in Sweden fairly directly reflect national economic policies. This is accomplished by forcing taxpayers who wish to claim any of the important subsidies and incentives to book them fully. Thus, taxable income in Sweden is basically book income. Looked at from a distance, one might say that Swedish tax laws and special national economic policies have a stranglehold on financial accounting and reporting in this Nordic country.

To the extent that Swedish accounting is not preempted by tax and national economic policies, it is responsive to four authoritative influences:

1. The latest Companies Act, which came into effect in 1977
2. The Swedish Accounting Law dated March 25, 1976 (effective from January 1, 1977)
3. The Swedish Accounting Standards Board, which is a government agency operating since July 1, 1976
4. The Swedish Institute of Authorized Public Accountants—Föreningen Auktoriserade Revisorer (FAR)

At present, there are approximately 750 authorized public accountants in Sweden. There are several other licensed classes of auditors with lower levels of professional qualifications. To date FAR has issued about a dozen recommendations on accounting practices and three on auditing.

The Companies Act requires companies' annual reports to include an administration report, balance sheet, income statement, statement of changes in financial position, and notes to the financial statements. The last four items are required for each company individually and, when appropriate, on a consolidated basis as well.

The most unusual feature of Swedish accounting practice is the presence of untaxed reserves. These reserves represent the accumulation of charges, which are allowed for tax purposes, but do not represent "ordinary and necessary" business events and transactions. Such reserves occur in connection with:

Inventories
Payrolls
Future investments
Accelerated depreciation
Blocked deposits with the Bank of Sweden

Deferred income taxes are typically not recognized in Sweden, nor are actuarially computed future pension liabilities. The latter are typically included among footnote disclosures as contingent liabilities.

There are no generally accepted practices with regard to extraordinary items. Companies include or exclude them from respective income statements more or less at will but usually disclose them in footnotes.

Some other significant practices concern the possibility of reevaluating property, plant, and equipment, subject to certain restrictions contained in the Companies Act. Depreciation is sometimes reported at two levels—in income statements toward the determination of operating income and in transfers to or from special reserves. As pointed out already, such reserves are typically untaxed income. Companies may capitalize R & D expenditures but few of them

TABLE 3.3   Swedish Föreningen Guide to Restate Swedish Financial Statements to U.S. Generally Accepted Accounting Principles

A comprehensive restatement of a set of Swedish financial statements to reflect the application of, for example, accounting principles generally accepted in the U.S. (known as GAAP), requires an in-depth investigation of the principles which have been applied over a period of years. The guidelines given below do not purport to give a short-cut to a GAAP restatement, but they do cover the most significant adjustment in the vast majority of cases, the reclassification of untaxed reserves, as well as some other items which it may be possible to adjust for on the basis of disclosures made in the annual report.

	TO ADJUST	
	NET INCOME	STOCK HOLDERS' EQUITY
Net income or stockholders' equity as reported in financial statements	x x x	x x x
ADJUSTMENTS:		
Untaxed reserves:		
Add 45% of balance sheet item		x x x
Add (deduct) 43% of year's transfer to (from) reserves	x x x	
Unprovided pensions:		
Deduct 43% of unprovided amount		x x x
Interests in associated companies:		
Add equity in year's undistributed earnings	x x x	
Add equity in accumulated undistributed earnings		x x x
Deferred exchange gains (losses):		
Add (deduct) 43% of deferred gains (losses)	x x x	x x x
Adjusted amounts	x x x	x x x

Notes:
1. The current effective tax rate is 57%. A normal cumulative effective tax rate (covering the period of buildup of the untaxed reserves) is 55%.
2. There would normally be insufficient information about the effect of unprovided pensions on net income on which to base an adjustment.
3. The adjustment for Swedish associated companies should of course include the equity in their untaxed reserves, etc.

Source: Föreningen Auktoriserade Revisorer (FAR), *Key To Understanding Swedish Financial Statements 1981*, Stockholm: FAR, 1982, p. 5.

do for tax reasons. When capitalized, such expenditures are subject to a maximum five-year amortization period.

Price level accounting is not generally practiced in Sweden. Translation of foreign currencies utilizes mainly the monetary-nonmonetary translation method, although the use of the current rate method for all financial statement items is gaining acceptance. Accounting for foreign exchange transaction and translation "gains and losses" is widely varied. At the time of this writing, FAR exposure drafts on both price level accounting and foreign currency translations are pending.

Similarly unresolved is the equity accounting issue. A 1980 FAR exposure draft would have prohibited equity accounting methods as contrary to existing provisions of the Swedish Accounting Law. At the same time, footnote disclosure of the equity in undistributed earnings of subsidiary companies was recommended. This apparent compromise is also unresolved as yet.

Beginning in 1980, FAR issues an annual *Key to Understanding Swedish Financial Statements.* The 1981 version contains a "guide" for restating Swedish financial statements to reflect accounting principles generally accepted in the United States—in broad-brush general terms. This guide is reproduced in Table 3.3.

Limited liability companies, branches of foreign corporations, and cooperative societies are required to be audited. While there are no mandatory auditing standards in Sweden, the auditing recommendations issued by FAR are binding on its members. While the subject of professional auditing is discussed at greater lengths in Chapter 9, it is noteworthy to observe here that the typical independent auditor's report in Sweden goes beyond the representations typically made in other countries. It includes a statement to the effect "that the board of directors and the managing director be [or not be] discharged from liability for 19XX."

Switzerland

A striking feature of Swiss financial reporting, especially by large multinational enterprises domiciled in Switzerland, is that many reports significantly exceed the minimal requirements contained in the applicable paragraphs of corporate law and securities regulations (see Table 3.2). This difference between financial reporting practices and statutory and regulatory norms is undoubtedly caused by international marketing pressures on the products and operations of Swiss companies, as well as by keen competition in the international financial capital markets.

Technical accounting developments originating outside of Switzerland are impacting the profession at an increasing rate. Many nations trading with Switzerland are directly affected by the current implementation phase of the EEC accounting-related directives—which in turn affect Swiss financial and commercial practices. Then there are the OECD and the U.N. guidelines that affect Swiss multinationals, especially those operating in Third World countries. While the Swiss multinationals are really neither more nor less affected than multinational enterprises domiciled elsewhere, the geographic and economic smallness of Switzerland simply makes these effects more visible. Several of the large Swiss-based multinational companies have created specific staffs in their controllers' and/or treasurers' departments to prepare their companies to cope with the various international financial reporting and disclosure recommendations, guidelines, or requirements already on the horizon.

In their annual reports, Swiss companies disclose few, if any, of the accounting policies they utilize. Consolidated financial statements generally are not published, since they are not required by statute. The dozen or so large Swiss companies that do publish consolidated financial statements publish them unaudited. From a multinational point of view, that is a major drawback.

On the positive side, a number of Swiss companies are actively experimenting with inflation accounting methods. For example, Ciba-Geigy has adopted a form of replacement cost accounting. Sulzer states fixed assets at current values. Other companies make supplemental disclosures of limited price level–adjusted data and, in one or two instances, selected nonmonetary assets (e.g., inventories and depreciable assets) are adjusted for the effects of purchasing power changes.

In Switzerland corporate law emanates from the Code of Obligations. Sections of the Code dealing with accounting, auditing, and financial reporting are so broad as to provide little substantive guidance for effective corporate financial reporting.

The most troublesome aspects of the existing statutory provisions are the following:

1. Unfettered use of undisclosed (i.e., secret) reserves
2. Lack of requirements for consolidated financial statement preparation
3. Use of statutory audits in all but a few large enterprise situations

Long before the accounting profession in North America and elsewhere recognized the desirability of multitiered professional organizations, the Swiss organized their Schweizerische Treuhand- und Revisionskammer into the following three groups:

1. Institute of Certified Public Accountants
2. Association of Public Trust and Auditing Companies
3. Society of Associations and Bank Auditing Firms

In Group 1, there are about 1,000 individual members, approximately one-fourth of whom work as individual practitioners. Local city or cantonal chapters organize the majority of professional activities, including continuing education programs.

Approximately 50 trust and auditing companies are members of Group 2. Together they employ some 4,000 professionals. The Association's organizational activities consist primarily of the preparation of industry statistics and lobbying.

Group 3 is a special-interest group whose activities are closely regulated by the Swiss Banking Commission. Nevertheless, the members are independently practicing professionals who benefit from meetings at which they can exchange experiences and from other professional development activities.

The Institute's publications program is fairly extensive.

At the time of this writing, an official Financial Accounting Standards Board is being organized by the Swiss Institute.

Accounting is not a major discipline at Swiss universities. Consequently, only a minority of practicing accounting professionals in Switzerland hold university degrees. The most typical entry into the accounting profession in Switzerland is via commercial junior colleges, although a small percentage of professional entrants hold only high school degrees.

With respect to opinion audits by independent auditors, statutory requirements limit them to the following situations:

1. Corporations with a legal capital of SF 5 million or more
2. Companies having bonds or debentures outstanding
3. Institutions appealing to the public to obtain money deposits

Aside from the foregoing independent audit requirements, each company must have one or more statutory auditors. These auditors have to satisfy themselves that the financial statements are in agreement with the books, that the books have been properly kept, and that the presentation in the financial statements of the results of operations and financial position is in accordance with all applicable provisions of the law. Statutory auditors need not be professionally certified or independent, but they may not be directors or employees of the company to be audited. The statutory auditors report to the annual stockholders' meeting. On the other hand, independent auditors, where their services are specifically required by law, report directly to the board of directors and the statutory auditors. Independent audit reports are "long form" in nature and quite detailed. They are not available to the stockholders.

United Kingdom

In the United Kingdom, company affairs, including financial accounting and reporting requirements, are primarily governed by statutes termed Companies Acts. These are national laws. Currently in force is the Companies Act of 1948 together with substantial amending Acts of 1967, 1976, and 1980. However, the legislation does not contain specific accounting standards and principles beyond the general "true and fair" financial reporting requirements. Thus the Institute of Chartered Accountants in England and Wales began to issue recommendations on accounting principles in 1942. These statements were not binding, however. When a number of financial failures occurred in the late 1960s, the British profession had no option other than taking a more definitive approach to accounting principles.

In 1970, the Accounting Standards Steering Committee (ASSC) was organized in association with most other professional accountancy bodies in the British Isles. After various reorganizations, the committee is now known as the Accounting Standards Committee (ASC). It has 22 members appointed by a senior committee of the U.K. Consultative Committee of Accountancy Bodies. In a 1982 departure from earlier practices, different professional accounting specialists (e.g., industry, practice, public sector, auditing) and some nonaccountants serve on the ASC.

The ASC issues formal Statements of Standard Accounting Practice (SSAP) that are binding upon the members of all the professional bodies making up the ASSC. Much as in the United States, some titles of standards issued are as follows:

1. Accounting for the Results of Associated Companies
2. Disclosure of Accounting Policies
3. Earnings per Share
4. The Accounting Treatment of Government Grants
5. Accounting for Value-Added Tax
6. Extraordinary Items and Prior Year Adjustments
. . . . .
10. Statements of Source and Application of Funds
11. Accounting for Deferred Taxation
. . . . .
13. Research and Development Costs
. . . . .
16. Current Cost Accounting

The details of British accounting standards need not be elaborated here since they permeate much of the English-language accounting literature and are thus readily available. Suffice it to say that these standards are by and large similar to those prevailing in North America, that published financial statements in Great Britain reflect a fair amount of financial disclosure, and that British accountants of late are innovation-minded, as in their support of current cost accounting measurements.[11]

The five principal accountancy bodies in the United Kingdom are the following:

1. The Institute of Chartered Accountants in England and Wales (ICAEW)
2. The Association of Certified Accountants
3. The Institute of Chartered Accountants of Scotland
4. The Institute of Cost and Management Accountants
5. The Chartered Institute of Public Finance and Accountancy

These five bodies are linked and individually and jointly strengthened through the Consultative Committee on Accountancy Bodies which was formed in May

[11] For those interested in U.K.-U.S. comparisons, an excellent source is F. R. Barfuss, R. D. Musson, and D. C. Bennett, "Some Significant Differences in U.S. and U.K. Reported Net Income," *CPA Journal*, February 1982, pp. 44–48.

1974 and to which the Institute of Chartered Accountants in Ireland also belongs.

The five U.K. professional accountancy bodies referred to above have a combined membership in excess of 100,000, approximately 45,000 of whom are in public practice. Companies incorporated under the Companies Act must appoint independent auditors even though there is no general statutory requirement that financial statements be audited. Audit requirements sometimes are imposed by certain special legislation. Taxation authorities normally insist on audited statements where these are already required by the Companies Acts. Consequently there is a significant amount of opinion auditing in the British Isles that supports the membership statistics just cited. The relatively heavy incidence of professional auditing in Great Britain prompts the inevitable comparison with other countries and the resulting research question of how much an economy or a social system really benefits from broadly applied professional auditing activities.

United Kingdom auditing standards and guidelines are issued by the Audit Practices Committee of the Consultative Committee referred to earlier. There are fewer such standards and guidelines in the United Kingdom than are found in the United States. Chapter 9 provides additional discussion on the subject of auditing.

Despite its long and numerous accounting traditions, the United Kingdom devotes only modest resources (at least by North American norms) to accounting research and policy making. The ICAEW does not require university or college degrees of aspiring new members. In 1979, 28 percent of persons signing training contracts with firms of chartered accountants did not possess a degree, 21 percent had a relevant degree (accounting major or equivalent), and the remaining 51 percent were holders of "nonrelevant" degrees.

From an accounting vantage point, the United Kingdom is presently being pulled toward the EEC on the one hand and yet steadfast in its Anglo sympathies and "ways of doing things" on the other. This dichotomy creates friction. We expect that the next decade will be one of many changes for U.K. accounting.

United States

United States accounting is sometimes maligned as "big bully." *Accountancy Age* characterized it as "overpaid, overrated, over there."[12] This tabloid review describes the AICPA as "weak, ineffectual, and largely irrelevant."[13] The Big Eight accounting firms are referred to as "robber barons" and the competition taking place within the U.S. accounting profession as instrumental to the effect that "there is a general undermining of standards."[14] From an international perspective U.S. accounting is often approached in love-hate fashion.

---

[12] Anthony Hilton, "Overpaid, Overrated, Over There" *Accountancy Age*, February 11, 1982, pp. 17–18.

[13] Ibid., p. 17.

[14] Ibid., p. 18.

Earlier on we pointed out that a shared power system exists in the United States with respect to financial accounting policy making. In this shared system, probably half of the balance of power rests with the public sector—for example, the Securities and Exchange Commission (SEC), the Internal Revenue Service (IRS), and a number of regulatory commissions. The other half rests with the private sector, represented by the FASB as independent standard setters, professional organizations like the AICPA, the Financial Executives Institute (FEI), the National Accountants Association (NAA), and the American Accounting Association (AAA) as representatives of professional accounting organizations, and stock exchanges, bankers associations, and business and industrial groups standing in for the business community at large. The key link allowing this mixed system to work effectively is the 1973 SEC Accounting Series Release (ASR) No. 150. According to this release:

> The Commission intends to continue its policy of looking to the private sector for leadership in establishing and improving accounting principles. For purposes of this policy, principles, standards, and practices promulgated by the FASB in its statements and interpretations, will be considered by the Commission as having substantial authoritative support, and those contrary to such FASB promulgations will be considered to have no such support.[15]

Another important trait of the U.S. system is the absence of general legal requirements for publication of periodic audited financial statements. Each of the 52 states and territorial jurisdictions of the United States has more or less superficial corporation statutes requiring that different books and records be kept and certain periodic financial reports rendered. However, many of these statutes are not rigorously enforced and reports rendered to local agencies are unavailable to the public. The state of Delaware, where many U.S. corporations are incorporated, makes no mention of record-keeping or financial reporting requirements in its state corporation laws.

Thus, annual audit and financial reporting requirements realistically exist only at the federal level. These requirements pertain to companies whose stock is listed on stock exchanges, and those companies whose stock is sold over the counter, and that have more than 500 shareholders and assets of over $1 million. The SEC administers these requirements and applies them currently to approximately 10,000 companies. Consequently, the vast majority of U.S. companies are not required to have annual audits or report their financial affairs publicly. Nonetheless, despite the absence of formal requirements to do so, many small companies have annual audited financial statements prepared at the request of banks or other financial credit sources, corporate boards of directors, senior company management, or in response to plain good business practice.

A third important dimension of the U.S. accounting scene is its fervor for

---

[15] Securities and Exchange Commission, *Statement of Policy on the Establishment and Improvement of Accounting Principles and Standards*, Accounting Series Release No. 150. Reprinted in *The Development of SEC Accounting*, G. J. Previts, ed. (Reading, Mass.: Addison-Wesley, 1981), p. 228.

detailed accounting regulations. Even ignoring the very voluminous tax accounting regulations supporting income, turnover, property, and excise tax systems, there are probably more detailed financial accounting and auditing regulations in the United States than in the rest of the world put together. This mass of rules, guidelines, recommendations, standards, generally accepted accounting principles, generally accepted auditing standards, regulatory accepted accounting practices, and so forth, must be carefully categorized and prioritized to be properly supportive of professional accounting activities.

Yet another major element of U.S. financial accounting practice is its segmentation and specialization. One aspect of this phenomenon was mentioned earlier in that only larger companies whose securities are publicly traded are subject to compulsory annual auditing and financial reporting. Some accounting principles are equally differentiated. For instance, FAS No. 14 mandating segmented reporting does not apply to private companies; FAS No. 33 requiring supplemental disclosures of current costs and general price level effects applies only to about the 1,000 largest corporations; and FAS No. 52 dictates different foreign exchange translation rules depending upon the economic circumstance of the functional currency of a particular foreign subsidiary (see Chapter 4 for details). In similar fashion, generally accepted auditing standards distinguish between opinion audits, audit reviews, and compilations (see Chapter 9 for details). Still other differentiations occur between industry-specific practices, for instance, revenue recognition in the moving picture industry, current cost calculations in the extractive and forest product industries, mergers in the savings and loan industry, and so forth.

The overview approach adopted for this chapter precludes mention of all U.S. accounting rules and regulations now in force. Major items are the FASB's conceptual framework project described in Chapter 2 and the SEC trend, beginning in 1981, toward deregulation instead of the previous regulation overload. Active participation in financial accounting policy making by nonaccounting interest groups is also noteworthy.

In the practice area, widespread use of LIFO inventory measurements, internationally unique rules on corporate poolings of interest and foreign exchange translations, plus comprehensive capitalization of financial leases and measurable pension obligations stand out.

United States professional auditing practices are referenced in Chapter 9. The typical short-form auditor's report is premised on the concepts of "fair presentation" in all financial statements covered and "conformity with generally accepted accounting principles consistently applied."

Deviation from an "unqualified" opinion is required if the professional auditor is unable to satisfy himself or herself as to any of the statements made therein.

SELECTED REFERENCES

AMERICAN INSTITUTE OF CERTIFIED PUBLIC ACCOUNTANTS, *Professional Accounting in 30 Countries*, New York: AICPA, 1975, 792 pp.

AUSTRALIAN RESEARCH FOUNDATION, *Australian Company Financial Reporting,* Sydney: ARF, 1981.

BEENY, J. H., *European Financial Reporting—France,* London: Institute of Chartered Accountants in England and Wales, 1976, 290 pp. (mimeographed).

BENSTON, GEORGE J., "Public (U.S.) Compared to Private (U.K.) Regulation of Corporate Financial Disclosure," *Accounting Review,* July 1976, pp. 483–498.

CANADIAN INSTITUTE OF CHARTERED ACCOUNTANTS, Accounting Standards Committee, *CICA Handbook* (Toronto: CICA, various dates), looseleaf.

CHOI, FREDERICK D. S., and VINOD B. BAVISHI, "Diversity in Multinational Accounting," *Financial Executive,* August 1982, pp. 45–49.

COOPERS & LYBRAND (USA), *International Financial Reporting and Auditing: A Guide To Regulatory Requirements,* New York, 1979, 173 pp.

DELOITTE HASKINS & SELLS (USA), *Doing Business in the United States of America—A Guide for the Foreign Investor,* New York, 1981, 133 pp.

ERNST & WHINNEY, *Switzerland* (International Series), New York, 1980, 8 pp.

FITZGERALD, R. D., A. D. STICKLER, and T. R. WATTS, eds., *International Survey of Accounting Principles and Reporting Practices,* Scarborough, Ont., Canada: Price Waterhouse International, 1979, unpaginated (distributed by Butterworths).

FÖRENINGEN AUKTORISERADE REVISORER, *Key To Understanding Swedish Financial Statements 1981,* Stockholm: FAR, 1982, 5 pp.

JAPANESE INSTITUTE OF CERTIFIED PUBLIC ACCOUNTANTS, *Corporate Disclosure in Japan,* Tokyo: JICPA, 1982, 67 pp.

KLAASSEN, JAN, "An Accounting Court: The Impact of the Enterprise Chamber on Financial Reporting in the Netherlands," *Accounting Review,* April 1980, pp. 327–341.

LAFFERTY, MICHAEL, *Accounting in Europe,* Cambridge, England: Woodhead, Faulkner, Ltd., 1975, 425 pp. (published in association with National Westminster Bank).

LAFFERTY, MICHAEL, and DAVID CAIRNS, *Financial Times World Survey of Annual Reports 1980,* London: Financial Times Business Information Ltd., 1980.

NOBES, CHRISTOPHER, and ROBERT PARKER, eds., *Comparative International Accounting,* Homewood, Ill.: Richard D. Irwin, Inc., 1981, 379 pp.

OLDHAM, K. MICHAEL, *Accounting Systems and Practice in Europe* (2nd ed.), Westmead, Farnborough, Hampshire, U.K.: Gower Press, 1981, 288 pp.

ORGANIZATION FOR ECONOMIC COOPERATION AND DEVELOPMENT, *Accounting Practices in OECD Member Countries,* Paris: OECD, 1980, 250 pp.

ROBINSON, CHRIS, "Country Profile—Canada," *World Accounting Report,* June 1982, pp. 7–10

TRIPARTITE ACCOUNTING STANDARDS COMMITTEE, *Netherlands Accounting Guidelines,* Amsterdam: TASC, 1981, 152 pp.

DISCUSSION QUESTIONS

1. The Choi and Bavishi (1982) survey results are not fully consistent with the Price Waterhouse International (Fitzgerald, 1979) survey results. Speculate on likely explanations of differences in international survey results regarding national financial accounting and reporting practices.

2. Deliberate understatement of assets and/or overstatement of known liabilities leads to the creation of so-called "secret reserves." Why are secret reserves frowned upon in British-American financial accounting practice?

3. What is the effect of world accounting diversity upon comparative (i.e., transnational) financial ratio analysis?

4. What are some possible consequences of international financial information overload? Is there any evidence that national financial accounting and reporting practices impinge on the operations of securities markets?

5. Based on the information presented in Table 3.2, which are the three most commonly used accounting principles among the ten countries, and which are the three least common such principles?

6. Distinguish between the terms *capital reserve* and *revenue reserve* as these terms are used in Australia.

7. In France, financial accounting standards and practices originate primarily from three authoritative sources: (a) companies legislation (Plan Comptable), (b) professional opinions and recommendations (L'Ordre National des Experts Comptables and Conseil National de la Comptabilité), and (c) stock exchange regulations (Commission des Opérations de Bourse). Which of these three has the greatest influence on day-to-day French accounting practice? Can you identify a specific instance of French accounting influence upon actual or proposed EEC accounting regulations?

8. In Japan, CPAs may express an "unqualified opinion" with respect to financial statements prepared in conformity with Japanese tax laws, even though such statements may not be in conformity with financial accounting principles generally accepted in Japan. Would you support adoption of this approach into international practice? Specify five other countries in which tax accounting rules heavily influence financial reporting practices.

9. In the Netherlands, financial accounting and reporting practices are highly developed and professional and ethical rules governing Dutch independent auditors are "as strict as any in the world." At the same time there are very few officially established financial accounting standards in Holland. How do you explain this seeming paradox?

10. In the United States some private and/or small public companies are exempted from compliance with certain specified FASs. This seems likely to lead eventually to full distinction between "big GAAP" and "little GAAP." Considered from an international vantage point, is this development desirable? Why or why not?

EXERCISES

1. Among other things this chapter provides synopses of national accounting practice systems in ten developed countries.
    Required:
    Utilizing the information provided in the chapter and referring to additional sources, as far as they are available, list for each country:
    A. The name of the national financial accounting standard setting board or agency.

    B.   Title of a standard recently published and the year of publication.

    C.   The name of the agency, institute, or other organization charged with the enforcement of published national financial accounting standards.

2.   There is some discussion in the chapter about the differential effects of accounting standards and practices upon business decisions. These effects seem particularly pronounced in multinational business operations.

Required:

    A.   From the perspective of multinational business decision making, list five distinct advantages and five distinct disadvantages of existing worldwide accounting diversity.

    B.   Specify as best you can the effects of international accounting diversity upon (a) multinational foreign exchange decisions, (b) international business mergers, and (c) effects on stock prices of MNCs.

    C.   As far as you can judge, which of the ten countries has the most benign financial accounting environment in terms of multinational business operations, and from the perspective of corporate management.

3.   Reread Chapter 3 and its Discussion Questions.

Required:

    A.   As you go through this material, prepare a list of 20 expressions, terms, or short phrases unfamiliar or unusual in your home country.

    B.   Write a concise definition or explanation of each item.

4.   Drawing upon personal, family, or educational experiences, take a developing country with which you are somewhat familiar.

Required:

For the country chosen prepare a synopsis of its national accounting and financial reporting practice system.

5.   Analyze the ten national accounting practice systems summarized in the chapter.

Required:

    A.   For each of the ten countries treated in the chapter, select the most important financial accounting practice or principle at variance with "world-class" accounting.

    B.   For each selection you make, state briefly your reasons for its inclusion on your list.

CASE

Restating Financial Statements

This case consists of excerpts from the 1981 annual report of a major Swedish multinational enterprise. In addition to the basic consolidated financial statements, selected notes on accounting policies and elaborations on financial statement items are also furnished.

EXHIBIT 3.1   Excerpts from the 1981 annual report of a Swedish multinational company

---

Stora Kopparbergs Bergslags AB

THE GROUP

Consolidated Profit and Loss Account
(SEK millions)

		1981	1980
Operations	Sales	4,621.4	4,121.4
	Other operating income	143.8	146.6
		4,765.2	4,268.0
	Operating expenses...........................	−3,926.1	−3,361.0
	Operating income before depreciation	839.1	907.0
Planned depreciation (Note 3)		− 244.7	−214.4
	Operating income after planned depreciation	594.4	692.6
Financial income and expense	Dividends received	14.1	12.3
	Interest income	95.4	117.7
	Interest expense	− 117.6	− 163.6
		− 68.1	− 33.6
	Interest expense on provisions for pensions	− 42.4	− 39.4
	Exchange loss on loan debt	− 20.5	− 9.5
		− 131.0	− 82.5
	Income after financial income and expense	463.4	610.1
Extraordinary income	Gain on sale and scrapping of fixed assets	10.7	26.7
and expense (Note 4)	Other extraordinary income	6.4	6.0
	Devaluation loss on loan debt	− 27.1	−
	Other extraordinary expense	− 5.3	− 42.7
		− 15.3	− 10.0
	Income before appropriations and taxes	448.1	600.1
Appropriations	Depreciation in excess of planned	− 180.9	− 187.0
	Change in inventory reserve	− 85.6	40.7
	Withdrawal from reserve in connection with		
	the sale of fixed assets	6.0	6.0
	Transfer from investment reserves		
	and similar reserves	80.2	5.4
	Appropriation to investment reserve	—	− 107.6
		− 180.3	− 242.5
Appropriation to compulsory investment reserves		−	− 109.1
Income before taxes		267.8	248.5
Taxes		− 119.0	− 125.7
Minority interest in profits		− 0.8	− 2.2
Group profit for the year		148.0	120.6

(continued)

EXHIBIT 3.1   (*continued*)

Stora Kopparbergs Bergslags AB

THE GROUP

Consolidated Balance Sheet December 31 (SEK millions)

ASSETS		1981	1980
Current assets	Cash and bank balances	281.8	282.3
	Short-term deposits	19.0	364.4
	Own bonds	28.0	30.5
	Bills receivable	27.7	33.1
	Accounts receivable	891.4	766.7
	Prepaid expenses and accrued income	29.6	50.4
	Other receivables	151.5	203.0
	Felling rights	65.6	68.2
	Inventories	1,092.6	729.8
	Advances to suppliers	25.6	25.7
		2,612.8	2,554.1
Blocked accounts with Bank of Sweden for investment reserves		69.9	13.5
Fixed assets	Shares and participations	668.0	871.7
	Long-term receivables	190.5	219.1
	Group goodwill	39.2	29.7
	Costs carried forward for development work		
	and similar items	3.0	8.0
	Advances to suppliers	79.1	15.9
	Construction in progress	186.7	171.8
	Machinery and equipment	1,868.9	1,689.7
	Buildings	595.4	566.4
	Land and other fixed property	973.9	959.4
		4,604.7	4,531.7
Total assets		**7,287.4**	7,099.3
Assets pledged (Note 8)		**1,583.6**	1,594.2

EXHIBIT 3.1 *(continued)*

Stora Kopparbergs Bergslags AB

THE GROUP

LIABILITIES AND STOCKHOLDERS' EQUITY		1981	1980
Current liabilities	Drawing account	33.2	25.9
	Due to suppliers	612.4	458.0
	Current maturities of long-term debts	256.8	127.5
	Accrued taxes	6.2	97.0
	Accrued expenses and prepaid income	181.4	185.6
	Short-term loans	138.2	13.6
	Other current liabilities.........................	193.7	222.6
		1,421.9	1,130.2
Long-term debt	Bonds	483.4	528.9
	Mortgage loans	208.6	227.9
	Debenture loans	60.1	66.7
	Other loans...................................	838.8	814.7
	Provisions for pensions (Note 9)	658.6	607.4
		2,249.5	2,245.6
Minority interests in subsidiaries		15.9	19.6
Reserve for shares (Note 4)		—	454.0
Untaxed reserves	Inventory reserve	501.4	341.2
	Investment reserves and similar reserves	57.8	136.5
	Compulsory investment reserve	107.7	109.1
	Accumulated depreciation in excess		
	of planned	1,454.8	1,276.4
		2,121.7	1,863.2
Stockholders' equity (Note 10)			
Restricted equity	Share capital (7,302,750 shares, par value		
	SEK 100 each)	730.3	730.3
	Statutory reserves	455.2	449.8
		1,185.5	1,180.1
Unrestricted equity	Free reserves	144.9	86.0
	Net profit for the year	148.0	120.6
		292.9	206.6
Total liabilities and stockholders' equity		7,287.4	7,099.3
Dividend		102.6	91.6
Contractual commitments and contingent liabilities		209.5	330.6

(continued)

EXHIBIT 3.1 (*continued*)

NOTES TO THE CONSOLIDATED FINANCIAL STATEMENTS
(Amounts in SEK millions unless otherwise stated)
Accounting and Valuation Principles
The consolidated accounts include all companies in which the Parent Company, Stora Kopparberg, directly or indirectly owns more than 50 percent of the shares.

The past equity method is applied in consolidating the balance sheets of the Parent Company and subsidiaries. Differences between the cost of shares in subsidiaries and stockholders' equity in the subsidiaries at date of acquisition have been allocated to fixed assets or goodwill. To the degree that these fixed assets are subject to a decrease in value, they have been reduced through planned depreciation.

Shares acquired prior to 1970 have in most instances been written down to 0. These write-downs, made for purposes of consolidation, are included among "Statutory reserves."

The income and balance sheets of foreign subsidiaries are translated at year-end exchange rates, with the exception of Nova Scotia Pulp Limited whose values have been calculated as follows: monetary items have been translated using the closing rate of exchange and non-monetary items in accordance with the rate at the date of the transaction. The income statements have been translated using the average exchange rates during the year except for depreciation, for which the rate at the date of transaction was used. Exchange differences have been transferred directly to stockholders' equity.

The Swedish companies' current receivables and short-term liabilities in foreign currency have been translated at year-end exchange rates or, in cases where the rate is guaranteed by forward exchange operations, at the forward rate. Long-term liabilities have been translated at the higher of the rate when the liability was incurred and the year-end rate. If all receivables and liabilities had been stated at year-end exchange rates, income would have improved by SEK 7 m.

Unrealized exchange losses and gains have been offset against each other. The excess loss has been charged against income. Losses that apply to operating liabilities and receivables are included in operating income while losses on loan liabilities are included in the accounts as financial expense, with the exception of the portion caused by the devaluation of the Swedish krona in 1981. This exchange loss is included among extraordinary expense.

Raw materials and fuel have been valued at the lower of cost or replacement value. Semifinished and finished goods have been valued at the lower of manufacturing cost and sales value, after deducting selling costs.
Definitions
Profitability
Profitability is calculated in the following manner:
1.   **Nominal profitability**
a)   on stockholders' equity:
       Operating income after financial income and expense charged with taxes (50%) in relation to the average stockholders' equity (= net capital + untaxed reserves minus latent tax liability).
            This profit concept is also the basis for calculating adjusted profit per share.
b)   on total capital:
       Operating income before financial income and expense in relation to average total capital (= balance sheet total with deductions for operating liabilities).

EXHIBIT 3.1   (*continued*)

   2.   **Real profitability**
   Operating income before financial expense, less price changes on ingoing inventories and adjusted to reflect calculated excess depreciation, in relation to total capital as defined in 1. b) above but using calculated residual values instead of planned residual values for fixed assets.
Profit per share
Profit calculated as stated in 1. a) above, divided by current number of shares.
Effects of inflation
The Group's profit and financial position are expressed in nominal terms, in accordance with traditional accounting theories. During times characterized by large changes in prices, however, this accounting practice is insufficient. Therefore, some effects of inflation should be pointed out.

	1981		1980
Nominal profit after financial income and expense		463.4		610.1
Adjustments for inflation				
Calculated excess depreciation	−183.6		−153.5	
Price changes on inventories at beginning of period	− 99.4		− 62.3	
Inflationary gains on net liabilities . . .	+ 65.9		+116.0	
		−217.1		− 99.8
Operating profit after financial income and expense, adjusted to reflect effects of inflation		246.3		510.3

It should be noted, however, that in calculating operating profit adjusted to reflect effects of inflation, inflationary increases in the value of assets is [sic] not taken into consideration. This is a substantial item for companies with extensive real assets.
Calculated excess depreciation
Planned depreciation is based on historical value. To express resource consumption for the period in real terms, depreciation is based on calculated current acquisition values (calculated depreciation).
     The difference between planned and calculated depreciation (calculated excess depreciation) is thus the calculated depreciation requirement with regard to changes in monetary values.
Price changes on inventories at beginning of the year
The Group's operating profit includes the effects on income of price rise gains/losses that arise when inventories from the beginning of the period are sold off and price increases mean the inventories are sold at higher prices at the same time as raw materials and components must be bought at higher prices. The price change is expressed as the difference between the ingoing and outgoing price of inventories multiplied by the consumed volume of ingoing inventories.
Inflationary gain on net liabilities
Changes in monetary values cause changes in the purchasing power of monetary assets and liabilities. The Company's monetary assets, primarily receivables and liquid funds, decline in value when prices rise while the repayment of liabilities requires a decreasing degree of purchasing power. When liabilities at the beginning of the year exceed monetary assets, inflationary gains arise. The change in monetary values corresponds to increase in the consumer price index calculated for each year.

(*continued*)

EXHIBIT 3.1   (*continued*)

NOTE 1   Personnel and labor costs

National Social Insurance Board standards have been used in calculating the number of employees in all personnel categories, as stated in the Annual Report.

The average number of employees and the amounts paid in wages, salaries and social costs are shown below:

Number of employees	Group		Parent Company	
	1981	1980	1981	1980
Sweden	8,806	8,754	5,601	5,494
Norway	27	29		
Denmark	20	21		
England	54	55		
West Germany	14	13		
France	8	9		
Italy	8	8		
Canada	987	1,037	˙987	1,037
U.S.A.	1	1		
Ireland	4	4		
	9,929	9,931	6,588	6,531
Number of work sites in Sweden . . .	57	55	26	24

The distribution of employees by work site is shown in a special list accompanying the accounts. A copy of the list can be obtained free of charge from the Company.

Personnel costs	Group		Parent Company	
	1981	1980	1981	1980
Wages and salaries				
Board of Directors[1] and Managing				
Director	1.7	1.5	1.7	1.4
Others				
Sweden	665.4	615.4	427.3	393.6
Norway	2.7	2.2		
Denmark	1.9	2.0		
England	4.6	4.4		
West Germany	2.6	2.2		
France	1.4	1.2		
Italy	1.2	1.0		
Canada	116.1	82.9	116.1	82.9
U.S.A.	0.3	0.2		
Ireland	0.4	0.5		
	798.3	713.5	545.1	477.9
Provisions for pensions and other so-				
cial costs	354.5	301.1	239.5	197.9

1. Includes bonuses of SEK 1.0 m. in 1981 and SEK 0.9 m. in 1980.

NOTE 9   Provision for pensions

The liability corresponds to the calculated Pension Reserve, except for SEK 8.6 m. (7.7), which is included under Contingent Liabilities. The commitment includes SEK 550 m. (504), of which the Parent Company's share is SEK 469 m. (430), covering obligations to the Pension Registration Institute (PRI).

EXHIBIT 3.1 (*continued*)

NOTE 10   Change in stockholders' equity

Group	Restricted stockholders' equity		Unrestricted stockholders' equity	Total
	Share capital	Restricted reserves		
Balance, Jan. 1, 1981	730.3	449.8	206.6	1,386.7
Profit allocation approved by Annual Meetings		0.1	− 91.4	− 91.3
Profit, 1981			148.0	148.0
Transfers		5.3	− 5.3	—
Exchange and translation differences in foreign subsidiaries			35.0	35.0
Balance at year-end	730.3	455.2	292.9	1,478.4

Parent Company	Restricted stockholders' equity		Unrestricted stockholders' equity		Total
	Share capital	Legal reserve	General reserve	Retained earnings	
Balance, Jan. 1, 1981	730.3	263.1	8.0	108.0	1,109.4
Profit allocation approved by Annual Meeting				− 91.3	− 91.3
Profit, 1981				105.0	105.0
Balance at year-end	730.3	263.1	8.0	121.7	1,123.1

It is proposed that SEK 72,000 of unrestricted stockholders' equity in the Group be allocated to restricted stockholders' equity.

NOTE 13   Specification of financial income and expense

	1981		1980	
Dividends on shares and participations				
From subsidiaries	9.9		9.8	
From others	10.3	20.2	8.9	18.7
Interest income				
From subsidiaries	33.4		19.9	
From others	58.4	91.8	93.7	113.6
Interest paid				
To subsidiaries	20.2		17.3	
To others	134.6	154.8	115.6	132.9

(*continued*)

EXHIBIT 3.1   (*continued*)

NOTE 14   Specification of funds provided from operations

	Group		Parent Company	
	1981	1980	1981	1980
Income after financial income and expense	463.4	610.1	356.6	415.8
Depreciation charged against income	244.7	214.4	147.8	128.7
Extraordinary items	− 25.4	− 33.3	− 23.5	− 31.7
Group contribution	−	−	− 35.4	53.6
Taxes	−119.0	−125.7	− 73.7	−115.0
Withdrawals from/deposits in blocked accounts	− 56.4	11.1	− 58.3	10.7
Dividends	− 91.6	− 80.6	− 91.3	− 80.3
Total funds provided from operations	415.7	596.0	222.2	381.8

Required

Using the format outlined in Table 3.3, restate the "group profit for the year" and stockholders' equity as of December 31, 1981 from the amounts reported in terms of accounting principles generally accepted in Sweden to amounts broadly reflecting U.S. GAAP. Be sure to note any assumptions made or special procedures applied.

4

Foreign Currency Translation

Accounting for foreign currency translation is without doubt one of the most controversial technical issues facing multinational enterprises that find it necessary to prepare consolidated financial statements incorporating the results of both domestic and foreign operations. Many of the problems associated with currency translation stem from the fact that foreign exchange rates used to effect the translation process are seldom fixed. As a consequence, operating results can vary, often markedly, from financial results owing to differences in translation rates employed and the accounting dispositions of resultant financial effects.

While most technical issues in accounting tend to resolve themselves over time, currency translation has proven to be an exception. That this trend will continue is supported by such developments as the demise of the dollar as a currency of unwavering strength, government-sanctioned gyrations in currency values, and the increased emphasis on transnational corporate financial disclosure (see Chapter 7 for a discussion of specific disclosure issues). Developments such as these have considerably heightened the interest of financial executives, accountants, and the financial community in the importance and economic consequences of foreign currency translation. Let us now examine the nature and development of this international accounting conundrum.

REASONS FOR
TRANSLATION

Companies with significant operations abroad cannot prepare consolidated financial statements unless their accounts as well as those of their subsidiaries are expressed in terms of a homogeneous currency. Thus, one cannot add Mexican pesos, Japanese yen, Swiss francs, and New Zealand dollars and obtain meaningful results. Accordingly, a single currency framework is required and this, traditionally, has been the reporting currency of the parent company. The process of restating various foreign currency balances to single currency equivalents is called *translation.*

Additional reasons for foreign currency translations are (a) recording foreign currency transactions, (b) reporting international branch and subsidiary activities, and (c) reporting the results of independent operations abroad.

The need to translate foreign currency transactions is similar to the need for consolidation procedures; namely, financial statements cannot be prepared from accounts that are expressed in various currencies. A company whose exports or imports are invoiced in terms of a foreign currency unit must translate those amounts to their domestic currency equivalents before entering the transactions in its books of account. Despite separate record keeping on the basis of local currency units, accounting reports resulting from such records must often travel internationally and be understood and used in countries other than those in which the reports are originally prepared.

Branch and subsidiary activities are another case in point. Branch activities are normally quite closely planned, administered, and controlled by the parent organization. Since both branch and parent are integral parts of a closely knit whole, it makes little sense to view the accounts of either by themselves. They must be combined so that a fair and complete total financial picture evolves. Again, foreign currency translation procedures are called for.

In contrast to branch activities, subsidiary companies enjoy a greater degree of autonomy by virtue of their separate legal existence. Nevertheless, foreign currency translation procedures are required. Parent company consolidation requirements are often in effect for subsidiary companies. In addition, parent companies must continually monitor the performance of foreign subsidiary operations and thus need accounting information that allows intercountry comparisons between subsidiaries' results as well as with those of the parent. Also, planning and administrative functions of parent company management cannot be performed effectively unless accounting information has substantially the same basis as that of the parent.

It is important to note, in this connection, that subsidiaries in other countries are quite likely to rely heavily on local management talent. This means there is a strong need for accounting information prepared according to local accounting concepts and practices and in terms of local currency units. This is the type of information that local managers are accustomed to and need for their own management purposes. Also, evaluation of local competitive conditions and comparisons with similar local firms are difficult unless locally oriented accounting information is available. Therefore, accounting information requirements of a parent company should generally not be allowed to overshadow local accounting information requirements. In effect, two distinct sets of information requirements exist and they require translation and reconciliation back and forth.

Finally, the expanded scale of international investment activities increases the need to convey accounting information about an independent company domiciled in one country to readers in another. This occurs, for example, when a company wishes to have its shares listed on a foreign stock exchange, contemplates a foreign acquisition or joint-venture arrangement, or simply desires to communicate the results of its operating performance and financial position to its foreign stockholders. Under these circumstances, a parent company translates its financial statements in their entirety from the domestic currency to the currency of the statement recipient's domicile.

Translations of accounts of independent companies are fundamentally distinct from translations of branch or subsidiary accounts. The former serve information purposes only. They are executed primarily for the convenience of a firm's foreign financial reporting audiences-of-interest and do not involve any restatement of accounting principles or adaptation of the original data base (see further discussion on this point in Chapter 7). In short, financial statements translated solely for information purposes have a single accounting domicile— the country in which the translated accounts are originally prepared.

TERMINOLOGY

Translation is not synonymous with *conversion.* Conversion is the physical exchange of one currency for another. Thus, a U.S. citizen vacationing in Rome would convert dollars into lira if he or she were interested in purchasing Italian goods. Translation is simply a change in monetary *expression,* as when a balance sheet expressed in British pounds is restated to U.S. dollar equivalents. No physical exchange occurs, no accountable transaction takes place. Indeed, the concept of foreign currency translation is analogous to translating a book from the Norwegian language to one written in English.

THE PROBLEM

The traditional medium for translating foreign currency amounts is the foreign exchange rate. This rate denotes the price of a unit of foreign currency in terms of the domestic or reporting currency. If foreign exchange rates were relatively stable, the translation process would be straightforward and no more difficult than, say, translating inches or feet to their metric equivalents. Exchange rates, however, are seldom stable as their values tend to vary in response to rather complex forces of supply and demand.

Until recently, the complex supply and demand factors were controlled, to some extent, by rather predictable governmental interactions in the foreign exchange market. Under the Bretton Woods system, currencies of countries that adhered to the International Monetary Fund (IMF) agreement were anchored to a common standard of value, namely, gold and certain "reserve currencies" that were readily convertible into gold. Governments of the IMF member countries committed themselves to limiting the fluctuation of their exchange rates within certain prescribed limits. When it appeared that the limits were likely to be exceeded, the monetary authorities of the nations concerned intervened in a number of ways to stabilize respective exchange rates. If the exchange rate movement could not be contained, the country whose currency was under pressure devalued or revalued its currency relative to other currencies. *Devaluation* means that more units of the devalued currency are needed to acquire a given number of units of another currency. *Revaluation* means just the opposite.

The Bretton Woods system came to an unexpected and abrupt end in late 1971 when fixed exchange rates were abandoned. Today the currencies of most industrialized countries are free to find their own values relative to one another, with governmental intervention much more constrained and unpredictable relative to these fluctuations. A system of *floating* exchange rates now prevails, creating, in turn, difficulties in multinational companies' foreign exchange translation and conversion procedures.

Fluctuating exchange values increase the number of translation rates that can be used to implement the translation process. Currency gyrations also give rise to exchange gains and losses that complicate the evaluation of multinational operations.

In a world of floating rates, at least three translation rates can be distinguished. First, there is the *current* rate, which is the exchange rate prevailing as of the financial statement date, for example, the rate in effect on December 31 for companies reporting on a calendar year basis. Second, there is the *historical* rate, which refers to the exchange rate prevailing when a foreign currency asset was first acquired or a foreign currency liability first incurred. Finally, there is the *average* rate comprising a simple or weighted average of either current or historical exchange rates. As average rates are simply variations of current or historical rates, the following discussion focuses on the latter.

What are the financial statement effects of using historical as opposed to current rates of exchange as foreign currency translation coefficients? Historical exchange rates generally preserve the original cost equivalent of a foreign currency item in the domestic currency statements. From the perspective of a U.S. parent company, assume that an item of inventory is acquired by a foreign subsidiary for 1,000 foreign currency (FC) units when the exchange rate is FC 2 = $1. This asset would appear in the U.S. consolidated statements at $500. Now assume that the exchange rate declines from FC 2 = $1 to FC 4 = $1 by the next financial statement date and that the inventory item is still on hand. Will the U.S. dollar equivalent of the inventory now change to $250? Clearly not. As long as we translate the original FC 1,000 cost at the rate that prevailed when the asset was acquired (historical rate), it will appear in the U.S. financial statements at $500, its historical cost expressed in U.S. dollars. The point is that use of historical exchange rates shield financial statements from foreign currency translation gains or losses, that is, from increases or decreases in the dollar equivalents of foreign currency balances due to fluctuations in the translation rate between reporting periods. It is the use of current rates that gives rise to translation gains or losses. Thus, in our previous example, translating the FC 1,000 piece of inventory at the current rate (FC 4 = $1) would yield a translation loss of $250 (FC 1,000 ÷ 2 − FC 1,000 ÷ 4).

At this point, a distinction should be drawn between *translation* gains and losses, such as that illustrated immediately above, and *transaction* gains and losses, both of which fall under the common rubric, "exchange gains and losses."

Foreign currency transactions occur whenever an enterprise purchases or sells goods for which payment is made in a foreign currency or when it borrows or lends foreign currency. Translation is necessary to maintain the accounting records in the currency of the reporting enterprise.

There are two types of transaction adjustments. The first, "gains and losses on settled transactions," arises whenever the exchange rate used to book the original transaction differs from the rate used to record settlement. Thus, if a U.S. parent company borrows FC 1,000 when the exchange rate is FC 2 = $1 and then converts the proceeds to dollars, it will receive $500 and record a liability of such on its books. If, at the time of repayment, the foreign exchange rate rises to FC 1 = $1, the U.S. company will actually have to pay out $1,000 to discharge its FC 1,000 debt. A $500 conversion loss has taken place.

The second type of transaction adjustment, "gains or losses on unsettled transactions," arises whenever financial statements are prepared prior to transaction settlement. In the preceeding example, assume that the FC 1,000 borrowing takes place during year 1 and is repaid during year 2. If the exchange rate prevailing at the end of year 1, the financial statement date, is FC 1.5 = $1, the dollar equivalent of the FC 1,000 loan will rise to $667, creating an exchange loss of $167. Until the foreign currency debt is actually extinguished, however, this unrealized exchange loss is similar in nature to a translation loss as it results from a restatement process. The distinction between tansaction and translation gains and losses is depicted schematically in Figure 4.1. Differences in exchange rates in effect at the various dates shown give rise to the various types of exchange adjustments discussed above.

When considering exchange gains and losses, the reader must be careful to distinguish between transaction gains and losses and translation gains and losses. Here lies the rub! In the case of losses (gains) on realized (settled) transactions, a real loss (gain) has occurred. This loss has been realized and accountants generally agree that such losses (gains) should be reflected immediately in income. In contrast, translation adjustments (including gains or losses on unsettled transactions) may be thought of as "unrealized" (i.e., "paper" items) that result from the application of different translation rates to individual for-

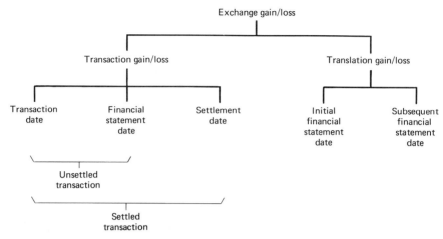

FIGURE 4.1   Types of Exchange Adjustments

eign currency account balances as in our earlier inventory translation example. In this instance, the appropriate accounting disposition is less obvious. Should translation gains and losses receive the same accounting treatment as conversion (settled transaction) gains or losses? Should the former be deferred in the balance sheet and taken into income in one or more future accounting periods? Or, should they never be brought into the income statement at all?

Fluctuating exchange rates give rise to two major issues in the area of accounting for foreign currency translation:

1. Which exchange rate should be used to translate foreign currency balances to domestic currency?
2. How should translation gains and losses be accounted for?

These two issues are treated at some length in the balance of this chapter. We begin by examining the issue of accounting for foreign currency transactions. We then address the problem of translating foreign currency financial statements.

FOREIGN CURRENCY TRANSACTIONS

A foreign currency transaction is one requiring settlement in a currency other than the primary currency in which an entity conducts its business. Examples include purchases and sales of goods and services whose prices are expressed in a foreign currency, borrowing or lending foreign currencies, and forward exchange contracts. The latter is an agreement to purchase or sell a specified amount of foreign currency at a fixed rate (the forward rate) on an agreed date in the future.

In October 1975, the U.S. Financial Accounting Standards Board (FASB) issued *Statement of Financial Accounting Standards No. 8* (FAS No. 8) providing, for the first time, authoritative guidance on accounting for foreign currency transactions. Paragraph 7 of that pronouncement mandated the following treatment for foreign currency transactions:

1. At the *transaction date* [italics added], each asset, liability, revenue or expense arising from the transaction shall be translated into (that is, measured in) dollars by use of the exchange rate (rate) in effect at that date, and shall be recorded at that dollar amount.
2. At each *balance sheet date* [italics added], recorded dollar balances representing cash and amounts owed by or to the enterprise that are denominated in foreign currency shall be adjusted to reflect the current rate.[1]

On this basis, a foreign exchange adjustment (i.e., gain or loss on a settled transaction) is necessary whenever the exchange rate changes between the transaction and settlement dates of a foreign currency payable or receivable to reflect the difference between the amount originally recorded and the settlement amount. Should financial statements be prepared prior to settlement, the accounting adjustment (i.e., gain or loss on an unsettled transaction) will equal the difference between the amount originally recorded and the amount presented in the financial statements.

The FASB rejected the view that a distinction should be drawn between gains and losses on settled and unsettled transactions arguing such distinctions to be incapable of practical application. Accordingly, it decided the latter should be accounted for in the same manner as the former. In this regard, two accounting treatments for transaction gains and losses are possible.

Single-Transaction Perspective

Under a "single-transaction" perspective, exchange adjustments (both settled and unsettled) would be treated as an adjustment to the original transaction accounts on the premise that a transaction and its subsequent settlement are a single event. This is illustrated in the example that follows.

On December 1, 1984, a U.S. manufacturer sells, on account, goods to a French importer for $20,000 when the dollar/franc exchange rate is U.S. $1 = FF 4. The franc receivable is due in 60 days and the U.S. company operates on a calendar year basis. Prior to collection of the receivable, the franc begins to depreciate. By year-end, the dollar/franc exchange rate is $1 = FF 4.5; on February 1, 1985, it is $1 = FF 5.0. These transactions are posted in Table 4.1.

In this illustration, the initial dollar amount recorded for both Accounts Receivable and Sales is considered an estimate until the account is collected, to be subsequently adjusted for changes in the dollar/franc exchange rate.

---

[1] Financial Accounting Standards Board, "Accounting for the Translation of Foreign Currency Transactions and Foreign Currency Financial Statements," *Statement of Financial Accounting Standards No. 8* (Stamford, Conn.: FASB, October 1975), p. 4.

TABLE 4.1   U.S. Company's Record—Single-Transaction Perspective

		FOREIGN CURRENCY (decrease)	U.S. DOLLAR EQUIVALENT (decrease)
12/1/84	Accounts Receivable	FF 80,000	$20,000
	Sales		20,000
	(To record credit sale)		
12/31/84	Sales		(2,222)
	Accounts Receivable		(2,222)
	(To adjust existing accounts for initial exchange rate change; FF 80,000/FF 4 minus FF 80,000/FF 4.5)		
2/1/85	Retained Earnings		(1,778)
	Accounts Receivable		(1,778)
	(To adjust accounts for additional rate change; FF 80,-000/FF 4.5 minus FF 80,000/FF 5.0)		
2/1/85	Cash		16,000
	Accounts Receivable	(80,000)	(16,000)
	(To record settlement of outstanding foreign currency receivable		

Further depreciation of the franc between the financial statement date (December 31) and the settlement date (February 1) would entail additional adjustments.

Two-Transaction Perspective

Under a "two-transaction" perspective, collection of the franc receivable is considered a separate event from the sale giving rise to it. In the previous illustration, the export sale and related receivable would be recorded at the exchange rate in effect at that date. Depreciation of the franc between December 1 and December 31 would result in an exchange loss (i.e., loss on an unsettled transaction) and would not affect the previously recorded revenue figure. Settlement of the foreign currency receivable on February 1, 1985, at the even lower exchange rate would result in a further exchange loss (i.e., loss on a settled transaction). See Table 4.2.

In the interest of uniformity, FAS No. 8 required the two-transaction method of accounting for foreign currency transactions. This treatment appears to be consistent with international practice. A survey by Fitzgerald, Stickler, and Watts suggests that this treatment is the prescribed or predominant practice in a majority of the 64 countries examined.[2]

[2] R. D. Fitzgerald, A. D. Stickler, and T. R. Watts, eds., *International Survey of Accounting Principles and Practices* (New York: Price Waterhouse International, 1979).

TABLE 4.2   U.S. Company's Record—Two-Transaction Perspective

		FOREIGN CURRENCY (decrease)	U.S. DOLLAR EQUIVALENT (decrease)
12/1/84	Accounts Receivable	FF 80,000	$20,000
	Sales		20,000
	(To record credit sale at 12/1/84 exchange rate)		
12/31/84	Foreign Exchange Loss		2,222
	Accounts Receivable		(2,222)
	(To record effect of initial rate change)		
2/1/85	Cash		16,000
	Foreign Exchange Loss		1,778
	Accounts Receivable	FF (80,000)	(17,778)
	(To record settlement of foreign currency receivable)		

Forward Exchange Contracts

Forward exchange contracts are generally used by importers or exporters at the time goods, invoiced in foreign currencies, are purchased from or sold to foreign parties. The purpose of the forward contract is to offset the risk of transaction gains or losses arising whenever exchange rates fluctuate between the transaction and settlement dates. Forward contracts are also employed to hedge anticipated foreign currency payables or receivables (foreign currency commitments), to offset the effects of translation gains and losses, and to speculate in foreign currencies.

As a special type of foreign currency transaction, forward exchange contracts can give rise to two types of adjustments—gains or losses on the forward contract and discounts or premiums. To illustrate, assume that on June 1, 1985, a U.S. manufacturer sells goods valued at 1 million Swedish kroner (Skr.) to a Swedish importer on account. Payment is to be received in three months. On June 1, the exchange rate for immediate delivery of currencies (spot rate) is $.24 = Skr. 1. If the spot rate remains unchanged through September 1, the U.S. exporter will expect to receive no less than $240,000 for the Skr. 1,000,000 owed. To avoid the risk of receiving less than $240,000, should the krona depreciate in value relative to the dollar, the U.S. exporter acquires a forward contract on June 1 to exchange Skr. 1,000,000 for U.S. dollars on September 1, 1985, at a forward contract rate of $.23 = Skr. 1. Under these circumstances, kroners can be sold only at a discount as the spot rate is greater than the forward rate. The total discount on the forward contract is $10,000 ($.24 spot rate − $.23 forward rate × Skr. 1,000,000 contract amount). If the exchange rate prevailing on September 1, 1985 (future spot rate) is $.21 = Skr. 1, the U.S. exporter realizes a gain of $30,000 ($.24 spot rate − $.21 future spot rate × Skr. 1,000,000). Had the company not purchased this forward contract, it would have received only $210,000 upon conversion.

Accounting entries for the foregoing example are provided below assuming that financial statements are prepared on June 30, prior to settlement of the kroner transaction. On June 30, the current exchange rate is $.23 = Skr. 1. The following treatment assumes that gains or losses on foreign currency contracts are reflected immediately in current income. Discounts or premiums are amortized over the life of the contract. Furthermore, in keeping with the two transaction perspectives mentioned earlier, should financial statements be prepared prior to settlement, translation gains or losses on foreign currency payables or receivables are reflected in current income.

It should be noted at the outset that forward exchange contracts are executory in nature; that is, two contracting parties agree to exchange currencies in the *future*. Since the forward contract is "unperformed" at the contract date (June 1 in our example), it would not be formally recorded in the U.S. manufacturer's accounts. As an aid to understanding the nature of forward contracts and their accounting treatment, a dual analysis is provided in Table 4.3. Journal entries appearing in the first column reflect generally accepted treatment of executory transactions. The second column contains a T-account analysis of entries that would be made if executory transactions were booked.

If the foregoing transaction took the form of a foreign currency commitment, a different accounting treatment would be required. In our previous example, assume that the U.S. manufacturer enters into a sales agreement on June 1 to receive Skr. 1,000,000 from the Swedish importer for goods delivered on September 1 (as opposed to June 1). If exchange rate movements mirror those in our previous example, a $30,000 gain would be recognized on a forward contract to hedge the Skr. 1,000,000 commitment. This time, however, the $30,000 gain would be deferred and included in the dollar basis of the foreign transaction. Discounts (premiums) on the forward contract would be amortized over the duration of the contract. The portion amortized during the commitment period may be included in the dollar basis of the related foreign currency transaction. A dual analysis of this foreign currency commitment is shown in Table 4.4 (pp. 122–24).

Gains or losses on forward contracts incurred to hedge (offset) balance sheet translation gains or losses would be recognized in income of the period in which they occur (per FAS No. 8). Discounts or premiums would be amortized over the duration of the contract. Gains or losses as well as discounts or premiums on forward contracts entered into for speculative purposes are recognized in current income.

FOREIGN CURRENCY
TRANSLATION

Companies operating internationally use a variety of methods to express, in terms of their domestic currencies, the assets, liabilities, revenues, and expenses that are stated or have been quantified in a foreign currency. These translation methods can be classified into two types: those employing a *single* translation

TABLE 4.3 U.S. Company's Record—Forward Exchange Contract

CONVENTIONAL ENTRIES	EXECUTORY CONTRACT BOOKED

CONVENTIONAL ENTRIES

6/1	Accounts receivable	$240,000
	Sales	$240,000

6/30	Foreign exchange loss	10,000
	Accounts receivable	10,000

EXECUTORY CONTRACT BOOKED

Accounts Receivable
6/1 240,000

Sales
6/1 240,000

(To record sales transaction at spot rate)

Forward ($)
Contract Receivable
6/1 230,000

Forward (Skr.)
Contract Payable
6/1 240,000

Deferred Discount
6/1 10,000

(To record agreement to exchange Skr. 1,000,000 with a dollar equivalent of $240,000 for $230,000 in three months)

Exchange loss
6/30 10,000

Accounts receivable
6/1 240,000 | 6/30 10,000

(To record translation loss on foreign currency receivable due to change in current rate between transaction date and financial statement date)

(continued)

119

TABLE 4.3 (*continued*)

CONVENTIONAL ENTRIES	EXECUTORY CONTRACT BOOKED

EXECUTORY CONTRACT BOOKED

CONVENTIONAL ENTRIES

Suspense account ... 10,000
   Foreign exchange gain ... 10,000

Discount expense ... 3,333
   Suspense account ... 3,333

9/1 Cash ... 230,000
   Foreign exchange loss ... 20,000
   Forward exchange gain ... 20,000
   Accounts receivable ... 230,000

EXECUTORY CONTRACT BOOKED

Forward (Skr.)

Contract payable		Exchange gain	
6/30 10,000	6/1 240,000		6/30 10,000

(To record gain resulting from reduced dollar equivalent of forward contract payable)

Discount expense		Deferred discount	
6/30 3,333		6/1 10,000	6/30 3,333

(Amortization of deferred discount for one month)

Cash		Exchange loss	
9/1 210,000		6/30 10,000	
		9/1 20,000	

Accounts receivable	
6/1 240,000	6/30 10,000
	9/1 230,000

(To record Skr. 1,000,000 payment by Swiss importer at 9/1 spot rate)

TABLE 4.3 (continued)

Forward (Skr.)

Contract payable			Cash	
6/30 10,000	6/1 240,000		9/1 210,000	9/1 210,000
9/1 230,000				

Exchange gain

	6/30 10,000
	9/1 20,000

(To record delivery of Skr. 1,000,000 per forward agreement at 9/1 dollar equivalent (Skr. 1,000,000 x $.21)

Forward ($)

Contract receivable			Cash	
6/1 230,000	9/1 230,000		9/1 210,000	9/1 210,000
			9/1 230,000	

(To record receipt of $230,000 cash per forward contract)

Discount expense			Deferred discount	
6/30 3,333			10,000	6/30 3,333
9/1 6,667				9/1 6,667

(To record amortization of deferred discount balance).

9/1	Discount expense	6,667
	Suspense account	6,667

TABLE 4.4 Dual Analyses of Foreign Currency Commitment

CONVENTIONAL ENTRIES	EXECUTORY CONTRACT BOOKED

CONVENTIONAL ENTRIES

6/1 Deferred discount   10,000
     Suspense account   10,000

6/30 Suspense account   10,000
     Deferred gain   10,000

EXECUTORY CONTRACT BOOKED

Forward ($)
Contract receivable
| 6/1 230,000 | |

Forward (Skr.)
Contract payable
| | 6/1 240,000 |

Deferred discount
| 6/1 10,000 | |

(To record agreement to exchange Skr. 1,000,000 with a dollar equivalent of $240,000 for $230,000 in three months)

Forward (Skr.)
Contract payable
| 6/30 10,000 | 6/1 240,000 |

Deferred gain
| | 6/30 10,000 |

(To record decrease in dollar equivalent of forward contract payable. Gain to be included in dollar basis of sales transaction)

Deferred sales adjustment
| 6/30 3,333 | |

Deferred discount
| 6/1 10,000 | 6/30 3,333 |

(Amortization of deferred discount. Also to be included in dollar basis of sales transaction)

TABLE 4.4 (continued)

		Accounts receivable		Sales	
9/1 Cash	230,000	9/1	210,000		9/1 210,000
Sales	210,000				
Deferred gain	20,000				

(To record dollar equivalent of Skr. 1,000,000 sales transaction upon delivery of goods valued at spot rate)

Cash		Accounts receivable	
9/1 210,000		9/1 210,000	9/1 210,000

(To record dollar equivalent of Skr. 1,000,000 received at prevailing spot rate of $.21 = Skr. 1)

Forward (Skr.)

Contract payable			Cash	
6/30 10,000	6/1 240,000		9/1 210,000	9/1 210,000
9/1 230,000				

Deferred gain	
	6/30 10,000
	9/1 20,000

(To record delivery of Skr. 1,000,000 per forward agreement at 9/1 dollar equivalent of Skr. 1,000,000 x $.21. Difference of 20,000 represents an additional gain to be included in dollar basis of sales transaction)

(continued)

123

TABLE 4-4 (*continued*)

CONVENTIONAL ENTRIES

9/1	Deferred gain	30,000	
	Suspense account		3,333
	Deferred discount		6,667
	Sales		20,000

EXECUTORY CONTRACT BOOKED

Forward ($)

Cash		Contract receivable	
9/1 210,000	9/1 210,000	6/1 230,000	9/1 230,000
9/1 230,000			

(To record receipt of $230,000 cash per forward contract)

Deferred gain		Deferred sales adjustment	
9/1 30,000	6/30 10,000	6/30 3,333	9/1 3,333
	9/1 20,000		

Deferred discount		Sales	
6/1 10,000	6/30 3,333		9/1 210,000
	9/1 6,667		9/1 20,000

(To adjust dollar basis of sales for exchange gain on forward contract and amortization of deferred discount)

TABLE 4.5   Exchange Rates Employed in Different Translation Methods for Specific Balance Sheet Items

	CURRENT	CURRENT – NONCURRENT	MONETARY – NONMONETARY	TEMPORAL
Cash	C	C	C	C
Accounts receivable	C	C	C	C
Inventories				
Cost	C	C	H	H
Market	C	C	H	C
Investments				
Cost	C	H	H	H
Market	C	H	H	C
Fixed assets	C	H	H	H
Other assets	C	H	H	H
Accounts payable	C	C	C	C
Long-term debt	C	H	C	C
Common stock	H	H	H	H
Retained earnings	*	*	*	*

Note: C = currrent rate; H = historical rate; and * = residual, balancing figure representing a composite of successive current rates.

rate to restate foreign balances to their domestic currency equivalents and those employing *multiple* rates. Table 4.5 summarizes the treatment of specific balance sheet items under the major translation methods described here.

Single Rate Method

Perhaps the simplest of all methods, this translation option applies a single exchange rate, the current or closing rate, to all foreign currency assets and liabilities. Foreign currency revenues and expenses are generally translated at exchange rates prevailing when these items are recognized. However, for purposes of expediency, these items are typically translated by an appropriately weighted average of current exchange rates for the period.

As all foreign currency financial statement items are, in effect, multiplied by a constant, this translation method preserves in the consolidated statements the original financial results and relationships (e.g., financial ratios) of the individual consolidated entities. Only the form, not the nature, of the foreign accounts is changed under the current rate method.

Despite its conceptual appeal and simplicity, the current rate method is faulted by some for violating the basic purpose of consolidated financial statements, which is to present for the benefit of parent company shareholders the results of operations and financial position of a parent and its subsidiaries from a single currency perspective (i.e., retain the reporting currency of the parent company as the unit of measure). Under the current rate method, consolidated results would reflect the currency perspectives of each country whose results made up the consolidated totals. For example, if an asset is acquired by a foreign subsidiary for FC 1,000 when the exchange rate is FC 1 = $1, its historical cost measured from a dollar perspective is $1,000; from a local currency perspective, also $1,000. If the exchange rate changes to FC 5 = $1, the historical cost of the asset from a dollar perspective (historical rate translation) would continue to be $1,000. If the local currency is retained as the unit of measure, the asset's value would be expressed as $200 (current rate translation).

The current rate method also errs by presuming that all local currency assets are exposed to exchange risk (i.e., assuming that their fluctuating domestic currency equivalents, caused by fluctuating current translation rates, are indicative of shifts in their underlying intrinsic values). This is seldom the case, however, as inventory and fixed asset values abroad are generally supported by local inflation. Indeed, translated asset values make little sense in the absence of local price level adjustments prior to translation. In addition, translation of a historical cost number by a current market-determined exchange rate produces a result that neither resembles historical cost nor current market value. For example, if a foreign operation purchases as an investment 1,000 shares of another company's common stock (a nonmonetary asset) for FC 100,000 when the exchange rate is FC 1 = $1, the historical cost of that investment is equivalent to $100,000. If the investment is carried at cost by the foreign operation, treating the investment as a nonmonetary item and translating it at the historical rate is appropriate. Translating it at the current market rate produces questionable results. Thus, if the market value of the investment rises to FC 150,000 and the current exchange rate increases to FC 1 = $1.25, translating the FC 100,000 using the current rate produces a figure of $125,000, which neither resembles a current value equivalent in dollars (FC 150,000 × $1.25 = $187,500) nor the historical cost in dollars (FC 100,000 × $1.00 = $100,000). Finally, translating all foreign currency balances by the current rate gives rise to translation gains and losses every time exchange rates change. Reflections of such exchange adjustments in current income could significantly distort reported measures of performance. Many of these gains and losses may never be fully realized as exchange rates often reverse their direction before realization takes place.

Multiple Rate Methods

Multiple rate methods utilize a combination of historical and current exchange rates in the translation process. Three such methods are discussed in turn.

Current-noncurrent method. Under the current-noncurrent approach, a foreign subsidiary's current assets and current liabilities are translated into their parent company's reporting currency at the current rate. Noncurrent assets and liabilities are translated at historical rates.

Income statement items, with the exception of depreciation and amortization charges, are translated at average rates applicable to each month of operation or on the basis of weighted averages covering the whole period to be reported. Depreciation and amortization charges are translated at the historical rates in effect when the related assets were acquired.

This methodology, unfortunately, suffers from a number of shortcomings. For example, it lacks adequate conceptual justification. Present definitions of current and noncurrent assets and liabilities do not explain why such a classification scheme should determine which rate to use in the translation process. Furthermore, fluctuating exchange rates may produce translations that distort operating results between accounting periods. Inventories are a case in point.

Under conditions of a deteriorating exchange rate, assume that inventories shipped from a U.S. parent company to one of its foreign subsidiaries during the last quarter of year 1 when the prevailing rate of exchange was FC 1 = $1. Assume also that these inventories remain unsold at year-end, the date of the financial statements. The inventories have a U.S. dollar cost of $100,000. Thus, the foreign subsidiary would record this transaction on its books at FC 100,000. The subsidiary operates with a 50 percent markup on cost, which leads to a selling price of FC 150,000 for the inventory.

Now assume that the foreign exchange rate falls to FC 1 = $.90 by year-end. Under the current-noncurrent translation method, the FC 100,000 of inventories are translated at the current rate, which yields a translated figure in U.S. dollars of $90,000. A translation loss of $10,000 would typically appear in the accounts and year 1 earnings would, therefore, be reduced by the same amount.

If the inventories in question are then sold for FC 150,000 during the first quarter of year 2, and the average rate of exchange during this quarter is FC 1 = $.95, the sale transaction yields approximately $142,500. The gross margin on the sale is then reported at $52,500 in year 2, whereas it should be reported at $42,500—the actual difference between cost and selling price in terms of U.S. dollars. In this example, some would argue

1. There really is no foreign exchange "loss" in year 1. The decline in the foreign exchange rate simply reduces the originally anticipated gross profit margin.
2. Reported operating results for both years 1 and 2 are distorted because of an unrealistic foreign exchange translation method.

Stated somewhat differently, use of the year-end rate to translate current assets implies that foreign currency cash, receivables, and inventories are equally exposed to exchange risk regardless of their form. Yet, in those instances where local price increases are possible following devaluation, inventory values are protected from currency erosion. Accordingly, the $10,000 write-down of inventories in the preceding example would not be warranted. On the other hand, translation of long-term debt at the historical rate shields interim periods from the impact of fluctuating currencies while burdening the year of settlement with what could amount to significant currency gains or losses. Many consider this to be at odds with reality.

Monetary-nonmonetary method.   Like the current-noncurrent method, the monetary-nonmonetary method uses a balance sheet classification scheme to determine appropriate translation rates. Originally espoused by the late Professor Samuel R. Hepworth in a research monograph entitled *Reporting Foreign Operations*,[3] *monetary* assets and liabilities—representing rights to receive or obligations to pay a fixed number of foreign currency units in the future (cash, receivables, and payables, including long-term debt)—are translated at the current rate. *Nonmonetary* items—fixed assets, long-term investments, and inventories—are translated at the historical rate. Income statement items are translated under procedures similar to those described for the current-noncurrent framework.

In contrast to the current-noncurrent method, this translation option relates exchange rate risk to the composition of a firm's current assets. It also reflects changes in the domestic currency equivalent of long-term debt in the period in which they occur, producing what many consider to be more timely indicants of exchange rate effects.

Note, however, that the monetary-nonmonetary method, like its predecessor, relies on a classification scheme to determine appropriate translation rates. Since translation is concerned with measurement and not with classification, the characteristics of assets and liabilities that determine their financial statement classification are not necessarily relevant for selecting appropriate translation rates. The monetary-nonmonetary method may also be criticized in that

> ... no comprehensive principle of translation can be derived solely from the monetary-nonmonetary distinction. Nonmonetary assets and liabilities are measured on different bases (for example, past prices or current prices) under different circumstances, and translation at a past rate does not always fit. Translating nonmonetary items at a past rate produces reasonable results if the items are stated at historical cost, but not if they are stated at current market price in foreign currency.[4]

Consider our earlier example of the FC 100,000 stock investment. If the current market value of the investment is FC 150,000 and the current exchange rate is FC 1 = \$1.25, translating FC 150,000 into \$150,000 using the historical rate of FC 1 = \$1 does not result in the current market value measured in dollars (FC 150,000 × \$1.25 = \$187,500) or the historical cost in dollars (FC 100,-000 × \$1.00 = \$100,000). To continue the previous quote:

> The monetary-nonmonetary method can produce ... a current market value only if it is recognized that, under the method, the current rate is the applicable historical rate for nonmonetary assets carried at current prices. The point has been confusing enough to cause some proponents of the monetary-nonmonetary method to argue that nonmonetary assets, such as investments and inventories, should become monetary assets if they are carried at market price.[5]

Unfortunately, this translation method also masks inventory risk whenever local pricing adjustments following a currency devaluation are con-

---

[3] Ann Arbor, Mich.: University of Michigan, 1956.

[4] Financial Accounting Standards Board, *Statement of Financial Accounting Standards No. 8*, pp. 58–59.

[5] Ibid.

strained by government price controls or local competitive pressures (i.e., translation of inventories at the historical rate preserves a dollar value in the consolidated results that may actually have been impaired). Another perceived distortion arises under the monetary-nonmonetary method from matching sales at current prices and translation rates against cost of sales measured at historical costs and translation rates. Exchange rate changes in this regard often result in distorted profit margins owing to the lag in inventory turnover rates. For instance, during a period when a given foreign currency appreciates relative to the dollar, cost of goods sold expressed in the given foreign currency will be translated at a lower historical exchange rate than foreign currency revenues, thereby producing a jump in dollar gross profits. The reverse occurs when a foreign currency depreciates relative to the dollar; that is, cost of sales are translated at a higher historical exchange rate than foreign currency revenues, thereby producing a depressing effect on reported gross margins.

Temporal method. According to the temporal approach, currency translation is a measurement conversion process (i.e., a restatement of a given value). As such, it cannot be used to change the attribute of an item being measured; it can only change the unit of measure. Translation of foreign balances, for example, restates the currency denomination of these inventories but not their actual valuation. Under U.S. generally accepted accounting principles, the asset cash is measured in terms of the amount owned at the balance sheet date. Receivables and payables are stated at amounts expected to be received or paid in the future. All other assets and liabilities are measured at money prices that prevailed when the items were acquired or incurred. In short, there is a time dimension associated with these money values.

According to Lorensen, the best way to retain the accounting bases used to measure foreign currency items is to translate their foreign money amounts by exchange rates in effect at the dates to which the foreign money measurements pertain. The temporal principle thus states that

> Money, receivables, and payables measured at the amounts promised should be translated at the foreign exchange rate in effect at the balance sheet date. Assets and liabilities measured at money prices should be translated at the foreign exchange rate in effect at the dates to which the money prices pertain.[6]

Under this principle, then, cash, receivables, and payables are translated at the current rate. Assets carried on the foreign statements at historical cost are translated at the historical rate. Assets carried at current values are translated at the current rate (see Table 4.5). Revenue and expense items are translated at rates that prevailed when the underlying transactions took place, although average rates are suggested when revenue or expense transactions are voluminous.

Under historical cost valuation, the translation procedures resulting from the temporal principle are virtually identical to those produced by the mone-

[6] Leonard Lorensen, "Reporting Foreign Operations of U.S. Companies in U.S. Dollars," *Accounting Research Study No. 12* (New York: American Institute of Certified Public Accountants, 1972), p. 19.

tary-nonmonetary method. Translation procedures differ, however, if other asset valuation bases, such as replacement cost, market values, or discounted cash flows are adopted.

Being a more general case of the monetary-nonmonetary method, this translation approach shares most of the advantages and disadvantages of the former. In deliberately ignoring local inflation as part of the translation process, this method shares a limitation common to all translation methods discussed above.

In practice, variations of each of the foregoing translation methods are often introduced to accommodate particular operating circumstances and management philosophies. As examples, some international companies adhere to the current rate method yet translate fixed assets at historical rates. Others subscribe to the current-noncurrent method but translate inventories at rates prevailing at the date of acquisition. Companies preferring the monetary-nonmonetary method have been observed to translate long-term debt at historical as opposed to current rates while companies employing the temporal method often translate inventories at current rates.

Financial Statement Effects

Tables 4.6 and 4.7 highlight the financial statement effects of the major translation methods described. The balance sheet of a hypothetical Mexican subsidiary of a U.S.-based multinational enterprise appears in pesos in the first column of Table 4.6. The second column depicts the U.S. dollar equivalents of the Mexican peso (P) balances when the exchange rate was P 1 = $.03. Should the peso depreciate by 33⅓ percent (P 1 = $.02 in relation to the dollar (in 1982 the peso actually devalued by more than 67%!), a number of different accounting results are possible.

Under the current rate method, exchange rate changes affect the dollar equivalents of the Mexican subsidiary's *total* foreign currency assets (TA) and liabilities (TL) in the current period. Since their dollar values are affected by changes in the current rate, they are said to be *exposed, in an accounting sense,* to foreign exchange risk. Accordingly, under the current-rate method, an exposed peso net asset position (TA > TL) would result in a translation loss should the Mexican peso depreciate in value, and an exchange gain should the peso increase in value. An exposed peso net liability position (TA < TL) produces a translation gain in the event of a Mexican peso devaluation and a loss if the peso increases in value. In our example, current rate translation yields a $150 translation loss (000s omitted) since the dollar equivalent of the Mexican subsidiary's net asset position *after* the peso depreciation is $300 (P 15,000 × $.02) whereas the dollar equivalent *before* the depreciation is $450 (P 15,000 × $.03).

Under the current-noncurrent method, the U.S. company's accounting exposure is measured by its peso net current asset or liability position (a positive P 9,000 in our example). Under the monetary-nonmonetary method, exposure is measured by its net peso monetary asset or liability position (a

TABLE 4.6 Mexican Subsidiary Balance Sheet

	PESOS	U.S. DOLLARS BEFORE PESO DEVALUATION ($.03 = P1)	U.S. DOLLARS AFTER PESO DEPRECIATION ($.02 = P1)			
			Current Rate	Current-Noncurrent	Monetary-Nonmonetary	Temporal
Assets						
Cash	P 3,000	$ 90	$ 60	$ 60	$ 60	$ 60
Accounts receivable	6,000	180	120	120	120	120
Inventories	9,000	270	180	180	270	180[a]
Fixed assets (net)	18,000	540	360	540	540	540
Total	P 36,000	$1,080	$720	$900	$990	$900
Liabilities & Owners' Equity						
Short-term payables	P 9,000	$ 270	$180	$180	$180	$180
Long-term debt	12,000	360	240	360	240	240
Stockholders' equity	15,000	450	300	360	570	480
Total	P 36,000	$1,080	$720	$900	$990	$900
Accounting exposure (P)			15,000	9,000	(12,000)	(3,000)
Translation gain (loss) ($)			(150)	(90)	120	30

Note: If the exchange rate remained unchanged over time, the translated statements would be the same under all translation methods.

[a] Assume inventories are carried at lower of cost or market. If they were carried at historical cost, the temporal balance sheet would be identical to the monetary-nonmonetary method.

TABLE 4.7 Mexican Subsidiary Income Statement (in thousands)

	PESOS	U.S. DOLLARS BEFORE PESO DEVALUATION ($.03 = P1)	U.S. DOLLARS AFTER PESO DEPRECIATION ($.02 = P1) Current Rate	Current-Noncurrent	Monetary-Nonmonetary	Temporal
Sales	P 40,000	$1,200	$800	$800	$800	$800
Cost of sales	20,000	600	400	400	600	600[a]
Depreciation[b]	1,800	54	36	54	54	54
All other expenses	8,000	240	160	160	160	160
Income before tax	10,200	306	204	186	(14)	(14)
Income tax (30%)	3,060	(92)	(61)	(56)	—	—
Translation gain (loss)[c]	—	—	(114)	(90)	120	30
Net income (loss)	P 7,140	$ 214	$ 29	$ 40	$106	$ 16

Note: This example assumes that the income statement is prepared the day after devaluation.

[a] Assumes that inventories were written down to market at period's end.

[b] Estimated life of fixed assets is assumed to be ten years.

[c] This example reflects what reported earnings would look like if all translation gains or losses were immediately reflected in current income.

132

negative P 12,000). Exposure under the temporal principle depends on whether the Mexican subsidiary's inventories or other assets are valued at historical cost (and therefore not exposed) or some other valuation basis (a negative P 3,000 in our example). The reader is encouraged to work through the example until all translation gains or losses that are produced by each of the remaining constructs can be traced. (For a further discussion of exposure management see Chapter 10.)

To summarize, the different translation methods illustrated offer a wide array of accounting results, ranging from a $150 loss under the current rate method to a $120 gain under the monetary-nonmonetary method. This is quite a variation in light of the fact that all the results presumably describe the same factual situation! What is more, operations reporting respectable profits before translation at the new rates may very well end up reporting losses or significantly reduced earnings statistics after translation, and conversely (see Table 4.7).

Which Is Best?

The quest for a single comprehensive translation methodology has engaged the energies of accountants for many years. Numerous writers have suggested their particular ideal translation modes to end the confusion that has characterized this aspect of international financial reporting. Most have premised their constructs on the traditional assumption that a single translation method can be appropriate for all circumstances in which translations occur and for all purposes which translation serves. We feel that the assumption just cited is categorically wrong. First, circumstances underlying foreign exchange translation differ widely. Translating accounts from a stable to an unstable currency (e.g., from Swiss francs to Argentine pesos) is not the same as translating accounts from an unstable currency to a stable one (e.g., from Chilean escudos to U.S. dollars). Likewise, there is little similarity between translations involving import- or export-type transactions and those involving a permanently established affiliate or subsidiary company in another country that reinvests its local earnings and does not contemplate repatriating any of its funds to the parent company in the near future.

Second, translations are undertaken for different purposes. Translating the accounts of a foreign subsidiary for purposes of consolidating such accounts with those of the parent company has very little in common with translating the accounts of an independent company primarily for the convenience of various foreign audiences-of-interest.

The problem of translation procedure thus has three dimensions:

1. Is it reasonable to employ more than a single translation method?
2. If so, what should the acceptable methods be and under what conditions should they be applied?
3. Are there situations in which translations should not be undertaken at all?

With respect to the first question there seems little doubt that, given the underlying conditions of multinational business today, a single translation methodology cannot logically serve equally well translations occurring under different conditions and serving different purposes. Thus, more than one translation method seems warranted.

Regarding the second question, three different translation approaches seem called for: (1) the historical method, (2) the current method, and (3) no translation at all.

Financial accounts of some or all foreign entities can be translated either in terms of a parent company perspective or in terms of a local perspective. Under the former, foreign operations are viewed as extensions of parent company operations and exist, in large measure, as sources of domestic currency cash flows. Interest centers on the remittable domestic utility of foreign resources rather than their local utility.[7] Accordingly, the object of translation is to change the unit of measure for financial statements of foreign subsidiaries from one defined in terms of a foreign currency to one defined in terms of the domestic currency. Another objective is to make the foreign statements conform to accounting principles generally accepted in the country of the parent company. These objectives, in the opinion of the authors, are best accomplished by the use of translation methods incorporating historical rates of exchange. While several historical rate method combinations have been identified and described, we continue to prefer the temporal principle as it generally retains the accounting principles used to measure assets and liabilities originally expressed in foreign currency units.[8] Since foreign statements under a parent company perspective are first adjusted to reflect parent company accounting principles (*before* translation), the temporal principle is appropriate as it changes only a measurement in foreign currency into a measurement in domestic currency without changing the basis of measurement. This is the key rationale of FAS No. 8, which the authors support.

Because the historical rate translation method inherently involves a conceptual dimension, it is easily adapted to processes that make accounting adjustments in the course of the translation. When this is the case, adjustments for differences between two or more sets of accounting concepts and practices are made in addition to the translation of currency amounts. For example, inventories or certain liabilities may be restated according to accounting practices different from those originally used. The temporal principle can accommodate any asset valuation framework whether it be historical cost, current replacement price, or net realizable values.

While the primary purpose of historical rate translation is the consolidation of the financial statements of an international branch or subsidiary company with those of a parent company, this method also serves additional accounting purposes. For example, the method is useful for special management information or administrative reports. Furthermore, it is useful in compiling national statistics about international investments and about

[7] Dennis H. Patz, "The State of the Art in Translation Theory," *Journal of Business Finance and Accounting,* Vol. 4, No. 3, 1977, p. 316.

[8] See Frederick D. S. Choi and Gerhard G. Mueller, *An Introduction to Multinational Accounting* (Englewood Cliffs, N.J.: Prentice-Hall, Inc., 1978).

international balance of payments questions as they concern individual countries.

We now turn to some evaluation of the current rate method of translation. This method, it should be noted, has no accounting orientation. It simply changes a medium of expression. It is straightforward translation (restatement) from one "language" to another. There is no change whatever in the nature of the accounts. Only their particular form of expression is changed.

The current rate method is first of all appropriate when the accounts of foreign subsidiaries are translated in a fashion that retains the local currency as the unit of measure; that is, all foreign entities are viewed from a local, as opposed to a parent, company perspective. This view recognizes that a foreign-based operation is a separate business unit whose business transactions are effected in a foreign currency. Interest centers on the status and performance of local operations in the host environment. Translation at the current rate, furthermore, does not change any of the initial relationships (e.g., financial ratios) in the foreign currency statements as all account balances are simply multiplied by a constant. This approach is most useful when the accounts of an independent company are merely translated for the convenience of foreign stockholders or other external user groups.

A second use of the current rate method comes about when price level–adjusted accounts are to be translated to another currency. If reliable price level adjustments have been introduced into a given set of accounts and if the domestic price level changes for the currency involved are reflected closely in related foreign exchange rate movements, then the current rate translation of price level–adjusted data yields results that are comparable to translating historical cost accounts under the historical rate translation method. This topic is covered in Chapter 5.

Now to repeat a question raised earlier, Are there situations in which translations should not be undertaken at all? We would argue in the affirmative. No translation is appropriate between highly unstable and highly stable currencies. Translation of one into the other will not produce meaningful information under any translation method. For example, historical dollar costs of inventories carried by an Argentine or Chilean subsidiary are a poor guide to pricing decisions in the face of heavy recent inflation in those countries.

No translation would also mean nonconsolidation of financial statements. This seems to be a reasonable conclusion. If a currency turns so soft as to put account translations into question, it should also act as a bar to financial statement consolidation. Should reporting of operations in extremely volatile currency areas be necessary, separate reports might be rendered. There is no reason why several rather soft currency operations could not be combined into a single report as long as this report is separate and clearly distinct from the main report.

No translation is necessary when financial statements of independent companies are issued for purely informational purposes to residents in another country that is in a comparable stage of economic development and has a comparable national currency situation. For example, a Canadian company reporting to U.S. stockholders should not be required to translate its accounts provided, of course, that it fully discloses the expression of monetary amounts in Canadian dollars.

Finally, translation should not take place for certain special management reports. Effective international managers should be able to evaluate situations and reach decisions in terms of more than a single currency unit. They need to develop "multilingual" capabilities with reference to different national currencies. Hence some internal company reports may well have several different columns of monetary amounts, each in a different currency unit. Certain other reports, for instance those on a possible international acquisition, may leave no choice about translation because historical foreign exchange rate information may simply not be available—even if subsequent consolidation or other accounting procedures would eventually require use of (often reconstructed!) historical rates. Still other types of reports may translate current or monetary items only and leave other items untranslated.

Appropriate current rate.   Thus far we have referred to rates of exchange used in various translation methods as either *historical* or *current*. Average rates are often employed in income statements for purposes of expediency. In practice, the choice of an appropriate exchange rate is not clear-cut because there are a number of exchange rates in effect for any given currency at any one point in time. There are buying rates and selling rates, spot rates and forward rates, official rates and free-market rates, witth numerous gradations of rate differentials in between. While this list is far from exhaustive, it does illustrate the problem that arises in trying to identify an appropriate rate when foreign currencies trade at significantly different rates depending on types of transactions and temporal dimensions involved. It is not difficult to cite examples of currencies whose official rates have varied significantly above or below free-market rates. At one time, a single U.S. dollar would officially buy 1,000 Brazilian cruzeiros, while the free market would offer more than twice that amount. And remember, today's current rate becomes tomorrow's historical rate!

In our present world of floating exchange rates, there are few limits to permissible degrees of fluctuations in currency values. Under these circumstances, Parkinson recommends the use of a standard bookkeeping rate that would approximate actual exchange rates for converting foreign currencies. He doubts whether the precise exchange rate prevailing at any specific date is particularly relevant for translation purposes.

To quote Parkinson directly,

> As a general rule, the accounts of a foreign subsidiary should be translated to Canadian currency at bookkeeping rates of exchange which need only approximate actual rates for converting the foreign currency. Once established, a bookkeeping rate should not be changed until, because of changes in actual exchange rates, it becomes clearly inappropriate; a new translation rate should be selected as soon as practical after a currency revaluation, as distinct from a mere currency fluctuation.[9]

[9] MacDonald R. Parkinson, *Translation of Foreign Currencies* (Toronto: Canadian Institute of Chartered Accountants, 1972), p. 26.

While foreign exchange translation is only a distant cousin of foreign exchange conversion, your authors feel that an appropriate translation rate should seek to achieve the greatest possible correspondence to economic and business reality. Thus the rate selected should be the free-market rate quoted for spot transactions in the country where the accounts to be translated originate. This is the only rate that appropriately measures current transaction values. For example, if the translation of the financial position of a Philippine subsidiary company were to be accomplished for the purpose of consolidation with the financial position of its U.S. parent company, the free U.S. dollar spot rate quoted by a major Philippine bank at or near the date of the financial statements should be used as the appropriate current translation rate.

In attempting to achieve certain national objectives, a country may apply different exchange rates to different transactions. At times, different simultaneous exchange rates occur for payments of imports, receipts for exports, dividend remittances, and so forth. In these situations, a choice from several existing rates must again be made. Several possibilities have been suggested: (a) use of dividend remittance rates, (b) use of free-market rates, and (c) use of any applicable penalty or preference rates, such as those associated with imports or exports.

Your authors are of the opinion that free-market rates are preferable with one exception. In cases where specific exchange controls are in effect (i.e., when certain funds are definitely earmarked for specific transactions to which specific foreign exchange rates apply), the specifically applicable rates should be utilized. For instance, if a Latin American subsidiary of a U.S. parent has received permission to import certain goods from the United States at a favorable rate and has set aside certain cash funds to do so, the earmarked funds should be translated to dollars at the special preference rate. The current year-end free-market rate should, of course, be applied to the balance of the foreign cash account. This procedure has the effect of translating portions of a foreign currency cash account at two or more different translation rates. Nothing is wrong with this as long as economic reality is properly and fully reflected thereby.

Translation Gains and Losses

Table 4.7 illustrated four respective translation adjustments resulting from the application of various translation methods to foreign currency financial statements. Accounting treatments accorded these adjustments internationally are as diverse as the underlying translation procedures. Hence, reasonable solutions to the problem of how to treat these translation "gains or losses" are urgently needed.

Approaches to accounting for translation adjustments range from deferral to no deferral with hybrid treatments in between.[10]

[10] For additional treatment of the issues discussed here, see Financial Accounting Standards Board, "An Analysis of Issues Related to Accounting for Foreign Currency Translation," *FASB Discussion Memorandum* (Stamford, Conn.: FASB, February 21, 1974), pp. 79–102.

Major deferral.   Inclusion of translation adjustments in current income is generally opposed on the grounds that they are merely the product of a re-statement process. Accordingly, changes in the domestic currency equivalents of a foreign subsidiary's net assets are "unrealized," having no effect on the local currency cash flows generated by the foreign entity which may be currently reinvested or remitted to the parent. Inclusion of such adjustments in current income would, therefore, be misleading. Under these circumstances translation adjustments should be accumulated separately as a part of consolidated equity. Parkinson offers additional reasons in support of deferral:

> On the one hand it can be argued that the gain or loss relates to a very long-term investment—perhaps even a permanent investment—of a . . . parent in a foreign subsidiary; that the gain or loss will not become realized until the foreign operation is closed down and all the net assets are distributed to the parent; that at or before such time the change in the exchange rate may have reversed—i.e. that no gain or loss will ever be realized. It can also be argued that operating results recorded in the periods following the currency revaluation (and translated at the then current exchange rate) will be indicative of the increased or decreased worth of the foreign operation and that in these circumstances there is no need to record a one-shot translation gain or loss in the income statement—that in fact the recording of such a gain or loss might be misleading.[11]

Deferral, however, may be opposed on grounds that exchange rates do not reverse themselves. Even if they did, deferral of exchange adjustments are premised on exchange rate predictions, a most difficult undertaking in practice. Situations could arise where operating results are misstated solely due to forecasting errors. To some, deferring translation gains or losses masks the behavior of exchange rate changes; that is, rate changes are historical facts and financial statement users are best served if the effects of exchange rate fluctuations are accounted for when they occur. According to FAS No. 8 (par. 199), "Exchange rates fluctuate; accounting should not give the impression that rates are stable."

Deferral and amortization.   Some favor deferring translation gains or losses and amortizing these adjustments over the life of related balance sheet items. As an example, assume that a U.S. parent's Finnish subsidiary, whose accounts are expressed in markkas, has a net exposed liability position. Appreciation of the markka relative to the dollar between consolidation dates produces a translation loss. On the assumption that the cost of an asset includes the sacrifice required to discharge related liabilities, the translation loss would be treated as part of the related asset's cost (single transaction perspective) and amortized to expense over the asset's useful life. This accounting disposition is also justified on the grounds that an exposed net liability position is, in effect, covered by foreign currency assets valued at cost. *Cover* is the difference between the dollar equivalent of a foreign currency asset translated at the current rate versus its cost translated at the historical rate. Since fixed assets are gen-

---

[11] Parkinson, *Translation,* pp. 101–102.

erally translated at historical rates, depreciation charges that are lower than what they would have been if translated at current rates offset or "cover" the reduction in income from amortizing the deferred translation loss over the asset's life.

Not only is this treatment incompatible with a duel transaction perspective, it is also logically inconsistent. According to Lorensen

> Under the deferral procedure, a change in the dollar value of net monetary liabilities is offset against a change in the dollar value of nonmonetary assets. Since changes in the dollar value of nonmonetary assets are not recognized under generally accepted accounting principles, offsetting is accomplished by *not* recognizing changes in the dollar value of net monetary liabilities. The argument for deferral says in effect that changes in the dollar value of one item should not be recognized because changes in the dollar value of the other item are not recognized. However, if offsetting is accomplished at all, it should be accomplished by changing generally accepted accounting principles to recognize changes in the dollar value of both items. Accomplishing the offsetting by not recognizing changes in the dollar value of either item introduces an aberration into accounting for foreign operations that no accountant would tolerate for domestic operations. That aberration is the same as not recognizing a $1 million loss from embezzlement in California because the company owns land in California worth $100 million that it bought for $10 million.[12]

An alternative disposition would be to include any gains or losses stemming from the translation of a net exposed liability position as an adjustment of the carrying value of foreign currency liabilities. Amounts so deferred would be amortized over the remaining life of the long-term liabilities by treating translation gains or losses as an adjustment of interest expense. Such treatment can be defended on the grounds that management typically assesses the likelihood of exchange rate changes when evaluating the costs and benefits of domestic versus foreign currency borrowings. However, is it appropriate to account currently for the expected effects of future rate changes on interest and principal payments? Assuming this issue is resolved, should all of the translation gains or losses in question be allocated over the remaining life of the foreign currency debt or should some portion be treated as an adjustment of interest recorded in previous periods? Should a limit be placed on interest rate adjustments following an exchange rate change if the resulting effective interest rate grossly exceeds that normally incurred by the company? Questions such as these make interest expense adjustments highly suspect.

No deferral. A third option in accounting for translation gains and losses is to recognize them in the income statement immediately. Deferral of any type is widely regarded as artificial and misleading. Moreover, deferral criteria are often attacked as impossible to implement and internally inconsistent. Thus, the traditional approach has been to recognize losses as soon as they occur but to recognize gains only to the extent realized. While conservative, deferring a translation gain solely because it is a "gain" denies that a rate

---

[12] Lorensen, "Reporting Foreign Operations," pp. 58–59.

change has occurred. Moreover, deferral of translation gains while recognizing translation losses is internally inconsistent. Another problem with this approach has been the absence of any explicit criteria to determine when realization of a translation gain occurs. In addition, those favoring deferral of translation gains are at a loss to determine how much should be deferred. In the past, companies have followed a procedure of netting current gains against prior losses and deferring the difference. But this implies that translation gains or losses are not period items and are expected to wash out over the longer run. If this were indeed the case, deferrals would be a questionable practice.

Inclusion of translation gains and losses in current income, unfortunately, introduces a random element to earnings that could result in significant earnings gyrations every time exchange rates change. Moreover, inclusion of such "paper" gains and losses into reported earnings can be misleading to statement readers as these adjustments do not always provide information that is compatible with the expected economic effects of rate changes on an enterprise's cash flows. Alas, it appears we have come full circle.

Where are we?   In view of our earlier comments on translation procedures, it is clear that the objectives of translation have an important bearing on the nature of any potential translation adjustment. Accordingly, if a local currency perspective is maintained (local company perspective), reflection of a translation adjustment in current income is unwarranted. Recall that a local company viewpoint calls for use of the current rate translation method—the purpose being to preserve relationships existing in the foreign currency statements. Increasing or decreasing current income by any translation gains or losses would, in our opinion, distort original financial relationships and possibly mislead rather than enlighten users of such information. Translation gains or losses should be treated here as adjustments to owners' equity much like those made when accounting for the effects of general price level changes. Here, owners' equity is simply "rolled forward," that is, restated to its end-of-period purchasing-power equivalent owing to changes in the general purchasing power of the monetary unit during the period.

If the reporting currency of the parent company is used as the unit of measure for the translated financial statements (parent company perspective), immediate recognition of translation gains or losses in income is advisable. Under a parent company perspective, a foreign subsidiary is viewed as an extension of the parent. Accordingly, maximization of the parent company's domestic currency equity in the foreign operation is a paramount concern. Under these circumstances, translation gains and losses reflect increases or decreases in the domestic currency equity of the foreign investment and should be recognized in consolidated income, properly labeled. No deferrals should be effected and no separate realization conditions should be imposed. Among other things, this treatment is fully consistent with such generally accepted practices as the equity method of accounting for certain intercompany investments.

TRANSLATION ACCOUNTING
DEBATES

Translation accounting practices have varied in response to increasing complexity of multinational operations and changes in the international monetary system. While accountants in many countries are engaged in debates over foreign currency translation, U.S. responses to the evolving translation problem are as indicative as those in any other country. To better understand recent developments on the U.S. translation accounting front, a brief history of U.S. foreign currency accounting is presented.

Pre-1965.   Prior to 1965, the translation practices of many U.S. companies were guided by *Accounting Research Bulletin No. 4* (ARB No. 4),[13] subsequently reissued as Chapter 12 of ARB No. 43.[14] This pronouncement advocated use of the current-noncurrent method described earlier. Transaction gains or losses were to be taken directly to income. Translation gains or losses were netted during the period. Net translation losses were recognized currently in the interest of conservatism while net translation gains were deferred in a balance sheet suspense account and used to offset translation losses in future accounting periods.

The effect of balance sheet deferral was to shield the bottom line of multinational companies from exchange rate fluctuations. Suppose, for example, that a U.S. parent company experienced a large translation gain during a given period that would significantly boost reported earnings that year. Rather than book the translation gain, the company could defer it to enable its earnings to assume a more normal appearance. If, in the following year, the company experienced a huge translation loss that would significantly depress reported earnings, it could offset the translation loss with the deferred translation gain, thus enabling earnings to continue a stable pattern.

1965–1975

To accommodate the needs of reporting enterprises, Chapter 12 of ARB No. 43 permitted certain exceptions to the current-noncurrent methodology. Under special circumstances, inventory could be translated at historical rates. Long-term debt incurred in connection with the acquisition of long-term assets just before a substantial and presumably permanent change in the exchange rate could be restated at the current rate. Any accounting difference owing to debt restatement was treated as part of the asset's cost. Translating *all* foreign currency payables and receivables at the current rate was officially sanctioned

[13] American Institute of Certified Public Accountants, Committee on Accounting Procedure, "Foreign Operations and Foreign Exchange," *Accounting Research Bulletin No. 4* (New York: AICPA, 1939).

[14] American Institute of Certified Public Accountants, Committee on Accounting Procedure, "Restatement and Revision of Accounting Research Bulletins," *Accounting Research Bulletin No. 43* (New York: AICPA, 1953).

in 1965 with the issuance of *Accounting Principles Board Opinion No. 6.*[15] This modification to ARB No. 43, in effect, added yet another translation option to a company's currency translation tool kit.

1975-1981

To end the diversity of treatments permitted under previous translation pronouncements, the FASB issued in October 1975 its controversial FAS No. 8. This pronouncement significantly altered U.S. practice as well as that of foreign companies subscribing to U.S. generally accepted accounting principles (GAAP) by mandating adherence to the temporal principle of translation. Equally significant, deferral of translation gains and losses was no longer permitted. Exchange gains and losses, both translation as well as transaction, had to be recognized in income during the period of the rate change.

The direct implication of this sweeping pronouncement was clear. In the absence of some protective device, earnings of multinational companies would fluctuate every time exchange rates varied. And, fluctuate they did! Consider, for example, ITT's experience in 1981.[16] In the first quarter, the company, whose annual sales revenue exceeded $23 billion, reported a reduction in earnings from the previous year of 45 percent. However, excluding translation effects, ITT's earnings were actually unchanged from the preceding year. In the following quarter, ITT reported an earnings improvement of 109 percent, but if translation gains were excluded, its earnings had actually declined by 29 percent. In the third quarter, the company's reported earnings were down 119 percent despite the fact that operating results had actually *increased* by 2 percent!

From the very beginning, corporate reaction to FAS No. 8 was mixed. While some applauded the pronouncement for its definitive properties, many condemned it for the distortions it caused in reported corporate earnings. The standard was criticized for producing accounting results not in accord with "economic reality." In addition, the yo-yo effect on corporate earnings of the FASB's ruling caused concern among executives of multinational companies. They worried that reported earnings of their companies would appear more volatile than those of purely domestic entities, and depress their stock prices. Despite evidence to the contrary,[17] the statement had a significant effect on corporate management practices. Studies on the economic impact of FAS No. 8 by the FASB,[18] Financial Executives Research Founda-

---

[15] American Institute of Certified Public Accountants, "Status of Accounting Research Bulletins," *Accounting Principles Board Opinion No. 6* (New York: AICPA, 1965).

[16] Raymond H. Alleman, "Why ITT Likes FAS 52," *Management Accounting*, July 1982, pp. 23–29.

[17] Roland Dukes, *An Empirical Investigation of the Effects of Statement of Financial Accounting Standards No. 8 on Security Return Behavior* (Stamford, Conn.: FASB, December 1978).

[18] T. G. Evans, W. R. Folks, and M. Jilling, *The Impact of Financial Accounting Standards No. 8 on the Foreign Exchange Risk Management Practices of American Multinationals: An Economic Impact Study* (Stamford, Conn.: Financial Accounting Standards Board, 1978).

tion,[19] and others[20] found management, in many instances, incurring current and/or potential cash costs to minimize noncash (translation) adjustments, including the opportunity costs of management time diverted away from mainstream operating problems.

1981–Present

In May 1978, the FASB invited public comment on its first 12 pronouncements which had been in effect for at least two years. Of the 200 letters received most related to FAS No. 8 and were unanimous in urging that it be changed. Responding to the expressed dissatisfaction with FAS No. 8, the FASB added to its agenda a project to reconsider the pronouncement. After numerous public meetings and two exposure drafts, the FASB issued *Statement of Financial Accounting Standards No. 52.*[21] It officially supersedes, in addition to FAS No. 8, FAS No. 20,[22] FASB Interpretation No. 15,[23] and FASB Interpretation No. 17.[24]

FEATURES OF STANDARD NO. 52

The basic objectives of translation under this new pronouncement differ substantially from those under FAS No. 8. The latter adopted a parent company perspective by requiring that foreign currency financial statements be presented as though all transactions had taken place in U.S. dollars. Standard No. 52 adopts a situational approach and recognizes a local company perspective as a valid reporting framework. The new translation rules are thus designed to:

1. Reflect in consolidated statements the financial results and relationships measured in the primary currency in which each consolidated entity conducts its business (its "functional currency")
2. Provide information that is generally compatible with the expected economic effects of an exchange rate change on an enterprise's cash flows and equity

[19] J. K. Shank, J. F. Dillard, and R. J. Murdock, *Assessing the Economic Impact of FASB 8* (New York: Financial Executives Research Foundation, 1979).

[20] F.D.S. Choi, H. D. Lowe, and R. G. Worthley, "Accountors, Accountants, and Standard No. 8," *Journal of International Business Studies*, Fall 1978, p. 84.

[21] Financial Accounting Standards Board, "Foreign Currency Translation," *Statement of Financial Accounting Standards No. 52* (Stamford, Conn.: FASB, 1981).

[22] Financial Accounting Standards Board, "Accounting for Forward Exchange Contracts," *Statement of Financial Accounting Standards No. 20* (Stamford, Conn.: FASB, 1978).

[23] Financial Accounting Standards Board, "Translation of Unamortized Policy Acquisition Costs by a Stock Life Insurance Company," *Interpretation No. 15* (Stamford, Conn.: FASB, 1977).

[24] Financial Accounting Standards Board, "Applying the Lower of Cost or Market Rule in Translated Financial Statements," *Interpretation No. 17* (Stamford, Conn.: FASB, 1977).

These objectives are premised on the notion of a "functional currency," which mirrors the currency perspective adopted by management for consolidated entities. The functional currency of a particular foreign entity is defined as the currency of the primary economic environment in which it operates and generates cash flows. If a foreign entity's operations are relatively self-contained and integrated within a foreign country (i.e., an operation that is not an extension of the parent company) its functional currency would ordinarily be its local currency (e.g., cruzeiros in the case of a Brazilian subsidiary of a U.S. parent). If a foreign entity is merely an extension of a U.S. parent company, its functional currency would be the U.S. dollar. Table 4.8 identifies circumstances justifying use of either the local or the U.S. currency as an entity's functional currency.

Determination of the functional currency is a key feature of FAS No. 52 as it determines the choice of translation method and disposition of exchange gains and losses. If the foreign currency in which the foreign entity's records are maintained is deemed to be the functional currency, its financial statements are *translated* to dollars using the current rate method. Translation gains or losses arising therefrom are disclosed in a separate component of consolidated equity. This preserves the financial statement ratios as measured in the local currency statements. However, if the U.S. dollar is determined to be the functional currency, a foreign entity's financial statements are "remeasured" to a

TABLE 4.8   Functional Currency Criteria

ECONOMIC FACTORS	CIRCUMSTANCES FAVORING PARENT CURRENCY AS FUNCTIONAL CURRENCY	CIRCUMSTANCES FAVORING LOCAL CURRENCY AS FUNCTIONAL CURRENCY
Cash flows	Directly impact parent's cash flows and are currently remittable to the parent	Primarily in the local currency and do not impact parent's cash flows
Sales price	Responsive to changes in exchange rates and determined by worldwide competition	Largely irresponsive to exchange rate changes and governed primarily by local competition
Sales market	Largely in the parent country and denominated in parent currency	Largely in the host country and denominated in local currency
Expenses	Primarily related to productive factors imported from the parent company	Incurred primarily in the local environment
Financing	Primarily from the parent or reliance on parent company to meet debt obligations	Primarily denominated in local currency and serviced by local operations
Intercompany transactions	Frequent and extensive	Infrequent nor extensive

Source: Financial Accounting Standards Board, *Statement of Financial Accounting Standards No. 52* (Stamford, Conn.: FASB, 1981), Appendix A.

dollar perspective using the former temporal method prescribed by FAS No. 8. Here all translation gains or losses arising from the translation process are included in determining current income.

In those instances where an entity has more than one distinct and "separable" operation (e.g., a branch or division) each operation may be considered an entity, each with a different functional currency designation. Thus, a U.S. parent might have a self-contained manufacturing operation in West Germany designed to serve the European market as well as a separate sales outlet for the parent company's exported products. Under these circumstances, financial statements of the manufacturing operation would be translated to dollars using the current rate method. The deutschmark statements of the sales outlet would be remeasured in dollars according to the temporal method.

Once the functional currency for a foreign entity has been determined, FAS No. 52 requires that it be used consistently unless changes in economic circumstances clearly indicate that the functional currency has changed. If a reporting enterprise can justify the change in conformity with Accounting Principles Board Opinion No. 20, "Accounting Changes," the accounting change need not be accounted for retroactively.

Foreign Currency Financial Statements

The purpose of translation is to restate foreign currency financial statements to a common reporting currency (e.g., the U.S. dollar). Under FAS No. 52, procedures for translating foreign currency statements to dollars depend not only on the functional currency designation for a particular foreign entity but also on whether its records are originally maintained in its functional currency. Figure 4.2 flow charts alternate translation procedures.

Translation when local currency is the functional currency.   When the local currency of a foreign entity is its functional currency, and its records are maintained in that currency, the following current rate procedures are employed:

1. All foreign currency assets and liabilities are translated to dollars using the exchange rate prevailing as of the balance sheet date; capital accounts are translated at the historical rate.
2. Revenues and expenses are translated using the exchange rate prevailing on the transaction date, although weighted average rates can be used for expediency.
3. Translation gains and losses are reported in a separate component of consolidated stockholders' equity. These exchange adjustments bypass the income statement until the foreign operation is sold or the investment is perceived to have suffered a permanent diminution in value.

Translation adjustments under the current rate method arise whenever (a) year-end foreign currency balances are translated at a current rate that differs from that used to translate ending balances of the previous period, and (b) for-

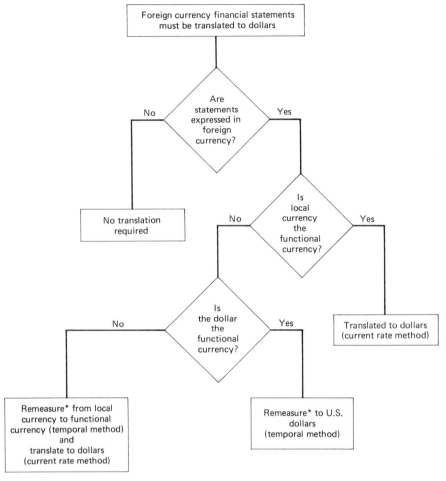

*The term *remeasure* means to translate so as to change the unit of measure from a foreign currency to the functional currency.

FIGURE 4.2   Translation Procedure Flowchart

eign currency financial statements are translated at a current rate that differs from exchange rates used during the period. The translation adjustment is calculated by (a) multiplying the beginning foreign currency net asset balance by the change in the current rate during the period and (b) multiplying the increase or decrease in net assets during the period by the difference between the average exchange rate and end of period exchange rate.

To illustrate, comparative foreign currency balance sheets at December 31, 1984 and 1985, and a statement of income for the year ended December 31, 1985, are presented in Table 4.9 for C&M Corporation, a wholly owned U.S. subsidiary. The statements conform with U.S. generally accepted accounting principles prior to translation to U.S dollars.

Capital stock was issued and fixed assets acquired when the exchange

TABLE 4.9   Financial Statements of C&M Corporation

BALANCE SHEET	12/31/84	12/31/85
Cash	FC 300	FC 500
Accounts receivable (net)	1,300	1,000
Inventories (lower of FIFO cost or market)	1,200	1,500
Fixed assets (net)	9,000	8,000
Total assets	FC 11,800	FC 11,000
Accounts payable	FC 2,200	FC 2,400
Long-term debt	4,400	3,000
Capital stock	2,000	2,000
Retained earnings	3,200	3,600
Total liabilities and owner's equity	FC 11,800	FC 11,000

INCOME STATEMENT	YEAR ENDED 12/31/85	
Sales		FC 10,000
Expenses		
Cost of sales	5,950	
Depreciation (straight-line)	1,000	
Other	1,493	8,443
Operating income		FC 1,557
Income taxes		467
Net income		FC 1,090

rate was FC 1 = $.17. Inventories at January 1, 1985, were acquired during the fourth quarter of 1984. Purchases (FC 6,250), sales, other expenses, and dividends (FC 690) occurred evenly during 1985. Exchange rates for calendar 1985 were as follows:

January 1, 1985	FC 1 = $.23
December 31, 1985	FC 1 = $.18
Average during 1985	FC 1 = $.22
Average during fourth quarter 1984	FC 1 = $.23
Average during fourth quarter 1985	FC 1 = $.19

Application of the FAS No. 52 translation process to the foregoing figures is depicted in Table 4.10.

Translation when U.S. dollar is the functional currency.   When the U.S. dollar is a foreign entity's functional currency, its foreign currency financial statements are remeasured (translated) to dollars using the temporal method originally advocated by FAS No. 8. Specifically:

1. Monetary assets and liabilities are translated using the rate prevailing as of the financial statement date; nonmonetary items including capital accounts are translated at historical rates.

TABLE 4.10   Current Rate Method of Translation (local currency is functional currency)

	FOREIGN CURRENCY	EXCHANGE RATE	DOLLAR EQUIVALENTS
Balance Sheet Accounts			
Assets			
Cash	FC 500	$ .18	$ 90
Accounts receivable	1,000	.18	180
Inventories	1,500	.18	270
Fixed assets	8,000	.18	1,440
Total	FC 11,000		$1,980
Liabilities and Stockholders' Equity			
Accounts payable	FC 2,400	.18	$ 432
Long-term debt	3,000	.18	540
Capital stock	2,000	.17	340
Retained earnings	3,600	a	404
Translation adjustment (cumulative)		b	264
Total	FC 11,000		$1,980
Income Statement Accounts			
Sales	FC 10,000	.22	$2,200
Cost of sales	5,950	.22	1,309
Depreciation	1,000	.22	220
Other expenses	1,493	.22	328
Income taxes	467	.22	103
Net income	FC 1,090		$ 240
Retained earnings 12/31/84	3,200		316
Dividends	690	.22	152
Retained earnings	FC 3,600		$ 404

[a] See statement of income and retained earnings.

[b] The translation adjustment for the year can be derived as follows. Assuming calendar 1985 is the first year in which the current rate method is adopted (previous translation method was a multiple rate method per FAS No. 8) a one-shot translation adjustment is calculated as of January 1, 1985. This figure approximates the amount by which beginning stockholders' equity would differ in light of the translation switch. It is derived by translating C&M Corporation's January 1, 1985, foreign currency net asset position at the current rate prevailing on that date. The beginning-of-period capital stock and retained earnings accounts retain their original translated amounts as of that date (i.e., carried over from the previous year's balance sheet). The resulting difference (calculated below) is C&M Corporation's beginning-of-period cumulative translation adjustment.

Net assets, 12/31/84		FC 5,200
Exchange rate, 12/31/84 (FC 1 = $.23)		× $.23
		$ 1,196
Less (as reported stockholders' equity, 12/31/84):		
Capital stock	$340	
Retained earnings (per FAS No. 8)	316	656
Cumulative translation adjustment		$ 540

(*continued*)

TABLE 4.10   (*continued*)

Given this information the following steps yield the translation adjustment for calendar 1985:

1. Net assets, 12/31/84	FC 1 = $.23	FC 5,200	
Change in current rate during year:			
Rate, 12/31/84	FC 1 = $.23		
Rate, 12/31/85	FC 1 = $.18	× $(.05)	$(260)
2. Change in net assets during year (net income less dividends)		FC 400	
Difference between average and year-end rate:			
Average rate	FC 1 = $.22		
Year-end rate	FC 1 = $.18	× $(.04)	$(16)
Total			$(276)
3. Cumulative translation adjustment, 1/1/85			540
4. Cumulative translation adjustment, 12/31/85			$ 264

2. Revenues and expenses are translated using average exchange rates for the period save those items related to nonmonetary items (e.g., cost of sales and depreciation expense), which are translated using historical rates.

3. Translation gains and losses are reflected in current income.

Table 4.11 illustrates application of the FAS No. 52 remeasurement process when the dollar is the functional currency.

Translation when foreign currency is the functional currency.   If a foreign entity's records are not maintained in its functional currency, remeasurement into the functional currency is required prior to dollar translation. For example, if a Hong Kong subsidiary's functional currency is the British pound but it maintains its records in Hong Kong dollars, remeasurement (translation) of its statements into pounds employing the temporal method would be necessary prior to dollar translation at the current rate. Remeasurement into the functional currency (e.g., British pounds) employs procedures identical to those enumerated in Table 4.11.

Foreign Currency Transactions

Foreign currency transaction rules under FAS No. 52 are similar to those under the previous FAS No. 8 with two major exceptions. Transaction adjustments—conversion gains or losses on settled transactions as well as translation gains or losses on unsettled transactions—are reported in a separate component of stockholders' equity when (1) the adjustment relates to transactions between a parent company and an affiliate that are of a long-term nature, and (2) the foreign currency transaction (including a forward contract) is intended as a hedge of a foreign operation's exposed net asset or liability position.

Intercompany transactions.   If an intercompany transaction is deemed by management to be of a long-term nature (i.e., intercompany payables or re-

TABLE 4.11 Temporal Method of Translation (U.S. dollar is functional currency)

	FOREIGN CURRENCY	EXCHANGE RATE	DOLLAR EQUIVALENTS
Balance Sheet Accounts			
Assets			
Cash	FC 500	$ .18	$ 90
Accounts receivable	1,000	.18	180
Inventories	1,500	.19	285
Fixed Assets	8,000	.17	1,360
Total	FC 11,000		$ 1,915
Liabilities and Stockholders' Equity			
Accounts payable	FC 2,400	.18	$ 432
Long-term debt	3,000	.18	540
Capital stock	2,000	.17	340
Retained earnings	3,600	a	603
Translation adjustment			
Total	FC 11,000		$ 1,915
Income Statement Accounts			
Sales	FC 10,000	.22	$ 2,200
Cost of sales	5,950	c	1,366
Depreciation	1,000	.17	170
Other expenses	1,493	.22	328
Aggregate exchange gain (loss)	—	b	206
Income taxes	467	.22	103
Net income	FC 1,090		$ 439
Retained earnings 12/31/84	3,200		316
Dividends	690	.22	152
Retained earnings 12/31/85	FC 3,600		$ 603

[a] See statement of income and retained earnings.

[b] 1. 12/31/84 Monetary assets − monetary liabilities × change in current rate
    = FC 1,600   − FC 6,600   × (.18 − .23) = $250

2. Change in net monetary asset position:
   12/31/84 FC (5,000)
   12/31/85 FC (3,900)
            FC 11,000
   Composition of change:
       Sources of monetary items × difference between year-end and average rate:
           Net earnings   FC 1,090
           Depreciation   FC 1,000
                            2,090 × (.18 − .22)   = $ (84)
       Uses of monetary items × difference between year-end and average rate:
           Increase in inventories   FC 300
           Dividends   FC 690
                            990 × (.18 − .22)   = $40

3. Aggregate translation adjustment:
       $250 − $84 + $40 = $206

[c] Beginning inventories   FC 1,200 at $.23 = $ 276
   Purchases   FC 6,250 at $.22 = $ 1,375
   Cost of goods available for sale $ 1,651
   Ending inventories   FC 1,500 at $.19 = $ 285
   Cost of sales $ 1,366

ceivables are not expected to be settled within the foreseeable future), exchange adjustments relating to these transactions now bypass income and are included in a separate component of consolidated equity. Transactions of this nature are considered to be part of a parent company's net investment in the foreign entity.

Parties to long-term intercompany transactions will generally be the U.S. parent and the foreign entity. Depending on the functional currency employed, the intercompany transaction could be a foreign currency transaction of the parent, the foreign subsidiary, or both. Using Denmark as an example, if a Danish subsidiary's functional currency is the Danish krone, a krone-denominated intercompany transaction would be a foreign currency transaction only of the U.S. parent. If the intercompany payable or receivable is denominated in dollars, it would be a foreign currency transaction of the Danish subsidiary. If the Danish entity's functional currency is the U.S. dollar, a krone-denominated intercompany account would be a foreign currency transaction of *both* parent and subsidiary. An intercompany transaction denominated in dollars would not be a foreign currency transaction of either.

The requirement that long-term intercompany transaction gains and losses be disclosed in stockholders' equity is applicable only when the foreign entity's functional currency is the local currency. In the case of our Danish operation, if the Danish entity's functional currency is the krone, either the U.S. parent's transaction adjustment (krone-denominated account) or the Danish entity's transaction adjustment (dollar-denominated account) is made to the separate component of stockholders' equity. If the Danish subsidiary's functional currency is the dollar, FAS No. 8's original prescription would apply and neither company would have a foreign currency transaction if the account is denominated in dollars. If the intercompany balance is denominated in krone, both entities would have a foreign currency transaction and the transaction adjustment of each would be reflected in current income.

Transactions intended as hedges.   Under FAS No. 52, foreign currency transactions can be used to hedge or offset other exchange gains and losses that would normally be reflected in reported earnings. Such exchange adjustments include, but are not limited to, gains or losses on foreign currency commitments (e.g., long-term purchase contracts or leasing agreements) and translation gains or losses arising from restating foreign currency financial statements.

Gains or losses on transactions intended to hedge foreign currency commitments are limited to the extent of expected exchange adjustments on the future commitments. Any excess translation gains or losses must be charged to current income. As an example, assume that on January 1, 1985, a U.S. company orders 4,000 color television sets from a South Korean manufacturer at a cost of 600,000,000 won (W) to be delivered and paid for in six months. The spot exchange rate is W 750 = $1. The following day the importing company acquires a time deposit in a South Korean bank by depositing $900,000 or W 675,000,000 ($900,000 × W 750). If the exchange rate on July 1, 1985, increases to W 700 = $1, the exchange loss experienced by the U.S. importer would be offset by an exchange gain on the won bank deposit. The latter, in turn, would be accounted for as follows:

Deferred portion	W 600,000,000/W 700 − W 600,000,000/W 750 =	$ 57,143
Included in income	W 75,000,000/W 700 − W 75,000,000/W 750 =	7,143
Total adjustment	W 675,000,000/W 700 − W 675,000,000/W 750 =	$ 64,286

Payment of the purchase commitment on July 1, 1985, at the spot rate of W 700 = $1 would be recorded as follows:

Cost of television shipment	W 600,000,000/W 700 =	$ 857,143
Less deferred gain on foreign currency transaction		57,143
Net cost of purchase		$ 800,000

Gains or losses on transactions intended as hedges of an exposed net asset or liability position are accumulated in consolidated equity to the extent of expected translation gains or losses. Thus, a U.S. parent company with a 268,-500,000 Argentine peso exposed net asset position in its Argentine subsidiary might borrow an equivalent amount of pesos as an offset. Should the peso devalue by 20 percent the translation loss on the subsidiary's net assets would be offset by the gain on the peso loan. Recording the transaction gain in shareholders' equity leaves consolidated income unscathed by the devaluation.

Forward exchange contracts.   Forward exchange contracts, defined earlier, may be secured to (1) hedge an existing or anticipated foreign currency payable or receivable (a foreign currency commitment), or (2) hedge an exposed net asset or liability position of a foreign operation, or (3) speculate in foreign currencies. Under FAS No. 8, each of these categories dictated a differ-

TABLE 4.12   Accounting Adjustments under FAS No. 8

	GAINS/LOSSES	DISCOUNT/PREMIUM
Identifiable foreign currency commitments	Deferred and included in dollar basis of foreign currency transaction[a]	Amortized over duration[b]
Exposed net asset or liability position	Recognized in income of period in which they occur	Amortized over duration of contract
Speculation	Recognized in income of period in which they occur[c]	Recognized in current income

[a] The amount deferred is limited to the amount of the related commitment, on an after-tax basis.

[b] The portion that is amortized during the commitment period may be included in the dollar basis of the related foreign currency transaction.

[c] Gains/losses in this category are a function of the difference between the forward rate available for the remaining period of the contract and the contracted forward rate (or the forward rate last used to measure a gain or loss on that contract for an earlier period).

TABLE 4.13 Conditions Qualifying a Forward Contract as a "Commitment" Hedge

FAS NO. 8	FAS NO. 52
1. Life of the forward contract must match that of the related foreign currency commitment.	1. Forward contract must be intended and designated as a hedge of a foreign currency commitment.
2. Forward contract must commence at the commitment date.	2. Forward contract need not commence at the commitment date.
3. Forward contract must be denominated in the same currency as the foreign currency commitment	3. Forward contract must be denominated in the same currency as the foreign currency commitment or in a currency that moves in tandem with it.
4. Foreign currency commitment must be firm and uncancelable.	4. Foreign currency commitment must be firm.

ent accounting treatment for discounts, premiums, gains, or losses on contracted forward exchange. Table 4.12 illustrates how these accounting adjustments were reported under FAS No. 8.

The scheme in Table 4.12 is modified by FAS No. 52 in that gains or losses related to a hedge of an exposed net asset or liability position are now reported in a separate component of stockholders' equity rather than in periodic income. Conditions qualifying a forward contract as a hedge of an identifiable foreign currency commitment under FAS No. 8 and the new FAS No. 52 (less stringent) are listed in Table 4.13.

THE CONTROVERSY CONTINUES

While FAS No. 52 is designed to still many of the criticisms leveled at FAS No. 8, new issues stir new controversies, a perhaps inevitable result given the complexity of multinational operations and the many purposes of translation. Several basic issues are dimensioned below.

Reporting Perspective

In adopting the notion of functional currency, FAS No. 52 accommodates both a local as well as a parent company reporting perspective in the consolidated financial statements. The first adopts the currency of the foreign operation's domicile as functional; the second, the U.S. dollar. However, several questions may be posed. First, are financial statement readers better served by incorporating two different reporting perspectives and, therefore, two different currency frameworks in a single set of consolidated financial statements? For example, let us assume that a U.S. parent company has two majority-owned subsidiaries in Latin America, one located in Brazil, the other in Mexico. If the Mexican subsidiary's functional currency is the U.S. dollar, its peso statements would be translated to dollars using the temporal method and any translation adjustments included in current income (as per FAS No. 8). If the Brazilian subsidiary's functional currency is deemed to be the cruzeiro, its cruzeiro statements would be translated to dollars using the current rate method and any resulting translation adjustments disclosed in a separate component of consolidated equity. Yet, is a translation adjustment produced under the temporal method any different in substance from that produced under the current rate method? If not, is any useful purpose served by disclosing some translation adjustments in income and others in stockholders' equity? Is FAS No. 8's concept of a single consolidated entity and a single unit of measure (the parent company's reporting currency) the lesser of two evils?

Concept of Income

Under FAS No. 52, adjustments arising from the translation of foreign currency financial statements and certain transactions are made directly to shareholders' equity, thus bypassing the income statement. The apparent intention was to provide statement readers with more accurate and less confusing income numbers, that is, translated results that are "directionally sympathetic" with the economic effects of exchange rate movements. Some, however, dislike the idea of "burying" translation adjustments, heretofore disclosed. They fear possible reader confusion as to the effects of fluctuating exchange rates on a company's worth. Equity adjustments, moreover, violate the *all-inclusive concept of income*,[25] which requires that companies disclose (1) operating revenues and expenses, and (2) all unusual, nonoperating, and infrequently occurring items in the computation of income, the latter category being reported separately in the income statement. This provision was designed to provide statement readers with all information bearing on a firm's "profitability." Which income concept is right?

Misleading Information?

While a multiple currency perspective, permitted by the FASB's translation standard may prove *confusing* to some readers, there are those who feel that FAS No. 52 could prove to be *misleading*. E. I. Du Pont de Nemours & Company explains that under FAS No. 52, foreign operations that appear profitable from a local currency perspective may actually turn out to be unprofitable from a U.S. dollar perspective.[26] As an illustration, assume that a U.S. parent makes a $1,000 equity investment in a Canadian subsidiary at the start of period 1. The subsidiary immediately uses the funds to purchase a $1,000 fixed asset with an estimated useful life of five years when the exchange rate is C$1 = $1.00. The exchange rate subsequently devalues to C$1 = US$.80 at the start of period 2 and remains unchanged thereafter. Annual revenues of the Canadian subsidiary are C$230, depreciation is straight-line, and there are no

---

[25] American Institute of Certified Public Accountants, "Reporting the Results of Operations," *Accounting Principles Board Opinion No. 9* (New York: AICPA, December 1966).

[26] Stanely R. Wojciechowski, "Du Pont Evaluates FAS 52," *Management Accounting*, July 1982, pp. 31–35.

TABLE 4.14   Distortive Effects of FAS No. 52

	PERIOD 1 (C$1 = US$1)			PERIOD 2 (C$1 = US$.80)			FIVE-YEAR TOTAL		
	Canadian dollars	U.S. dollars		Canadian dollars	U.S. dollars		Canadian dollars	U.S. dollars	
		T	C		T	C		T	C
Revenues	230	230	230	230	184	184	1,150	966	966
Expense (depr.)	200	200	200	200	200	160	1,000	1,000	840
Income	30	30	30	30	(16)	24	150	(34)	126

Note: T = temporal method; C = current rate method.

other transactions during each period. Cash is repatriated annually to the U.S. parent. Operating results over the five-year period are summarized in Table 4.14.

In this example, the consolidated entity would report a cumulative net cash outflow (loss) of $34 under the temporal method. The temporal method also reveals that the company did not recover the fixed asset investment in U.S. dollars. This is not evident under the current rate method. Indeed, the latter procedure suggests a cumulative profit of $126 even though there was a net cash outflow of $34 over the life of the investment. The $34 loss would be disclosed in consolidated equity until the investment is sold or completely liquidated, a remote possibility in many instances.

To Smooth or Not to Smooth?

Under FAS No. 8, treatment of exchange gains and losses includes minimization of a smoothing option permitted by the earlier use of balance sheet reserves to account for net translation gains. Ironically, FAS No. 52 reintroduces smoothing opportunities. Consider, once again, the notion of functional currencies. When a foreign entity's functional currency is not readily apparent, its determination is left to management. Once determined, the functional currency is expected to be used consistently, unless management ascertains a change in the underlying circumstances. Ernst & Whinney states that "a change in the functional currency would not be considered a change in accounting principle under APB Opinion No. 20, 'Accounting Changes.' We believe a change in the functional currency of a foreign entity would be viewed as a change to reflect new events or economic circumstances."[27] This means that the cumulative effect of a functional currency change, computed for all prior periods to the beginning of the period in which the change is made, would not have to be disclosed.

As an example of a smoothing opportunity, assume that a U.S. parent company has a manufacturing subsidiary in Switzerland whose functional currency is the U.S. dollar. The U.S. parent wishes to borrow Swiss francs for use in its Geneva operations. If the parent were to take out the franc loan, an ap-

[27] Ernst & Whinney, "Foreign Currency Translation," *Financial Reporting Developments*, October 1980, p. 12.

preciation of the franc by the repayment date would be reflected in consolidated income. However, if the Swiss *subsidiary* borrowed the funds and the franc were designated as its functional currency, an exchange adjustment, stemming from a rise in the franc's value, would bypass consolidated income and appear in stockholders' equity instead.

Assume now that the U.S. parent desired use of the franc loan proceeds. Again, borrowing Swiss francs through the Swiss subsidiary would shield consolidated income from the effects of a fluctuating franc/dollar exchange rate. Under FAS No. 52, transactions between an investor and investee of a long-term nature are viewed as increases or decreases in a parent company's foreign investment. Accordingly, foreign exchange adjustments, whether attributed to settled or unsettled transactions, are treated as adjustments to stockholders' equity. Alternatively, if the Swiss subsidiary has a net exposed asset position, the U.S. parent could designate the Swiss franc borrowing as a hedge of the Swiss subsidiary's positive exposure. In this instance, a transaction loss incurred on a rise in the franc's value vis-à-vis the dollar would flow to consolidated equity as an offset to the positive translation adjustment stemming from consolidation.

Foreign Currency Translation and Inflation

An inverse relationship between a country's rate of inflation and its currency's external value has been empirically demonstrated. Consequently, use of the current rate to translate the cost of nonmonetary assets, located in inflationary environments, will eventually produce domestic currency equivalents far below their original measurement bases. At the same time, translated earnings would be greater because of correspondingly lower depreciation charges. Such translated results could easily mislead rather than inform. Lower dollar valuations would usually understate the actual earning power of foreign assets supported by local inflation and inflated return on investment ratios of foreign operations could create false expectations of future profitability.

Rather than address the foregoing issue, the FASB decided against inflation adjustments prior to translation believing such adjustments to be inconsistent with the historical cost valuation framework employed in basic U.S. statements. As a preliminary solution, FAS No. 52 requires use of the U.S. dollar as the functional currency for foreign operations domiciled in hyperinflationary environments, that is, those countries in which the cumulative rate of inflation exceeds 100 percent over a three-year period. This procedure would hold constant the dollar equivalents of foreign currency assets as they would now be translated at the historical rate (per temporal method).

This accounting treatment, however, is not without limitations. To begin with, translation at the historical rate is meaningful only if differential rates of inflation between the subsidiary's host country and parent country are perfectly negatively correlated with exchange rates. Failing this, the dollar equivalents of foreign currency assets in inflationary environments will also be misleading. In addition, should inflation rates in the hyperinflationary economy subside in the future (e.g., fall below 100 pecent), switching to the current rate method (local currency would now be the functional currency) could produce a significant translation adjustment to consolidated equity as exchange rates may have changed significantly during the interim. Under these circumstances, charging stockholders' equity with translation losses on foreign currency fixed assets could have a significant effect on financial ratios with stockholders' equity in the denominator. Indeed, Business International reports that some U.S. companies that adopted FAS No. 52 early are worried about the reactions of investment analysts and especially the reactions of banks with which they have loan-covenant agreements on minimum debt to equity ratios.[28] At issue is whether the equity impact of FAS No. 52 will affect the evaluation of companies by creditors, shareholders, and credit-rating agencies.

TRANSLATION METHODS
AND PRACTICES OUTSIDE
THE UNITED STATES

The problem of translating foreign currencies is not unique to the United States. The problem of foreign currency translation has assumed global proportions as more and more countries host business entities whose operating activities transcend national boundaries. Examination of selected foreign currency translation pronouncements outside the United States is thus helpful in monitoring how other countries are dealing with this elusive problem. Moreover, an international survey provides a useful perspective for gauging domestic translation policies.

EEC Countries

The European Economic Community's Fourth Directive governing the content and publication of annual financial statements is silent as to methods of currency translation to be followed or how they are to be shown in the accounts. So is the proposed Seventh Directive concerning the preparation and audit of consolidated accounts. Both Directives merely require that exchange rates used to translate foreign currency balances be disclosed. In the absence of any definitive requirement, one must look to national pronouncements, legislation and enterprise practices for guidance.

Germany. There is no governmental or professional accounting requirement covering foreign currency translation processes in Germany. The German Institut der Wirtschaftsprüfer, however, recommends that the translation method as well as exchange adjustments resulting from the translation process be disclosed. The latter are to have no effects on reported earnings.

---

[28] "BIMR Survey Shows Applying FAS No. 52 Generally Boosted Earnings," p. 122.

German corporate translation practices generally reflect variations of the current rate method. Consider some examples.

Hoechst translates

all items in the balance sheet and the net income for the year and its appropriation at rates ruling on the balance sheet date;
all income and expenses, as well as movements of fixed assets and stockholders' equity, at weighted average annual rates.[29]

For Schering

The items of the local currency accounts of the foreign companies are converted into D-Marks at the average rate on the balance sheet date. The fixed assets and the related depreciation, however, are shown at the rates valid at the time of purchase. If there are separate import rates the liabilities affected are valued at these rates. Expenses and income, with the exception of depreciation based on historical rates, are converted at the average for the year.[30]

Differences arising from translating foreign currency financial statements also reflect a variety of treatments. Excerpts from the annual reports of Hoechst and Volkswagenwerk follow:

Hoechst. The method of translation because of changes in the value of the Deutschmark ... resulted in an increase in the value to be rated in Deutschmarks, of Hoechst AG's share of the equity of the companies consolidated. Within the scope of elimination of intercompany investments and net equities, this has reduced the balance due to consolidation correspondingly, without affecting the net income for the year (see ... "Balance Due to Consolidation").[31]
    The differences arising from the application of different rates in the statement of income is included in "Other Expenses."[32]
Volkswagenwerk. Differences incurred by translating balance sheet items have been entered direct in the reserve from capital stock surplus. They have not affected the net earnings for the report year. Differences incurred by translating the items of the statement of earnings were balanced so that the net earnings were not influenced by these either.[33]

The Netherlands.   In the absence of definitive rules concerning the translation of foreign currencies for purposes of consolidation, one must look to Dutch reporting modes for guidance. Despite the lack of governmental or professional guidelines, Dutch translation practices are strikingly similar with most companies employing a variant of the current rate method and taking exchange gains and losses to reserves. Thus, whereas companies like Oce-van der

---

[29] Hoechst *1980 Annual Report*, p. 72.
[30] Schering *1980 Annual Report*, p. 49.
[31] Hoechst, *Annual Report*, p. 72.
[32] Ibid.
[33] *Volkswagenwerk 1980 Annual Report*, p. 63.

Grinten and Thyssen-Bornemisza translate balance sheet items at the year-end rate, Buhrman-Tetterode and Elsevier-NDU except fixed assets which are translated at historical rates. The translation policies of Philips are reproduced below as a standard of comparison.

> In the Combined Statement of Financial Position, amounts in foreign currency are converted into guilders at the official exchange rates ruling on the balance sheet date.
> The medium rate is used as a rule for currencies with a fixed relation to the guilder or to another currency.
> Exchange differences due to the conversion into guilders of property, plant and equipment and stocks are offset against Revaluation Surplus for the relevant country; in so far as such Revaluation Surplus is insufficient for this purpose, the deficiency is included as a miscellaneous charge in the profit and loss account.
> Exchange differences due to the conversion into guilders of nominal assets and liabilities are likewise included as miscellaneous income/charges in the profit and loss account.
> In the Combined Statement of Results, sales and results in foreign currencies are converted at the rates applicable in the relevant periods.
> The balances of the relevant profit and loss accounts are converted at the end of the year at the rates applied in the Combined Statement of Financial Position. The resultant difference is included under miscellaneous income/charges in the profit and loss account.[34]

United Kingdom.   As we go to press, there is no mandatory accounting method for foreign currency translation in the United Kingdom. However, U.K. Exposure Draft No. 27, "Accounting for Foreign Currency Translations," is expected to be released as an authoritative standard. The U.K. exposure draft resembles in most major respects FAS No. 52. A brief overview of ED No. 27 is provided below.

Exposure Draft No. 27 divides foreign operations into those that operate as separate or quasi-independent entities and those that are direct extensions of the parent company. Where foreign operations are viewed as extensions of the parent, ED No. 27 requires use of the temporal method to translate foreign currency financial statements. Exchange gains or losses should be reflected in current income. Where the foreign operation is viewed as a separate or quasi-independent entity, the closing rate method is to be used with translation gains or losses recorded as a movement in reserves.

If foreign currency borrowings have been used to finance or hedge investments in foreign operations, exchange gains or losses on the borrowing may be offset, as reserve movements, against exchange differences arising from the translation of foreign currency financial statements provided that:

1. The relationship between the parent company and the foreign affiliate justifies the use of the closing rate method for consolidation purposes.
2. In any accounting period, the exchange adjustments stemming from foreign currency borrowings do not exceed translation gains and losses.

---

[34] *Philips 1980 Annual Report*, p. 36.

3. The aggregate foreign currency borrowings, on which the exchange gains or losses have arisen, are restricted to the total amount of cash expected to be generated by the net investments.
4. The accounting treatment is applied consistently.

At present, British companies appear to favor the closing rate method or a variant that applies the average rate to revenue and expense items. While most companies take exchange differences to reserves, some reflect such adjustments in current income.

Selected Other Countries

Switzerland.   There are no legal requirements for Swiss MNCs to prepare consolidated financial statements. If consolidation occurs, any translation method is permissible.

As is true elsewhere in Europe, most Swiss companies employ the current rate method of currency translation. Many vary this treatment by using historical rates for fixed assets and depreciation. Accounting for translation gains and losses, however, varies from company to company. Two examples follow:

> *Nestle.* Adjustments resulting from the annual translation into Swiss francs of the various balance sheet items are not charged to the profit and loss account but are transferred directly to consolidated shareholders' funds, showing separately differences arising from the working capital and those relating to the fixed assets (see "Movement of the Consolidated Shareholders' Funds").[35]
>
> *Sandoz.* Currency translation gains and losses affecting the current assets and liabilities of our foreign subsidiaries are included together with other exchange rate gains or losses. Gains are carried forward to be offset against any losses due to currency translation and exchange rate movements in the following accounting periods. If these losses exceed the available provisions, they will be shown as expenditure in the Consolidated Statement of Income.[36]

Canada.   In September 1978, Canada's Accounting Research Committee (ARC) issued Section 1650, "Translation of Foreign Currency Transactions and Foreign Currency Financial Statements." It recommended that Canadian multinationals adopt a translation premised on the temporal method set out in FAS No. 8. In light of the FASB's recent revision of FAS No. 8, the ARC issued new currency translation rules effective January 1, 1983. In keeping with FAS No. 52, integrated foreign operations (i.e., those viewed as extensions of the parent company) must now be translated under the temporal method whereas self-sustaining foreign operations must be translated using the current rate method. The major difference between the Canadian and U.S. translation pronouncements is that the Canadian rules require that:

1. Exchange gains and losses relating to long-term monetary items of the reporting enterprise that are dominated in a foreign currency, and adjustments arising on translation of long-term monetary items of integrated foreign op-

---

[35] *Nestle 1980 Annual Report*, p. 8.
[36] *Sandoz 1980 Annual Report*, p. 22.

erations be deferred and amortized over the life of the related asset and liability.

2. Deferred income taxes be translated at the historical rate.

Japan. Owing to the growth of Japanese overseas investments, Japan's Business Accounting Deliberation Council issued, in June 1979, an accounting standard for foreign currency translation. Interestingly, the pronouncement incorporates features of both the temporal and current-noncurrent methods. Specifically, foreign currency financial statements are translated using temporal rates save long-term monetary assets and liabilities, which are translated at historical rates. Moreover, translation gains and losses are to be taken to a translation adjustment account in the asset or liability sections of the balance sheet. However, flexibility is accorded companies operating under extraordinary currency situations whereupon "other reasonable methods of accounting and reporting may be employed."

In examining Japanese reporting practices, a distinction is drawn between those companies subscribing to U.S. generally accepted accounting principles (GAAP) and those adhering to principles generally accepted in Japan. Companies subscribing to U.S. accounting norms, such as Matsushita, Toshiba, Honda, and Mitsubishi Electric, employ the temporal method with translation gains and losses reflected in current income. Companies following Japanese GAAP employ a variety of methods reflecting the diversity that characterizes current practice in Japan.

Current Trends

Table 4.15 provides a global summary by country of translation methods employed. At first blush, it appears that the current rate or closing rate method is more prevalent today than multiple rate methods. Closer examination, however, suggests that global translation methods are really grouping themselves into two basic trends. While a conceptual distinction exists between the mone-

TABLE 4.15 Translation Methods Around the World (predominant practice)

COUNTRY	CURRENT	CURRENT-NONCURRENT	MONETARY-NONMONETARY	TEMPORAL
Argentina				X
Australia	X			
Austria				X
Bahamas			X	
Bermuda				X
Bolivia				X
Botswana	X			
Canada	X			X
Chile				X
Colombia	X			
Costa Rica			X	
Denmark	X			
Dominican Republic				X

(*continued*)

TABLE 4.15   (*continued*)

COUNTRY	CURRENT	CURRENT-NONCURRENT	MONETARY-NONMONETARY	TEMPORAL
Equador				X
El Salvador		X		
Fiji	X			
Finland			X	
France	X			
Germany	X			
Greece	X			
Guatemala			X	
Honduras			X	
Hong Kong	X			
India	X			
Iran		X		
Ireland	X			
Ivory Coast	X			
Jamaica				X
Japan	X			
Kenya	X			
Korea			X	
Malawi		X		
Malaysia	X			
Netherlands	X			
New Zealand		X		
Nicaragua			X	
Norway	X			
Pakistan		X		
Panama				X
Paraguay	X			
Peru				X
Philippines			X	
Senegal	X			
Singapore	X			
South Africa		X		
Sweden			X	
Switzerland	X			
Taiwan			X	
United Kingdom	X			X
United States	X			X
Venezuela				X
Zambia		X		
Zimbabwe	X			

Source: Fitzgerald, Stickler, and Watts, *International Survey*, unpaginated, and F.D.S. Choi and V. Bavishi, "Financial Accounting Standards: A Multinational Synthesis and Policy Framework," *International Journal of Accounting*, Fall 1982, pp. 76, 78, 79, 81, 83, 174.

tary-nonmonetary method and the temporal method, that distinction, for all practical purposes, largely vanishes when foreign currency non-monetary assets are valued under the historical cost principle. Since this is indeed the case in most countries of the world, the temporal method is really a more general case of the monetary-nonmonetary method. Therefore, if these methods are grouped together, they appear to be as prevalent as the current rate approach.

That this is indeed the case can be seen in recent accounting standardization efforts at the international level. The 46-nation member International Accounting Standards Committee (IASC), headquartered in London, has issued a steady stream of pronouncements aimed at harmonizing accounting and reporting standards. Its recent International Accounting Standard No. 21, "Accounting for the Effects of Changes in Foreign Exchange Rates," supports the use of the current rate method or the temporal method depending on the operational and financial characteristics of a parent's foreign operations. In this regard, IAS 21 mirrors to a large extent the foreign currency translation provisions embodied in U.S. FAS No. 52 as well as U.K. ED No. 27. Specifically, foreign currency transactions entered into by a company should be translated to their domestic currency equivalents using the exchange rate ruling on the date at which the transaction occurred. At the balance sheet date, monetary assets and liabilities denominated in foreign currencies should be converted at the exchange rate ruling on that date or at the exchange rate effective in forward exchange contracts. Gains or losses arising from these transactions, with a few exceptions, should be included in current income.

The current or closing rate translation method is required for foreign operations that are not considered integral to the operations of the parent; the temporal method is recommended for those that are. Under the former, translation adjustments arising from the restatement process are to be taken to Stockholders' Equity. Under the latter, gains and losses are to be reflected in current income except that (a) gains and losses relating to long-term monetary items may be deferred and amortized over the remaining lives of the monetary items and (b) gains or losses arising from severe devaluations may be offset against the carrying value of the assets concerned, provided that the adjusted value of the assets does not exceed the lower of replacement cost and the amount recoverable from the use or eventual sale of the assets. These exemptions are not permitted by U.S. FAS No. 52 or U.K. ED No. 27.

Upon implementation, U.S. FAS 52 and IAS 21 permit but do not require restatement of comparative information with respect to prior years. Restatement of comparative data is required upon implementation of U.K. ED No. 27.

SELECTED REFERENCES

ACCOUNTING STANDARDS COMMITTEE, "Accounting for Foreign Currency Translations," *Exposure Draft 27*, London: ASC, 1980, unpaginated.

ALLEMAN, RAYMOND H., "Why ITT Likes FAS 52," *Management Accounting*, July 1982, pp. 23–29.

AMERICAN INSTITUTE OF CERTIFIED PUBLIC ACCOUNTANTS, "Status of Accounting Research Bulletins," *Accounting Principles Board Opinion No. 6*, Paragraph 18, New York: AICPA, 1965, p. 42.

AMERICAN INSTITUTE OF CERTIFIED PUBLIC ACCOUNTANTS, Committee on Accounting Procedure, "Restatement and Revision of Accounting Research

Bulletins," *Accounting Research Bulletin No. 43*, Chapter 12, "Foreign Operations and Foreign Exchange," New York: AICPA, 1953, pp. 111–116.

BENDER, DOUGLAS E., ed., "Foreign Currency Translation—FAS 52, Parts I, II, III," *CPA Journal*, June, July, August 1982, var. pp.

BUSINESS INTERNATIONAL, *New Directions in Managing Currency Risk: Changing Corporate Strategies and Systems Under FAS No. 52*, New York, 1982.

CHOI, FREDERICK D. S., "Accounting for Multinational Operations," in *Handbook of International Business*, eds. Ingo Walter and Tracy Murray, New York: John Wiley & Sons, Inc., 1982, pp. 23.1–23.49.

COOPERS & LYBRAND, *Foreign Currency Translation: An Implementation Guide*, New York, January 1982, 94 pp.

DELOITTE HASKINS & SELLS, *Foreign Currency Translation*, New York, December 1981, 35 pp.

ERNST & WHINNEY, "Foreign Currency Translation," *Financial Reporting Developments*, Cleveland, January 1982, 66 pp.

FINANCIAL ACCOUNTING STANDARDS BOARD, "Accounting for the Translation of Foreign Currency Transactions and Foreign Currency Financial Statements," *Statement of Financial Accounting Standards No. 8*, Stamford, Conn.: FASB, October 1975, 103 pp.

FINANCIAL ACCOUNTING STANDARDS BOARD, "Foreign Currency Translation," *Statement of Financial Accounting Standards No. 52*, Stamford, Conn.: FASB, December 1981, 78 pp.

HEPWORTH, SAMUEL R., *Reporting Foreign Operations*, Ann Arbor, Mich.: University of Michigan, 1956, 211 pp.

IJIRI, YUJI, "Foreign Currency Accounting and Its Transition," in *Managing Foreign Exchange Risk*, ed. Richard J. Herring, n.p.: Cambridge University Press, forthcoming.

INTERNATIONAL ACCOUNTING STANDARDS COMMITTEE, "Accounting for the Effects of Changes in Foreign Exchange Rates," *International Accounting Standard Exposure Draft 23*, London: IASC, March 1, 1982, unpaginated.

LORENSEN, LEONARD, "Reporting Foreign Operations of U.S. Companies in U.S. Dollars," *Accounting Research Study No. 12*, New York: American Institute of Certified Public Accountants, 1972.

PATZ, DENNIS H., "The State of the Art in Translation Theory," *Journal of Business Finance & Accounting*, Vol. 4, No. 3, 1977, pp. 311–325.

RATCLIFFE, THOMAS A., and PAUL MUNTER, "Currency Translation: A New Blueprint," *Journal of Accountancy*, June 1982, pp. 82–90.

SHANK, JOHN K., JESSE F. DILLARD, and RICHARD J. MURDOCK, *Assessing the Economic Impact of FASB No. 8*, New York: Financial Executives Research Foundation, 1980.

WOJCIECHOWSKI, STANLEY R., "Dupont Evaluates FAS 52," *Management Accounting*, July 1982, pp. 31–35.

DISCUSSION QUESTIONS

1. Briefly explain the nature of foreign currency translation as (a) a *restatement* process and (b) a *remeasurement* process.

2. Should a multinational company with a partially owned foreign subsidiary in, say, the Philippines disclose its ''foreign exchange gains and losses'' in financial reports to its Philippine shareholders?

3. How does the treatment of ''exchange gains and losses'' differ between FAS No. 52 and its predecessor, FAS No. 8?

4. Explain the rationale underlying the disposition of transactions gains and losses in current income?
5. What is a forward contract? How does the FASB's new foreign currency translation pronouncement alter their accounting treatment?
6. Describe the conceptual underpinnings of the functional currency notion, a key ingredient of FAS No. 52.
7. Compare and contrast features of the major foreign currency translation methods introduced in this chapter. Which do you feel provides statement readers with more useful information? Please explain.
8. What lessons, if any, are there to be learned from an examination of the history of foreign currency translation in the United States?
9. FAS No. 52 can be viewed as a practical compromise to the foreign currency translation problem. Do you think the FASB's new pronouncement will, at long last, end the great foreign currency translation debate?
10. What trends can you discern from our international survey of foreign currency translation practices?

EXERCISES

1. On April 1, A.C. Corporation, a U.S. electronics manufacturer, purchases 24 million yen worth of computer chips from the Sando Company paying 10 percent down, the balance to be paid in three months. Interest at a rate of 16 percent per annum is payable on the unpaid foreign currency balance when the yen payable is extinguished. The U.S. dollar/Japanese yen exchange rate on April 1 was $1.00 = ¥ 240; on July 1 it stood at $1.00 = ¥ 250.

    Required: Prepare dated journal entries in U.S. dollars to record the incurrence and settlement of this foreign currency transaction assuming (a) A.C. Corporation adopts a single-transaction perspective, and (b) the company employs a two-transactions perspective.

2. On December 15, A.C. Corporation acquires 100 percent of the net assets of the Sando Company based in Tokyo, Japan, for ¥ 18,-750,000,000. At the time, the exchange rate was $1.00 = ¥ 250. The acquisition price is traceable to the following identifiable assets:

Cash	¥ 2,500,000,000
Inventory	5,000,000,000
Fixed Assets	11,250,000,000

    Being a calendar year company, A.C. Corporation prepares consolidated financial statements every December 31. However, by the consolidation date, the Japanese yen devalues such that the new spot rate is $1.00 = ¥ 260.

    Required: Assuming no transactions took place prior to consolidation, what would be the translation gain or loss if Sando's balance sheet were translated to dollars by the temporal rate method? How does the translation adjustment you derive differ from that calculated in Exercise 1?

3. On June 1, ACL International, a U.S. confectionary products manufacturer, purchases on account bulk chocolate from a Swiss supplier for 222,222 Swiss francs (SF) when the spot rate is $.45 = SF 1. The Swiss franc payable is due on September 1. To minimize its exposure to an exchange loss, should the franc appreciate relative to the dollar, ACL International acquires a forward contract to exchange $100,000 for francs on September 1 at a forward rate of $.47 = SF 1.

Required: Given the following exchange rate information, provide journal entries for June 1, June 30, and September 1. The company closes its books quarterly.

June 30 spot rate $.46 = SF1
September 1 spot rate $.48 = SF1

4. Manzana S.A., the Chilean affiliate of a U.S. manufacturer, has a balance sheet as shown in Table 4.16. The current exchange rate is $.02 = E 1 (50 escudos to the dollar).

TABLE 4.16   Balance Sheet of Manzana S.A.

ASSETS			LIABILITIES		
Cash	E	6,000	Accounts payable	E	18,000
Accounts receivable		12,000	Long-term debt		24,000
Inventories[a] (cost = 24,000)		18,000			
Fixed assets, net		36,000	Stockholders' equity		30,000
Total assets	E	72,000	Total liabilities	E	72,000

[a] Inventories are carried at the lower of cost or market.

Required:
A.   Translate the escudo balance sheet of Manzana S.A. into dollars at the current exchange rate of $.02 = E 1. All monetary accounts in Manzana's balance sheet are denominated in escudos.
B.   Assume the escudo devalues from $.02 = E 1 to $.015 = E 1. What would be the translation effect if Manzana's balance sheet were translated by the current-noncurrent method? By the monetary-nonmonetary method?
C.   Assume instead that the escudo strengthens to $.026. What would be the translation effect under each of the two methods?

5.   Using the information provided in Exercise 4:
Required:
A.   What would be the translation effect if Manzana's balance sheet were translated by the temporal method assuming

escudo devaluation of 25 percent? By the current rate method?
B. Assuming the escudo appreciates by 30 percent, what would be the translation effects under each of the two methods in part A?
C. Based on your calculations above and in Exercise 4, which translation method—current-noncurrent, monetary-nonmonetary, temporal, or current—do you feel provides statement readers with the more meaningful information?

CASE

Cranfield Corporation

Cranfield Corporation is a recently acquired U.S. manufacturing subsidiary located on the outskirts of London. Its products are marketed principally in the United Kingdom with sales invoiced in pounds and prices determined by local competitive conditions. Expenses (labor, materials, and other production costs) are mostly local although a significant quantity of components are imported from the U.S. parent. Financing is primarily in U.S. dollars and provided by the parent.

With the recent issuance of FAS No. 52 in the United States, headquarters management is faced with the decision of choosing a functional currency designation for its London operation; that is, should it be the U.S. dollar or the British pound? You are asked to advise management on the appropriate currency designation as well as its relative financial statement effects. Prepare a

TABLE 4-17   Cranfield Corporation Financial Statements

BALANCE SHEET	12/31/84	12/31/85
Assets		
Cash	£ 1,150	£ 1,060
Accounts receivable	3,290	2,800
Inventory (FIFO)	3,200	3,000
Fixed assets	4,500	4,800
Accumulated depreciation	520	820
Intangible asset (patent)		70
Total	£11,620	£10,910
Liabilities and Stockholders' Equity		
Accounts payable	£ 3,490	£ 3,140
Due to parent	1,960	2,075
Long-term debt	4,000	3,200
Deferred taxes	90	120
Capital stock	1,600	1,600
Retained earnings	480	775
	£11,620	£10,910

(*continued*)

TABLE 4–17   (*continued*)

INCOME STATEMENT		YEAR ENDED 12/31/85
Sales		£15,600
Expenses		
Cost of sales	£12,400	
General and administrative	1,300	
Depreciation	300	
Interest	380	14,380
Operating income		£ 1,220
Transaction gain (loss)		(115)
Income before taxes		£ 1,105
Income taxes		
Current	£ 580	
Deferred	30	610
Net income		£ 495
Retained earnings at 12/31/84		480
		975
Dividends		200
Retained earnings at 12/31/85		£ 775

Exchange rate information and additional data:
   1. Exchange rates:

December 31, 1984	$1.80 = £1
December 31, 1985	$1.70 = £1
Average during 1985	$1.76 = £1
Average during fourth quarter 1984	$1.84 = £1
Average during fourth quarter 1985	$1.72 = £1

   2. Common stock was acquired, long-term debt issued, and original fixed assets purchased when the exchange rate was $1.90 = £1.
   3. Due to parent account is denominated in U.S. dollars.
   4. Exchange rate prevailing when the intangible asset (patent) was acquired and additional fixed assets purchased was $1.74 = £1.
   5. Purchases and dividends occurred evenly during 1985.
   6. Of the £300 depreciation expense for 1985, £20 relates to fixed assets purchased during 1985.
   7. Deferred taxes are translated at the current rate.
   8. Inventory represents approximately three months of production.

report that supports your recommendations and identify any policy issues uncovered by your analysis.

Comparative balance sheets for Cranfield Corporation at December 31, 1984 and 1985, and a statement of income for the year ended December 31, 1985, are presented in Table 4.17. The statements conform with U.S generally accepted accounting principles prior to translation to dollars.

5

Accounting
for Inflation

Fluctuating currency values, the subject of Chapter 4, are today an integral feature of the international business scene. Equally complex and perplexing is the phenomenon of inflation. Accounting for the effects of changing prices is especially germane to managers of multinational enterprises as rates of inflation vary substantially from country to country, thereby increasing the potentially distortive effects of inflation on reported results of operations. Local inflation, in turn, impacts exchange rates used to translate foreign currency balances to their domestic currency equivalents. As we shall see, it is difficult to separate the issue of foreign currency translation from the issue of inflation when accounting for foreign operations.

COPING WITH INFLATION

The subject of changing price levels is not new. What is new is the fact that inflation today has assumed global dimensions. Rising prices not only continue to plague the economies of the less developed countries but now engulf many nations of the industrialized world as well. National commitments to rapid economic growth and full employment, together with the secular rise in the cost of energy, account for a goodly portion of the world's current inflationary tendencies.

The international consequences of severe global inflation are disturbing in the extreme. As inflation erodes the standards of living of those on fixed incomes and significantly complicates business decision making, widespread political and social unrest are likely outcomes. Economic resentments undoubtedly account for many political upheavals that have characterized world politics in recent years.

Unfortunately, while agreement generally exists about the nature of the inflation problem, little has happened by way of solutions. Governments the world over have experimented with a number of potential inflation remedies. Included in this category are restrictive fiscal and monetary policies, mandatory wage and price controls, and other regulatory activities. All of these policies have been less than successful in containing for very long any national inflation malady.

A direct implication of the foregoing, for business at least, is that inflation is a phenomenon largely beyond management control and one with which managers must learn to cope. Rational pricing, productivity, and asset management programs are valuable management tools in this regard. Effective inflation management techniques are, in turn, largely dependent on an information system that enables managers to gauge the distorting effects of inflation on enterprise performance and elements of financial position. Accounting data that reflect the effects of changing prices thus are both necessary and appropriate.

To date, accepted accounting principles in the United States and many other countries have been premised on the assumption of stable price levels. In the former, for example, the general price level remained relatively constant from the time of the American Revolution to the beginning of World War II, a period of 150 years. Under these circumstances, a measurement framework based on historical cost appeared justified. However, the magnitude and persistence of inflation since that time is bringing the historical cost valuation framework increasingly into question. Matching revenues realized during an inflationary period against the historical costs of resources acquired in the past when price levels were lower generally results in overstatements of enterprise income. Figure 5.1 demonstrates in graphic fashion the magnitude of this overstatement during the decade of the 1970s for U.S. manufacturing enterprises. Further to our point, while after-tax profit of U.S. nonfinancial corporations were at an all-time high at the start of the 1980s, real earnings (after adjusting for the effects of inflation) were actually 46 percent less on the average.[1] Overstatements of enterprise income, in turn, may lead to:

1. Increases in proportionate taxation
2. Requests by shareholders for more dividends
3. Demands for higher wages by labor or their representatives
4. Actions by host governments not in the best interests of multinational operations (e.g., imposition of price controls and excess profit taxes)
5. Reduced confidence in the credibility of enterprise accounting reports

---

[1] Arthur Young & Company, *Financial Reporting and Changing Prices: A Survey of How 300 Companies Complied with FAS 33* (New York, August 1980), p. 8.

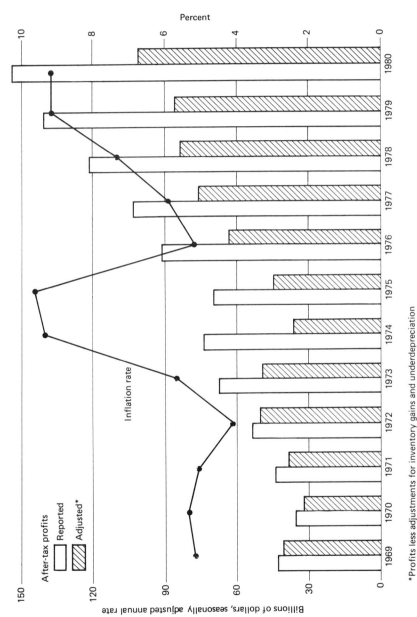

FIGURE 5.1 How Rising Inflation Distorts Corporate Earnings

Source: U.S. Department of Commerce, "Gross Domestic Product of Corporate Business in Current Dollars and Constant Dollars," *Survey of Current Business* (Washington, D.C.: U.S.D.O.C. Bureau of Economic Analysis, various issues).

171

Should a firm actually distribute all of its overstated earnings in the form of higher dividends, wages, and the like, there is always the danger that it may not preserve sufficient resources internally with which to replace specific assets whose prices have risen. Inventories and plant and equipment are important asset categories here. Furthermore, failure to adjust corporate financial statements for changes in the purchasing power of the monetary unit makes it difficult for statement readers to interpret and compare reported operating performances of companies both within and between countries. Purchasing power gains and losses that arise from holding monetary items are also ignored under conventional accounting procedures. This further distorts business performance comparisons during inflationary periods.

Many external users of financial statements are cognizant of the need to consider price changes when interpreting historical cost-based statements. Nevertheless, explicit recognition of inflation's effects for external readers is useful for several reasons:

1. The effects of changing prices depend partially on the transactions and circumstances of an enterprise, and users do not have detailed information about those factors.

2. Alleviation of the problems caused by changing prices depends on a widespread understanding of the problems; a widespread understanding is unlikely to develop until business performance is discussed in terms of measures that explicitly allow for the effects of changing prices.

3. Statements by managers about the problems caused by changing prices will have greater credibility when enterprises publish financial information that addresses those problems.[2]

TYPES OF INFLATION ADJUSTMENTS

When it comes to accounting for price level changes, we must be careful to distinguish between general and specific price movements. In the past the term *inflation* has been applied indiscriminately to both.

A *general price level change* occurs when, on the average, the prices of all goods and services in an economy move from an earlier position; that is, the purchasing power of the monetary unit changes in terms of its ability to command goods and services in general. A *specific price level change,* on the other hand, refers to a change in the price of a specific commodity. In the context of a business enterprise, it refers to changes in the specific prices of a firm's resources, for example, inventories, plant and equipment, and supplies.

Statistical series that measure changes in both general and specific prices do not generally move in parallel fashion. For example, while the Wholesale Price Index (measuring average changes in prices of about 2,200 commodities

[2] Financial Accounting Standards Board, "Financial Reporting and Changing Prices," *Statement of Financial Accounting Standards No. 33* (Stamford, Conn.: FASB, September 1979).

sold in primary markets in the United States) rose about 5.8 percent between mid-1981 and mid-1982, the relative price changes of some of its specific components exhibited the following pattern: machinery and equipment, up 16.3 percent; transportation equipment, up 15.3 percent; but metals and metal products, up only 1.7 percent; hides, skins, and leather, up only 1.1 percent; while pulp, paper, and allied products, down 16.4 percent; and fuels and related products, down 30.2 percent.[3] These data apply only to the United States. The dispersion of specific price changes internationally would probably be even greater.

In addition, each type of price change has a differing effect on measures of a firm's financial position and operating performance and should be accounted for, consequently, with different objectives in mind. Hereafter, accounting for the financial statement effects of general price level changes is referred to as the *historical cost–constant dollar model.* Accounting for specific price changes is referred to as the *current cost (value) model.*

General Price Level Adjustments

In explaining the accounting objective of the historical cost–constant dollar model, let us briefly review the concept of enterprise income. From a balance sheet perspective, income represents that portion of a firm's wealth (net asset) position that can be disposed of during an accounting period without decreasing its original wealth position. To illustrate, assume that a U.S. merchandiser starts the calendar year with $100 in cash (no debt), which is immediately converted into salable inventory. The entire inventory is sold uniformly throughout the year at a 50 percent markup on cost. Assuming stable prices, enterprise income would equal $50 measured as the difference between the ending and beginning net assets ($150 − $100), or revenue minus expenses (cost of goods sold). In this case, a dividend distribution of $50 would leave the firm with as much money capital at the end as it had at the beginning, namely, $100.

Once we depart from the assumption of stable prices, the $50 may no longer represent the amount of a firm's disposable wealth. The historical cost–constant dollar model takes this into account by measuring income in such fashion that it represents the maximum amount of resources that could be distributed to various income claimants during a given period while preserving the firm's ability to command as many goods and services, *in general,* at the end of the period as it could at the beginning.

Using the previous example, assume now that the general level of prices, as measured by an appropriate price index, increased from 100 at the beginning of the period to 121 at the end, averaging 110 during the year. This implies that it takes $121 at year-end to purchase, in general, what $100 would have purchased at the beginning. Income under the historical cost–constant dollar model would be measured thusly:

---

[3] U.S. Department of Commerce, "Commodity Prices," *Survey of Current Business,* August 1982, p. S6.

	NOMINAL DOLLARS	ADJUSTMENT FACTOR	CONSTANT DOLLARS
Revenues	$ 150	121/110	$ 165
Less: Expenses	100	121/100	121
Price level-adjusted operating income			$ 44
Less: Monetary loss			15
Price level-adjusted net income			$ 29

In this example, sales are made uniformly throughout the year. Hence revenues are translated to their end-of-period purchasing power equivalent by multiplying $150 by the end-of-period index over the average index. Expenditures for inventory were made at the start of the period; hence, the use of the beginning-of-period index when restating $100 to end-of-period dollars. As sales were made for cash, cash was received evenly throughout the year. Owing to inflation, the firm in question would ideally like to end with a cash balance of $165 ($150 × 121/110). In fact, the firm's cash balance will amount to no more than $150. Hence, it experiences a $15 loss in general purchasing power (a monetary loss) having held a monetary asset during a period of inflation. Disbursing no more than $29 would help assure that the company could commend as many goods and services, in general, at the end of the period as it could at the beginning. (Proof: Net assets at period's end of $150 − $29 = $121, the amount necessary to command what $100 could purchase at the beginning.)

It is possible to convert measurement of historical cost to their beginning-of-period purchasing power equivalents by multiplying the foregoing figures by the ratio of the general price level index at the beginning of the period to the price index prevailing at the end. Either method, if used consistently, is satisfactory.

Current Cost Adjustments

The current cost model views income as the amount of resources that could be distributed during a given period, barring tax considerations, while maintaining a company's productive capacity or physical capital. One way to achieve this is to adjust a firm's original net asset position using appropriate specific price indexes or direct pricing to reflect changes in an item's current cost equivalent during the period. In our example, if, during the same period, prices of the firm's inventories increased by 40 percent (it would now take $140 to replace inventories that originally cost $100), the firm would increase (debit) the value of existing inventories and increase (credit) owner's equity by $40. The adjustment accomplishes two things. It communicates to statement readers that the firm must retain an additional $40 in the business to enable it to replace higher-priced inventories. In effect, the $40 equity adjustment establishes a higher criterion level of beginning net assets ($140) against which to compare ending net assets ($150) in measuring income. The inventory revaluation also increases the cost of resources consumed (cost of goods sold). Thus, current revenues are matched with the current economic sacrifice incurred to generate those revenues. In our example, current cost-based net income would be measured as $150 − $100 × 140/100 or $10. The $150 figure could represent ending net assets or sales revenues; the $100 × 140/100 figure, beginning net assets or cost of goods sold adjusted to its current cost equivalent. Distributing no more than $10 would help ensure that the firm would preserve sufficient resources internally to enable it to replace specific assets whose prices had risen during the period. Thus, whereas the objective of general price level adjustments is to preserve the general purchasing power of an enterprise's original money capital, the current cost model attempts to preserve a firm's physical capital or productive capacity.

The Great Debate

Financial statement distortions caused by changing prices together with the latter's persistence and probable continuation have today created a general awareness that some form of inflation accounting is desirable. The major issue facing financial executives and accountants in the 1980s, therefore, is not a matter of whether to or not, but rather of how.

Proponents of the historical cost–constant dollar model argue that the current cost model violates the historical cost measurement framework, is too subjective, and is difficult to implement in practice. In ignoring changes in the general purchasing power of money, it not only impairs the interpretability of interperiod comparisons but also fails to consider monetary gains or losses from holding monetary items such as debt. Those favoring current cost adjustments argue that businesses are not affected by general inflation; they are affected instead by increases in specific operating costs and plant expenditures. In many instances, recording purchasing power gains from holding debt during inflation could be misleading. Highly levered firms could show large monetary gains while on the brink of bankruptcy.[4] An additional fear expressed by companies with foreign operations is the possible politicization of general price indexes. Concern over the accuracy of Brazilian price level statistics is a case in point.[5]

Disenchantment with the historical cost–constant dollar and current cost models in their pure forms has garnered some support for another measurement framework incorporating features of both.[6] Here, current cost amounts are converted to their end-of-period purchasing power equivalents to facilitate comparisons of current income with those of prior periods. Moreover, mone-

---

[4] R. Vancil, "Inflation Accounting—The Great Controversy," *Harvard Business Review*, March–April 1976, pp. 58–67.

[5] Alan H. Seed III, *Inflation: Its Impact on Financial Reporting and Decision Making* (New York: Financial Executives Research Foundation, September 1978).

[6] Robert R. Sterling, "Relevant Financial Reporting in an Age of Price Changes," *Journal of Accountancy*, February 1975, pp. 42–51.

tary gains or losses, generally ignored by the current cost model, are factored into the measurement process. Described as the current cost–constant dollar model, this measurement approach boasts informational benefits claimed by the other two. Unfortunately, it also shares several of their drawbacks as well, including subjectivity, lack of comprehensibility, and cost of implementation. In short, the debate on inflation accounting is far from over.

INTERNATIONAL PERSPECTIVE ON INFLATION ACCOUNTING

Rather than await the outcome of the inflation accounting debate on a priori grounds, several countries have begun to experiment with alternative inflation accounting constructs. Premised on the conceptual underpinnings of the models previously described, actual practices also reflect pragmatic considerations such as the severity of national inflation and the views of those directly affected by inflation accounting numbers. Examination of selected countries' responses to accounting for changing prices is helpful in assessing the current state of the art as well as future trends.

U.S. Response

In September 1979, the Financial Accounting Standards Board (FASB) issued *Statement of Financial Accounting Standards No. 33* (FAS No. 33), "Financial Reporting and Changing Prices." It is the result of intermittent efforts by the U.S. accounting profession to integrate inflation adjustments into U.S. annual reports. Highlights of the lengthy standard follow.

Major provisions.   Applicable for fiscal years ending after December 23, 1979, FAS No. 33 requires disclosure of both historical cost–constant dollar and current cost information. The FASB concluded that preparers and users of financial reports should have further practical experience with inflation accounting. Hence the required disclosures *supplement* rather than *replace* historical cost as the basic measurement framework for primary financial statements.

The statement presently applies to public U.S. enterprises that have *either* (1) inventories and property, plant, and equipment (before deducting accumulated depreciation) of more than $125 million, *or* (2) total assets amounting to more than $1 billion (after deducting accumulated depreciation). Assets include those in foreign locations. The statement also applies to publicly held non-U.S. companies that prepare their basic financial statements in U.S. dollars and in accordance with U.S. generally accepted accounting principles (GAAP), such as the Royal Dutch–Shell Group when reporting to their U.S. shareholders.

A comprehensive review of FAS No. 33 by the FASB is contemplated no later than September 1984. In the meantime, the Board intends to assess the usefulness of the inflation disclosures as a basis for possible future revision.

Supplementary disclosure requirements of FAS No. 33 are summarized below.

INFORMATION FOR THE CURRENT YEAR

Historical Cost–Constant Dollar Basis

Income from continuing operations (i.e., cost of sales and depreciation, depletion, and amortization expenses restated to constant dollars)

Purchasing power gain or loss on net monetary items

Current Cost Basis (beginning in 1980)

Income from continuing operations (i.e., cost of sales and depreciation and amortization expense of property, plant and equipment measured at current cost)

Current cost amounts of inventory and property plant and equipment at year-end

Increases or decreases in the current cost amounts of inventory and property, plant, and equipment, net of inflation (general price level changes)

INFORMATION FOR EACH OF THE FIVE MOST RECENT YEARS

Net Sales and Other Operating Revenues

Historical Cost–Constant Dollar Information

Income from continuing operations

Income per common share from continuing operations

Net assets at year-end

Current Cost Information

Income from continuing operations

Income per common share from continuing operations

Net assets at year-end

Increases or decreases in the current cost amounts of inventory and property, plant, and equipment, net of inflation

Other Information

Purchasing power gain or loss on net monetary items

Cash dividends declared per common share

Market price per common share at year-end

Level of the consumer price index used to measure income from continuing operations

Explanations of the information disclosed and discussions of the significance of the information in the circumstances of the reporting enterprise

Firms are allowed and encouraged to experiment with statement presentations of the required information. Exxon Corporation offers a useful reporting format that exceeds FAS No. 33's disclosure minima. It appears in Exhibit 5.1.

Compliance with FAS No. 33 requires that a firm adjust, at a minimum, inventory, fixed assets, and their related charges to income, using the U.S. Con-

EXHIBIT 5.1   Exxon Corporation's 1982 Disclosure

Supplemental Information on Inflation Accounting*

Background

During 1982, inflation slackened to a more modest rate, but continued to further erode the purchasing power of the dollar. This trend causes a distortion in the conventional measures of financial performance.

Inflation affects monetary assets, such as cash and receivables, which lose a part of their purchasing power during periods of inflation since they will purchase fewer goods or services in the future. Conversely, holders of liabilities benefit during periods of inflation because less purchasing power will be required to satisfy these obligations in the future. Thus, a 1972 debt of one dollar can be satisfied with a payment of a 1982 dollar which has the equivalent purchasing power of $.43.

Inflation also affects plant and equipment, which is reflected in the financial statements at the amounts expended in the years in which the investments were made rather than in today's costs. This tends to understate depreciation charges in the current year, and thus overstate earnings.

The information on this and the following page is presented in an experimental fashion in an attempt to overcome these shortcomings of historical cost accounting.

General Methodology

The supplemental data presented here include adjustments made in accordance with Financial Accounting Standards Board Statement No. 33–Financial Reporting and Changing Prices, as modified by Statements No. 39 and No. 70. The method used provides the effect of changes in specific costs.

This method adjusts for the current, or specific, costs of inventory and plant and equipment. Current replacement costs have been used for these items. That is, specific prices that would have to be paid currently have been used as replacement costs for the inventory of crude oil and products and for property, plant and equipment.

For the most part, the specific cost data used here represent replacement in-place and in-kind. No consideration has been given to possible replacement of assets of a different type, at a different location or with improved operating cost efficiencies. The specific costs used, while believed reasonable, are necessarily subjective. They do not necessarily represent amounts for which the assets could be sold or costs which will be incurred, or the manner and extent in which actual replacement of assets will occur.

More specifically, land, other than oil and gas acreage, has been valued based on appraisal or estimated current market prices. Oil and gas acreage costs have been updated using the U.S. Consumer Price Index (CPI). Development costs of oil and gas properties were measured by use of appropriate indices or estimates of current

drilling, material and equipment costs. Other plant and equipment, for the most part, was updated by use of internally developed construction cost indices. Items such as automotive equipment and office buildings were costed at current market prices.

Supplemental Data

Table I shows the results of operations in 1982 as reflected in the Consolidated Statement of Income (page 22) and as adjusted for specific costs. Adjustments reflect an increase in the 1982 cost of goods sold as shown in the income statement for the $1,886 million before tax profit realized on sales of quantities from LIFO inventories. An additional depreciation charge of $2,596 million is necessary to reflect the increases of the specific costs of the facilities over the financial statement values. The depreciation adjustment maintains the same methods, useful lives and salvage value assumptions as used in computing financial statement depreciation. After these adjustments, specific cost basis income from continuing operations is a loss of $296 million.

Statement No. 33 requires that income taxes not be modified for the effects of specific cost adjustments. Therefore, the 51 percent effective tax rate for the financial statement earnings becomes an effective 107 percent for the specific cost results. This indicates the restriction on capital recovery caused by the hidden additional tax that results from inflation.

Table I also shows changes in shareholders' equity, other than income from continuing operations, which occurred during the year as a result of inflation. The first of these is a gain resulting from the effect of the decline in the purchasing power of the dollar on the net monetary amounts owed by the company. Most of the company's current assets, except inventories, and the current liabilities and long-term debt are considered to be monetary items. This gain represents the decline in the amount of purchasing power required at the end of 1982 to pay these net liabilities versus the amount that would have been required to pay them at the end of 1981.

The second change in shareholders' equity represents the additional increase during the year in the specific prices for inventory and property, plant and equipment over the increase attributed to the effects of general inflation as measured by the CPI. This additional cost of plant and equipment is charged to income from continuing operations by means of the increased depreciation charge previously mentioned.

Table II presents a summarized balance sheet at year end 1982 based on the Consolidated Balance Sheet shown on page 21 and as adjusted for specific costs.

*All data for 1980 and 1981 have been restated, where applicable, for the change in 1982 in the method of accounting for foreign currency translation. See Note 2, page 25

(*continued*)

sumer Price Index for All Urban Consumers to restate these data to a constant dollar basis. Greater flexibility is permitted when obtaining information on current cost equivalents, including the use of specific price indexes or direct pricing.

Financial Accounting Standard No. 33 replaced Accounting Series Release (ASR) No. 190 (March 1976) of the U.S. Securities and Exchange Commission (SEC), which called for footnote disclosures of certain replacement cost data by large U.S. enterprises in their 10-K filings with the Commission. Accounting Series Release No. 271 removed this,requirement for fiscal years

EXHIBIT 5.1 (*continued*)

Table I–Income from continuing operations and changes in shareholders' equity adjusted for changing prices
For the year ended December 31, 1982

	As reported on page 22	Adjusted for specific costs
	(millions of dollars)	(millions of average 1982 dollars)
Income from continuing operations		
Total revenue	$103,559	$103,559
Costs and other deductions		
Crude oil and product purchases	56,084	57,970
Depreciation and depletion	3,333	5,929
Other costs and deductions	18,513	18,513
Income, excise and other taxes	21,443	21,443
Total costs and other deductions	99,373	103,855
Income from continuing operations	4,186	(296)
Gain from decline in the purchasing power of net amounts owed		557
Excess of increase in specific prices over general inflation		
Inventories		443
Property, plant and equipment		4,777
Net income	**$ 4,186**	
Net change in shareholders' equity from above	$ 4,186	**$ 5,481**

The Table II categories of "All other assets" and "Total liabilities" have been restated from the year-end 1982 dollar amounts to average 1982 dollar amounts using the CPI.

The sum of all the foregoing balance sheet adjustments results in the restatement of shareholders' equity–the investment base. The adjustments for specific costs increase the shareholders' equity to a basis of $69 billion.

Table II–Summarized balance sheet adjusted for changing prices at December 31, 1982

	As reported on page 21	Adjusted for specific costs
	(millions of dollars)	(millions of average 1982 dollars)
Assets		
Inventories	$ 5,536	$ 14,256
Property, plant and equipment	38,982	70,804
All other assets	17,770	17,605
Total assets	62,288	102,665
Total liabilities	33,848	33,511
Shareholders' equity	**$ 28,440**	**$ 69,154**

In other words, it would take $69 billion (1982 dollars) to provide the same purchasing power as the $28 billion represented in the financial statements.

Table III summarizes the earnings results, shareholders' equity and returns over a five-year period. In this table, the financial statement data, shown unadjusted for inflation in the first section, for the years 1978 through 1981 have been adjusted for specific costs in the same manner as has been discussed for the year 1982. Income from continuing operations is composed of the same factors as shown in Table I. The returns on average shareholders' equity are considerably lower than reflected in the financial statements when the results and the investment base are adjusted for specific costs. These decreases in returns show the erosion that has taken place in the capital base of the company from the continuing inflation faced by the general public, the oil and gas industry, and Exxon.

Table III–Summary of income, shareholders' equity and return (millions of dollars except per share amounts)

	Years ended December 31				
	1978	1979	1980	1981	1982
Unadjusted for inflation					
Income from continuing operations (net income)	$ 2,763	$ 4,295	$ 5,350	$ 4,826	$ 4,186
Per share*	3.10	4.87	6.15	5.58	4.82
Foreign currency translation adjustment	—	—	(217)	(1,248)	(819)
Shareholders' equity at year-end	20,229	22,552	26,627	27,743	28,440
Return of net income on average shareholders' equity, percent	**14.0**	**20.1**	**21.8**	**17.8**	**14.9**
Adjusted for specific costs (average 1982 dollars)					
Income (loss) from continuing operations	1,655	3,178	3,254	1,608	(296)
Per share*	1.85	3.61	3.74	1.86	(.34)
Gain from decline in purchasing power of net amounts owed	821	1,328	1,414	1,137	557
Excess of increase (decrease) in specific prices over general inflation	(501)	3,589	4,419	3,432	5,220
Net change in shareholders' equity, from above	1,975	8,095	9,087	6,177	5,481
Per share*	2.22	9.18	10.44	7.14	6.31
Foreign currency translation adjustment	—	—	(898)	(3,693)	(3,203)
Shareholders' equity at year-end	58,792	64,189	68,701	68,003	69,154
Return of net change in shareholders' equity on average shareholders' equity, percent	**3.3**	**13.2**	**13.7**	**9.0**	**8.0**

Table IV–Supplementary data adjusted for general inflation (average 1982 dollars)

	1978	1979	1980	1981	1982
Total revenue (millions)	$96,298	$112,990	$129,077	$121,969	$103,559
Dividends per share*	2.44	2.59	3.16	3.18	3.00
Market price at year-end, per share*	35	34⅝	45⅛	32⅛	29⅜
Average consumer price index (1967 = 100)	195.4	217.4	246.8	272.4	289.1

*Restated. See Note 13, page 31.

ending on or after December 25, 1980, when the FASB's current cost disclosures became mandatory.

The International Response

The worldwide nature of the problem of disclosing the effects of changing prices has led to active development of inflation-accounting proposals internationally. Some major developments are briefly sketched. Addresses of organizations that will provide further information are noted with each subsection (also refer to Chapter 12 for full descriptions of the activities of these organizations).

International Accounting Standards Committee. Established with the objective of harmonizing accounting standards internationally, the International Accounting Standards Committee (IASC) has maintained an accommodating posture in the area of inflation accounting. *International Accounting Standard 6* (IAS No. 6), "Accounting Responses to Changing Prices," summarized major inflation-accounting alternatives in a preface. The standard merely stated that

> enterprises should present in their financial statements information that describes the procedures adopted to reflect the impact on the financial statements of specific price changes, changes in the general level of prices, or of both. If no such procedures have been adopted that fact should be disclosed.[7]

Standard No. 6 became operative for financial statements covering periods on or after January 1, 1978.

In November 1981, the IASC issued IAS No. 15 "Information Reflecting the Effects of Changing Prices." This pronouncement, which supersedes IAS No. 6, recommends that large publicly traded enterprises disclose the following information using any method that adjusts for the effects of changing prices:

1. The amount of the adjustment to, or the adjusted amount of, depreciation of property, plant, and equipment
2. The amount of the adjustment to, or the adjusted amount of, cost of sales
3. A financing adjustment(s), if such adjustment(s) is generally part of the method adopted for reporting information on changing prices
4. The enterprise results recomputed to reflect the effects of the items described in (1) and (2) and, where appropriate, (3), and any other items separately disclosed that the method adopted requires

If a current cost method is adopted, the current cost of inventories and of property, plant, and equipment should be disclosed. Disclosure of methods used to compute the inflation adjustments is also required.

The foregoing information should be disclosed on a supplementary basis unless inflation-adjusted accounts constitute the basic financial statements. It should be provided in financial statements covering periods beginning on or after January 1, 1983.[8]

Other international accounting organizations. In an effort to harmonize financial disclosures among member countries of the European Economic Community (EEC), the EEC Commission issued its Fourth Directive in 1978. In the area of asset measurement, the directive retains the historical cost principle as its basic valuation method. However, it allows member states to autho-

---

[7] International Accounting Standards Committee, "Accounting Responses to Changing Prices," *International Accounting Standard 6* (London: IASC, 1977), par. 17.

[8] For more information contact International Accounting Standards Committee, 3 St. Helen's Place, London EC3 6DN, England.

rize the use of replacement value measurements or other methods based on current or market values. Any differences between historical cost valuations and replacement cost or current market valuations must be aggregated and separately disclosed as an item of "revaluation reserve" in Owners' Equity. The summarized revaluation reserves must be disaggregated according to the main asset categories to which they pertain.[9]

The U.N. Working Group of Experts on International Standards of Accounting and Reporting (GEISAR), whose major aim is harmonizing the disclosure practices of transnational corporations, has not yet concerned itself with accounting measurement rules. In a 1977 report *International Standards of Accounting and Reporting for Transnational Corporations,* the U.N. Group simply calls for the disclosure of accounting policies including overall valuation methods such as historical cost, replacement value, general price level adjustments, or any other valuation basis.[10]

The Organization for Economic Cooperation and Development (OECD), which serves as a policy forum for its 26 member nations, has thus far adopted a posture similar to that of the U.N. group.[11]

The United Kingdom. In a development pattern paralleling that in the United States, the U.K. Accounting Standards Committee (ASC) issued *Statement of Standard Accounting Practice No. 16* (SSAP No. 16), "Current Cost Accounting," in March 1980 on a three-year experimental basis. Effective for financial reporting periods beginning on or after January 1, 1980, the U.K. standard differs from FAS No. 33 in two major respects. First, whereas the U.S. standard requires both constant dollar and current cost accounting, SSAP No. 16 adopts only the current cost method for reporting. Second, whereas U.S. inflation adjustments have an income statement focus, the U.K. current cost statements must include both a current cost income statement and balance sheet, together with explanatory notes. The U.K. standard may be complied with by using only one of the following three practices:

1. Presenting current cost accounts as the basic statements with supplementary historical cost accounts
2. Presenting historical cost accounts as the basic statements with supplementary current cost accounts
3. Presenting current cost accounts as the only accounts accompanied by adequate historical cost information

Standard No. 16 applies to all listed companies and unlisted companies that satisfy any two of the following criteria: sales of £5 million or more, total assets of £2.5 million or more, and 250 or more employees.

Although concepts of and methods for determining current costs are

[9] For more information contact European Economic Community, U.S. Office, 245 East 47th Street, New York, N.Y. 10017.

[10] For more information contact Center on Transnational Corporations, United Nations, Box 20, Grand Central P.O., New York, N.Y. 10017.

[11] For more information contact Organization for Economic Cooperation and Development, U.S. Office, Suite 1207, 1750 Pennsylvania Avenue, N.W., Washington D.C. 20006.

roughly similar in both FAS No. 33 and SSAP No. 16, the latter differs in its treatment of gains and losses related to monetary items. Whereas FAS No. 33 requires separate disclosure of a single figure derived by applying a *general* price level index to a firm's *net* monetary asset or liability position, SSAP No. 16 requires two figures, both mirroring the effects of *specific* price changes and included in measuring period income. The first, called a monetary working capital adjustment (MWCA) recognizes the effect of specific price changes on the total amount of working capital (basically trade receivables less trade payables) employed by the business in its day-to-day operations. The second adjustment reduces the *total* of the adjustments made to reduce historical cost–based income for the higher cost equivalents of depreciation expense and cost of goods sold, including the MWCA. Based on the ratio of total debt to total capitalization, the "gearing adjustment" acknowledges that it is unnecessary to recognize in the income statement the additional replacement cost of assets to the extent they are financed by debt. An illustrative example of supplementary disclosures conforming to SSAP No. 16 appears in Table 5.1.

A special meeting of the Institute of Chartered Accountants in England and Wales was called in July 1982 to consider a resolution calling for the immediate withdrawal of SSAP No. 16. Although the inflation accounting standard survived by a slim voting margin, it appears that SSAP No. 16 will be modified, suggesting an additional period of experimentation in the United Kingdom.[12]

Argentina.   A 1972 pronouncement of the Argentine Technical Institute of Public Accountants now mandates, in certain provinces, that publicly held corporations with paid-in capital exceeding 5 million pesos present complete restatement of all nonmonetary items using a general price index. The supplemental information may be disclosed in (1) a second column in the basic financial statements, (2) footnotes to the basic statements, or (3) a complementary set of financial statements.

More recently (September 1980), the Argentine Professional Council of Economic Sciences of the Federal District, which regulates the public accounting profession in Buenos Aires, declared that basic financial statements should, in the future, disclose historical cost–constant dollar figures in one column and historical cost in another.[13]

Australia.   Inflation-accounting developments in Australia have proceeded in several phases. In phase 1, a provisional accounting standard (October 1976) was issued recommending current cost accounting to be applied to fixed assets and inventories in the basic financial statements. In phase 2, attention turned to the required treatment of purchasing power gains and losses, culminating in the issuance (August 1979) of an exposure draft, *The Recogni-*

[12] For more information contact Institute of Chartered Accountants, Chartered Accountant's Hall, P.O. Box 433, Moorgate Place, London EC2P 2 BJ, England.

[13] For more information contact Federacion Argentina de Colegios de Graduados en Ciencias Economicas, Avenida Cordoba 1261, 2 Piso 1055, Buenos Aires, Argentina.

TABLE 5.1   UK Limited: Example of Current Cost Accounts per SSAP No. 16 (£ thousands)

YEAR ENDED 12/31/84		INCOME STATEMENT	YEAR ENDED 12/31/85	
36,000		Turnover		40,000
4,840		Profit before interest and taxes on a historical cost basis		5,800
		Less current cost operating adjustments		
	800	Cost of sales	920	
	140	Monetary working capital	200	
2,640	1,700	Depreciation	1,900	3,020
2,200		Current cost operating profit		2,780
	(340)	Gearing adjustment	(332)	
	360	Interest payable less receivable	400	
20				68
2,180		Current cost profit before taxes		2,712
1,220		Taxation		1,460
		Current cost profit attributable to shareholders		
960				1,252
800		Dividends		860
		Retained current cost profit for the year		
160				392

YEAR ENDED 12/31/84		BALANCE SHEET	YEAR ENDED 12/31/85	
		Assets employed		
36,260		Fixed assets		39,060
		Net current assets		
	6,400	Stock	8,000	
	1,400	Monetary working capital	1,600	
	7,800	Total working capital	9,600	
	(800)	Proposed dividends	(860)	
	(1,200)	Other current liabilities (net)	(1,140)	
5,800				7,600
42,060				46,660
		Financed by		
		Share capital and reserves		
	6,000	Share capital	6,000	
	24,700	Current cost reserve[a]	28,808	
	7,460	Other reserves and retained profit	7,852	
38,160				42,660
3,900		Loan capital		4,000
42,060				46,660

[a] Current cost reserve:

Balance at January 1		24,700
Revaluation surpluses reflecting price changes		
Land and buildings	400	
Plant and machinery	2,860	
Stocks and work in progress	980	
	4,240	
Monetary working capital adjustment	200	
Gearing adjustment	(332)	
		4,108
Balance at December 31		28,808

Source: Accounting Standards Committee, SSAP No. 16 (1980).

tion of Gains and Losses on Holding Monetary Items in the Context of Current Cost Accounting. In phase 3, Australian accounting bodies have issued an "omnibus" exposure draft extending current cost provisions to other financial statement categories including those denominated in foreign currencies.

In the most recent phase, Australia's Current Cost Accounting Standards Committee of the Australian Accounting Research Foundation issued a proposed standard replacing pronouncements issued in phases 1–3. Beginning in 1983, all listed companies with total assets exceeding A$20 million and government businesses with assets over A$100 million were to introduce supplementary income statements and balance sheets reflecting current cost adjustments for depreciation, cost of sales, and gains or losses on monetary items. Reporting entities may elect to present current cost accounts as their primary statements. In this event, supplementary financial statements based on a historical cost basis are required. While the proposed standard resembles that issued in the United Kingdom, a major distinction lies in its exclusion of a gearing adjustment. In addition, Australia's calculation of monetary gains and losses (as in the United Kingdom) differs from that of the United States in the use of specific, as opposed to general, price indexes.[14]

Belgium.   An October 1976 *Royal Decree on Financial Statements of Enterprises* permits use of current cost data with respect to inventories, fixed assets, cost of goods sold, and depreciation in the basic financial statements by means of footnote disclosure. Valuation differences are to be charged or credited to a revaluation account.[15]

Brazil.   In the face of double- and frequently triple-digit rates of domestic inflation (120% in 1981), Brazilian accounting principles have for many years attempted to record the effects of inflation on enterprise statements for both book and tax purposes. The amended Brazilian corporation law now revises previous practice.[16] Effective January 1, 1978, companies are required to adjust both permanent assets (land, buildings, equipment, deferred assets, and investments, including investments in subsidiaries and affiliated companies) and equity accounts (capital, reserves, and retained earnings) for changes in the general price level using the ORTN, a Brazilian government treasury bond index, as a deflator. Depreciation is also restated and netted against the asset adjustment. Price level–adjusted depreciation is deductible for taxes.

Inflation adjustments for permanent assets and owners' equity are netted with the excess reflected directly in current income. A permanent asset adjust-

---

[14] For more information contact Australian Accounting Research Foundation, 170 Queen Street, Melbourne, Victoria 3000.

[15] For more information contact Institut des Reviseurs d'Enterprises, Rue Caroly 17, 1040 Brussels, Belgium.

[16] Robert Fleming, "New Concepts in Brazilian Accounting for Inflation," *The Accountant's Magazine*, April 1979, pp. 162–165.

ment that exceeds the equity adjustment is treated as a gain to the benefits of leverage and conversely. While a loss stemming from the balance sheet adjustment is tax deductible, a gain is recognized in taxable income only to the extent that it exceeds exchange losses on foreign currency accounts and charges for monetary correction of certain accounts in local currency (e.g., long-term debt in Brazil is indexed for inflation). Table 5.2 illustrates in general fashion the Brazilian approach to accounting for inflation. Bear in mind that inflation-adjusted statements constitute the basic as opposed to supplementary financial statements.[17]

Canada. Having aired the relative merits of both the historical cost–constant dollar and current cost models, the Accounting Research Committee (ARC) of the Canadian Institute of Chartered Accountants (CICA) issued a new CICA Handbook section (replacing a December 1979 proposal, *Current Cost Accounting*) in December of 1982 entitled "Reporting the Effects of Changing Prices." While referencing constant dollar information, the CICA recommendations emphasize current cost adjustments. Applicable to large public companies with inventories and fixed assets of at least C$50 million or total assets of at least C$350 million, the recommendations call for supplementary disclosure of (a) the current cost of goods sold and depreciation expense, (b) a financing adjustment similar in nature to the U.K. gearing adjustment, (c) income attributable to shareholders on a current cost basis, and (d) current and deferred taxation. Additional disclosures include (e) changes in the current cost equivalents of inventory and property plant and equipment during the period, (f) changes in the foregoing attributed to general inflation, (g) purchasing power gains or losses on monetary items, and (h) the current cost equivalent of property, plant, and equipment as well as net assets at year end. The new CICA Handbook section is to be reviewed after five years of operation at which time a mandatory system of inflation accounting in the basic financial statements will be entertained.[18]

France. Listed companies in France were required to reflect in their basic financial statements the current replacement costs of fixed assets in 1978. Asset revaluation adjustments were to be disclosed in Stockholders' Equity. Mandated by the French Finance Acts of 1977 and 1978, the disclosures were restricted to fixed assets and did not take into account the effects of inflation on debt and cost of goods sold. The disclosure requirements were also limited to the current report year.

More recently, French accountants have been successful in initiating a dual reporting experiment among some 20 firms in various industrial sectors. The firms agreed to supplement their official historical cost accounts with an-

---

[17] For more information contact Instituto dos Auditores Independentes do Brazil, Rua Antonia de Godoi, 83-16 Andar, Conjunto 161, Sao Paulo, Brazil.

[18] For more information contact The Canadian Institute of Chartered Accountants, 150 Bloor Street West, Toronto, M5S 2Y2, Canada.

TABLE 5.2 Inflation Adjustments Brazilian Style

HISTORICAL AMOUNTS

BALANCE SHEET	1/1/85	12/31/85
Current assets	150	450
Permanent assets	1,600	1,600
Provision for depreciation	(200)	(300)
Total	1,550	1,750
Current liabilities	50	50
Long-term debt	400	400
Equity		
Capital	800	800
Reserves	300	300
Profit of period		200
Total	1,550	1,750

INFLATION-CORRECTED AMOUNTS ASSUMING 25% RATE OF INFLATION

		12/31/85
Current assets		450
Permanent assets		2,000
Provision for		
Depreciation	300	
Correction	75	
Correction of historical charge to P + L	25	(400)
Total		2,050
Current liabilities		50
Long-term debt		400
Equity		
Capital		800
Capital reserve		200
Reserves		375
Profit of period		225
Total		2,050

TABLE 5.2 (*continued*)

INCOME STATEMENT

	YEAR ENDED 12/31/85		YEAR ENDED 12/31/85	
Operating profit		500		500
Depreciation of period	100		100	
Correction of depreciation			25	125
(historical)				
Trading profit		400		375
Inflationary loss				
Exchange loss foreign debt	(100)		(100)	
Monetary correction local debt	(100)		(100)	
Gain on correction of balance sheet			50[a]	(150)
Net profit		200		225

Source: Adapted from Robert Fleming, "New Concepts in Brazilian Accounting for Inflation," *The Accountant's Magazine*, April 1979, pp. 162–165.

[a] Gain on correction of balance sheet:

Correction of permanent assets	400	
Correction of depreciation allowance	75	325
Correction of capital	200	
Correction of reserves	75	275
		50

187

other indexed for inflation. Specifically, the replacement costs of ending inventories are being recalculated using a retail price index while cost of sales is being determined on a last-in, first-out (LIFO) basis. Depreciation and fixed assets are also being adjusted to their current cost equivalents using appropriate indexes. Experiences gained during this experiment, soon to be expanded, are expected to provide the basis for formal legislation.[19]

Japan. With the exception of the early 1950s, when land and certain depreciable assets were revalued by legislative initiative, valuation principles in Japan have been based on historical cost. Owing to accelerating rates of inflation, especially in the area of property values, the Japanese Institute of Certified Public Accountants and the Business Accounting Deliberation Council are actively studying the issue. No formal pronouncement has yet been issued.[20]

The Netherlands. Despite the absence of any formal requirements to do so, a generally accepted accounting principle in the Netherlands is the inclusion of current replacement value measurements in annual accounts. Influenced by the replacement value theory developed in the 1920s by Professor Th. Limperg of the University of Amsterdam, larger Dutch companies, Philips being a noted example, carry certain inventory and depreciable fixed assets at their current replacement values with corresponding replacement value-based depreciation and cost of sales expenses in income statements, and replacement valuation "reserves" in the Owner's Equity section of balance sheets. Support for this practice is contained in a note accompanying reissue of the IASC exposure draft, "Accounting for Changing Prices," by the Council of Netherlands Instituut van Registeraccountants in January 1976.[21]

New Zealand. In March 1982, the New Zealand Society of Accountants issued *Current Cost Accounting Standard No. 1* (CCAS No. 1), "Information Reflecting the Effects of Changing Prices." While the standard does not depart significantly from those of other Commonwealth countries alluded to earlier (CCAS No. 1 mirrors in many respects prescriptions of SSAP No. 16), it is notable for the process by which it evolved. As early as 1975, the New Zealand profession worked closely with the University of Waikato on an inflation accounting project in which academia, government, and industry cooperated in examining and experimenting with alternative measurement options. Operative for periods beginning on or after April 1, 1982, the resultant CCAS No. 1 stipulates three supplementary adjustments to historical cost–based operating income to arrive at current cost operating profit. These include adjustments for

[19] For more information contact La Documentation Francaise, 31 Quai Voltaire, Paris.

[20] For more information contact The Japanese Institute of Certified Public Accountants, the Kabuki Building, 4-12-15 Ginza, Chuo-Ku, Tokyo, Japan.

[21] For more information contact Netherlands Instituut van Registeraccountants, Mensinge 2, Postbus 7984, Amsterdam 1011, Netherlands.

cost of sales, depreciation, and the amount of additional (or reduced) funds needed for monetary working capital (basically trade receivables less trade payables) as a result of specific price changes as they affect the business.[22]

West Germany.   As a result of a 1975 professional accounting recommendation, "Accounting for the Purpose of Maintaining the Substantialistic Value of An Enterprise," public companies in West Germany are encouraged to supplement their basic financial statements with information disclosing the effect on earnings of cost of goods sold and depreciation restated to their replacement cost equivalents. However, that portion of inventories and fixed assets that is considered to be financed by debt, as opposed to equity, is excluded in determining such effect. Current cost adjustments are premised on the assumption that shareholders' equity is first used to finance fixed assets and then inventory. Fixed assets are restated using government-supplied indexes while the inventory adjustment is a function of the relative price increase during the year related to ending inventory multiplied by the value of beginning inventory. Possible application of this recommendation is illustrated in Table 5.3. To date, no major West German corporations have availed themselves of the recommendation in their published financial statements.[23]

PROBLEM AREAS

Country initiatives in accounting for inflation suggest that, with the exception of Argentina, Brazil, and other South American countries, where general price level-adjusted statements have been adopted as primary, most countries including the United States continue to adhere to the historical cost model supplemented by inflation-adjusted data. While the current cost (value) model appears to be gaining international favor, most countries have not accepted it in its pure form. Notice the frequency with which the term *changing prices* is used in the titles of most national and international pronouncements suggesting the inclusion of both general and specific price information.

Why are not more countries following the U.S. example? The answer is that there are many accounting problems that have yet to be resolved when it comes to effective and comprehensive inflation accounting. Which types of price changes should be accounted for? While Brazil has chosen to account for general price level movements, is this really the best way to go? Even if we answer in the affirmative, which statistical price series would we employ—an index of consumer prices, an index of wholesale prices, or some other statistical construct? Then, how often should we adjust accounts—annually, semiannually, monthly, or weekly? What about gains and losses from holding monetary

---

[22] For more information contact New Zealand Society of Accountants, Willbank House, 57 Willis Street, P.O. Box 11342, Wellington, New Zealand.

[23] For more information contact Institut der Wirschaftsprüfer in Deutchland e.V., 4 Dusseldorf 30, Cecilienallee 36, West Germany.

TABLE 5.3   Current Cost Accounting as Recommended in West Germany

Assume that the following values existed on December 31, 1985:

	Historical Cost	Replacement Cost
Depreciable assets	6,000	8,000
Other fixed assets	4,000	N/A
Shareholders' equity	11,000	N/A
Depreciation expense	600	800

Assume that the following facts applied to inventory valuations for 1985:

Closing inventory at December 31, 1985 prices	2,400
Closing inventory at January 1, 1985 prices	2,000
Opening inventory at historical cost	1,800
Closing inventory at historical cost	2,200

The adjustment with regard to depreciation expense is initially calculated as 200, the difference between replacement cost and historical cost–based amounts (800 − 600).

The adjustment with regard to inventory is initially

The extent of price changes represented in closing inventory

$$\frac{2400 - 2000}{2000} = 20\%$$

This percentage price rise applied to opening inventory
20% × 1800

$$= 360$$

The total adjustment initially determined is 560 (200 + 360).

Since the shareholders' equity exceeds the amount of fixed assets the adjustment related to depreciation expense is the entire 200. Since the excess of shareholders' equity over fixed assets is 1,000 (11,000 − 10,000) and this represents 1,000/2,200 of inventory, the recommended profit and loss correction associated with inventory would be 164 (i.e., 1,000/2,200 × 360).

Source: Adapted from IASC Discussion Paper, "Treatment of Changing Prices in Financial Statements: A Summary of Proposals," March 1, 1977.

items? Should these be reflected in current operating income or simply disclosed as a separate figure? Should financial statements of earlier periods be restated in terms of current-period price levels (i.e., rolled forward) when prior statements are presented for comparative purposes? If so, will a single overall adjustment suffice? And how should the accounts of foreign subsidiaries and branches be consolidated with those of the parent? Should they first be adjusted for foreign inflation and then translated to their domestic currency equivalents or vice versa? This catalogue of questions is endless.

Many of these issues parallel those discussed in connection with the foreign currency translation problem. For example, both price level restatements and foreign currency translations have a common denominator problem, both have similar difficulties with the methodology of restatement, and both face a dilemma in classifying and disposing of restatement "gains or losses." The similarities, however, are more apparent than real. That is to say, the theoretical accounting considerations involved in the two processes are not the same. Foreign exchange translation is largely a unit-of-account (measurement unit) problem. Price level adjustment is primarily concerned with the distinction between capital and income and, therefore, has predominantly valuation (measurement process) implications.

Specific effects also differ in the two processes. A cash account translated from one currency to the next is not particularly problematical, whereas a price level adjustment of a cash account is. Historical accounts properly translated from one currency to another are *not* automatically price level-adjusted because foreign exchange rates are seldom perfectly negatively correlated with price level changes and, as we have seen, single accounts in a balance sheet may be successfully adjusted for inflation effects. On the other hand, translation of an inflation-adjusted foreign currency balance could result in a "double charge" for inflation.

With these distinctions in mind, let us now examine three inflation accounting issues that have proved especially troublesome to accountants. They are (1) the question of whether constant dollars or current costs provide a better measurement of the effects of inflation, (2) the accounting treatment of "inflation gains and losses," and (3) accounting for foreign operations. To confine our scope, issue (1) is discussed in conjunction with issue (3).

Inflation Gains and Losses

Treatment of gains and losses on monetary items (i.e., cash, receivables, and payables) is a controversial issue. Our survey of various country practices reveals important variations in this respect.

In the case of the United States, gains or losses on monetary items are determined by restating in constant dollars the beginning and ending balance of, and transactions in, all monetary assets and liabilities (including long-term debt). The resulting figure is intended to provide a useful basis for assessing the performance of an enterprise in maintaining the general purchasing power of investors (FAS No. 33, pars. 150–152). Rather than being included in reported earnings it is disclosed as a separate stand-alone item. This treatment signals that the FASB views gains and losses in monetary items as different in nature than other types of earnings.

In the United Kingdom, gains and losses on monetary items are partitioned into a monetary working capital and a gearing adjustment. Both figures, it should be recalled, are determined in relation to specific as opposed to general price changes. Underlying the former, the following rationale is offered (SSAP No. 16, pars. 11–13): When sales are made on credit, the firm in effect ties up working capital (i.e., finances changes in the replacement cost of its inventories) until the related trade receivables are collected. Conversely, when inventories and other supplies are purchased on account, specific price changes related to these items are essentially financed by the supplier during the credit period. This releases working capital of the buyer for other uses. Since these phenomena relate to inventories, they are calculated using the same specific price indexes and are viewed as an extension of the current cost of sales adjustment in arriving at adjusted operating income of the enterprise.

The gearing adjustment indicates the benefit (or cost) to shareholders from debt financing during a period of changing prices. This figure is added (deducted) to current cost operating profit to arrive at a disposable wealth measure entitled Current Cost Profit Attributable to Shareholders.

A third approach, that of Brazil, does not adjust current assets and liabilities explicitly as these amounts are "expressed in current values."[24] However, as indicated in Table 5.3, the adjustment from netting price level–adjusted permanent assets and owners' equity represents the general purchasing power gain or loss in financing working capital from debt or equity. A permanent asset adjustment that exceeds an equity adjustment represents that portion of permanent assets being financed by debt, giving rise to a purchasing power gain. Conversely, an equity adjustment greater than the permanent asset adjustment denotes the portion of working capital being financed by equity. A purchasing power loss is recognized for this portion during an inflationary period.

While other treatments no doubt exist, your authors are sympathetic with the general notions embodied in SSAP No. 16. In addition to inventories and plant and equipment, an enterprise needs to increase its net nominal monetary working capital under upward price pressures so as to maintain its operating capability. It also experiences an increase in well-offness when debt is employed during inflation. However, the magnitude of these phenomena should not be measured in general purchasing power terms for the simple reason that a firm rarely, if ever, invests in an economy's market basket. Nor do we feel that the purpose of inflation accounting is to measure and communicate the maintenance of the general purchasing power of investors. Rather the object is to measure the performance of an *enterprise* which will, in turn, facilitate the assessment of the amounts, timing, and uncertainty of future cash flows.[25] Interpretation of the significance or value (general purchasing power) of those amounts is best left to others.

In another piece, one of your authors has advocated the use of an index that measures a firm's command over specific goods and services to calculate its monetary gains and losses.[26] As the construction of firm-specific purchasing power indexes may not be feasible for all enterprises, the British approach appears to be a good practical alternative. However, rather than disclosing the gearing adjustment or some such facsimile either as an element of income or as an offset to interest expense (the latter being a function of general price level trends rather than specific price changes), we prefer to treat it as a reduction of the current cost adjustments for depreciation, cost of sales, and monetary working capital. In our view, current cost charges to restate historical cost income during inflation are offset by the reduced burden of servicing debt used to finance those operating items (see Table 5.4 for an illustration of our disclosure preference).

[24] Fleming, "New Concepts."

[25] Financial Accounting Standards Board, "Objectives of Financial Reporting by Business Enterprises," *Statement of Financial Accounting Concepts No. 1* (Stamford, Conn.: FASB, November 1978), par. 37.

[26] Frederick D. S. Choi, "Foreign Inflation and Management Decisions," *Management Accounting*, June 1977, pp. 21–27.

TABLE 5.4 Alternative Current Cost Monetary Disclosures

SSAP NO. 16 (ALT. 1)

Historical cost-based operating income		2,900
Less: Current cost adjustments		
Cost of sales	(460)	
Monetary working capital	(100)	
Working capital	(560)	
Depreciation	(950)	(1,510)
Current cost operating income		1,390
Gearing adjustment	166	
Interest payable less receivable	(200)	(34)
Current cost profit before taxation		1,356
Taxation		(730)
Current cost profit attributable to shareholders		626

SSAP NO. 16 (ALT. 2)

Historical cost-based operating income		2,900
Less: Current cost adjustments		
Cost of sales	(460)	
Monetary working capital	(100)	
Working capital	(560)	
Depreciation	(950)	(1,510)
Current cost operating income		1,390
Interest payable less receivable		(200)
		1,190
Taxation		(730)
		460
Gearing adjustment		166
Current cost profit attributable to shareholders		626

SUGGESTED METHOD

Historical cost-based operating income		2,900
Less: Current cost adjustments		
Cost of sales	(460)	
Depreciation	(950)	
Monetary working capital	(100)	
Gearing adjustment	166	(1,344)
Current cost-based operating income		1,556
Interest payable less receivable		(200)
Current cost-based net income before taxes		1,356
Taxes		(730)
Current cost-based net income		626

Holding Gains and Losses

A major feature of current value accounting is its division of total earnings into two parts: (1) operating income reflecting the difference between current revenues and the current cost of resources consumed and (2) unrealized holding gains that result from the possession of nonmonetary assets that rise in replacement value during an inflationary period. While the measurement of holding gains is straightforward, their accounting disposition is less clear. Should portions of, let us say, raw materials inventory gains be "realized" in periods when the respective inventories are turned into finished goods and sold? Are there ever "unrealized" adjustment gains or losses that should be deferred? Or, should all such gains or losses simply be lumped together and disclosed in a special new section within stockholders' equity?

Our position is that increases in the replacement cost of operating assets (e.g., higher projected cash outflows to replace equipment) do not represent gains, realized or unrealized. Whereas current cost-based income is an approximate measure of a firm's disposable wealth, increases or decreases in the current cost of inventory, plant, and equipment, and other operating assets are revaluations of owners' equity representing the portion of earnings which must be retained in the business to preserve the physical capital (or productive capacity) of the enterprise. Assets held for speculation, such as vacant land or marketable securities, do not need to be replaced to maintain productive capacity. Hence, should current cost adjustments be extended to these items, increases or decreases in their current cost (value) equivalents (not to exceed their realizable values) should be reflected directly in income properly labeled as to their nature and source.

Accounting for Foreign Inflation

The issue presented here arises whenever a company consolidates the accounts of foreign affiliates domiciled in inflationary environments. Recall that all of the foreign currency translation methods described in Chapter 4 basically ignore the effects of foreign inflation in the consolidation process. To remedy this shortcoming, some writers advocate restating foreign account balances to reflect changes in the local purchasing power of the foreign currency unit and then translating the adjusted amounts to their domestic currency equivalent. Purported advantages of the "restate-translate" proposal are as follows:

1. It enables statement readers to assess ordinary operating results in terms of the local currency as well as the separate effects of inflation on these results.
2. It enables management to gauge better the performance of a subsidiary after providing for "maintenance" of the subsidiary's financial assets.
3. It enables management to evaluate the performance of a subsidiary in terms of the environment in which the subsidiary's assets are domiciled.
4. In enables management to ascertain the full effect of any currency devaluation on a subsidiary's operating results if devaluation occurs.

Critics of the restate first and then translate approach argue that this method results in a unit of measure that reflects multiple standards in terms of general purchasing power. For example, a U.S. parent company consolidating the results of ten foreign subsidiaries (each domiciled in a country experiencing different rates of inflation) would obtain financial statements in U.S. dollars. These dollar amounts, however, would really reflect the purchasing power of ten different countries. This is criticized as highly undesirable, especially for statement readers in the United States who necessarily have a parent company (i.e., a U.S. dollar) perspective on the consolidated statements. Moreover, as we pointed out earlier, foreign exchange rates contain an element of inflation effects. To this extent any local inflation is counted "double" under the restate-translate methodology.

Restate-translate critics support the adoption of what may be called the *translate-restate approach*. Under this process, foreign accounts are first translated to the domestic currency of the parent company and then restated to their domestic general purchasing power equivalents.

Proponents of the latter approach argue that it is easier for parent companies to translate all foreign operations into domestic currency units and then do one inflation restatement than to restate affiliate accounts in each foreign country. Moreover, the translate-restate option not only reveals the financial statement effects of changes in foreign currency exchange rates but also discloses the effect of domestic inflation on the prospective returns to domestic investors. In short, consolidated accounts prepared according to the translate-restate proposal are expressed in terms of a single standard of measure, namely, dollars of domestic purchasing power. And that is what counts!

The differential effect of the translate-restate approach versus the restate-translate approach on consolidated results can be significant. To illustrate, Table 5.5 presents comparative foreign currency balance sheets for January 1 and December 31, 1985, and a statement of income for Cruzeiro Corporation, a Brazilian subsidiary of a U.S.-based MNC. Results under the translate-restate

TABLE 5.5   Cruzeiro Corporation Financial Statements (Cr. thousands)

BALANCE SHEET	1/1/85	12/31/85
Cash	Cr. 5,000	Cr. 3,600
Inventory		1,000
Fixed assets		5,000
Accumulated depreciation		500
Total assets	Cr. 5,000	Cr. 9,100
Notes payable		4,000
Owners' equity	5,000	5,100
Total liabilities & owners' equity	Cr. 5,000	Cr. 9,100

INCOME STATEMENT	YEAR ENDED 12/31/85
Revenues	Cr. 5,000
Cost of sales	2,000
Gross margin	Cr. 3,000

(continued)

TABLE 5.5   (*continued*)

INCOME STATEMENT			YEAR ENDED 12/31/85	
Operating expenses				
Wages	Cr.	1,600		
Depreciation	Cr.	500		
Interest		800		2,900
Net income			Cr.	100

Notes:
1. Cruzeiro Corporation was formed on January 1, 1985 with a U.S. parent company cash investment of $100,000
2. Exchange rates on 1/1/85: $.02 = Cr. 1; on 12/31/85: $.015 = Cr 1; average rate during the year: $.0175 = Cr. 1.
3. During the year, the Brazilian general price level increased from 120 to 180, averaging 150 during the year.
4. The U.S. general price level index increased 10 percent during the same period.
5. Plant and equipment were acquired on Jan. 2 for Cr. 5,000,000 in return for Cr. 1,000,000 down and a 20 percent three-year mortgage note with interest payable each 12/31.
6. Inventory costing Cr. 3,000,000 was purchased on 1/2/85.
7. Sales and wage transactions were incurred uniformly throughout the year.
8. The cruzeiro is deemed to be the functional currency. (see Chapter 4 for details).

option are illustrated in Table 5.6. The restate-translate alternative is portrayed in Table 5.7.

Excluding monetary gains and losses, the translate-restate method produces a significantly higher dollar operating income than the restate-translate method, in our example a $209 profit as opposed to a $7,050 loss. If monetary gains and losses are considered, the restate-translate option produces a bottom line about 130 percent higher than translate-restate.

How do we choose between these competing constructs? Debates on the issue thus far have generated more heat than light. Our feeling is that the controversy can only be resolved by addressing it from a decision-oriented framework.

Generally, and in brief, investors are interested in a firm's dividend-generating potential since the value of their securities investment is ultimately related to future dividends. A firm's dividend-generating potential, in turn, is directly related to its capacity to produce goods and services. Unless a firm preserves its productive capacity and thereby its earning power, dividends are a moot consideration.

A direct implication of this argument is that investors are interested in specific rather than general price level-adjusted statements. Why? Because specific price level adjustments (our current cost model) determine the maximum amounts of resources that can be paid out as dividends (disposable wealth) without reducing a firm's productive capacity.

What does this conclusion imply about the restate-translate versus trans-

TABLE 5.6 Translate-Restate Method Illustration

	HISTORICAL	×	EXCHANGE RATE	=	TRANSLATED	×	PRICE INDEX	=	RESTATED
Balance Sheet, 1/1/85									
Cash	Cr. 5,000,000		.02		$ 100,000		—		$ 100,000
Owners' equity	5,000,000		.02		100,000		—		100,000
Income Statement, 12/31/85									
Sales	Cr. 5,000,000		.0175		$ 87,500		110/105		$ 91,667
Cost of Sales	2,000,000		.0175		35,000		110/100		38,500
Wages	1,600,000		.0175		28,000		110/105		29,333
Depreciation	500,000		.0175		8,750		110/100		9,625
Interest	800,000		.0175		14,000		110/110		14,000
Net income	Cr. 100,000				$ 1,750				$ 209
Net monetary gains					—				2,072[a]
Owners' equity 1/1/85	5,000,000		.02		100,000		110/100		110,000
Owners' equity 12/31/85	Cr. 5,100,000				$ 101,750				$ 112,281
Balance Sheet, 12/31/85									
Cash	Cr. 3,600,000		.015		$ 54,000		110/110		$ 54,000
Inventory	1,000,000		.015		15,000		110/100		16,500
Fixed assets	5,000,000		.015		75,000		110/100		82,500
Accumulated depreciation	500,000		.015		7,500		110/100		8,250
Total	Cr. 9,100,000				$ 136,500				$ 144,750
Notes payable	Cr. 4,000,000		.015		$ 60,000		110/110		$ 60,000
Owners' equity	5,100,000				101,750		—		112,281
Equity adjustment from translation[b]	—				(25,250)		110/100		(27,775)
Total	Cr. 9,100,000				$ 136,500				$ 144,506[c]

(continued)

TABLE 5.6 *(continued)*

^a Monetary gains and losses:

	Cash	×	Exchange Rate	=	Translated	×	Price Index	=	Restated
1/1 Orig. Investment	Cr. 5,000,000	×	.015	=	$ 75,000	×	110/100	=	$ 82,500
1/2 Down payment, P & E	(1,000,000)		.015		(15,000)		110/100		(16,500)
1/2 Inventory purchase	(3,000,000)		.015		(45,000)		110/100		(49,500)
1/3–12/31 Cash sales	5,000,000		.015		75,000		110/105		78,571
1/3–12/31 Wages	(1,600,000)		.015		(24,000)		110/105		(25,143)
12/31 Interest	800,000		.015		(12,000)		110/110		(12,000)
	Cr. 3,600,000				$ 54,000				$ 57,928
									54,000
					Monetary loss				$ (3,928)

	Notes payable	×		=	Translated	×	Price Index	=	Restated
1/1	Cr. 4,000,000		.015		$ 60,000		110/100		$ 66,000
					60,000				$ 60,000
					Monetary gain				$ 6,000

Net monetary gain = $6,000 − $3,928
= $2,072

^b Beginning net assets   Cr. 5,000,000 × (.015 − .02)   = $ (25,000)
Increase in net assets   Cr. 100,000 × (.015 − .0175) = $ (250)
$ (25,250)

^c Difference due to rounding.

TABLE 5.7 Restate-Translate Method Illustration

	HISTORICAL	×	PRICE INDEX	=	RESTATED	×	EXCHANGE RATE	=	TRANSLATED
Balance Sheet, 1/1/85									
Cash	Cr. 5,000,000		—		Cr. 5,000,000		.02		$ 100,000
Owners' equity	5,000,000		—		5,000,000		.02		100,000
Income Statement, 12/31/85									
Sales	Cr. 5,000,000		180/150		Cr. 6,000,000		.015		$ 90,000
Cost of Sales	2,000,000		180/120		3,000,000		.015		45,000
Wages	1,600,000		180/150		1,920,000		.015		28,800
Depreciation	500,000		180/120		750,000		.015		11,250
Interest	800,000		180/180		800,000		.015		12,000
Net income	Cr. 100,000				Cr. (470,000)				$ (7,050)
Net monetary gains	—				820,000[a]		.015		12,300
Owners' equity, 1/1/85	5,000,000		180/120		7,500,000		.02		150,000
Owners' equity,	Cr. 5,100,000				Cr. 7,850,000				$ 155,250
Balance Sheet, 12/31/85									
Cash	Cr. 3,600,000		180/180		Cr. 3,600,000		.015		$ 54,000
Inventory	1,000,000		180/120		1,500,000		.015		22,500
Fixed assets	5,000,000		180/120		7,500,000		.015		112,500
Accumulated depreciation	(500,000)		180/120		(750,000)		.015		(11,250)
Total	Cr. 9,100,000				Cr. 11,850,000				$ 177,750
Notes payable	Cr. 4,000,000		180/180		Cr. 4,000,000		.015		$ 60,000
Owners' equity	5,100,000				7,850,000				155,250
Equity adjustment from translation	—						—		(37,500)[b]
Total	Cr. 9,100,000				Cr. 11,850,000				$ 177,750

(continued)

199

TABLE 5.7 (*continued*)

[a] Net monetary gains:

	Cash	Restated	Translated
1/1 Equity investment	Cr. 5,000,000	180/120	Cr. 7,500,000
1/2 Down payment, P & E	(1,000,000)	180/120	(1,500,000)
1/2 Inventory purchase	(3,000,000)	180/120	(4,500,000)
1/3–12/31 Cash sales	5,000,000	180/150	6,000,000
1/3–12/31 Wages	(1,600,000)	180/150	(1,920,000)
12/31 Interest	800,000	180/180	(800,000)
	Cr. 3,600,000 →		Cr. 4,780,000
			3,600,000
	Monetary loss		Cr. (1,180,000)

	Notes payable	Restated	Translated
1/1 Balance	Cr. 4,000,000 →	180/120	Cr. 6,000,000
			4,000,000
	Monetary gain		Cr. 2,000,000

Net monetary gain = Cr. 2,000,000 − 1,180,000
= Cr. 820,000

[b] Beginning net assets Cr. 7,500,000 (.015 − .02) = $ (37,500).

late-restate dilemma? It implies that the dilemma is trivial. The reason is that both processes are based on a valuation framework that has little to recommend it—historical cost. Neither restatement for general price level changes abroad and translation to domestic currency amounts nor translation to domestic currency amounts and restatement for domestic inflation changes that valuation base. In other words, the historical cost model, adjusted for changes in the general purchasing power of the monetary unit, whether it be foreign general purchasing power or domestic general purchasing power, is still the historical cost model!

The price level adjustment procedure that seems appropriate from our point of view is as follows:

1. Restate the financial statements of all subsidiaries, both domestic and foreign, as well as the statements of the parent, to reflect changes in specific price levels (e.g., current costs).
2. Translate the accounts of all foreign subsidiaries into domestic currency equivalents using a constant (e.g., the current or a base-year foreign exchange rate).

Restating both foreign and domestic accounts to their specific current price equivalents produces information that is decision-relevant. This information encodes the maximum amount of realistic potential dividend flows to investors. It also facilitates predictions of future cash flows. Moreover, comparisons and evaluations of the consolidated results of all firms would be a much easier task than it now is.

Although we have not explicitly considered the decision models of management, the proposal advocated here should also be germane to them. For instance, with current cost-based information generated throughout the enterprise, headquarters management should be in a better position to evaluate the relative performance of its subsidiaries since enterprise results would be comparable not only nationally but internationally as well. And since managers are concerned with the maintenance of productive capacity, our proposal should further facilitate more equitable resource allocations within any national or multinational corporate system—especially when general and specific price levels do not move in parallel.

While the U.S. experiment with supplementary disclosures of both current cost and general price level adjustments is expected to continue at least through 1984, recent developments suggest that the restate (current cost)–translate model advocated here is gaining support. By way of background, FAS No. 33 was originally based on the method of accounting for foreign currency translation mandated by FAS No. 8. Under these circumstances, U.S. multinationals subject to FAS No. 33's current cost provisions were required to restate foreign currency assets to their current cost equivalents prior to dollar translation. In keeping with the parent company perspective embodied in FAC No. 8, the translate-restate approach described earlier was permitted when presenting historical cost–constant dollar information.

To conform FAS No. 33's disclosure requirements with the local company perspective now permitted by FAS No. 52, the FASB issued *Statement of*

Financial Accounting Standards No. 70 (FAS No. 70), "Financial Reporting and Changing Prices: Foreign Currency Translation" in December 1982. This statement has no effect on the reporting of inflation disclosures by enterprises for which the U.S. dollar is the functional currency for all significant foreign operations. Under the original terms of an exposure draft leading up to FAS No. 70, firms measuring foreign operations in a functional currency other than the U.S. dollar were to provide historical cost–constant dollar information by restating foreign currency assets for foreign general price level changes prior to translation. Responding to expressed dissatisfaction with the historical cost–constant dollar aspect of FAS No. 33, the FASB revised its exposure draft. Enterprises measuring a significant part of their foreign operations in functional currencies other than the U.S. dollar are now exempted from FAS No. 33's requirement to present historical cost information in units of constant purchasing power, provided that current cost information is disclosed. As a means of facilitating interperiod comparisons, current cost information is to be measured either in units of U.S. general purchasing power or units of foreign general purchasing power. Although advocating what is in effect a choice of either *restate-translate-restate* or *restate-restate-translate* methodology (a proposal that is sure to generate additional reporting controversies) the basic valuation framework is one premised on current costs.

Internationally, our restate-translate formulation is an integral feature of SSAP No. 16[27] and most proposals calling for supplementary current cost disclosures. In the Netherlands, the restate-translate method has been practiced by the Philips Lamp Company for over 25 years.[28] What is unique about the Philips approach is that the restated current cost information is not only disclosed for external reporting purposes but constitutes an integral feature of the company's management information system. Indeed, the company does not simply conform its internal reporting to its external reporting system, which is a common practice in many companies. Rather, it does just the opposite. Philips basic reporting philosophy is perhaps best reflected in the remarks of Dewey R. Borst, Comptroller of Inland Steel Company:

> Management seeks the best current information to monitor how they have done in the past, and to guide them in their current decision-making. Outsiders value financial statements for the same general purpose of determining how the firm has done in the past and how it is likely to perform in the future. Therefore, there is no legitimate need to have two distinct sets of data and methods of presentation of financial information. The same data now available through the development of managerial accounting is also suitable for outsiders.[29]

---

[27] Accounting Standards Committee, *Guidance Notes on SSAP No. 16: Current Cost Accounting* (London: Institute of Chartered Accountants in England and Wales, 1980).

[28] R. C. Spinosa Cattela, "An Introduction into Current Cost Accounting and Its Application within Philips," *Philips Administrative Review*, December 1977; reprinted in F. D. S. Choi and Gerhard G. Mueller, *Essentials of Multinational Accounting* (Ann Arbor, Mich.: University Microfilms International, 1979, pp. 59–65.

[29] "Accounting vs. Reality: How Wide Is the 'GAAP'," *The Week in Review*, July 13, 1982, p. 1.

SELECTED REFERENCES

ACCOUNTING STANDARDS COMMITTEE, "Current Cost Accounting," *Statement of Accounting Practice No. 16,* London: Institute of Chartered Accountants in England and Wales, March 1980, 19 pp.

ACCOUNTING STANDARDS COMMITTEE, *Guidance Notes on SSAP 16: Current Cost Accounting,* London: Institute of Chartered Accountants in England and Wales, 1980, 69 pp.

ARTHUR YOUNG & COMPANY, *Financial Reporting and Changing Prices: A Survey of How 300 Companies Complied with FAS 33.* New York, August 1980, 83 pp.

ARTHUR YOUNG & COMPANY, *Financial Reporting and Changing Prices: A Survey of Preparers' Views and Practices,* New York, August 1981, 34 pp.

BELL, PHILIP W., "Public Policy Objectives in a Market Economy and Function and Structure in Accounting," paper presented at the Fourth Annual Meeting of the European Accountants Association in Aahrus, Denmark, April 5–7, 1982, 88 pp.

CATTELA, R. C. SPINOSA, "An Introduction into Current Cost Accounting and Its Application within Philips," *Philips Administration Review,* December 1977; reprinted in Frederick D. S. Choi and Gerhard G. Mueller, *Essentials of Multinational Accounting: An Anthology,* Ann Arbor, Mich.: University Microfilms International, 1979, pp. 59–65.

CHOI, FREDERICK D. S., "Foreign Inflation and Management Decisions," *Management Accounting,* June 1977, pp. 21–27.

FINANCIAL ACCOUNTING STANDARDS BOARD, "Financial Reporting and Changing Prices," *Statement of Financial Accounting Standards No. 33,* Stamford, Conn.: FASB, September 1979, 127 pp.

FINANCIAL ACCOUNTING STANDARDS BOARD, "Financial Reporting and Changing Prices: Foreign Currency Translation—An Amendment of FASB Statement No. 33," *Proposed Statement of Financial Accounting Standards,* Stamford, Conn.: FASB, December 22, 1981, 24 pp.; revised ed., August 19, 1982, 39 pp.

FLEMING, ROBERT, "New Concepts in Brazilian Accounting for Inflation," *The Accountant's Magazine,* April 1979, pp. 162–165.

INTERNATIONAL ACCOUNTING STANDARDS COMMITTEE, "Information Reflecting the Effects of Changing Prices," *International Accounting Standard 15,* London: IASC, November 1981, unpaginated.

LAFFERTY, MICHAEL, ed., "World Accounting Report," London: *The Financial Times Limited,* various issues.

LORENSEN, LEONARD, and PAUL ROSENFIELD, "Management Information and Foreign Inflation," *Journal of Accountancy,* December 1974, pp. 98–102.

REVSINE, LAWRENCE, "A Capital Maintenance Approach to Income Management," *The Accounting Review,* April 1981, pp. 383–389.

SEED, ALAN H., III, *Inflation: Its Impact on Financial Reporting and Decision Making,* New York: Financial Executives Research Foundation, September 1978, 137 pp.

STERLING, ROBERT R., "Relevant Financial Reporting in an Age of Price Changes," *Journal of Accountancy,* February 1975, pp. 42–51.

TODD, KENNETH R., "How One Financial Officer Uses Inflation-Adjusted Accounting Data," *Financial Executive,* October 1982, pp. 13–19.

VANCIL, R., "Inflation Accounting—The Great Controversy," *Harvard Business Review,* March-April 1976, pp. 58–67.

WALTON, PETER, ed., *International Accounting and Financial Report,* London: Institute for International Research Ltd., various issues.

WYMAN, HAROLD E., JESSE F. DILLARD, and FREDERICK D. S. CHOI, "Response to 'Financial Reporting and Changing Prices: Foreign Currency Translation. An Amendment to FASB Statement No. 33,' original and revised editions dated December 22, 1981 and August 19, 1982, respectively," *Report of the Sub-*

committee of the Committee on Financial Accounting Standards of the American Accounting Association, Sarasota, Fla.: American Accounting Association, April 1, 1982, 9 pp. plus appendices; October 1, 1982, 8 pp. plus appendices.

DISCUSSION QUESTIONS

1. In what respects does accounting for inflation resemble the process of accounting for foreign currency translation? In what respects does it differ?

2. Following are the remarks of a prominent American Congressman:

    > The plain fact of the matter is that inflation accounting is a premature, imprecise, and underdeveloped method of recording basic business facts. To insist that any system of inflation accounting can afford the accuracy and fairness needed for the efficient operation of our tax system is simply foolish. My years on the Ways and Means Committee have exposed me to the many appeals of business—from corporate tax "reform" to the need for capital formation—which have served as a guise for reducing the tax contributions of American business. In this respect, I see inflation accounting as another in a long line of attempts to minimize corporate taxation through backdoor gimmickry.[30]

    Explain why you agree or disagree with the foregoing quote.

3. Professional accountancy bodies the world over generally agree that the degree of inflation may become so great that conventional financial statements will lose much of their significance and price level-adjusted statements will clearly become more meaningful. Since domestic rates of inflation vary significantly from country to country, at what point do price level-adjusted financial statements become "more meaningful"? How does one determine whether the benefits of price level-adjusted accounting information exceed the costs involved?

4. Briefly describe the nature of the historical cost–constant dollar and current cost models. In what ways are they similar? In what ways do they differ?

5. This chapter describes various approaches being taken around the world to account for the effects of changing prices. What conclusions do you draw as to the current state of the art and apparent inflation accounting trends?

6. Compare and contrast the major similarities and differences between U.S. FAS No. 33 and U.K. SSAP No. 16. Which approach do you feel provides the more useful information to external readers?

7. How does the Brazilian approach to accounting for monetary gains and losses resemble that under FAS No. 33? In what ways does it differ?

[30] Taken from Haskins & Sells, *The Week in Review*, July 23, 1976, pp. 7–8.

8. As a potential investor in the shares of multinational enterprises, which inflation construct—restate-translate or translate-restate— would provide you with consolidated information most relevant to your decision needs? Which information set is most optimal from the viewpoint of the foreign subsidiary's shareholders?

9. How does accounting for foreign inflation differ from accounting for inflation domestically?

10. "For accounting purposes, our Italian subsidiary does not revalue its assets to reflect changes in the general level of prices in Italy. Accounting for the financial statement effects of changing prices would mean an increase of about 25–30 people in their accounting department. Besides, they maintain that translating their financial reports into dollars automatically reflects the impact of inflation." Do you agree with the last statement in this quote?

EXERCISES

1. Sobrero Corporation, a Mexican affiliate of a major U.S.–based hotel chain, starts the calendar year with 1 billion peso (P) cash equity investment. It immediately acquires a refurbished hotel in Acapulco for P 900 million. Owing to a favorable tourist season, Sobrero Corporation's rental revenues totaled P 144 million for the year. Operating expenses of P 86,400,000 together with rental revenues were incurred uniformly throughout the year. The building, comprising 80 percent of the original purchase price (balance attributed to land), has an estimated useful life of 20 years and is being depreciated in straight-line fashion. By year-end, the Mexican consumer price index rises to 420 from an initial level of 263, averaging 340 during the year.
    Required: Prepare financial statements for Sobrero Corporation's first year of operations in terms of (a) the historical cost model and (b) the historical cost–constant dollar model. Compare and evaluate the information content of rate of return statistics computed using each alternative information base.

2. Based on the operating information provided in Exercise 1, assume now that Mexico's construction cost index increased by 80 percent during the year while the price of vacant properties adjacent to Sobrero Corporation's hotel increased in value by 90 percent.
    Required: Using this information to restate the value of the company's nonmonetary assets, what would Sobrero Corporation's financial statements look like under the current cost model?

3. Assume that Sobrero Corporation, described in Exercise 1, is a Brazilian entity.
    Required: Based on the information provided in that exercise, calculate Sobrero Corporation's monetary gain or loss (i.e., "gain on correction of balance sheet") and contrast the resulting figure with that derived under U.S. FAS No. 33.

4. Microdata do Brazil, a U.S. subsidiary, begins and ends its calendar

year with an inventory balance of Cr. 500 million. The dollar/cruzeiro exchange rate on January 1 was $.02 = Cr. 1. During the year, the U.S. general price level advances from 180 to 198 while the Brazilian general price level doubles. The exchange rate on Dec. 31 was $.015 = Cr. 1.

Required:

A. Employing the temporal method of translation, calculate the dollar equivalent of the inventory balances using the restate-translate method described in this chapter.

B. Repeat the exercise using the translate-restate method.

C. Which dollar figure do you feel provides the more useful information?

D. If dissatisfied with either result, suggest an alternative approach that would overcome the limitations of method A and method B.

5. Cappucino Enterprises, S.A., a U.S. subsidiary domiciled in Italy, accounts for its inventories on a FIFO basis. The company translates its inventories to dollars at the current rate. Year-end inventories are recorded at 10,920,000 lira (L). During the year, the replacement cost of inventories increases by 20 percent. Inflation and exchange rate information were as follows:

January 1:   Specific price index = 100
                $1 = L 1,400
December 31: Specific price index = 120
                $1 = L 1,820

Required: On the basis of this information, calculate the *dollar* current cost adjustment for cost of sales while avoiding a "double charge" for inflation.

CASE

Jayson Enterprises

Jayson Enterprises, a Belgian paint manufacturer, begins the calendar year with the following Belgian franc (BF) balances:

Cash	920,000	Accounts payable	420,000
Inventory	640,000	Owners' equity	1,140,000

During the first week in January, the company acquires additional paint supplies costing BF 2,400,000 on account and a warehouse for BF 3,200,000 paying BF 800,000 down and signing a 20-year, 10 percent note for the balance. The warehouse (assume no salvage value) is depreciated straight-line over the period of the note. Cash sales amounted to BF 6,000,000 for the year; selling and administrative expenses, including office rent, were BF 1,200,000. Payments on account totaled BF 2,200,000 while inventory on hand at year-end was BF 480,000. With the exception of interest expense, paid on December

31, all other cash receipts and payments took place uniformly throughout the year.

On January 1, the U.S. dollar/franc exchange rate stood at $.025 = BF 1; at year-end it was $.02 = BF 1. The average exchange rate during the year was $.022. Starting at a level of 128, the Belgian consumer price index rose to 160 by December 31, averaging 144 during the year. At the new financial statement date, the cost to replace paint supplies had increased by 30 percent; the cost to rebuild a comparable warehouse, as judged from the construction cost index, would be approximately BF 4,480,000.

Required

1. Assuming beginning inventories were required when the general price index level was 128, prepare Jayson Enterprises' financial statements (i.e., income statement and balance sheet) under the (a) conventional original transactions cost model, (b) historical cost–constant franc model, and (c) current cost model.
2. Comment on which financial statement set provides Belgian readers with the more useful performance and wealth measures.
3. Assume now, that Jayson Enterprises' U.S. headquarters management is interested in seeing the Belgian franc statements in U.S. dollars. Two price level–foreign currency translation procedures are requested. The first is to translate Jayson's unadjusted franc statements to dollars (use the current rate method) and then restate the resulting dollar amounts for U.S. inflation (the U.S. general price level at the financial statement date stood at 108, up 8 percent from the previous year). The other procedure is to restate the Belgian franc statements for inflation (e.g., using the historical cost–constant franc model), then translate the adjusted amounts to dollars using the current rate. Comment on which of the two resulting sets of dollar statements you feel is preferable for use by American readers. (The U.S. general price level averaged 104 during the year.)

6

Further
Technical
Issues

Foreign currency translation and accounting recognition of inflation effects are without doubt the two most important international accounting technical issues of the day. A full chapter is devoted to each of these topics in order to put into full focus the sizable scope of each topic, the long histories of thought and practical experimentation characteristic of each, plus the current status and likely new developments surrounding them. In an important sense these two technical aspects alone are full justification for serious attention to the international accounting field.

This chapter extends the technical discussions of international financial accounting issues to eight additional topics. These eight were chosen judgmentally and without reference to formal surveys like the 1980 Scott Troberg Delphi evaluation entitled *Eighty-eight International Accounting Problems in Rank Order of Importance.*[1] The central aspect of the eight choices is that they are very different from one another. All have received recent attention in the literature and all have unresolved elements. All are essentially accounting measurement issues; reporting and disclosure matters are covered in Chapter 7. Some issues are ever present, like the consolidation of financial statements, while others occur sporadically, like foreign property expropriations. Some have a geographic focus, like value-added reporting, while others are global, like accounting for taxes on income. By design, the issues selected for this

[1] Sarasota, Fla.: American Accounting Association.

chapter cover the full range of technical international financial accounting problems.

Consolidated Financial Statements and Equity Method Accounting

Consolidated financial statements essentially convey the results of operations and the financial position of a group of companies as if they were a single economic unit regardless of any legal distinctions that exist among the separate corporate entities. Principles of consolidating foreign accounts are similar in most respects to those followed in consolidating purely domestic subsidiaries. Hence, accounts of the parent company and its foreign subsidiaries are generally combined on a line-by-line basis by adding together like items of assets, liabilities, revenues, and expenses. Intercompany transactions, including intercompany sales, charges, and dividends, are eliminated.

Consolidated statements appeared first in the United States around the turn of the century, became general practice in the United Kingdom in the 1930s, and are a postwar innovation in much of Continental Europe. As pointed out in Chapter 3, the accounting standard requiring preparation of consolidated financial statements in Japan was not passed until 1975. Worldwide, approximately 25 countries presently have mandatory consolidation standards.

In an effort to move world accounting closer to general consolidation practice, the International Accounting Standards Committee (IASC) put the topic on its early agenda and produced IAS No. 3 (effective for financial statements covering periods beginning on or after January 1, 1977) simply entitled "Consolidated Financial Statements." Highlights of IAS No. 3 include the following:

> A parent company should issue consolidated financial statements, except that it need not do so when it is a wholly owned subsidiary.
>
> A subsidiary should be excluded from consolidation if: (a) control is temporary, or (b) the subsidiary operates under conditions in which severe long-term restrictions on the transfer of funds impair control by the parent company over the subsidiary's assets and operations.
>
> Uniform accounting policies should preferably be followed by companies in the consolidated financial statements. . . .
>
> Investments in associated companies . . . and in subsidiaries which are not consolidated . . . should be included in the consolidated financial statements under the equity method of accounting.[2]

The important issue then, until recently, was not really the underlying conceptual structure of consolidations nor the technical refinements of application. It was purely and simply the question of whether there should be consolidation at all. Professor L. J. Seidler, in a forceful discussion on technical

---

[2] International Accounting Standards Committee, *Consolidated Financial Statements,* International Accounting Standard No. 3 (London: IASC, 1976), Para. 34, 36, 39, 40.

issues, rates consolidation (along with translation and inflation accounting) as one of the three most significant technical problems in international accounting today.[3] Among other observations, he finds that in West Germany consolidated financial statements are found but the methodology is frequently abused. For Japan, he points to Byzantine combinations of industrial, banking, and trading operations most reluctant to disclose their consolidated financial affairs.

Consolidation criteria.   In the United States, subsidiaries are commonly excluded from consolidation in circumstances where the ability of the U.S. parent to control the financial operating policies of the foreign subsidiary is limited. Control is usually presumed to exist if the U.S. parent owns more than 50 percent of the voting shares of the subsidiary. In other countries, it is often considered appropriate to exclude from consolidation any subsidiary whose business activities are so dissimilar to those of the parent that combined financial statements would not be meaningful (e.g., when banks and insurance companies are subsidiaries of industrial companies). Additional grounds for nonconsolidation of foreign accounts include impracticality of consolidation, insignificance of foreign accounts in terms of amounts involved, the likelihood of disproportionate expense or delay in preparing consolidated statements, or the opinion of the company's directors that the effects of consolidation would be misleading or harmful to its business.

Companies electing not to consolidate the accounts of foreign subsidiaries may account for these investments in one of two ways: the cost method or the equity method. Under the cost method, an investment in the shares of a foreign investee is recorded at cost. The parent company subsequently recognizes income from such an investment only to the extent that dividends are distributed by the investee. In most cases, however, recognition of income on the basis of dividends received is not an adequate measure of the income actually earned. Dividends received may bear little relation to the real performance of the investee; that is, dividend distributions can be varied to meet the income or cash needs of the parent.

This state of affairs is largely eliminated under the equity method of accounting for investments whereby the carrying value of the investee is adjusted to reflect the investor's proportionate share of the investee's profits or losses. Dividends received from an investee are treated, in turn, as reductions in the carrying value of the parent's investment (see the journal entry illustration later in this section).

Individual consolidation techniques, for example, eliminations of intercompany investments and markups on intercompany transfers, are treated at length in most intermediate financial accounting textbooks and a plethora of financial accounting handbooks. There is no need to repeat these details here. The use potential of consolidated financial statements is well established in the finance literature. Active users include shareholders, creditors, regulators, managers, attorneys, public policy makers, labor union representatives, and others.

---

[3] Seidler, "Technical Issues," p. 43.

From an economic standpoint, there seems little question that the information content of consolidated financial statements is high. Again, we see no need to regurgitate the interests and objectives of the various statement users.

Areas of controversy. While many countries are still struggling to adopt consolidation procedures de novo, others find that maturity generates some undesirable side effects. In West Germany, for instance, foreign subsidiaries may be excluded from consolidation. Ownership control is defined differently in France, and combined statements of subconsolidation groups are acceptable in the Netherlands. The level of information aggregation inherent in consolidated financial statements is thought to be so mammoth in the United States that "decomposition" in the form of business segment disclosures was introduced at the strong urging of financial analysts.[4] Indeed there appear to be instances where U.S. accounting may have overreached its rationality. It is instructional to read Professor H. P. Hill's comments about consolidated financial statements:

> The entire process of consolidating the worldwide accounts of every multinational company can be criticized from the standpoint of rational behavior. So many assumptions go into the translation and consolidation process that the results are sometimes more a tribute to the ingenuity of the accountants than they are a measure of the achievements of the management. Stockholders looking for the amount of their dividend coverage will not find it in the consolidated statements of a company doing business in Indonesia or Argentina. Stockholders in a U.S.-denominated company expect a certain portion of the profits to be distributed to them, and who can say this expectation is irrational? But if the profits are locked in a foreign country with inflation measured in triple digits and with the inevitable exchange controls that accompany such inflation, real doubt exists that such profits should really be considered profits to U.S. shareholders.
>
> Some of the entries in consolidated financial statements made to reflect minority interests are so esoteric as to create strong doubt that the public is aware of their nature. Suppose, for example, a multinational company with wholly owned subsidiaries bows to the pressures being exerted by Mexico and sells shares in its Mexican subsidiary to Mexican nationals. Suppose, further, these shares are additional shares used to finance expansion of the Mexican business, not unlikely since a government enacting this kind of requirement is hardly thinking of sending investors' money to the U.S. Presumably, such shares would be sold at their market value, not at the lower book value of the existing shares. We can guess that not even knowledgeable investors are aware that such a transaction, by which the parent company shareholders merely maintain the value of their investment, results in a book profit when the new book value of the Mexican company is apportioned between the majority and minority shareholders. Nor is it rational that increasing the size of an organization with no return to the shareholders results in a book profit in their financial statements.[5]

In a similar vein, when the Financial Accounting Standards Board (FASB) requested comments on its initial group of Financial Accounting

---

[4] B. S. Neuhausen, "Consolidation and the Equity Method—Time for an Overhaul," *Journal of Accountancy*, February 1982, pp. 54ff.

[5] H. P. Hill, "Rational Expectations and Accounting Principles," *Journal of Accountancy*, April 1982, p. 44.

Standards, Touche Ross & Co. developed a list of ten consolidation-related problems. In question form, this list may be summarized as follows:

1. To what extent should nonhomogeneous, foreign or special-risk subsidiaries and/or affiliates be included in consolidations—especially finance subsidiaries which might be instrumental in off–balance sheet financing possibilities if they are excluded from consolidations?
2. Under what conditions are combined financial statements preferable to consolidated financial statements?
3. Are all transactions between or among related intercorporate parties "tainted" (i.e., to be eliminated in consolidation), even if the relationship is distant, uncontrolled, and the transactions economically reasonable?
4. Why is it that when a parent company sells some of its investment in an investee, there results a gain or loss; when the investee sells some of its stock (resulting in the same proportionate change in ownership of the investor), it is strictly a capital transaction?
5. Under what conditions is it reasonable to prepare and publish parent company financial statements separate from (or in addition to) consolidated financial statements?
6. How should one account for stock dividends issued by controlled subsidiaries?
7. Is it economically defensible to eliminate intercompany profit in proportion to legal ownership?
8. Should accounting recognition be accorded to some state laws which do not recognize equity method accounting [see next section] and thereby limit dividend distributions arising from equity method-based retained earnings?
9. Is it appropriate to "push down" some parent company costs into the financial statements of subsidiaries when the latter prepare separate financial statements?
10. If substantially all of the minority interest in a subsidiary is represented by outstanding nonconvertible preferred stock, should the related preferred dividend be classified as interest expense in consolidated financial statements?[6]

The foregoing enumeration of problems is simply illustrative of the stormy weather in which consolidation accounting finds itself internationally.

The equity method debacle.   Accounting Principles Board Opinion No. 18 stipulates equity method accounting in the United States. It applies to common stock investments in domestic and foreign unconsolidated subsidiaries and corporate joint ventures. Typically, equity method accounting is appropriate when the investor parent company has the ability to exercise significant influence over the operating and financial policies of other entities in which it has an ownership interest of 20 percent or more. Where the ownership interest exceeds 50 percent, equity method accounting cannot be substituted for consolidation procedures when the latter are appropriate.

Under equity method accounting, the consolidated net income of the in-

[6] Touche Ross & Co., "ARB 51—Consolidated Financial Statements," *Open Line*, A Letter to Accounting Educators, February 1979.

vestor company includes the proportionate share of any net income or loss reported by unconsolidated (but influenced!) subsidiaries or affiliates for periods subsequent to acquisition. The effect of this treatment is that the parent company's net income for any period and stockholders' equity at the end of the period are reported as though consolidation had occurred. Dividends received by the parent company are treated as reductions of the Investments in Subsidiaries and Affiliates account.

By way of an example, assume that on December 31, 19X4, PAM Corporation acquired 40 percent of the outstanding common stock of MAP Corporation for $5 million. The acquisition occurred at book value. The following entry is made to record it on PAM Corporation's books:

	DR	CR
12/31/X4 Investment in MAP Corporation	$5,000,000	
Cash (or Payables)		$5,000,000
(To record intercorporate investment in MAP Corporation—40 percent ownership.)		

On December 31, 19X5, MAP Corporation reports $1.5 million of net income after taxes. Using the equity method of accounting, PAM Corporation recognizes its share in MAP's net earnings as follows:

	DR	CR
12/31/X5 Investment in MAP Corporation	$600,000	
Investment Income		$600,000
(To record 40 percent of MAP Corporation's net income after taxes for 19X5.)		

Later on, effective March 15, 19X6, MAP Corporation declares a $500,-000 cash dividend. Receipt of 40 percent of it is recorded on PAM Corporation's books as follows:

	DR	CR
4/1/X6 Cash	$200,000	
Investment in MAP Corporation		$200,000
(To record receipt of company's share of cash dividend paid by MAP Corporation.)		

In West Germany, the equity method is effectively disallowed by statute. In most other Continental countries it is tolerated but seldom used. The French method of application involves calculation of proportionate shares of net assets of an investee. This, in effect, excludes any elements of goodwill from equity method recognition. Effective dates for mandated use of the equity method in consolidated financial statements are postponed again and again in Japan. The most recent effective date published is April 1, 1983.

Application of the equity method sometimes causes consternation. Jardine Matheson and Hongkong Land report that each company exercises significant management control over the other.

> When a matter is to be discussed which affects both companies, such as dividend policy, each board meets separately to formulate its policy. A joint meeting is then held at which the final decision is taken and, given the overlap in board representation, each company can be said to be exerting an influence over the other.[7]

Each of the two companies owns 40 percent of the other. Since both employ equity method accounting, Hongkong Land gets, let us say, 40 percent of the earnings of Jardine Matheson into its financial statements but then "gives back" 40 percent of the consolidated total to Hongkong. The financial press in Hong Kong alluded to the situation as "trying to find the final reflection in a room full of mirrors." Obviously, crossholdings are a major unresolved equity accounting issue.

An illustration from B. F. Neuhausen indicates how a 50-50 joint venture can produce significantly different results depending upon whether the equity method or the proportionate consolidation method is used. Exhibit 6.1 reprints Neuhausen's illustration of the point.

Your authors favor the continued employment of the equity method of accounting although with significantly greater policy guidance on this matter, especially regarding international applications. At the time of this writing the FASB has placed the subject of financial statement consolidation on its active agenda.

Limits of MNC entities.   The earlier quote from Professor Hill's 1982 article makes the point that consolidated financial statements of MNCs are such a conglomeration of restatements, translations, adjustments, eliminations, and allocations that the economic reality of these statements has become a question of considerable substance. Procedures appropriate for domestic consolidations are conceivably inappropriate for multinational consolidations. In the international realm far-flung operations are likely to be subject to highly diverse economic risks, dissimilar national rates of inflation, differential legal constraints, dissimilar public controls and policies and a host of other such factors. This has prompted some observers to question outright the rationality of single consolidation of heterogeneous multinational operations. Others feel that multiple subconsolidations might be appropriate—for example, by reporting financial positions and results of operations in multiple-column format according to economic risk classifications. There is also the possibility that translation of all functional currencies into a single reporting currency may be misleading. At the present state of the art, mammoth multinational consolidations of financial statements are at best precarious.

One reason for the existing turmoil surrounding MNC consolidations is the absence of a clear concept of what constitutes a multinational business en-

---

[7] Lawrence Foulds, "Equity Accounting Footnote," *World Accounting Report*, November 1981, p. 16.

EXHIBIT 6.1   Accounting Effects of Different Forms of Organization for Joint Ventures

Assume that two oil companies desire to share equally in a new refinery. One option is to establish a corporate joint venture to construct and operate the refinery, with each company owning 50 percent of the stock and entitled to use 50 percent of the refinery's capacity. Another option is to establish a 50/50 partnership to construct and operate the refinery, with each partner entitled to use 50 percent of the refinery's capacity. The investment in the corporate joint venture must be accounted for by the equity method, while the investment in the partnership could be accounted for either by the equity method or by proportionate consolidation. If the refinery costs $500 million, financed by $200 million in cash from the venturers and by $300 million in loans to the joint venture, the balance sheets of the venturers would be affected as follows (000's omitted):

	Venturer's balance sheet*		
	Before joint venture	Equity[a] method	Proportionate[b] consolidation
Current assets	$ 450	$ 350	$ 350
Property, plant and equipment	550	550	800
Investment in joint venture	—	100	—
	$1,000	$1,000	$1,150
Current liabilities	$ 280	$ 280	$ 280
Long-term debt	240	240	390
Stockholders' equity	480	480	480
	$1,000	$1,000	$1,150

*An illustration of the effect on the income statement would require additional assumptions and is, therefore, omitted for simplicity.

[a Reduce cash by $100,000 and increase investment by like amount: nonconsolidation option.

b Reduce cash by $100,000, increase long-term debt by $150,000 and increase PP&E by $250,000: consolidation option.–Ed.]

The economic substance of the two options is similar—each venturer has use of 50 percent of the new refinery's capacity. The difference in legal form does affect the rights and obligations of the parties: partners bear unlimited liability, while stockholders' liabilities are limited to the amount of their investment. That difference may be more theoretical than real, however, because in arrangements of this type shareholders usually directly or indirectly guarantee debt of a corporate joint venture, and the shareholders might have equitable or moral obligations to satisfy liabilities of their corporate joint venture. The key question is whether the difference in the balance sheet (and income statement) is warranted.

B. F. Neuhausen, "Consolidation and the Equity Method—Time for an Overhaul," *Journal of Accountancy*, February 1982, p. 60.

tity. Do host country interests and controls extend far enough to invalidate the possibility of a single homogeneous worldwide business entity? To what limits can one reasonably push the notion of a single unique reporting currency to cover any and all events and transactions? If accounting standards and practices influence management decisions, how realistic is it to restate summary data prepared on the basis of one set of accounting rules to an arbitrarily selected different set, and retain the original information content of the data? At the present stage of international accounting development, we barely know what questions to ask about MNC consolidations, let alone conduct appropriate research or proposing approaches to possible resolutions of the perceived dilemmas!

Conceived, in part at least, out of frustration about the shortcomings of present MNC consolidation practices, the Commission of the European Economic Community (EEC) published, on April 29, 1976, a first draft of a proposed directive on consolidated financial statements (see also the related portions of Chapter 12). The draft encountered substantial opposition and was finally adopted as the EEC's *Seventh Council Directive* on June 13, 1983. Due to its controversial nature, the full implementation of the Directive by the EEC member states may be delayed until 1990.

Among many other provisions, the Seventh EEC Directive requires consolidation when "dominant influence" is present, irrespective of the degree of legal ownership. For example, an undertaking exercises "dominant influence" if it can appoint more than half of the members of another undertaking's supervisory body pursuant to contract.

Still more at variance with present practices is the member state option for horizontal consolidation of all entities operating within the EEC subject to a determined "dominant influence." For most MNCs this would mean at least one subconsolidation on a geographic basis. Such subconsolidation might include not only incorporated enterprises, but also partnerships, joint ventures, or other forms of business organization. If nothing else, the Directive has triggered major discussions of likely goals for multinational consolidations and techniques appropriate to such goals.

Major changes loom on the horizon of multinational financial statement consolidations. Only the timing of such changes remains an open question.

Business Combinations

Accounting for business combinations, or mergers, is among the thornier issues of the international accounting scene. In the business community the "urge to merge" shows no signs of abatement even though divestitures, spinoffs, and sell-offs also seem to occur with increasing frequency. One question is whether permissive accounting practices have actually fostered otherwise unattractive mergers. Another question is whether particular merger accounting rules give certain domicile companies competitive advantages over companies domiciled elsewhere and subject to different rules. There is also the issue of "representational faithfulness," which is one of the qualitative characteristics of accounting information called for in the FASB's *Statement of Financial Accounting Concepts No. 2.* Has merger accounting, internationally, become so creative that it no longer represents attendant economic realities?

The accounting substance of the issues surrounding business combinations concerns (a) how balance sheet items should be recognized subsequent to a merger, (b) whether goodwill recognition should be a part of merger accounting, and (c) whether merger activities should produce accounting effects upon subsequent income statements of the combined entities. Pooling of interest methodology combines items at existing book values and thereby avoids goodwill recognition and effects upon income measurements during subsequent accounting periods. As stated in Chapter 3, pooling of interest is seldom found outside the United States.

The purchase and the new entity methods (see descriptions below) restate assets and liabilities at the time of a merger to their respective fair market values and thereby create accounting "differences" (i.e., "purchased" goodwill). This goodwill may either be written off directly to stockholders' equity or amortized into income statements of subsequent periods. The larger the differences between total consideration offered in a business combination and *book values,* the larger are differential accounting effects.

Three accounting alternatives.   In September 1981, the IASC issued its Exposure Draft No. 22 dealing with the subject. The three alternative practice methods allowed by No. 22 were characterized by *World Accounting Report* as follows:

1. THE PURCHASE METHOD

Identifiable assets to be restated to their assigned values at the date of acquisition.

Goodwill representing primarily a payment in anticipation of future income to be amortised systematically over its useful life.

Negative goodwill representing an expectation of future losses to be held as deferred income and released to income over the period of anticipated losses.

Negative goodwill representing a bargain purchase may be allocated to individual monetary assets in proportion to their fair values.

When purchase consideration is mainly securities and there is evidence that goodwill is neither a result of a bargain purchase nor an expectation of profits or losses, it may be adjusted against shareholders' funds immediately.

The consideration should include any noncash element at fair value.

The acquirer's direct purchase expenses to be included in the acquisition cost.

Further rules governing additional payments that are contingent on future events.

2. THE POOLING OF INTEREST METHOD

The assets and liabilities of combining companies and the revenue and expenses to be simply added together as if combined from start of period.

Comparatives to be similarly restated.

Direct costs of pooling to be written off immediately.

3. THE NEW ENTITY METHOD

>   Individual assets and liabilities of combining companies to be restated to their fair values at the date of combination.

>   Direct costs of combining to be written off immediately.[8]

On the pooling of interest method, the only minimum criteria laid down for its acceptance are (1) the underlying business combination should represent a realistic "uniting of interests," and (2) the basis of the transaction should be an exchange of common voting stock. These criteria are much softer than, for instance, the 1971 U.K. proposal (never ratified!), which would have allowed the pooling of interests alternative only if (1) the substance of the main businesses of the constituent companies continued, (2) the voting rights of the amalgamated undertaking not give any of the former companies more than three times the power of any of the others, (3) 90 percent of the offer be in shares with identical voting rights to those of the shares replaced, and (4) the offer to combine had been accepted by holders of at least 90 percent of the total equity capital.

In the United States, Accounting Principles Board Opinion No. 16 spells out even more specific conditions necessary for a pooling of interests. Examples of applicable criteria are (1) the parties to a combination may not have investments greater than 10 percent in one another, nor may they be owned or majority controlled by another corporation, (2) there can be no significant distributions, within two years of an effective merger date, to stockholders of the separate companies or the resultant combined entity, (3) an issuing company may exchange only its voting common stock for 90 percent or more of the voting common stock of a combining company, (4) the exchange ratio between the common voting stocks affected must be known, (5) consumation of the combination must occur as a single transaction or plan within one year of initiation, (6) the combination must be fully resolved at consumation, that is, when the exchange of shares takes place, and (7) there must be an absence of negating future transactions, that is, conversion of exchange shares into cash. Under the authoritative rules in the United States, if any of the 12 conditions specified for pooling of interests treatment cannot be met, the merger must be treated as a purchase.

Illustration.   Assume the balance sheets shown in Table 6.1 for July 1, 19X4, the date of a proposed business combination between entities R, S, and T.

Now assume:

   (a)   T company pools R and S Companies and issues $2,500 new common stock to the former owners of R and S Companies. Under this approach, the book values of assets and liabilities of all three companies stay intact.

   (b)   T Company "purchases" R and S Companies by assuming all of their existing liabilities at fair market values and issuing $10,000 worth of additional

---

[8] Peter Mantle, "IASC Acts on Merger Accounting," *World Accounting Report*, September 1981, p. 11.

TABLE 6.1   Balance Sheets of Combining Companies

ITEM	R COMPANY Book amounts	R COMPANY Fair market values	S COMPANY Book amounts	S COMPANY Fair market values	T COMPANY Book amounts	T COMPANY Fair market values
Cash	$ 500	$ 500	$ 50	$ 50	$ 600	$ 500
Accounts receivable (net)	800	750	200	250	1,400	1,500
Inventories	1,200	1,750	2,450	3,700	3,000	2,500
Plant & properties	2,500	4,000	3,300	4,000	4,000	3,500
Total assets	$5,000	$7,000	$6,000	$8,000	$9,000	$8,000
Accounts payable	$ 500	$ 800	$1,000	$1,000	$ 500	$ 500
Accrued expenses	0	700	500	300	0	500
Long-term debt	2,000	2,000	2,500	2,200	3,000	3,000
Common stock	1,000	—	1,200	—	2,500	—
Retained earnings	1,500	—	800	—	3,000	—
Total liabilities & owners' equity	$5,000		$6,000		$9,000	

common stock. Here the assets of R and S Companies are conveyed at their respective fair market values.

(c)   A new entity, RST Company, is created. All assets and liabilities are carried at their respective fair market values and new common stock in the amount of $10,000 is issued.

The resulting balance sheets are shown in Table 6.2.

Even though the illustration in Tables 6.1 and 6.2 is quite simplified and abbreviated, it puts into focus the differential effects of the three alternatives available to account for business combinations.

Practice patterns.   In 1981, Professor Misako Nakagawa published "A Comparative Study of Merger Accounting Systems in Eleven Countries."[9] He concluded that three different patterns prevail, namely:

1.   British-American
2.   French
3.   West German

The British-American system is a mixed system that includes other English-speaking countries as well. Constrained by its case law, this system utilizes predominately purchase method accounting and tolerates pooling of interests accounting under carefully specified conditions.

The French pattern, also found in Brazil, conceives mergers narrowly. Here, one or more companies transfer their assets and liabilities as a whole to

[9] Misako Nakagawa, "A Comparative Study of Merger Accounting Systems in Eleven Countries," *Kanto Gakuin University Economic Review*, March 1981, pp. 1–9.

another and go into dissolution. The transfer may also be to a newly established company. Hence, mergers involve liquidation procedures and "contributions in kind" to a new enterprise. Appraisers are appointed to determine current market values of assets transferred. While this procedure is similar to purchase method accounting, the dissolution, or liquidation aspect, is absent from the latter. French companies sometimes use the merger routine to achieve asset write-ups occasioned by inflation effects.

Professor Nakagawa found the German pattern comparable to those prevailing in Argentina, Japan, Mexico, Spain, and Switzerland, among others. While the pattern is similar to British-American purchase accounting, it is based on legal rather than economic considerations. A concept of union of de juris entities is applied. While mandatory valuation provisions do not exist, the overriding consideration appears to be that all items for the surviving entity be valued on an internally consistent and comparable basis. "It seems that the *sine qua non* of the union of juristic persons theory is to evaluate the assets of all the constituents on the same basis, whether at their book values or at their current values, and that all other matters are considered incidental."[10] Special rules about legal and other reserves prevail, as well as amounts available for eventual distributions to shareholders. Goodwill is redetermined in German accounting practice at each successive financial statement date. Hence the question of goodwill amortization is moot.

From a perspective of natural sovereignty and other political considerations, it is likely that various acceptable methods of accounting for business

TABLE 6.2   Balance Sheets After Combination

	MERGER METHOD		
ITEM	Pooling: T Company Survives (a)	Purchase by T Company (b)	New Entity: RST Company (c)
Cash	$ 1,150	$ 1,150	$ 1,050
Accounts receivable (net)	2,400	2,400	2,500
Inventories	6,650	8,450	7,950
Plant & properties	9,800	12,000	11,500
Goodwill	0	2,000	0
Total assets	$20,000	$26,000	$23,000
Accounts payable	$ 2,000	$ 2,300	$ 2,300
Accrued expenses	500	1,000	1,500
Long-term debt	7,500	7,200	7,200
Common stock	5,000	12,500	10,000
Paid-in capital	0	0	2,000
Retained earnings	5,000	3,000	0
Total liabilities & owners' equity	$20,000	$26,000	$23,000

[10] Ibid., p. 4.

combinations will exist side by side for some time to come. The economic effects-based purchase method has the support of your authors.

Pensions

Accounting for the cost of pension plans is another international problem of sizable dimensions. At the time of this writing, all accounting standard-setting bodies around the world have this topic under active consideration. While Table 3.2 reports that in each of the ten countries covered company pension fund contributions are provided regularly, there is considerable diversity in the measurement and reporting of these contributions. There are problems with determining and assigning to individual periods the costs of past services covered and changes in pension agreements. Equally difficult is the question of how contingent pension liabilities ought to be reported. Again, referring to Table 3.2, nine of the ten countries exclude pension fund assets and liabilities from their regular financial statements. Yet compound interest accumulation rates assumed for pension fund assets significantly affect estimates of future sizes of these funds and thereby levels of current company pension contributions. The later point was illustrated succinctly in an article entitled "Pension Accounting Magic."[11] For example, by changing its assumed interest accumulation rate (for reporting purposes) from 7 percent in 1979 to 10 percent in 1980, U.S. Steel Corporation cut its $1 billion reported 1979 pension liability to zero for 1980. Similarly, Ford Motor Company changed its respective rates from 6 percent to 7 percent and likewise decreased its reported pension liability from $1.92 billion in 1979 to zero for 1980.

The essence of the problem was outlined by the FASB in its 1980 background paper *Accounting for Pensions by Employers*. The four key considerations identified are:

1. What is the employer's obligation related to pensions? What portion, if any, of that obligation should be recognized as a liability?
2. How should that obligation be related to accounting periods in determining periodic pension costs?
3. What measurement methods and assumptions are most appropriate for estimating those obligations and periodic pension costs?
4. How should the unique accounting problems of multiemployer plans be dealt with?[12]

One view from the United Kingdom is that "A central problem in the field of pensions is that it is already very much the preserve of another group of professionals—the actuaries."[13] Actuaries, it is said, have the luxury of great flexibility and subjectivity in the judgments they make. Their assumptions ad-

---

[11] Arlene Hershman with G. Bruce Knecht, "Pension Accounting Magic," *Dun's Review,* May 1981, pp. 78, 80, 82.

[12] Financial Accounting Standards Board, *Accounting for Pensions by Employers,* A Background Paper (Stamford, Conn.: FASB, 1980), p. 8.

[13] Barry Riley, "Pension Accounting: The Tricky Path Ahead," *World Accounting Report,* February 1982, p. 20.

dress such items as probable returns on pension fund assets, mortality rates among persons covered in the plan, average retirement age, and the number of employees who will leave a company before retirement age. "Actuaries are reluctant to standardize these assumptions, arguing that circumstances can differ substantially from company to company. But it is apparent that by choosing a stronger or a weaker basis of valuation the actuary can come to widely differing conclusions about the adequacy of contributions."[14]

Accountants, on the other hand, are required to treat pension costs consistently from period to period and allocate the actual cost of retirement benefits over the working life of an employee. Are unfunded pension contributions riskier pension fund assets than, let us say, those portions invested in real properties? How should special pension contributions be accounted for? Should there be a possibility of a "pension contribution holiday" in circumstances in which a company may experience temporary financial difficulties even though its pension plans are comfortably funded? Should companies be allowed to smooth their reported income by manipulating pension contributions? And how should all this be disclosed in financial statements?

A view from North America was expressed in a 1982 speech by the Chairman of Price Waterhouse USA, Joseph E. Connor, delivered to the Machinery and Allied Products Institute. Here are three relevant paragraphs:

> Fitting pensions into the traditional accrual accounting system is no easy task. Conceptual issues tend to become confused with measurement difficulties. Legal implications, actuarial concepts, and the proper influence of financial practice need to be considered in charting a sound accounting course in the pension environment.
>
> There is basic disagreement on whether a promise to pay pensions to employees at some far-off future date creates a present liability—which ought to be recorded—or a present contingency—which need not be. If there is a present liability, is it discharged by remitting the annual contribution to a trusteed plan or only when present employees receive the promised pensions? Who owns the burgeoning billions of dollars in assets resting in the pension funds established by U.S. companies? The possibility that the Board may find a conceptual basis for loading these assets into the balance sheets of the plan sponsors as an offset for the pension liability accumulated to date is still a mere straw in the wind. But neither can that possibility be arbitrarily dismissed.
>
> My view is that pensions are a form of compensation, the cost of which should be allocated to the periods in which services are rendered. Past service costs arising on initial plan adoption and plan changes creating increased benefits should be accounted for prospectively—as they generally are now. Under this approach, the balance sheet pension liability includes only cumulative pension expenses, together with interest equivalents, less amounts contributed to the plan.[15]

Mr. Connor's assessment proved to be prophetic. In November 1982, the FASB issued its *Preliminary Views on Employers' Accounting for Pensions and Other Postemployment Benefits.* Exhibit 6.2 provides an illustration of the proposed balance sheet effects.

[14] Ibid.

[15] Joseph E. Connor, *Building a Better World of Financial Reporting,* Brochure (New York: Price Waterhouse & Co., 1982), p. 6.

EXHIBIT 6.2

ABC Company Balance Sheet,
December 31, 19X5
(in Millions)

Assets		Liabilities & Owners' Equity	
Cash	$100	Accounts Payable	$150
Receivables	200	Net Pension Liability (See Note)	190
Deferred Pension Plan Cost	50	Long-term Debt	100
Property, Plant, and Equipment	210	Stockholders' Equity	120
Total	$560	Total	$560

Note to Financial Statements:

Pensión benefit obligation	$300
Pension plan assets	−100
Measurement valuation allowance	− 10
Net pension liability	$190

The *deferred pension cost* is an intangible asset representing expected economic benefits to be realized by the employer as a result of past plan amendments or the initiation of a plan. Presumably, an increased pension benefit obligation is incurred with the expectation that the employer will realize economic benefits in future periods. Those future economic benefits underlie the intangible asset which will be amortized by charges to periodic pension cost in future periods. Under the proposal, a plan amendment or initiation would not immediately change the amount of shareholders' equity.

The proposal specifies the use of a *single method* to measure the *pension liability* and the *amount of pension cost*. For plans that define benefits in terms of the employee's future salary (final-pay or career-average-pay plans), the pension benefit obligation would be measured by the actuarial present value of projected credited benefits, which recognizes estimated future salary levels.

Investments held by the pension plan would be carried at *fair value*. Any operating assets would be valued at cost less accumulated depreciation.

The *measurement valuation allowance* results from certain changes in the measures of the pension benefit obligation and plan assets. Measurement changes affecting the pension benefit obligation are experience gains and losses and effects of changes in actuarial assumptions. The measurement change affecting plan assets is the net appreciation or depreciation in fair value of investments (including both realized and unrealized gains and losses), to the extent that the change in fair value differs from the appreciation implicit in the assumed rate of return for the period. Measurement changes would be recognized prospectively—through amortization of the measurement valuation allowance—in measuring the net pension liability and periodic pension cost.

Amortization of both the measurement valuation allowance and the intangible asset would be computed each year by multiplying the unamortized balance at the end of the period by a percentage equal to 100 divided by the average remaining service period of active plan participants. For example, if the average remaining service period is 20 years, the amortization percentage would be 5%.

Adapted from Deloitte Haskins & Sells, *The Week in Review*, November 26, 1982.

The proposal in Exhibit 6.2 goes a long way toward resolving existing disparities—at least in the United States and if it is indeed eventually adopted. It might provide a basis for national and international standard setters to communicate with one another to the point of consensus on the actuarial cost method advanced. This will require compromise since unique conceptual solutions are clearly not obtainable in the pension area. Your authors agree with Mr. Connor, who concluded:

> The method established should require pension cost estimate calculations to include explicit assumptions as to expected change in plan benefits, including assumptions as to the effect of inflation. If original estimates include all appropriate types of assumptions, later changes in those estimates should create less distortion. . . . What we should hope for is a rational methodology which provides meaningful results in most, if not all, circumstances.[16]

Leases

Accounting for long-term financial leases is internationally as diverse as accounting for pension costs. However, there is a big difference between these two topics. In the pension area, underlying concepts, rationales and pragmatically useful practices, as well as appropriate reporting and disclosure techniques, are all largely unresolved. They represent, according to one report caption, a "tricky path ahead."

In the area of financial leases, there are few technical accounting aspects left to be resolved. Most interested parties appear to have a good general understanding of the issue and know the consequences of alternative treatments. The nucleus of the entire problem is whether one accounts for long-term financial lease transactions on the basis of their economic substance or their legal form. Slowly but surely, the substance over form preference is gaining support very much along lines of FAS No. 13 (issued in 1976) and IAS No. 17 (issued in 1982 and effective January 1, 1984). Belgium and Canada also have long-term financial lease capitalization requirements along these lines. Australia, the Netherlands, and the United Kingdom have exposure drafts of accounting standards covering financial lease capitalization in final stages of adoption.

To refresh readers' understanding of the mechanics of long-term financial lease capitalization, we offer below a brief review example. As with subsequent issues raised in the chapter (e.g., research and development, comprehensive income tax allocation), the numerical aspects involved do not have inherent international accounting dimensions. Individual application and policy-setting aspects, though, may be fully international in scope.

MicroReach Co., a Seattle company, leases some computing equipment from the Japanese Fuwa Corporation. It is a three-year noncancelable lease, and MicroReach guarantees a $5,000 residual value at the end of the lease term. Annual lease payments of $15,000 are made at the end of each year, and a 12 percent underlying interest rate has been negotiated.

The present value of this long-term financial lease is as follows:

[16] Ibid., pp. 6–7.

Present value of 3 yearly payments (12%)	$36,000
Present value of end-of-lease guarantee (12%)	3,560
Total lease asset and lease liability (MicroReach books)	$39,560

Selected balances of related accounts of MicroReach (the lessee) are shown in Table 6.3.

To convey some flavor of the requirements actually published in lease accounting standards, one illustrative paragraph is excerpted from each of the seven substantive sections of IAS No. 17 and reprinted immediately following (original paragraph numbers are retained):[17]

Accounting for Leases in the Financial Statements of Lessees

44. [*Finance Leases.*] A finance lease should be reflected in the balance sheet of a lessee by recording an asset and a liability at amounts equal at the inception of the lease to the fair value of the leased property net of grants and tax credits receivable by the lessor or, if lower, at the present value of the minimum lease payments. In calculating the present value of the minimum lease payments the discount factor is the interest rate implicit in the lease, if this is practicable to determine; if not, the lessee's incremental borrowing rate is used.

47. [*Operating Leases.*] The charge to income under an operating lease should be the rental expense for the accounting period, recognised on a systematic basis that is representative of the time pattern of the user's benefit.

Accounting for Leases in the Financial Statements of Lessors

48. [*Finance Leases.*] An asset held under a finance lease should be recorded in the balance sheet not as property, plant and equipment but as a receivable, at an amount equal to the net investment in the lease.

51. [*Operating Leases.*] Assets held for operating leases should be recorded as property, plant and equipment in the balance sheet of lessors.

Accounting for Sale and Leaseback Transactions

54. If a sale and leaseback transaction results in a finance lease, any excess of sales proceeds over the carrying amount should not be immediately recognised in income in the financial statements of a seller-lessee. If such an excess is recognised, it should be deferred and amortised over the lease term.

Disclosure

57. [*Disclosure in the Financial Statements of Lessees.*] Disclosure should be made of the amount of assets that are the subject of finance leases at each balance sheet date. Liabilities related to these leased assets should be shown separately from other liabilities, differentiating between the current and long-term portions.

60. [*Disclosures in the Financial Statements of Lessors.*] Disclosure should be made at each balance sheet date of the gross investment in leases reported as finance leases, and the related unearned finance income and unguaranteed residual values of leased assets.

[17] International Accounting Standards Committee, *Accounting for Leases,* IAS 17 (London IASC, 1982).

TABLE 6.3 Selected Balances of MicroReach Lease-Related Accounts

YEAR	LEASE LIABILITY (BEGINNING OF YEAR)	RENTAL PAYMENTS (END OF YEAR)	ANNUAL INTEREST EXPENSE (AT 12%)	ANNUAL LEASE EXPENSE "AMORTIZATION"	LEASE LIABILITY (END OF YEAR)
1	$39,560	$15,000	$ 4,760	$10,240	$29,320
2	29,320	15,000	3,530	11,470	17,850
3	17,850	15,000	2,150	12,850	5,000
		$45,000	$10,440	$34,560	

According to conference materials published in 1980 by Deloitte Haskins & Sells (Switzerland),[18] countries that tolerate lease capitalizations without mandatory requirements to that effect include Denmark, Germany, Japan, South Africa, Sweden, and Switzerland. Countries where lease capitalization is prohibited outright (i.e., those still insisting on a form over substance argument) include France, Italy, and Spain. In those countries capitalization is impossible until legal title to an asset has been acquired.

It is your authors' judgment that reasonably complete international harmonization of capitalization of long-term financial leases is merely a matter of time. Where national tax incentives favor the leasing of capital assets (e.g., Canada, the United Kingdom, and the United States), leasing activities will continue to flourish and homogeneous accounting treatment grow because there is simply no opposition to it. France, West Germany, and Japan also have large domestic leasing markets but less favorable tax treatments. Hence they are more likely to be attracted to leases as off–balance sheet financing devices and therefore less receptive to accounting capitalization. Of course, countries without significant leasing activities (e.g., many of the developing countries) really do not have much of a stake either way.

Probably the largest benefit from internationally harmonized lease accounting policies accrues from increased comparability among firms. Airlines, construction firms, shipping companies, computer service firms, real estate enterprises, and many other economic units now lease significant portions of their capital assets. To them, long-term financial leases are simply one of several different forms of acquiring the continual services of certain specific assets. Why should an airline that buys its flight equipment through long-term credit agreements show different financial ratios and different funds, earnings, liabilities and assets totals than a similar airline working with long-term flight equipment leases throughout?

FAS No. 13 mandates that "a lease that transfers substantially all of the benefits and risks incident to the ownership of property should be accounted for as the acquisition of an asset, and the incurrence of an obligation, by the lessee and as a sale or financing by the lessor."[19] Tell-tale criteria for lease capitalization are the following:

1. Ownership of the lease property transfers to the lessee at the end of the lease term.
2. The lessee has the option to purchase the property at a bargain price.
3. The term of the lease extends over 75 percent or more of the estimated useful life of the property.
4. The present value of the minimum lease payments totals at least 90 percent of the fair market value of the lease property.

Your authors agree with the foregoing definition and classification criteria. Barring unforeseen developments, long-term financial lease accounting is

[18] Deloitte Haskins & Sells, *Accounting for Leases Internationally* (Zürich/Geneva, 1980).

[19] Financial Accounting Standards Board, *Accounting Standards,* Vol. 2 (New York: McGraw-Hill, 1982), p. 29141.

likely to disappear in a few years from enumerations of critical international accounting issues.

Research and Development

The capacity to engage in effective pure or applied research and develop new products or services is limited. As industrialization proceeds, research and development (R & D) expenditures assume greater significance. Postindustrial society may well make R & D one of its major endeavors. The problem of accounting for research and development is contemporary, thoroughly international, and of increasing significance to accountants.

In the United States, FAS No. 2 (excerpted later in this section) makes the technical aspects of R & D accounting a relatively straightforward matter in that it mandates a current expensing approach with very few specified exceptions. It is the basic accounting measurement characteristic of *conservatism* which comes to play here. In general, a high degree of uncertainty attaches to most R & D activities with regard to identifying resulting future benefits. At the time R & D activities are performed, it is generally impossible to measure future success.

One of the best discussion papers on the topic is that of W. J. McGregor.[20]

He identifies five basic factors that require consideration and resolution in the determination of appropriate accounting measurement rules for R & D. These factors are as follows:

1. Activities to be identified as R & D for financial accounting and reporting purposes
2. Elements of costs to be identified with R & D activities
3. Accounting for R & D costs
4. Disclosures of R & D information in financial statements
5. Amortization of deferred R & D costs (if prior capitalization occurred)

While rigorous international comparisons are not available, it would appear that the nature of R & D costs from country to country are probably as homogeneous as any other category of costs. Thus it is surprising that different accounting standards setting bodies have arrived at different conclusions with regard to their recommendations in the face of very similar conceptual premises and underlying economic facts.

In the United States FAS No. 2 mandates that "all research and development costs encompassed by this statement shall be charged to expense when incurred."[21] The only exception to this requirement is "the costs of research

---

[20] W. J. McGregor, *Accounting for Research and Development Costs,* Discussion Paper No. 5 (Melbourne: Australian Accounting Research Foundation, 1980). See especially Chapter 4, "Analysis of the Basic Factors," and Chapter 5, "Analysis of Current Practice." A useful review of this monograph appeared in the January 1982 issue of *The Accounting Review.*

[21] Financial Accounting Standards Board, *Accounting Standards,* Vol. 2 (New York: McGraw-Hill, 1982), p. 38849.

and development activities conducted for others under a contractual arrangement."[22] Unique activities in the extractive industries are also excluded.

On the other hand, IAS No. 9 prescribes expensing of R & D costs except when

1. The product or process is clearly defined and the costs attributable to the product or process can be separately identified.
2. The technical feasibility of the product or process has been demonstrated.
3. The management of the enterprise indicated its intention to produce and market or use the product or process.
4. There is a clear indication of a future market for the product or process or, if it is to be used internally rather than sold, its usefulness to the enterprise can be demonstrated.
5. Adequate resources exist or are reasonably expected to be available to complete the project.[23]

In other words, the IASC recommendation allows significantly greater amounts of deferral than the FASB's counterpart.

Statement of Standard Accounting Practice No. 13 (SSAP No. 13), (1977) is the relevant recommendation of the Accounting Standards Committee in Great Britain. It adopted a compromise position between the two foregoing extremes by suggesting, on grounds of the matching principle, that costs of development of new and improved products (clearly identifiable, separable expenditures, technical feasibility and commercial liability) may be deferred.

Australian practice parallels British practice. The former is based on AAS No. 9 (1972) entitled "Expenditure Carried Forward to Subsequent Accounting Periods."

When it comes to actual corporate reporting practices, most major corporations worldwide appear to expense their R & D costs currently and disclose both this policy and the cost classifications affected. Judging from available surveys of corporate financial reporting practices, probably 95 percent of all publicly reporting companies fall into the "expense R & D immediately" column. In the limited cases where R & D costs are capitalized, specific amortization rules apply—for example, the maximum of five years in Germany.

IAS No. 9 includes the following list as to the nature of R & D costs:

1. The salaries, wages, and other related costs of personnel engaged in research and development activities.
2. The costs of materials and services consumed in research and development activities.
3. The depreciation of equipment and facilities to the extent that they are used for research and development activities.
4. Overhead costs related to research and development activities

---

[22] Ibid., p. 38847.

[23] International Accounting Standards Committee, *Accounting for Research and Development Activities,* IAS 9 (London: IASC, 1978), para. 17.

5. Other costs related to research and development activities such as the amortization of patents and licenses.[24]

If R & D costs are as comprehensively defined as just enumerated, there is at least a conceptual question whether all such costs should be expensed in the periods incurred regardless of any future benefit considerations. Your authors view the IASC recommendation as the most realistic in economic terms and the most defensible conceptually. But additional cost-benefit analyses must be undertaken, additional cause-and-effect relationships identified, and potential implementation problems analyzed before one could urge the IASC solution upon all other standard setters worldwide.

Taxes on Income

Worldwide accounting for taxes on income is in disarray. Major British-American multinational companies have received qualified opinions from their joint U.K.-U.S. independent auditors on consolidated financial statements since comprehensive income tax allocation standards in the United Kingdom and the United States are contradictory. The most common practice worldwide is still the traditional taxes payable method, that is, recognition of a current liability for actual taxes estimated to be currently payable. Increasingly though, tax effect accounting is advocated and adopted into practice. Of the 62 countries covered in the 1979 international survey by Price Waterhouse International,[25] the taxes payable method (flow through method) is common practice in 46 countries and tax effect accounting characterizes 14 countries.

When it comes to tax effect accounting, one can either employ the deferral (U.S. APB No. 11) or the liability (U.K. SSAP No. 15) method. The difference between these two approaches often is substantial. A brief numerical example illustrates the point.

In the United Kingdom, The BOC Group reported data shown in Table 6.4 in its annual report for 1981.

As it stands, the deferred tax "liability" of the BOC Group on September 30, 1981 was 2.8 percent of total common shareholders' equity at the same date. If U.S. accounting standards had been employed (i.e., all potential future tax liabilities recognized), this percentage would have been 17.1 percent. A significant difference indeed!

TABLE 6.4   BOC Group Deferred Tax Liability (£ millions)

1981 provision for tax on a full deferred tax basis	£	39.9
Deferred tax not payable in the foreseeable future		(2.3)
1981 provision for tax used in profit & loss account	£	37.6
Total common shareholders' equity, September 30, 1981	£	784.6
Deferred tax, September 30, 1981	£	22.1
Total potential deferred tax, September 30, 1981	£	133.9

---

[24] Ibid., para. 15.

[25] R. D. Fitzgerald, A. D. Stickler, and T. R. Watts, eds., *International Survey of Accounting and Reporting Practices* (Scarborough, Ont., Canada: PWI, 1979).

Both the full deferral and the foreseeable future liability methods are sanctioned in IAS No. 12, the effective date of which was January 1, 1981. The first six paragraphs of the standard read as follows:

> The tax expense for the period should be included in the determination of net income of the enterprise.
>
> The taxes on income relating to an item that is charged or credited to shareholders' interests should be accounted for in the same manner as the relevant item and the amount should be disclosed.
>
> The tax expense for the period should be determined on the basis of tax effect accounting, using either the deferral or the liability method. The method used should be disclosed.
>
> The tax effect accounting method used should normally be applied to all timing differences. However, the tax expense for the period may exclude the tax effects of certain timing differences when there is reasonable evidence that these timing differences will not reverse for some considerable period (at least three years) ahead. There should also be no indication that after this period these timing differences are likely to reverse. The amount of timing differences, both current and cumulative, not accounted for should be disclosed.
>
> The tax effect of timing differences that result in a debit balance or a debit to the deferred tax balance should not be carried forward unless there is a reasonable expectation of realisation.
>
> Deferred tax balances should be presented in the balance sheet of the enterprise separately from the shareholders' interests.[26]

As the use of tax effect accounting has gained momentum, sharp criticism of the method is also spreading. In the United States the companies included in the Dow Jones Industrial Index provided deferred taxes averaging 12 percent of their pretax income from continuing operations for 1981. Their balance sheets report deferred income tax amounts in the billions of dollars and these amounts are growing.

Another set of data is available for the Canadian scene. C. S. R. Drummond and Seymour L. Wigle surveyed the financial statements of 70 Canadian companies listed as the largest public companies by *The Financial Post* (Canada).[27] For these companies, deferred taxes as a percentage of shareholders' equity grew 85.9 percent from 1970 to 1980. The same percentage in terms of total assets grew 41.4 percent during the same period. In grouping the data by industries, real estate companies had 54.49 percent of their 1980 shareholders' equity equal to the reported deferred tax amount. Paper and publishing companies reported deferred taxes equal to 10.03 percent of their 1980 total assets. These deferred tax "liabilities" are so staggeringly large and growing at such a rate that the relative size and growth factors alone can be taken as an indication that not all is well with the respective financial accounting principle.

Of course there is also a flip side to the concern just expressed. Eight of the ten countries covered in Table 3.2 require tax effect accounting and have

---

[26] International Accounting Standards Committee, *Accounting for Taxes on Income,* IAS 12 (London: IASC, 1979), para. 40–45.

[27] C. S. R. Drummond and Seymour L. Wigle, "Let's Stop Taking Comprehensive Tax Allocations for Granted," *CA Magazine,* October 1981, pp. 56–61.

thereby institutionalized it. For instance, many regulated companies and many cost-plus contracts now recognize deferred taxes as a period expense. If tax effect accounting were abandoned, these companies would suffer severe negative economic consequences because they would have to redefine their costs of doing business and convince regulatory commissions and contracting agencies and officers that a fundamental shift would need to be made in calculating effective total costs of doing business.

The Canadian researchers referred to earlier assert that "comprehensive tax allocation contravenes both the going concern concept and the standard on the recognition of contingencies."[28] They further argue that the term *deferred credit* is a play on words with no real substance. Other authors have indicted tax effect accounting for its lack of economic reality, absence of conceptual logic, and flagrant inconsistency from a balance sheet perspective.

The present world state of accounting for income taxes is not good. Your authors support tax effect accounting when attendant events and circumstances make it reasonably certain that tax timing differences will affect the actual flow of funds in the foreseeable future. We do not condone unquestioned comprehensive tax allocation. It appears likely that IAS No. 12 will be among the first to experience a substantial revision by the IASC in due course.

Property Expropriations

The notion of sovereignty is difficult in modern political affairs. Traditionally, the term connoted the absolute independence of nation states. In other words, the sovereign country will not tolerate any jurisdiction from without. It cannot be forced to comply with anyone else's laws—even international laws as far as they exist.

Sovereignty allows for the possibility of property expropriation in the multinational business arena. Expropriation occurs when host governments seize foreign-owned properties. If foreign owners are not compensated for their former properties, expropriation turns into confiscation. Since host governments typically assume ownership of expropriated properties, one can also speak of such acts as "nationalization." Concepts and analysis of political risk measurement and management plus economic costs and other consequences of property expropriations are widely covered in the international business and political science literature.[29]

Accounting issues associated with expropriation are troublesome. When foreign assets are forced into ownership changes, it is normally difficult to determine the amount of the resulting economic effect. Book values, whether conventionally determined or, let us say, price level-adjusted, are notoriously poor indicators of current economic values. Since forced divestment is generally accompanied by a politically unstable situation, market or liquidation

---

[28] Ibid., p. 60.

[29] See, for example, David K. Eiteman and Arthur I. Stonehill, *Multinational Business Finance*, 3rd ed. (Reading, Mass.: Addison-Wesley, 1982), Chapter 8, "Political Risk Management," pp. 288–339.

values are difficult to estimate. Discounted future earnings are similarly precarious in these situations and, of course, comparisons with recent similar investments or replacement investments cannot be made since comparison situations are likely to be completely unavailable (forced divestment prospects eliminate or sharply reduce new direct foreign investments in the country concerned).

So how does one measure the amount or value of an expropriation? Most often, it has to occur on the basis of adjusted book values simply because of the very limited availability of any alternatives. Since book values of assets are a consequence of particular financial accounting policies selected and taxation methods applied, they may bear little or no relationship to the actual economic significance of the event. Estimates of expropriation losses are usually highly subjective.

An additional complication is introduced if it can be established that current economic values, at the time of the expropriation, were in excess of net book values. In such situations, should a gain be recognized on the premise that expropriation constituted a form of "realization"? If the real economic impact of an expropriation event is to be measured and financially reported, a prior adjustment of book values is quite likely to be needed and, therefore, a gain or loss recognition unavoidable.

Assume that a West German MNC has built a pharmaceutical laboratory in Nari to store, package, label, and market certain drugs, vitamins, health care products, and hospital supplies. The inventories and property, plant, and equipment totals on December 31, 19X6 are shown in Table 6.5.

Now assume that early in 19X7 a full-scale revolution occurs in Nari. The new revolutionary government summarily expropriates all foreign properties in Nari. The historical cost-based net book value of the lost laboratory is DM 18 million. Obviously the property had no current market value immediately prior to the revolution.

Since historical cost is the sole acceptable basis of accounting measurement in West Germany (see Chapter 5), the loss to be reported should be DM 18 million less any prior provisions set up to cover such contingencies. Had the company been a U.K. MNC using current cost accounting, it would have recognized a production capacity maintenance adjustment (i.e., current replacement cost—used) and an expropriation loss correspondingly higher.

Forced divestments or expropriations seldom have a "record date." Sometimes they can be linked to a political revolution, an election, or some

TABLE 6.5   Values Pertaining to Laboratory Assets (DM millions)

Historical cost	DM 30
Depreciation and amortization	12
Current replacement cost (new)	75
Current replacement cost (used)	60
Current market value	0
Current insured value (political revolution *not* covered)	80

other definite event. But takeover control over enterprise assets may come gradually or step by step. Should parent company managements have discretion about when to recognize an expropriation? Could such divestments be recognized piecemeal? How might one time recognition of loss if, for instance, a newly established foreign government issues its own long-term bonds in exchange for certain business assets and these bonds have zero current market value? These and other questions must be resolved in timing the accounting recognition of expropriation events. With respect to reporting of earnings, should expropriation losses (or gains) be shown among operating items? On the one hand, one can argue that wealth deprivations in other countries are a normal risk of multinational business and, therefore, should be anticipated with contingency reserves or similar other provisions regularly charged against multinational operations. On the other hand, one might argue that risk assessment in connection with future forced divestments is impossible and that their occurrence should be viewed more as a natural disaster or other outright loss. The latter view suggests treatment of such events as extraordinary gain or loss situations in the period of recognition.

In the United States expropriation losses must be reported net of any tax effects and classified as extraordinary items. Thus, in FASB terms, they are of a character "significantly different from the ordinary and typical activities of the enterprise" and they would not be "reasonably expected to recur in the foreseeable future."[30] Earnings per share data are therefore not affected by any expropriation losses.

The U.S. situation is unusual in that most other countries permit the treatment of expropriation losses as charges to equity reserves or direct write-offs to owners' equity. Hybrid practices are common internationally. Of special interest to financial statement users is the fact that external financial statements seldom disclose expropriations specifically and even less frequently disclose specific amounts of gains or losses. Footnote disclosure of expropriations is also rarely found.

Parenthetically we call attention to the fact that expropriations often impinge on a firm's overall profitability and future earning power, and may necessitate costly capacity or product substitutions and cause breaks in personnel, production, or marketing chains. Thus, indirect as well as direct costs are associated with expropriation activities.

With the internationally increasing frequency of property expropriations by host governments, accounting treatment in the extraordinary items category is difficult to defend. Treatment as direct (and typically material) losses seems more logical. Also, the general lack of adequate disclosure creates financial reporting reliability problems for multinational enterprises—whether they had expropriation losses in a given reporting period or not. The leadership of IASC in focusing attention on this international accounting issue would probably go a long way toward resolving it.

---

[30] Financial Accounting Standards Board, *Accounting Standards*, Vol. 2, Current Text as of June 1, 1982 (New York: McGraw-Hill, 1982), p. 24469.

Value Added

National income accounting has a long and consistent history of utilizing value-added measurements. Enterprise or business accounting, on the other hand, has traditionally relied on individual transaction measurements and thus shunned value-added thinking.

One origin of bringing a value-added dimension to corporate financial reporting is the latest (1965) German Corporations Act. While British-American income statements can be called "sales oriented," German income statements then introduced are "manufacturing oriented." This is accomplished by adding increases or decreases in inventories of finished and unfinished products as well as other expenses capitalized during a reporting period to net sales to come to a "total effort" or "total output" measure at the head of an income statement. All German companies subject to the 1965 Corporation Act report in this fashion.

More explicit recognition of value-added measuring and reporting by individual enterprises came with the 1975 publication of *The Corporate Report* in the United Kingdom.[31] This report unequivocally recommended publication of individual company statements of value-added performance. This recommendation was justified in the following terms:

> The simplest and most immediate way of putting profit into proper perspective vis-a-vis the whole enterprise as a collective effort by capital, management and employees is by presentation of a statement of value added. . . . It usefully elaborates on the profit and loss account and in time may come to be regarded as a preferable way of describing performance. . . .
>
> From value added must come wages, dividends and interest, taxes and funds for new investment. The interdependence of each is made more apparent by a statement of value added. . . . The statement of value added provides a useful measure to help in gauging performance and activity. The figure of value added can be a pointer to the net output of the firm, and by relating other key figures (for example, capital employed and employee costs) significant indicators of performance may be obtained.[32]

As of the date of this writing, individual enterprise value-added data are totally absent from the North American financial accounting and reporting scene.

Definitions and uses. Professors S. J. Gray and K. T. Maunders have produced a study which is, as far as your authors are aware, the most comprehensive research on the subject of value-added accounting to date.[33] For purposes of their study, they establish a working definition to the effect that the most usable and useful value-added representation for an enterprise and for a

---

[31] Accounting Standards (Steering) Committee, *The Corporate Report* (London: ASC, 1975).

[32] Ibid., pp. 49–50.

[33] S. J. Gray and K. T. Maunders, *Value Added Reporting: Uses and Measurements* (London: Association of Certified Accountants, 1980).

particular period is the difference between total output value (including but not necessarily limited to sales revenue) and corresponding input value (material and services obtained from other enterprises). The difference so determined is "net output" or value added. Naturally, adding factor payments to employees, providers of capital, and governments is another way of measuring "net output."

When it comes to uses of value-added reports or statements, Gray and Maunders hold unequivocally to the proposition that without testable hypotheses about how value-added information may be used, it is not possible to establish logically supportable measurement and reporting rules. After appropriate analysis they conclude that four direct uses can be attributed to value-added information:

1. For predicting "managerial efficiency"
2. For evaluating "relative equity among stakeholders within companies"
3. As an indicator of "ability to pay" in relation to productivity issues arising in collective bargaining negotiations
4. As a basis for evaluating the "social performance" of a company

The researchers, though much more tentatively, also postulate possible impacts on union and employee behavior and thereby indirect usefulness of value-added information for predicting expected earnings of a company and risks attaching to these.

Principles and practices.   Rather than paraphrase the major findings of the researchers, whose work we found particularly useful in the present context, we reproduce below a summary of their recommendations:

a. The measurement of value added on a production rather than a sales basis appears desirable and worthy of experiment.
b. Value added should be measured and disclosed on both a gross and net basis if it is to serve a wide range of uses. Depreciation should not be treated as a distribution of value added.
c. Inflation adjustments are necessary if net value added is to be meaningful.
d. Non-operating items should be disclosed separately below the calculation of value added. They should not be excluded from the value added statement. There is a pressing need for a more comprehensive and systematic approach to disclosure and presentation.
e. The segmentation of the value added statement is desirable and at the least should involve a geographical segmentation between the U.K. and overseas activities of the firm.
f. The disclosure of relative shares in the distribution of value added should be made on a more systematic basis. The share of employees and government should be disclosed on the basis of amounts actually payable. In the case of shareholders the amount of profit attributable, as well as payable in the form of dividends, should be disclosed as their share.[34]

[34] Ibid., p. 37.

EXHIBIT 6.3   Value-Added Statement Format

STATEMENT OF VALUE ADDED		
		£M
Turnover		XX
Bought-in materials and services		XX
Value added		XXX
Applied the following way		
to pay employees		
wages, pensions and fringe benefits		XX
To pay providers of capital		
interest on loans	X	
dividends to shareholders	X	XX
To pay government		
corporation Tax Payable		XX
To provide for maintenance and		
expansion of assets		
depreciation	X	
retained profits	X	
		XX
Value added		£XXX

Source: Accounting Standards (Steering) Committee, *The Corporate Report* (London: ASC,¹ 1975).

EXHIBIT 6.4   Swedish Value-Added Statement

STATEMENT OF GROUP VALUE ADDED (SEK millions)				
Calculation of value added		1981		1980
Sales and other operating income		4,765		4,268
Cost of operations, including wages and salary				
expenses		3,048		2,561
Value added		1,717		1,707
Distribution of value added				
To employees:				
Wages and salaries after tax deduction		471		438
To lenders:				
Costs of loans raised		220		203
To shareholders:				
Proposed dividend		102		91
To the national and municipal governments:				
Withholding tax and social service charges on				
behalf of employees	652		576	
Company tax on profit for the year	119	771	126	702
Retained within the business for consolidation				
and expansion		153		273
Total		1,717		1,707

Source: Stora Kopparbergs Bergslags AB, *Annual Report 1981*.

Actual value-added reporting practices are discussed in Chapter 7. We note here parenthetically that value-added statements are now required as a part of mandatory social responsibility reporting in France. Partial reference appears on West German income statements as described earlier. In all other instances value-added reporting is entirely voluntary. Recent surveys in the United Kingdom indicate that approximaely 25 percent of the listed companies included in *The Times One Thousand Survey* present value-added statements to the readers of their annual financial reports. Exhibit 6.3 shows the statement format suggested in the U.K. *Corporate Report.* Exhibit 6.4 portrays a recent reporting example from Sweden.

It is important to recognize that the value-added topic has both measurement and reporting dimensions like all topics treated in Chapters 4, 5, and 6. Its relative newness at the micro level of financial measurement and reporting prompted us to allocate space to the topic both in this chapter and the next. In this chapter the emphasis is on its measurement aspects with mere mention of reporting—mostly via a brief illustrative example. In the next chapter the topic is treated as a part of the larger social responsibility reporting issue, and illustrated more completely in that context.

SELECTED REFERENCES

BRADLEY, DAVID G., "Managing against Expropriation," *Harvard Business Review,* July-August 1977, pp. 75–83.

CHOI, FREDERICK D. S., *Multinational Accounting: A Research Framework for the Eighties,* Ann Arbor, Mich.: UMI Research Press, 1981, 248 pp.

DELOITTE HASKINS & SELLS (Switzerland), *Accounting for Leases Internationally,* Zurich/Geneva, 1980, 30 pp.

DRUMMOND, CHRISTINA S. R., and SEYMOUR L. WIGLE, "Let's Stop Taking Comprehensive Tax Allocation for Granted," *CA Magazine,* October 1981, pp. 56–61.

FINANCIAL ACCOUNTING STANDARDS BOARD, *Financial Reporting By Private and Small Public Companies,* Stamford, Conn.: FASB, 1981, 39 pp. (Invitation to Comment).

GIBSON, KEATH P., "Accounting for the Cost of Defined Benefit Pension Plans," *Financial Executive,* March 1981, pp. 36–43.

GRAY, S. J., and KEITH T. MAUNDERS, *Value Added Reporting: Uses and Measurement,* London: Association of Certified Accountants, 1980, 71 pp. (ACA Research Study).

JENSEN, A. W., and LARRY W. PAPERNICK, "Impact of the New Recommendations on Accounting for Leases," *CA Magazine,* April 1979, pp. 42–46.

KELLEY, THOMAS P., "Accounting Standards Overload—Time for Action?" *CPA Journal,* May 1982, pp. 10, 12–14, 16, 17.

McGREGOR, WARREN J., *Accounting for Research and Development Costs* (Discussion Paper No. 5), Melbourne: Australian Accounting Research Foundation, 1980, 97 pp.

MORLEY, MICHAEL F., "Value Added: The Fashionable Choice for Annual Reports and Incentive Schemes," *Accountant's Magazine* (Scotland), June 1979, pp. 234–236.

MULLER, MAARTEN H., "Compensation for Nationalization: A North-South Dialogue," *Columbia Journal of Transnational Law,* No. 1, 1981, pp. 35–78.

NAKAGAWA, MISAKO, "A Comparative Study of Merger Accounting Systems in 11 Countries," *Kanto Gakuin University Economic Review*, March 1981, pp. 1–9.
NEUHAUSEN, BENJAMIN S., "Consolidation and the Equity Method—Time for an Overhaul," *Journal of Accountancy*, February 1982, pp. 54–56, 59, 60, 62, 64, 66.
NOBES, CHRISTOPHER, and ROBERT PARKER, eds., *Comparative International Accounting*, Homewood, Ill.: Richard D. Irwin, Inc., 1981, 379 pp.
RILEY, BARRY, "Pension Accounting: The Tricky Path Ahead," *World Accounting Report*, February 1982, p. 20.
TROTMAN, KEN T., "An Evaluation of Accounting for Construction Contracts: An International Comparison," *International Journal of Accounting*, Spring 1982, pp. 151–166.
WALKER, R. G., "International Accounting Compromises: The Case of Consolidation Accounting," *Abacus*, December 1978, pp. 97–111.
WYLD, RICHARD, "Merger Accounting—Legally Dead, But Will It Lie Down?" *Accountancy*, August 1980, pp. 49–50.
YOSHIDA, HIROSHI, and KAZUTOYO SUMITA, *An Introduction to International Accounting*, Tokyo: Zeimukeiri Kyokai, 1982, 273 pp.

DISCUSSION QUESTIONS

1. The practice of consolidating the accounts of foreign subsidiaries, while varying from country to country, is on the increase. Three frequently mentioned rationales for consolidation are geographic location, degree of ownership, and homogeneity of business activities. Comment on the limitations of these consolidation criteria and suggest at least three alternative standards that might better facilitate a parent company's decision to include a foreign subsidiary in the consolidation process.

2. In their standard "Consolidated Financial Statements and the Equity Method of Accounting," the IASC recommends consolidation of all subsidiaries except "where control is likely to be temporary or where severe long-term restrictions on the transfer of funds jeopardize the parent's exercise of control." This provision, however, conflicts with the well-established U.S. practice that permits non-consolidation of banking, finance, and insurance subsidiaries. Which position do you support? What does the conflict imply about the objectives of consolidated financial statements?

3. Identify the three main accounting alternatives available for recognition of business combinations. Country by country, do existing practice patterns correspond to one or the other of the three distinguishable accounting approaches?

4. Why are companies generally reluctant to report the total of measurable future pension obligations and liabilities in their balance sheets? Analyze the differences and similarities between the FASB's proposed "net pension liability" and the customary U.S. "deferred taxes"?

5. Capitalization of long-term financial leases is sometimes referred to as "padding the balance sheet" of lessees. There is also the argument that long-term financial lease capitalization leads to double counting—the same item appearing on both lessors' and lessees'

books. Identify the underlying accounting concepts that support lease capitalization as discussed in the text.

6.   ''The question of what to include in or exclude from R & D costs is significantly more difficult than the accounting decision between expensing and capitalizing.'' Do you agree with this statement? Why or why not?

7.   The measurement of deferred tax liabilities differs significantly between the United Kingdom and the United States. This is illustrated by way of an example in the text. Assuming that some deferred tax recognition is desirable, which of the two approaches do you favor? Be prepared to defend the position you take on conceptual grounds.

8.   In the United States, several financial accounting standards involve a two-tiered measurement and reporting system which distinguishes between privately held companies and large public companies. In the international arena, the distinction is likely to come between MNCs and large uninational companies. Are the arguments pro and con the same for both situations? Is the question predominantly a measurement or a reporting issue?

9.   Develop a rationale for a petition to the IASC to place accounting measurement and reporting of property expropriation in nondomestic instances on its active agenda.

10.   Statements of Value-Added are becoming increasingly popular in U.K. financial reporting while they remain totally absent from the United States scene. Speculate on the reason(s) for this difference. What interest groups are likely to find such statements useful?

EXERCISES

1.   Company K, a U.S. parent company, makes a $2 million investment in 30 percent of the shares of the Swiss Q Company. Attendant circumstances are such that K Company uses the equity method of accounting to present this investment in its financial statements. A Swiss franc/U.S. dollar exchange rate of 2 to 1 is appropriate for all transactions in this exercise.
Required: Prepare accounting journal entries to present the following transactions and events concerning K Company:
A.   U.S. funds are transfered to make the investment.
B.   At the end of year 1, Q Company reports net income after taxes of 1 million Swiss francs based on Swiss accounting principles. Had U.S. accounting principles been used, the reported net income figure would have been SFR 1.5 million.
C.   During the ensuing year, Q Company suffered a major expropriation loss and reported a $10 million loss in terms of U.S. GAAP.
D.   Since Q Company has significant cash reserves, it pays a cash dividend of SFR 600,000 early in the following year.
E.   What is the balance in the Investment in Q Company account on K Company's books after transactions A to D? How should this

balance be reported in consolidated financial statements prepared shortly after transaction D?

2.   Refer to the RST Company example in the text section on business
     combinations. Assume that U Company has the balance shown in
     Table 6.6 on July 1, 19X4:

TABLE 6.6   Balance Sheet for U Company

ITEM	BOOK AMOUNTS	FAIR MARKET VALUES
Cash	$ 3,000	$ 3,000
Accounts receivable (net)	2,000	2,000
Inventories	1,500	1,500
Plant and properties	2,500	2,500
Total assets	$ 9,000	$ 9,000
Accounts payable	$ 500	$ 500
Accrued expenses	—	—
Long-term debt	1,000	1,000
Common stock	1,500	—
Retained earnings	6,000	—
Total liabilities & owners' equity	$ 9,000	—

Required: U Company together with R, S, and T Companies are
combining to form a new entity. This new entity issues common
stock with a par value of $15,000. Prepare the opening balance
sheet for the new entity.

EXHIBIT 6.5   Consolidated Balance Sheet of the Akzo Group

after allocation of profit (1981) and loss (1980)				
IN HFL MILLION	DECEMBER 31, 1981		DECEMBER 31, 1980	
noncurrent assets				
property, plant and				
equipment	3,673.4		3,440.4	
investments in non-				
consolidated com-				
panies	351.5		356.9	
other noncurrent				
assets	134.5		119.4	
		4,159.0		3,916.7
current assets				
inventories	2,506.5		2,454.8	
short-term receivables	2,570.4		2,288.9	
prepaid expenses	62.8		67.7	
cash and marketable				
securities	897.5		882.6	
		6,037.2		5,694.0
total assets		10,196.2		9,610.7

(continued)

EXHIBIT 6.5   (*continued*)

Group equity				
Akzo N.V. stockhold-ers' equity	2,448.7		2,266.2	
minority interest in Group equity	406.8		392.8	
		2,855.5		2,659.0
long-term liabilities				
provisions	1,335.1		1,328.7	
subordinated loans	75.0		25.0	
other long-term debt	2,715.2		2,716.8	
		4,125.3		4,070.5
current liabilities				
bank borrowings and overdrafts	613.2		573.7	
other current liabilities	2,602.2		2,307.5	
		3,215.4		2,881.2
total Group equity and lia-bilities		10,196.2		9,610.7

Provisions in respect of pension rights

Most Group companies have arranged appropriate pension plans for their employees, with due observance of the statutory regulations and customs in the countries concerned, including the computational methods and interest rates used. The ensuing liabilities and the required contributions and admission fees are generally computed on an actuarial basis.

The item salaries, wages and social charges in the consolidated statement of income includes Hfl 340 million (1980: Hfl 320 million) for pension expense.

At December 31, 1981, as at December 31, 1980, the present value of the pension benefits was on balance fully covered by:

—provisions, in the aggregate amount of Hfl 435 million (at December 31, 1980: Hfl 412 million), made by Group companies in their balance sheets;

—the funds accumulated in independent pension funds through payment of contributions.

3. Exhibit 6.5 is the actual consolidated balance sheet of the AKZO Group (headquartered in the Netherlands) as of December 31, 1981. The corresponding note on "Provisions in respect of pension rights" is also shown.
   Required: As far as you can determine from the information given, would the "net pension liability" as proposed by the U.S. FASB (see text section on pensions) be larger or smaller than reported for the AKZO Group on December 31, 1981?

4. Table 6.7 is an incomplete long-term financial lease amortization schedule similar to the one appearing in the text.
   Required: Complete the foregoing schedule by filling in the 14 blank spaces.

TABLE 6.7   Lease Amortization Schedule

YEAR	LEASE LIABILITY (BEGINNING OF YEAR)	RENTAL PAYMENT (END OF YEAR)	ANNUAL INTEREST EXPENSE (AT 12%)	ANNUAL LEASE EXPENSE "AMORTIZATION"	LEASE LIABILITY (END OF YEAR)
1	$95,025	$ 24,000	$ _____	$ _____	$82,428
2	$ _____	$ 24,000	$9,891	$ _____	$ _____
3	$ _____	$ 24,000	$ _____	$15,802	$52,518
4	$ _____	$ 24,000	$ _____	$ _____	$ _____
5	$34,821	$ 24,000	$ _____	$19,821	$15,000
		$120,000			

5.   Obtain a copy of the 1982 annual report of the IBM Corporation. *Required:* Prepare a statement of value added for IBM for 1982 as best you can from the data provided in the published annual report. Use the value-added statement format shown in Exhibit 6.3.

CASE

Consolidation of a Foreign Direct Investment[35]

This case presents data on a direct foreign investment in New Zealand by a U.S. parent company. The case is presented in two parts and should be completed in sequence.

PART A

On 1/1/X1, P Company purchased 80 percent of S Company's common stock from S Company stockholders for US$100,000 cash. S Company is located in New Zealand. The balance sheets of P Company and S Company as of January 1, 19X1, appear in Table 6.8. Note that P Company has recorded the US$100,000 investment in S Company. Assume that the book values of S Company's assets and liabilities are the same as their fair values; however they are denominated in New Zealand dollars. The current rate of exchange is NZ$1 = US$.80. There are no intercompany receivables or payables between the two companies.

Required

Complete the January 1, 19X1 consolidated balance sheet shown in Table 6.8.

[35] Prepared at Pacific Lutheran University, Tacoma, Wash.

TABLE 6.8   Consolidated Balance Sheets for P and S Companies (January 1, 19X1)

ITEM	P COMPANY (US$)	S COMPANY (NZ$)	S COMPANY (US$)	CONSOLIDATED (US$)
Current assets	$120,000	$ 75,000		
Investment in S	100,000			
Goodwill	0	0		
Plant (net)	280,000	250,000		
Total assets	$500,000	$325,000		
Current liabilities	$ 50,000	$ 50,000		
Bonds payable	180,000	125,000		
Minority interest				
Capital stock	150,000	62,500		
Paid-in capital	50,000	37,500		
Retained earnings	70,000	50,000		
Total equities	$500,000	$325,000		

PART B

During 19X1, P Company sold raw materials inventory to S Company at a sales price of US$20,000 (NZ$25,000). S Company processed all of these raw materials into finished goods and sold the finished products to its customers during 19X1. On December 31, 19X1, S Company still owed P Company US$5,000 (NZ$6,250) for these purchases. Thus S Company has accounts payable of NZ$6,250 and P Company has accounts receivable of US$5,000 on their respective books. The exchange rate between US$ and the NZ$ remained the same. The 19X1 financial statements for P and S Companies are shown in Table 6.9.

Required

Complete the consolidated financial statements for the year ended December 31, 19X1.

TABLE 6.9   Financial Statements for P and S Companies

ITEM	P COMPANY (US$)	S COMPANY (NZ$)	S COMPANY (US$)	CONSOLIDATED (US$)
Income Statement				
Sales	$480,000	$250,000		
Dividend income	8,000	0		
Total revenues	488,000	250,000		
Cost of goods sold	$260,000	$137,500		
Operating ex-				
penses	160,000	81,250		
Minority interest				
Total expenses	420,000	218,750		
Net income	$ 68,000	$ 31,250		
Retained earnings				
1/1/X1	$ 70,000	$ 50,000		
Net income	68,000	31,250		
	138,000	81,250		
Dividends	24,000	12,500		
Retained earnings				
12/31/81	$114,000	$ 68,750		
Balance Sheet				
Current assets	$125,000	$ 81,250		
Investment in S				
Company	100,000	—		
Goodwill	0	0		
Plant (net)	295,000	256,250		
Total assets	$520,000	$337,500		
Current liabilities	$ 46,000	$ 43,750		
Bonds payable	160,000	125,000		
Minority interest	—	—		
Capital stock	150,000	62,500		
Paid-in capital	50,000	37,500		
Retained earnings	114,000	68,750		
Total equities	$520,000	$337,500		

Financial
Reporting
and Disclosure

Previous chapters addressed some of the technical issues in international accounting. While the topics covered ranged from foreign currency translation to accounting for expropriation, all had a common focus, namely, accounting *measurement*. This chapter extends our earlier discussion by examining the *transmission* of accounting measurements to foreign readers.

MEASUREMENT VERSUS DISCLOSURE

Financial reporting may be thought of as a *process*. Bedford conceptualizes this process as consisting of four procedural steps:

1. *Perception* of the significant activity of the accounting entity or in the environment in which the entity performs. Implicit in the traditional perception is the belief that financial transactions represent the significant activities.
2. *Symbolizing* the perceived activities in such fashion that a data base of the activities is available that can then be analyzed to grasp an understanding of the interrelationships of the mass of perceived activities. Conventionally, this symbolization has taken the form of recordings in accounts, journals, and ledgers using well-established bookkeeping and measurement procedures.
3. *Analysis* of the model of activities in order to summarize, organize, and lay bare the interrelationships among activities and to provide a status picture or map of the entity. Traditionally, this analysis process has been viewed as one

of developing accounting reports to provide insights into the nature of entity activities.

4. *Communication* (transmission) of the analysis to users of the accounting product to guide decision makers in directing future activities of the entity or in changing their relationship with the entity.[1]

Steps 1 and 2 constitute the process of accounting *measurement,* the "assignment of numerals to an entity's past, present, or future economic phenomena on the basis of observation and according to rules."[2] Implicit in this conception are the requirements that (a) there exist some attribute or feature of a business-related object or event (e.g., the value of an asset) worthy of measurement and (b) there exist a means of making the measurements (e.g., the use of exchange prices to value enterprise assets). Steps 3 and 4 of the financial reporting process constitute *disclosure,* the communication of accounting measurements to some user of that information to facilitate a decision.

In theory, it is questionable whether information generated from the measurement process can or should be distinguished from the disclosure of that information. Without disclosure, accounting measurements in and of themselves serve no useful purpose. Yet disclosure cannot take place until the information has been developed. Thus, measurement and disclosure articulate with one another to give corporate financial reporting its substance.

In practice, there are a number of disclosure issues that stand apart from purely measurement issues, particularly in the international setting. Accordingly, for purposes of this chapter, we deem it useful to separate accounting measurement from disclosure issues. Still the interrelationships between the two should not be overlooked.

Available disclosure literature leads us to assert that (a) disclosure is not only fundamental to financial reporting but is, at the same time, its most qualitative aspect and (b) the nature and extent of disclosure needed in individual reporting situations is determinable only by expert professional judgment. The qualitative nature of disclosure often renders its format indeterminate. For instance, disclosure can occur directly within financial statements by appropriate statement captions, various parenthetical disclosures, or procedures such as listing items even though monetary amount balances may be zero. As an example, it is customary in West Germany to disclose fully all fixed asset movements directly within balance sheets proper.

In Anglo-American countries, disclosure occurs predominantly by means of footnotes to financial statements. This development was probably influenced heavily by requirements established through the various U.S. Securities Acts and their amendments. Right or wrong, there are many financial reports published in North America and in the United Kingdom in which the total space devoted to footnotes exceeds that devoted to the financial statements themselves.

When financial reporting is restricted to the transmission of accounting

---

[1] Norton M. Bedford, *Extensions in Accounting Disclosure* (Englewood Cliffs, N.J.: Prentice-Hall, Inc., 1973).

[2] American Accounting Association, Committee on Foundations of Accounting Measurement, *Accounting Review Supplement,* 1971, p. 4.

measurements, the allocation of accounting information among various user groups becomes a major policy issue. As the provision of accounting information is not costless, judgments as to appropriate disclosures for various foreign audiences-of-interest often require consideration of the different interests and competing demands of each group. Disclosures helpful to one group often prove harmful to others, so that accountants and managers alike must balance the claims of a number of interested parties and a variety of costs and benefits.

EVOLUTION OF CORPORATE DISCLOSURE

Before examining its international facets, let us briefly sketch the evolution of corporate disclosure. The following discussion provides a framework for assessing current disclosure issues related to MNCs.

Capital Market Influences

In a competitive economy, corporate disclosure exists as a means of discharging a corporation's accountability to providers of money capital (investors) and to facilitate the allocation of resources to their most productive uses.[3] In fulfilling society's material wants, corporations need to attract large sums of money capital to finance extensive production and distribution activities. In the face of internal financing constraints, corporations depend heavily on external capital markets, comprising all of the individuals and institutions through which savings are pooled and made available to corporate borrowers. Unfortunately, investors are seldom in a position to observe personally whether savings entrusted to the corporation are utilized efficiently or effectively. As a result, investors expect and are provided with an accounting for the stewardship of monies entrusted to the corporate entity. If corporate disclosures were not available, investors would have no basis on which to judge a security's merits and would be reluctant to part with their savings. That managers and directors accept seriously the accountability phase of their stewardship, or at least recognize in self-interest that disclosure delegates part of the responsibility for assessing the corporation's status and progress to users of financial reports, is evidenced by the trend toward more and more disclosure.[4]

Another developmental force behind corporate disclosure is the fact that corporations not only compete with each other in the capital markets, but attempt to obtain external financing as cheaply as possible. The conceptual link between expanded disclosure and a firm's cost of capital draws on the theory of investment behavior under uncertainty. To wit:

---

[3] Morris Mendelson and Sidney Robbins, *Investment Analysis and Securities Markets* (New York: Basic Books, Inc., 1976).

[4] Stephen Zeff, "Greater Disclosure Fever Spreading across the Globe," *World Accounting Report*, February 1979, p. 2.

1. In a world of uncertainty, investors regard the returns from security investments as any monies received as a consequence of ownership.
2. Because of uncertainty, these returns are viewed in a probabilistic sense, that is, as expected values of subjective probability distributions.
3. Investors use some measure of dispersion of a security's expected returns and the correlation of those returns with those of other securities as measures of the risk associated with a security.
4. Investors prefer a higher expected return for any level of risk or a lower level of risk for any given expected return.
5. A security's value is positively related to its expected return streams and inversely related to the riskiness associated with those returns.

Increased firm disclosure improves the subjective probability distributions of a security's expected returns in the mind of an investor by reducing the uncertainty (risk) associated with that return stream. Moreover, for firms performing above their industry average, improved disclosure tends to increase the relative importance that investors place on favorable firm data relative to other information (e.g., industry data and general economy data) utilized in making judgments with respect to the firm. Both of the foregoing effects will entice an individual to pay a larger amount for a given security than he or she would otherwise, thus lowering a firm's cost of capital.[5]

Nonfinancial Influences

While corporate accountability has historically been associated with the capital formation process, there is today a growing worldwide trend of holding corporations accountable to the public at large for both their policies and actions. Gray and Perks have offered a number of reasons behind this movement:[6]

1. The development and growth of the influence of trade unions in most developed countries, both at the level of the corporation (through various methods of "participation" and/or extensions of collective bargaining) and at the national level.
2. The increase in what has been called the "democratic imperative" with the demand for recognition of the view that those who are significantly affected by decisions made by institutions in general must be given the opportunity to influence those decisions.
3. The postwar rejection by many governments of classical economic premises such as the belief that the unregulated pursuit of private gain maximizes societal welfare.
4. The substantial growth in industrial concentration, which has given rise to corporations large enough to assert a significant influence on national economic and social policies of host countries.

In the latter regard, smaller nation-states tend to see the multinationals as a direct challenge to their national sovereignties. Labor unions assert that the

---

[5] Frederick D. S. Choi, "Financial Disclosure in Relation to a Firm's Capital Costs," *Accounting and Business Research*, Autumn 1973, pp. 282–292.

[6] Rob Gray and Bob Perks, "How Desirable Is Social Accounting?" *Accountancy*, April 1982, pp. 101–102.

multinational enterprise is able to "import" or "export" jobs. Publics at large have become concerned because they are told that even general standards of living in a given country may well be affected by the collective influence of multinational business activities. The foreign exchange value of their country's currency may be significantly affected by direct foreign investment strategies decided in a very small number of boardrooms around the world. Public welfare may be influenced by arbitrary allocations of corporate tax payments between countries, by substantial under-the-table payments to officials in other countries, and by a long string of still other asserted multinational corporate manipulations. Many of these concerns translate directly into demands for expanded corporate disclosures, both financial and nonfinancial in tenor.

While shareholders and creditors will undoubtedly continue to be the major targets of corporate disclosure, "nonfinancial shareholders" such as labor unions (interested in the terms, conditions, security, and location of employment), governments (interested in the macroeconomic impacts of corporate operations), and general public groups (interested in the environmental and social effects of enterprise decisions) are emerging as the new audiences-of-interest. Recent disclosure proposals of the United Nations Commission on Transnational Corporations are illustrative of this new trend (see Chapter 12 for a full discussion of the organizational aspects of the U.N. effort. Table 7.1 illustrates items of nonfinancial disclosure currently being called for by the United Nations for (a) the multinational enterprise as a whole and (b) individual member companies of a multinational group.[7] In drafting its list of minimum disclosures, the U.N. Group of Experts apparently felt the need to extend the scope of required disclosures beyond purely financial disclosures. Information on the social and economic impact of the transnational corporations was considered necessary to satisfy the growing interest of various user groups, the general public, local communities, as well as the international community.

Table 7.1 is suggestive. The view that corporate disclosure *to investors* adequately discharges a corporation's responsibility to society is increasingly questioned. While some may consider this to be an aberration of the financial reporting process, it seems more realistic to view such developments as a reflection of the evolution of the corporation into a multinational and multifunctional institution with enlarged and diffused responsibilities to those dependent upon or affected by it.

Corporate Response

Expanded information demands such as those enumerated have thus far been received with mixed emotions. Some companies have embraced expanded disclosure requests as a positive dimension of their external relations programs. Others have been less than enthusiastic. Those opposed to greater corporate transparency argue that such requests are often (a) discriminatory

---

[7] United Nations Economic and Social Council, *International Standards of Accounting and Reporting for Transnational Corporations* (New York: UN, 1977), pp. 76–79.

TABLE 7.1   U.N. Disclosure Proposals

SECTION B. INDIVIDUAL MEMBER COMPANY

List of minimum items for general purpose reporting of an individual member company (including the parent company) of a group of companies comprising a transnational corporation

*1. Labour and employment
  *(a) Description of labour relations policy
    *(i) Trade union recognition
    *(ii) Complaints and dispute settlement mechanism and procedure
  *(b) Number of employees as at year end, and annual average (for the parent company—breakdown by geographic area and line of business if feasible).
  (c) Number employed by function (professional, production, etc.)
  (d) Number of women employees by function
  (e) Number of national employees by function
  (f) Average hours worked per week
  (g) Labour turnover, annual rate
  (h) Absenteeism—working hours lost (number and as percentage of total working hours per year)
  (i) Accident rate (describe basis)
  (j) Description of health and safety standards
  (k) Employee costs
    (i) Total wages, salaries, and other payments to employees (before tax)
    (ii) Social expenditures paid to institutions and Government for benefit of workers (excluding pension schemes reported in the profit and loss statement)
    (iii) Summary description and cost of training programmes
*2. Production
  (a) Description of practices regarding acquisition of raw materials and components (indicate percentage acquired from intercompany foreign sources and percentage from all foreign sources)
  (b) Indicate average annual capacity utilization in accordance with normal industrial practice
  *(c) Physical output by principal lines of business in accordance with normal industrial practice
  *(d) Description of significant new products and processes
*3. Investment programme
  *(a) Description of announced new capital expenditure
  *(b) Description of main projects including their cost, estimated additions to capacity, estimated direct effect on employment
  *(c) Description of announced mergers and takeovers, including their cost and estimated direct effect on employment
*4. Organizational structure (For the parent—description of management structure)
  *(a) Names of members of board of directors and, where applicable, the supervisory board and a description of their affiliations with companies outside the group
  *(b) Number of owners or shareholders, and where known, the names of the principal owners or shareholders
*5. Environmental measures
  Description of types of major or special environmental measures carried out, together with cost data, where available

---

* Disclosures also required of the parent company.
Source: UNESC, International Standards, pp. 77–79.

(e.g., discriminate against MNCs versus purely domestic concerns), (b) premature, given the absence of a demonstrated need for suggested disclosures, and (c) costly, not only in terms of preparation but also in terms of competitiveness whenever required disclosures deprive a company of an existing competitive advantage, or give a competitive advantage to others.[8] Notwithstanding arguments to the contrary, information demands of a corporation's enlarged reporting constituency cannot be ignored if the corporation is to continue to enjoy the degree of freedom it has been granted in the past in managing a significant portion of a nation's scarce resources. Failure to adequately respond to expressed information needs increases the likelihood of greater control over corporate reporting. As a national example, the emergence of the Securities and Exchange Commission (SEC) in the United States is often attributed to the lag by U.S. corporations in providing adequate disclosures to individual investors prior to the 1930s. In parallel fashion, a number of international organizations have adopted operating postures aimed at increasing their regulatory grip on transnational disclosure practices. These include but are not limited to the following (again see Chapter 12 for more complete descriptions):

1. United Nations Center on Transnational Corporations (UNCTC), an information-gathering agency of the United Nations Economic and Social Council, charged with building a comprehensive information system on transnational enterprises to facilitate monitoring of their activities.
2. Organization for Economic Cooperation and Development (OECD), a 24-nation body that provides a framework for harmonizing national policies in many fields (including disclosure).
3. European Economic Community (EEC), a regional economic union aimed at harmonizing economic, social, fiscal, and monetary policies among its member countries.
4. International Accounting Standards Committee (IASC), an international professional accounting organization established to promulgate worldwide accounting principles.
5. International Confederation of Free Trade Unions (ICFTU), one of several multinational labor organizations serving to monitor MNC behavior that bears on present and future employment effects.

The foregoing discussion suggests that the modern corporation can expect to face an acceleration rather than a diminution in the demands for corporate transparency. While competition for capital will continue to be a motivating force, management must increasingly weigh the negative sanctions of government controls in the corporate disclosure decision.

There is no objective, verifiable economic calculus by which the costs and benefits of disclosure can be measured. . . . Thus, disclosure policy necessarily involves value judgments and the selection of what should be disclosed is a political/social choice which may be resolved either through the response of MNC management

[8] R. K. Mautz and William G. May, *Financial Disclosure in a Competitive Economy* (New York: Financial Executives Research Foundation, 1978).

to market and interest group pressures or by means of regulation, governmental or private, i.e., professional/stock exchange, in circumstances where the market is viewed as inadequate or inappropriate.[9]

Let us now consider selected disclosure issues in the area of transnational reporting. These issues arise whenever a multinational enterprise needs to (a) communicate the results of its operations to foreign audiences-of-interest or (b) communicate the results of its foreign operations to domestic readers.

REGULATORY DISCLOSURE REQUIREMENTS

Today, a growing number of MNCs around the world are listing their securities on foreign exchanges. Motivating this practice is a number of perceived advantages. By exposing the company to local investment communities, a foreign listing increases a corporation's international image and, concomitantly, its avenues for future financing. A broader stock distribution together with a larger trading volume also facilitates the acquisition of foreign companies through an exchange of shares. In addition to increasing the market for its products (would a General Motors stockholder purchase a Toyota?), practices that broaden the availability of its stocks to local investors, including foreign employees, promote the local acceptance of an MNC's activities as well as tempering nationalistic sentiments so prevalent in many countries. In a recent case study of the Novo Corporation (domiciled in Denmark), Stonehill and Dullum demonstrated that a foreign listing can significantly reduce a company's cost of capital largely owing to disparities in the investor information base.[10]

As a basis of investor protection, most securities exchanges, in conjunction with professional or governmental regulatory bodies such as the SEC in the United States, the Ministry of Finance in Japan, and the Commissione Nazionale per le Societa e la Borsa (CONSOB) in Italy, impose disclosure requirements for both domestic and foreign companies seeking access to their securities markets. All are concerned with assuring that investors are provided with a minimum of disclosures that will permit them to intelligently appraise a company's past performance and future prospects. Nowhere is this concern more evident than in the United States where disclosure standards are generally considered to be the most stringent in the world. An examination of these requirements as they pertain to foreign companies follows. Along a similar vein, an excellent guide to regulatory disclosure requirements outside the United States is contained in Coopers & Lybrand's *International Financial Reporting and Auditing: A Guide to Regulatory Requirements.*[11]

[9] Gray and Perks, "How Desirable?" p. 101.
[10] Arthur I. Stonehill and Kare B. Dullum, *Internationalizing the Cost of Capital in Theory and Practice* (New York: John Wiley & Sons, 1982).
[11] New York: Coopers & Lybrand, 1979.

SEC Requirements

Initial issues of securities in the United States are regulated by authority of the Securities Act of 1933. Trading of securities on organized exchanges are regulated by authority of the Securities Exchange Act of 1934. Embodied in these acts is the philosophy that U.S. investors are best protected by full and fair disclosure of a company's affairs. Approval by the SEC does not mean approval or disapproval of the *investment value* of securities. An imprudent investor could very well suffer a loss yet have no recourse to the SEC.

In dealing with foreign issues in the U.S. markets, the SEC's policy has officially been to provide U.S. investors with protections equal to those provided when they deal in securities of U.S. companies. This policy, however, raises difficult questions of compliance given differences in national laws, business practices, and accounting principles. In light of jurisdictional problems and respect for national sovereignties, should U.S. regulators impose on foreign issuers the same standards as those applied to domestic issuers? Although a negative response to this question would seem justified in light of the discussion in Chapter 2, such a response would have to be tempered by another question. Should U.S. investors be provided with any less disclosure just because a reporting company happens to be domiciled outside the geographic limits of the United States. The following discussion describes the SEC's recent accommodative posture to foreign investors.[12] Underlying this posture is a desire to encourage the internationalization of the U.S. securities markets while providing U.S. investors with protections as equal as reasonably and practically possible to those provided in relation to U.S. issuers. In the absence of specific criteria, the reader must judge for himself whether the SEC policies achieve the proper balance between U.S. investor and foreign issuer rights.

Foreign firms are subject to SEC regulations and disclosure when the following conditions are present:

1. The foreign firm issues securities for original sale to the U.S. investing public.
2. The foreign firm wishes to trade its existing outstanding securities on an organized U.S. exchange.
3. The foreign firm's stock is traded over the counter in the United States but it has assets in excess of $1 million, more than 500 shareholders worldwide, of which 300 or more reside in the United States.

Although the regulatory authority and philosophy of full disclosure behind it affects both domestic and foreign firms equally, practical considerations have led the SEC to use two sets of forms, one set for domestic firms and another one for foreign firms. The forms for foreign firms are as follows:

1. *Form 20* has been the form authorized for use by most foreign firms under the Securities Exchange Act of 1934 to register initially securities for pur-

[12] Frederick D. S. Choi and Arthur I. Stonehill, "Foreign Access to U.S. Securities Markets: The Theory, Myth, and Reality of Regulatory Barriers," *The Investment Analyst*, July 1982, pp. 17–26.

poses of listing on an exchange under Section 12b or for trading over the counter under Section 12c. The comparable domestic form is *Form 10*.

2. *Form 20-K* has been the annual reporting form filed by each foreign issuer with the SEC. This is comparable to *Form 10K* for domestic firms.

3. *Form 6-K* is the form that foreign security issuers file quarterly. This corresponds to *Form 8-K* and *Form 10-Q* for domestic firms.

4. *Form S-1* is used to register a first-time public offering by either foreign or domestic issuers under the Securities Act of 1933. It consists of a prospectus to be given to investors and supplemental information which would be available to investors at the SEC office. Contents of the prospectus are governed by three provisions. Form S-1 details the items to be disclosed in the prospectus. Regulation S-K explains the content of the business description in the prospectus and Regulation S-X details the corresponding financial disclosures.

In general the forms used by foreign issuers have been less detailed and require less disclosure than the corresponding form for domestic U.S. issuers. Among the reasons for this are the following:

1. Foreign firms were not disclosing certain facts to their own shareholders, such as individual executive remuneration, industry segment reporting, five-year financial summaries, material transactions between the firm and its management, and insider trading.

2. It would be extremely costly for foreign firms to publish financial statements using U.S. generally accepted accounting principles (GAAP).

3. It would also be costly for foreign firms to translate into English all press releases and other documents given to their stockholders.

Responding to complaints that foreign companies enjoy preferential treatment in accessing the U.S. capital markets, the SEC issued in 1977 a series of proposals designed to bring its disclosure requirements for foreign firms more in line with those required of U.S. companies. Subsequent hearings and written comments were almost universally opposed to many of the proposed changes. As a result of the negative reception, the SEC adopted new Form 20-F which combines and replaces Forms 20 and 20-K. Form 6-K is also amended. New Form 20-F is a compromise, requiring more narrative disclosure than Forms 20 and 20-K but less than their domestic equivalent Form 10-K. The most controversial items, in the SEC Release No. 34-16371 pertain to the following requirements:

1. Foreign firms are required to disclose industry segment results only on a revenue basis with a narrative discussion only if revenue and profit contributions of the industry segments differ significantly. This is far less complete than the industry segment reporting required of domestic firms under Regulation S-K. It was a significant concession on the part of the SEC compared to their 1977 proposed changes.

2. The proposed requirement for a five-year summary of operations and related management discussion was not adopted.

3. Foreign firms involved in oil and gas operations must provide general information about their quantities of reserves and production.

4. If the foreign firm's voting securities are in registered form (rather than bearer form), they must disclose beneficial owners of more than 10 percent of their stock as well as the aggregate ownership of directors and officers as a group. This requirement is similar to the one for domestic firms except the percentage is 10 percent rather than 5 percent for domestic firms.

5. Foreign firms need only disclose a list of the names and positions with the firm for each director and officer. This compares to the requirement that domestic firms disclose the business experience and general background of their directors and officers.

6. Remuneration of individual directors or officers of foreign firms need not be disclosed unless the firm already discloses this information to its own stockholders or the public. Foreign firms are permitted to disclose remuneration for directors and officers in the aggregate. This was another significant concession by the SEC, motivated mainly by the negative comments they received in the various hearings following the SEC 1977 Proposals.

7. Foreign firms are required to disclose pending legal proceedings except for environmental litigation.

8. Foreign firms must describe the principal trading market outside the United States for their securities.

9. Foreign firms need to disclose material transactions between their managements and the firms only if required pursuant to foreign laws or otherwise. In general, foreign laws are more permissive on such disclosures than U.S. law.

10. Foreign firms filing financial statements as part of Form 20-F need not comply with U.S. GAAP, or Regulation S-X. They do need to discuss differences in the principles they use compared to U.S. GAAP and Regulation S-X. This is a significant cost relief for foreign firms and meets one of their principal objections to the SEC 1977 Proposals.

11. Foreign firms need not disclose in Form 20-F a list of all parents and subsidiaries but would need to provide such a list upon request to the SEC. This is particularly favorable for Japanese and Korean firms because of the large number of affiliated companies related by cross-ownership or group business ties.

12. Documents submitted as part of Form 6-K need to be translated into English only if they are distributed to security holders or if they contain material press releases. Other types of information and documents need be furnished only if English translations already exist. This meets the objection of foreign firms to the heavy cost of preparing translations, as well as potential legal liability for faulty translations.

13. Rule 3a 12-3, which exempts foreign firms from the proxy and insider trading rules, is revised to ensure that foreign firms are subject to SEC regulation as it applies to acquisitions or tender offers.

14. Foreign firms may continue to file their annual reports on Form 20-F with a six-month time lag rather than the four-month time lag suggested by the SEC 1977 proposals. This was conceded due to the fact that foreign firms must first comply with their own regulations, which typically allow more than four months time.

The SEC's latest modifications to foreign firms' disclosure rules are reprinted in Appendix 7A. The net result has been to relax some requirements but tighten others. Principal changes include the following:

1. *Segmental reporting.* Foreign issuers qualifying as "world-class" companies (i.e., those with at least $300 million in voting securities held by those unaf-

filiated with the company's management and filing annual reports with the SEC for at least three years) are exempted from disclosing profits for each major geographic and industrial segment of their operations. However, companies issuing stock or debt securities are still affected.

2. *Accounting principles.* Foreign issuers may prepare their financial statements in accordance with foreign GAAP but must qualify material differences between those and U.S. GAAP.

3. *Abbreviated prospectuses.* World-class foreign companies are now permitted to file abbreviated prospectuses for their securities. They are now able to refer purchasers to other documents already on file with the SEC, rather than having to duplicate them in the prospectus.

4. *Inflation accounting.* Under certain prescribed conditions, companies that do not normally account for inflation's effects are required to provide supplementary information to *quantify* or *indicate* the effects of changing prices on their financial position and operating income statements.

Stock Exchange Requirements

In the United States the securities of foreign firms trade in three main markets, namely, the New York Stock Exchange (NYSE), American Stock Exchange (ASE), and the over-the-counter market (NASDAQ). Registration with the SEC is required prior to trading on the NYSE or ASE in accordance with the Securities Exchange Act of 1934. No SEC registration is required for NASDAQ quotation. Disclosure and reporting requirements for listing do not normally exceed those required by the SEC on Forms 20-F and 6-K. Therefore additional listing requirements relate more to the nature of a company's size, profitability, and trading liquidity.

In recent years considerable energy has been expended to encourage a common worldwide standard for disclosure and listing requirements. This effort is still proceeding under the auspices of the Federation Internationale des Bourses de Valeurs. Table 7.2 illustrates what disclosure requirements look like for foreign issuers listing their shares on exchanges outside the United States.

SPECIAL REPORTS

In the transnational reporting sphere, special reports abound. They are not very different from their domestic cousins, but naturally many of them address problems that do not exist on a uninational plane.

Two brief examples will suffice to make the point. The first might be taken from the annals of the Boeing Company when it provides aircraft and various spare parts and training services to the small flag-carrying airlines of the developing countries. Typically, Export-Import Bank financing is sought in these situations. But before such financing can be obtained, the financial statements of the respective airlines have to be restated to a common denominator so that they (a) become comparable to financial statements of other airlines and (b) can serve as a basis for some financial forecasting. The resulting financial statements are clearly special reports.

TABLE 7.2 Survey of Information Required for Nondomestic Companies

IS THE FOLLOWING INFORMATION REQUIRED?	AMSTERDAM	FRANKFURT	LONDON
(1) General information			
(a) Capitalization—designation of each class of stock, par value, authorized capital, issued or outstanding capital, past changes in capital, etc.	Yes	Yes	Yes
(b) History of the company	Yes	Yes	Yes
(c) Outline of business	Yes	Yes	Yes
(d) Future business outlook	Yes	Yes	Yes
(e) Retail of subsidiary and affiliate companies	Yes	Yes	Yes
(f) Principal financers or banks	Yes	No	Yes
(g) Description of facilities or properties	Yes	Yes	Yes
(h) Names, titles, careers of directors, officers, etc.	Yes	Yes	Yes
(i) Number of shares owned by directors, officers, etc.	No	No	Yes
(j) Employees—labor relations	Yes	Yes	Yes
(k) Options given to directors, officers, etc.	No	No	Yes
(l) Bonus, profit participation, pension plans, etc.	No	Yes	Yes
(2) Financial information			
(a) Annual reports	Yes	Yes	Yes
(b) Balance sheets	Yes	Yes	Yes
(c) Other financial information (if necessary)	Yes	Yes	Yes
(d) Consolidated/Unconsolidated/Either	Consolidated	Either	Consolidated
(e) Prepared according to accounting principles in the country of origin/National accounting principles/Either	Either	Country of origin	Either
(f) Disclosure of differences between accounting principles in the country of origin and national accounting principles (when former are used)	No	No	Yes
(g) Audit report or certificate prepared by accountants in the country of origin/By national accountants/Either	Either	Country of origin	Either
(h) Dividend information	Yes	Yes	Yes
(3) Legal information			
(a) Outline of company law, tax law, foreign exchange control laws, accounting rules, etc. of the country of origin	Yes	Yes	Yes
(b) Certification by competent authority to the effect that the company is duly established under law of the country of origin	Yes	Yes	Yes
(c) Pending litigation, if any	Yes	Yes	Yes
(d) Certified copy of charter and bylaws	Yes	Yes	Yes
(4) Particulars of stock for which listing is sought			
(a) Description of stock class, par value, rights and privileges, etc.	Yes	Yes	Yes
(b) Number of shares outstanding	Yes	Yes	Yes
(c) Number of shares owned by company	Yes	Yes	Yes
(d) Number of shares owned by resident nationals	No	No	No
(e) Number of shareholders (total)	No	No	Yes
(f) Identification and number of shares held by largest shareholders	Yes	Yes	Yes
(g) Names of stock exchanges on which stock is listed	Yes	Yes	Yes
(h) Price range on home exchange	Yes	Yes	No
(i) Trade volume on home exchange	Yes	No	No
(j) Names of transfer or fiscal agents	Yes	Yes	Yes

Source: *Business International Money Report*, February 1978.

ZURICH	PARIS	BRUSSELS	LUXEMBOURG	TORONTO	TOKYO	NYSE
Yes	Yes	Yes	Yes	Yes	Yes	Yes
Yes	Yes	Yes	Yes	Yes	Yes	Yes
Yes	Yes	Yes	Yes	Yes	Yes	Yes
Yes	Yes	Yes	No	No	Yes	Yes
Yes	Yes	Yes	Yes	Yes	Yes	Yes
No	No	Yes	No	No	No	Yes
Yes	Yes	Yes	Yes	Yes	Yes	Yes
Yes	Yes	Yes	Yes	Yes	Yes	Yes
No	No	No	No	No	Yes	Yes
No	Yes	No	Yes	Yes	Yes	Yes
No	Yes	Yes	Yes	Yes	Yes	Yes
No	No	Yes	Yes	Yes	Yes	Yes
Yes	Yes	Yes	Yes	Yes	Yes	Yes
Yes	Yes	Yes	Yes	Yes	Yes	Yes
Yes	Yes	Yes	Yes	Yes	Yes	Yes
Either	Consolidated	Consolidated	Consolidated	Consolidated	Consolidated	Consolidated
Either	Either	Either	Either	Either	Country of origin	Either
No	Yes	Yes	No	No	Yes	Yes
Country of origin	Either	Either	Either	Either	Country of origin	Either
Yes	Yes	Yes	Yes	Yes	Yes	Yes
Yes	No	Yes	Yes	No	Yes	Yes
Yes	Yes	Yes	Yes	Yes	Yes	Yes
Yes	Yes	Yes	Yes	Yes	Yes	Yes
Yes	Yes	Yes	Yes	Yes	Yes	Yes
Yes	Yes	Yes	Yes	Yes	Yes	Yes
Yes	Yes	Yes	Yes	Yes	Yes	Yes
Yes	Yes	No	Yes	Yes	Yes	Yes
Yes	Yes	No	No	Yes	Yes	No
Yes	Yes	No	No	Yes	Yes	Yes
Yes	Yes	Yes	No	Yes	Yes	Yes
Yes	Yes	Yes	Yes	Yes	Yes	Yes
No	Yes	Yes	No	Yes	No	No
No	Yes	No	Yes	Yes	No	No
Yes	Yes	Yes	Yes	Yes	Yes	Yes

Another illustration might be taken from the operations of the International Finance Corporation (IFC), which is an international investment institution established to assist industrial development in the Third World through investments in productive private enterprises. National governments are agreement members of the IFC. The capital base of the IFC exists by virtue of quota contributions from all member governments.

Investments of the IFC are spread throughout the economically less developed countries of the Free World. Since IFC borrowers normally are independent private industrial or commercial enterprises, they are subject to the laws of the respective countries in which they are domiciled. Hence the accounting and financial reporting of each borrower are subject to applicable local laws.

Notwithstanding locally binding statutes, the IFC requires periodic financial reporting from the borrower firms so that the investments can be properly monitored. This means that some form of transnational financial reporting has to be involved for meaningful analysis possibilities at IFC headquarters. The IFC has published manuals that specify both its accounting and financial reporting requirements and the independent audit reports it expects. These are best seen as special reports within the larger area of transnational financial reporting.

MULTIPLE DISCLOSURES

When corporate securities are held totally within the country in which the issuing firm is incorporated, dissemination of financial information to investors and others concerned with accounting data is generally covered by accounting standards and principles generally accepted in that country. Both the preparers and the consumers of the information have the responsibility of being familiar with applicable rules. While this state of affairs does not guarantee effective communication in all cases, a mutual understanding of the ground rules that apply at least minimizes distortion.

International ownership of corporate securities presents a new problem. Past, present, and future securities owners in various countries outside the corporate domicile differ from one another not only in their cultural and social attitudes, their life-styles, and general behavior patterns, but also in the understanding they have of the accounting principles underlying the financial statements that they encounter. Under these circumstances, expanded corporate disclosures are helpful in classifying the information content of financial statements. The challenge here is effective communication of intended messages to foreign readers. Failure could mean higher capital costs and other disadvantages.

Reporting Requirements

At present, little formal attention has been accorded the transnational reporting dimension. As mentioned earlier, non–U.S. companies seeking a U.S.

listing must conform to the disclosure requirements of the SEC. In seeking comparability in financial statements issued to U.S. investors, the SEC permits foreign issuers to prepare their financial statements in accord with accounting principles generally accepted in their home countries. Material differences between foreign and U.S. GAAP must now be reconciled by way of footnotes to the financial statements. Table 7.2 suggests that other countries permit foreign listors to submit financial statements based either on the reporting principles of the country of origin or that of the country in which listing is sought. Japan and Germany appear satisfied with statements prepared only according to the reporting company's country of domicile. With the exception of foreign operations disclosures, to be discussed in a subsequent section, international organizations such as the IASC, the United Nations, and the OECD have also been silent on the subject of reporting to foreign readers.

In the absence of enforceable transnational disclosure norms, one must look to existing practice for guidance. Four distinguishable approaches are observed.

Convenience Translations

The nationalistic orientation, which so strongly permeates much accounting thinking and many of the rules by which accounting is applied, is probably responsible for the attitude that basically expects investors in other countries to fend for themselves as far as transnational reporting goes. In other words, companies will make copies of annual reports available to investors wherever they happen to reside or have a mailing address, but no special efforts are made to assist such foreign users with understanding and interpreting financial reports prepared on a basis often significantly different from what the reader may be accustomed to.

For instance, quite a few U.S. corporations have convinced themselves that U.S. accounting and reporting standards are qualitatively higher than they are elsewhere in the world and that the English language and reports expressed in terms of U.S. dollars are so universal that any translations or reporting adaptations are simply not needed. Consequently, securities holders the world over simply receive copies of annual reports and other financial information just as U.S. investors do. French companies are equally nationalistic as a rule. All of their communications are typically in the French language, expressed in French francs, and prepared on the customary French basis.

A modest concession to multinational financial reporting audiences-of-interest is made when companies translate at least the language portion of their reports to the national idiom of major groups of addressees. For instance, Proctor & Gamble slipsheets their annual reports mailed to France with French translations of all annual report textual materials. Many Dutch, German, Swedish, and Swiss companies regularly publish their annual reports in as many as six foreign language editions—Dutch, English, French, German, and Spanish, plus the home language (e.g., Swedish or, let us say, Italian in the case of an Italy-based multinational enterprise).

Many companies go a step further. In addition to language translations, monetary amounts are translated as well (usually at the year-end foreign exchange rate throughout). Thus, L. M. Ericsson, the large Swedish telephone company, prepares its U.S. convenience statements by showing translated U.S. dollar amounts only and prominently displaying on every page the proviso that "The United States dollar amounts shown in the above statement represent translations from Swedish kroner at the official parity (date) of Skr. (rate) to $1." Fujitsu, the giant Japanese computer manufacturer, presents its monetary expressions in dual columns, for example, U.S. dollars and Japanese yen, when reporting to American readers. The dual column notion perhaps finds its greatest expression in Chile where companies such as Corporacion Nacional del Cobre de Chile presents its annual report, cover to cover, in twin columns with Spanish text and peso amounts in one column and English text and dollars in another.

Although convenience translations lend an international appearance to primary statements and may offer some public relations benefits, they may also mislead. For example, language and/or currency translations often give the foreign reader the impression that the accounting principles underlying the convenience statements have been translated as well. If such is not the case, erroneous conclusions are a likely result. Another big problem is that financial analysts and others in the financial community tend to interpret convenience-type statements as comparable in substance to domestically prepared statements for purposes of financial comparisons and securities analysis. Of course, the translated statements cannot be so used, and once again a high potential for misuse is created.

Differences in underlying independent auditing standards and practices also often lead to a misinterpretation of the degree of third-party reliability that may be placed upon these convenience statements.

These problems may be minimized by disclosures that specifically identify the national accounting principles, reporting domicile, and auditing standards underlying convenience statements. Until then, convenience translations represent at best an evolutionary step in the development of multinational disclosure practice.

Special Information

Recognizing that probably not every multinational portfolio investor can be conversant with all existing national accounting standards and principles, and understand and interpret their respective applications correctly, a small number of multinational companies have made an effort to explain to readers in other countries the particular accounting standards and practices forming the basis for their reporting. For instance MNCs domiciled in Sweden now typically include a copy of the most recent edition of the Foreningen Auktoriserade Revisorer (FAR) information booklet entitled *Key to Understanding Swedish Financial Statements* with each copy of their financial statements mailed to non-Swedish addressees (see the section on Sweden in Chapter 3).

The foregoing practice, while laudable, is not without its limitations. Underlying the explanations in accounting principles booklets is the presumption that foreign readers possess the technical expertise to quantitatively reconcile disclosed accounting differences. Unfortunately, this is seldom the case.

Limited Restatements

A partial remedy to the understandability problem just described is used by several Netherlands-based multinationals. For instance, in addition to language translations, the Philips Company estimates what earnings adjustments would be required if accounting principles generally accepted in the United States rather than in the Netherlands were followed. A direct result is that Dutch investors see earnings and per-share numbers that are consistent with local accounting practices, while their U.S. counterparts are at least provided with earnings numbers that are readily understood and can be used comparatively. The disadvantage of partial restatements is fairly obvious; that is, rate-of-return comparisons are hardly meaningful when earnings restated to U.S. GAAP are compared with total assets and other financial statement categories that reflect Dutch accounting norms.

Primary-Secondary Statements

In its February 1975 study entitled *International Financial Reporting*, the Accountants International Study Group (AISG) recommends that two kinds of financial statements be recognized as part of formal (or official) generally accepted accounting standards and principles.[13] *Primary* financial statements would be prepared according to financial accounting principles generally accepted in a company's country of domicile and in that country's language and national currency. Independent auditors would express opinions on primary financial statements—again according to both the generally accepted financial accounting principles and the generally accepted auditing standards of the domicile country.

Secondary financial statements would be prepared specifically for financial reporting audiences-of-interest in other countries. Such secondary financial statements would have one or more of the following characteristics:

1. The reporting standards of a foreign country would have been followed.
2. The statements would have been translated into a foreign currency.
3. The statements would have been translated into a language that is not the language of the reporting company's country of domicile.
4. The independent auditor's report would be expressed in a form not commonly used in the reporting company's country of domicile.

If the primary statements include sufficient information to satisfy the information requirements of financial reporting audiences-of-interest in other

[13] Accountants International Study Group, *International Financial Reporting* (Toronto: AISG, 1975).

countries, the primary statements themselves will serve multiple purposes and secondary statements are unnecessary. The AISG recommendation presumes that all companies prepare primary statements and that the majority of companies with financial reporting audiences-of-interest in more than a single country will also prepare secondary statements (at least until greater worldwide harmony of financial accounting standards evolves).

Secondary statements have notably been embraced by Japanese multinationals such as Hitachi and Honda in reporting to their North American readers.

Advantages.   A primary-secondary system of transnational reporting allows full recognition of national points of view parallel with other national or possibly even international viewpoints. Specific recognition of reader audiences for primary and secondary reports should increase the information content (and therefore quality) of both types of financial statements. The degree of generality of published corporate reports would be reduced by a dual system, and thus the likelihood of more useful relevant information entering economic and decision channels would be greater.

Multiple transnational reporting explicitly recognizes that the nature of multinational business and finance differs in several important respects from strictly uninational business and finance. This difference is not only a matter of degree but of organizational structure, business policy, and nature of business transactions as well. Since the multinational enterprise is a full economic reality in our day and age, institution of a multiple reporting system would be a first step toward more realism in recognizing accounting effects resulting from the multinational business phenomenon.

Furthermore, it seems reasonable to assume that primary-secondary transnational reporting will encourage the growth of broad and active international money capital markets. One of your coauthors has demonstrated through his research that increased financial disclosure by firms performing above average in their respective industries lowers their respective capital costs when they source long-term money capital in the relatively unregulated international capital market.[14] These findings permit the assertion that the increased amount of financial disclosure resulting from dual reporting is likely to benefit firms entering, or active in, international financial markets. In turn, the international capital market should be stimulated into further growth and should be able to increase its relative economic efficiency.

Disadvantages.   Aside from considerations of production cost, a substantial difficulty with the primary-secondary reporting proposal is that it runs counter to the so-called "single domicile for financial statements" point of view. The substance of this viewpoint is that business managers make a great many business decisions with at least an awareness of how these decisions are

---

[14] Frederick D. S. Choi, "Financial Disclosure and Entry to the European Capital Market," *Journal of Accounting Research,* Autumn 1973, pp. 159–175.

later mirrored in their financial statements. Thus corporate mergers, equipment leasing policies, and investments involving foreign exchange exposure (FAS No. 52 implications) are often made with a half an eye to corresponding financial statement effects. If different financial accounting rules would apply, then possibly some business decisions would be made differently. And if this is so, realistic financial reporting results are unobtainable when a set of "alien" accounting rules is imposed upon a set of specific business decisions and their financial consequences.

The single-domicile viewpoint, therefore, holds that financial statements can present only a single representation of financial decisions and results of operations—only for a given time, under a given set of rules, and for a given purpose. When business decisions are made under these conditions, they ought to be reported only in terms of the same conditions.

Potential reader confusion is another difficulty. If we accept the proposition that accounting principles are shaped by a particular social, economic, and legal environment (see Chapter 2), and that national accounting environments differ, translation of financial statements from one set of accounting principles to another could distort the original message. Even if accounting principles between two countries are similar, business and financial mores that govern the interpretation of accounting-based financial statement ratios may vary internationally (see Chapter 8). This could lead to further message distortion. As an example high debt ratios, viewed with alarm in the United States, are an accepted part of the business scene in South Korea.

The solution to the reader confusion problem must be sought in terms of disclosure. In fact, the AISG study takes it as one of its specific recommendations that "a public company which has significant international ownership or financing interests and presents a summary of its accounting policies should identify the nationality of the accounting principles followed."[15] Footnote disclosures of the main differences between accounting principles of the reporting company's and reader's countries of domicile, together with their effect on net income and financial position, would also be helpful, as would environmental disclosures that assist readers in properly interpreting secondary statement information. Several Japanese companies have begun to provide such disclosures in their registration filings with the U.S. SEC as a result of past misunderstandings.

FOREIGN OPERATIONS
DISCLOSURES

With the advent of floating exchange rates, global inflation, increased nationalism, and political uncertainty, investors the world over have become very interested in the nature of a firm's foreign operations and the implications of such activities for the risk and return dimensions of their investments. Proponents of

---

[15] Accountants International Study Group, *International Financial Reporting*, par. 65.

special foreign operations disclosures argue that consolidated financial statements (discussed in Chapter 6), while desirable for their synergistic insights, do not enable investors and other analysts to accurately assess the returns and risks associated with their security investments.[16] Both domestic and, particularly, foreign operating segments of a multinational entity often experience patterns of profitability, growth, and risk that differ from consolidated trends. Geographic area disclosures of consolidated statistics such as sales and operating assets are intended to enable financial statement users to assess the effect that operations in major areas of the world may have on the enterprise as a whole. At the same time, increased concern over the social and economic impact of MNCs on host countries, especially those classified as "developing," has resulted in demands for greater disclosure of multinational operations to the general public. A compelling argument in this respect is provided by the United Nations in its *International Standards of Accounting and Reporting.*[17]

Opponents of such disclosures express concern that foreign operations disclosures may be (a) harmful to a reporting company's competitive position, (b) too detailed for general purpose financial statements, and (c) confusing to statement readers. A common rejoinder, however, is that such disclosures are no more onerous than information currently provided in conventional accounting reports.

Arguments notwithstanding, there is today a push at both national and international levels to require more disclosure of a firm's foreign operations—such disclosures being viewed as useful supplements to consolidated information.[18]

Reporting Requirements

Foreign operations disclosure requirements are commonly treated in conjunction with reporting for business segments. In the United States, *Financial Accounting Standard No. 14* (FAS No. 14), "Financial Reporting for Segments of a Business Enterprise,"[19] is the authoritative pronouncement. In addition to information concerning industry segments, the FAS No. 14 requires separate information disclosures of an enterprise's foreign operations, which can be done in an aggregate fashion, or, if appropriate, by geographic area. Such separate disclosures are only required, however, if foreign operations contribute 10 percent or more of consolidated revenues, or the assets identifiable with the foreign operations are 10 percent or more of consolidated assets. Excluding unconsolidated subsidiaries and investees, a foreign operation is defined as a revenue-producing operation located outside the United

---

[16] Malcolm C. Miller and Mark C. Scott, *Financial Reporting by Segments* (Melbourne: Australian Accounting Research Foundation, 1980).

[17] New York: United Nations Center on Transnational Corporations, October 1977; further referenced in Chapter 12.

[18] Ingo Walter and Tracy Murray, *Handbook of International Business* (New York: John Wiley & Sons, 1982).

[19] Stamford, Conn.: Financial Accounting Standards Board, December 1976.

States (for U.S. enterprises) that generates revenues either from sales to unaffiliated customers or from intercompany sales or transfers between geographic areas. Information sought by FAS No. 14 for foreign operations includes:

1. Revenues, with separate disclosures of (a) sales to unaffiliated customers, (b) sales or transfers between geographic areas, and (c) transfer pricing bases used
2. Operating income, net income, or some other measure of profitability in between, as long as a consistent measure is used for all geographic areas
3. Identifiable assets

The U.S. Securities and Exchange Commission conformed its earlier line-of-business reporting rules with FAS No. 14.[20] Now all SEC filings must contain revenue, income and identifiable assets information for foreign operations as required in FAS No. 14.

Foreign operations disclosure provisions, similar to those of FAS No. 14, are also contained in International Accounting Standard No. 14 (IAS No. 14) "Reporting Financial Information by Segment."[21] Finalized in March 1981, its intended purpose is "to enable users of financial statements to assess the effect that operations in different industries and in different geographical areas may have on the enterprise as a whole."[22] Companies whose securities are publicly traded and other "economically significant" entities including subsidiaries are encouraged to report the following information for industry and geographic segments considered significant to the enterprise:

1. Sales or other operating revenues, distinguishing between revenue derived from customers outside the enterprise and revenue derived from other segments
2. Segment result
3. Segment assets employed, expressed either in money amounts or as percentages of the consolidated totals
4. The basis of intersegment pricing

When both parent company and consolidated financial statements are presented, segment information need be presented only on the basis of consolidated financial statements.

Governmental interest in foreign operations disclosures manifests itself in a number of disclosure documents issued by international agencies whose concerns span both financial and nonfinancial effects of multinational operations. The EEC's Fourth Directive requires that sales be disaggregated by categories of activity and geographic markets to the extent that these categories and markets differ substantially from one another.[23] The OECD's *Guidelines for Mul-*

[20] Stamford, Conn.: Financial Accounting Standards Board, December 1976.

[21] London: International Accounting Standards Committee.

[22] Ibid., par. 5.

[23] Commission of the European Communities, *Amended Proposal for a Fourth Council Directive for Co-ordination of National Legislation Regarding the Annual Accounts of Limited Liability Companies* (Brussels, 1974).

TABLE 7.3   UN's Foreign Operations Disclosure Proposals

Segment and Disclosure Geographically:
Sales to unaffiliated customers
Transfers to other geographical areas (eliminated in consolidation)
Operating results, such as profit before general corporate expenses, interest expense,
    taxes on income and unusual items
(Does not prohibit segmenting net income as well)

To the Extent Identifiable with a Geographic Area, Disclose:
Total assets or net assets or total assets and total liabilities, and at least:

  Property, plant and equipment, gross
  Accumulated depreciation
  Other long-term assets
New investment in property, plant and equipment
Describe principal activities in each geographical area or country
Disclose the basis of accounting for transfers between areas or countries
Disclose exposure to exceptional risks of operating in other countries
Comments: (1) Preference is expressed for segmenting assets according to the loca-
                tion of the assets and not necessarily the location of the records, and
                attributing revenue to the geographical area of the last significant value
                added by operations.
           (2) Amounts disclosed should aggregate to the total of the item shown in
                the consolidated financial statements, or reconciling amounts should
                be given.
Segment and Disclose by Line of Business
Sales to unaffiliated customers
Transfers to other lines of business (eliminated in consolidation)
Operating results, such as profit before general corporate expenses, taxes on income
    and unusual items
  (Does not prohibit segmenting net income as well)
To the Extent Identifiable with a Line of Business, Disclose:
Total assets or net assets or total assets and total liabilities, and at least:
  Property, plant and equipment, gross
  Accumulated depreciation
  Other long-term assets
Net investment in property, plant and equipment
Describe the principal products and services in each line of business
Disclose the basis of accounting for transfers between lines of business
Note: Amounts disclosed should aggregate to the total of the item shown in the consoli-
        dated financial statements or reconciling amounts should be given.

Source: United Nations Center on Transnational Corporations, *Towards International Standardization of Corporate Accounting and Reporting* (New York: UNCTC, 1982), pp. 72–74.

tinational Enterprises calls for a number of pertinent disclosures which are
listed in the relevant sections of Chapter 12.[24]

The most comprehensive disclosure "package" yet to be proposed on the
international front is that originally recommended by the U.N. Group of Experts on International Standards of Accounting and Reporting (GEISER).[25]
Not yet finalized, the proposal contains extensive lists of minimum financial

---

[24] Paris: Organization for Economic Cooperation and Development, 1976.
[25] United Nations, *International Standards*, pp. 53–79.

and nonfinancial disclosure "requirements" some of which are detailed in Table 7.1. The proposed U.N. foreign operations disclosures generally exceed those of the U.S. SEC and FASB, and of the IASC, the EEC, and the OECD. Table 7.3 lists the disclosure items applicable to the enterprise as a whole. Similar provisions also apply to individual member companies of the multinational parent as well.

Foreign Operations Disclosures: Current Practice

While disclosure requirements play a role in establishing disclosure minima, the absence of such requirements does not necessarily preclude companies from volunteering desired information or exceeding existing disclosure standards. Survey findings with respect to foreign operations disclosures by 270 European and non-European multinationals are detailed in Table 7.4.

To summarize, multinational companies based in Europe are generally forthright when it comes to disclosing foreign revenues in the aggregate or by geographic area. Lower geographic revenue statistics appearing in Table 7.4 may be due to the fact that sales by geographic areas may not be significant enough to warrant separate disclosure. Revenue disclosure patterns evidenced in Europe are also characteristic of the United States and Canada and, to a lesser extent, Japan.

In contrast to revenue data, profitability disclosures, either in the aggregate or by geographic area, are not prevalent in Europe excluding the United Kingdom and France. Within Europe, West Germany and Switzerland are least forthcoming with regard to foreign income. Outside Europe, Japanese multinationals are the most reluctant group. Even lower levels of disclosure by both European and Japan-based MNCs were discerned for foreign assets.

European multinationals fared better in the areas of exports and capital expenditures and, notwithstanding intragroup differences (e.g., France, the Netherlands, and Switzerland), disclosure of exports from the home country averaged 42 percent in Europe as a whole versus 25 percent and 27 percent for the United States and Canada, respectively. Whereas Japanese multinationals revealed more about their exports than those from North America, their capital expenditure disclosure patterns were no better.

Policy Issues

Numerous problems characterize the area of foreign operations disclosures. Consider the area of classification criteria.

Segmentation of operating results geographically is premised on the belief that operations in different parts of the world are subject to different degrees of risk, rates of growth, and thus profit opportunities. While such disclosures are potentially useful, identification of meaningful geographical reporting categories has proven extremely difficult. Thus, a U.S. subsidiary located in Latin America (e.g., El Salvador) may generate the bulk of its revenues from exports to the EEC. The appropriate geographical classification,

TABLE 7.4   Foreign Operations Disclosures by Multinational Corporations—Geographic Area Disclosures

DISCLOSURE ITEM	European						North American		
	United Kingdom (N = 58)	West Germany (N = 28)	France (N = 13)	Netherlands (N = 9)	Sweden (N = 13)	Switzerland (N = 11)	United States (N = 94)	Canada (N = 11)	Japan (N = 34)
Foreign sales	93%	90%	87%	89%	100%	91%	100%	100%	65%
Sales by geographic areas	93	71	87	67	100	91	86	91	29
Foreign income	74	7	87	33	23	0	98	73	12
Income by geographic areas	67	0	40	22	23	0	84	64	0
Foreign assets	19	10	40	22	31	18	92	91	15
Assets by geographic areas	17	0	13	22	15	18	85	46	3
Exports from home country	78	61	13	11	62	10	25	27	53
Exports by geographic areas	14	10	0	0	8	0	5	18	21
Capital expenditures: foreign	19	36	20	33	39	46	15	9	15
Capital expenditures by geo. areas	19	23	20	33	15	46	11	9	3
Avg. no. of geo. areas reported	6.3	3.5	4.1	4.6	10.6	5.8	3.2	4.0	3.9

Source: F. D. S. Choi and V. Bavishi, "A Cross-National Assessment of Management's Geographic Disclosures," paper presented at the Fourth Annual Meeting of the European Accounting Association, Barcelona, Spain, March 1981.

assuming the El Salvadorean operation is significant, is unclear. Whereas the foreign operation's primary revenue base may be in Europe, its political riskiness may be ultimately tied to its Latin American domicile. The issue is complicated even further by the temporal nature of environmental risks.

At the present time, geographical classification criteria suggested by accounting standard setters have been less than definitive. At the international level, the OECD stands alone in recommending that factors such as geographic proximity, economic affinity of operations, or similarities in business environments be considered in determining geographic areas. Nationally, the United States suggests classification criteria similar to those of the OECD. Canada simply specifies a geographic segment as a single operation or groups of operations located in a particular geographical area with domestic operations considered to be a separate geographic segment. Although no formal requirements exist in Japan with regard to geographic disclosures, a geographic area is defined "according to administrative purposes of the competent authorities."

A recent disclosure survey suggests that geographic categories currently employed by many U.S. companies are arbitrary and possess limited information content.[26] European companies tend to fare somewhat better in this regard. In the international survey, reported in Table 7.4, Choi and Bavishi subjectively ranked geographic classifications employed in decreasing order of informativeness. On the basis of this ranking scheme and despite within-group variances, most European companies employed geographic classifications that were considered informative. As a region, approximately 77 percent of European-based MNCs presented geographic categories either in terms of (a) individual countries, (b) individual countries and regions, separately disclosed, or (c) individual regions. In contrast, only 68 percent of American multinationals and 47 percent of Japanese MNCs employed similar categories.

In the absence of more specific institutional guidance, geographic classifications must necessarily rely on subjective interpretations of existing guidelines. Specification of meaningful geographical reporting categories is an area in dire need of research activity.

Other segmental disclosure problems relate to (a) materiality criteria and (b) corporate allocations. Regarding the former, a particular geographic area per FAS No. 14 is considered a separate reporting unit if area revenues from sales to unaffiliated customers or identifiable assets are 10 percent or more of worldwide totals. In addition to being completely arbitrary, the 10 percent criterion could suppress useful risk and return disclosure by limiting the number of segments reported on. Under the 10 percent rule, a company whose multinational operations comprise less than 30 percent of group totals is limited to two geographic segments; one, if multinational operations are less than 20 percent. Table 7.4 indicates that U.S. companies limit the number of geographic reporting categories to 3.2 on the average. In contrast, the average for Europe

[26] Vinod B. Bavishi and Harold E. Wyman, "Foreign Operations Disclosures by U.S.-based Multinational Corporations: Are They Inadequate?" *International Journal of Accounting,* Fall 1980, pp. 153–168.

as a whole is 5.8 categories. Swedish companies are the best performers in this respect, reporting 10.6 geographic categories on average.

In requiring disclosure of foreign operations' profitability by significant geographic areas, paragraph 10 (d) of FAS No. 14 requires that "operating expenses incurred by an enterprise that are not directly traceable to specific geographic areas should be allocated on a reasonable basis among those reporting segments." To the extent that such expense allocations are arbitrary, disclosed operating results will vary in their objectivity and relevance. Reporting entities must thus decide whether to (1) further improve upon the information being provided, or (2) in the absence of any theoretically correct or cost-efficient solution, alert statement readers to the data's limitations. Until further experience is gained on reporting foreign operations, the latter alternative, perhaps by means of a cautionary note, would appear to be a logical expedient.

All in all, experience in the United States and Europe suggests that foreign operations disclosure is still at an early stage of development. Nevertheless, heightened interest in the foreign operations of multinational companies ensures that further reporting innovations are definitely in the offing.

SOCIAL RESPONSIBILITY DISCLOSURES

Corporate operations, for the most part, concern themselves with production processes and technological innovation. These activities, however, do not take place in a social vacuum and corporations both domestic and multinational are being called upon to account for social responsibilities that transcend purely "bottom line" concerns.

Social accounting means different things to different people. To an economist the term has long been associated with national income accounting, that is, accounting for the performance of an entire nation. Here, the term refers to the measurement and communication of information about a firm's effects on employee welfare, the local community, and the environment.[27] Emphasis tends to be on nonfinancial as opposed to strictly financial performance measures.

The call for social responsibility disclosures is premised on several arguments. First, society grants corporations the freedom to manage a significant portion of its scarce resources. In return for this privilege, corporations have the responsibility to render periodic accountings to society on its effectiveness and efficiency in managing those resources. This tacit understanding constitutes, if you will, a social contract between the corporation and the body politic. More ideological in tone is the argument that individuals, including organizations of individuals, possess a hierarchy of needs. Once basic needs for survival are satisfied, individuals and organizations strive to satisfy higher social and self-esteem needs. Social responsibility disclosures are an integral feature of this behavioral phenomenon. Finally, corporations should recognize in

[27] Gray and Perks, "How Desirable?"

self-interest the importance of anticipating public opinion on matters of social concern. A reputation of being an enlightened employer with a sincere regard for environmental responsibilities translates directly into future economic dividends such as low levels of industrial disputes and favorable host government relations.

Despite the growing interest in the social aspects of corporate accountability, the field is still at a nascent stage of development. Fundamental questions of *what, how, who,* and *when* are still substantially unanswered. The following paragraphs examine the current state of the art.

Reporting Requirements

The most far-reaching social responsibility disclosure proposals to date are those put forth by GEISAR. An offshoot of the U.N. Center on Transnational Corporations, the activities of the GEISAR group are consistent with the U.N. effort to formulate a code of conduct for transnational corporations. Disclosure provisions of the proposed code are reproduced in Table 7.5. Specific elements of the nonfinancial disclosures proposed by the GEISAR group are contained in Table 7.1.

Nonfinancial disclosure provisions of the OECD are contained in its *Guidelines for Multinational Enterprises* mentioned earlier in the chapter. In contrast to the U.N. initiative, the OECD disclosure suggestions simply stipulate information on the average number of employees in each geographical area. In similar fashion, the EEC Fourth Directive requires disclosure of the average number of employees as well as annual personnel costs for each category (undefined) of employees. In an attempt to upgrade disclosures of direct consequence to employees, the EEC has recently proposed (in a document known as the Davignon-Vredeling Proposal, after its principal Commission sponsors) expanded disclosure requirements for MNCs operating in Europe. Included here are information disclosures on economic and financial positions, production and sales trends, investment and production programs, rationalization schemes, introduction of new working methods, and any procedures with the potential to substantially affect employee interests. In certain instances, such as the shutdown of a plant, information would have to be provided within 60 days of a decision taking effect. Welcomed by the European Trade Union Confederation, the proposals have thus far drawn strong protests from organized groups representing EEC employers' interests.

In its *Multinational Charter of Trade Union Demands for the Legislative Control of Multinational Companies*, the International Confederation of Free Trade Unions (ICFTU) specifies the following employee disclosure provisions in its list of public accountability requirements via company annual reports.

> Public reporting must cover . . . a breakdown of employment figures for individual companies and establishments.
>
> There must be a list of fundamental items which allow an appropriate comparative view covering all the various companies that make up the group structure. This list comprises:

TABLE 7.5 Information Disclosure Recommendations Contained in the U.N. Draft Code of Conduct for Transnational Corporations, 1982

43. Transnational corporations should disclose to the public in the countries in which they operate by appropriate means of communication, clear, full and comprehensible information on the structure, policies, activities and operations of the transnational corporation as a whole. The information should include financial as well as non-financial items and should be made available on a regular annual basis, normally within six months and in any case not later than twelve months from the end of the financial year of the corporation. In addition, during the financial year, transnational corporations should wherever appropriate make available a semi-annual summary of financial information.

The financial information to be disclosed annually should be provided where appropriate on a consolidated basis, together with suitable explanatory notes and should include, inter alia, the following:

(1) a balance sheet;
(2) an income statement, including operating results and sales;
(3) a statement of allocation of net profits or net income;
(4) a statement of the sources and uses of funds;
(5) significant new long-term capital investment;
(6) research and development expenditure.

The non-financial information referred to in the first paragraph should include, inter alia, the following:

(1) the structure of the transnational corporation, showing the name and location of the parent company, its main entities, its percentage ownership, direct and indirect, in these entities, including shareholdings between them;
(2) the main activity of its entities;
(3) employment information including average number of employees;
(4) accounting policies used in compiling and consolidating the information published;
(5) policies applied in respect of transfer pricing.

The information provided for the transnational as a whole should as far as practicable be broken down:

—by geographical area or country, as appropriate, with regard to the activities of its main entities, sales, operating results, significant new investments and numbers of employees;
—by major line of business as regards sales and significant new investment.

The method of breakdown as well as details of information provided should be determined by the nature, scale and interrelationships of the transnational corporations' operations, with due regard to their significance for the areas or countries concerned.

The extent, detail and frequency of the information provided should take into account the nature and size of the corporation as a whole, the requirements of confidentiality and effects on the transnational corporation's competitive position, as well as the cost involved in producing the information.

The information herein required should, as necessary, be in addition to information required by national laws, regulations and administrative practices of the countries in which transnational corporations operate.

United Nations Economic and Social Council, "Draft United Nations Code of Conduct on Transnational Corporations," *Report of the Ad Hoc Intergovernmental Working Group of Experts on International Standards of Accounting and Reporting* (New York: UN EcoSoc, 1982), par 43.

> Social data and indicators must be an integral part of the public accountability of multinationals: concise information should be given on employment and wages. . . .
> Information on employment should cover total employment, world-wide, by subsidiary companies and by individual plant units. It should be further broken down into manual and non-manual workers; men and women; skilled, semi-skilled and unskilled; indigenous workers, nationals from the parent company and other foreign workers.
> Information on employment and other relevant social data is to be given by main product groups belonging to particular industries. This industrial or major product data should include . . . employment figures with their breakdown into categories. . . .[28]

At the national level, social responsibility disclosures perhaps find their greatest expression in France. Following the recommendations of the Sudreau report on French Company Law reform, a new French Company Decree requires all enterprises employing more than 750 employees to supply their works councils,[29] union representatives, and the inspecteur du travail (an official of the French Labor Administration) with an annual social report covering in great detail matters such as employment, wages, social costs, working conditions, and training and industrial relations. As an example, one subcategory alone—"Other Working Conditions"—contains over 23 disclosure items ranging from the numbers of workers older than 50 with night versus day jobs to the number of employees subjected to noise levels in excess of 85 decibels! In addition, a special social report must be presented for each separate enterprise unit employing a minimum of 300 workers. In 1982, firms employing more than 300 employees had to prepare their first social report covering activities of the previous year.

Although French companies are not required to furnish these special reports for external consumption, it is highly likely that such reports will be influential in light of the growing practice of French firms to supply their shareholders with social data.

Current Practices

With the exception of special-purpose reports such as those required under the new Company Decree in France or industrial census reports required by national departments of commerce or bureaus of economic analysis, social responsibility disclosure requirements are either in the developmental stage or voluntary. This is due, no doubt, to the absence of conceptually sound and definitive systems of social responsibility measurement and reporting. Nevertheless, a growing number of corporations have begun to experiment individually with social responsibility disclosures, not the least of which are MNCs. This is

---

[28] International Confederation of Free Trade Unions, *Multinational Charter of Trade Union Demands for the Legislative Control of Multinational Companies* (Brussels: ICFTU, 1975), pp. 34–36.

[29] Works councils are special committees mandated by law for companies with more than 50 employees. The committee consists of elected employees and one or two senior management executives. It serves as a forum for discussing employee issues and economic problems, such as investments and layoffs.

an area in which multinationals may very well become accounting innovators and practice leaders.

A recent survey by Lafferty and Cairns sheds some light on the social disclosure practices of the world's largest industrial corporations.[30] Among the social disclosures scrutinized were employment reports, value-added statements, and environmental statements.

Approximately one-half of the corporations surveyed devoted separate sections of their annual reports to employee data. Companies revealed a wide variety of employee information. Also disclosed were information on numbers employed as well as analytical breakdowns by location, sex, qualifications, age, length of service, and job. In terms of extent and quality, French companies (e.g., Moet-Hennessy) were exemplary. Informative disclosures were also found among West German (e.g., Daimler-Benz) and Swedish (e.g., Svenska Cellulosa) companies. Appendix 7B presents an excerpt of employee disclosures provided by Daimler-Benz, the German automobile manufacturer.

Value-added statements, rarely found in North American reports, were discerned in the reports of European-based MNCs, notably those from the United Kingdom and West Germany. Value-added accounting is among the special technical issues covered in Chapter 6. Value-added disclosures are a prime example of a multinational reporting innovation as legal or professional disclosure requirements in this respect are nonexistent. The consolidated value-added statement from the BOC Group in the United Kingdom is illustrated in Exhibit 7.1. Consistent with our discussion in Chapter 5, BOC presents its comparative value-added statements on a current cost basis.

In contrast to employee and value-added disclosures, the *Financial Times* survey discerned scant disclosures with respect to the environment. Notable exceptions were generally company-specific, with a wide variation in the extent and quality of environmental disclosures across countries and industries.

Information disclosure regarding number of employees has proven to be of great interest to the United Nations. To begin, number-of-employees disclosure by geographic area affords host governments information as to the impact of transnational corporations on their aggregate employment base. Limited employment in certain geographic areas revealed by such disclosures could conceivably reflect problems requiring government attention. Employee disclosure by line of business, in turn, helps identify those industries and activities that are deemed economically attractive to foreign direct investors. Should these activities conflict with host country employment objectives, for example, if a foreign investor confines its activities to labor-intensive operations that expand unskilled employment as opposed to more technology-oriented pursuits that expand skilled-labor employment, the host government could take appropriate measures to encourage foreign investment activities in desired directions. Segmented data by functional categories carry the analysis of employment structure a step further. Combined with geographical and/or line-of-business

---

[30] Michael Lafferty and David Cairns, *1980 Financial Times Survey of Annual Reports* (London: Financial Times, 1980).

EXHIBIT 7.1   Consolidated Statement of Value Added (Years ended 30th September)

	1982 £ million	%	1981 £ million	%
Turnover	1 534.2		1 521.7	
Bought in materials, services and depreciation	(955.1)		(961.4)	
Value added	579.1		560.3	
Investment income	2.8		3.5	
Extraordinary items	6.0		0.6	
	587.9		564.4	
Applied as follows:				
To employees as pay or as contributions to pensions and welfare schemes	446.8	76.0	429.8	76.2
To banks and other lenders as interest	65.3	11.1	65.7	11.6
To governments as taxes on profits	24.0	4.1	35.0	6.2
To partners in companies not wholly owned by the Group	7.6	1.3	6.5	1.2
To shareholders	19.5	3.3	16.9	3.0
	563.2	95.8	553.9	98.2
Amount retained within the Group	24.7	4.2	10.5	1.8
	587.9	100.0	564.4	100.0

Regional analysis:	Value added 1982 Total £ million	Per employee £	Value added 1981 Total £ million	Per employee £
Europe	203.7	13 500	184.3	10 400
Africa	47.2	8 900	52.2	9 600
Americas	251.2	18 300	240.8	17 100
Asia	2.3	2 200	2.7	3 000
Pacific	74.7	14 400	80.3	15 800
	579.1	14 300	560.3	13 000

Value added is a measure of the amount of wealth that the Group creates by its activities throughout the world. This statement shows the value added in 1982 and how it has been shared among those contributing towards its creation.

The amounts are stated on the current cost accounting basis. The 1981 figures have been restated as a result of changes in accounting policies

reporting, employee disclosure by function enables governments and labor groups to examine whether employment practices of transnational corporations are consistent with local norms. Examples include the hiring of women and other minorities, age structure and seniority patterns, nationals versus expatriates, and salaried as opposed to nonsalaried employment patterns.

Tabulated results of a U.N. study on number-of-employees disclosures appears in Table 7.6. With the exception of Sweden and the United Kingdom, which leaned toward yearly averages, most countries disclose employee numbers in terms of year-end totals. Data for two years were common, although the

TABLE 7.6 Number of Employees: An International Comparison

	CANADA (N = 7)	WEST GERMANY (N = 18)	JAPAN (N = 17)	SWEDEN (N = 15)	SWITZERLAND (N = 8)	UNITED KINGDOM (N = 43)	UNITED STATES (N = 147)
Measurement base							
None	28	22	47	60	25	28	45
Yearly average	—	28	6	27	12	35	18
Year-end	72	39	47	13	62	20	36
Monthly average	—	5	—	—	—	—	—
Yearly average plus year-end	—	5	—	—	—	2	—
Weekly average	—	—	—	—	—	14	—
Number of years							
1	—	—	23	—	16	40	17
2	83	46	54	60	16	50	34
3–4	—	6	8	—	—	—	—
5	17	27	15	40	50	10	46
6–9	—	18	—	—	16	—	2
10	—	—	—	—	—	—	—
11+	—	—	—	—	—	—	—
Line of business							
Disclosure	14	28	6	27	25	5	4
Nondisclosure	86	72	94	73	75	95	96
Geographical area							
Disclosure	14	22	6	27	38	19	3
Nondisclosure	86	78	94	73	62	81	97
Domestic/worldwide							
Disclosure	14	17	—	40	12	32	8
Nondisclosure	86	83	100	60	88	68	92

Adapted from United Nations Economic and Social Council, *Information Disclosure: Number of Employees* (New York: UN, E/C.10/Ac.3/8, 1980), p. 27.

United States and Switzerland tend to favor five-year statistics. West Germany, Sweden, and Switzerland are more inclined to disclose segmental employee numbers whereas Japan and the United States appear least inclined to do so.

Some Issues

Nonfinancial and expanded social disclosures being suggested for MNCs by international organizations such as the United Nations and the OECD raise a number of issues. To begin with, many of the disclosure items called for are items for which measurement constructs do not yet exist. Take, for example, the nonfinancial disclosure category "Number of employees by geographical and business segments." Accurate measurement of the term "Number of employees" may encompass full-time, part-time, temporary, or contract employees; it may also include year-end, yearly average, month-end, or monthly average head counts. Other measurement problems include (1) accounting for transfers of employees from one industry or geographical segment to another, (2) allocating general and administrative service employees to lines of business, and (3) even measuring the number employed within a geographic area. As an illustration of the latter, assume that an MNC acquires 51 percent of the shares of a going concern in country X. In this case, should the acquiring company include 51 percent of the employees of the acquired company as its own? Or, should it include 100 percent? Similar questions arise in connection with multinational joint-venture arrangements as well as nonconsolidated affiliates where the parent company's ownership interest is less than 50 percent. Under these circumstances, is it meaningful to recommend the international adoption of nonfinancial disclosures before an adequate measurement framework is in place? Is this a case of "putting the cart before the horse"?

Even if nonfinancial measurement rules existed, a number of issues would still remain. First, nonfinancial measurement rules would inevitably vary internationally to reflect environmental circumstances peculiar to individual nation-states. Studies advocating uniform measurement rules thus seem called for. At the same time, however, uniform measurement rules could destroy the utility of resulting measurements. Consider, for example, the U.N. disclosure items "Average hours worked" and "Number of women employees—by function." Since collective bargaining is currently undertaken on a local or national basis and since the number of hours worked or women employed can only have reference to the socioeconomic and cultural mores of a particular society, what meaning would uniform measurements have for consolidation or comparative purposes?

A closely related issue is that of objectives and purposes. Whereas financial disclosures have traditionally been oriented toward shareholders and creditors, social disclosures appear to be oriented toward noninvestor groups. At the present time there have been few formal studies aimed at identifying who these noninvestor groups are and the nature of their information needs. If, for example, nonfinancial disclosures are intended to produce redistributional effects to satisfy certain political aims as opposed to greater corporate transparency, then the effort to establish transnational reporting and disclosure standards is fraught with political and economic considerations that have not seriously entered the debate in accounting. Examining the costs and benefits of transnational disclosure from the vantage point of political economy as opposed to microeconomics would appear to be a promising research area.

CONCLUSION

Developments highlighted in this chapter suggest that the interest in transnational reporting and disclosure has attained new highs. That this trend will continue is supported by three general observations.[31]

First, disclosure holds relatively little emotional content for accountants (even though this may not be the case for business people and bankers who feel that a certain degree of business secrecy is an essential ingredient of a competitive system). In contrast, accounting measurements are much more controversial. Disagreements will no doubt continue over such issues as who should be given proprietary responsibility for the preparation and issuance of financial statements or the nature of environmental disclosures. These debates, however, pale when compared to emotional accounting issues such as the accounting treatment of foreign currency translation gains and losses, the use of current values in making accounting measurements, or the measurement of social benefits and costs.

Second, changes in disclosure requirements are more easily implemented than changes in measurement rules. The latter directly impact user decisions and consequent behavior patterns for individual employees to large industrial corporations to international government agencies. A change in a disclosure requirement, on the other hand, does not require changes in an underlying measurement system. Hence, it is more easily tolerated if its merit is appealing or the authority of its sponsor clearly recognized.

Third, notwithstanding the well-intentioned work of international accounting organizations such as the IASC, a comprehensive set of internationally accepted and enforceable accounting principles does not yet exist. Moreover, it is increasingly clear that a single set of accounting measurement rules may not serve equally well under every known social, economic, and legal system. Thus, efforts to standardize accounting have met with much frustration. Yet, this same frustration is what adds to the appeal of more and better disclosure. A company can disclose and "be with it" without giving up its national accounting "roots." Disclosure may well be the solution to the international accounting dilemma.

In light of these trends we offer some broad guidelines in relation to the disclosure needs for transnational reporting. These guidelines are as qualitative as the disclosure process itself.

[31] Gerhard G. Mueller, "An International View of Accounting and Disclosure," *The International Journal of Accounting*, Fall 1972, pp. 117–134.

General Interest

Since there is a broad awareness of and general public interest in multinational business affairs, disclosure of a company's multinational involvements should become a standard item of financial reporting. As a minimum, each publicly owned company should report regularly (a) all exchanges on which its securities are listed or admitted for trading, (b) an estimate of the number and percentage of ownership holders not residing in the company's country of domicile, and (c) the full extent of a company's multinational business involvement—whether it extends only to minor export-import activities, multinational business based on direct foreign investments or joint-venture arrangements, or transnational sourcing of capital. Even if a company were not involved at all with any type of multinational activities, it appears that present social and economic climates dictate that investors be so informed explicitly. Disclosure is (at present) the only vehicle by which this can be achieved.

Type of Disclosure

Effective disclosure should relate directly to the financial statements in question. This means that referenced footnotes or elaboration reports tied directly to financial statement items constitute the most desirable type of disclosure. Disclosure is least effective when it occurs in documents or media entirely separate from an annual report or when specific disclosure occurs in a manner that appears to disassociate it from corresponding financial statements.

Nature of Disclosure

Several qualitative objectives for financial statements are spelled out in FAS No. 2, including relevance, understandability, verifiability, neutrality, comparability, and timeliness (see Figure 2.3). These qualitative standards are directly relevant to disclosure in transnational financial reporting. For instance, verifiability is comparatively more difficult when financial reports cross national borders, and therefore appropriate disclosures may be even more important here than in counterpart domestic reporting. The same applies to neutrality. Accounting neutrality vis-à-vis business transactions and events is not a foregone conclusion or general condition. Relatively more disclosure in international circumstances can help to render financial information more neutral.

Comparability and timeliness can never be achieved entirely. Nonetheless, as their accomplishment seems very elusive in most transnational situations, particular attention should be paid to them.

Quantification

Any national set of generally accepted accounting standards and principles constitutes a language. And languages are means of communication serving specified information purposes. But different national users of financial statements do not always understand each other's accounting principles language. While disclosure facilitates international financial communications somewhat, resorting to a more commonly understood language may prove desirable. Such a language may be the quantitative expressions that are a part of the general accounting language. While quantification should be used as widely as possible as a tool of disclosure in transnational reporting, nonquantifiable expressions should not be precluded if they improve the communicative effect of accounting messages. This is likely to be the case when accounting for multinational corporate social responsibilities. New reporting dimensions must be charted when responding to the information needs of nontraditional audiences-of-interest.

APPENDIX 7A

New SEC Disclosure Requirements for
Non-U.S. Issuers (approved November 18, 1982)

Introduction
The following rules apply to registration, under the U.S. Securities Act of 1933, of securities offerings by foreign issuers, except for North American companies (e.g.—Canadian or Mexican issuers). The rules are designed as part of the Commission's integrated disclosure system, by which registration statements under the U.S. Securities Act of 1933 utilize, to the maximum degree feasible, annual reports submitted on Form 20-F, under the U.S. Securities Exchange Act of 1934.

Three new forms are also prescribed for use by foreign issuers filing Form 20-F. All would be distinct from the forms used by domestic issuers. Thus, any future changes in rules and forms used by domestic issuers would not automatically apply to foreign issuers.

Disclosure Requirements
The registration statements of foreign issuers continue to be subject to the disclosure requirements for textual material set forth in Regulation S-K of the Commission, and the disclosure requirements for financial statements set forth in Regulation S-X of the Commission. However, several significant changes proposed for foreign issuers include:

Financial Statements: A foreign registrant may prepare its financial statements in accordance with generally accepted accounting principles of its home country. However, the registrant is required to identify the body of accounting principles followed and to quantify the material differences between those principles and U.S. Generally Accepted Accounting Principles (GAAP). In addition, unless one of the exceptions outlined below is available, the registrant is required to disclose all other information required by U.S. GAAP and Regulation S-X, including segment reporting, pension information, reserve recognition accounting and other supplemental information.

Exceptions: Disclosure of all information required by U.S. GAAP and Regulation S-X is *not* required in:

Annual reports on Form 20-F;

Offerings of certain non-convertible debt securities that are rated in one of the four highest rating categories for debt by at least one nationally recognized rating organization; and

Rights, dividend reinvestment plans and certain other offerings to shareholders or employees.

(However, quantification of material differences between U.S. and foreign GAAP is still required in all three of these exceptions.)

Segment Reporting: Unless an exception is available, foreign issuers would be required—as are domestic issuers—to disclose revenues and profits (or losses) for each industry segment.

Exceptions are comparable to those available for financial statements—i.e., annual reports on Form 20-F, offerings of specified highly rated non-convertible debt securities, and certain offerings to shareholders or employees. (The modified segment provisions in Form 20-F are retained, requiring disclosure by industrial segment only on a revenue basis, accompanied by a narrative discussion only if the revenue contributions of segments differ materially from their contributions to profits or losses.)

Management Disclosure: A foreign issuer is required to disclose only the aggregate amount of remuneration paid to all officers and directors as a group, unless relevant information relating to individuals has previously been disclosed to shareholders or otherwise made public.

Similarly, a foreign issuer must disclose the interest of officers or directors in certain transactions only if that information is disclosed to shareholders or otherwise made public.

Management Discussion and Analysis: The SEC recently amended Regulation S-K to require management to comment on the registrant's liquidity, capital resources and operations. The amended requirement must be included in Form 20-F.

The New Forms
As revised, Form 20-F will provide the basis for an integrated disclosure system for eligible issuers wishing to file registration statements. Eligibility to use proposed new Forms F-1, F-2, and F-3 will vary with the status of the registrant.

Form F-3:
Integration: A registrant may incorporate Form 20-F information in the prospectus by reference, but must deliver Form 20-F on request.

Eligibility: A registrant must have been a reporting company for at least 36 months. Voting stock held by nonaffiliates must have aggregate market value, worldwide, equivalent to at least $500 million, $150 million of which is owned beneficially or of record by U.S. residents. (Exception: For highly rated non-convertible debt securities only the 36-month reporting requirement applies.)

Transactions: Eligible registrants may use this form:

If securities are offered for cash and the registrant's latest Form 20-F filing discloses all information required by U.S. GAAP and Regulation S-X;

If certain highly rated non-convertible debt securities are offered for cash (even without all GAAP and S-X information);

For rights offerings, dividends or interest reinvestment plans and conversions or warrants (even without all GAAP and S-X information).

Form F-2:
Integration: A registrant may deliver Form 20-F with the prospectus, in lieu of including the Form 20-F information in the prospectus.

Eligibility: A registrant must have securities registered under Sections 12(b) or 12(g) of the Securities Exchange Act of 1934, or be required to file reports pursuant to Section 15(d) of that Act and have either:

Filed all required reports for at least the past 36 months, or

Filed at least one Form 20-F and the aggregate market value, worldwide, of voting stock held by non-affiliates is the equivalent of at least $500 million, $150 million of which is owned beneficially or of record by U.S. residents.

Transactions: Eligible registrants may use this form to register securities offered in any transactions except exchange offers.

Form F-1:
No Integration: A registrant must include in the prospectus all information required by Form 20-F, plus additional information.

Eligibility: This form must be used when a foreign issuer is not eligible to use either Form F-3 or F-2.

Transactions: This form may be used for any offering. It is also the only form that may be used to register securities in an exchange offer. (Foreign issuers may wish to comment on whether forms F-3 and F-2 should also be available for exchange offers.)

Timeliness of Financial Statements
Under the Commission's new ruling, foreign issuers who are eligible to use Form 20-F submit, in the filing of the registration statement, audited financial statements from two prior years if:

The filing is made within six months after the end of the issuer's most recent fiscal year;

At the time of the filing, the audited financial statements for the most recent fiscal year are not yet available, and

On the effective date of the registration statement, the issuer provides an unaudited financial statement as of a date no later than five months before the effective date of the registration statement.

The Commission also permits that in the case of certain offerings to shareholders, such as pro rata rights offerings, the financial statements may be up to one year old at the effective date of the registration statement. Statements in these instances now may be up to 18 months old.

Currency Translations
The SEC believes that exchange rates and the rate of inflation are of material importance to investors. Under current practice, many foreign registrants present "convenience translations," whereby foreign currency amounts are translated into U.S. currency on the basis of the exchange rate in effect on a specified date or the average exchange rate during each report period.

However, noting that volatile exchange rate fluctuations can make "convenience translations" misleading, the Commission requires foreign issuers to indicate the relevant monetary situation:

Currency In Which Financial Statements Are Presented
A foreign issuer is required to present its primary financial statements in the currency of the country in which it is incorporated or organized, unless it conducts a majority of its business and keeps its books and records in another currency.

A foreign issuer must present selected information in the same currency used in the primary financial statement and reconcile that information with U.S. GAAP and Regulation S-X.

The Commission would not object if the registrant also chooses to translate the selected data or its financial statement into U.S. currency for the most recent fiscal year and any subsequent interim period.

Effects of Inflation
Although the SEC has not asked foreign issuers to comply with SFAS-33, the general standard for inflation accounting by U.S. issuers, it requires alternative means of disclosing the effects of inflation. If the financial statements are denominated in the currency of a country that has experienced inflationary effects exceeding a total of 100% over the most recent three fiscal years, and have not been recast or otherwise supplemented to provide information on a constant currency or current cost basis, the issuer is required to provide either supplementary information to quantify, or supplementary financial statements to indicate, the effects of changing prices on its financial condition and operating results.

Exchange Rates and Dividends
The Commission requires foreign issuers to provide a history of exchange rates for the most recent 5-year period and a 5-year summary of dividends per share, stated in both the currency in which the financial statements are presented and U.S. currency, based on the exchange rates at each respective payment date.

Source: New York Stock Exchange.

APPENDIX 7B

Employee Disclosures

Emphasis of our Personnel Policy. The central objective of our personnel policy in 1981 continued to be the assurance of steady employment to the greatest possible extent in all areas of our company. In view of the labor market problems, we consider our ability to add about 2,800 new jobs of significance for the whole economy.

Of increasing significance for our labor policy is the continuing adaptation of working conditions in production and administration to the employee's needs, while at the same time maintaining technical and economic efficiency. To achieve this, additional effort must be invested in training and education, both basic and advanced, as well as in individual career development and the maintenance of good relations between management and employees.

Constructive cooperation with the general and plant works councils based on mutual trust acquires an even greater significance in view of the growing tasks. We are very happy, therefore, that we can again report having reached a consensus in talks on all major issues of mutual concern during the year 1981, despite frequent differences in our initial positions.

Labor Contracts. In the metal working industry, wage and salary increases of 4.9% became effective on April 1, 1981. A lump-sum of DM 160 was paid for each of the months of February and March, 1981. In addition, the next-to-last stage on the way to a contractual six-week vacation for all employees took effect as provided for in the 1979 agreement. The average vacation entitlement of our employees already passed the 30-day mark last year, including the contractual and statutory vacation supplement for high seniority employees and disabled persons.

Social Welfare Law. The increase in the social security contribution rate and in the social security wage base (to DM 4,400), with proportionate effects on unemployment and health insurance, contributed to a further rise in personnel expenses in 1981. Some 150 employees were active as employer or employee representatives on committees dealing with pension, health and accident insurance and labor administration.

Employees. In the last five years, our company has created about 22,000 new jobs in the Federal Republic of Germany. Of significance for the whole economy is, above all, the fact that the steady growth of employment at our Company was not only possible in areas with comparatively low unemployment rates, such as the Middle Neckar region, but, to our satisfaction, also in economically depressed regions.

Daimler-Benz AG 1981: 148,361 Employees.

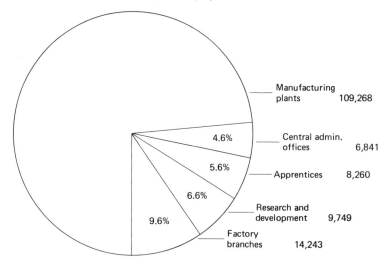

	Manufacturing plants	109,268
4.6%	Central admin. offices	6,841
5.6%	Apprentices	8,260
6.6%	Research and development	9,749
9.6%	Factory branches	14,243

It was our endeavor again in 1981 to differentiate job status solely on the basis of function. Accordingly, the differentiation between wage earners and salaried employees plays an increasingly smaller role. Meanwhile, nearly a third of all wage earners have the so-called "monthly wage" contracts; in this way, a far reaching assimilation of job status between wage earners and salaried employees has been achieved.

YEAR-END FIGURES—DAIMLER-BENZ AG

Figures at year-end	1972	1973	1974	1975	1976	1977	1978	1979	1980	1981
Group	143,793	150,014	149,175	149,742	155,003	163,302	167,165	174,431	183,392	187,961
Foreign	19,498	21,638	25,135	26,597	27,985	31,088	31,890	32,267	37,069	38,865
Domestic	124,295	128,376	124,040	123,145	127,018	132,214	135,275	142,164	146,323	149,096
of which:										
Daimler-Benz AG	122,601	126,855	122,899	122,775	126,652	131,807	134,437	141,401	145,532	148,361
of which:										
Main office	6,100	6,735	6,599	6,533	6,728	7,220	7,649	8,180	8,810	9,487
Plants										
Untertuerkheim	22,794	23,411	22,469	22,095	22,950	24,115	24,495	25,054	25,565	25,573
Sindelfingen	30,567	31,580	30,682	30,955	33,232	34,359	34,558	36,551	37,194	38,353
Mannheim	12,373	12,730	12,863	12,900	12,901	13,383	13,584	14,053	14,619	14,521
Woerth	7,458	8,201	8,400	8,687	8,430	8,853	8,774	9,622	10,192	11,055
Gaggenau	7,968	8,397	8,704	8,680	8,603	8,696	8,860	9,177	9,354	9,707
Bremen	4,099	3,923	3,496	4,099	4,293	4,727	5,994	6,571	6,515	6,309
Duesseldorf	4,652	4,712	4,476	4,401	4,572	4,664	4,621	4,954	5,118	5,058
Kassel	3,795	4,012	3,774	3,838	3,931	4,089	3,969	4,086	4,341	4,359
Berlin	2,504	2,754	2,723	2,886	2,895	3,065	3,054	3,191	3,252	3,473
Hamburg-Harburg	2,065	1,875	1,706	1,736	2,184	2,265	2,385	2,475	2,535	2,613
Bad Homburg	860	696	685	692	715	736	767	814	855	881
Branches	16,537	17,162	15,689	14,705	14,693	15,157	15,727	16,673	17,182	16,972

Disabled Persons. More than 8,300 of our employees were recognized as disabled at the end of 1981. That is about 6% of our work force. We also place a large number of orders with workshops for the handicapped. The total volume of such orders was about DM 13 million in 1981.

Foreign Employees. The proportion of foreign employees in the work force of 21.8% is essentially unchanged from last year's 21.7%. We have further expanded educational programs for foreign employees, particularly for young "second-generation foreigners.''

Social Security. In 1981, DM 127 million were disbursed for current benefits to 31,493 pensioners, widows and children. Payments to employees who retired in 1981 averaged DM 539 monthly. At the end of 1981, 1,886 former employees who had resigned—more than half of them foreigners—had vested pension rights. In 150 cases, pension benefits are already being paid. Pensioners, or their survivors, received transition payments totaling DM 15 million. Moreover, we were able to assist 6,000 employees in individual cases with one-time payments. It is particularly gratifying that the proportion of disability cases has declined among new pension recipients.

Health, Job Safety. The health services at our factories were further extended through construction of new and alteration of existing buildings as well as improvements in medical facilities and equipment. At the end of 1981, 155 physicians and medical assistants were employed at Daimler-Benz, to which the private physicians under contract by our branches and sub-branches must be added.

For each million productive man-hours, only 69 accidents occurred, with an average of nine workdays lost per accident. The 1981 accident rate was cut by more than 4% from 1980.

In 1981, the sickness level trend changed direction for the first time in years. In relation to the number of hours that should have been worked, the overall sickness level declined from 8.7 to 8.5% (wage earners 9.8%, salaried employees 4.9%).

SUMMARY OF PERSONNEL EXPENSES—DAIMLER-BENZ AG

	1981		1980		1981 to 1980
	millions of DM	in % of wages and salaries (basic expenditure)	millions of DM	in % of wages and salaries (basic expenditure)	Change in %
Wages and salaries (basic expenditure)	4,234.3	100.0	3,954.3	100.0	+ 7.1
Paid vacation and other time off	1,693.0	40.0	1,558.9	39.4	+ 8.6
Normal paid vacation (Union contract)	665.6		600.1		
Additional paid vacation	324.6		293.3		
Holiday pay	203.5		190.1		
Wage and salary continuation pay during illness	352.4		339.9		
Other time off and convalescence	146.9		135.5		

SUMMARY OF PERSONNEL EXPENSES (*continued*)

	1981		1980		1981 to 1980
	millions of DM	in % of wages and salaries (basic expenditure)	millions of DM	in % of wages and salaries (basic expenditure)	Change in %
Contribution for employee benefits	960.8	22.7	879.1	22.2	+ 9.3
Medical and social security contributions	893.3		817.5		
Contributions to employee trade associations	60.3		58.1		
Contributions to Pension Insurance Association	7.2		3.5		
Special payments	469.1	11.1	430.1	10.9	+ 9.1
Christmas and special remuneration	363.7		328.1		
Formation of personal capital	105.4		102.0		
Pay during training periods[1]	188.6	4.4	170.8	4.3	+10.4
Social services[1]	166.1	3.9	157.7	4.0	+ 5.3
deduct-amounts included twice	− 122.4	− 2.9	−111.4		+ 9.9
Personnel expenses (without old-age pensions)	7,589.5	179.2	7,039.5	178.0	+ 7.8
Old-age pensions	688.1	16.3	1.680.5	42.5	•
of which: extraordinary pension provisions	—	—	1,408.0	35.6	•
Total personnel expenses[2]	8,277.6	195.5	7,312.0	184.9	+13.2
of which: shown under "other expenses"	17.6		15.4		•
Personnel expenses as shown in "Statement of income"	8,260.0		8,704.6		− 5.1

[1] without allocated overhead. [2] in 1980, without extraordinary pension provisions

Employee Capital Formation. In addition to the contractually guaranteed DM 624, every employee received a voluntary payment of DM 156 for capital-forming investments in 1981. Employees were able to choose between employee shares and company debt certificates. We are happy to say that the number of employee shareholders increased still more and now numbers 74,800 (last year 62,100). Our employees have purchased some 270,000 employee shares since 1973. Over 9,000 employees took company debt certificates in 1981.

We specifically promoted personal capital formation by our employees in the form of home or apartment purchases again in 1981. In all, we extended loans totalling DM 33.4 million for the construction of about 1,650 employee-owned apartments or homes in 1981.

Shift Work, Working Conditions. We systematically carried on our vigorous efforts to improve working conditions in 1981. Our program, focusing on specific objectives, included the following measures:

We want to raise the quality of workplace planning: aspects of workplace design, more human work flow and job environment are already taken into account in the early phases of planning.

The know-how and experience in workplace design are incorporated during installation of new manufacturing facilities. This involves a number of measures ranging from greatest possible reduction of so-called overhead work to rational use of industrial robots and from buffering to removal of preparatory operations from assembly line production.

In view of the age structure of our work force, we will increase our efforts to provide more jobs for older workers and employees with reduced job efficiency.

The comprehensive exchange of information on new approaches to workplace design will be intensified.

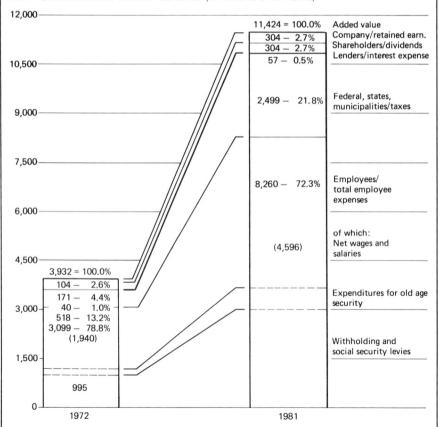

Added Value Statement–Daimler-Benz AG (in millions of D-Marks)

Suggestion Program. The promotion of the Company suggestion program remains an important tool of management. Just under 7,000 employees submitted some

14,500 suggestions in 1981, for which awards totalling DM 3.2 million were paid. *Educational Policy.* We continued our efforts to further differentiate the training opportunities offered by us according to Company requirements and the applicants' prior education. Today we offer training in 35 technical and eight commercial occupations, in vocational lecture courses for high school students, and at the Baden-Wuerttemberg Vocational Academy for high school graduates.

We again increased the number of openings for apprentices in 1981. With 2,500 youngsters commencing training, the total number of apprentices and students undergoing practical training reached its highest level ever at the end of 1981 at 8,260. In addition, about a third of our managerial staff took part in continuing management training courses.

Daimler-Benz AG 1981 Annual Report.

SELECTED REFERENCES

BAVISHI, VINOD B., and HAROLD E. WYMAN, "Foreign Operations Disclosures by U.S.-Based Multinational Corporations: Are They Inadequate?" *International Journal of Accounting,* Fall 1980, pp. 153–168.

BEDFORD, NORTON M. *Extensions in Accounting Disclosure,* Englewood Cliffs, N.J.: Prentice-Hall, Inc., 1973, 208 pp.

CHOI, FREDERICK D. S., "Financial Disclosure in Relation to a Firm's Capital Costs," *Accounting and Business Research,* Autumn 1973, pp. 282–292.

CHOI, FREDERICK D. S., and ARTHUR I. STONEHILL, "Foreign Access to U.S. Securities Markets: The Theory, Myth and Reality of Regulatory Barriers," *The Investment Analyst,* July 1982, pp. 17–26.

FINANCIAL ACCOUNTING STANDARDS BOARD, "Financial Reporting for Segments of a Business Enterprise," *Statement of Financial Accounting Standards No. 14,* Stamford, Conn.: FASB, 1976, 58 pp.

GRAY, ROB, and BOB PERKS, "How Desirable Is Social Accounting?" *Accountancy,* April 1982, pp. 101–102.

GRAY, S. J., and K. T. MAUNDERS, *Value Added Reporting: Uses and Measurement,* London: Associations of Certified Accountants, 1980.

GRAY, S. J., J. C. SHAW, and L. B. McSWEENEY, "Accounting and Information Disclosure," unpublished manuscript, University of Glasgow, October 1981, 141 pp.

LAFFERTY, MICHAEL, and DAVID CAIRNS, *1980 Financial Times World Survey of Annual Reports,* London: Financial Times, 1980, 334 pp.

LEES, FRANCIS A., *Reporting Transnational Business Operations,* New York: The Conference Board, Inc., 1980, 43 pp.

MAUTZ, R. K., and WILLIAM G. MAY, *Financial Disclosure in a Competitive Economy,* New York: Financial Executives Research Foundation, 1978, 286 pp.

MENDELSON, MORRIS, and SIDNEY ROBBINS, *Investment Analysis and Securities Markets,* New York: Basic Books, Inc., 1976, 755 pp.

MILLER, MALCOLM C., and MARK R. SCOTT, *Financial Reporting by Segments,* Melbourne: Australian Accounting Research Foundation, 1980, 120 pp.

MUELLER, GERHARD G., "An International View of Accounting and Disclosure," *The International Journal of Accounting,* Fall 1972, pp. 117–134.

MUELLER, GERHARD G., and LAUREN M. WALKER, "The Coming Age of Transnational Financial Reporting," *Journal of Accountancy,* July 1976, pp. 67–74.

SCHREUDER, HEIN, "Employees and the Corporate Social Report: The Dutch Case," *The Accounting Review,* April 1981, pp. 294–308.

STONEHILL, ARTHUR I., and KARE B. DULLUM, *Internationalizing the Cost of Capital in Theory and Practice,* New York: John Wiley & Sons, 1982, 157 pp.

UNITED NATIONS CENTER ON TRANSNATIONAL CORPORATIONS, *Towards International Standardization of Corporate Accounting and Reporting,* New York: United Nations, 1982, 104 pp.

WALTER, INGO, and TRACY MURRAY, *Handbook of International Business,* New York: John Wiley & Sons, 1982, 1230 pp.

ZEFF, STEPHEN, "Greater Disclosure Fever Spreading Across the Globe," *World Accounting Report,* February 1979, p. 2.

DISCUSSION QUESTIONS

1. Briefly explain the distinction between accounting measurements and accounting disclosure. Which of the two reporting processes do you feel promises substantial innovative advances during the balance of this decade? Why?

2. Why is corporate financial disclosure so important in a competitive world economy?

3. Identify at least four reasons why multinational corporations are increasingly being held accountable to audiences-of-interest beyond traditional investor groups.

4. Multinational corporations have viewed the trend toward more and varied corporate disclosures with mixed emotions. Discuss the nature of these concerns and present your evaluation of their legitimacy.

5. "Foreign companies seeking to issue securities in a domestic capital market such as the U.S. markets should be required to disclose no less than their domestic counterparts." Explain whether you agree with this statement and support your argument with a country example.

6. Financial statements are said to have a single "reporting domicile." Explain what is meant by this expression and its implications for transnational financial reporting.

7. Is there a difference between special purpose reports and secondary financial statements as advocated by the AISG?

8. What is the purpose of foreign operations disclosures and what formal guidance exists internationally with respect to this reporting development?

9. Several empirical studies have concluded that foreign operations disclosures of both U.S. and non-U.S.-based MNCs are far from adequate. What is the basis for such conclusions? Can you suggest any criteria that may be helpful in improving the current state of the art?

10. What is meant by the term *social responsibility disclosure?* What purposes does it serve internationally and why is it still at a nascent stage of development?

EXERCISES

1. Using the data provided in Table 7.2, partition the extent of the ten countries' disclosure requirements into three categories—"high disclosure," "medium disclosure," and "low disclosure." What are the implications of your classification scheme for international investors? Foreign issuers?

2. Construct a table that contrasts the foreign operations (segmental) disclosure requirements of the various international accounting organizations mentioned in this chapter including those of the United States (per FAS No. 14). Column headings should read IASC, UNCTC, OECD, EEC, United States, and any other country for which such information is readily available. Row headings should list various disclosure items, for example, revenues by geographic area, assets by geographic area, and so forth. Using checkmarks in each matrix cell to denote the presence or absence of a given requirement, discuss the implication of your tabulation for the international standards movement, that is, which organization(s) appears to be exerting a leadership role in the area of foreign operations disclosures?

3. Set out in columnar format the various multiple disclosure formats discussed in this chapter (i.e., convenience translations, special information, limited restatements, and secondary statements) that are being employed by MNCs as a means of resolving the transnational reporting problem.
    Required:
    A. List at least two positive and two negative attributes associated with each.
    B. Identify the reporting mode you feel is most helpful from a foreign reader's perspective.
    C. If you are unsatisfied with all of the options, suggest and defend a reporting framework you feel is more optimal.

4. Refer to the BOC Group's value-added statements reproduced in Exhibit 7.1. Using the information provided for 1981, rearrange the format to produce a traditional multiple-step income statement. On the basis of your restatement, identify what you feel are the major conceptual differences between the value-added statement and the income statement.

5. Reproduced in Table 7.7 is a condensed income statement of the Dutchgirl Paint Company, a U.S.-based manufacturer, including selected notes to the financial statements appearing in the company's 1985 annual report.
    The Dutchgirl Paint Company has a sizable shareholder group domiciled in the Netherlands. Accordingly, it would like to restate its income statement to Dutch guilders (DG) and in conformity with Dutch accounting principles. Information provided in Chapter 3 suggests that the valuation of nonmonetary assets at their current replacement values is generally accepted in the Netherlands. While fixed assets are depreciated in straight-line fashion for external re-

TABLE 7.7   Dutchgirl Paint Company Income Statement for the Year Ended December 31, 1985 (amounts in thousands)

Net sales[a]		$ 580,000
Cost of goods sold[b]		329,000
Gross margin		251,000
Operating expenses		
Wages	100,000	
Depreciation[c]	40,000	
Amortization of goodwill[d]	2,500	
Other	15,500	158,000
Net operating income		$ 93,000
Income tax		42,780
Net income		$ 50,220

[a] Sales volume during the year (in physical units) totaled 29,000 units, up 9 percent from the preceding year.

[b] Inventories are accounted for on a FIFO basis.

DECEMBER 31 (000s)	1985	1984
Raw materials and work in process	$13,000	$11,000
Finished goods	10,000	9,000
	$23,000	$20,000

Dealer catalogs suggest that the replacement cost of similar units averaged $13 per unit at year-end. Our lowered average unit costs are a result of improvements in our production efficiency.

[c] Depreciable plant was acquired in 1980 for $800,000,000 when the construction index stood at 80. The plant is being depreciated on a straight-line basis. At the end of 1985 the construction index was 128.

[d] Purchased goodwill, reflecting a business acquisition during the year, is being amortized over a ten-year period.

porting purposes, intangibles are generally written off to retained earnings in the year of acquisition.

Required: As the company's accountant, perform the convenience restatement assuming that the dollar/guilder exchange rate on December 31, 1985, is $.36 = DG 1.

CASE

Social Responsibility Disclosure

This case involves a practical assessment of the social responsibility disclosures of a major multinational corporation. The methodology employed is that of content analysis.

Required

Using the information provided in Tables 7.1 and 7.6 for starters, construct a checklist of employee disclosure items that you feel would prove useful to a socially conscious reader. You may assign weights to each disclosure item you select to reflect differences in perceived user importance or you may disregard a weighting scheme altogether. Implicit in this assignment is the need to develop some criterion or criteria of "usefulness" which by its very nature is user-specific (i.e., an investor may attach a different degree of importance to, say, "number of employees" than would an employee representative). Be sure to state the assumptions underlying your checklist construction.

On the basis of your disclosure checklist, numerically quantify the extent of social responsibility disclosures contained in the excerpt from Daimler-Benz's annual report reproduced in Appendix 7B. You are encouraged to examine similar sections of annual reports of other multinationals preferably in the automobile manufacturing industry such as Ford (U.S.), Honda (Japan), or British Leyland (U.K.).

In arriving at a disclosure score for Daimler-Benz, identify the major problems you encountered in (a) constructing your checklist and (b) assigning a disclosure score to the excerpt appearing in Appendix 7B.

8

Analyzing Foreign Financial Statements

Investor interest in foreign securities is growing very rapidly. The U.S. Securities Investors Association estimates that American investors bought and sold a record of $17.8 billion in foreign securities in the first year of this decade, up 77 percent from the preceding year. In similar fashion, investors domiciled outside the United States traded a record $75 billion in U.S. securities, a run-up of 72 percent!

What accounts for these increases? For one thing returns on foreign securities, comprising both dividends and capital gains, often exceed those available domestically. As illustrated in Figure 8.1, security returns in the United States during the 1970s generally trailed those in Hong Kong, Singapore, Japan, Canada, and the United Kingdom. When the effects of foreign exchange rate changes are included (e.g., Swiss shares, together with any dividends thereon, are worth more in U.S. dollars if the Swiss franc appreciates in relation to the U.S. dollar—see Chapter 4 for details), Dutch, Swiss, and French securities also outperformed those in the United States during the last decade.

Foreign securities also afford domestic investors—individual, institutional, and corporate—a means of diversifying their securities holdings internationally, thus reducing the risks of concentrating on a single country. Evidence suggests that movements of securities prices in different countries are not closely related.[1] Thus, while securities in one country are doing worse than

[1] H. Levy and M. Sarnat, "International Diversification of Investment Portfolios," *American Economic Review*, September 1970, pp. 668–675.

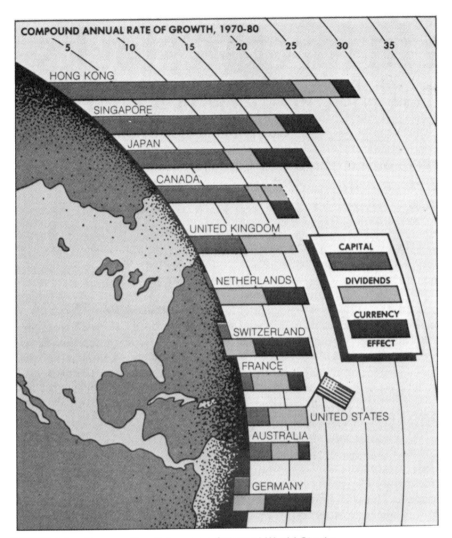

FIGURE 8.1   Comparative Returns on Selected World Stocks

Source: "The Boom in Foreign Stocks: How to Get a Piece of It," *Changing Times,* August 1981, p. 22.

anticipated, those in another might be doing better. By investing in stocks of different countries portfolio risks, measured in terms of variability of returns, are reduced.[2] Finally, domestic investors have moved into foreign securities to take advantage of special opportunities such as the expansion of the Japanese electronics industry, the development of mineral resources in Australia or the real estate boom in Hong Kong, to name but a few.

Whether investors participate in foreign companies by purchasing corpo-

_____

[2] Bruno H. Solnik, "Why Not Diversify Internationally Rather than Domestically?" *Financial Analysts Journal,* July–August 1974, pp. 48–54.

rate securities in a foreign country or acquiring foreign securities traded domestically,[3] their buy or sell decisions are ultimately based on information
contained in a company's financial statements. This is especially the case internationally as competing sources of information, prevalent in broadly based
capital markets such as those in the United States or the United Kingdom, are
less readily available. Accordingly, this chapter synthesizes information presented in Chapters 2 through 7 by examining several problems that executives
and investors can expect to encounter when analyzing foreign financial statements. All differ in terms of their relative magnitude; all vary in degree of trac-
tability. Avenues for coping with such problems are identified whenever
possible.[4]

Data Accessibility

The ability to properly analyze investment information is a major attribute of successful investors. In order to undertake such analysis, however, security analysts must have access to necessary data. In a country such as the
United States, sources of data for investment analysis abound.[5] In addition to
corporate annual reports that are sent to shareholders and other interested parties, the provision of interim financial statements and special statistical supplements affording better insights into a company's operations is common.
Corporate filings with the U.S. Securities and Exchange Commission (SEC)
are rich sources of financial information as are data provided by (1) various financial services such as Moody's Investor Services, Standard and Poor's Corp.,
and Value Line; (2) computerized data banks such as COMPUSTAT (Standard and Poor's), CRSP (Center for Research on Security Prices at the University of Chicago), and NAARS (National Automated Accounting Research
System); (3) governmental publications such as those published by the U.S.
Treasury Department, the Department of Commerce, and the Federal Trade
Commission; (4) economic research organizations such as the Conference
Board, the National Bureau of Economic Research, and the Brookings Institution; (5) indexes of security prices such as the Dow-Jones Averages, Standard
and Poor's Stock Price Index, and the NASDAQ Over-the-Counter Indexes;
and (6) business and financial publications including the news media which are
too numerous to mention.

    While the availability of published corporate information in the United
States is extremely high, parallels to various U.S. information sources can gen-

---

[3] For example, as of June 1982, there were approximately 41 foreign companies listed
on the New York Stock Exchange, 54 on the American Stock Exchange and 142 trading in
the over-the-counter markets.

[4] Observations on various corporate reporting practices are based on a content analysis
of the annual reports of 1,000 companies representing over 20 individual groupings in 20
countries. See Vinod B. Bavishi, Frederick D. S. Choi, Hany A. Shawky, and Jean-Pierre
Sapy-Mazella, *Analyzing Financial Ratios of the World's 1,000 Leading Industrial Corporations* (New York: Business International Corporation, 1981).

[5] Morris Mendelson and Sidney Robbins, *Investment Analysis and Securities Markets*
(New York: Basic Books, Inc., 1976).

erally be found in most countries around the world, although to a much lesser extent. What differs here is that foreign access to *local* information sources is much more problematic. A tour of most national public libraries will reveal limited information on nondomestic companies.

As investor interest in foreign securities continues to grow, information services that meet investors' needs for information can be expected to materialize quickly. Indeed, several developments in this regard are already underway. Several large brokerage houses such as Merrill Lynch, with branch offices in Japan, and Daiwa Securities Co., Ltd., with offices in the United States, make available to their clients *analysts' guides* detailing information on respective domestic companies. Financial information services are also beginning to increase the international supply of corporate financial data. Included here are concerns such as *Moody's Investor Services* in New York, which recently began publishing an *International Reference Manual* as a complement to its domestic data services; *Extel Card Services in London*, which provides comprehensive financial summaries on Australian, European, and North American companies; *Information Internationales* in Paris, which provides financial and operating summaries for some 700 large global companies; and *Capital International Perspectives* in Geneva, which provides financial analysis based on stock prices and dividend data on 1,500 companies worldwide. On the university front, computerized data bases containing information gleaned from foreign annual reports of the world's leading industrial enterprises are currently being assembled at such institutions as the University of Connecticut and New York University. Last but not least, users interested in financial data for specific companies may often obtain annual reports directly from companies of interest. Corporate directories of foreign enterprises are available in the reference sections of most major libraries.

Timeliness of Information

Delays in the receipt of foreign information presents a problem for domestic readers that is distinct from its availability. In South Korea, for example, companies whose shares are listed on the national stock exchange must file their annual accounts for public inspection with the Korean Securities and Exchange Commission within 45 to 60 days after year-end. In the United States, the timetable is 90 days.[6] In other countries, regulatory requirements afford companies more leeway. In the United Kingdom, annual reports of publicly held companies must be filed with the government within seven months of year-end; listed companies must submit these reports to the London Stock Exchange within six months. While annual accounts in France must be submitted within 15 days prior to the annual shareholders' meeting, such meetings can be held up to six months after the company closes its books. It is also common practice for French companies to publish parent company statements before

---

[6] Coopers & Lybrand, *International Financial Reporting and Auditing* (New York, 1979).

TABLE 8.1   Average Delay between Year-End Date and Date of Auditor's Report

NUMBER OF DAYS	COUNTRIES
1–30	None
31–60	Brazil
	Canada
	United States
61–90	Australia
	Denmark
	Finland
	Netherlands
	Norway
	Sweden
91–120	Belgium
	France
	West Germany
	India
	Malaysia
	South Africa
	Switzerland
	United Kingdom
121 and over	Austria
	Italy

publishing consolidated accounts. Similar time lags are associated with the publication of language translations that are more suitable for foreign audiences.

An insight into comparative information delays can be obtained by examining the number of days that elapse between the year-end date associated with published financial statements and the date of the auditor's report appearing thereon. The information assembled in Table 8.1 presumes that the auditor's dateline is a reasonable indication of when corporate financial information first becomes available for public consumption. Actual information delays on the average range from 30 to 60 days for Brazilian, Canadian, and American companies to over 120 days for Australian and Italian companies.

Information delays, together with other information disparities described later, have significant implications for capital market efficiency. A typical assumption in finance theory is that investors, both domestic and foreign, have ready and immediate access to all relevant information about a firm. Given this happy state of affairs, share prices of a given company will immediately reflect such information and be the same in whichever market the shares are traded. The evidence presented in this chapter makes this assumption highly suspect.

Language and Terminology
Barriers

Information barriers commonly associated with foreign financial statements include those of language and terminology. Companies domiciled in non-English-speaking countries will naturally publish their accounts in their

TABLE 8.2   Language of Financial Statements of Leading Non-U.S. Industrial Companies

PREDOMINATELY ENGLISH-LANGUAGE (0–10% OF REPORTS NON-ENGLISH)	CONSIDERABLE % NON-ENGLISH (10%–50%)	PREDOMINATELY NON-ENGLISH (50% OR MORE)
Australia	Belgium	Austria
Canada	Brazil	France
Denmark	Italy	Mexico
Finland	West Germany	South Korea
India		Spain
Ireland		
Japan		
Malaysia		
Netherlands		
Norway		
South Africa		
Sweden		
Switzerland		
United Kingdom		

national idiom. Then too, accounting terminology differences may easily confuse. Thus, the term *stock* would immediately be associated with certificates of corporate ownership by a U.S. reader. A U.K. analyst, on the other hand, would associate the term with a firm's inventory of unsold goods. Other examples of terminology differences include *turnover* (sales revenue), *debtors* and *creditors* (accounts receivable and payable), and *hire purchase* (leased assets).

An obvious remedy to the language barrier is the development of multilingual capabilities on the part of the foreign analyst. This is not an uncommon practice in many parts of the world. Most Danish investors, for example, are generally fluent in at least four languages—Danish, English, French, and German. Most Brazilians are comfortable with Spanish, Portuguese, and English.

While familiarity with languages other than one's native tongue is beneficial, a survey of the financial reports of the world's 600 leading industrial companies outside the United States suggests that language may not be the insurmountable problem that it is normally thought to be. Table 8.2 identifies countries whose companies supply English-language translations of all or portions of their annual reports. Table 8.2 indicates that English is becoming an accepted medium of international business communications. In a majority of the cases examined, the entire annual report was translated into English or an abridged version of the local language report was supplied in English (see Chapter 7 for a discussion of convenience translations). In some cases, English language translations supplemented the original text. In others they were confined to the financial statements and explanatory notes.

Additional avenues for coping with language as well as terminology barriers include the following:

1. The use of accounting lexicons to translate foreign language account titles and terms into English or other languages. The *Lexique UEC*[7] facilitates Danish, Dutch, English, German, Italian, Portuguese, and Spanish translations—see also Chapter 12.
2. The use of professional translators on a one-time basis to translate key account titles and terms when lexicons covering a given language are not available.
3. The construction of a terminology matrix using an English translation of a foreign language report as a guide. This is especially feasible in those instances where non-English-speaking nations utilize script alphabets, and account titles as well as report formats are uniform within given countries.
4. Reliance on investment advisory services with in-house foreign language capabilities.

Foreign Currency Statements

While language translations of foreign annual reports are occurring with increasing frequency, currency translations remain an exception. The vast majority of companies around the world denominate their financial accounts in the currency of their country of domicile.

To a U.S. reader accustomed to dealing in dollars, analysis of accounts expressed in Dutch guilders may appear confusing. A normal inclination is to translate foreign currency balances to domestic currency. However, aside from questions of convenience and personal preference, foreign currency reports are largely troublesome in appearance only. Financial ratios that transform nominal (interval) measurements to percentage relationships are independent of the currency of denomination. A current ratio computed from a Dutch balance sheet expressed in guilders or a Brazilian balance sheet expressed in cruzeiros is no different from a current ratio computed from the same financial statement translated into dollars. For example, consider the following year-end balance sheet accounts of a British company:

	1983	1984	1985
Current assets	£ 12,500	£ 12,200	£ 12,800
Current liabilities	£ 8,333	£ 7,625	£ 8,000

Assuming year-end dollar/pound exchange rates of $2.10, $2.20, and $1.60 for 1983, 1984, and 1985, respectively, the current ratio will be 1.5 to 1 for 1983, 1.6 to 1 for 1984, and 1.6 to 1 for 1985 whether expressed in British pounds or U.S. dollars. Local currency (e.g., pound) balances are especially appropriate when analyzing financial trends.

Readers preferring a domestic currency framework when analyzing foreign currency accounts may use convenience translations rates (discussed in Chapter 7) consisting of year-end exchange rates as illustrated above. One must be careful, however, when analyzing translated trend data. Use of convenience rates to translate foreign currency accounts can distort underlying fi-

[7] Union Européene des Experts Comptables Economiques et Financiers, *Lexique UEC*, rev. ed. (Dusseldorf: UEC, 1980).

nancial patterns in local currency. To illustrate, assume the following three-year sales revenue pattern for our British concern.

	1983	1984	1985
Sales revenue	£ 23,500	£ 28,650	£ 33,160

Convenience translations using the year-end exchange rates employed earlier (i.e., $2.10 for 1983, $2.20 for 1984, and $1.60 for 1985) yield a U.S. dollar sales increase of 7.5 percent ($53,056 − $49,350/$49,350) over the three-year period. The sales gain in pounds, however, is 41 percent (£33,160 − £23,500/£23,500).

The foregoing problem can be remedied by scaling prior-year data for exchange rate differentials between years. Alternatively, foreign currency data can be translated to domestic currency using a single base year's exchange rate. But, which base-year exchange rate should be used? In our example, should the three years' pound-denominated sales figures be translated using the 1983 exchange rate, the 1985 exchange rate, or some other year's convenience rate? Use of a base-year rate will yield a trend analysis consistent with that in local currency. This is illustrated in Table 8.3.

While your authors prefer the analysis of foreign statements in local currency, use of the most recent year's exchange rate as a convenience translator is advocated for readers favoring domestic currency statistics. Use of the most current year-end rate provides a reference point that spans time to the decision point, namely, the present. An exception, however, is warranted if the foreign currency financial statements have been adjusted for changes in the general purchasing power of the foreign currency unit (see Chapter 5 for a discussion of this treatment). If foreign currency balances are expressed in base-year purchasing power equivalents, year-end exchange rates associated with the given base year should be employed. In our example if sales revenues were expressed in pounds of 1983 general purchasing power, the 1983 exchange rate would have been an appropriate translation rate. As another example, if sales revenues were expressed in 1970 pounds, the 1970 dollar/pound exchange rate would be appropriate.

Differences in Statement Format

Differences in balance sheet and income statement formats can also prove bothersome. In countries such as the United States, most companies adopt the account form of balance sheet with assets appearing on the left and

TABLE 8.3   Trend Analysis with Base-Year Exchange Rate

	SALES REVENUE			PERCENT CHANGE		
	1983	1984	1985	1983/84	1984/85	1983/85
Pounds	23,000	28,650	33,160	21.9%	15.7%	41.1%
Dollars						
Using 1983 base rate	49,350	60,165	69,636	21.9%	15.7%	41.1%
Using 1985 base rate	37,600	45,840	53,056	21.9%	15.7%	41.1%

equity claims on the right. In Commonwealth countries such as South Africa, the format is often just the reverse. Readers in North America are also accustomed to seeing assets displayed in decreasing order of liquidity and liabilities listed in increasing order of maturity. Designed to afford readers a glimpse of the current debt-paying ability of a company, this practice is seldom followed in European and Commonwealth countries. There the most liquid assets and the shortest-term liabilities appear at the foot of the balance sheet.

Classification differences also abound internationally. For example, accumulated depreciation is reported as a contra-asset account in the United States. In West Germany, depreciable assets are usually reported net of accumulated depreciation, but all current period changes in long-term asset accounts are shown directly in the balance sheet. Whereas treasury stock (reacquired shares) is generally treated as reductions of stockholders' equity in countries such as Canada and the Philippines, it is typically shown as an asset in Portugal and Italy. In most countries, the distinction between a current and noncurrent liability is a year. In West Germany it is often four years. Handbooks like the AICPA's *Professional Accounting in 30 Countries*[8] may be consulted for a detailed treatment of other classification differences prevailing in individual countries.

Financial statement format differences, while troublesome, are seldom "critical." Owing to the pervasiveness of the double-entry bookkeeping system around the world, the underlying structure of financial statements is quite similar. Accordingly, most format differences can usually be reconciled with a little effort. Initial reader disorientation is normally the extent of such reporting idiosyncracies.

Extent of Disclosure

A problem of greater import to security analysts is the quantity of information revealed in foreign financial statements. Levels of disclosure normally taken for granted in the Netherlands, the United States, and the United Kingdom are seldom found elsewhere. As examples, Austrian companies seldom disclose sales revenue or cost of goods sold figures in their income statements. Typically, Austrian earnings statements begin with net operating income and proceed from there. Statements of changes in financial position that provide useful insights into a company's financing and investing activities are still rarely presented by reporting entities in such industrialized countries as Denmark, Germany, Japan, and Switzerland.[9] Descriptions of accounting policies customarily appearing in the "notes" section of Anglo-American annual reports are limited or nonexistent in those of most Italian, Spanish, and Swiss companies.

More comprehensive evidence of international disclosure disparities is

[8] New York: American Institute of Certified Public Accountants, 1975.

[9] R. D. Fitzgerald, A. D. Stickler, and T. R. Watts, eds., *International Survey of Accounting Principles and Reporting Practices* (Scarborough, Ont.: Price Waterhouse International, 1979).

TABLE 8.4   Disclosure Items Desired by U.S. Security Analysts (and seldom found in actual disclosure practices)

Factors which affect next year's worldwide profitability
Reporting of nonfinancial information
Whether material part of business depends on a single customer
Interim reports dealing with foreign currency gains and losses
Line of business sales where 10% concentrations exist
Interim reports disclosing percent foreign sales and earnings
Description of exceptional risks from operating outside United States
Line of business sales by type of customer
Financial statements of unconsolidated subsidiaries
Foreign currency exposure in overseas subsidiaries
Foreign ownership of company's common stock
Brief description of nature of foreign currency uncertainties
Amount of foreign exchange forward contracts outstanding
Forecasts of next year's worldwide earnings and profitability
Foreign earnings not remitted to U.S. parent
Extent of intercompany receivables and payables
Parent's unconsolidated statements
Percentage of sales of domestic products to foreign affiliates
Inventory valuation methods used in overseas subsidiaries

Source: Francis A. Lees, *Reporting Transnational Business Operations* (New York: The Conference Board, Inc., 1980), p. 35.

provided by Barrett.[10] His examination of disclosure practices of 103 large firms located in France, Germany, Japan, the Netherlands, Sweden, the United Kingdom, and the United States revealed wide variances between disclosure levels of U.S. and U.K. firms and those from other countries in the sample. However, while U.S. sample firms exhibited better average levels of disclosure than any other national sample, save for the United Kingdom, they were not uniformly better in terms of specific categories of disclosure (e.g., segmental disclosures). Similar conclusions were reached by S. J. Gray.[11] In examining the provision by European companies of financial ratio and other analytical data desired by European security analysts, Gray found disclosures of British companies superior to those on the European continent but not in all categories. Hence, his suggested scope for improvement.

Insights into specific disclosure improvements sought by financial analysts are provided by Francis A. Lees.[12] He reports that U.S.-based multinational companies disclose only one-half of the information perceived to be important by professional readers of financial statements. Disclosure items contained in financial analysts' "wish lists" but not often found in published disclosures of the U.S. companies surveyed appear in Table 8.4. While surveys

---

[10] M. Edgar Barrett, "The Extent of Disclosure in Annual Reports of Large Companies in Seven Countries," *International Journal of Accounting*, Spring 1977, pp. 1–25.

[11] S. J. Gray, "Statistical Information and Extensions in European Financial Disclosure," *International Journal of Accounting*, Spring 1978, pp. 27–40.

[12] Francis A. Lees, *Reporting Transnational Business Operations* (New York: The Conference Board, Inc., 1980).

such as those just described acknowledge significant improvements in corporate disclosures over time, gaps remain between information sought and information provided.

While there is little that individual investors can do to mitigate the problem of inadequate disclosure, institutional pressures for improved corporate transparency are mounting. At the international level, the International Accounting Standards Committee (IASC) has already issued a number of pronouncements specifying minimum levels of corporate disclosures (see Chapter 12). International governmental organizations such as the United Nations, the Organization for Economic Development (OECD), and the European Economic Community (EEC) are also contributing to the pressures (see Chapters 7 and 12).

At the same time, market forces are likely to succeed where bureaucrats are likely to fail. The availability of new capital to international borrowers is likely to depend on the attainment of disclosure levels comparable to those that international investors have become accustomed to receiving from successful and forthright borrowers in the past. While these disclosure responses are voluntary, competition for access to limited supplies of money capital will assure that the trend toward improved disclosure continues.[13] A good country example of this phenomenon is Sweden.[14]

Influenced by a civil law system stressing creditor protection and a system of tax incentives requiring that external financial reports conform to tax law, Swedish income statements have traditionally conveyed a distorted picture of a company's actual operating performance (see Chapter 3 for a description of various tax-induced reserves in Swedish financial reporting). As a consequence, Swedish companies faced a dilemma. On the one hand, it would be foolish to sacrifice potential tax savings in order to report more realistic earnings figures. On the other hand, potential capital suppliers, particularly those domiciled outside Sweden, would continue to receive a misleading picture of enterprise performance given extant reporting rules. In the face of limited domestic supplies of greatly needed capital, this was a problem of no small proportion. Yet, a solution was found through increased disclosure. Following the lead of Sweden's larger multinationals such as Volvo and L. M. Ericsson, several Swedish companies voluntarily evolved a reporting format providing income numbers conforming to both Swedish and U.S.-style generally accepted accounting principles (GAAP). Exemplifying the primary-secondary reporting format discussed in Chapter 7, these companies now report an operating income figure based on internationally accepted accounting principles. From this figure are subtracted various reserves and deductions permitted by Swedish tax and civil law to yield a bottom-line figure fully in accord with Swedish reporting rules. A highly simplified example of this contemporary Swedish reporting format as applied to a hypothetical income statement is illustrated in Table 8.5.

---

[13] Frederick D. S. Choi, "Financial Disclosure and Entry to the European Capital Markets," *Journal of Accounting Research*, Autumn 1973, pp. 159–175.

[14] The authors acknowledge appreciatively Professor Sven-Erik Johansson's helpful insights provided on this matter.

TABLE 8.5   Traditional Versus Selectively Used Contemporary Swedish Income
Statement Formats

ITEM		AMOUNT
Traditional Statement		
Sales		1,000
Cost of goods sold (generally overstated by excessive inventory writedown)		(900)
Income before depreciation		100
Depreciation (accelerated)		(70)
Income before taxes		30
Taxes		15
Net income (distorted by tax incentives and hidden reserves)		15
Contemporary Format		
Sales		1,000
Cost of goods sold (per internationally accepted GAAP, e.g., FIFO)		(870)
Income before depreciation		130
Normal depreciation (straight-line)		(50)
Income before appropriations (per internationally accepted GAAP)		80
Appropriations		
Increase of inventory reserve	(30)	
Depreciation in excess of normal	(20)	(50)
Income before taxes		30
Taxes		(15)
Net income (per Swedish GAAP)		15

Such a reporting mode offers yet another promising model for bridging the gap between domestic and international user needs. Together with the reporting modes identified in Chapter 7, there now are at least three "primary-secondary" reporting formats for communicating with transnational audiences-of-interest:

1. Single statement (Sweden).
2. Supplemental schedule (Philips in the Netherlands).
3. Completely separate financial statements (Japan).

Accounting Principles Differences

While disclosure practices such as the Swedish example are laudable, they unfortunately remain the exception. For the vast majority of countries, statement readers must in large measure fend for themselves when it comes to understanding national accounting and reporting practices. As Chapters 2–7 have demonstrated, differences in accounting principles from country to country remain the order of the day despite ongoing attempts to harmonize such. Consequently, a major hurdle facing readers of foreign financial statements is the need to reconcile major differences in measurement principles when comparing financial statement data *between* countries. Observed differences in accounting-based financial ratios between countries may be influenced as much by differences in accounting principles as by differences in the underlying attributes these ratios are trying to measure.

Fortunately, numerous published information sources that afford insights into a country's accounting practices are available. As mentioned in Chapter 1, many international public accounting firms publish international business/accounting reference guides describing locally accepted accounting and reporting principles. National professional accounting societies, governmental agencies, as well as several large international banks do likewise. Specialized newsletters such as *World Accounting Report* (Financial Times), *International Accounting and Financial Report* (London), and *Business International Money Report* (New York) also enable statement readers to keep abreast of recent additions or changes in national accounting principles as do various professional and academic accounting journals.

Financial statement reconciliations are very important in facilitating "apple to apple" numerical comparisons between countries. The process can also be extremely complex and challenge the technical expertise of the most astute analyst. Notwithstanding its importance, the mechanistic process of financial statement reconciliation should never override the equally important process of understanding the business and financial environment that gives rise to accounting principles in the first place. Remember, the whole purpose of financial statement analysis is to give meaning and significance to reported or reconstructed numbers to facilitate proper interpretation. Proper interpretation, in turn, requires an understanding of the environmental context from which accounting numbers are derived. The balance of this chapter is devoted to illustrating this important point.[15]

International Ratio Analysis

Financial ratio analysis is today a well-established tool for financial performance evaluation, credit analysis, and security analysis.[16] Ratios commonly used by investors, security analysts, and bond rating services are listed in Table 8.6. While financial ratios may be appropriate measures of risk, efficiency, and profitability for U.S. firms, they are often misused when applied to foreign firms. This is due partly to explainable differences in accounting principles. A more serious problem, however, is that even when ratios are based on U.S. GAAP, they may be misinterpreted because the investor does not understand a particular foreign environment that influences all financial ratios in that environment.

Consider the case of Japan. An initial comparison of the aggregate finan-

---

[15] The following discussion is excerpted from a recently completed two-and-a-half-year, three-nation study with collaborators in Japan, Korea, and the United States. We wish to acknowledge the cooperation of Messrs. Hisaaki Hino of Morgan Guaranty Trust Company, Junichi Ujiie of Nomura Securities Company, Ltd., Professors Sang Kee Min and Sang Oh Nam of Seoul National University, and Professor Arthur I. Stonehill of Oregon State University.

[16] James O. Horrigan, ed., *Financial Ratio Analysis: An Historical Perspective* (New York: Arno Press, 1978).

cial ratios of manufacturing enterprises in Japan with those in the United States reveals striking differences. As can be seen in Table 8.6, Japanese companies generally appear less liquid, less solvent, less efficient, and less profitable than their U.S. counterparts. The ratios of the Japanese companies, however, are based on Japanese as opposed to U.S. accounting principles. Adjusted ratio differences between Japanese and U.S. companies reflecting common accounting measurement rules suggest that accounting restatements do have some effect on observed ratio differences. In most instances, however, these effects explain only a minor portion of observed ratio differences.

**TABLE 8.6   Mean Differences in Aggregate Financial Ratios.
United States versus Japan**

RATIO	ALL MANUFACTURING COMPANIES		
	U.S.	JAPAN	% DIFFERENCE
Current ratio current assets current liabilities Used to analyze the ability to meet short-run debt commitments.	1.9 to 1	1.1 to 1	40%
Inventory turnover cost of goods sold average inventory	6.8 times	5.0 times	26%
Average collection period avg. receivables sales per day Used to analyze the "staleness" of receivables.	43 days	86 days	(102%)
Debt ratio total debt total assets Used to analyze the ability to meet long-run debt commitments.	47%	84%	(77%)

Times interest earned
         earnings before int. & taxes (EBIT)
         interest charges
Used to analyze ability to service fixed debt charges.
	6.5 times	1.6 times	75%

Profit margin net profits sales Used to analyze competitive margins.	5.4%	1.3%	74%
Return on total assets EBIT avg. total assets Used to measure profit efficiency of total assets.	7.4%	1.2%	84%
Return on net worth net profit avg. net worth Used to measure profit efficiency of stockholders' funds.	13.9%	7.1%	49%

Source: Frederick D. S. Choi, "When Analysing Japanese Securities . . . Think Japanese," *NYU Business,* Fall 1982, p. 43.

Environmental considerations. The financial statistic that immediately captures the attention of U.S. security analysts is the apparent high leverage of Japanese companies. In aggregate ratio comparisons, debt ratios of Japanese concerns average an eye-opening 84 percent in comparison to only 47 percent for U.S. companies. Yet, when analyzed from a Japanese perspective, high debt ratios are rarely considered cause for alarm. Part of the reason is historical.

When the Japanese government ended Japan's 200 years of international isolation over a century ago (the Meiji Restoration), it embodied rapid economic growth and development as a national goal. To achieve what amounted to a national obsession, the government established an extensive banking infrastructure to supply industry with the bulk of enterprise financial requirements. The reliance of industrial companies on the banking "establishment" was heightened during the aftermath of World War II when the need to rebuild a war-torn economy in the absence of viable financial alternatives was particularly strong. Large enterprises evolved, with major commercial banks constituting the core of the new industrial groupings called *keiretsu*. Related through commercial and personal ties, as opposed to the majority stockholdings characteristic of the prewar *zaibatsu* (large holding companies), the relationship between banks and these related companies has become very close; so close, in fact, that a bank would seldom impose financial penalties on delayed debt repayment or call a delinquent loan. Instead, it would typically extend the terms of repayment and occasionally refinance the loan. The lending bank would even go so far as to install a key bank official as president or board member of a troubled company to provide it with helpful managerial assistance. Likewise, related companies would prepay receivables owed to the distressed firm and allow additional lag time for payables from that firm to related companies. With the ability to postpone interest and principal payments, long-term debt in Japan is more akin to equity.

With long-term debt assuming characteristics of preferred stock in Japan, interest can be likened to dividends. Accordingly, interest-coverage ratios, which are considerably lower in Japan (average 1.6 times) than in the United States (6.5 times), are not viewed with much concern. In the context of Japanese business, earnings over and above those needed to cover what in effect are "captive" loan charges are of modest perceived benefit to the bank. When a loan is negotiated, a general agreement, seldom disclosed, also stipulates that the company stands ready to provide the lending bank with collateral or guarantors upon the bank's request. Again at the bank's request, borrowing companies must submit their year-end proposed appropriation of income (including dividends) before it can be submitted to shareholders for approval. Compensating balances, though illegal, are customarily insisted upon with 20–50 percent of company borrowings reportedly kept with the bank in the form of time or other deposits. Under these conditions, low interest coverage does not necessarily mirror high default risk.

Institutional and cultural factors also cause liquidity ratios to differ without necessarily changing the basic financial risk characteristics being measured.

For example, the lower current ratios of Japanese companies, reflecting large current debt positions relative to current assets, signal a relatively weaker short-term debt-paying ability to an American reader. In Japan, however, a lower current ratio is seldom indicative of corporate illiquidity because short-term debt assumes a different meaning. From a company's perspective, short-term borrowing is attractive since interest rates on shorter-maturity obligations are typically lower than those on long-term obligations. Moreover, short-term borrowings are seldom liquidated but are normally renewed or "rolled over." Banks are more than willing to renew such loans as this affords them an opportunity to adjust their interest charges to reflect changing market conditions. Consequently, short-term debt in Japan operates more like long-term debt elsewhere. Indeed, while officially granted for working capital purposes, the use of short-term debt to finance long-term assets appears to be the rule rather than the exception in Japanese financial management practices.

Longer average collection periods (86 days in Japan versus 43 days in the United States) also reflect differences in business customs. Purchases, for example, are rarely made for cash. Instead, postdated checks with maturities ranging between 60 to 90 days are common. The Japanese tradition of lifetime employment also influences collection policies to some extent. Companies will often go to great lengths to accommodate their commercial customers. During business downturns, repayment terms will be extended to avoid placing the buyer in a financial bind, thereby threatening an otherwise stable employment base. In return, continued patronage helps to assure employment stability for the selling enterprise. Moreover, lower inventory turnover statistics in Japan are affected by the lifetime employment tradition. During slack periods, manufacturing companies prefer to continue production and accumulate inventories rather than idle workers.

Differences in relative profit margins and rate of return ratios between Japanese and American companies, as cited earlier, are significant. Here again, one must look to the environment to interpret properly apparent lower profitability of Japanese entities.

In Japan, managers are not as concerned with short-term profits as their U.S. counterparts. One reason is that management security in Japan is higher than in the United States. Corporate shares of Japanese companies are largely held by related commercial banks, trade suppliers, and corporate customers. These "stable" shareholders, in turn, are more interested in maintaining the strengthening functional business ties than in short-run stock market gains. Accordingly, corporate shares are normally held on a long-term basis regardless of short-term market performance.

Embracing sales growth as their primary objective, corporate managers in Japan believe that increased market share will assure profits in the long-run. Moreover, growing sales contribute to higher employment and job security and are therefore consistent with the tradition of lifetime employment. With increased sales as a common goal among Japanese enterprises, price competition is severe, resulting in low profit margin and profitability statistics. This is especially the case for large companies that typically sell heavily in extremely competitive export markets.

To conclude, are Japanese companies more risky, less efficient, and less profitable than their U.S. counterparts? Not necessarily, especially when analyzed from the environmental context in which business transactions underlying accounting measurements are effected.

In Europe, also, profit measurement appears to be highly correlated with national characteristics.[17] Thus large companies in France and Germany tend to be more conservative or pessimistic in their profit measurement behavior than large companies in the United Kingdom. Environmental considerations such as the influence of tax laws and different user orientations (i.e., investor vs. creditor) are offered as partial explanatory variables.

Thus, when analyzing foreign financial statements, readers must not only have a working knowledge of major differences in accounting principles between investor and investee countries, they must also understand national business and financial mores underlying reported accounting numbers to assure interpretation within the proper environmental context. While direct experience with a country is an invaluable means of acquiring environmental awareness, directed reading programs, enrollment in university international business programs, or participation in continuing education seminars offer alternative sensitizing opportunities.

Another option is to compile appropriate country and industry norms aggregated from individual company ratios.[18] As national environmental characteristics are reflected in country or industry ratio aggregates, these constructs afford statement readers useful and cost efficient standards against which to compare and thereby interpret company ratios on a global basis.

Conclusion

For the unwary reader, analyzing the financial statements of foreign companies can be fraught with pitfalls. Nevertheless, with proper caution and insight, many of these problems are manageable. While problems relating to data availability and timeliness are very real, foreign financial information services are steadily increasing in response to investor demands. As a last resort, users can secure annual reports directly from the specific company in question. Language, terminology, currency, and statement format problems are largely mechanical in nature and readily resolved with the help of accounting lexicons and language translations, format restatements, and year-end currency transformations.

Problems relating to accounting and disclosure differences are more serious and less easily remedied. Professional and academic publications, however,

---

[17] S. J. Gray, "The Impact of International Accounting Differences from a Security-Analysis Perspective: Some European Evidence," *Journal of Accounting Research*, Spring 1980, pp. 64–76.

[18] Bavishi et al., *Analyzing Financial Ratios.*

provide significant amounts of information on the accounting principles and practices between countries, permitting at least ball-park reconciliations. Activities aimed at harmonizing accounting and disclosure standards are also at an all-time high. Together with influences such as the competition for external capital and the geographic spread of public accounting firms internationally, gaps in accounting and disclosure are narrowing. Once accounting differences have been reconciled, national environmental differences must still be analyzed if information gleaned from foreign financial statements is to be properly interpreted. Efforts to better understand the environments of reporting foreign enterprises are essential and worthwhile.

SELECTED REFERENCES

AMERICAN INSTITUTE OF CERTIFIED PUBLIC ACCOUNTANTS, *Professional Accounting in 30 Countries,* New York: AICPA, 1975, 792 pp.

BARRETT, M. EDGAR, "The Extent of Disclosure in Annual Reports of Large Companies in Seven Countries," *International Journal of Accounting,* Spring 1977, pp. 1–25.

BAVISHI, VINOD B., FREDERICK D. S. CHOI, HANY A. SHAWKY, and JEAN-PIERRE SAPY-MAZELLA, *Analyzing Financial Ratios of the World's 1,000 Leading Industrial Corporations,* New York: Business International Corporation, 1981, 387 pp.

"THE BOOM IN FOREIGN STOCKS: HOW TO GET A PIECE OF IT," *Changing Times,* August 1981, pp. 21–24.

CHOI, FREDERICK D. S., "Financial Disclosure and Entry to the European Capital Markets," *Journal of Accounting Research,* Autumn 1973, pp. 159–175.

CHOI, FREDERICK D. S., "Primary-Secondary Reporting: A Cross-Cultural Analysis," *International Journal of Accounting,* Fall 1980, pp. 83–104.

CHOI, FREDERICK D. S., SANG KEE MIN, SANG OH NAM, HISAAKI HINO, JUNICHI UJIIE, and ARTHUR I. STONEHILL, "Multinational Finance: The Use and Misuse of International Ratio Analysis," *Journal of International Business Studies,* Spring-Summer 1983, pp. 113–131.

COOPERS and LYBRAND, *International Financial Reporting and Auditing,* New York, 1979, 173 pp.

DRURY, D. H., "Effects of Accounting Practice Divergence: Canada and the United States," *Journal of International Business Studies,* Fall 1979, pp. 75–87.

FISHER, ANDREW, "Financial Times World Survey of Annual Reports 1980," *World Accounting Report,* July 1980, pp. 3–5.

FITZGERALD, R. D., A. D. STICKLER, and T. R. WATTS, eds., *International Survey of Accounting Principles and Reporting Practices,* Scarborough, Ontario: Price Waterhouse International, 1979, 47 pp. plus tables.

GRAY, S. J., "The Impact of International Accounting Differences from a Security-Analysis Perspective: Some European Evidence," *Journal of Accounting Research,* Spring 1980, pp. 64–76.

GRAY, S. J., "Statistical Information and Extensions in European Financial Disclosure," *International Journal of Accounting,* Spring 1978, pp. 27–40.

HAMPTON, ROBERT, III, "A World of Difference in Accounting and Reporting," *Management Accounting,* pp. 14–18.

HORRIGAN, JAMES O., ed., *Financial Ratio Analysis: An Historical Perspective,* New York: Arno Press, 1978, 271 pp.

JONES, EDWARD H., "Decision-Making Based on Foreign Financial Statements," *Financial Executive,* February 1981; pp. 32–35.

LEES, FRANCIS A., *Reporting Transnational Business Operations,* New York: The Conference Board, Inc., 1980, 43 pp.

MENDELSON, MORRIS, and SIDNEY ROBBINS, *Investment Analysis and Securities Markets,* New York: Basic Books, Inc., 1976, 755 pp.

SOLNIK, BRUNO H., "Why Not Diversify Internationally Rather Than Domestically?" *Financial Analysts Journal,* July-August 1974, pp. 48–54.

WHITTINGTON, GEOFFREY, "Beware Efficient Markets Theory," *The Accountant's Magazine,* April 1979, pp. 145–146.

DISCUSSION QUESTIONS

1. What are four considerations that explain the growing interest of investors in foreign securities?

2. One version of the popular efficient markets hypothesis is that the market fully impounds all publicly available information as soon as it becomes available. Thus it is supposedly not possible to "beat the market" if fundamental financial analysis techniques are applied to publicly available information such as a firm's published accounts. Why might this hypothesis be more tenable in the United States as opposed to some international capital markets?

3. While English-language translations of foreign annual reports are occurring with increasing frequency, there are still occasions when a reader will receive a foreign report expressed in the language and accounting terminology of the reporting company's domicile country. Suggest in a paragraph or two some of the ways in which you could deal with this problem.

4. How does the translation of foreign currency financial statements differ from the foreign currency translation process described in Chapter 4?

5. Explain three ways in which differing foreign financial information statement formats might prove confusing and possibly misleading to statement readers.

6. Highlight some of the forces contributing to improved corporate financial disclosures for international investors. Which of these forces do you feel promises to be effective in the long run?

7. Describe several factors that need to be taken into account when comparing the reported profitability of companies between countries.

8. Aside from changed operating conditions locally, what environmental factors might limit the comparability of a foreign entity's reported performance over time?

9. The *quick* or *acid-test* ratio is frequently used to assess the short-term debt paying ability of a business enterprise. Commercial lenders often view a ratio of at least 1 to 1 to be satisfactory as a rule of thumb. Why might it be inappropriate to apply this standard when evaluating the liquidity position of a foreign company?

10.   ABC Company, a U.S.-based MNC, uses the temporal translation method (see Chapter 4) in consolidating the results of its foreign operations. Translation gains or losses incurred upon consolidation are reflected immediately in reported earnings. Company XYZ, a Dutch MNC, employs the current rate method with translation gains and losses being reflected in owners' equity. Identify several financial ratios that would be affected by these divergent accounting principles and outline their implications for security analysts.

EXERCISES

1.   Your investment portfolio currently consists of stocks selected exclusively from the United States. You wish to diversify your investment portfolio by including securities from other countries.

    Required: Using the information provided in Figure 8.1 and Tables 8.1, 8.2, and 3.2, which three countries appearing in Table 8.1 would you be inclined to include in your portfolio selection decision set? (Ignore tax considerations.) Explain the rationale underlying your country selections.

2.   Condensed comparative income statements of Visical do Brazil for the years 1983 through 1985 are presented below (000s cruzeiros):

	1983	1984	1985
Sales	91,600	114,300	138,900
Gross margin	15,500	20,500	27,700
Net income	8,500	10,800	15,900

You are interested in gauging the past trend in dividends paid by Visical do Brazil from a U.S. dollar perspective for purposes of comparison. The company's payout ratio (ratio of dividends paid to reported earnings) has averaged 30 percent. Foreign exchange rates during the three-year period were as follows:

1983	1984	1985
$1 = Cr. 4.7	$1 = Cr. 5.4	$1 = Cr. 6.0

    Required: Prepare a trend of dividends paid by Visical do Brazil from a U.S. perspective assuming (a) there are no restrictions on the payment of dividends to U.S. investors and (b) Visical do Brazil's accounting practices are similar to those in the United States.

3.   Table 8.4 contains a list of items that financial analysts regard highly in assessing the nature of a company's international operations.

    Required: As a newly chartered financial analyst, rank these items in decreasing order of importance in terms of their relevance to forecasting a company's financial performance.

4.   The financial statements of Dot-son Enterprises (Japan) and Lincoln Enterprises (U.S.) are presented in Table 8.7.
       Required: Reconcile Dot-son Enterprises' financial statements with those of Lincoln Enterprises for the benefit of a U.S. security analyst.

5.   This exercise is based on information provided in Exercise 4 and assumes that the balances in asset and equity accounts at year-end approximate the average balances in effect during the year.
       Required: Using traditional financial ratio analysis, compare the profitability, solvency, and liquidity of the two companies. Based on the material presented in this chapter, which company appears to be the better investment candidate? State specific reasons for your choice.

CASE

Financial Statement Analysis

Having invested in American stocks for many years, you decide to diversify your investment portfolio internationally. You have heard that yields on foreign stocks often exceed those domestically. Moreover, a recent *Wall Street Journal* article suggested that the inclusion of foreign securities in a U.S. stock portfolio could very well reduce the overall riskiness of that portfolio, especially if foreign stock market returns are less than perfectly positively correlated with those in the United States.

For starters, you decide to analyze the financial statements of the well-known German chemical company, BASF. The company's principal financial statements together with explanatory notes appear in Exhibit 8.1.

You suspect that international accounting principles differences can have a significant impact on financial ratios and other financial statistics aimed at shedding some light on a firm's risk and return dimensions. To your delight, a week's stint in your university's graduate library reveals the existence of an analyst's guide for restating the accounts of German companies to a basis more consistent with Anglo-American accounting norms. Published by the German Association of Investment Analysts, the restatement guide is reproduced in Table 8.8.

To facilitate your financial analysis and to serve as a standard of comparison, the aggregate financial ratios of the major manufacturing enterprises in the U.S. are reproduced in Table 8.9.

On the basis of the information provided, as well as any other information you deem pertinent, evaluate the risk and return features of BASF as a potential investment candidate.

TABLE 8.7 Financial Statements of Dot-son Enterprises and Lincoln Enterprises

	DOT-SON ENTERPRISES[a] (¥ THOUSANDS)	LINCOLN ENTERPRISES[b] ($ THOUSANDS)
Income Statements for the Year		
Sales	¥ 2,464,000	$ 12,000
Less expenses		
Cost of sales	1,971,200	5,600
Selling & administrative	295,680	2,320
Other operating	81,840	40
Interest	49,280	760
Taxes	41,888	656
Total expenses	¥ 2,439,888	$ 10,032
Net income	¥ 24,112	$ 12,000
Balance Sheets As of Year-End		
Cash	¥ 220,000	$ 100
Accounts receivable (net)	897,600	800
Inventory	686,400	1,500
Investments	343,200	5,600
Plant and equipment (net)	492,800	4,000
Total assets	¥ 2,640,000	$ 12,000
Short-term payables	¥ 290,400	$ 344
Short-term debt	924,000	656
Other current liabilities	158,400	—
Long-term debt	924,000	4,000
Reserves	158,400	—
Capital stock	132,000	4,000
Owners' equity	52,800	3,000
Total liabilities and owners' equity	¥ 2,640,000	$ 12,000

[a] Notes to Dot-son's financial statements:

1. The balance sheet and income statement are prepared in accordance with the Japanese Commercial Code and related regulations.
2. Investments in subsidiaries and affiliated companies are stated at cost.
3. Inventories are stated at LIFO cost. Ending inventories restated to a FIFO basis would have been ¥198,000 higher.
4. Fixed assets are carried at cost. Depreciation, with minor exceptions, is computed by the sum-of-the-years'-digits method. Plant and equipment, purchased two years ago, have an estimated useful life of four years.
5. Purchased goodwill of ¥112,000 during the year is classified under Other Operating Expenses. Under U.S. GAAP, it would have been amortized over a ten-year period.
6. Dot-son is allowed to set up "special purpose" reserves (i.e., government-sanctioned charges against earnings) equal to a certain percentage of total export revenues. This year's charge (included in Other Operating Expenses) was ¥ 26,400,000. Similarly, this year's addition to general-purpose reserves totaled ¥ 30,800,000.
7. The ¥/$ exchange rate at year-end was ¥220 = $1.

[b] Notes to Lincoln Enterprises' financial statements:
1. The balance sheet and income statement are based on U.S. GAAP.
2. Inventories are stated at FIFO cost.
3. Plant and equipment is depreciated in straight-line fashion.

317

EXHIBIT 8.1   BASF Group

1981 Financial Statements
Balance Sheet of the BASF Group as of December 31, 1981

Assets	Dec. 31, 1981 1,000 DM	Dec. 31, 1980 1,000 DM
I. FIXED ASSETS		
A. PROPERTY, PLANT AND EQUIPMENT	7,977,197	7,723,382
B. PATENTS, TRADEMARKS, FRANCHISES	98,583	102,255
C. INVESTMENTS		
1. Investments in affiliates	380,991	337,922
2. Long-term loans to affiliates	32,036	30,945
3. Other investments and long-term loans	315,198	314,049
	728,225	682,916
	8,804,005	8,508,553
II. CURRENT ASSETS		
A. GOODS ON LEASE	148,170	125,071
B. INVENTORIES	5,104,692	4,305,331
C. UNCOMPLETED CONTRACTS	146,911	172,391
D. NOTES AND ACCOUNTS RECEIVABLE		
1. Notes receivable	196,974	262,382
2. Accounts receivable-trade	4,018,858	3,593,664
3. Other receivables	454,977	381,336
4. Allowance for doubtful receivables	(253,253)	(209,612)
5. Receivables from affiliates	264,486	206,713
	4,682,042	4,234,483
E. CASH AND CASH ITEMS		
1. Marketable securities	150,163	101,036
2. Cash	575,002	569,160
	725,165	670,196
	10,806,980	9,507,472
III. DEFERRED CHARGES AND PREPAID EXPENSES	273,333	266,229
	19,884,318	18,282,254

EXHIBIT 8.1 (*continued*)

Capital and Liabilities	Dec. 31, 1981 1,000 DM	Dec. 31, 1980 1,000 DM
I. STOCKHOLDERS' EQUITY		
A. PAID-IN CAPITAL		
1. Capital stock of BASF Aktiengesellschaft	2,032,478	1,997,971
2. Paid-in surplus	1,906,997	1,844,207
	3,939,475	3,842,178
B. EARNED SURPLUS		
1. As of January 1	3,018,439	2,964,593
2. Dividend of BASF Aktiengesellschaft (previous year)	(279,716)	(315,353)
3. Net income	366,779	358,747
4. Other changes	373	10,452
5. As of December 31	3,105,875	3,018,439
EQUITY OF BASF GROUP	7,045,350	6,860,617
II. BALANCE ARISING FROM CONSOLIDATION	16,576	45,245
III. MINORITY INTERESTS	118,473	131,999
IV. SPECIAL RESERVES	736,096	698,508
V. LONG-TERM RESERVES		
1. Pension reserves	2,482,290	2,269,207
2. Other long-term reserves	1,094,759	944,659
	3,577,049	3,213,866
VI. LONG-TERM LIABILITIES		
1. Bonds and promissory notes	863,781	1,056,515
2. Long-term liabilities to banks	564,689	368,724
3. Other long-term liabilities	460,685	417,944
4. Long-term liabilities to affiliates	76,845	84,516
	1,966,000	1,927,699
VII. CURRENT LIABILITIES AND ACCRUALS		
1. Accounts payable-trade	2,145,587	2,040,224
2. Notes payable	558,728	337,951
3. Short-term liabilities to banks	804,229	684,970
4. Advances received	213,901	215,227
5. Accrued taxes and tax liabilities	780,241	672,329
6. Other accrued charges	755,656	660,363
7. Other short-term liabilities	1,039,676	696,927
8. Short-term liabilities to affiliates	90,113	70,566
	6,388,131	5,378,557
VIII. DEFERRED INCOME	36,643	25,763
	19,884,318	18,282,254

(*continued*)

EXHIBIT 8.1 (*continued*)

**Statement of Income of the BASF Group
for the Year Ended December 31, 1981**

	1981 1,000 DM	1980 1,000 DM
NET SALES		
To third parties	30,864,953	26,985,299
To non-consolidated affiliates	900,871	745,311
TOTAL	31,765,824	27,730,610
Cost of sales	25,862,333	22,304,998
GROSS PROFIT	5,903,491	5,425,612
Administrative, selling and other costs	4,095,948	3,594,421
INCOME FROM OPERATIONS	1,807,543	1,831,191
OTHER EXPENSES AND INCOME		
Expenses for non-consolidated affiliates	68,158	14,818
Other income from investments	54,837	63,609
Interest income	178,974	151,061
Interest expense	564,480	402,968
Write-downs of investments	19,759	6,193
Gains on currency transactions (net)	7,306	(90,260)
Other expense (net)	105,959	260,904
TOTAL	(517,239)	(560,473)
INCOME BEFORE INCOME TAXES AND MINORITY INTERESTS	1,290,304	1,270,718
Income taxes	909,001	891,411
INCOME AFTER TAXES	381,303	379,307
Minority interests in income	14,524	20,560
NET INCOME	366,779	358,747

We have examined the balance sheets of the BASF Group as of December 31, 1981 and 1980 and the related statements of income for the years then ended. Our examinations were made in accordance with auditing standards generally accepted in Germany and in the United States of America and, accordingly, included such tests of the accounting records and such other auditing procedures as we considered necessary in the circumstances. We did not examine the financial statements of certain BASF subsidiaries and affiliates, which statements reflect assets constituting 23% and 24%, respectively, of Group assets as of December 31, 1981 and 1980 and revenues constituting 33% and 36%, respectively, of Group revenues for the years ended December 31, 1981 and 1980. These financial statements were examined by other auditors whose reports thereon have been furnished to us, and our opinion expressed herein, in so far as it relates to the amounts included for such companies, is based solely upon the reports of the other auditors.

As discussed in the notes to the Financial Statements of the BASF Group, the financial statements of German companies are prepared and included in the Group Financial Statements in accordance with the accounting and valuation principles legally prescribed in Germany. The financial statements of the foreign companies are included in accordance with generally accepted accounting principles commonly followed by companies in the United States of America except that interest was not capitalized as required under such principles; the capitalization of such interest would increase the BASF Group property, plant and equipment by DM 105.8 million in 1981 and DM 45.5 million in 1980; increase stockholders' equity by DM 75.4 million in 1981 and DM 32.6 million in 1980; and increase net income by DM 42.8 million in 1981 and DM 32.6 million in 1980, net of tax effects.

**Schitag
Schwäbische Treuhand-
Aktiengesellschaft**
Wirtschaftsprüfungsgesellschaft
Steuerberatungsgesellschaft

Dr. Frey　　　　　Prof. Dr. Csik
Wirtschaftsprüfer　Wirtschaftsprüfer

Reference is also made to the notes to the Group Financial Statements for descriptions of and the effects of the major differences between German accounting principles and those generally accepted in the United States.

In our opinion, based upon our examinations and the reports of other auditors, except for the aforementioned effects of the foreign companies not capitalizing interest, the above mentioned Financial Statements of the BASF Group present fairly its financial position at December 31, 1981 and 1980 and the results of its operations for the years then ended in conformity with the accounting principles referred to in the preceding paragraph, applied on a consistent basis.

Stuttgart/Washington, D. C.
April 6, 1982

Deloitte Haskins & Sells
Certified Public Accountants

J. M. Crawford　　T. F. Bluey
Partner　　　　　Partner

EXHIBIT 8.1   *(continued)*

Notes to the 1981 Financial Statements of the BASF Group with comparisons to 1980

Companies included in the Financial Statements

The consolidated Financial Statements of the BASF Group include the Financial Statements of BASF Aktiengesellschaft, its significant subsidiaries and, on a proportional consolidation basis, the significant fifty-percent-owned affiliates. The Group consolidation thus includes BASF Aktiengesellschaft, 102 subsidiaries and 8 fifty-percent-owned affiliates. Subsidiaries and 50-percent-owned affiliates not consolidated as well as the significant less than 50-percent-owned affiliates are included using the equity method of accounting.

BASF Química da Bahia S. A., Camaçari-Bahia, which started operations during the year, was newly included in the consolidation. Other changes in the number of consolidated companies were due to reorganizations and mergers of companies. These changes had no material effect upon the Group Financial Statements.

Principles of accounting and valuation

The financial statements of German companies are prepared and included in the Group Financial Statements in accordance with the accounting and valuation principles legally prescribed in Germany.

The financial statements of the foreign companies are included in accordance with the generally accepted accounting principles commonly followed by companies subject to the requirements of the Securities and Exchange Commission (SEC) in the United States. However, not included is interest cost in the acquisition or production cost of qualifying assets, as prescribed in accordance with these principles, starting with the fiscal year 1980.

Had the Financial Statements of the German companies also been included on the basis of U.S. accounting principles, and had the capitalization of interest cost been applied by all BASF Group companies, the stockholders' equity and net income would have changed as follows:

Increase of stockholders' equity as of December 31, 1981 and 1980 by DM 1,493.5 million and DM 1,425.8 million, respectively; increase of income after taxes for 1981 and 1980 by DM 67.7 million and DM 49.0 million, respectively.

These differences result primarily from the valuation of investments acquired by issuing shares, when the issued shares are accounted for at nominal value as permitted by German law, the application of special tax regulations to the valuation of property, plant and equipment and investments, appropriations to and from special reserves, the non-application of the capitalization of interest cost as prescribed by U.S. accounting principles, and the immediate charge to income in 1974 as a result of the change to the discounted value method for the determination of pension reserves rather than amortization of the charge over an extended period.

Also, U.S. principles would require additional disclosures and explanations: The presentation of sales, income and assets in different business segments and foreign operations, additional income tax disclosures, certain disclosures of leased assets and lease commitments, certain disclosures of the effects of changes in purchasing power, certain disclosures of proved and developed crude oil and natural gas reserves and the separate reporting of extraordinary items. These additional disclosures would have no effect upon stockholders' equity or net income.

Principles of currency conversion

Foreign currency financial statements are translated into DM for the purpose of inclusion in the Group Financial Statements as follows:

a) Revenue and expenses – at quarterly average rates, except for depreciation, depletion, the disposal of fixed assets and inventories consumed in cost of sales which have been translated at historical rates.

b) Property, plant and equipment, intangible assets, deferred charges, investments in affiliates and inven-

tories – at rates in effect at the date of acquisition or production (historical rates).

c) All other assets and liabilities – at rates existing at the close of the year. Changes in value due to currency fluctuations are charged or credited to income.

(continued)

EXHIBIT 8.1   (*continued*)

Notes to the 1981 Financial Statements of the BASF Group with comparisons to 1980

Property and depreciation

Property, plant and equipment is generally stated at cost less accumulated depreciation. In case of permanent diminution of value, special depreciation is made. Additions, betterments and renewals are capitalized. Maintenance and repair costs are charged to income. In general, depreciation is computed under the declining balance method where permitted, otherwise under the straight-line method. The annual rates are based on estimated useful lives for the various types of property. Special accelerated depreciation of fixed assets as permitted under special tax regulations is taken by the German companies to the fullest extent allowable within available time limits. Fixed asset acquisitions of low value are charged against income in the year of acquisition. Gains or losses realized when assets are sold or otherwise disposed of are taken into income, unless special German tax regulations permit a deferral of such gains, in which case the amount is credited to certain new additions or temporarily deferred as special reserves in the balance sheet. Costs to drill and equip producing oil and gas wells are capitalized and amortized within 1 to 8 years.

Geophysical expenditures, including exploratory and dry hole costs, are charged against income. Concession acquisition costs are capitalized and amortized over the expected term.

Property, plant and equipment is summarized as follows:

million DM	December 31, 1981	1980
Land	590.1	568.3
Buildings	5,319.8	5,003.9
Machinery and equipment	19,252.2	18,094.3
Construction in progress, including advances	1,134.3	1,014.6
	26,296.4	24,681.1
Accumulated depreciation	18,319.2	16,957.7
Property, plant and equipment, net	7,977.2	7,723.4

Provision for depreciation for the years 1981 and 1980 amounted to DM 1,733.0 million and DM 1,592.2 million, respectively.

Inventories

Inventories are stated at acquisition or production cost or at the lower market value. The lower market value represents replacement cost in case of raw materials and supplies and in case of semi-finished and finished products the expected sales proceeds less costs to be incurred prior to sale. Cost includes direct costs and an appropriate portion of the production overhead including depreciation charges. Generally, cost is determined under the average cost method. However, certain inventories have been determined by the Lifo-method (last in – first out) aggregating DM 874.1 million in 1981 and DM 700.8 million in 1980. The aggregate value determined at average cost or at the lower market value would amount to DM 1,271.8 million and DM 954.5 million in 1981 and 1980, respectively.

Cash and cash items

Marketable securities are carried at cost or market value, whichever is lower.

Cash is summarized as follows:

million DM	December 31, 1981	1980
Time deposits	297.9	337.8
Cash on hand and demand deposits	277.1	231.4
	575.0	569.2

Paid-in capital

Paid-in capital includes the total of capital stock of BASF Aktiengesellschaft, the premiums paid for capital stock and the reserves contributed from the decartelization of IG Farbenindustrie Aktiengesellschaft. Changes in these items resulting from the issuance of shares during 1981 and information concerning conditionally authorized capital are shown in the notes to the Financial Statements of BASF Aktiengesellschaft.

Earned surplus

The earned surplus consists of the free reserves appropriated from profits and the profit available for dividend of BASF Aktiengesellschaft and the undistributed earnings or losses since dates of acquisition of the consolidated subsidiaries and affiliates and the proportional earnings of the investments carried under the equity method of accounting.

EXHIBIT 8.1   *(continued)*

**Balance arising
from consolidation**

Balances arising from consolidation result from differences between the recorded costs of acquisition of investments in consolidated companies and the underlying net assets at the time of acquisition.

Debit balances represent acquired goodwill together with any excess of the fair value over the book value of net assets at the acquisition date which has not been allocated to other Group balance sheet items. Debit balances are amortized on a regular basis.

Credit balances arise from acquisitions made by issuing shares for investments when such shares were accounted for at nominal value as permitted by German law, and from permitted valuation adjustments of investments under German tax regulations.

In 1980, an amount equivalent to the gain from sale of an investment has been taken as a special write-off against the investment in Fritzsche, Dodge & Olcott Inc. and is included in other expense (net).

Individual debit and credit balances are netted and result in a net credit excess.

**Special reserves and
long-term reserves**

Special reserves relate primarily to reserves for price increases of inventories and similar reserves or deferrals of gains as permitted under German tax regulations. Other long-term reserves consist mainly of amounts provided for risks and probable losses in connection with oil, gas and mining operations.

Long-term liabilities

Bonds and promissory notes, due after one year, are summarized as follows:	million DM December 31,	
	1981	1980
BASF Aktiengesellschaft:		
8¹/₂% Bonds of 1974 with detachable stock warrants, due 1983–1986	328.5	328.5
6³/₄% promissory notes, maturing serially between 1975–1982	—	5.0
Subsidiaries and 50-percent-owned affiliates:		
6¹/₂% Swiss Franc Bonds of BASF Finance Europe N. V. of 1976, due 1991	124.3	110.4
7¹/₂% U. S. Dollar Notes (private placement) of BASF Overzee N. V. of 1978, due 1982	—	98.0
Redeemable preferred shares with cumulative preferred dividends of BASF Canada Inc. of 1978, repayable through 1985	42.8	45.4
9³/₄% U. S. Dollar Bonds of BASF Finance Europe of 1979, due 1983	67.5	58.8
7¹/₂% French Franc Bonds of BASF Transatlantica S. A. of 1972, due 1974–1987	22.4	24.5
8³/₄% Swiss Franc Bonds of BASF Overzee N. V. of 1975, due 1985	25.0	22.2
Various promissory notes, insurance loans, bonds and mortgages at 5¹/₄–10¹/₄% interest, maturing serially between 1965–2002	253.3	363.7
	863.8	*1,056.5

(continued)

EXHIBIT 8.1   *(continued)*

Notes to the 1981 Financial Statements of the BASF Group with comparisons to 1980

8½% Bonds with detachable stock warrants of 1974/1986:

Each 8½% bond with a nominal value of DM 300 (smallest denomination) has 2 detachable stock warrants granting the right to purchase for each of these 1.05 shares of capital stock of BASF Aktiengesellschaft at a price of DM 117.60 per share or a total of up to 2,799,955 shares at a nominal value of DM 50 at December 31, 1981. The right expires on May 31, 1986.

Fixed assets of DM 263.2 million and DM 259.1 million in 1981 and 1980, respectively, were pledged as collateral to long-term liabilities.

The interest rates of long-term bank loans, excluding South American borrowings, are principally between 6 and 17.5 percent.

Other long-term liabilities consist principally of amounts due to employee benefit organizations.

The short-term portions of all long-term liabilities amounting to DM 391.7 million and DM 131.6 million at December 31, 1981 and 1980, respectively, are classified with the appropriate current liabilities.

The maturities of all long-term liabilities from 1983 through 1986 are as follows:

	million DM
1983	479.3
1984	160.1
1985	186.6
1986	202.8

In February 1982, BASF Overzee N. V. floated 165.0 million U.S. Dollar bonds, bearing interest at 11% and due in 1988. Each bond with a nominal value of 1,000 U.S. Dollar has bearer-stock warrants granting the right to purchase 20 shares of capital stock of BASF Aktiengesellschaft of a nominal value of DM 50 at a price of DM 133.00 per share. In total, up to 3,300,000 shares may be issuable. The right expires on February 29, 1988.

Short-term liabilities to banks

This caption includes short-term bank borrowings plus current maturities of long-term liabilities to banks amounting to DM 69.1 million and DM 83.9 million in 1981 and 1980, respectively. In addition, the unused lines of credit aggregated DM 406.7 million and DM 364.8 million at December 31, 1981 and 1980, respectively. The maximum amount of short-term bank borrowings in 1981 was DM 1,619.4 million. The weighted average effective interest rate for such borrowings as of December 31, 1981 was 14.3 percent excluding South American borrowings and 20.2 percent including such borrowings.

Research and development

Research and development costs are charged to operations as incurred. Such expenses amounted to DM 1,094.3 million in 1981 and DM 992.8 million in 1980.

Pension plans

In accordance with legal requirements, employees in various countries are covered by compulsory insurance laws. Employees of certain companies are also entitled to pensions provided by company agreements. These latter pension benefits have been adequately provided for in accordance with actuarial computations or by company-sponsored old age employee benefit organizations. In the case of certain foreign companies the amounts are funded through pension funds or insurance contracts. The total cost of compulsory insurances and the various pension plans amounted to DM 956.4 million in 1981 and DM 865.0 million in 1980.

Other expense (net)

Other expense (net) in the Statements of Income of the BASF Group includes, at the respective DM amounts, charges in connection with the shut-down of various production facilities at BASF Systems Corporation during 1981, in the amount of 13.3 million U.S. Dollars, and at BASF Wyandotte Corporation during 1980, in the amount of 74.5 million U.S. Dollars.

Income taxes

Income taxes include corporation tax, trade income tax or similar income-related taxes and are provided on the basis of taxable income, taking into account any loss carryforwards of individual companies as prescribed by local tax statutes. Taxes on oil producing operations, payable in certain countries at rates of up to 84 percent of taxable income in those countries, are included in income tax expense; such taxes amounted to DM 466.2 million in 1981 and DM 388.0 million in 1980. Property tax, trade capital tax, real estate tax or similar non-income related taxes are not included as income taxes but as operating costs.

Source and application of funds

Source and application of funds of the BASF Group is shown under "Finance" on page 4.

Contingent liabilities and commitments

There are various pending legal actions arising in normal business operations for which adequate provisions have been made. Also, in the ordinary course of business, the companies have incurred contractual commitments pursuant to terms of leases and other contracts or pension plans, and are contingently liable as guarantor or endorser of notes. Adequate provision has been made for any losses and uncertain liabilities which may be reasonably foreseen.

TABLE 8.8 Financial Analysis in Germany—Summary of the DVFA Method of Adjusting the Accounts of German Companies

The main items of these adjustments are listed below. Except where indicated the items adjusted are allowed for or charged to both Trade Income Tax and Corporation Tax, and consequently the tax charge must be altered as well, if the net trading profit is to be arrived at. Thus only 41.3% of the adjustments are in fact added to or subtracted from the profits, unless the items concerned are tax-free. This figure is calculated as follows:

	gross adjustment	100
less	Trade Tax (average rate)	13
		87
less	Corporation Tax	
	52.53% x 87	45.7
		41.3

Adjustments

(1) Add back extraordinary and prior period expenditure; deduct similar receipts (in the case of prior year tax payments or receipts no adjustment is made for tax of course).

(2) Add back special depreciation (*Sonderabschreibungen*), write-off of small value items, and transfers to special accounts with a reserve element (*Sonderposten mit Rücklageanteil*) because these are purely tax matters and do not affect the real profit; *deduct* any write-back of such items, including the depreciation which would have been charged in any year but for the fact that owing to tax concessions it had been charged in earlier years (but had been adjusted in their calculations by the investment analysts). This latter part of the recommendations has not been adopted to any great extent in practice owing to the difficulties involved.

(3) Add back any increase in the reserves contained in the stock valuation, and in particular the reductions below cost of the value of imported raw materials specifically allowed by Income Tax Ordinance 80.

(4) Add back any increase in the level of the pension provision—not because these are not a genuine liability, but because not all companies provide fully for them.

(5) Add back any increase in the level of medium and long-term provisions (short-term provisions it will be recalled are what would be called accruals in this country). Three reasons are adduced for this:
  (a) because the size of them is in a considerable measure at the discretion of the company;
  (b) because the size depends on the kind of industry concerned;
  (c) because they frequently turn out to be too high, as the item "receipts from the write-back of provisions" in many companies' profit and loss accounts shows.

(6) Equalisation of Burdens Levy   Add back any increase in the provision, again because not all companies provide for it. (No tax adjustment required—because creation of the provision is not allowable for tax). Deduct any decrease.

(7) Add back any depreciation on investments, or (without adjusting for tax) any special depreciation charged but not allowed for tax. Neither are normal trading costs.

(8) Add back any increase in the level of the general bad debt provision, because standards for provisions are not always similar. In practice the whole item in the profit and loss account "depreciation of current assets other than stock" is added back.

(9) Deduct any profits from the sale of fixed assets and add back losses. Deduct profit from the write-back of provisions. Deduct revaluations, which are generally caused, as had been shown, by retroactive adjustments. None of these are trading income.

(10) Deduct tax-free grants (*Investitionszulagen*) generally included in "other receipts," without adjusting for tax. They are not trading income.

325

TABLE 8.8   (*continued*)

(11) Add back capital increase costs and taxation, without adjusting for tax, as they are
not allowable. They are not trading expenditure.

Source: J. H. Beeny, *European Financial Reporting: West Germany*, a General Education
Trust publication of the Institute of Chartered Accountants in England and Wales, London,
1975.

TABLE 8.9   Aggregate Financial Ratios for Major U.S. Manufacturers (1981)

Current ratio	1.9 times	Fixed assets turnover	3.9 times
Quick ratio	1.1 times	Total asset turnover	1.4 times
Debt ratio	47%	Profit margin	5.4%
Times interest earned	6.5 times	Return on total assets	7.4%
Inventory turnover	6.8 times	Return on net worth	13.9%
Average collection period	43 days		

Source: Frederick D. S. Choi, Hisaaki Hino, Sang Kee Min, Sang Oh Nam, Junichi Ujiie, and
Arthur I. Stonehill, ''Multinational Finance: The Use and Misuse of International Ratio Analysis,'' *Journal of International Business Studies*, Spring-Summer 1983, p. 116.
parison, the aggregate financial ratios of the major manufacturing enterprises in the U.S. are
reproduced in Table 8.9.

On the basis of the information provided, as well as any other information you deem
pertinent, evaluate the risk and return features of BASF as a potential investment candidate.

9

Auditing

Independent auditors perform the attest function in financial reporting. As competent outside experts, they review financial information and then attest to its reliability, fairness, and other aspects of quality. This process establishes and maintains the integrity of financial information.

Investors have a big stake in such attestation since they can make decisions with better expected outcomes if they have relatively better information available. The public is also involved. Incomplete, unreliable, or even misleading financial information may well have a negative effect on capital formation processes within an economy. Moreover, scarce resources may be misdirected into socially less desirable channels or wasted through excessive rates of bankruptcy. Sensitivity to the attest function is probably higher in multinational settings than it is in single country situations.

Aside from decision and public interest effects, independent audits introduce efficiency into financial reporting processes. If users of financial information had to obtain and verify this information item by item and user by user, an immensely costly process would unnecessarily be repeated over and over.[1] As it stands, division of responsibilities produces net benefits. Management is most efficient in preparing and offering financial representations needed by outsiders. Independent auditors function to ensure that these representations are by

[1] R. G. May, G. G. Mueller, and T. H. Williams, *A New Introduction to Financial Accounting*, 2nd ed. (Englewood Cliffs, N.J.: Prentice-Hall, 1980).

and large free of bias and "present fairly . . . in conformity with generally accepted accounting principles applied on the basis consistent with that of the preceding year." In this fashion, then, we have an economically more efficient information process both for the providers and for the users of the information.

In an award-winning monograph Professor W. A. Wallace explores market evidence on the audit function against conceptual frameworks like agency theory, information economics, the demand for and the supply of audits, audit products attributes, and insurance and information hypotheses.[2] Her basic conclusion is that "economic incentives exist for parties to have and to supply an audit."[3] According to Professor Wallace the audit fulfills three explicit demands: (1) a demand for a monitoring mechanism, (2) a demand for information production to improve investors' decisions, and (3) a demand for insurance to protect against losses from distorted information. Moreover, a long list of joint products of the audit is developed. This list includes cost savings in operations stemming from suggestions by auditors for improved operating efficiency, lower cost from property and bonding insurance, reduced loss from errors, lower costs for complementary services, and regulatory compliance.

Considerable evidence similar to that referenced in the foregoing paragraphs supports the proposition that independent audits are economically efficient, public interest effective, and decision relevant. This proposition holds internationally as well as in domestic settings.

The American Institute of Chartered Public Accountants (AICPA) has provided a generalized description and analysis of the independent audit function in *A User's Guide To Understanding Audits and Auditors' Reports.*[4] Section headings in this guide are as follows:

1. Financial statement whys and wherefores
2. Financial statements and the accounting process
3. What is an audit?
4. The auditor's standard report: What it says and what it means
5. Modifications of the standard audit report
6. In summary . . .
7. Appendix: Generally accepted auditing standards

A technically more formal definition codified by the AICPA is as follows:

The objective of the ordinary examination of financial statements by the independent auditor is the expression of an opinion on the fairness with which they present financial position, results of operations, and changes in financial position in conformity with generally accepted accounting principles. The auditor's report is the medium through which he expresses his opinion or, if circumstances require, disclaims an opinion.[5]

---

[2] W. A. Wallace, *The Economic Role of the Audit in Free and Regulated Markets* (New York: Touche Ross & Co., Aid to Education Program, 1980).

[3] Ibid., p. 49.

[4] New York: AICPA, 1982.

[5] American Institute of Certified Public Accountants, *Statement on Auditing Standards No. 1* (New York: AICPA, 1973), p. 1.

Professors E. Stamp and M. Moonitz, concerned with the international aspects of independent audits, have defined auditing as follows:

> An audit is an independent, objective, and expert examination of a set of financial statements of an entity along with all necessary supporting evidence. It is conducted with a view to expressing an informed and credible opinion, in a written report, as to whether the financial statements portray the financial position and progress of the entity fairly, and in accordance with generally accepted accounting principles. The purpose of the independent expert opinion, which should be expressed in positive and not negative terms, is to lend credibility to the financial statements (the responsibility for whose preparation rests with management).[6]

The two definitions just cited are similar in substance. This is the case for most such definitions adopted by institutes or associations of independent auditors the world around. Auditing is a technical issue. Stamp and Moonitz are quite correct in their analysis when they observe that

> Laymen, by and large, tend to leave technical issues to the technicians, and call them to account only when there is some notorious and blatant breakdown in the system. As a result, if left to work out the problem by themselves, auditors in different countries should come up with similar solutions to similar technical problems, just as engineers in different countries tend to come up with similar solutions to the technical problems of road construction or bridge-building.[7]

INTERNATIONAL AUDIT ENVIRONMENT

Even though the technical aspects of auditing (i.e., definition, objectives, framework, standards, and procedures) are internationally more homogeneous than their financial accounting and reporting counterparts, there are some important variations that suggest more attention be devoted to international auditing harmonization. These variations range from procedural aspects (e.g., emphasis on long-form audit reports in Continental Europe versus short-form reports and elaborate working paper techniques in the English-speaking countries) to philosophies of appropriate auditor qualifications (e.g., the requirement of at least a Master's degree in West Germany to no higher education requirement at all in the United Kingdom). The section entitled *Some Issues* later in the chapter brings into closer focus more of the existing multinational variations of professional auditing.

As a way to describe the international audit environment, we selected three of its dimensions for somewhat closer scrutiny. Historical points, comparative characteristics, and language of auditors' reports are highlighted in the remainder of the present section. These portrayals are illustrative. They do not reflect judgments on characteristics of vulnerability to third-party liabilities,

---

[6] Edward Stamp and Maurice Moonitz, *"International Auditing Standards"* (Hemel Hempstead, Hertfordshire, U.K.: Prentice-Hall International, 1978), p. 27.

[7] Ibid., pp. 131–132.

potential for international professional development, or sensitivity to external social and political factors.

Origins and Growth of Multinational
Professional Accounting Service Firms[8]

The initial base for the formation of multinational accounting firms was the United Kingdom, which was the first country to have an organized accounting profession. Its growth during the nineteenth century was encouraged by the enactment, in 1845, of a requirement that companies keep accounts, which had to be audited by persons other than directors. John L. Carey has pointed out that while many auditors initially were untrained amateurs, the companies laws "made inevitable the development of an organized profession of accounting whose practitioners are competent and independent."[9]

The earliest accounting body was The Society of Accountants in Edinburgh, which was granted a Royal Charter in 1854. This Society was renamed and reconstituted by charter in 1951 as the Institute of Chartered Accountants of Scotland, with members of bodies formed in Glasgow (1854) and Aberdeen (1867) also becoming members at that time. However, the first *national* accounting body was the Institute of Chartered Accountants in England and Wales (the English Institute), which was established in 1880, and by 1882 had 1,200 members and had initiated a series of examinations.

No less than four members of the English Institute's first Council are remembered in the names of large multinational accounting firms: Arthur Cooper, William Welch Deloitte, Samuel Lowell Price, and Frederick Whinney. A fifth Council member was a partner of William Barclay Peat. A further indication of the contribution of the United Kingdom to international accounting activity is seen in the fact that two Scotsmen of that era are Arthur Young (who emigrated to the United States) and George A. Touche.

In the late nineteenth and early twentieth centuries, the U.K. firms started establishing offices in other countries. For example, Deloitte, Dever, Griffiths and Co. (as it was then known) opened offices in 17 foreign cities between 1890 and 1914, including New York, Buenos Aires, Johannesburg, Mexico City, Rio de Janeiro, Montreal, and Moscow. The prime purpose for opening these offices appears to have been to serve the interests that their U.K. clients were developing throughout the British Empire and in other countries.

In the United States the American Association of Public Accountants was formed in 1887, with the encouragement and participation of English and Scottish Chartered Accountants who were living in the United States. In the absence of a statutory audit requirement initial growth was slow, with membership standing at 35 in 1892. However, by the time the name was changed to the Institute of Accountants in the United States of America in 1916, there were

---

[8] Dr. Alister K. Mason of Deloitte Haskins & Sells, Toronto, contributed significantly to this section.

[9] John L. Carey, *The Rise of the Accounting Profession* (New York: American Institute of Chartered Public Accountants, 1969), Vol. I, p. 19.

1,169 members.[10] Developments in 1913 and 1914 that spurred the demand for U.S. accountants were the imposition of federal income taxes and the establishment of the Federal Reserve Board and the Federal Trade Commission. Further impetus subsequently came, during the Depression years, with the formation of the Securities and Exchange Commission (SEC) and the requirement by the New York Stock Exchange that listed companies have audits. The Institute's name was changed to the American Institute of Accountants in 1917, and then to the American Institute of Certified Public Accountants in 1957.

While several of the early professional accountants in the United States were those sent by U.K. accounting firms, numerous firms without any U.K. connections were formed. Some of these established offices in several U.S. cities, and a few opened offices in Europe and Latin America as well. Rather than opening their own offices, others entered into arrangements with European firms; for example, in 1905 Haskins & Sells, who had opened their own offices in London in 1901, arranged with the Amsterdam firm of Van Dien, Van Uden & Co. "to represent us in accounting matters entrusted to our care in Holland and certain other European countries."[11] In addition, some initially independent U.S. firms later became associated with U.K. firms, with either an informal understanding to refer work to each other, or a more formal contractual arrangement.

(It is interesting to note, at this point, that there is little indication that accounting firms from Continental Europe established offices in the United Kingdom, the United States, or other parts of the world during this period. A prime explanation for this is that, although the Nederlands Instituut van Registeraccountants was formed in Holland in 1895, the accounting profession in many European countries was not generally organized until later. In Germany, for example, the Institut der Wirtschaftsprüfer was established in 1930, while in Spain—which for reasons of a common language might have been expected to be influential in Latin America—the first professional body dates only from 1944. Contributing factors might include the fact that English was the dominant language in the conduct of international commerce and finance.)

Over the years the strongest multinational links U.S. accounting firms have made have been with U.K. firms, and vice versa. In several cases a new name has evolved for use on both sides of the Atlantic, and elsewhere—sometimes after lengthy prior association under two or more names. An early example of a new "international" name was the agreement reached in 1925 between the U.K. firm of W. B. Peat & Co. and the U.S. firm of Marwick, Mitchell & Co. A more recent example is the 1979 agreement between Whinney Murray & Co. of the United Kingdom and Ernst & Ernst of the United States. However, in 1979, the major multinational firm of Klynveld Main Goerdeler & Co. (KMG) was formed, with the three-part name flowing from the Dutch, U.S., and German member firms—but *not* from Thomson McLintock, the large and

[10] Ibid., pp. 38–39, 124–127.

[11] Arthur B. Foy, *Haskins & Sells—Our First Seventy-Five Years* (New York: H & S, 1970), p. 129.

historic member firm from the United Kingdom, nor from Thorne Riddell, the even larger Canadian member firm.

Regardless of whether a common name is used, there have been increasing pressures in recent years for uniform professional standards to be followed by the multinational accounting service firms. The U.S.-originated practice of "peer review" has been the source of certain of these pressures. Another source has been concern within the firms that an audit report bearing a firm's name should be based on the same quality of work whether signed in Baltimore, Berlin, Bombay, Brisbane, or Bogota. While some firms claim to adhere to—or to be moving towards—uniform auditing standards and procedures, including a uniform policy on independence, the accounting principles followed in financial reports are usually determined by the client's jurisdiction of incorporation (i.e., *national* principles).

In discussing multinational accounting firms, attention is usually focused on the nine largest firms. The following listing is in order of size, based on published figures and on estimates for 1979 revenues:[12]

1. Coopers & Lybrand
2. Peat, Marwick, Mitchell & Co.
3. Klynveld Main Goerdeler & Co.
4. Arthur Andersen & Co.
5. Price Waterhouse & Co.
6. Deloitte Haskins & Sells
7. Ernst & Whinney
8. Arthur Young & Co.
9. Touche Ross & Co.

These firms all have annual revenues in excess of $500 million, have representation in all the main areas of the Western world, and between them play a leading role in many of the countries in which they operate. However, there are also several smaller multinational firms, perhaps with offices in only a few countries, and with varying degrees of formality and detail in their international agreements. Most of these have their oldest and largest member firms in the United Kingdom and/or the United States.

We have referred to the organizational arrangements under which firms may conduct their multinational operations. Professor K. W. Kubin has written about a "continuum of internationality" in considering accounting firms:

> At the one extreme, there are those accounting firms whose clients encounter some few international accounting problems which, however, do not require the auditor to travel abroad, let alone establish an office overseas. At the other extreme of the continuum are the large, prestigious accounting firms with their own offices in virtually all major business centers of the free world. In between these two extremes of internationality we find (1) firms which have only U.S. offices, but whose auditors frequently travel abroad to perform the necessary audit work

[12] List prepared by *Public Accounting Report* and reproduced in *Accountancy*, August 1980, p. 10. See Table 1.3 in Chapter 1 for 1980 and 1982 data.

for the foreign subsidiaries of their clients, (2) accounting firms which rely on an international network of correspondent firms to do all necessary accounting work abroad, and (3) a system of affiliate partnerships set up in foreign countries with local accounting firms.[13]

Two points regarding the foregoing quote should be emphasized: (1) a firm may rely on different arrangements in different countries, and (2) the arrangements in a particular country may evolve from the use of a correspondent firm to an affiliated partnership.

Auditing Environment in Germany, Japan, and the Netherlands

The three countries selected for *brief* commentary on different national environments are non-English-speaking countries. As we pointed out in the preceding section on the operations of multinational professional accounting service firms, the English-speaking countries are typically considered the cradle of professional auditing. Their auditing developmental periods are comparatively the longest and in general their auditing environments the most benign. One informal estimate has it that some 90 percent of currently practicing independent auditors have the English language as their mother tongue. So there is not much point in reiterating the more or less obvious!

Another reason for our selection emanates from the study conducted by Stamp and Moonitz.[14] They investigated the then-present state of auditing standards in nine different countries: Australia, Brazil, Canada, France, West Germany, Japan, the Netherlands, the United Kingdom and the United States. From among these nine, especially in terms of standard setting and enforcement in particular, and professional leadership in general, they concluded that Australia, Brazil, Canada, West Germany, the Netherlands, the United Kingdom, and the United States are "vital" countries. "Vital" was a characteristic attributed to those countries "without whose support an attempt to establish international auditing standards would no doubt fail."[15] France and Japan were excluded from this category. In terms of the Stamp and Moonitz categorization, we selected two vital and one nonvital country for comment. Note that some aspects of professional auditing and auditing standards are briefly referred to in the country-by-country discussion portion of Chapter 3.

West Germany. The West German accounting profession is characterized by high educational standards for admission, smallness of size (about 4,000 members), incredibly complex regulatory constraints, and significant international leadership, particularly with respect to affairs of the European Economic Community (EEC).

---

[13] Konrad W. Kubin, "The International Profession of Accountancy," *Collected Papers of the American Accounting Association's Annual Meeting, August 18–20, 1975* (Sarasota, Fla.: AAA, 1975), p. 124.

[14] Stamp and Moonitz, *International Auditing Standards.*

[15] Ibid., p. 138.

Professional organization in West Germany is two-pronged—by law all *Wirtschaftsprüfer* (WPs) must belong to the Chamber of Public Accountants. About 90 percent of them also belong to a voluntary body, The Institute of WPs. The Chamber is organized somewhat like U.S. bar and medical associations. It issues ethical rules and investigates complaints of unprofessional conduct. Ethical rules issued deal with topics like independence, privileged status of client relationships, and advertising and solicitation.

The Institute safeguards economic interests of the profession and acts as a partner in standard-setting processes. In the latter sense, it behaves somewhat like its U.S. counterpart. Regarding auditing, The Institute of WPs publishes expert opinions, position papers, and explanations. Typically the thrust of these recommendations is then adopted by governmental agencies in amending applicable corporate law. This process functions very much like the AICPA-SEC relationship in the United States.

Beginning in 1977, The Institute of WPs began to publish "Generally Accepted Standards for the Audit of Financial Statements." As one would expect, these standards are tied closely to applicable corporate and private companies law. This makes West Germany one of only a handful of countries with nationally established and enforced auditing standards.

Japan.   Professional auditing in Japan is inscrutable. Even though the Japanese CPA law was ratified in June 1948, and the Japanese Institute of CPAs founded in 1949, the profession in Japan still struggles with social acceptability. It is difficult to attract bright, promising university graduates into the profession. High-level civil servants enjoy considerably greater personal prestige than practicing CPAs. Numerical growth of the profession has at best been moderate. As of June 15, 1982, the total number of Japanese CPAs stood at 6,791.

The second major professional auditing-related difficulty in Japan is the fact that it is so multifaceted. Everything seems subject to multiplicity. There is companies law applicable to all Japanese companies and simultaneously SEC law for those corporations whose shares are traded publicly. Realistic independent audit requirements are limited to large companies and those whose shares are traded publicly. The Japanese corporations who have financed portions of their long-term capital requirements outside Japan typically follow British-American reporting and auditing standards. This adds yet a third simultaneous dimension.

Standard setting is similarly scattered. The Justice Ministry has a hand in it because it administers the Commercial Code applicable to all companies. The Finance Ministry is involved because it is in charge of the Japanese SEC legislation. The Institute of CPAs is involved because it wants to bring about greater influence on behalf of the profession. The Business Accounting Deliberation Council (an advisory body to the Ministry of Finance composed of government officials, professors, business executives, and CPAs) may be the real "power behind the throne." And the Japanese political (i.e., public interest) system has consistently held that any deviations from the general Commercial

Code or its special implementation decrees are to be considered as lacking conformity with generally accepted accounting principles. These multiple standards and their differential enforcement create major tensions for those practicing the profession.

A third concern surfaces over the current Japanese tendency to emulate U.S. practices and organizations. While this may be pleasant for U.S. egos, it is not conducive to coping with the Japanese infrastructure which, among other things, considers CPAs as outsiders everywhere, puts social homogeneity above individual performance, and thrives on interpersonal "reciprocal obligations." Fairly wholesale adoption of the U.S. style has simply not served Japanese professional interests well because the new style did not replace what had gone before, but was simply superimposed on it and now coexists along with it.

Finally, it is our observation that Japan is unwilling to innovate. The existing Japanese auditing standards are literally carbon copies of U.S. standards. In international councils and committees, Japan is most often siding with emerging consensus rather than pursuing its own point of view. Until Japan reduces some of its internal multiplicity, generates more political and social prestige for its practicing CPAs, and begins to exercise some independent leadership (in the Pacific region if nowhere else), we must agree with the Stamp and Moonitz assessment that the present importance of Japan in terms of international auditing processes "is less than it ought to be."[16]

The Netherlands.   The Dutch are amazing accounting professionals. They are at an international high water mark of professional and technical development. Yet at the same time they shun standard setting and rule making. There are really no nationally promulgated auditing standards in the Netherlands. The Dutch Institute (NIvRA) translates into the Dutch language the auditing statements issued by the Union Européenne des Experts Comptables Economiques et Financiers (UEC) discussed later in this chapter. As necessary, supplemental rules or comments relating specifically to practice in the Netherlands are added on. The latter are few and far between.

Effective 1967, the Registered Accountants Act began to protect the title *Register Accountant* and, in essence, made the Dutch Institute a creature of the state. Holland is the only country with a formal procedure for an administrative accounting court, where concerned parties can challenge each other over accounting and auditing matters. Despite all this governmental reach into professional affairs, the 4,000 plus members of NIvRA are fiercely independent and strictly auditing-oriented. Dutch Register Accountants may not engage in tax or administrative services work, nor may they perform consulting activities. Dutch professionals are really the only ones worldwide who are *exclusively* independent auditors.

Another unique aspect of the profession in the Netherlands is its close tie to universities and academic pursuits. Many leading practitioners also hold tenured professorial appointments and vice versa. It is a situation not unlike

[16] Ibid., p. 140.

the one found in the U.S. medical and law professions. Education and practical experience prerequisites in Holland are very high by international standards.

Dutch professional accountants enjoy high esteem both at home and abroad as well as across their national social spectrum, from labor unions to business executives, and from academics to politicians. Throughout the history of accounting and auditing, the Dutch have played worldwide leadership roles. In 1959, the then-president of the Dutch Institute addressed the annual meeting of the AICPA in San Francisco in order to argue for the creation of a formal mechanism to set international accounting standards. Fourteen years later, the International Auditing Standards Committee (IASC) got off the ground! Under the strong influence of Dutch accounting academics and practitioners, the largest Dutch corporation, N.V. Philips Industries, actually employed replacement cost accounting measurement methods and publicly reported portions of its operations on that basis for decades while the rest of the world considered a departure from historical cost measurement rules as outright heretical! Holland is clearly a nation of utmost professional auditing vitality.

Auditors' Reports

The language of auditors' reports differs greatly from country to country. These reports range from bare statements about compliance with legal requirements to fairly extensive prose about standards and procedures employed; scope covered; processes used in arriving at the opinion; conformity with identified accounting standards; consistency of accounting, auditing, and reporting standards employed; discharge of management from its fiduciary duties; and similar other points. To give the reader a flavor of actual auditors' reports published, three such reports were randomly selected from three non-U.S. sets of financial statements, covering the reporting year 1981. These reports are reproduced in Exhibits 9.1, 9.2, and 9.3.

The Dutch and Japanese reports resemble standard U.S. short-form reports. The most concise language occurs in the opinion from the Netherlands, whereas the Japanese report is quite descriptive. Regarding the latter, it is noteworthy that auditing standards observed are those "generally accepted in Japan," and financial accounting standards applied are "in conformity with

EXHIBIT 9.1   Auditors' Report from the Netherlands

AUDITORS' REPORT

We have examined the foregoing 1981 financial statements of Akzo N.V., Arnhem. For the purpose of our examination we also have made use of the reports of other independent auditors with respect to a number of subsidiaries. In our opinion, these financial statements present fairly the financial position of Akzo N.V. at December 31, 1981, and the results of its operations for the year then ended.

Arnhem, March 30, 1982

Klynveld Kraayenhof & Co.

EXHIBIT 9.2   Auditors' Report from West Germany

AEG-TELEFUNKEN
AKTIENGESELLSCHAFT

The Consolidated Financial Statement and the Annual Report were duly verified and found by us to comply with the law.

Deutsche Warentreuhand- und Kontinentale Treuhand-Aktiengesellschaft Wirtschaftsprüfungsgesellschaft, Steuerberatungsgesellschaft

Hamann   Neukirchen
Wirtschaftsprüfer   Wirtschaftsprüfer

Berlin and Frankfurt (Main), April 19, 1982

EXHIBIT 9.3   Auditors' Report from Japan

OPINION OF INDEPENDENT ACCOUNTANTS

To the Board of Directors of Mitsubishi Heavy Industries, Ltd.

We have examined the consolidated balance sheet (expressed in yen) of Mitsubishi Heavy Industries, Ltd. and consolidated subsidiaries as of March 31, 1982 and 1981, and the related consolidated statement of income and retained earnings for the years then ended. Our examinations were made in accordance with auditing standards generally accepted in Japan, and accordingly included such tests of the accounting records and such other auditing procedures as we considered necessary in the circumstances. The financial statements of Mitsubishi Motors Corporation, a consolidated subsidiary, which statements reflect total assets and net sales constituting 11 percent and 14 percent, respectively, for the year ended March 31, 1982, and 12 percent and 21 percent, respectively, for the year ended March 31, 1981, of the related consolidated totals, were examined by other auditors.

In our opinion, the accompanying consolidated financial statements present fairly the financial position of Mitsubishi Heavy Industries, Ltd. and consolidated subsidiaries at March 31, 1982 and 1981 and the results of their operations for the years then ended, in conformity with accounting principles generally accepted in Japan consistently applied during the period subsequent to the changes, with which we concur, made as of April 1, 1980, in the method of valuing marketable securities, the method of recognizing revenue on specific long-term contracts which meet certain conditions, and the method of translating the accounts of foreign subsidiaries and affiliates as described in Note 1. c), f), and h) of the Notes to Consolidated Financial Statements.

The accompanying consolidated financial statements expressed in United States dollars have been translated into dollars solely for the convenience of the reader. We have reviewed the translation and, in our opinion, the consolidated financial statements expressed in yen have been translated into dollars on the basis set forth in Note 2 of the Notes to Consolidated Financial Statements.

Showa Audit Corporation

Tokyo, Japan
July 31, 1982

accounting principles generally accepted in Japan." Conformity with applicable laws is the essence of the West German report.

Present auditors' reports around the world cause much unnecessary confusion. While there may be some commonalities in substance, there are clearly major differences in underlying audit objectives, referenced accounting and auditing standards, and general format. These differences alone support the case for strong international harmonization efforts in auditing.

WORLDWIDE
HARMONIZATION

Earlier in the chapter we pointed out that auditing is a technical activity whose development, standards, and procedures are the domain of the technicians themselves. Wisely, we believe, political and social forces and special-interest groups have remained distant from audit standard-setting activities. Courts of law have intervened occasionally, as have management representatives like the audit committees of corporate boards of directors. Spectacular fraud cases have influenced some audit procedures, like physical inventory observation as a consequence of the well-known McKesson-Robbins swindle. Overall though, professional auditors have been the "stewards of their own house."

The intensity of national auditing standard-setting activities varies from country to country. In the United States this activity is intense, voluminous, supported by considerable research and, from a practical point of view, quite detailed. In the Netherlands, on the other hand, no indigenous auditing standards exist despite a very high level of professional development. Most national auditing standards environments fall toward the end of the spectrum representing little or no formal auditing standard-setting activity. International auditing standard setting will surely foster significant national follow-up.

Stamp and Moonitz have identified seven specific benefits they believe will flow from the promulgation and enforcement of international auditing standards:

1. The existence of a set of international auditing standards, which are known to be enforced, will give readers of audit reports produced in other countries justifiable confidence in the auditor's opinion. By thus lending credibility to the work of the foreign auditor they enable that auditor to lend credibility to the financial statements upon which he is reporting.
2. International auditing standards will reinforce the benefits that are already flowing from the existence of international accounting standards, by providing readers with greater assurance that the accounting standards are being adhered to.
3. International auditing standards, by adding strength to international accounting standards, will assist readers in making international financial comparisons.
4. International auditing standards will provide further incentives to improve and extend the set of international accounting standards.

5. The existence of international auditing standards will assist in the flow of investment capital, especially to underdeveloped areas.
6. The development of an international set of standards will make it easier for underdeveloped countries to produce domestic auditing standards, and this will be of benefit to them.
7. Effective and credible auditing is necessary in all instances where there is a separation between management (who produce financial reports) and outsiders (who use the reports). The need is all the greater in the case of multinational enterprises since management is separated from the outsiders by greater differences in culture, political and economic systems, geographical boundaries, etc. Thus international auditing standards are, in this respect, even more important than national ones.[17]

Today's international auditing standard setting is spearheaded by IFAC (the International Federation of Accountants) and the UEC (more fully discussed in Chapter 12). While IFAC is the more global of these two organizations, it is thought to represent predominantly British-American interests and viewpoints. There is much debate whether this is in fact so. Regardless, many Europeans consider the UEC an important "counterweight" to the IFAC. For the time being, the side-by-side existence of these two professional organizations serves positive purposes.

IFAC Guidelines and Statements of Guidance

The IFAC's organizational structure is addressed in Chapter 12. In the present context we limit our attention to the IFAC's International Auditing Practices Committee (IAPC). This senior committee is empowered to develop and issue recommendations directly and without review on behalf of the IFAC Council. Interestingly enough, IAPC recommendations are called *Guidelines* rather than *Standards*. The nature, authority, and scope of these guidelines is defined by the Council as follows:[18]

International Auditing Guidelines. Within each country, local regulations govern, to a greater or lesser degree, the practices followed in the auditing of financial information. Such regulations may be either of a statutory nature, or they may be in the form of statements issued by the regulatory or professional bodies in the countries concerned, or in both.

The statements on auditing already published in many countries differ in form and content. IAPC takes cognizance of such statements and differences and, in the light of such knowledge, issues International Auditing Guidelines which are intended for international acceptance.

The Authority Attaching to the Guidelines. International Auditing Guidelines issued by IAPC do not override the local regulations referred to . . . above governing the audit of financial information in a particular country. To the extent

---

[17] Ibid., p. 146.

[18] International Federation of Accountants, *Preface to International Auditing Guidelines of the International Federation of Accountants* (New York: IFAC, July 1, 1979), para. 3–7.

that International Auditing Guidelines conform with local regulations on a particular subject, the audit of financial information in that country in accordance with local regulations will automatically comply with the International Auditing Guideline in respect of that subject. In the event of local regulations differing from, or being in conflict with, International Auditing Guidelines on a particular subject, member bodies, in accordance with the Constitution of IFAC, should work towards the implementation of the Guideline issued by IAPC, when and to the extent practicable.

The Scope of the Guidelines. International Auditing Guidelines apply whenever an independent audit is carried out: that is, in the independent examination of financial information of any entity, whether profit oriented or not, and irrespective of its size, or legal form, when such an examination is conducted with a view to expressing an opinion thereon. International Auditing Guidelines may also have application as appropriate, to other related activities of auditors.

Any limitation of the applicability of a specific International Auditing Guideline is made clear in the introductory paragraph to that Guideline.

In addition to the *Preface* quoted above, the IAPC had covered the following topics as of 1982:

INTERNATIONAL AUDITING GUIDELINES

1.	Objective and Scope of the Audit of Financial Statements	January 1980
2.	Audit Engagement Letters	June 1980
3.	Basic Principles Governing an Audit	September 1980
4.	Planning	February 1981
5.	Using the Work of an Other Auditor	July 1981
6.	Study and Evaluation of the Accounting System and Related Internal Controls in Connection with an Audit	July 1981
7.	Control of the Quality of Audit Work	September 1981
8.	Audit Evidence	January 1982
9.	Documentation	January 1982
10.	Using the Work of an Internal Auditor	July 1982
11.	Fraud and Error	October 1982

EXPOSURE DRAFTS

E-12.	The Auditor's Report on Financial Statements	February 1982
E-13.	Analytical Review	July 1982
E-14.	Other Information in Documents Containing Audited Financial Statements	October 1982
E-15.	Auditing in an EDP Environment	October 1982
E-16.	Events after the Balance Sheet Date	January 1983

Since professional ethics is directly related to independent audit activities, the status of IFAC pronouncements in the ethics area is relevant and simply listed here in terms of the issues covered. Please note that the ethics *Guidelines* and *Statements* are prepared by the IFAC Ethics Committee but must be approved by the Council of the IFAC prior to publication. As with all

IFAC pronouncements, the "approved text" is published in the English language.

GUIDELINES

Professional Ethics for the Accountancy Profession	July 1980

STATEMENTS OF GUIDANCE

1.	Advertising Publicity and Solicitation	September 1981
2.	Professional Competence	September 1981
3.	Integrity, Objectivity and Independence	September 1982
4.	Confidentiality	September 1982

UEC Statements

As set forth in greater detail in Chapter 12, the UEC began its international auditing standards-setting activity about one year earlier than the IAPC. The direction of work for the two groups has been highly similar as is evident from a comparison of the auditing issues which both groups have addressed since each commenced work. While the IAPC draws from a larger membership and has at its disposal a greater amount of other resources as well, the UEC has the advantage of a more focused thrust for its work (i.e., auditing in Europe) plus the likelihood of more ready acceptance of its recommendations "at home."

Nevertheless, the IAPC and the Auditing Statements Board (ASB) of the UEC have officially agreed to avoid duplication of their respective work programs. This dimension of the two international auditing standard-setting groups is covered more fully in Chapter 12.

The ASB of the UEC issues neither "standards" nor "guidelines"—it issues *Statements*. The titles of both auditing and professional ethics statements issued so far, plus those of respective exposure drafts outstanding in 1983, are as follows:[19]

AUDITING STATEMENTS BOARD (ASB)

- Preface; Policy Statement; Policy Paper on its Tasks and Methods.
- Statements

ASB 1: Object and Scope of the Audit of Annual Financial Statements
ASB 2: The Use of Another Auditor's Work
ASB 3: The Auditor's Working Papers
ASB 4: Audit Considerations Regarding the Going Concern Basis
ASB 5: The Audit of Foreign Exchange Contracts of Credit Institutions
ASB 6: Quality Control—Ensuring and Improving the Quality of Audits
ASB 7: Effect of an Internal Audit Function on the Scope of the Independent Auditor's Examination
ASB 8: The Audit Report

[19] Personal letter from UEC Secretariat dated June 29, 1983.

ASB   9:   Review by an Independent Accountant of the Interim Statements of an Enterprise

ASB 10:   The Auditor's Attendance at Physical Stocktaking

ASB 11:   Management Representations to the Auditor

ASB 12:   The Detection of Fraud Within the Scope of an Audit of Financial Statements

ASB 13:   Audit Considerations in Respect of Post Balance Sheet Events

ASB 14:   The Audit of Financial Statements of Small Enterprises

- Exposure Drafts

ED 15:   The Confirmation of Debtor Balances as an Audit Technique

ED 16:   The Auditor and Corresponding Amounts in Financial Statements

ED 17:   Audit Procedures Relating to Contingencies

ED 18:   Audit Considerations Relating to the Director's Report

PROFESSIONAL ETHICS COMMITTEE

- Statements—Essential Rules

Ethics 1:   Independence

Ethics 2:   Advertising

Ethics 3:   Professional Work

Ethics 4:   Confidentiality

Ethics 5:   Relations with Colleagues

- Exposure Drafts

ED 6:   Clients' Monies

ED 7:   Essential Rule for Accountants Other Than Those in or Employed in Public Practice

Illustration of an International Statement/Guideline

Both the IAPC and the ASB published their respective first sets of recommendations under "Objective and Scope" titles. For present purposes it is useful to compare these two statements. Since the ASB came forth with its statement in March 1978 (the IAPC's is dated January 1980) selected paragraphs from its text are reproduced first. Paragraph numbers shown correspond with those appearing in the official texts.

ASB Auditing Statement No. 1[20]

2. **The Object of an Audit.** The object of an audit of financial statements[21] is an expression of an opinion as to whether or not these statements show a true and fair view of the state of affairs of the enterprise at the balance sheet date

[20] Auditing Statements Board (UEC) *Object and Scope of the Audit of Annual Financial Statements* (Munich: ASB, 1978).

[21] Normally financial statements will cover a period of one year. In some instances a shorter or longer period may be covered. In the context of this statement financial statements include balance sheet, income statement and if appropriate fund statements, notes and other statements and explanatory material which are identified as being part of the financial statements.

and of its results for the financial year, having regard to the law and conventions of the country in which the enterprise is registered.

3. **The Scope of an Audit.** The audit should be organized in such a way that it covers adequately all aspects of the enterprise as far as they are relevant to the financial statements being audited.

    The scope will vary from country to country depending on local legal and professional requirements and standards. . . .

5. **Principal Features of an Audit.** An audit may be sub-divided into the following features:

    5.1. *The Study and Evaluation of the Accounting Systems of the Enterprise.* . . .
    5.2. *The Examination of the Financial Statements.* . . .

IAPC International Auditing Guideline No. 1[22]

Objective of an Audit

2. The objective of an audit of financial statements,[23] prepared within a framework of recognized accounting policies,[24] is to enable an auditor to express an opinion[25] on such financial statements.

3. The auditor's opinion helps establish the credibility of the financial statements. The user, however, should not assume that the auditor's opinion is an assurance as to the future viability of the entity nor an opinion as to the efficiency or effectiveness with which management has conducted the affairs of the entity. . . .

Scope of an Audit

5. The auditor normally determines the scope of an audit of financial statements in accordance with the requirements of legislation, regulations, or relevant professional bodies. . . .

10. In forming his opinion on the financial statements, the auditor carries out procedures designed to obtain reasonable assurance that the financial statements are properly stated in all material respects. Because of the test nature and other inherent limitations of an audit, together with the inherent limitations of any system of internal control, there is an unavoidable risk that

---

[22] International Auditing Practices Committee, *Objective and Scope of the Audit of Financial Statements* (New York: IAPC, 1980).

[23] The term "financial statements," as defined by the International Accounting Standards Committee, covers balance sheets, income statements or profit and loss accounts, statements of changes in financial position, notes, and other statements and explanatory material which are identified as being part of the financial statements.

[24] Fundamental accounting assumptions and considerations governing the selection and application of accounting policies, as well as other standards to be observed in the presentation of audited financial statements, are issued by the International Accounting Standards Committee. Many national professional bodies also issue pronouncements on such matters. Legislation or regulations within a country often contain further accounting and disclosure requirements.

[25] There is a variety of terminology used in different countries by auditors in expressing an opinion on financial statements. The actual wording used reflects concepts determined by local legislation, by rules issued by professional bodies, or by the development of general practice within the country. Wordings frequently used to reflect these concepts are "present fairly in accordance with generally accepted accounting principles," "give a true and fair view," and "in conformity with the law." This guideline does not address the wording to be used by an auditor in expressing his opinion on financial statements.

even some material misstatement may remain undiscovered. However, any indication that some fraud or error may have occurred which could result in material misstatement would cause the auditor to extend his procedures to confirm or dispel his suspicions.

11. Constraints on the scope of the audit of financial statements that impair the auditor's ability to express an unqualified opinion on such financial statements should be set out in his report, and a qualified opinion or disclaimer of opinion should be expressed, as appropriate.

Comparing the two sets of recommendations reveals much similarity. While this duplication appears redundant, it is in fact beneficial since each of the two organizations has its own sphere of influence and group of "followers." Together these two standards promote a single international thrust and are likely to achieve greater international harmony than one of the two sets of standards could on its own. Of course, if internationalization of the auditing profession continues to progress, there will come a time when only a single international auditing standard-setting body is needed.

Let us now mention a few of the differences between the excerpts quoted. The IAPC guideline makes it clear that the auditor normally determines the scope of an audit "in accordance with the requirements of legislation, regulations, or relevant professional bodies." The ASB seems to have the auditor somewhat more in the background. It states that audit scope "will vary from country to country depending on local, legal and professional requirements and standards." For the ASB, these differences are unassailable fact. For the IAPC, the auditor determines appropriate scope "in accordance with." In the first instance, the local requirements become the main determinants of what happens. In the second instance, the auditor "determines."

When the ASB refers to "financial statements" it means a balance sheet, an income statement and, *if appropriate,* funds statement, notes, and other statements and explanatory material that are identified as being part of the financial statements (emphasis added). There is no clue as to what the phrase "if appropriate" connotes. The IAPC guideline allows no discretion in this matter.

The ASB utilizes the term "enterprise" where IAPC uses "entity." The former puts considerable emphasis on "verification." The latter repeatedly alludes to "judgment." The possibility of fraud is directly mentioned by the IAPC. It would lead to extended audit procedures. The ASB is concerned that systems weaknesses "be brought to the attention of the client."

There is no need to belabor the point that the two recommendations are highly similar. They exhibit many more commonalities than differences. In terms of the goal of full international harmonization, considerable benefits flow from this common "wavelength."

CRITICAL ISSUES

As one would expect, international auditing faces a number of unresolved issues just like international accounting and transnational financial reporting.

Chapters 4, 5, and 6 are devoted entirely to presently unsettled international accounting measurement issues. Transnational financial disclosure (i.e., reporting) matters are brought to the fore in Chapter 7. Now is the time to identify and describe briefly several of the important issues discernible in the international auditing environment.

Basic Principles

Defined fields of endeavor (or areas of inquiry, or separable intellectual subject matter) appear to develop best and achieve important practical usefulness when they are well structured and conceptualized. Various approaches to the conceptual development of the field of international accounting are described and analyzed in Chapter 2.

The IAPC's International Auditing Guideline (IAG) No. 3 sets forth a score of *basic principles* for the field of auditing.[26] These basic principles represent as high a level of abstraction as appears to be reachable for the field of auditing at the present time. Broadly speaking, the basic principles are for auditing what the conceptual framework is for the financial accounting standards of the Financial Accounting Standards Board (FASB). It is our assessment that the IAG No. 3 principles are so universal and pervasive that they are likely to become the underlying terms of reference for national professional auditing groups and institutes throughout the Western world. These principles have "constitutional" characteristics. Their substantive components cover topics like

1. Integrity, Objectivity and Independence
2. Confidentiality
3. Skills and Competence
4. Work Performed by Others
5. Documentation
6. Planning
7. Audit Evidence

The issue is of course whether the IAPC's basic principles will in fact achieve worldwide acceptance. In the affirmative case, major professional integration and scope for technical development would be at hand.

Auditor's Report

The illustration earlier in this chapter of selected auditors' reports from various nations makes the point convincingly that reporting format and language are anything but internationally uniform. Auditors' reports are probably widely misunderstood internationally.

In a first step toward solving this dilemma, IAPC published its Exposure Draft No. 12 (ED No. 12) on February 1, 1982, entitled *The Auditor's Report on Financial Statements.* Paragraphs 3 through 13 of this ED address "Basic Ele-

---

[26] IAPC, *Basic Principles Governing an Audit,* 1980.

ments of the Auditor's Report." Also covered are proposals regarding (a) types of opinions, (b) circumstances that may result in other than an unqualified opinion, and (c) reference to other auditors. An appendix contains illustrative examples of the auditor's report.

Premised on the "Basic Elements" proposed in ED No. 12, Professors V. B. Bavishi and M. E. Hussein undertook a survey study covering 696 of the world's largest industrial companies with reasonable representation of both the developed and the developing nations. Companies whose auditor's report was not provided in the English language were excluded from the study. The survey covered primarily published financial statements for periods ending in 1980. The object of the survey was to compare the auditor's report as proposed in ED No. 12 with actual current worldwide practices. The data displayed in Table 9.1 report the results of this effort.

Weighting the evidence in terms of countries covered rather than the number of companies included in the study, an auditor's signature on a report was the most common practice observed. Least common is identification of the report addressee. Dating of reports and disclosing the dates or periods of the financial statements covered also achieved high scores, whereas reference to the consistent application of underlying accounting principles and report indexing appear not very harmonized throughout the world.

Overall, the results of the research cited support our contention that there exists a considerable need for more international auditing standardization. At least with respect to the auditor's report, present international practices are a mixed bag.

Professional Independence

Despite a considerable amount of international writing and speech making about various aspects of professional independence, the subject continues as an international auditing issue of major proportions. It seems generally agreed that CPAs in the United States are subject to the highest order of independence requirements that exist internationally. In some nations, auditors may sit on corporate boards of directors or own small financial interests in companies their firms audit. On the Continent, many large audit firms are owned, at least in part, by large banks. This does not mean that European auditors are necessarily dependent in fact or in appearance. Rather, it means that a thoroughly different organization of the independent auditing profession prevails. While a non-U.S. person may hold that an audit firm performing management advisory services and tax advocacy for a client cannot possibly be independent, U.S. auditors would argue that bank equity ownership of an audit firm (though carefully separated from audit operations) impairs independence. Who is right?

The auditor independence question often raises some operational problems in multinational engagements. Auditor independence is a concept not only entrenched in professional ethics codes in the United States but anchored in administrative SEC regulations such as their basic Regulation SX and Ac-

TABLE 9.1   Present International Conformity with IAPC ED No. 12 (Percent)

COUNTRY		N	Title Given	Addressee Identified	Auditor Signed	Auditor's Address	Report Dated	Scope & Opinion in Separate Paragraphs	Report Indexed	Report's Location (% by itself)
FAR EAST & ASIA:	Australia	N=25	100	4	100	88	100	88	52	12[D]
	India	N=20	100	5	100	95	100	100	85	80[A]
	Japan	N=76	95	84	100	91	100	97	59	47[D]
	Malaysia	N=20	100	0	100	95	100	100	90	70[D]
	Philippines	N=9	100	67	100	100	100	89	67	67[Mixed]
	Singapore	N=5	100	0	100	100	100	100	60	40[D]
	Taiwan	N=7	86	57	71	73	85	100	29	43[D]
	Thailand	N=6	88	88	100	87	100	100	13	100[A]
AMERICAS:	Brazil	N=6	50	50	100	100	100	100	50	67[D]
	Canada	N=40	100	88	100	100	100	100	47	30[Mixed]
	Mexico	N=7	71	71	100	100	100	71	0	100[D]
	United States	N=125	98	87	100	100	100	81	55	14[D]
EUROPE:	Austria	N=8	0	0	100	100	100	0	0	0[C]
	Belgium	N=13	100	8	85	85	85	100	62	69[D]
	Denmark	N=14	86	0	100	100	100	77	21	29[Mixed]
	Finland	N=20	100	0	100	100	100	95	100	55[D]
	France	N=46	100	4	98	83	95	96	63	57[A]
	Germany	N=60	10	0	100	100	100	7	5	15[B]
	Ireland	N=10	100	0	100	100	100	100	100	90[A]
	Italy	N=8	75	50	50	25	37	44	37	100[A]
	Netherlands	N=25	100	4	100	100	100	100	76	72[D]
	Norway	N=10	90	20	100	90	100	100	80	10[D]
	Spain	N=11	82	82	91	9	73	91	64	55[D]
	Sweden	N=34	100	3	100	30	100	100	79	35[D]
	Switzerland	N=19	95	21	100	19	100	100	79	90[D]
	United Kingdom	N=60	100	0	100	57	100	97	95	50[A]
AFRICA:	South Africa	N=10	100	0	100	80	90	70	80	10[A]

(continued)

TABLE 9.1 (*continued*)

COUNTRY		SCOPE				OPINION		
		Company's Name	Financial Statements Identified	Date/Period Covered	Reference to Auditing Standards	True and/or Fair	Conformity	Consistently Applied
FAR EAST & ASIA:								
Australia	N=25	92	68	96	0	100	96	4
India	N=20	95	30[E]	100	55	95	100	5
Japan	N=76	100	100	100	100	100	99	96
Malaysia	N=20	10	100	100	5	100	100	0
Philippines	N=9	100	100	100	100	100	100	100
Singapore	N=5	20	100	100	100	100	100	0
Taiwan	N=7	100	86	100	86	86	86	86
Thailand	N=8	100	100	100	100	100	100	100
AMERICAS:								
Brazil	N=6	100	100	100	100	100	100	83
Canada	N=40	98	97	100	100	100	100	100
Mexico	N=7	100	29[E]	100	86	86	100	86
United States	N=125	99	100	100	100	100	100	100
EUROPE:								
Austria	N=8	0	0[F]	0	88	0	100	0
Belgium	N=13	46	46[EF]	100	77	39	100	15
Denmark	N=14	57	36[E]	100	79	29	93	0
Finland	N=20	95	0[F]	100	95	0	100	0
France	N=46	52	71	100	65	22	76	35
Germany	N=60	5	0[F]	4	93	2	100	2
Ireland	N=10	50	100	100	40	100	100	0
Italy	N=8	25	87	75	25	13	63	25
Netherlands	N=25	100	20[E]	100	8	96	12	0
Norway	N=10	90	0[E]	100	90	20	100	0
Spain	N=11	91	27[EF]	100	18	0	64	18
Sweden	N=34	24	3[F]	97	56	6	100	0
Switzerland	N=19	37	42[E]	100	53	11	90	11
United Kingdom	N=60	25	98	100	88	100	98	2
AFRICA:								
South Africa	N=10	10	100	90	10	100	80	0

[A] Report located before financial statements [B] In between financial statements [C] After financial statements [D] After financial statements & footnotes [E] Uses the phrase "annual report." [F] Uses the phrase "financial statements." [EF] Both of these phrases used

Source: Vinod B. Bavishi and Mohamed E. Hussein, "The Auditor's Report: Proposed IFAC Guideline and Current Worldwide Practices," paper presented at Annual Meeting of the American Accounting Association, San Diego, Calif., 1982.

counting Series Release No. 126. Therefore, independent auditors of publicly held U.S. parent companies have the responsibilities of assuring themselves that foreign subsidiary companies are all audited by persons who meet U.S. definitions of auditor independence. This is not always a simple matter when audits abroad are conducted by associated or correspondent firms rather than by a firm's own branch offices. The situation may be even more vexing in those countries where local rules require that independent audits be performed only by local nationals.

Professors Stamp and Moonitz have identified professional independence as one of two key areas of difficulty (enforcement of standards being the other area) encountered in the international auditing field.[27] It is their contention that stormy waters lie ahead for the strengthening of professional independence in the multinational context. "The steps taken are likely to be those that will preserve the outward form of 'independence, objectivity and integrity' without necessarily preserving its essence."[28] Your authors agree.

Audit Conditions

Independent audits may be legally required in some cases and voluntarily submitted to in others. Regulatory agencies may have control over them or stock exchanges may stipulate them as a condition to listing a company's securities or simply admitting given securities for trade on an exchange. Audit fees may be legally prescribed in one country and left to market forces in another. In some places auditors only audit, while in others they engage in executive placement, financial investment management, tax advocacy, and other professional-type services.

Auditing procedures are somewhat less uniform multinationally than one might expect at first blush. The extended U.S. procedures of confirming trade accounts receivable and observing physical inventory counts are still not commonly practiced elsewhere, although there seems to be a trend toward greater use of these procedures in several countries. By contrast, trade accounts payable are sometimes confirmed in a number of countries but not in the United States. This is also the case for legal titles to real properties. Although auditing procedures among countries seem to vary more than respective auditing standards, both still do not vary nearly so much as accounting principles.

Certain audit practices also have a multinational dimension. West German independent auditors are known for relatively brief audit working papers and at the same time for rather long-winded formal long-form reports. There is an apparent tendency to show as much as possible of the audit work performed directly in an audit report. On the other hand, typical audit working papers are quite voluminous in North American practice, and audit reports are often held to the so-called short-form report.

Detailed figure checking for all material amounts occurs in some coun-

---

[27] Edward Stamp and Maurice Moonitz, "International Auditing Standards," *CPA Journal,* June 1982, pp. 24, 26, 28–30; July 1982, pp. 48–53.

[28] Ibid., p. 32.

tries, while sampling and different statistical methods are used in others. Professional conduct is regulated by law in some countries, while elsewhere there are only recommendations from professional institutes to which professional auditors must belong in order to achieve professional recognition and acceptance. This is the case in Switzerland, for instance. Several countries have laws excluding professional auditors from other countries from making their services available for local statutory financial reporting purposes. Professional reciprocity also varies widely from country to country.

Issues surrounding audit conditions are receiving direct attention from the two international auditing standard-setting bodies. For instance, IAG No. 9 addresses "Documentation," and ASB No. 3 covers "The Auditor's Working Papers." Specific efforts of the foregoing type are hopefully reducing the worldwide inventory of issues relating to independent audit execution. Your authors believe that significant progress on this issue is now observable and likely to continue without much impediment.

Professional Qualifications

Another difficulty with auditing in the multinational setting lies in recognizing the status of an auditor rendering an opinion. Most countries register or certify several classes of auditors; often only one and, in exceptional cases, two, types of auditors have the professional qualifications and the necessary independence to render meaningful opinions on financial statements that might be used in other countries.

France is an example in point. Several classes of bookkeepers and accountants may obtain government licenses to practice their respective trades and professions. Yet only the French Expert Comptable is in a position to render a professional opinion on financial statements.

To make matters even more confusing, some certificates on French financial statements are signed by so-called "Commissaires." These parties are statutory auditors whose appointments are mandatory under French commercial law. They are required to oversee in very general terms a company's bookkeeping and accounting and then to report annually to the stockholders' meeting. The law does not specify any professional qualifications for Commissaires. Often one or several stockholders serve in this capacity. Consequently, a statement of an opinion by a Commissaire has a completely different meaning and premise from a possibly similar statement or opinion by an Expert Comptable.

Educational requirements are another ingredient of professional qualifications. We have already pointed out that educational requirements for professional qualification are modest in the United Kingdom and substantial in West Germany. On the other hand, practical experience requirements are substantial in Britain and the Netherlands, but are no longer required at all in some jurisdictions of the United States. Again, as indicated previously in this chapter, these matters are addressed by the IFAC's Ethics Committee and its Education Committee. Similarly, the UEC channels its involvement here through a Professional Ethics Committee. Your authors are of the view that recent international development efforts augur well for some near-term reduction of the store of problems and issues relating to professional qualifications internationally.

Politicization

Any enumeration of prevailing international auditing issues would be incomplete without reference to ongoing political tugs of war. In the literature this dimension is often sensationalized and therefore must be assessed cautiously. It is in essence the "conflict" between English-speaking and non-English-speaking members of the profession. We alluded to the existing dichotomy earlier when we discussed redundancy between the IFAC and the UEC. The matter was also discussed in Chapter 2, and will again be raised in Chapter 12.

The issue was put most bluntly in *World Accounting Report:*

> The IFAC is becoming seen by many as an organization heavily influenced—some would even say manipulated—by the North American profession. The location of the IFAC headquarters in New York and the indefinite appointment of an American Secretary General are the factors cited most often to support this point of view. . . . What matters is appearances. And there are signs that IFAC's "appearance" is increasingly viewed by European and other accountants as tainted with an American bias.[29]

Should the charge of "British-American bias" in international accounting and auditing professional organization and standard setting be ignored? Your authors would answer with a resounding no. But all parties concerned must also recognize the fact that international organization and standard setting are matters of politics and diplomacy first and technical auditing and accounting second. Irrespective of the fact that accounting and auditing are most highly developed and practiced in English-speaking countries, major European, Scandinavian, and Far Eastern contributions cannot be brushed aside. Continuing the quote from *World Accounting Report*, "In dealing with auditing and ethics, there is . . . a huge variety of attitudes and practices, especially in Europe. Any attempt to impose an Anglo-American norm will inevitably be resented."[30]

From a political perspective then, the issue is threefold: (1) The appearance must be avoided that the English-speaking nations dominate and run international professional auditing affairs, (2) British-American norms should not be imposed stroke by stroke upon the rest of the world, and (3) professional leaders around the globe and in academic, governmental, industrial, as well as professional practice pursuits must assertively advocate the realistic benefits of international involvement. So long as international accounting and auditing are perceived, in some quarters at least, as latter-day manifestations of British-American colonialism, no effective progress is possible. The international polit-

---

[29] Peter Mantle, "IFAC and the Internal Political Threat," *World Accounting Report*, December 1982, p. 2.

[30] Ibid.

ical dimension cannot be wished away. It is very real and an issue probably as large as the most complex technical item.

Research

The postscript to Chapter 2 dealt briefly with accounting research methodologies. In general, the same types of research are applicable to auditing. Yet, in the field of auditing there exists a relative paucity of rigorous research. It has only been in the last decade or two that auditing research has found full-fledged academic recognition. Prior to that time, auditing was considered exclusively a professional, applied field wherein rigorous research had no place. Today, annual auditing research symposia (e.g., University of Illinois), auditing conferences (e.g., University of Kansas), a large special interest section of the American Accounting Association, and a special division of the AICPA provide auditing research of high caliber in the United States. It is also significant that the foundations of several major international professional accounting service firms have allocated significant cash and human resources to auditing research. For instance, the Peat, Marwick, Mitchell Foundation, between 1976 and 1982, funded 65 individual outside auditing research projects at a total cost of $1,212,100. Grants of such size naturally attract research attention!

Notwithstanding our earlier discussion of perceived undue North American influences upon accounting and auditing, we observe that to date North America is carrying the lion's share of rigorous theoretical and applied auditing research. In your authors' view this is unfortunate. Auditing is a worldwide endeavor subject to many national cultural, legal, and political constraints. They all merit serious research attention.

The critical issue is whether international auditing standards, professional ethics, educational prerequisites, and a host of other audit conditions can be specified or even mandated without due prior research. As it stands, the international profession appears to leave itself wide open to criticism by making largely judgmental pronouncements. Appropriately specified research in auditing clearly warrants international attention.

Enforcement of Standards

We indicated above that Stamp and Moonitz regard enforcement of standards as one of two key areas of difficulty in the international auditing field. The issue is also addressed in Chapter 12 with respect to international accounting standards. Time and again, the enforcement issue is highlighted as the least satisfactory aspect of international standard setting. Since professionally developed standards lack the force of law, the possibility of economic sanction, and, more generally, international political and diplomatic recognition, enforcement of standards is by and large left to the profession itself. Insistence upon tight or tightening auditing standards invariably produces adverse economic consequences for clients (i.e., increased audit service fees), which in turn leads to competitive pressures among independent auditors. This whole matter is complex, emotional and unlikely to be resolved in the near future.

Stamp and Moonitz have recommended that the best enforcement strategy is to take preventative measures within the profession. Possible ex ante courses of action include educational prerequisites, training, comprehensive examination procedures, and continuing professional education. Disciplinary ex post measures seem best dealt with by the courts and other outside parties. The IFAC is urged to put forth a continuing and substantive effort to monitor and rate national professional organizations, even though it is powerless to apply direct sanctions. "Nevertheless, its impact on events, and its ability to shape and influence progress, is potentially great if it would be willing to publicize evidence of shortcomings revealed by the monitoring and rating process suggested herein."[31] Your authors endorse these recommendations.

INTERNAL AUDITING

The internal audit function in multinational business operations is increasing in every dimension. Its recognition as a professional activity and the reliance senior management is placing upon it are at all time highs. Business International Corporation grouped the profound changes now taking place in internal auditing into three main categories:[32]

1. Increase in scope of work
2. Recognition of internal auditing as a profession by independent auditors
3. Pressures from outside for increased accountability by management, and for extension of auditing functions

Many explanations have been advanced concerning the recent rise of internal auditing. One is the phenomenal growth of audit committees of corporate boards of directors. These audit committees often rely on internal audit functions as their direct instrumentality and in turn have conveyed much prestige and direct access to top management to internal auditing.

Another salient feature is the unprecedented growth in corporate control needs. Security problems inherent in today's computerized information systems make effective internal auditing a "must" activity. The question if illicit payments by MNCs has ushered in yet another generation of specific tasks for internal auditing. In the United States, for instance, the 1977 Foreign Corrupt Practices Act triggered major expansions of internal audit departments of most larger U.S. corporations.

One U.S.–based MNC, which publicly acknowledged unauthorized foreign payments, *doubled* its total internal and external auditing expenses between 1977 and 1978. During 1976 Lockheed Aircraft Corporation's Board of

---

[31] Stamp and Moonitz, "International Auditing Standards," p. 53.

[32] Business International Corporation, *International Accounting, Auditing and Tax Issues* (New York, 1979).

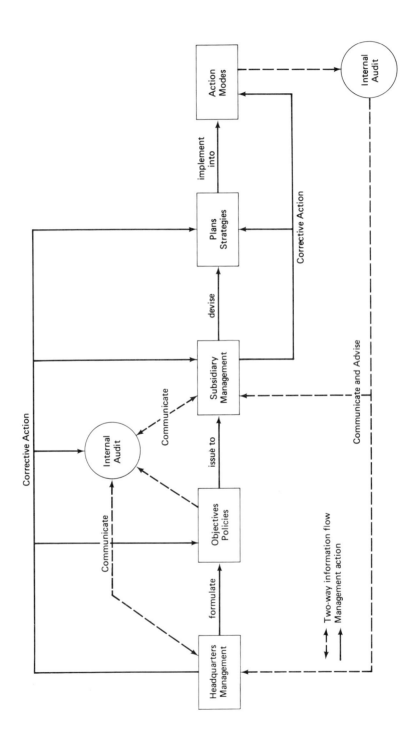

FIGURE 9.1   Control Dimensions of Internal Auditing in Multinational Operations

be suggested. The external perspective offered by the audit staff can also help to identify problems to which local managers may have become myopic. Management services of this nature can play a significant part in persuading overseas managers to identify with the worldwide organization and its control system.

Local versus Headquarters Staffing

Internal auditors can thus play a significant role in multinational financial control systems. But should this function necessarily be performed by headquarters staff or can another group do as well or better? While the use of parent company audit teams seems logical, worldwide auditor travel is generally expensive. It is probably no exaggeration to state that stationing a U.S. national abroad generally costs a company twice as much as if a local national were employed instead, especially in light of recent U.S. tax legislation. The high cost of domestic audit teams is compounded by the difficulty of attracting qualified personnel for the task, except at a premium, because of extensive travel and long absences from home. Another consideration is that domestic auditors with a limited foreign language capacity are frequently handicapped when auditing foreign subsidiaries.

A likely solution to this problem lies in using some combination of both domestic and foreign nationals in the control process. One variant is to deploy a small team of internal auditors from domestic headquarters as a supplement to auditing personnel in the field. Another is to employ audit teams that specialize in servicing subsidiaries domiciled in a particular geographic region. One large U.S.-based chemical MNC maintains a separate international audit staff in Europe. This regional unit reports directly to regional headquarters in Europe, subject to guidelines framed by the parent company's corporate internal auditing department. Other arrangements are possible. In any case, various possible tradeoffs merit careful consideration.

Hierarchical Relationships

The organizational relationship between the internal audit staff and enterprise management is another issue. Specifically, should the internal audit specialist report directly to (a) headquarters management of the parent company or (b) managers of the foreign subsidiaries whose performance is being reported upon?

Reporting to top management of the parent company, say the group controller, offers a number of advantages. To begin with, it strengthens the position and credibility of the internal auditor vis-à-vis local management. Advice and counsel of the audit specialist is less likely to be ignored by local personnel. Under these circumstances, the auditor becomes an important channel for the communication and enforcement of headquarters policy. A policy of reporting directly to top management also reduces the likelihood of incongruent behavior on the part of local managers. Knowing that independent audit procedures will eventually test their financial representations, local managers are less prone to mask the effects of suboptimal behavior than might otherwise be the case. Finally, reporting to headquarters management achieves greater uniformity and consistency in internal reporting formats.

A major disadvantage of having audit reports bypass local managers is the possible ill will created at the subsidiary level. Internal auditors are easily cast as agents or spies of upper management by local personnel and therefore seen collectively as external threats. Resultant perceptions, deserved or not, contribute to communications barriers already made difficult by distance and culture.

Reporting directly to local managers also has its pluses and minuses. On the plus side, local reporting enables issues and performance deviations to be settled quickly and "on the spot." Moreover, internal auditors are then seen as part of the local management team rather than as some external threat to be guarded against. In this kind of atmosphere, communications are likely to be freer, making it easier for the internal audit staff to identify potential trouble spots in financial control sooner than otherwise.

The major disadvantage of this reporting scheme is self-evident. In the absence of reliable feedback on the status of its multinational operations, the whole concept of financial control becomes academic. Data submitted to headquarters could easily be colored by the internal auditor's allegiance to local management groups. Local managers might also exhibit more reluctance to solicit help from headquarter's staff in view of their quasi-independence. In short, headquarter's management could quickly lose control.

How then might one proceed? Reexamination of the limitations identified with either of the two reporting modes just discussed suggests that the limitations probably are more apparent than real. Properly administered, internal reporting to both headquarters and local managers is a normal and, indeed, essential feature of a multinational control system. The paradigm of financial control illustrated in Figure 9.1 suggests that internal audit communiques to both headquarters and local management personnel are part of a closed-loop information system that rejuvenates the entire control process. In short, continual feedback at both the enterprise and subsidiary levels is the critical ingredient that allows the total organization to adapt readily to its ever-changing environment.

SELECTED REFERENCES

AMERICAN ACCOUNTING ASSOCIATION, *Report of the 1980-81 International Accounting and Auditing Standards Committee,* Sarasota, Fla.: AAA, 1981, 76 pp. (mimeographed).

AMERICAN INSTITUTE OF CERTIFIED PUBLIC ACCOUNTANTS, *A User's Guide to Understanding Audits and Auditors' Reports,* New York: AICPA, 1982, 28 pp.

BASU, B. K., *An Insight Into Auditing,* Calcutta, India: Book Syndicate Private Ltd., 1981, 748 pp. (Reviewed in *Journal of Accountancy,* August 1982, p. 99.)

BAVISHI, VINOD B., and MOHAMED E. HUSSEIN, "The Auditor's Report: Proposed IFAC Guideline and Current Worldwide Practices," paper delivered at annual meeting of American Accounting Association, San Diego, Calif., 1982.

BUSINESS INTERNATIONAL CORPORATION, "Internal Auditing—Concepts and Practices," pp. 179–220 in *International Accounting, Auditing and Tax Issues*, New York, 1979.

CAREY, JOHN L., *The Rise of the Accounting Profession*, 2 vols., New York: AICPA, 1969, 387 pp., 545 pp.

DEFLIESE, PHILIP L., KENNETH P. JOHNSON, and RODERICK K. MACLEOD, *Montgomery's Auditing* (9th ed.), New York: Ronald Press, 1975, 869 pp.

FANTL, IRVING L., "Control and the Internal Audit in the Multinational Firm," *International Journal of Accounting*, Fall 1975, pp. 57–65.

INTERNATIONAL FEDERATION OF ACCOUNTANTS, *International Auditing Guideline*, New York: IFAC, various numbers, dates, and exposure drafts.

KUBIN, KONRAD W., "The International Profession of Accountancy," *Collected Papers of the American Accounting Association's Annual Meeting* (August 18–20, 1975), pp. 123–135.

MAY, ROBERT L., "The Harmonization of International Auditing Standards," in *The Internationalization of the Accountancy Profession*, ed. W. John Breman, Toronto: The Canadian Institute of Chartered Accountants, 1979, pp. 58–64.

SAWYER, LAWRENCE B., *The Manager and the Modern Internal Auditor*, New York: AMACOM, 1979, 466 pp.

SCOTT, GEORGE M., and BART H. WARD, "The Internal Audit: A Tool for Management Control," *Financial Executive*, March 1978, pp. 32–37.

SNELL, DONALD M., "The International Auditing Practices Committee," *CA Magazine*, November 1979, pp. 78, 80, 82.

STAMP, EDWARD, and MAURICE MOONITZ, *International Auditing Standards*, Hemel Hempstead, Hertsfordshire, U.K.: Prentice-Hall International, 1978, 159 pp.

STAMP, EDWARD, and MAURICE MOONITZ, "International Auditing Standards," *CPA Journal*, June 1982, pp. 24, 26, 28–30, 32; July 1982, pp. 48–53.

STOKES, DONALD J., "The Nature and Extent of Contemporary Audits of Directors' Reports," *Abacus*, June 1982, pp. 70–82.

UNION EUROPÉENE DES EXPERTS COMPTABLES ECONOMIQUES ET FINANCIERS, *Auditing Statement*, Munich, West Germany: UEC, various numbers, dates, and exposure drafts.

WALLACE, WANDA A., *The Economic Role of the Audit in Free and Regulated Markets*, New York: Touche Ross & Co. Aid to Education Program, 1980, 51 pp.

WYMAN, HAROLD E., and VINOD B. BAVISHI, "The Structure of the Auditing Profession in the European Economic Community and Europe," paper delivered at annual meeting of European Accounting Association, Aarhus, Denmark, 1982.

DISCUSSION QUESTIONS

1. The chapter cites, in its early pages, Professor W. A. Wallace to the effect that "Economic incentives exist for parties to have and to supply an audit." What are three explicit demands for an audit?

2. Do you consider auditing to be primarily an economic, legal, political, social, or technical process? Be sure to consult dictionary definitions in making your choice.

3.   In the United Kingdom, auditing developed on the basis of require-
     ments written into companies laws. What are the key factors under-
     lying the rise of auditing in the United States?

4.   Multinational professional accounting service firms typically operate
     offices in many countries. Firms who must service international cli-
     ent needs but have only domestic offices must "internationalize" in
     alternative ways. Identify three organizational approaches through
     which this can be accomplished.

5.   From a comparative perspective, would you rather operate a me-
     dium-sized local CPA firm in Japan, the Netherlands, or West Ger-
     many? What are some key reasons for your choice?

6.   Enumerate the seven specific benefits stated in the chapter that one
     might expect from the establishment and enforcement of interna-
     tional auditing standards.

7.   What do the IFAC and the UEC have in common? With regard to au-
     diting, what are some important differences between these two in-
     ternational professional organizations?

8.   Critically appraise the statement made in the text to the effect that
     the basic principles stated in IAG No. 3 have "constitutional" char-
     acteristics.

9.   What are the cornerstones of the importance of the internal audit
     function to the operations of the MNCs?

10. A policy dilemma facing MNC managers is the question of whether
     to employ home country or host country internal auditors in control
     processes of multinational operations. What are the major trade-offs
     involved?

EXERCISES

1.   *Comparative evaluation.* This chapter identifies and briefly dis-
     cusses eight international auditing issues. Elsewhere in the book
     accounting measurement and disclosure (i.e. financial reporting)
     issues are brought to the fore.
     Required:
     A.   Using only topical headings, list the issues identified each for
          (a) accounting measurement, (b) disclosure, and (c) auditing.
     B.   Compare and contrast the three lists compiled under (A).
          Make your comparisons in terms of the following qualitative
          characteristics:
          1.   Degree of abstractness
          2.   Technical complexity
          3.   Overlap with corresponding U.S. domestic issue
          4.   Relative importance to practicing professionals
          5.   Likelihood of early satisfactory resolution
     C.   Report the results of your work in schedule form, placing the
          issues into a vertical column and the characteristics along the
          horizontal axis. Using a numerical rating scale from 1 (very

low) to 7 (very high), provide a numeric rating for each issue in relation to each characteristic.

2. With a probable view toward *political sensitivities,* the IFAC elected a West German citizen as its first president in 1977 and a Canadian to follow in that office. At the International Congress of Accountants in Mexico in 1982, an eminent citizen of the Philippines became the third IFAC president (the length of an IFAC presidential term of office is two and a half years).
   Required:
   A. List and briefly discuss some other actions IFAC may take to avoid the charge of a serious British-American bias.
   B. Some home countries of IFAC member bodies are listed in the case at the end of Chapter 12. Utilizing the information thus provided in Chapters 9 and 12, draft a press release (250 to 350 words) to be sent to all major financial newspapers around the world (e.g., *Wall Street Journal)* to assure editors and readers of these papers that the IFAC is in fact, spirit, and appearances a truly international representative of the accounting profession.

3. *International consistency in auditors' reports.* In Table 9.1, 15 different dimensions of auditors' reports are surveyed in terms of actual present-day reporting practices of nearly 700 of the world's largest industrial companies.
   Required:
   A. Ignore all footnotes. On the basis of the individual numbers reported (column by column and row by row), note the two most consistent and the two least consistent dimensions as well as countries.
   B. Restate all of the percentages in Table 9.1 by appropriately weighting them for the number of companies included for each country. For example the weight coefficient for the United States would be 125/696, to be multiplied by each of the percentages now listed. Carry all calculations to two decimal points.
   C. Using the weighted data computed under (B), repeat the procedure required under (A).
   D. Did weighting improve the information content of the data furnished? Write a concise paragraph in defense of your answer.

4. *Enforcement of international accounting, auditing and reporting standards.* Standards set in the private sector on a voluntary basis are by nature difficult to enforce. Chapter 9 discusses this difficulty in terms of auditing standards and Chapter 12 in terms of financial accounting and reporting standards.
   Required:
   A. Are international accounting and reporting standards easier to enforce than international auditing standards? Cite specific reasons in support of your answer.
   B. Is international enforcement of standards easier when there are just a few standards to enforce or when standards cover a

field fairly completely; that is, is enforcement easier now with 11 IAGs in place than it might be if definitive IAGs numbered 50? Again furnish well-reasoned arguments in support of your answer.

C.   Draft a memorandum (250 to 350 words) to the Board of Directors of the AICPA urging that the present reference to "generally accepted auditing standards" in standard short-form U.S. auditor's reports be changed to "international auditing guidelines."

5.   *Mirror mirror on the wall.* Based on 1979 revenue data, this chapter provides a size ranking of the nine largest multinational professional accounting service firms. Table 1.3 at the end of Chapter 1 provides comparable revenue data for 1980 and 1982.
Required:
A.   Compare the size rankings for 1979, 1980, and 1982. List ten variables that might influence worldwide revenue changes for the firms identified.

B.   For each firm compute the percentage change of worldwide revenues from 1980 to 1982. Write a concise paragraph of your opinion explaining the highest as well as the lowest rate of change observed.

CASE

Words Words Words . . .

Exposure Draft No. 12 of the International Auditing Practices Committee of the International Federation of Accountants states specifically that "This Guideline does not provide standard report wording because of the variety of terminology used in different countries and because of the different circumstances encountered around the world." In other words, no agreement could be reached on a worldwide standard text for an independent auditor's report.

Nevertheless, in its appendix, the ED sets forth an illustrative example, among several others, of a report with an unqualified opinion that refers to a "true and fair view" and to regulations and statutory requirements. This text is reproduced in Exhibit 9.4.

The second text, reproduced in Exhibit 9.5, is the standard report suggested by the AICPA in its 1982 *User's Guide* mentioned earlier in the chapter.

The third alternative, Exhibit 9.6, was launched as a "trial balloon" by the AICPA in September 1980 in exposure draft format and as a follow-up to the recommendations of its prestigious Cohen Commission.

EXHIBIT 9.4   IAPC Standard Auditor's Report

Auditors' Report to the Members of ABC Company, Ltd.
We have audited the financial statements on pages xx to xx in accordance with approved Auditing Standards.
In our opinion the financial statements give a true and fair view of the state of the company's affairs at 31 December 19xx and of its profit and source and application of funds for the year then ended and comply with the Companies Act 1948 and 1967.

/S/ UK & Company
London
March 15, 19XX

EXHIBIT 9.5   AICPA Standard Auditors' Report (1982 *User's Guide*)

To RMW Corporation, Its Directors, and Shareholders:
We have examined the balance sheets of RMW Corporation as of December 31, 19X2 and 19X1, and the related statements of income, retained earnings, and changes in financial position for the years then ended. Our examinations were made in accordance with generally accepted auditing standards and, accordingly, included such tests of the accounting records and such other auditing procedures as we considered necessary in the circumstances.
In our opinion, the financial statements referred to above present fairly the financial position of RMW Corporation as of December 31, 19X2 and 19X1, and the results of its operations and the changes in its financial position for the years then ended, in conformity with generally accepted accounting principles applied on a consistent basis.

March 7, 19X3

Rachel & Company
Certified Public Accountants

EXHIBIT 9.6   AICPA Proposed Auditor's Report (1980 draft)

(Addressee)
The accompanying balance sheet of X Company as of December 31, 19XX, and the related statements of income, retained earnings and changes in financial position for the year then ended are management's representations. An audit is intended to provide reasonable, but not absolute, assurance as to whether financial statements taken as a whole are free of material misstatements. We have audited the financial statements referred to above in accordance with generally accepted auditing standards. Application of those standards requires judgment in determining the nature, timing and extent of testing and other procedures, and in evaluating the results of those procedures.
In our opinion, the financial statements referred to above present the financial position of X Company as of December 31, 19XX, and the results of its operations and the changes in its financial position for the year then ended in conformity with generally accepted accounting principles.

Dateline

/S/
CPA Firm

Required

1. Review the illustrative actual auditors' reports shown in the text and note   5 major items or phrases which appear in the actual report examples but do not appear in the "standard reports" shown above.
2. What are the essential differences between the report texts appearing in Exhibits 9.5 and 9.6?
3. From among the actual examples shown in the chapter and the illustrations reported in the case, which report text do you consider most suitable for use by MNCs irrespective of given headquarters' domiciles? Why?
4. Without regard to your answer in (3), draft an auditor's report that you deem especially suitable for MNC use. Be sure that you can justify your draft.

10

Managerial Accounting

Previous chapters dwelled on financial reporting for external users of enterprise data. We now shift our attention to accounting for managerial decisions, particularly as it relates to the multinational enterprise.

The concept of managerial accounting entertained here does not incorporate the traditional notions of accounting for enterprise costs. While the origins of managerial accounting are found in cost accounting, the latter, today, encompasses little beyond the determination of inventory values for financial reporting purposes. Moreover, cost accounting concepts are, to a large extent, the same both domestically and internationally. Attention is therefore focused on the newer strategic area of managerial planning and control systems. It is here that significant international challenges are making themselves felt.

The foregoing implies that managerial accounting exists to provide information inputs to managerial decision processes. Accordingly, accounting issues are examined from the perspective of a management decision framework.

Financial Management of
Multinational Entities

The spread of business internationally has fostered mutations of domestic management specialties. This development has been necessitated by additional variables and constraints that typify the multinational dimension. Foreign currency exchange risks, restrictions on fund remittances across national borders, diverse national tax laws, interest rate differentials between various national financial markets, the global shortage of money capital, and the effects of worldwide inflation on enterprise assets, earnings, and capital costs are just examples of variables calling for specialized knowledge among multinational financial executives.

A direct response to such environmental complexities is the emergence of the international financial management function. One Conference Board study reveals that more than half of the companies queried reported having a specially designated executive in charge of arranging the financial decisions of its international operations. The trend in this direction, furthermore, is on the increase.[1]

In view of the emergence of this managerial specialty, a description of some of the major international financial management issues along with their accounting implications is provided in this chapter. Needless to say, a viable set of financial decisions and policies cannot be produced nor the attainment of enterprise objectives properly gauged without adequate and timely information. Managerial accounting thus commands a strategic role in the development of information support systems for financial decisions within the multinational entity.

To limit the scope of our discussion, managerial accounting issues are divided into two broad areas: financial planning and financial control. Specific subtopics include (a) foreign investment analysis, (b) foreign exchange risk management, (c) management information systems, and (d) financial control including performance evaluation of foreign operations. Foreign inflation, currency fluctuations and sovereign risk are discussed in relation to the performance evaluation issue.

FOREIGN INVESTMENT ANALYSIS

The decision to invest abroad is a principal means of implementing the global strategy of a multinational company. Direct investment beyond national boundaries, however, typically involves an enterprise in a commitment of enormous sums of capital to an uncertain future. In this respect, risk is inevitable. The added risk dimension is compounded by an unfamiliar international environment that is distant and complex and in a constant state of change. Under these circumstances, formal planning becomes highly desirable and is normally performed within a capital budgeting framework, that is, a framework that compares both the benefits and costs of any contemplated activity.

Owing to significant advances in domestic capital budgeting theory, sophisticated approaches to investment decisions are now available. Procedures exist for determining a firm's optimum capital structure, measuring a firm's

---

[1] Irene W. Meister, *Managing the International Financial Function* (New York: The Conference Board, 1970), pp. 1–2.

cost of capital, and evaluating investment alternatives under conditions of uncertainty. Normative decision rules for investment choice typically call for the discounting of an investment's risk-adjusted cash flows at an appropriate interest rate, namely, the firm's weighted average cost of capital. In the absence of capital rationing, a firm increases the wealth of its owners if it accepts independent investment projects promising positive net present values. When considering mutually exclusive options, rational behavior dictates selection of alternatives promising the maximum net present value.

When we enter the international arena, investment planning quickly becomes a "mission impossible." Different tax laws, differential rates of inflation, risks of expropriation, fluctuating exchange rates, exchange controls, restrictions on the transferability of foreign earnings, and language and intercultural differences all introduce a degree of complexity not usually found under more homogeneous and stable domestic conditions. Add to this the difficulty of quantifying such data, and the problem is quickly magnified. Modifications of domestic capital budgeting theory that accommodate these additional environmental complexities are thus called for.

Multinational adaptations of traditional investment planning models have taken place in at least three major areas and are discussed below. These include (1) determination of the relevant return from a multinational investment, (2) measurement of expected cash flows, and (3) calculation of the multinational cost of capital.

Financial Return Perspectives

In assessing a foreign investment opportunity, we must address the question of what constitutes the *relevant return*. Should the international financial manager evaluate expected investment returns from the perspective of the foreign project or that of the parent company? (Note that this issue parallels in many respects the problem of currency perspectives associated with foreign currency translation discussed in Chapter 4.) Returns from the former perspective could differ significantly from the latter owing to (a) governmental restrictions on repatriation of earnings and capital, (b) license fees, royalties, and other payments that provide income to the parent but are expenses from the project viewpoint, (c) differential rates of national inflation, (d) changing foreign currency values, and (e) differential taxes to name a few.

One might argue that, ultimately, return and risk considerations of a foreign investment should be on behalf of the parent company's stockholders. This is consistent with domestic capital budgeting doctrine as cash flows to the parent ultimately provide the basis for dividend payments and other uses which support parent company objectives. On the other hand, arguments can be made that such an ethnocentric posture is no longer appropriate. To begin with, investors in the parent company are increasingly drawn from a worldwide community. Thus investment objectives should reflect a much more cosmopolitan outlook than before. Observation also suggests that many companies, in true multinational fashion, possess long-run as opposed to short-run investment horizons. Funds generated abroad tend to be reinvested there rather than repatriated to the parent company. Under these considerations, returns from a host country perspective seem appropriate. Emphasis on local project returns is consistent with the objective of maximizing consolidated earnings of the group. As mentioned in Chapter 6, earnings of majority-owned affiliates are generally consolidated with those of the parent. Earnings of less than majority owned affiliates are typically accounted for either under the equity or cost methods.

Another response to the original question of appropriate return standards might be, "it all depends." Planned reinvestment of funds in the original host country would justify a local country perspective; planned deployment of the funds elsewhere would justify a parent country perspective. In short, consideration of the financial returns should vary depending on how a given foreign investment fits into a multinational company's foreign investment portfolio now and in the future.[2]

An appealing solution is offered by Eiteman and Stonehill.[3] Drawing on a behavioral theory of the firm, they posit that there is a multiplicity of goals that financial managers must satisfy, depending on the aspiration levels of both investor and noninvestor groups comprising the organization and its environment. In the case of a foreign investment, the host country government is one such group. To assure some congruity between the goals of the multinational investor and the host government, at least two financial return calculations are proposed: one from the host country perspective and the other from the parent country perspective. Calculation of the former is based on the assumption that, if a foreign investment promises to be profitable, the foreign investor would not be misallocating the host country's scarce resources. For example, a country enjoying full employment of its resources would probably not look favorably on a proposed foreign investment promising a 12 percent return on assets employed when investments of comparable risk elsewhere in the country are yielding 18 percent. Evaluation of an investment opportunity from a local perspective also provides useful information to the parent company. If a foreign project cannot promise a risk-adjusted return that exceeds those of locally based competitors, parent company shareholders would be better off by investing directly in the shares of local companies instead.

In practice, financial managers appear divided over the issue of whose returns should be considered. In a recent survey of 156 U.S.-based multinationals, 21 percent of the responding firms emphasized, for foreign investment evaluation purposes, returns from the viewpoint of the parent company, 42 percent stressed returns from the perspective of the local project, while 37 percent employed both local and parent company perspectives.[4]

At first glance, the accounting implications of multiple rate of return cal-

[2] Rita M. Rodriguez and E. Eugene Carter, *International Financial Management* (Englewood Cliffs, N.J.: Prentice-Hall, Inc., 1976), p. 342.

[3] David K. Eiteman and Arthur I. Stonehill, *Multinational Business Finance,* 3rd ed. (Reading, Mass.: Addison-Wesley Publishing Co., Inc., 1982).

[4] Vinod B. Bavishi, "Capital Budgeting Practices at Multinationals," *Management Accounting,* August 1981, p. 34.

culations appear straightforward. After all, dual rate of return calculations would simply involve a doubling of data requirements, would they not? Nothing could be further from the truth. In the earlier discussion, project rate of return calculations were assumed to be a proxy for host country evaluations of a foreign investment. In practice, the analysis is much more complicated. For example, proposals submitted to host country officials probably have to reflect various macro considerations. Thus, would project rate of return calculations really reflect a host country's opportunity costs? Are the expected returns from a foreign investment limited to projected cash flows or are there additional social externalities to be considered? If there are additional benefits, how are these measured? Does a foreign investment require any special overhead expenditures by the host government? What is risk from a host country viewpoint and how can this aspect of a foreign investment be measured? Questions such as these indicate a geometric as compared to an arithmetic expansion in the information requirements associated with this aspect of foreign investment analysis.

Measuring Expected Returns

Measuring the expected cash flows associated with a foreign investment is a challenging exercise. Examples of international considerations that account for this state of affairs are examined first from a local project perspective and then from a parent company perspective. Assume for purposes of discussion that a U.S. multinational corporation is considering acquisition of 100 percent ownership of a manufacturing facility in Israel in lieu of U.S. exports to that country. One-half of the investment is financed by the U.S. parent in the form of cash and equipment. The balance is financed by local bank borrowing at market rates. The Israeli subsidiary imports one-half of its raw materials and components from the U.S. parent and exports one-half of its output to Greece. As a means of repatriating funds to the parent company, the Israeli subsidiary pays the U.S. parent a licensing fee, royalties for use of parent company patents, and technical service fees for management services rendered. Earnings of the Israeli subsidiary are remitted to the parent in the form of dividends. A diagram of prospective cash flows that need to be measured is provided in Figure 10.1.

The basic methodology of estimating projected cash flows associated with the Israeli operations is not unlike that employed for a domestic company. Expected receipts are based on sales projections and anticipated collection experiences. Operating expenses, converted to their cash equivalents, and local taxes are similarly forecast. Additional elements of return, have to be considered, however. They include the following:[5]

1. The additional operating income of the overseas unit resulting from the merger of its own capabilities with those of the investing corporation.

[5] Paul O. Gaddis, "Analysing Overseas Investments," *Harvard Business Review*, May-June 1966, p. 119.

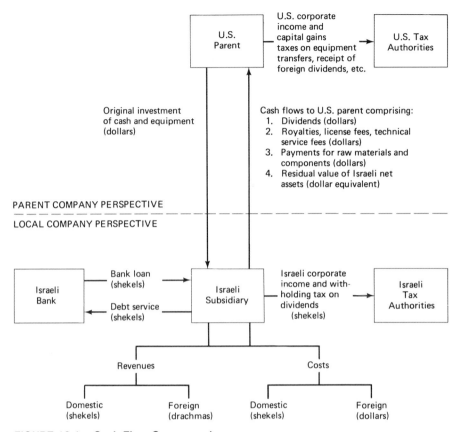

FIGURE 10.1   Cash Flow Components

2. Additional income from increased export sales resulting from the proposed investment action, including (a) additional export income at each U.S. operating unit that manufacturers products related to those that will be produced overseas, and (b) additional earnings from new export activity at the overseas operating unit resulting from its increased capabilities to sell beyond the boundaries of its traditional national markets.

3. Additional income from increased licensing opportunities shown on the books of both the affected U.S. units and the overseas unit.

4. Additional income from the importation to U.S. operating units of technology, product design, or hardware from the overseas operating unit.

Another distinguishing feature of this process is the need to consider the impact of changing prices and fluctuating currency values on expected foreign currency returns. Focusing for the moment on the latter, if local currency cash flows were fixed, for example, if the Israeli venture took the form of a bond investment, the measurement of exchange rate effects would be straightforward. In this instance, depreciation of the Israeli shekel relative to the U.S. dollar would reduce the dollar equivalent of future interest income. When foreign currency income is generated by an ongoing manufacturing enterprise, the analysis is more complicated as net operating cash flows are themselves influenced by exchange rate changes. Accordingly, accounting measurements of exchange rate effects for each class of activity such as domestic versus export sales, domestic versus imported costs as well as their cumulative effects on projected cash flows are necessary.

The foregoing measurement processes are built into the assumptions underlying the following example, which illustrates the effects of both changing prices and currency values on expected returns for the first two years of a six-year investment project. Assume that our Israeli subsidiary is expected to sell 100,000 units of its manufactured product in the local market at an initial unit price of 3,333 Israeli shekels (S). Another 100,000 units will be exported to Greece and priced in drachmas (D) reflecting the shekel base price. Thereafter, changes in local selling prices are tied to annual rates of inflation in Israel and Greece, which are expected to average 20 percent and 10 percent, respectively. Unit sales, both domestic and foreign, are expected to increase each year by 10 percent. Owing to inflation differentials between the two countries, the shekel is forecast to depreciate relative to the drachma by 10 percent per annum. Variable costs of production (raw materials and labor) also reflect local inflation rates. As 50 percent of the Israeli manufacturer's raw materials are imported from the United States, imported raw material prices are expected to increase by 10 percent each year in keeping with anticipated U.S. inflation. Anticipated depreciation of the shekel relative to the U.S. dollar is 5 percent. Licensing and other fees are targeted to average 10 percent of gross revenues while selling and administrative expenses are expected to increase by 15 percent each year from an initial year level of S 80,000,000. Assuming an annual depreciation expense of 100,000,000 and a 40 percent Israeli corporate income tax, the projected annual cash flow pattern will increase from S 151,924,000 to S 201,656,200 in local currency. Measured in U.S. dollars, net cash flows increase from $4,557,720 to $5,747,202. This is illustrated in Table 10.1.

In this example, a depreciating local currency had a positive effect on projected local cash flows owing to the structure of the foreign operation's product and factor markets.

Once a parent country perspective is employed, we find that cash flows to the U.S. parent company need not parallel those of the Israeli subsidiary. This seems strange indeed, as cash generated from, say, a Hawaiian subsidiary is immediately available to its California parent. The explanation for this phenomenon lies in the various constraints that foreign governments can impose on the flow of funds across national boundaries. Owing to balance of payments considerations, some countries, for example, limit the repatriation of dividends to a certain proportion of a company's capital that has been formally registered with the host government. Others do not allow repatriation of cash flows made possible by tax-deductible depreciation as these are not a part of reported earnings which form the basis of dividend declarations. This consideration alone would reduce the repatriable cash flows of our previous Israeli subsidiary example by 66 percent and 50 percent for each of the two years examined.

Accordingly, cash flows that can be repatriated to the parent company

TABLE 10.1   Cash Flows from Israeli Subsidiary

	YEAR 1	YEAR 2
Sales (units)		
Domestic	100,000	110,000
Foreign	100,000	110,000
Price (per unit)		
Domestic	S 3,333	S 4,000
Foreign	S 3,333	S 4,033
	(D 11,110)	(D 12,221)
Gross revenues		
Domestic	S 333,300,000	S 440,000,000
Foreign	S 333,300,000	S 443,630,000
	(D 1,111,000,000)	(D 1,344,310,000)
Total	S 666,600,000	S 883,630,000
Raw Materials (cost per unit)		
Domestic	S 667	S 800
Foreign	S 667	S 772
	$ (20)	$ (22)
Labor (cost per unit)	S 333	S 400
Variable cost (per unit)	S 1,667	S 1,972
Total variable costs	S 333,400,000	S 433,840,000
Licensing fees, royalties, etc.	S 66,660,000	S 88,363,000
Depreciation expense	S 100,000,000	S 100,000,000
Selling and administrative expense	S 80,000,000	S 92,000,000
Total expenses	S 580,060,000	S 714,203,000
Net operating income	S 86,540,000	S 169,427,000
Corporate income tax at 40%	S 34,616,000	S 67,770,800
Net income	S 51,924,000	S 101,656,200
Depreciation	S 100,000,000	S 100,000,000
Net cash flow (shekels)	S 151,924,000	S 201,656,200
Net cash flow (dollars)	S 4,557,720	S 5,747,202
	Exchange Rates	
	S .30 = D 1	S .33 = D 1
	S 33 = $ 1	S 35 = $ 1

must be identified and estimated, taking into account current and anticipated changes in foreign exchange rate behavior, restrictions of funds transfers, and other government constraints. In addition, while tax assessments under any given national jurisdiction tend to be uniform, this is not the case internationally. Consequently, differential tax levies between Israel and the United States as well as other costs of transferring funds to the U.S. parent have to be accounted for. (International tax considerations are dimensioned in Chapter 11.)

Multinational Cost of Capital

If foreign investments are evaluated in the context of the discounted cash flow model, then an appropriate discount rate must be developed. Capital budgeting theory typically employs a firm's cost of capital as this discount rate; that is, a project must yield a return at least equal to a firm's capital costs to be acceptable. This "hurdle rate" is, in turn, functionally related to the proportions of debt and equity in a firm's financial structure as follows:

$$k_a = k_e \frac{E}{S} + k_i (1 - t) \frac{D}{S},$$

where

k_a = weighted average after-tax cost of capital
k_e = cost of equity
k_i = cost of debt before tax
t = marginal tax rate
E = value of a firm's equity
D = value of a firm's debt
S = value of a firm's capital structure (E + D).

While the value of a firm's debt and equity can be measured in terms of conventional accounting book values, they are usually measured in terms of fair market values. This is especially appropriate when inflation causes book values to diverge significantly from market values.

To illustrate the calculation of a firm's weighted average cost of capital, assume that a firm's outstanding bonds, with an effective interest cost of 10 percent, have a market value of $30,000,000. Assume further that the market value of its common stock, bearing a cost of 14 percent, is $70,000,000. If the firm's marginal tax rate is 40 percent, its weighted average discount rate would be

$$k_a = \frac{30m}{100m} (1 - .40) .10 + \frac{70m}{100m} (.14)$$
$$= .018 \quad + .098$$
$$= 11.6\%.$$

Does the measurement of the cost of capital for a multinational entity differ very much from that of a purely domestic firm? Yes, indeed. In this regard Eiteman and Stonehill identify seven international variables that influence the overall cost of capital for a multinational firm.[6] Each opens up new vistas for both applied and basic research and is listed below.

1. The *availability of capital* is normally a given parameter domestically. It is an important variable in the international arena.
2. *Segmented national capital markets,* that is, those in which required returns of securities of comparable risk and return differ, can also distort capital costs for firms domiciled in these markets. A significant question facing international financial managers is whether firms residing in such markets can lower their cost of capital by sourcing capital in international markets.
3. Are investors willing to pay a premium for shares of multinational firms that promise to satisfy their *international portfolio diversification* needs?

[6] Eiteman and Stonehill, *Multinational Business Finance.*

4. Should firms adjust their overall cost of capital to reflect *foreign exchange* and *political risks?*
5. How should a firm incorporate *international tax considerations* in external financial sourcing and financial structure decisions?
6. How and to what extent does the amount of *financial disclosure* affect a company's access to international capital markets and thus its cost of capital?
7. How do multinational operations change a firm's *optimal financial structure?* Specifically, how does the added international availability of capital and ability to diversify cash flows internationally affect a firm's optimal debt ratio?

Eiteman and Stonehill provide an excellent analysis of these variables in their *Multinational Business Finance.* We limit our discussion to a brief on some measurement issues.

The cost of equity capital may be calculated in various ways. One popular measure is to combine the expected dividend yield with the expected dividend growth rate. Letting D_i = expected dividends per share at period's end, P_o = the current market price of the stock at the beginning of the period, and g = expected growth rate in dividends, the cost of equity is represented symbolically as $k_e = D_i/P_o + g$. While measurement of current stock prices is not a problem in most countries in which a multinational firm's shares are listed, measurement of the terms D_i and g is often troublesome. To begin, D_i represents an expectation. Expected dividends, in turn, are naturally dependent on the operating cash flows of the company as a whole. Measurements of these cash flows, unfortunately, are complicated by environmental considerations such as those mentioned in connection with our Israeli manufacturer. Moreover, measurement of the dividend growth rate, which is itself a function of expected future cash flows, is rendered difficult by exchange controls and other governmental constraints over multinational funds transfers.

Similar problems relate to the measurement of the debt component of the average cost of capital. In a uninational setting, the cost of debt is the effective interest rate multiplied by $(1 - t)$ as interest is generally a tax-deductible expense. When a multinational company borrows foreign currencies, however, additional factors enter the picture. The effective after-tax interest cost must now consider foreign exchange gains or losses that arise whenever foreign exchange rates fluctuate between the transaction and settlement dates (see Chapter 4). Assume that a U.S. multinational borrows 100,000 Dutch guilders for a year at 8 percent interest when the dollar/guilder exchange rate is $.38 = DG 1. Should the guilder appreciate to $.418 = DG 1 prior to repayment, the borrowing company will incur a transaction loss of $4,104 [DG 106,000 × ($.418 − $.380)]. This additional 10 percent cost of debt financing would be tax deductible. Assuming a corporate tax rate of 40 percent, the after-tax cost of debt would be .18 (1 − .40) or 10.8 percent as opposed to 4 percent in a purely domestic transaction.

Additional tax considerations come into play when a multinational borrows funds in several foreign capital markets. Account must be taken of current and prospective tax rates in each foreign market over the life of the loan. Assessment of the tax-deductibility status of interest payments would have to be made as not all national taxing authorities recognize interest deductions, particularly if they are between related entities in a multinational corporate network. Moreover, recognition of deferred taxes, which arise whenever income for tax purposes differs from income for external reporting purposes (see Chapter 6), is becoming a generally accepted practice among many industrialized countries in which MNCs operate. Being a "liability," on which no interest is paid, the question arises whether this represents an interest-free source of financing and should be included in the cost of capital determination. While this issue merits additional attention, we do not feel that it should be included in the cost of capital calculation. As discussed in Chapter 4, deferred taxes under the current rate method are translated at the current rate with any translation gains or losses taken to owners' equity and held in suspense until realization occurs. Under the temporal method they are translated at the historical rate. As current earnings are not burdened under either treatment with exchange rate effects, neither should the cost of capital be relieved by what in effect is an interest-free loan from a government.

Accounting Considerations

Despite the improvements and modifications undertaken to internationalize capital budgeting theory, the fact remains that little progress has taken place in the actual implementation of these conceptual refinements. One study of the methods used by multinational firms to evaluate foreign investments discloses that, in most cases examined, firms employ the same tools of analysis internationally as they do domestically.[7] A study of a similar nature concludes that not only do firms not modify existing tools when evaluating foreign investment opportunities but that the overall approach to foreign investment decision making is actually *less* sophisticated than that employed at home.[8] What accounts for such a phenomenon? The answer should come as no surprise to accountants. All the capital budgeting constructs that we have examined naively assume that the required information is readily available. Thus, given this happy state of affairs, all that remains to be done is for the financial manager simply to input the required numbers into some mechanical decision process and "crank out" the answers. Unfortunately, obtaining accurate and timely information is the most difficult and critical dimension of the entire capital budgeting decision, more so in the international sphere where different climates, culture, languages, and information technology complicate the generation of required intelligence. Until information systems are designed that promise to capture these extranational considerations, the present gap between investment theory and practice will continue.

---

[7] David J. Oblak and Roy J. Helm, Jr., "Survey and Analysis of Capital Budgeting Methods Used By Multinationals," *Financial Management,* Winter 1980, p. 38.

[8] James R. Piper, "How U.S. Firms Evaluate Foreign Investment Opportunities," *MSU Business Topics,* Summer 1971, pp. 11–20.

FOREIGN EXCHANGE RISK
MANAGEMENT

Foreign exchange risk refers to the risk of loss due to changes in the international exchange value of national currencies. Specifically, fluctuating exchange rates can affect the values of a firm's foreign assets and liabilities, its current profits and future cash flows. Thus, a U.S. parent company operating a wholly owned subsidiary in Norway (whose functional currency is the U.S. dollar) experiences an increase or decrease in the dollar value of its Norwegian net monetary assets whenever the exchange value of the krone appreciates or depreciates relative to the dollar. Since foreign currency amounts typically are translated to their domestic currency equivalents either for management review or external financial reporting purposes (see Chapter 4), resultant translation effects have a direct impact on reported profits. In an economic sense, fluctuating exchange rates also affect the discounted present value of the entire foreign investment by impacting future cash flows, that is, expected sales and cost streams. Cash flow effects are not limited to companies with foreign operations. Purely domestic companies with payables or receivables invoiced in foreign currencies will also experience cash flow effects whenever the exchange rates in question vary between transaction and settlement dates.

Now that foreign currencies of most major industrial nations are relatively free to find their own value levels in the international marketplace, the frequency of exchange rate changes has become almost a daily occurrence. Moreover, the magnitude of these exchange rate changes has been far from insignificant. As examples, for the 11-year period January 1971 through January 1982, the German mark appreciated by 62 percent vis-à-vis the U.S. dollar. Similarly, the Japanese yen appreciated by 64 percent while the British pound depreciated by 20 percent. Bear in mind that a 10-year perspective tends to mask day-to-day movements in currency values, which can be even more volatile. As a result, when we compare the percentage change between the high and low values during this same period, this figure was 60 percent for the British pound, 96 percent for the Japanese yen, and 112 percent for the German mark![9]

In view of such currency instability, a major objective of international financial management is to minimize financial losses caused by this phenomenon. Risk management techniques in this regard include (a) forecasting exchange rate movements, (b) measuring a firm's exposure to the risks of loss occasioned by currency movements and (c) designing strategies to hedge exchange risks.

Forecasting Exchange Rate
Changes

In developing an exchange risk management program, the financial manager should have a good idea of the potential direction, timing, and magnitude

---

[9] *International Financial Statistics,* various issues.

of exchange rate changes. Forewarned of such developments he or she can more efficiently and effectively arrange for appropriate defensive measures whenever the prospects of loss exceed the costs of such protection. Great disagreement, however, exists about the feasibility of predicting currency movements.

Those supporting exchange rate forecasting as a valid risk management tool operate on the premise that decision makers in the firm have the capability of outperforming the market as a whole when it comes to predicting exchange rate behavior.[10] This capacity is, in turn, premised on the existence of timely and comprehensive information on which to base such predictions. Information frequently used in formulating exchange rate forecasts (e.g. currency depreciation) relate to *changes* in:

1. *Inflation differentials.* Evidence suggests that a higher rate of inflation in a given country relative to another tends, over time, to be offset by an equal but opposite movement in the value of its currency.

2. *Monetary policy.* An increase in a country's money supply that exceeds the real growth rate of national output fosters inflation which, in turn, impacts exchange rates.

3. *Balance of trade.* Currency devaluations are often used by governments to cure an unfavorable trade balance (exports < imports).

4. *Balance of payments.* A country that spends (imports) and invests more abroad than it earns (exports) or receives in investments from abroad experiences downward pressure on its currency's value.

5. *International monetary reserves and debt capacity.* A country with a persistent balance of payments deficit can forestall a currency devaluation by drawing down its savings (i.e., level of international monetary reserves) or drawing on its foreign borrowing capacity. As these resources decrease, the probability of devaluation increases.

6. *National budget.* National deficits caused by excessive government spending also exacerbates local inflation.

7. *Forward exchange quotations.* A foreign currency that can be acquired for future delivery at a significant discount signals a reduced level of confidence in that currency.

8. *Unofficial rates.* Increases in the spread between official and unofficial or "black market" exchange rates are suggestive of increased pressure on governments to align their official rates with more realistic market rates.

9. *Behavior of related currencies.* Currency movements of countries with whom a given country has close economic ties will normally elicit a positive correlation in the behavior of the latter's currency.

While the foregoing items of economic intelligence are helpful inputs for predicting the direction of currency movements, they alone are usually insufficient for predicting the timing and magnitude of currency changes. The reason is that changes in currency parities for many countries have been and still are, to some extent, a function of political sentiments. Political responses to devaluation or revaluation pressures in the past have frequently manifested them-

---

[10] For some evidence on the track records of exchange rate forecasters, see Richard M. Levich, "How to Compare Chance with Forecasting Expertise," *Euromoney*, August 1981, pp. 61–78.

selves in a number of temporary alternatives other than exchange rate adjustments. These actions, which unfortunately treat the symptoms rather than the
underlying causes of the problem, include such measures as selective taxes, import controls, export incentives and exchange controls. (Mexico, in 1982, is a
case in point.) Nevertheless, indicants of the political frame of mind of a country whose currency is under pressure are at least useful in helping financial
managers to discern whether a particular government will lean toward market
intervention or rely on free-market solutions to remedy its currency disequili-
bria.

To others, however, exchange rate forecasting is a futile exercise. Foreign
exchange markets, in a world where exchange rates are free to fluctuate, are
said to be "efficient" markets.[11] Thus, current market rates (i.e., forward exchange rates) can be thought of as representing the consensus of all market participants about future rates of exchange. Underlying opinions are based on
interpretations of what currently available information means for future rates.
If a significant number of market participants were to receive information that
would lead them to expect a decline in the exchange rate in the future, they
would reduce their holdings of that currency by selling it in the exchange markets. This action, in itself, would drive the price of the currency down until the
market reflected the new opinions of all market participants, given the latest set
of information. In short, information that is generally available would immediately be impounded in current exchange rates by the market and thus have little value for predicting future exchange rate behavior. Under these conditions,
exchange rate changes are viewed as random events responding to new information or unforeseen events. Forward exchange rates become the best available estimates of future rates. Yet, longtime practitioners in the field observe
that foreign exchange markets in fact are made up of numerous participants
with varying degrees of information relating to future exchange rates. Accordingly, the randomness of exchange rate changes are a reflection of the diversity
of opinions on exchange values by participants who are less than fully informed.

What does all of this imply for management accountants? For one thing,
subscription to exchange rate forecasting as a valid risk-reduction technique
means that accountants must develop currency surveillance systems that are
capable of gathering and processing comprehensive yet accurate information
on variables correlated with exchange rate movements in timely fashion. Only
by so doing can accountants ensure financial managers of a "superior" source
of information on which to base their currency forecasts. At the same time, financial managers must have a clear understanding of the consequences of not
adopting alternative forecasting modes. Comparisons of decision outcomes
based on company projections versus market-based forecasts (i.e., forward exchange rates) provide useful information for gauging opportunity costs and
management performance.

---

[11] Gunter Dufey and Ian H. Giddy, "International Financial Planning: The Use of
Market-Based Forecasts," *California Management Review*, Fall 1978, pp. 69–81.

If the foregoing procedures are not possible or are economically unfeasible, then both financial managers and accountants should devote more attention to arranging a multinational company's affairs in such fashion that, regardless of exchange rate behavior, the detrimental effects of rate changes are minimized. This process is referred to as exposure management.

The Management of Foreign Exchange Exposure

Structuring a company's affairs to minimize possible adverse effects of exchange rate changes requires prior identification of its exposure to exchange rate risk. As a general concept, foreign exchange exposure exists whenever a change in foreign exchange rates alters the value of a firm's net assets, earnings, and cash flows. Traditional accounting measures of foreign exchange exposure have centered on two major types of exposure—translation and transaction.

Translation exposure. Translation exposure stems from the preparation of consolidated accounts and measures the impact of exchange rate changes on the domestic currency equivalents of a firm's foreign currency assets and liabilities. In terms of our discussion in Chapter 4, foreign currency items exposed to exchange rate risk are those items translated at current as opposed to historical exchange rates. Accordingly, translation exposure is measured by taking the difference between a firm's exposed foreign currency assets and liabilities. This process is conceptualized in Figure 10.2.

Exposed Assets > Exposed Liabilities = Positive Exposure

Exposed Assets < Exposed Liabilities = Negative Exposure

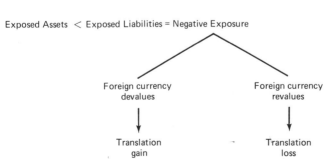

FIGURE 10.2   Translation Exposure

An excess of exposed assets over exposed liabilities (i.e., those foreign currency items translated at current exchange rates) gives rise to a net exposed asset position. Referred to as a *positive exposure,* devaluation of the foreign currency relative to the reporting currency (domestic currency) produces a translation loss as the domestic currency equivalents of the foreign currency net assets is less after devaluation than before. Revaluation of the foreign currency would produce a translation gain. Conversely, a firm experiences a net exposed liability position or *negative exposure* whenever exposed liabilities exceed exposed assets. In this instance, devaluation of the foreign currency gives rise to a translation gain as the domestic currency equivalents of the net foreign currency liabilities decrease following the devaluation. Revaluation of the foreign currency gives rise to a translation loss.

Owing to differences in foreign currency translation methods internationally, accounting measures of exposure will vary depending upon the translation method adopted. Chapter 4 distinguished four major translation options. Accordingly, specific measures of a firm's translation exposure can range from its net working capital position under the current-noncurrent translation method to its net asset position under the current rate method.

Table 10.2 reiterates the major translation options described in Chapter 4. The year-end balance sheet is that of a hypothetical Philippine subsidiary of a U.S. parent company. The second column depicts the U.S. dollar equivalents of the Philippine peso (P) amounts at a given exchange rate of $.10 = P 1. The peso is expected to devalue by 20 percent during the coming period. As inventories are stated at market values under the lower-of-cost-or-market rule, the monetary-nonmonetary and temporal translation methods produce different exposure measures and are treated separately. Assuming the U.S. parent designates the U.S. dollar as the subsidiary's functional currency, its potential foreign exchange loss on a positive exposure of P 1,200 million would be $24 million determined as shown in Table 10.3.

Alternatively, if the parent company designates the Philippine peso as the subsidiary's functional currency, the potential exchange loss would be $46 million based on a positive exposure of P 2,300,000 in keeping with the current rate method mandated by Financial Accounting Standard (FAS) No. 52. There is little question that FAS No. 52 will have a significant impact on the exposure management policies of U.S.-based MNCs.

The foregoing example assumed that the Philippine subsidiary's transactions were denominated solely in pesos. In most foreign operations, however, transactions are typically effected in multiple currencies. To capture the multicurrency dimensions of exchange risk (e.g., a receivable denominated in Finnish markkas is unlikely to have the same future value as a receivable in Portuguese escudos, even if both have the same face value at the time of sale) management accountants prepare a variety of exposure reports that distinguish among foreign currency assets and liabilities according to the currencies in which they are denominated. A multiple-currency exposure report along these lines is illustrated in Table 10.4. That illustration, reflecting the temporal method of translation, assumes that our Philippine subsidiary manufactures a

TABLE 10.2 Accounting Exposure Illustrated (in thousands)

	PESOS	U.S. DOLLARS BEFORE PESO DEVALUATION ($.10 = P 1)	U.S. DOLLARS AFTER PHILIPPINE PESO DEVALUATION ($.08 = P 1)			
			Current Rate	Current-Noncurrent	Monetary-Nonmonetary	Temporal
Assets						
Cash	P 500,000	$ 50,000	$ 40,000	$ 40,000	$ 40,000	$ 40,000
Accounts receivable	1,000,000	100,000	80,000	80,000	80,000	80,000
Inventories	900,000	90,000	72,000	72,000	90,000	72,000
Fixed assets (net)	1,100,000	110,000	88,000	110,000	110,000	110,000
Total	P 3,500,000	$ 350,000	$ 280,000	$ 302,000	$ 320,000	$ 302,000
Liabilities & owners' equity						
Short-term payables	P 400,000	$ 40,000	$ 32,000	$ 32,000	$ 32,000	$ 32,000
Long-term debt	800,000	80,000	64,000	80,000	64,000	64,000
Stockholders' equity	2,300,000	230,000	184,000	190,000	224,000	206,000
Total	P 3,500,000	$ 350,000	$ 280,000	$ 302,000	$ 320,000	$ 302,000
Accounting exposure (P)			2,300,000	2,000,000	300,000	1,200,000
Translation gain (loss) ($)			(46,000)	(40,000)	(6,000)	(24,000)

TABLE 10.3   Calculation of Potential Foreign Exchange Loss (in millions)

Exposed assets			
Cash	P 500		
Accounts receivable	1,000		
Inventories	900		P 2,400
Exposed liabilities			
Short-term payables	P 400		
Long-term debt	800		1,200
Positive exposure			P 1,200
Predepreciation rate	P 1,200	=	$ 120
($.10 = P 1)			
Postdepreciation rate	P 1,200	=	96
($.08 = P 1)			
Potential foreign exchange loss			($ 24)

durable good for sale in local, Australian, and American markets. Factor supplies are imported from Indonesia.

The format of the exposure report in Table 10.4 resembles that in Table 10.2 with the exception that, in the former, exposed assets and liabilities have been segregated by currency of denomination. Balance sheet items are typically expressed in U.S. dollars to facilitate an assessment of the relative magnitudes of the various items.

A multiple-currency exposure reporting format offers a number of advantages over its single-currency counterpart. For one thing, the information provided is more robust. Rather than disclosing a single net positive exposure figure of $120 million, the report in Table 10.4 shows that this figure is comprised of several different currency exposures each having differing exchange risk consequences for the U.S. parent. For example, from a U.S. perspective, the dollar column has no bearing on translation exposure as dollar-denominated balances of the Philippine subsidiary would simply be consolidated with those of the U.S. parent at their face values regardless of exchange rate changes. In addition, under a single-currency perspective, the positive exposure of $12,500 in Australian dollars is combined with the negative exposure of $12,500 in Indonesian rupiahs, suggesting a natural offset. This may indeed be true if both the Australian dollar and Indonesian rupiah move in tandem relative to the U.S. dollar. However, if they do not (e.g., if the Australian dollar depreciates and the Indonesian rupiah appreciates vis-à-vis the dollar) the translation effects could be significantly different.

A multiple-currency report also enables the parent company to aggregate similar exposure reports from all of its foreign subsidiaries and analyze, on a continual basis, its worldwide translation exposure by national currency. This presupposes a centralized control or monitoring function, typically administered from corporate or perhaps regional headquarters as a logical approach to analyzing both individual and aggregate exposure positions of the group. This is particularly helpful in those situations where the responsibility for protection against translation exposure is vested with local managers. One can easily

TABLE 10.4 Multiple-Currency Translation Exposure (in thousands)

	PHILIPPINE PESOS	AUSTRALIAN DOLLARS	INDONESIAN RUPIAHS	U.S. DOLLARS	TOTAL[a]
Exposed assets					
Cash	$ 50,000	—	—	—	$ 50,000
Receivables	45,000	$ 15,000	—	$ 40,000	100,000
Inventories	90,000			—	90,000
Total	$ 185,000	$ 15,000		$ 40,000	$ 240,000
Exposed liabilities					
Short-term payables	$ 20,000	$ 2,500	$ 12,500	$ 5,000	$ 40,000
Long-term debt	50,000			30,000	80,000
Total	$ 70,000	$ 2,500	$ 12,500	$ 35,000	$ 120,000
Net exposure	$ 115,000	$ 12,500	$ (12,500)		

[a] Stated in U.S. dollars at the spot rate effective on the date of the report.

383

imagine a situation where, say, a Philippine manager attempts to eliminate a positive exposure in Australian dollars, unaware that his London counterpart may be attempting to eliminate an equal but opposite exposure in the same currency. Multicurrency exposure reports enable a parent company to avoid hedging activities that can prove dysfunctional from a corporate-wide viewpoint.

Transaction exposure. The second facet of exchange rate risk, discussed extensively in Chapter 4, concerns exchange gains and losses that arise from the settlement of transactions denominated in foreign currencies. Unlike translation gains and losses, transaction gains and losses have a direct effect on cash flows.

A multicurrency transaction exposure report for our Philippine subsidiary appears in Table 10.5. While similar in many respects to a translation exposure report, it differs in that it includes items that normally do not appear in the body of conventional financial statements but that give rise to transactions gains and losses. Included here are items such as forward exchange contracts, future purchase and sales commitments, and long-term leases. These items are normally disclosed in footnotes to the financial statements as they are executory in nature. Excluded from the exposure report are items that do not directly relate to foreign currency transactions such as cash on hand. A transaction exposure report also differs from a translation exposure report in terms of perspective. Whereas the latter is viewed from the perspective of the parent company, the former is viewed from the perspective of the foreign operation. In Table 10.5, concern centers on what happens on the books of the Philippine affiliate if the peso devalues or revalues relative to the Australian dollar, the Indonesian rupiah, and the U.S. dollar. The peso column is of no concern as peso transactions are recorded and settled in pesos. A devaluation of the peso relative to the Australian and U.S dollars, however, will produce transaction gains owing to positive exposures in both currencies. A revaluation of the peso relative to the rupiah would produce a transaction gain as fewer pesos would be required to settle the Philippine subsidiary's foreign currency obligations. These transaction gains or losses, net of tax effects, directly impact U.S. dollar earnings upon consolidation.

As before, centralized control of a firm's overall exchange exposures is possible by having each foreign affiliate forward its multicurrency exposure reports to corporate headquarters on a continual basis. Once exposures have been aggregated by currency and country, centrally coordinated hedging policies that avert costly duplication of effort at the subsidiary level can be undertaken to offset potential losses. One such policy would be to enter into specific contractual arrangements to ensure against a given amount of loss. For example, one way of hedging the positive Philippine peso exposure of $115 million appearing in column 1 of Table 10.4 would be to enter into foreign exchange contracts to sell forward $115 million worth of pesos. Another policy option would be to reduce a firm's exposure to as close to zero as possible by adjusting both the levels and monetary denomination of a firm's exposed assets and lia-

TABLE 10.5 Multiple-Currency Transaction Exposure ($ thousands)

	PHILIPPINE PESOS	AUSTRALIAN DOLLARS	INDONESIAN RUPIAHS	U.S. DOLLARS	TOTAL
Exposed assets					
Receivables	$ 45,000	$ 15,000	—	$ 40,000	$ 100,000
Inventories	90,000	—	—	—	$ 90,000
Future sales	—	—	—	—	—
Commitments	—	10,000	—	—	10,000
Total	$ 135,000	$ 25,000	—	$ 40,000	$ 200,000
Exposed liabilities					
Short-term payables	$ 20,000	$ 2,500	$ 12,500	$ 5,000	$ 40,000
Long-term debt	50,000	—	—	30,000	80,000
Future purchase commitments	—	—	10,000	—	10,000
Leases	—	5,000	—	—	5,000
Total	$ 70,000	$ 7,500	$ 22,500	$ 35,000	$ 135,000
Net exposure	$ 17,500	$ 17,500	$ (22,500)	$ 5,000	

bilities. Referring again to Table 10.4, a natural hedge against the $115 million positive exposure would be to increase the Philippine subsidiary's peso borrowings by $115 million. This of course presumes that the excess cash generated thereby is remitted back to the parent or invested in nonexposed assets. Otherwise, the net exposed asset position would remain unchanged. Other specific methods of reducing a firm's exposure in a subsidiary located in a devaluation-prone country include the following:

1. Keeping local currency cash balances at the minimum level required to support current operations
2. Remitting profits in excess of those needed for planned capital expansions back to the parent company
3. Speeding up (leading) the collection of outstanding local currency receivables
4. Deferring (lagging) payments of local currency payables
5. Speeding up the payment of foreign currency payables
6. Investing excess cash in local currency inventories and other assets less subject to devaluation loss
7. Investing in strong currency foreign assets
8. Raising selling prices
9. Invoicing export sales in hard currencies
10. Engaging in currency swaps, that is, obtaining parent currency and exchanging it for local currency under an agreement with the host government to reverse the transaction at a similar rate in the future

Accounting versus economic exposure.   The reporting framework described above enables a financial manager to identify his or her company's consolidated exposure in an accounting sense. It may not, however, measure exposure in an economic sense. Although the previous framework highlights a firm's exposure to foreign exchange risk at a given point in time, it does little to identify the temporal dimensions of that risk. That is to say, it does not measure the effects of currency value changes on the future operating performance and, hence, future cash flows of the firm. In many instances, the future cash flow effects of exchange rate changes outweigh immediate accounting effects reported in the consolidated financial statements.

For example, assume that our Philippine subsidiary, described in connection with Table 10.2, obtains all of its labor and materials locally. In this instance, depreciation of the Philippine peso relative to all other foreign currencies (FC) could very well improve rather than worsen the subsidiary's position. A depreciated peso could increase the subsidiary's exports to Australia and the United States by making its goods cheaper in terms of their currencies. The subsidiary could either maintain its product prices in terms of the foreign currencies, thereby increasing its foreign currency receipts by the devaluation percentage, or it could lower its FC price and presumably increase its overseas sales volume. Domestic sales could also rise as the peso devaluation would make domestic sales competitive with imports of similar products. In turn, the devaluation would have no appreciable effect on the cost of its factor inputs as they are locally sourced. Thus, the future profitability of the Philippine subsidiary conceivably would increase rather than decrease because of the currency depreciation. Under these circumstances, "booking" a translation loss on a positive translation exposure would distort the economic implications of the peso devaluation.

As another example, Table 10.5 indicates that the Philippine subsidiary is long on Australian dollars; that is, exposed assets exceed exposed liabilities. On the basis of this report, a financial manager might decide to hedge this exposed position by selling $17.5 million worth of Australian dollars in the forward exchange market. Would this be the right decision? Probably not. Although the Philippine subsidiary is long on Australian dollars, not all the items appearing in the exposure report necessitate an immediate inflow or outflow of the Australian currency. Thus, the future sales commitment of $10 million will probably not entail a cash inflow until a subsequent accounting period. In addition, not all Australian dollar receipts or disbursements are included in the exposure report since future sales denominated in Australian dollars have not been considered. And, while Australian dollar receivables currently total $15 million, this figure will not remain stationary for long. From an *external* reporting perspective, these future cash flows should not be considered. From an *internal* reporting perspective, however, these future scenarios cannot be ignored.

The concept of economic exposure necessitates reporting formats that expand the boundaries of traditional accounting measures. Survey results suggest that multinational companies have devised or are currently experimenting with a number of internal reports which attempt to communicate this added dimension of exchange rate risk.[12] One modifies exposure reports such as that in Table 10.4 to reflect more specific economic considerations. Balance sheet items that are considered adequately hedged in terms of consolidated statements but that promise to affect the operations of the subsidiary or future income flows to the consolidated group are measured and reported. For example, some U.S. companies adhering to the temporal principle of foreign currency translation consider inventory (normally translated at historic exchange rates) as exposed. Others, adhering to the current rate method, omit fixed assets from the traditional exposure report (even if translated using current rates) as fixed assets tend to retain their intrinsic values regardless of exchange rate changes. Still others combine both translation and transaction exposure reports including off–balance sheet exposures. Since transaction gains or losses give rise to local tax effects, the net income effect of a currency devaluation or revaluation will differ from that calculated by multiplying traditional accounting exposures by the change in the exchange rate. These tax effects are considered in reporting exposures on an after-tax basis.

Still another reporting format goes a step further and differentiates between exposures that are static from those that are fluid in nature. Specifically, multicurrency cash flow statements are prepared which enable companies to

[12] Business International Corporation, *New Directions in Managing Currency Risk: Changing Corporate Strategies and Systems under FAS No. 52* (New York, 1982).

TABLE 10.6   Budgeted Cash Flows by Currency

Unit/Country: _____   Date: _____

BUDGET PERIODS

CURRENCY		January	February	March	April	May	June
PHILIPPINE PESOS	Receipts						
	Payments						
	Net						
AUSTRALIAN DOLLARS	Receipts						
	Payments						
	Net						
INDONESIAN RUPIAHS	Receipts						
	Payments						
	Net						
OTHER	Receipts						
	Payments						
	Net						

monitor monthly or quarterly cash receipts and disbursements for an annual period or longer for each currency in which business is transacted (See Table 10.6). Whereas a traditional exposure report considers the effects of exchange rate changes on account balances as of the financial statement date, the multi-currency cash flow statement emphasizes the significance of exposures generated by currency movements over the forthcoming budget period. Thus cash receipts for each national currency include the collection of current and anticipated credit sales, asset disposals, and other cash-generating activities. Similarly, multiple-currency cash disbursements incorporate those required for current and anticipated obligations, debt service, and other cash purchases.

Required—An Expanded Information Base

Ideally, financial managers of multinational enterprises should concentrate on managing their transaction and economic exposures of exchange risk, as these directly impact a firm's current and future cash flows. In a world where stock markets are perceived as less than totally efficient, however, executives are loathe to ignore translation exposure and incur the costs of having to report lower earnings to shareholders.

On the other hand, eliminating translation exposure can also prove expensive. For example, whenever the threat of devaluation is imminent, foreign subsidiaries in the country concerned are urged to minimize their local currency working capital balances—cash and receivables in particular. The subsidiaries are also encouraged to increase holdings of local currency debt. In many instances such policies prove to be disadvantageous. Increased export potential, made possible by more favorable international terms of trade, might call for an increased investment in working capital rather than a decrease. The opportunity cost suffered in terms of lost sales could far exceed any translation loss shown for the year. In addition, local currency borrowing prior to an expected fall in local currency values usually proves costly. Since other foreign companies have the same idea concurrently, the local banking system may accommodate such credit demands only at an exorbitant cost. Furthermore, bank credit during such periods is usually scarce since the economy is under severe credit restraint to counter the problems causing the devaluation pressures in the first place. The cost of borrowing under these circumstances often exceeds any protection provided.

Will FAS No. 52 resolve the issue of accounting versus economic exposure? Maybe yes; probably not. To see why, let us quickly review some of the changes occasioned by this new U.S. accounting pronouncement. Recall from Chapter 4 that FAS No. 52 mandates the use of the current rate translation method for foreign subsidiaries whose functional currency is deemed to be the local currency. Under this reporting option, translation gains and losses bypass income and flow directly to stockholders' equity. As a result of this treatment, U.S. dollar–denominated balances held abroad (e.g. those stemming from intercompany transactions) as well as other nonfunctional currency balances are now exposed to exchange risk. Under FAS No. 8, transaction gains or losses resulting from such nonfunctional currency balances were offset by related translation adjustments and, thus, had no effect on consolidated income. On the other hand, certain transaction gains and losses that used to appear in current income now flow to stockholders' equity, for example (a) transactions designated as hedges of a foreign subsidiary's positive or negative translation exposure and (b) intercompany transactions of a long-term investment nature.

Companies experiencing great swings in reported earnings under FAS No. 8 may experience even greater fluctuations in owners' equity under FAS No. 52. By increasing asset exposure (inventories and fixed assets are now translated at the current rate), many firms will experience a shift from negative to positive exposure positions—thus reversing the potential financial statement effects of a change in exchange rates.

The net result of FAS No. 52 is that many companies may very well redirect their attention from hedging translation exposure to hedging their cash flow (transaction) exposures. On the other hand, companies sensitive to fluctuations in stockholders' equity are unlikely to ignore their translation exposure. This, incidentally, will be more costly and difficult to accomplish as the size of a subsidiary's exposed net asset position is likely to be larger under FAS No. 52 than it was under FAS No. 8. Translation exposure will be especially important if a multinational parent plans to liquidate or sell a foreign operation, at which time the accumulated translation adjustment recorded in stockholders' equity will flow through reported earnings. Attention to translation will also continue for companies that define the U.S. dollar as the functional currency and/or translate the accounts of foreign affiliates whose books are not maintained in their functional currencies.

The foregoing discussion suggests that many corporate executives will continue to be concerned with *both* accounting and economic exposure. The perspective that is emphasized is likely to depend upon a myriad of considerations—including the nature of a foreign operation, the composition of its net assets, its liquidity position, the nature of local financing options, the character of its foreign currency transactions, the flexibility of local pricing policy to offset exchange losses, governmental constraints on the strategic positioning of corporate funds and, ultimately, management's risk and return preferences. Accordingly, accountants need to develop dual reporting systems that (a) measure and assess the impact of exchange rate changes under both exposure frameworks, (b) evaluate the expected outcomes of alternative defensive strategies, and (c) calculate the costs of implementation in terms of out-of-pocket expenditures and opportunities foregone. Only in this way will financial managers achieve a valid basis for arriving at an optimal exposure management posture.

MANAGEMENT INFORMATION SYSTEMS AND CONTROL

Previous sections of this chapter highlight some of the strategic planning issues faced by financial managers of multinational enterprises. Once questions of strategy have been decided, attention generally focuses on the equally important areas of financial control and performance evaluation. These considerations are especially important as they enable financial managers to:

1. Implement the global financial strategy of the multinational enterprise
2. Evaluate the degree to which the chosen strategies contribute to the attainment of enterprise objectives
3. Motivate management and employees to achieve the financial goals of the enterprise as effectively and efficiently as possible

Financial control systems are treated here as a special subset of the broader topic of management information systems. Accordingly, policy issues related to multinational business intelligence systems are examined first as a prelude to the more specialized topics of financial control in the multinational company.

Information and Information Systems

In the complex world of international business, executives manage largely on the basis of information. Here, as elsewhere, information may simply be defined as data relevant to managerial decisions. As intimated earlier, however, multinational managers typically require an expanded and more sophisticated information set than their domestic counterparts. For one thing, business decisions of the former are undertaken in a multinational as opposed to a single-country framework. Superimposed on this framework are a number of environmental complexities that impede simple and effective business information flows.

To illustrate the information needs of multinational executives, let us consider some of the information requirements of financial planners at the regional or corporate level. Their concern centers on both operating and environmental data. The quantity of information demanded of managerial accountants in the field will vary depending upon the degree of managerial responsibility vested in local managers. The greater the decision authority of local managers, the less information is transmitted, and conversely. In assuming the latter condition, Giannotti and Smith have identified four major classes of information that managerial accountants prepare for corporate consumption.[13] These are detailed in Table 10.7. For each set of data transmitted, corporate management must determine the relevant time frame of the reports, the level of accuracy required, the frequency of transmission, and costs of timely preparation and transmission in relation to expected benefits and transmission costs.

Environmental factors that complicate these and other information flows are conceptualized in Figure 10.3.

Distance is one of the complicating factors. Informal and instantaneous communication between a parent company and its subsidiaries is much more difficult when they are thousands of miles apart. Due to geographic circumstances, formal information flows in the form of written communications generally substitute for relatively frequent personal contacts between operating managers in local environments and headquarters management. Developments in teleprocessing and other electronic transmission networks promise to alleviate but not entirely eliminate this information constraint.

Another factor is the great diversity of external conditions that must be considered in multinational decision making. Included here are various legal, political, social, and cultural factors that bear upon financial decisions. For ex-

---

[13] John B. Giannotti and Richard W. Smith, *Treasury Management* (New York: John Wiley & Sons, Inc., 1981).

TABLE 10.7   Corporate/Regional Data Requirements for Financial Managers

COLLECTIONS	LIQUIDITY	OPERATING EXPENSES	DISBURSEMENTS
Credit control	Borrowings out-standing	Forecast of re-ceipts and dis-bursements by currency	Order placement
Major accounts outstanding, with history and credit limits	Investments made		Raw material in-ventory levels
	All investment/bor-rowing facilities available with rates applied	Forecast of exports and imports by country	Payments
Accounts receiv-able		Histogram data for all major curren-cies affecting the operating com-pany	Amounts paid in the period by currency
Aging report, in-cluding inter-company	Forecast of range of cash positions		Projected dis-bursements by currency
	Forecast of interest rate develop-ments		
Major delinquent accounts		Summary of all ex-posed positions and hedging ac-tions taken	Variance analy-sis of previous projections
Summary of days outstand-ing	Variance analysis of previous pro-jections		
Receipts		Variance analysis of previous pro-jections	
Amounts col-lected in the period by cur-rency			
Projected collec-tions by cur-rency			
Variance analy-sis of previous projections			

Source: John B. Giannotti and Richard W. Smith, *Treasury Management* (New York: John Wiley & Sons, Inc., 1981), p. 415.

ample, secrecy is much more prevalent in business dealings abroad than in the United States. Consequently, U.S. headquarters management must often rely on the use of internal auditors to monitor the affairs of its foreign subsidiaries. Economic considerations, such as competitive conditions abroad, international tax developments, transnational financing possibilities, foreign inflation, and fluctuating currency values, also need to be acknowledged in this regard.

Then there are information feedback requirements. An operation located halfway round the globe is more easily neglected than one closer to the domes-tic parent. It is especially important that all components of a multinational sys-

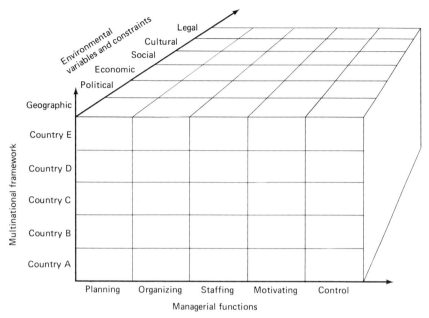

FIGURE 10.3   Decision Cells for International Managers

tem be systematically provided with timely and relevant information. Failing this, coordination of group activities is well nigh impossible.

Business information flows have traditionally assumed a vertical mode in organizational hierarchies; that is, information moves from lower to higher management echelons and conversely. Such information vectors are indeed appropriate where interorganizational dependence and cooperation is minimal. When organizational interaction is prevalent, as is often the case internationally, lateral information flows, such as between Far Eastern subsidiaries of a European multinational company, may be potentially as important as information flowing to and from company headquarters.

For all of these reasons, international managers are concerned (a) with the type and quantity of information they receive and (b) with the systems through which such information is created or collected and then transmitted to information users. It is important that the information itself not be confused with any particular information system through which it might flow.

Information issues.   Let us first think briefly about business information as such. Cross-cultural studies have established rather convincingly that managers in different environments have not only different ways of analyzing and resolving problems but also different information needs on which they base business decisions. Hence, we have a fundamental dilemma for the multinational enterprise. Local managers in host countries are likely to want different decision information than headquarters management is likely to want in the home country, for example, local currency versus home currency rate of return statistics. Under these circumstances, deliberate redundancy is often the only way in which different but parallel information needs can be met. We shall return to this point shortly.

A second major information problem is the question of translation, from one information code (language) to another. For example, in appraising the status of their overseas operations, U.S. managers generally express a preference for management reports stated in terms of U.S. dollars. Foreign investments are said to be originally sourced in dollars. Accordingly, foreign operations are typically translated to their domestic currency equivalents in order for U.S. headquarters managers to evaluate the returns produced by these "dollar investments." In translating foreign currency amounts for managerial review purposes, however, do we generally retain the same monetary relations after the translation process is completed as before?

A special feature of consolidated reports is that financial statements prepared according to foreign accounting principles are usually restated first to accounting principles of the parent country before being aggregated with other intracorporate accounts. In transliterating accounting effects from one set of accounting principles to the next, however, do we somehow alter the information content of the various components of a group consolidation?

Finally, can we simply transpose information such as, for instance, the word-for-word translation of a management report from English into French or the straight arithmetic restatement of U.S. dollar amounts in French franc amounts? Would a French manager receiving a report so transposed receive the same message (information content) as a financial manager in the United States on the basis of the original report? The recent experiences of several Japanese companies are suggestive in this regard. According to the Japan Overseas Enterprise Association (a trade group), a number of Japanese companies are using English as their official business language as their overseas operations generally employ local nationals who are rarely conversant in Japanese. While such a policy boasts a number of advantages, problems also arise. Messages sent by wire are encoded in the Latin alphabet. The same sounds, however, often have different meanings. For example, the Japanese word for *debentures* and for *credits* sounds the same—*saiken*—which often leads to confusion. *Tani* is another problem word that, in phonetic spelling in a financial report, could mean either a unit of money or the word *besides*. In financial affairs, this could make a lot of difference in the information content of transmitted messages. Furthermore, the Japanese language contains many words for which there are no English equivalents. As a result, technical communication in English is often an extremely difficult and precarious affair for Japanese managers.

Even if problems associated with encoding and decoding of internal messages could be solved, there would still be problems of coping with the phenomenon of information overload. The three-dimensional information matrix illustrated in Figure 10.3 displays the diversity of external variables that are brought to bear on financial decision making within the firm. Consider the information load if a company were to operate in 20 or 25 different countries. One estimate of the number of financial reports passing through the control-

ler's department of a major MNC each year as tabulated from the firm's accounting manual, reached 55,000![14]

Human information specialists tell us that there are definite limits to an
individual's information-processing capabilities. Once such limits are reached,
information filtering, sequencing, sampling, or even discarding are resorted to.
Because of this, multinational companies, attempting to optimize the use of information within the major constraints of human processing capabilities and
time, must increasingly weigh the benefits and costs of additional intelligence.
A technique already implemented by some firms is Planned Information Acquisition Analysis (PIAA).[15] This method attempts to measure the incremental
value of a new information source. Each new document or information service
the firm uses for information is reevaluated after a two-year interval. The number of times these sources have been used and found relevant as an information
input is compared to existing documents in a similar category. Based on the results of this comparison, the information source is either dropped or retained.
In this fashion, acquisition of new data may be limited to those items deemed
most useful to the firm.

Systems issues.   Quite apart from the issue of information per se,
there is the question of the type of system needed to facilitate multinational
business information flows. Opinions are divided on this issue. Some business
experts argue that information systems employed abroad should be no different from those used in a predominantly uninational setting. Others, however,
argue for tailor-made information systems that are developed to accommodate
the enlarged perspective of the multinational enterprise. Some would extend
this to its logical extreme and adopt a "fresh start" approach that would develop systems with truly global orientations (systems not oriented to decentralized parent country operations) almost from the ground up.

Your authors would approach this issue in a somewhat different way.
Rather than treat systems design as mutually exclusive options, we would
adopt a more fluid posture. That is to say, information systems need to be responsive to the organizational framework and the particular policies that are
implemented by managements of multinational business concerns. One writer
has discerningly classified multinational organization policies as (a) ethnocentric, (b) geocentric, or (c) polycentric.[16] This classification scheme seems appropriate for the purposes at hand.

An ethocentric or home country orientation is one in which home country
standards and attitudes are applied to overseas business. Foreign operations
typically do not enjoy independent existence and are tightly controlled from

---

[14] George C. Watt, Richard M. Hammer, and Marianne Burge, *Accounting for the
Multinational Corporation* (New York: Financial Executive's Research Research Foundation,
1977), p. 244.

[15] J. Alex Murray, "Intelligence Systems of the MNC's," *Columbia Journal of World
Business,* September-October 1972, pp. 63–77.

[16] Howard Perlmutter, "The Tortuous Evolution of the Multinational Corporation,"
Columbia Journal of World Business, January-February 1969, pp. 9–18.

corporate headquarters. From an accounting point of view, business events and transactions abroad are measured and communicated from the perspective of the home country. Management and control occur through home country standards and procedures, by means of home country measurement rules, and on the basis of the home country currency. Overseas activities might be characterized here as *foreign* as opposed to *multinational.* Under these circumstances, it would appear appropriate simply to transplant domestic information and control systems abroad. This would be a good starting point for firms just venturing into the international arena. It makes good sense from a financial consolidation perspective and is, no doubt, cheaper to install than an entirely new system.

A geocentric or world orientation is a second category into which a multinational company might fall. Here, global thinking and organization supplants a purely domestic point of view. From this enlargened perspective, foreign subsidiaries are not viewed as mere appendages or interdependent satellites of the parent company but as parts of an integrated network whose aims are to optimize global objectives. Productive resources are generally secured wherever in the world they are least expensive and employed where their productivity is greatest. This organizational philosophy, in turn, necessitates coordinative decisions and the design of information systems that support the global decision mode. Tailor-made or "from the ground up" approaches to systems design seem called for here.

Despite the conceptual appeal of the geocentric philosophy, the fact remains that this organizational state is still largely an ideal to be achieved. At present, polycentric or host country-oriented companies are becoming the most dominant form of international business. These organizations recognize and thrive on international diversity. Their policies permit substantial degrees of local autonomy for foreign affiliates, with communications being largely of the two-way variety. In these circumstances, local managers in host countries need different decision information than headquarters management is likely to require for control purposes. Therefore, what is needed are expanded accounting systems capable of satisfying different but parallel information needs.

Management accountants can aid in designing information systems that incorporate data retaining their local characteristics (e.g., inflation-adjusted foreign currency reports) and, at the same time can be aggregated (translated) to satisfy more global points of view. Practices instituted by some multinational companies permit information diversity at the subsidiary level but also require that such data and accompanying analyses be remitted to centralized data banks. Such "parallel" systems appear to be far better than the single, centralized global information configurations that are strange to everyone, particularly those at the subsidiary level.

The multiple transnational financial reporting scheme discussed and advocated in Chapter 7 is really an outgrowth of the polycentric viewpoint and a parallel financial information system of a fairly high order.

Issues in Financial Control

Management control systems may be defined as processes aimed at the accomplishment of enterprise objectives in the most effective and efficient manner. Financial control systems, in turn, are quantitative measurement and communication schemes (information systems) that facilitate control processes. This is typically achieved by (a) communicating financial goals to appropriate responsibility levels within the organization, (b) specifying criteria and standards for evaluating performance, (c) monitoring actual performance, and (d) communicating deviations between actual and expected performance to those responsible as a basis for corrective action.

A sound financial control system is a welcome management tool in any business organization. To begin with, it enables top management to target the objectives of its various subsidiary units toward a common end. This is accomplished through a system of operational and financial policies, internal reporting structures, operating budgets, and procedure manuals that are consistent with top management's expectations and aspirations. Suboptimal behavior, which typically occurs when a subunit strives to achieve its own ends at the expense of the combined entity, is thereby minimized. A timely reporting system that constantly monitors the activities of each subentity serves as a useful motivation device. A good control system also enables headquarters management to evaluate the strategic plans of the company and to revise them when environmental conditions warrant changes in their underlying premises. This is facilitated by an information system that keeps management apprised of any environmental changes that might significantly impact on a company's operations. Finally, a good control system enables top management to evaluate the performance of its subordinates at each responsibility level of the firm. This is accomplished by assuring that subordinates are held accountable only for those events within their control.

If a well-designed control system is useful to a uninational company, it is invaluable to its multinational counterpart. As we have repeatedly observed, conditions that impact on management decisions abroad are not only different but are in a continual state of change.

The importance of a well-functioning control system can be illustrated by examining the experience of a multinational company that apparently lacked such a system in the mid-1970s. France's Rhone-Poulenc, ranked among the world's largest chemical companies, ended its 1975 calendar year with a hefty $200 million loss. While a recession was partly to blame for this unusual event, a major contributing cause was a management squabble that frequently pitted chiefs of some of the company's scattered and newly acquired divisions against Paris headquarters.

For example, in an effort to streamline its financial controls, Rhone-Poulenc's 112 major subsidiaries, spread throughout 23 countries, were consolidated under eight central divisions. These plans, however, were resisted from the start. Independent-minded executives in charge of Rhone-Poulenc's far-flung operations reportedly ignored requests for information, engaged in trans-actions without proper authorization, and even furnished company headquar-ters with false reports. One company executive explained, "Managers feel more loyalty to their original companies than to the group, and each one still belongs to a local Mafia."

With recession eating into sales, an attempt was also made to lay off some of Rhone-Poulenc's 120,000 workers. French law, however, constrained the company from doing so. Hence its solution was to cut the hours of both its blue- and white-collar workers. The result was a minirevolt among Rhone-Poulenc's middle managers who complained that they were actually working just as long as before but for less money. The company's control system simply did not function properly.

Domestic versus multinational control system.   Given the impor-tance of a well-functioning control system, questions arise as to its design and implementation in a multinational entity. An issue in this regard is whether a parent company should use its domestic control system unaltered for its foreign operations as well.

Studies have revealed that the systems employed by a number of multi-national enterprises to control their foreign operations are identical in many respects to those used domestically. Items commonly transplanted abroad in-clude financial and budgetary control as well as the tendency to impose over-seas the standards developed for appraising domestic operations. In what is now a classic piece,[17] David Hawkins offers four basic reasons for this:

1. Financial control considerations are seldom a critical problem in the early stages of establishing a foreign operation.
2. It is normally cheaper to transplant as much of the domestic system abroad than create from scratch an entire system designed for the foreign operation.
3. To avoid a number of problems related to preparing and analyzing consoli-dated financial statements, the corporate controller's office insists that all operating subsidiaries use similar forms and schedules to record and transmit financial and operating data.
4. Former domestic executives heading the foreign operation, including their corporate superiors, feel more comfortable in their new role if they can con-tinue to use as much as possible of the domestic control system largely be-cause they reached the highest levels of management by successfully adapting to and using the domestic system.

The aforementioned research results have led some writers to posit that financial control systems abroad should be no different than those employed at home. We would concur with this position if the operating environments, orga-nizational structures, and objectives of foreign operations were identical to those domestically. Unfortunately, such "ceteris paribus" conditions rarely hold in practice. More to the point, it is difficult to believe that a central con-

---

[17] David F. Hawkins, "Controlling Foreign Operations," *Financial Executive*, Febru-ary 1965, pp. 25–32.

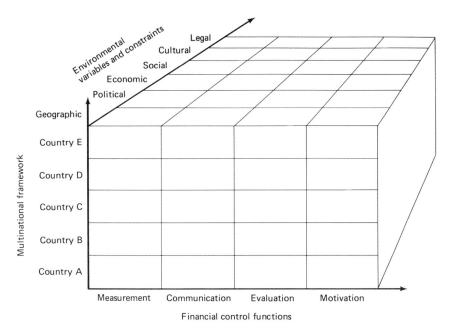

FIGURE 10.4   Framework for Multinational Financial Control

troller's staff could design a uniform and effective worldwide control system if for no other reason than that the multinational operating environment is so diverse. A simple transformation of Figure 10.3, replacing the horizontal vector with one that emphasizes various control functions, illustrates this point (see Figure 10.4).

The potential impact of environmental diversity, depicted in Figure 10.4, on the financial control process is briefly described in the paragraphs to follow.[18]

Earlier we observed that geographical distance often creates an impediment to traditional methods of communicating business directives and performance results between affiliates and company headquarters. While improved technology promises to ameliorate many of the negative effects of geographic distance on interorganizational communications, there exists a more subtle kind of distance whose effects on cross-national communications are less easily remedied. We are referring to cultural distance, which inevitably accompanies the widespread use of foreign nationals in managing overseas affiliates. Language difficulties, cross-cultural differences in attitudes toward risk and authority, differences in need-achievement levels, and other cultural attributes often result in a number of dysfunctional consequences. These may include (a) misunderstood directives, (b) lower tolerance to criticism, (c) unwillingness to discuss business problems openly or to seek assistance, (d) loss of

[18] For a concise discussion of specific environmental effects, see David Zenoff, *Management Principles for Finance in the Multinational* (London: Euromoney Publications, 1980), pp. 187–188.

confidence among foreign managers, (e) unwillingness to delegate authority, and (f) reluctance to assume responsibility.

Under these constraints, managers of multinational companies are confronted with a number of dilemmas. Therefore, should a separate and distinct communications system be implemented for foreign nationals only? Should foreign nationals be evaluated in terms of performance standards that differ from those for their domestic counterparts? Should motivational techniques applied overseas differ from those applied domestically? Answers to these questions necessarily entail modifications to extant control mechanisms.

Distribution channels, credit terms, industrial policies, financial institutions, and business etiquette (including in certain instances expectations of gratuities to secure favorable business treatment), all vary from country to country. These actually diverse business practices call for adaptive behavior on the part of international financial managers.

Consider, for the moment, the subject of business gratuities. Bribes to secure business favors have long been illegal in the United States. In many parts of the world, however, under-the-table payments are a fact of everyday business affairs. Subsidiaries of U.S. agribusiness corporations with large-scale growing operations in the so-called "banana republics" report that such payments are necessary to assure that containers of fruit waiting for export are placed in "active" positions in the loading queues for outbound shipping vessels. One executive comments, "If these payments were to be stopped, my bananas would just sit there on the docks and rot!" Another example is local mail delivery. Unofficial payments to mail carriers is quite often a prerequisite for timely delivery of inbound mail. Apart from any ethical issues, the question of business gratuities overseas confronts financial managers of U.S. multinational enterprises with a very real additional dilemma. If such payments are monitored and acknowledged in the formal financial control system, a U.S. parent company may open itself to legal action at home. If, however, such payments are kept outside the control system through bogus documentation and contrived accounting transactions, the entire control system is soon rendered ineffective. This problem continues to command the attention of the accounting and legal professions.

Companies with operating activities abroad must also adapt to a larger number of governmental regulations and restrictions. Exchange controls, restrictions on capital flows, joint ownership requirements, and a myriad of other specific business regulations are examples of this.

Hawkins offers a useful example of how governmental regulations and restrictions thwarted the application of unadulterated domestic control systems overseas in the case of one multinational company.[19] In this scenario, a business characterized by frequent and dramatic changes in production levels made it crucial for a farm equipment manufacturer to maintain a flexible manpower policy. Closely related to these production requirements was a need for the company to maintain tight control over the levels of its raw material inven-

[19] Hawkins, "Controlling Foreign Operations," p. 31.

tories. Accordingly, the entire management control system was geared to communicating to plant managers the need to control labor costs and inventory levels and to motivate managers to exercise this control. Overseas, however, this same control system proved useless.

As it turned out, foreign managers could not and would not lay off labor every time there was a lull in production. Local laws and customs in many countries either prohibited or discouraged laying off workers. Similarly, since many of the raw materials used in the production process abroad were imported, inventory levels were, in large measure, determined by the availability of foreign exchange. In those countries where foreign exchange was restricted, inventory policy was, in effect, controlled not by management decision but by government balance of payments policies. The control system simply did not recognize this operating reality, resulting, not surprisingly, in poor profit performance on the part of the manufacturer's overseas operations.

Of all the environmental considerations enumerated in Figure 10.4, perhaps the most influential on the design of overseas control systems are those related to the strength of a nation's currency. Internal rates of inflation and fluctuating currency values are the prime considerations here. Fluctuating currency values, for example, make budgetary goal setting an extremely difficult process overseas. Just imagine the frustration budgetary analysts experience every time sales and profit plans are carefully and painstakingly drawn and laid only to find such projections invalidated by overnight currency exchange rate changes (recent examples in Argentina and Mexico come to mind readily). To keep financial managers forewarned of such developments timely and comprehensive surveillance systems are needed. Yet, as we have seen, forecasting and communicating environmental changes are difficult owing to the politics of devaluation, let alone problems caused by geographic distances and language barriers.

A previous section of this chapter identifies a number of management techniques designed to minimize the adverse effects of fluctuating currency values. Often these practices deviate from asset management policies called for in more stable environments. Corporate control systems need to acknowledge these differences. Failing this, system inadequacies surface as a result of applying financial controls designed for a stable environment to one that is more stable.

Administration of the financial control function. Whether or not multinational companies modify their financial control systems when operating in foreign environments, one thing is clear. Most companies differ in their administration of financial controls.

In addition to differences in the corporate mission of overseas operations which are often strategic in nature (we shall return to this point subsequently), financial control policy is also related to management's organizational philosophy, particularly as it relates to the international financial function. Here, as elsewhere, opinions are divided as to a *best* organizational approach. Examine, for example, the remarks of a group treasurer of a medium-sized multinational company headquartered in San Francisco:

> We work very closely with our [local] financial managers and we expect them to follow very closely our policies and procedures. We consult with them, but when something critical comes up, we'll send out a cable directing them that immediately they are to hedge and such and such. But generally speaking, we have an opportunity to review the subject with them, suggest what we propose to do, and then give them a chance to react to it. I mean as a matter of courtesy, if nothing else. And many times, they can contribute in a very worthwhile way to whatever our plans may be. I don't like to say that our companies don't have any leeway. They are part of our team and we like to use their brains just like they were sitting right here; and we try to operate on this basis. But someone along the line has to say "this is what we do" and that's San Francisco.[20]

This viewpoint obviously favors *centralization* of the international financial function. Financial policy decisions are located at a high enough level in the organization so that sufficient perspective is gained to appreciate which courses of action best serve company-wide objectives.

Consider now a point of view expressed by a financial executive of a large diversified manufacturer of electrical consumer goods and industrial products that favors decentralization of international financial management:

> Although many U.S. corporations are decentralized in their domestic operations, they seem to be less so with regard to their foreign operations. One reason may be the concern as to whether foreign managers are sufficiently trained in some aspects of international finance such as foreign exchange exposure management. We feel this is essential training and our people get that training. Our foreign operations are as highly decentralized as our domestic operations.[21]

In this case, financial decisions are delegated to subsidiary managers who have a better "feel" for their operating environments.

How then do we choose between these opposing viewpoints? Does theory provide us with any answers? Unfortunately, no! Management scientists, for example, extol the many virtues of organizational patterns premised on a decentralized profit center orientation. We are also told, on the other hand, that the basic rationale for the multinational corporation is the many economic advantages that accrue from seeking out the most efficient combination of resources worldwide. The global planning and logistical coordination that this entails implies centralized administration and direction for the entire enterprise management system.

Where does this leave us? In the absence of viable theoretical norms, a pragmatic approach to the issue seems best. If we observe the behavior of multinational enterprises in this regard, we find that many are breaking their own ground on the matter. For example, a study analyzing the functional organiza-

---

[20] Sidney M. Robbins and Robert B. Stobaugh, *Money in the Multinational Enterprise: A Study in Financial Policy* (New York: Basic Books, Inc., 1973), p. 41.

[21] I. James Czechowicz, Frederick D. S. Choi, and Vinod B. Bavishi, *Assessing Foreign Subsidiary Performance: Systems and Practices of Leading Multinational Companies* (New York: Business International Corporation, 1982), p. 104.

tion patterns of 300 U.S.-based multinational companies suggests that several basic patterns are beginning to emerge, namely:[22]

1. Centralization of the international financial function at corporate headquarters
2. Centralization of the international financial function at international headquarters
3. Division of the international financial function between corporate and international headquarters

One interpretation of these findings is that there is no optimal pattern to the organization of the international financial function. A more plausible explanation is offered by Robbins and Stobaugh who conclude that the patterns observed are not random occurrences. Instead they tend to develop and evolve in a predictable fashion. Moreover, companies' sizes and degrees of international involvement are important determinants of organizational patterns and the resultant financial effects.[23]

Thus, empirical observations suggest that small firms typically run decentralized financial operations. With a small financial staff and a limited involvement in overseas pursuits, company headquarters typically has neither the time nor the required expertise to manage closely the financial affairs of its foreign subsidiaries. Key decisions are generally made by financial managers overseas, with little direction, if any, provided by parent company management.

As a company's foreign involvement grows, several developments occur. Increased company size is normally accompanied by a larger and more experienced financial staff, better attuned to the needs of the total system. The increased importance of overseas operations also encourages closer control by headquarters' personnel. Under these conditions, financial decision making becomes an increasingly centralized affair. Headquarters staff make strategic financial decisions for the entire system, and implementing decisions are made at the local level. The emphasis now shifts from a policy of "every tub on its own bottom" to one of systems optimization. Often, a stage is reached later on when a company becomes so large and complex that centralized decision making becomes extremely difficult. Whereas headquarters management would like to maintain tight control over financial decisions abroad, the greater number of financial options, resulting from an increased network of foreign subsidiaries, makes an overall systems approach well nigh impossible to achieve. Adaptations to evolving organizational constraints are thus effected by decentralizing financial decision making but within a framework of policy guidelines issued by central headquarters staff.

Where does this leave us? The organizational patterns just described can be seen as representing different stages of evolution along the path toward a more global organizational philosophy. Other patterns are likely to unfold as

---

[22] Meister, *Managing the International Finance Function.*
[23] Robbins and Stobaugh, *Money in the Multinational Enterprise*, pp. 37–44.

organizational philosophies attain the heights of geocentrism. The direct implication here is that financial control systems need to assume a chameleonic posture overseas. Financial control systems, in short, are not static concepts. Rather, they must remain ever responsive to changes in the organizational structure of the multinational enterprise, recognizing all the environmental variables and constraints under which its units operate.

PERFORMANCE
EVALUATION OF FOREIGN
OPERATIONS

The evaluation of enterprise performance is a central feature of an effective control system. As financial stratagems are implemented and executed, periodic surveillance is necessary to ensure that enterprise objectives are being accomplished to the fullest.

A properly designed performance evaluation system allows top management to (a) judge the profitability of existing operations, (b) spot areas that are not in control, (c) allocate limited corporate resources productively, and (d) evaluate managerial performance.

Developing an effective performance evaluation system for domestic operations remains as much of an art as it is a science, and the complexity increases when operations are located overseas. Performance evaluation of foreign operations must take into account such complicating international factors as exchange rate volatility, foreign inflation, transfer pricing, and a host of other environmental effects. If these factors are not considered, headquarters runs the risk of receiving distorted measures of operating results and may use inappropriate standards to appraise performance and motivate overseas managers to take actions not in line with corporate goals. A direct consequence is reduced corporate efficiency and, perhaps, reduced international competitiveness.

In the remaining sections of this chapter, we examine some major issues associated with the performance evaluation of foreign operations, describe the performance evaluation practices of leading MNCs and offer some general policy guidelines. Owing to the developmental nature of this subject, heavy reliance is placed on corporate experience gleaned from a major performance evaluation survey in which one of your authors was a principal investigator.[24]

Consistency

The penchant for enhanced corporate earnings is a phenomenon that does not appear to be limited to any one country. A cross-national study by

---

[24] I. James Czechowicz, Frederick D. S. Choi, and Vinod B. Bavishi, *Assessing Foreign Subsidiary Performance: Systems and Practices of Leading Multinational Companies* (New York: Business International Corporation, 1982).

Stonehill et al., for example, revealed a decided preference among executives in Europe, Japan, and the United States for an accounting-oriented financial goal of maximizing growth in corporate earnings as opposed to the theoretical ideal of maximizing shareholder wealth.[25] This objective is, in turn, consistent with that voiced in conjunction with multinational performance evaluation systems. Survey results indicate that a principal objective of performance evaluation is to assure adequate profitability.[26]

A potential conflict, however, arises in those instances where the performance evaluation system does not reflect the specific nature of a foreign operation that may emphasize targets other than short-run profits. To elaborate, MNCs establish operations abroad for a number of reasons. Companies whose existence is critically dependent on a steady supply of factor inputs, such as in the petroleum and steel industries, generally expand overseas to secure sources of raw materials. Others invest abroad to lower production costs. This is accomplished by gaining access to sources of less costly labor, power, or auxiliary services. When a company can no longer profitably service a market by exporting to it because of increased tariffs, it will often establish a local operation within the country concerned to circumvent such barriers. Other reasons for expanding abroad include the need to (a) avoid losing a foreign market to major competitors, (b) create markets for components and related products, (c) diversify business risks, (d) search for new markets, (e) satisfy government regulations, and (f) spread overhead costs among a larger number of producing units. A common feature of many of these objectives is their *strategic* as opposed to short-run nature.

Strategic considerations are less easily quantified than those related to short-run earnings gains. Hence the danger exists that the former may receive less attention than the latter when headquarters subsequently evaluates subsidiary results. Should this occur, the performance evaluation system will invariably produce misleading control signals.

Given the uniqueness of each foreign subsidiary's mission, performance evaluation systems need to be consistent with foreign objectives in relation to overall corporate goals. For example, if a foreign subsidiary's objective is to produce component parts for other units in the system, it should be evaluated in terms of price as well as production and delivery timetables relative to alternate sources of supply. In establishing unit objectives and designing evaluation systems for monitoring subsequent performance, consideration should also be accorded the viewpoints of both local and corporate managers. Foreign managers should participate fully and from the start with senior managers in the establishment of unit objectives. This participative approach helps to assure a known evaluation framework that is sensitive to local operating conditions yet consistent with overall corporate aspirations. Alternatively, companies should see to it that long-term objectives are not sacrificed because of foreign manag-

[25] William Persen and Van Lessig, *Evaluating the Financial Performance of Overseas Operations* (New York: Financial Executives Research Foundation, 1979, p. 16.

[26] Arthur I. Stonehill et al., "Financial Goals and Debt Ratio Determinants: A Survey of Practice in Five Countries," *Financial Management,* Autumn 1975, pp. 27–41.

ers' preoccupation with short-term results. This can be accomplished by conforming short-term performance goals and related management incentive schemes to the company's strategic plans.

Unit versus Managerial Performance

Following are the remarks of two multinational corporate controllers:

Controller A: I think generally we would look upon the manager's and unit's performance as about one and the same. The operation of the foreign unit is the responsibility of the manager and how the unit does is pretty much tied in with his evaluation.[27]

Controller B: In terms of evaluating the manager, it is very much related to how he is doing against his budget because he did present his budget which was approved by the executive office and this was his plan of action for the coming year. Now in terms of evaluating whether his unit is one that we want to continue or invest in or whether we should be looking at other alternatives, the return on investment becomes the significant factor.[28]

These differing viewpoints raise the issue of whether, in evaluating a foreign operation, a distinction should be made between the performance of the unit versus the manager of that unit. While some readers may be inclined to side with the viewpoint expressed by Controller A, this position is generally tenable only under very restrictive conditions.

To elaborate, the performance of a foreign operation may be affected by the actions of several parties, each with a stake in the affairs of the foreign entity. These stakeholders include, but are not limited to, local management, headquarter's management, the host government and the parent company's government.

Local managers have an obvious and direct influence on reported earnings by way of their operating decisions. Other aspects of foreign performance are attributed to decisions made at corporate headquarters. To protect the value of assets located in devaluation-prone countries, for example, corporate treasury will often instruct the foreign unit to transfer liquid funds to sister subsidiaries located in strong currency countries. This may be accomplished, in part, by increasing the transfer prices that a subsidiary in a devaluation-prone country must pay for imported goods from related subsidiaries. Interest charges on loans arranged by the parent company, royalty and management fees assessed by the parent for the use of patents and services (often unsolicited!), as well as the allocation of certain headquarter's expenses are additional examples in this regard.

Actions and policies of host governments can also directly affect the reported results of a foreign subsidiary for better or worse. Required minimum capitalization ratios in various countries often bias subsidiary rate of return

---

[27] Czechowicz et al., *Assessing Foreign Subsidiary Performance*, p. 25.

[28] Ibid., p. 26.

calculations by inflating the investment base against which earnings are compared. Foreign exchange controls that ration the availability of foreign currency to pay for needed imports will often have a depressing effect on a subsidiary's performance. Such policies generally necessitate the stockpiling of imported inventories and other supplies when foreign exchange is readily available, thus inflating storage and holding costs as well as the investment base for return on investment calculations. Government controls over wages and prices, which has become increasingly popular of late, is another policy variable that could prejudice the reported performance of local managers.

Closer to home, government restrictions on the payment abroad of certain business gratuities (e.g. the Foreign Corrupt Practices Act in the United States) could impact foreign performance. Domestic constraints on such payments, which might be a generally accepted practice on the local scene, could lead to orders lost to foreign competitors not so constrained, or higher local operating costs.

To properly motivate and assess the performance of foreign managers, it is important that a distinction be drawn between managerial and unit performance. That is, local managers should be evaluated only on the basis of those foreign currency assets, liabilities, revenues, and expenses that are "controllable," that is, those balance sheet and income statement items for which local managers are responsible and which they have the authority to influence. This can be accomplished in practice by partitioning each balance sheet and income statement item into controllable and noncontrollable components as illustrated in Table 10.8.

Under this framework, for example, a manager of a U.S. affiliate in Italy would not be held accountable for effective interest charges incurred with respect to a Swiss franc borrowing mandated by corporate treasury. As the borrowing decision is a headquarter's decision, headquarter's management rather than the Italian manager is responsible for the interest cost (i.e., the nominal interest rate in Switzerland plus the exchange risk incurred). However, since

TABLE 10.8   Partitioned Financial Statements (local currency)

	LOCALLY CONTROLLABLE	LOCALLY NONCONTROLLABLE
Balance Sheet		
Assets (detailed)	XX	XX
Liabilities (detailed)	XX	XX
Owners' equity (detailed)	XX	XX
Income Statement		
Revenues	XX	XX
Operating expenses	XX	XX
Interest	XX	XX
"Other"	XX	XX
Taxes	XX	XX
Net income	XX	XX

the affiliate derives some benefit from the loan proceeds it should bear an equitable interest cost. This can be accomplished by imputing a "capital charge" based on the cost that would have been incurred had the Italian manager borrowed locally or from the parent.

To return to our earlier quotes, Controller A would be correct in equating unit with managerial performance if, and only if, the latter has the ability to influence *all* events affecting the unit's performance during the period. In short, managers should be evaluated on *controllable* items. The unit should be evaluated on those factors *attributed* to it.

Performance Criteria

The comments of Controller B in the preceding section are insightful. First, they suggest that a single criterion is unlikely to capture all facets of performance of interest to headquarter's management. Second, they identify two of the more widely used financial performance criteria adapted by MNCs for evaluating their foreign operations. These criteria are return on investment (ROI) and budgeted performance. Whereas the former relates enterprise income to some specified investment base, the latter compares operating performance relative to a budget. The essence of budgetary control is that any difference between budget and actual performance can be traced to the manager or unit responsible. In an oft-cited *Harvard Business Review* article, Robbins and Stobaugh demonstrate the superiority of budget over ROI comparisons for evaluating managerial performance.[29] Accordingly, ROI measures may be more appropriate for measuring unit performance in relation to global resource allocation decisions while budget comparisons may be more useful for managerial and operating assessments.

At the outset, it should be noted that many companies do not confine their performance criteria to financial considerations. On the contrary, nonfinancial criteria reinforce financial measures by accounting for actions that may not contribute directly to profits in the short run, but may have significant implications for performance in the long run. This is especially important when distinguishing between managerial and unit performance.

Nonfinancial measures that are generally considered important include (a) market share as measured by sales or orders received as a percentage of total sales in a market, (b) personnel development (gauged in terms of number of people promoted in relation to the number of promotable employees), (c) employee morale (ascertained via in-house opinion surveys), and (d) productivity measurements (output in relation to factor inputs or conversely). At a time when MNCs are subject to increasingly vocal attacks by their critics, no less significant is performance in the areas of social responsibility and host government relations. Nonfinancial factors may well account for continued success abroad.

---

[29] Sidney M. Robbins and Robert B. Stobaugh, "The Bent Measuring Stick in Foreign Subsidiaries," *Harvard Business Review*, September-October 1973, pp. 80–88.

With regard to financial criteria, additional issues surface with respect to (a) the identification of the relevant components of both ROI and budget indicators and (B) their accounting measurement.

Variations in ROI and budget comparisons relate to appropriate elements of income and the investment base. Thus, should income constitute the difference between revenues and expenses as they appear in a subsidiary's conventional income statement, or should it incorporate additional dimensions? While conventional measures of income may be more reflective of a firm's efforts and accomplishments than a strictly cash flow measure, it can prove misleading in an international setting. To begin, net income may reflect allocations of corporate headquarter's expenses or transfer prices that are beyond the control of the unit manager. It may not reflect the strategic nature of the foreign unit's mission such as sourcing low-cost components for other sister units in the multinational network. In addition to differences in national accounting principles used to measure the bottom line, a subsidiary's reported results rarely reflect its total contribution to the MNC.

To remedy these shortcomings, corporate accountants need to specify as accurately as is feasible the returns specifically attributed to the foreign subsidiary's existence. Reported profits, therefore, should "add back" such things as (a) royalty payments, various service fees, and corporate allocations charged to the foreign subsidiary and (b) any profits on intracorporate sales to the subsidiary. If the sales mentioned in (b) are not made at arm's-length prices, the foreign subsidiary's profits should be adjusted for any transfer pricing subsidies (the subject of transfer prices is discussed more fully in Chapter 11).

While the foregoing procedure should prove helpful in identifying returns attributable to the foreign unit, elements of income for managerial evaluations should preferably include only those elements of revenues and expense that are controllable by the manager of that unit.

And what of the denominator in return on investment criteria? Should the investment base consist of shareholders' equity? Should it incorporate shareholders' equity plus total interest-bearing debt (alternatively, fixed assets plus net working capital)? Or, should it comprise total assets? If the latter, should the asset base include nonproductive resources that are carried because of local environmental constraints? Should it include assets that are allocated by corporate headquarters, for example, cash balances that are controlled by corporate treasury?

As with income, we feel that a distinction should be drawn wherever possible between unit and managerial evaluation. In the case of the latter, the investment base should comprise resources that are controllable by the unit manager. Thus excess inventories, stockpiled because of host government exchange control policies, should be eliminated as should intracorporate receivables and cash balances whose levels are largely outside the influence of foreign managers. In the case of the former, the investment base should include all capital employed in accomplishing the unit's stated objectives. Ultimately, however, definitions of unit performance as an economic investment are a function of management preferences. There is some evidence that national proclivities may have some bearing on this issue. Assume, as an example, that a foreign unit ends the year with the following foreign currency (FC) financial position. (Current liabilities are exclusive of any interest-paying debt including the current portion of long-term debt.)

Cash	FC	500	Current liabilities	FC	300
Accounts receivable		200	Long-term debt		800
Inventory		300			
Fixed assets		1,000	Owners' equity		900
	FC	2,000		FC	2,000

Assume further that earnings before interest and taxes (EBIT) amount to FC 200. Interest rates in the local environment average 12 percent.

We observe that many companies in the United Kingdom as well as the United States tend to compute an ROI by relating EBIT to fixed assets plus net working capital. In our example, this investment base would yield a performance statistic of 11.7 percent (FC 200/FC 1,700). The comparable figure for many Netherlands-based MNCs, however, is closer to 16.7 percent. Dutch companies typically remove the ending cash balance from the definition of capital employed as, operationally, cash on hand is considered a nonearning asset. On the other hand, the latter is used as a standard of comparison. That is, return on assets employed should at least exceed the return that would have been earned had cash been invested in the local capital market, a figure of 12 percent in our example. Otherwise funds invested in operating assets could have been better employed in local money-market instruments instead.

Measurement Issues—Accounting for Changing Prices

Aside from definitional questions, the designer of an evaluation system for foreign operations must also face the issue of accounting measurements. In countries where inflation is a significant force, should local currency asset values be adjusted for changing prices? Such restatements directly affect measures of various ROI components as well as performance statistics for budgeting purposes. For example, failure to account for inflation generally results in an overstatement of return on investment measures. As a result enterprise resources may not be channeled to their most promising use within the multinational network. Solutions to these problems are not readily formulated, however. Accountants and enterprise managers in many countries are still not agreed on whether the benefits of formally incorporating the effects of changing prices into the internal performance evaluation system exceed the costs. Even if they did, there would still be disagreement as to the method of accounting for inflation.

Our position on the merits of inflation accounting has been set forth in Chapter 5 and need not be repeated here. However, to provide some additional perspective on the usefulness and feasibility of inflation adjusted performance statistics, the performance evaluation practices of ICI, the U.K. chemical giant, are described next. (Other European MNCs, like AKZO of the Netherlands, follow highly similar performance evaluation procedures.)

Prior to 1973, ICI utilized performance measures based on historic cost. Owing to the oil crisis, ICI saw the price of one of its major raw materials shoot up by a factor of five times in a single year. As a result, top management, who had heretofore been satisfied with a historic rate of return standard of 15 to 20 percent, was informed that even a 50 percent standard was inadequate! In the words of one of ICI's deputy chief accountants: "We need to replace the old ratio with some new yardstick, and since our managers are intelligent men, we have to support our new yardstick with sound intellectual and common sense arguments for its use."[30]

An examination of the impact of inflation on historic accounts disclosed six adverse consequences: (1) cost of goods sold were understated compared to current sales, (2) capital employed was understated in relation to its current worth, (3) as a result of (1) and (2), returns on capital were "doubly" over-stated, (4) comparisons of divisional performance based on similar assets of different ages were spurious, (5) intercountry comparisons of subsidiary performance were meaningless and (6) performance comparisons over time were invalid.

To eliminate these distortions, ICI incorporated current cost adjustments (CCA) in its internal reporting system. According to a company spokesperson, "It was not adopted in bored response to a new and tiresome accounting standard; it provided a vitally needed management tool."[31]

ICI evaluates the performance of its European operations primarily by product line and secondarily by subsidiary. Outside Western Europe, where goods are manufactured and sold locally, such as subsidiaries in Brazil and Australia, operations are evaluated on a subsidiary basis. The reason is that Western Europe is effectively a free-trade area. There are no internal tariffs so manufacturing need not be locally based.

ICI divides its performance measures into two categories: long-term (at least one year) and short-term. The principal long-term measures are cash flow generation by product and return on investment (ROI). In its cash flow measure, the company seeks to determine whether a product will earn enough money to pay for its plant replacement, its share of corporate costs, and have some excess profit to finance a level of growth that headquarters feels is realistic. This calculation is modeled for each product line and gives a required return on investment needed to finance the growth. In modeling its operations, ICI discovered that the required rate of CCA return differed by country. For example, its operations in West Germany needed twice the U.K. rate of return to finance the same rate of growth. This is primarily due to tax factors.

ICI's measure of return on investment is the ratio of current cost operating profit (before interest, taxes, and dividends) over current cost fixed assets, plus net working capital. Assets are valued at replacement cost net of deprecia-

---

[30] Czechowicz et al., *Assessing Foreign Subsidiary Performance,* p. 124.
[31] Ibid.

tion for large businesses and at gross for smaller product lines to eliminate distortions due to the age of the assets (i.e., the I in ROI would decrease over time simply due to depreciation, thus raising the rate of return).

In Western Europe, profit is measured before interest and taxes because these expenses are headquarters' responsibility and it is difficult to relate a loan to a particular project or determine the actual tax paid when a product is made in one country and sold in several other countries. Where performance is evaluated on a subsidiary basis (e.g., Brazil and Australia), profit is measured post interest and tax. ICI does this because these subsidiaries do their own borrowing and investment decisions will be influenced by local taxes and tax incentives.

By using a current cost ROI as opposed to a historic cost return, ICI has made its measure of return fairly insensitive to local inflation. As a result, the company can compare businesses in different countries and at different times.

While ICI uses mainly cash flow generation and ROI to assess long-term performance, the firm's principal measure of short-term performance is comparing actual results against budget. This is true particularly with regard to financial ratios such as gross profit margin (i.e., profit before corporate costs). The company has a three-year plan and the plan's first year becomes that period's operating budget. Performance is tracked on a monthly and quarterly basis. Quarterly results are given greater significance.

Like most MNCs, ICI incorporates inflationary expectations in budgeting local selling prices and certain operating costs such as expected labor costs. While budgeting systems can incorporate either historical or current values as subparts, ICI prefers the latter and forecasts a replacement value for both cost of goods sold and depreciation.

The reason for this approach, according to ICI, is "to force management's attention to the fact that if a company is in a volatile cost set-up, as we are when the price of oil and derivatives can go up or down very fast, it has to use the cost it will incur to replace raw materials and factor that into its selling price. If it uses historic cost, the profit may not be adequate to continue purchasing oil at today's cost."[32]

Thus, performance is tracked using the actual cost of goods incurred that month. The unit's manager is held accountable for the variance (if any) because he is expected to react to unexpected (i.e., greater than forecasted) increases in cost by raising his prices. This assumes that his competitors suffered the same cost increases, which may not always be the case as a result of exchange rate factors.

A forecasted depreciation expense, based on local indexes reflecting the asset's replacement cost, is also included in the budget. The local manager is not held accountable for any variance (calculated quarterly) between forecasted and actual depreciation because of the difficulties of discerning and reacting to a change in forecasted depreciation. But the product manager is expected to make budgeted profit after actual depreciation.

---

[32] Ibid., p. 126.

ICI also includes a forecasted monetary working capital adjustment (MWCA) in its budget. (See Chapter 5 for a discussion of this concept.) However, ICI does not find the difference between forecasted and actual MWCA very meaningful because it is invariably due to changes in costs and selling prices and its impact shows up on the rest of the profit and loss account. Moreover, when there is a surge in the price of oil, the MWCA can exceed all other inflation adjustments and managers may not be able to meet their short-term profit goals unless they expect this increase and raise their prices before the increase.

The gearing adjustment on net, nontrading monetary liabilities, which is required by U.K. external reporting standards, is not incorporated into budgeting because raising funds is headquarters', not operating management's, responsibility.

Measurement Issues—Foreign Currency Translation

The financial performance of a foreign operation can be measured in terms of local currency, home country currency, or both. The currency framework employed can have a significant impact on the assessment of a foreign unit's performance as well as its manager's. Owing to fluctuating currency values, favorable operating statistics measured in terms of local currency can turn into losses when expressed in terms of home country currency.

Those favoring a local currency perspective feel that, since foreign transactions take place in a foreign environment and are effected in a foreign currency, a local currency viewpoint should prevail. When evaluation is done in local currency, foreign currency translation gains and losses are not considered. Thus, the foreign unit is evaluated on its ability to perform locally in local currency terms.[33] One company official holding such a view states:

> We evaluate our foreign operations primarily based on their local currency results. It is our belief that over the long run, the ability to achieve good performance in local currency terms will result in good performance in dollar terms. Good performance in local currency terms can only be achieved if prices are raised in line with local inflation, which over a period of time compensates for changes in the exchange rate.[34]

Those favoring a parent currency perspective argue that home country shareholders are ultimately interested in domestic rather than foreign currency returns. Since headquarters management is held accountable for domestic currency returns, so should their foreign managers. In the words of another corporate controller:

> We are a dollar-based company. We're concerned with dollar results, not francs or pounds. We want our subsidiary managers to run their operations with that in

[33] Helen G. Morsicato, *Currency Translation and Performance Evaluation in Multinationals* (Ann Arbor, Mich.: UMI Research Press, 1980).

[34] Czechowicz et al., *Assessing Foreign Subsidiary Performance*, p. 31.

mind. Furthermore, converting results into dollars makes it easier to evaluate and compare our subsidiaries.[35]

But then, even if dollars were a better yardstick of performance than local currency, problems would still remain. Currency exchange value changes that lag behind foreign rates of inflation due to local government intervention in the exchange markets could still distort performance measures. In a period of excessive inflation, local currency earnings and their dollar equivalents would increase. In the subsequent period in which the foreign currency depreciates, the dollar value of local earnings would fall despite any increase in local currency earnings. Under these circumstances, dollar measurements introduce a random element to foreign performance measures despite possible stable earnings patterns overseas.

In the long run, a foreign unit's attractiveness as an investment must be gauged in terms of home country currency. Accordingly, a parent currency perspective seems appropriate for strategic planning and long-term investment decisions. In evaluating periodic managerial performance, however, the currency framework employed is necessarily related to who *is* held accountable for exchange risks. Note that this is a separate question from the issue of who *should be* held accountable for exchange risks. If corporate treasury is responsible for managing exchange risks, both transaction and translation, then measuring foreign performance statistics in local currency is a logical tack. Alternatively, parent currency measures are just as valid so long as exchange gains and losses are abstracted when evaluating the performance of the foreign manager. If local managers are responsible for exchange gains and losses, and are given the necessary tools to hedge this environmental risk, then a parent currency measurement framework is justifiable. We observe for example that some MNCs that centralize exposure management at corporate treasury still hold the foreign manager accountable for translation gains and losses. The rationale appears to be one of instilling an exchange rate consciousness among foreign managers. A corporate treasurer explains:

> There are certain areas where responsibility falls to both treasury and operations jointly—for example, exchange exposure. The trouble in my experience is that when some companies say that's a joint area and we'll manage it jointly—that's a guaranteed way of assuring that no one makes a decision. What you've got to do is take common areas and divide up the responsibility so each gets a specific piece of responsibility. I don't want the local manager to feel his responsibility ends in local currency. He has to be responsible to his boss, who is a dollar shareholder. While he may not be given authority to hedge via forward contracts, he has control over inventory, accounts receivable and accounts payable. We set up a system that motivates the manager to make appropriate asset management steps in the context of his environment.[36]

Consider now some aspects of the budgetary process. Control over a network of domestic and foreign operations requires that foreign currency budgets

[35] Ibid.
[36] Ibid., pp. 40–41.

also be expressed in parent currency terms for comparative purposes. When this is done, a change in exchange rates used to establish the budget and to monitor or track actual performance gives rise to a variance over and above those due to other price and volume changes. Lessard and Lorange have identified three possible rates that can be employed in drafting the beginning of period operating budget: (1) the actual spot rate in effect at the time the budget is established, (2) a rate that is expected to prevail at the end of the budget period (projected rate) and (3) the actual rate at the end of the period if the budget is updated every time exchange rates change (ending rate).[37] Comparable rates can be used in tracking actual performance relative to the budget. Different exchange rate combinations used to set the budget and track performance give rise to differing allocations of responsibilities for exchange rate variations. Each, in turn, produces differing potential managerial responses. Let us consider some relevant possibilities.

1. *Budget and track performance at initial spot rate.* This approach is equivalent to examining operating results in local currency. Exchange rate changes have no effect on the evaluation of the foreign manager's performance. A negative consequence is that local managers have little incentive to incorporate anticipated exchange rate changes into their operating decisions.

2. *Budget at ending (updated) rate and track at ending rate.* This combination produces results similar to those described above. Local management is not encouraged to develop an exchange rate consciousness because the same rate is used for both budgeting and subsequent evaluation.

3. *Budget at initial rate and track at ending rate.* In this case, local managers bear the full responsibility for exchange rate changes during the period. Potentially negative consequences associated with this control design include "padding" of budgets by local managers or hedging actions that may not be optimal from the corporate point of view.

4. *Budget and track performance using projected exchange rates.* Under this system, which reflects a local currency perspective, foreign managers are encouraged to incorporate expected exchange rate changes into their operating plans but are not held responsible for unexpected rate changes, which are absorbed by the parent company.

5. *Budget at projected rate and track at ending rate.* This exchange rate combination, like the previous system, does not hold the local manager accountable for expected rate changes. Instead, managers are responsible for and thereby encouraged to hedge unanticipated exchange rate changes.

Which option is best for evaluating managerial performance? All of the five options enumerated above are found in practice. We focus here on the latter two. As an illustration, assume the following (LC = local currency):

Projected rate of exchange:	$.50 = LC 1	Actual end-of-period rate:	$.25 = LC 1
Budgeted earnings in LC:	800,000	Actual earnings in LC:	1,000,000
Budgeted earnings in $:	400,000	Actual earnings in $:	250,000

[37] Donald R. Lessard and Peter Lorange, "Currency Changes and Management Control: Resolving the Centralization/Decentralization Dilemma," *Accounting Review*, July 1977, pp. 628–637.

In this scenario, if the projected rate is used in monitoring performance, the dollar result is $500,000 or $100,000 above budget. The manager appears to have performed well. However, if the actual end-of-period rate is used, the dollar loss is $250,000, a negative variance of $150,000. The manager has performed poorly. If performance is measured in local currency the manager appears to have performed well. Should this manager get his bonus? Which rate should be used?

Most discussions in the literature seem to favor option 4, which in effect, adopts a local currency perspective. Lessard and Lorange, for example, favor the use of projected rates in both budgeting and tracking performance for a number of reasons. First, using the projected exchange rate in budgeting encourages managers to factor the effects of expected exchange rate movements into their operating decisions (e.g. changing invoice prices, currencies of denomination for export sales, sources of input, production schedules, or borrowing sources)—actions that are congruent with corporate objectives vis-à-vis expected rate changes. Use of the projected rate to monitor performance, in turn, shields local managers against unanticipated exchange rate changes that are beyond the control of foreign managers. Also, protection against exchange risk can be coordinated on a company-wide basis.

In our opinion, however, use of a projected exchange rate for budgeting and the actual ending rate for tracking performance also has merit. Like the previous option, the use of a projected rate in setting the budget encourages managers to incorporate the effects of anticipated exchange rate changes into their operating plans for the budget period. Holding managers (both local and corporate) accountable for unexpected rate changes encourages them to respond to exchange rate movements by deliberately deviating from original forecasts.[38] Just imagine what would happen if a foreign manager, anticipating a 30 percent local currency devaluation, experiences a 70 percent currency movement and does nothing to offset the unanticipated currency shift because his performance is monitored using the projected rate. (Mexico in 1982 is a prime example.) The described option 5 is especially useful when local operating plans can be changed to accommodate unanticipated currency developments. In those instances where any remaining variances between the actual and projected rates are put aside when evaluating local managers (i.e., the remaining variance is regarded as a forecasting error and the responsibility of corporate headquarters) this system offers additional benefits over its *projected-projected* counterpart.

When responsibility for exchange variances is divided between various levels in the management hierarchy, budget variances need to be analyzed by responsibility level. From our previous example, the foreign subsidiary's operating variance and exchange rate variance would be analyzed as shown in Table 10.9.

Specifically, the total budget variance of −$150,000 (LC 800,000 × $.50 −

---

[38] This presumes that local managers possess the authority to hedge exchange risks with some oversight function assumed by corporate treasury.

TABLE 10.9   Analysis of Exchange Rate Variances

	COMPUTATION		
RESPONSIBILITY	Operating Item	Exchange Rate	Variance
Local currency operations (Foreign management)	LC Budget × Budget − LC Actual × Budget		= Local-currency operating variance
Parent currency operations (Headquarters' management)	LC Actual × Budget − LC Actual × Actual		= Parent-currency exchange variance

LC 1,000,000 × $.25) would comprise a positive variance of $100,000 attributed to the foreign manager (LC 800,000 × $.50 − LC 1,000,000 × $.50) and a negative variance of −$250,000 attributed to corporate headquarters (LC 1,000,000 × $.50 − LC 1,000,000 × $.25).

Giannotti and Smith go a step further and provide a framework for analyzing budget variances when the responsibility for exchange variances is divided between an international division's operating management (parent currency variation) and corporate treasury (variance from budget rates).[39] This useful framework is illustrated in Table 10.10.

The framework assumes that local managers are responsible for domestic operating results. Ideally, the degree of the local manager's responsibility for exchange variances should be commensurate with his or her ability to react to exchange rate changes.

To repeat an earlier observation, the economic impact of changes in exchange rates on performance can be more profound than can be discerned through accounting measures alone. To fully assess the impact of inflation and currency volatility, and gauge their ability to react to these factors, companies need to analyze their competitive position in the market and the impact of cur-

TABLE 10.10   Three-Way Analysis of Exchange Rate Variance

	COMPUTATION		
RESPONSIBILITY	Operating Item	Exchange Rate	Variance
Local currency operations (Local management)	LC Budget × Budget − LC Actual × Budget		= Local-currency operating variance
Parent-currency operations (International division)	LC Actual × Budget − LC Actual × Actual		= Parent-currency operating variance
Foreign exchange variance from budget (Treasury)	LC Budget × Budget − LC Budget × Actual		= Exchange rate variance from budget

[39] Giannotti and Smith, *Treasury Management.*

rency changes on their costs and revenues vis-à-vis their competition. To shed additional practical light on this issue, we examine once again ICI's posture with regard to exchange rates and budgetary control.

ICI, like many MNCs, uses a forecasted rate of exchange in setting budgets and the actual end-of-period rate for tracking performance. But ICI, unlike a number of MNCs, feels that the variance that results when the actual exchange rate differs from the budget rate is not meaningful by itself. States its deputy chief accountant:

> We may have budgeted a rate for the French franc for our subsidiary in France and the end-of-the-month exchange rate turns out to be identical to the forecasted rate. There is no arithmetic variance but we may have lost some sales volume in France. The reason may be that our competitors are exporters from Germany and the Deutschemark has weakened against the French franc. As a result, the Germans may have a margin advantage against us and can lower their prices in French francs to maintain the same level of profits when converting to Deutschemarks.[40]

Thus, ICI feels that the impact of exchange rate changes is more substantial than the picture captured by accounting measures. It finds that further analysis is necessary to determine the real impact of currency fluctuations on performance to arrive at effective reactions and to determine to what extent the local manager is to be held accountable for protecting his budgeted profit in pounds sterling.

To achieve these objectives, ICI looks at the currencies in which both its costs and revenues arise in relation to those of its competitors. Here is an illuminating view from within the company:

> We buy oil and oil related products, which are basically dollar denominated, and we are not a price-maker but are in competition with other producers in Europe. Our oil costs are dollar denominated and our revenues are denominated in other European currencies. If the pound appreciates against all other currencies, then revenues arising from foreign sales, and even those from U.K. sales subject to competitive pressures, will be reduced. As partial compensation, raw material costs (dollar-denominated oil) will be lower, but on balance ICI is worse off because the decrease in raw material costs is less than the decrease in sales revenue in absolute terms. The figure can be significant because ICI is the U.K.'s largest single exporter. Currency movements in the opposite direction are, of course, possible and in fact have recently occurred. An appreciation of the U.S. dollar against all other currencies puts the same raw material cost pressures on our European competitors as on U.K. manufacturing operations so we will not suffer a comparative disadvantage. The comparative disadvantage would arise if there was a depreciation of the pound versus the dollar coupled with a depreciation of other European currencies against the pound, which happened in 1980. This would both reduce our income and increase our costs.[41]

This approach to analyzing the economic impact of currency movements affects ICI's evaluation of its managers, whose freedom to react to such exter-

[40] Czechowicz et al., *Assessing Foreign Subsidiary Performance*, p. 126.
[41] Ibid., p. 127.

nal circumstances is limited. In measuring the manager's performance, the company takes into account the extent to which he has been affected by factors beyond his control and also the extent to which he has been able to react to those factors.

Performance Standards

Once questions of measurement have been resolved, companies must develop meaningful standards against which to compare performance. But what standards are appropriate for a company with operations dispersed all over the globe? Let us enumerate some of the possibilities.

A company may have certain corporate-wide objectives, such as a minimum required ROI, that can be applied to individual subsidiaries or product lines; or it may set different ROI levels or other benchmarks (such as gross margin) for different subsidiaries or product lines. Such quantitative factors may be incorporated into the subsidiary's budget and subsequently can be compared with actual results. Performance can also be measured over time, and companies may require an improvement factor in specific ratios or income—say over the previous period or periods. Past performance is usually significant in developing the following period's budget. Finally, firms can compare their own overseas performance with that of competitors or compare different units within the parent company.

Comparison of the foreign units' performance against that of their competitors either in the same country or cross-border can be very useful. At the same time, however, such comparisons are subject to many pitfalls (see Chapter 8 for a more extensive discussion of problems associated with analyzing foreign financial statements). For example, when competitors are indigenous local firms, the problem of data availability and adequacy may be considerable, especially if competitor companies are privately held. Even if the data were available, comparability might be difficult. It may be impossible to determine competitors' transfer pricing policies as well as the accounting principles applied. Cross-border comparisons compound the problem even further.

Companies with other units of the parent company, either at home or abroad, must also be tempered with caution as questions of comparability again arise. Differences in subsidiary objectives will automatically bias performance comparisons unless directly accounted for (we shall return to this point shortly). Even if subsidiary objectives are the same, differences in country risk profiles would have to be allowed for. If one accepts the premise that higher levels of risk should be offset by higher levels of return, it is reasonable to expect higher profitability from operations in riskier countries. To date, however, little agreement exists regarding how these country risks should be incorporated in the assessment of subsidiary performance.

Many firms require a shorter payback period, adjust cash flow projections for risk, or raise the required rate of return when considering investments in "riskier" countries. The ROI measurement lends itself to adjustments for political risk since setting a desirable level can allow for a premium commensurate with risk in a given country to be offset to some extent by a reduction in risk that results from geographical diversification of a firm's portfolio of foreign operations.[42]

The assignment of risk premiums to an ROI target is ultimately subjective. However, the process can be made systematic. One approach is to adjust the corporate-wide ROI by a numerical risk index developed for each country of operation. For example, assume that a country-by-country risk assessment service, such as Business International, assigns a total score of 65 out of 100 possible points to Country Y (a higher number indicates a lower country risk profile). If a company's target ROI for each country is 15 percent, Country Y's risk-adjusted target ROI would be about 23 percent (15 divided by 65%). If Country Z's risk index were 75, its target ROI would be 20 percent (15 divided by 75%). Under this system, differences between a subsidiary's actual ROI and its budgeted ROI would be calculated and used to compare the performance of subsidiaries in different countries. Other things being equal, if Country Y unit's actual ROI was 23.5 percent and Country Z unit's ROI was only 21 percent, the latter unit will have outperformed the former as its variance from its budgeted ROI was a positive 1 percent versus only .5 percent for the unit in Country Y.

The foregoing construct is obviously not without limitations as an overall risk index may not reflect the risk to which a particular foreign unit is exposed. That is, the risk exposure of an oil company's subsidiary may differ from that of a consumer goods manufacturer. Thus, the risk index should be modified to reflect the specific risk to each unit. A more critical issue raised by the preceding example, however, is the question of whether or not a company-wide ROI standard should be applied at all.

Previous discussion in this chapter should have convinced the reader that performance evaluations based on a single company-wide standard are generally unsatisfactory. A brief example will refresh the point. In their bid to tap the resources of the multibillion Eurodollar market, many U.S. companies have established special offshore financing subsidiaries under appropriate enabling legislation. A major purpose of these subsidiaries has been to secure funds for profitable deployment elsewhere in a multinational corporate system. Evaluating the performance of these subsidiaries using company-wide ROI criteria necessarily proves misleading. Although a foreign financing subsidiary may not be profitable on its own, this cannot be taken at face value since its operation obviously contributes to profits elsewhere in the corporate system. In addition to the strategic nature of many foreign operations, we have also seen that actions by governments and corporate headquarters affecting the profitability of a foreign subsidiary are frequently beyond the control of foreign managers.

A more useful standard of comparison for multinational operations appears to be a performance budget. Budgets, realistically set, enable performance targets to incorporate organizational and environmental considerations

---

[42] Tamir Agmon and Donald Lessard suggest that investors value the international diversification provided by MNCs. See their "Investor Recognition of Corporate International Diversification," *Journal of Finance*, September 1977, pp. 1049–1055.

that are peculiar to a particular unit. Comparisons of performance relative to a budget also enables headquarters management to factor out those results for which subsidiary managers can be held responsible from those that are the result of decisions or actions beyond their control.

Following is a number of caveats that may serve as useful guidelines for those interested in appraising the results of foreign operations:

1. Foreign subsidiaries should not be evaluated as independent profit centers when they are really strategic components of a multinational system.
2. Company-wide return on investment criteria should be supplemented by performance measures attuned to the specific objectives and environments of each foreign unit being evaluated.

More specifically:

3. A set of specific goals, incorporated in performance budgets, should be targeted for each foreign subsidiary that takes into consideration each subsidiary's internal and external environment.
4. A subsidiary's performance should be evaluated in terms of departures from these objectives and the reasons therefore assessed considering managerial responses to unforeseen developments.
5. Subsidiary managers should not be held responsible for results that are beyond their control (at home and abroad); that is, a distinction should be drawn between managerial and unit performance.
6. Subsidiary managers whose performance is being measured should participate fully in the establishment of subsidiary objectives (at home and abroad).
7. Multiple measures of performance, both financial and nonfinancial, should be employed in the evaluation of foreign operations.

A Multinational Comparison

To provide an international perspective on the process of performance evaluation of foreign operations, we briefly describe the corporate practices of 88 leading MNCs in the United States and abroad (including the United Kingdom, Sweden, Switzerland, France, West Germany, and Japan). Survey findings are based on a multinational questionnaire survey, personal interviews, and executive roundtables with senior executives sponsored by Business International Corporation.[43]

System objectives.   Survey respondents, both U.S. and non-U.S., indicate that the primary purpose of their performance evaluation system is to ensure adequate profitability. The ability to identify possible problems (deviations from plan) and facilitate resource allocation decisions is also considered important. Evaluating the subsidiary manager was considered to be of secondary importance. This result could be due to the fact that managerial evaluation is performed at lower levels in the management hierarchy (most respondents were senior executives). It may also indicate that unit performance is an important ingredient in managerial evaluation.

---

[43] Business International Corporation, *New Directions in Managing Currency Risks.*

Performance criteria.   In practice, financial criteria tend to dominate performance evaluation systems. Both U.S. and non-U.S. MNCs indicate that the most important financial criterion used to evaluate the performance of overseas units is budgeted compared to actual profit, followed by return on investment. This contrasts with earlier studies that found ROI to be the sole performance criterion used by U.S. MNCs to judge their foreign subsidiaries. (Robbins and Stobaugh's thesis of the "bent measuring stick" apparently proved influential!) Also considered somewhat important are budget compared to actual sales, return on sales, return on assets, budget compared to actual return on investment, and operating cash flows. With regard to the latter, however, U.S-based multinationals tend to emphasize the importance of cash flows to the parent, whereas non-U.S. multinationals express a preference for cash flows to the foreign subsidiary, indicating a more local perspective. Interestingly, both groups attach little importance to the notion of residual income recommended in the literature.

Despite difficulties in measurement, some nonfinancial criteria are considered important in multinational performance evaluation systems. Market share is deemed most important. Also important are productivity improvement, relationships with host governments, quality control, and employee development and safety. Responses in this regard are similar for both U.S. and non-U.S. firms.

A noteworthy finding is the similarity in both financial and nonfinancial criteria employed by U.S. as well as European multinationals to evaluate both managerial and unit performance. The similarity also extends to domestic and foreign operations. Although many companies are aware of the importance of evaluating the manager somewhat differently than the unit, it appears that, for some companies at least, this distinction is blurred.

Despite the similarities in performance criteria employed internationally, measures of these criteria vary. Whereas U.S. companies are divided over using before-tax or after-tax numbers in computing ROI ratios, non-U.S. companies generally opted for before-tax calculations. U.S. multinationals are also split over deducting headquarters expenses and foreign exchange adjustments from the reports of foreign subsidiaries. Non-U.S. MNCs tend not to include them. The rationale many companies give as to why certain expenses are not included in their evaluations is that there are matters over which the manager often has no control. Other companies argue that some expenses cannot be attributed to a particular unit.

Currency volatility.   In terms of which currency perspective they employ for performance evaluation purposes, most U.S. companies surveyed adhere to a parent currency perspective. This is partially reflected in the currency translation method employed for external reporting purposes (most companies had not yet adopted FAS No. 52) as well as the U.S. dollar denomination of foreign operations' performance statistics. In contrast, non-U.S. multinationals generally prefer a local currency perspective when evaluating both the foreign unit and its manager. Although most non-U.S. MNCs also use the same translation method for both internal and external reporting purposes, most employ the current rate method which is consistent with a local currency perspective.

Both U.S. and non-U.S. multinationals are consistent in their treatment of transaction gains and losses. These currency adjustments are generally included in the performance measures of both the foreign unit and its manager. In the case of both respondent groups, holding the unit manager accountable for transaction gains and losses is generally consistent with the authority granted for hedging this form of exchange rate risk.

Principal differences between U.S. and foreign multinationals center on the treatment of translation adjustments. Companies in the United States tend to include translation "gains and losses" primarily in the performance measures of the foreign unit (56%) and corporate treasury (56%). A significant minority (38%), however, also hold foreign managers accountable for this item. Non-U.S. MNCs, on the other hand, generally absolve both the unit and its manager from accountability for such exchange adjustments, placing such responsibility higher up the corporate ladder. A possible explanation, cited earlier, is the preference among non-U.S. firms for a local currency perspective. Another may relate to the fact that most non-U.S. respondents do not have to immediately recognize translation gains and losses in income for external reporting purposes.

Survey results indicate that the majority of firms, both U.S. and non-U.S., use a projected exchange rate to establish budgets and end-of-period rates to track performance. In most instances, however, variances due to the use of these different exchange rates are seldom held against either the unit or the manager, as they are regarded as forecasting errors. Those (primarily U.S. companies) that do hold subsidiary managers accountable for these variances feel that local managers possess the authority and tools to achieve their targeted results.

Inflation and performance evaluation.   When asked whether they formally incorporate inflation adjustments into their performance evaluation systems, the overwhelming response from U.S. multinationals is that they do not. Even in Brazil, for instance, where government-supplied indexes are available for revaluing assets and inflation adjustments are made for local reporting purposes, most U.S. companies surveyed continue to utilize historical cost in assessing the performance of their Brazilian operations. When U.S. firms do make internal adjustments for inflation, the process is largely confined to budgeting. As with foreign exchange adjustments, such companies incorporate an anticipated inflation rate in setting the budget and then use the actual rate at the period's end to monitor performance.

In marked contrast, the consensus among European multinationals, particularly those based in the United Kingdom and Sweden, is that inflation adjustments—no matter how crude—provide more useful measures of performance than do unadjusted cost figures. A majority adjust their foreign units' assets for inflation and base depreciation and cost of goods sold on the restated amounts. In preparing consolidated accounts, these firms generally feel that foreign statements should first be restated for local inflation and then translated to the parent company currency.

Other environmental problems.   Governmental price controls, required minimum capitalization ratios, and differences in local business practices are identified by U.S. and non-U.S. multinationals as additional environmental considerations affecting the evaluation of operations in the industrialized countries. In less industralized environments, considerations such as those just enumerated as well as time delays in information generation, the shortage of local accounting expertise, and different concepts of control are frequently mentioned. Asked whether these and other socioeconomic and political considerations are taken into account when evaluating foreign operations, the general response by both MNC groups was negative.

Performance standards.   In rank-ordering various performance evaluation standards, performance relative to plan or budget is ranked first by both U.S. and non-U.S. firms. Historical comparisons of a unit's performance over time are also considered useful. Both MNC groups attach less importance to performance comparisons with competitors in the same country and with related units in the multinational system. Interestingly, non-U.S. MNCs attach more importance to the former than their U.S. counterparts. Only 40 percent of both survey groups adjust their performance standards for country risk. Those doing so tend to require a higher rate of return for riskier countries. However, U.S.-based MNCs tend to incorporate country risk into the budgeting process to a greater extent than non-U.S. MNCs.

Satisfaction with existing systems.   Despite the many unresolved issues associated with the evaluation of foreign operations, most multinationals queried expressed satisfaction with their existing systems. While only a minority of companies believe that their evaluation systems may induce foreign managers to engage in dysfunctional behavior, the percentage doing so, 14 percent for U.S. and 21 percent for non-U.S. companies, is noteworthy. When asked if they anticipate a need for future modifications to their existing performance evaluation systems, approximately one-fourth of the U.S. and one-third of the non-U.S. MNCs answered yes!

SELECTED REFERENCES

AL-HASHIM, DHIA, "Internal Performance Evaluation in American Multinational Enterprises," *Management International Review*, Vol. 3, pp. 33–39.
BUSINESS INTERNATIONAL CORPORATION, *New Directions in Managing Currency Risk: Changing Corporate Strategies and Systems Under FAS No. 52*, New York, 1982, 252 pp.
CZECHOWICZ, I. JAMES, FREDERICK D. S. CHOI, and VINOD B. BAVISHI, *Assessing Foreign Subsidiary Performance: Systems and Practices of Leading*

Multinational Companies, New York: Business International Corporation, 1982, 192 pp.

DUFEY, GUNTER, and IAN. H GIDDY, "International Financial Planning: The Use of Market-Based Forecasts," *California Management Review*, Fall 1978, pp. 69–81.

EITEMAN, DAVID K., and ARTHUR I. STONEHILL, *Multinational Business Finance* (3rd ed.), Reading, Mass: Addison-Wesley Publishing Co., Inc., 1982, 721 pp.

GEORGE, ABRAHAM M., "Cash Flow versus Accounting Exposures to Currency Risk," *California Management Review*, Summer 1978, pp. 50–55.

GIANNOTTI, JOHN B., and RICHARD W. SMITH, *Treasury Management*, New York: John Wiley & Sons, Inc., 1981, 508 pp.

KOBRIN, STEPHEN J., *Environmental Assessment in the International Firm: Politics as a Problem of Managerial Process*, Berkeley: University of California Press, 1982, 238 pp.

LESSARD, DONALD R., and PETER LORANGE, "Currency Changes and Management Control: Resolving the Centralization/Decentralization Dilemma," *Accounting Review*, July 1977, pp. 628–637.

McCOSH, ANDREW, EDWIN WHITING, and SYDNEY HOWELL, "Planning and Control Systems and Their Evaluation During Inflation," Working Paper Series No. 71, London: Manchester Business School and Centre for Business Research, 1981, 108 pp.

MORSICATO, HELEN G., *Currency Translation and Performance Evaluation in Multinationals*, Ann Arbor, Mich.: UMI Research Press, 1980, 176 pp.

PEASNELL, K. V., "On Capital Budgeting and Income Measurement," *Abacus*, June 1981, pp. 52–67.

PERSEN, WILLIAM, and VAN LESSIG, *Evaluating the Financial Performance of Overseas Operations*, New York: Financial Executives Research Foundation, 1979, 142 pp.

ROBBINS, SIDNEY M., and ROBERT B. STOBAUGH, "The Bent Measuring Stick for Foreign Subsidiaries," *Harvard Business Review*, September-October 1973, pp. 80–88.

SATO, SEICHI, KYOSUKE SAKATE, GERHARD G. MUELLER, and LEE H. RADEBAUGH, eds., *A Compendium of Research on Information and Accounting for Managerial Decision and Control in Japan*, Sarasota, Fla.: American Accounting Association, 1982, 159 pp.

SHAPIRO, ALAN C., "Evaluation and Control of Foreign Operations," *International Journal of Accounting*, Fall 1978, pp. 80–104.

SRINIVASAN, C. A., and HANNS-MARTIN W. SCHOENFELD, "Some Problems and Prospects in Design and Development of Corporate-wide Information Systems," *Management International Review*, Vol. 18, No. 2, 1978, pp. 15–20.

SRINIVASULU, S. L., "Classifying Foreign Exchange Exposure," *Financial Executive*, February 1983, pp. 36–44.

VAN BREDA, MICHAEL F., "Accounting Rates of Return under Inflation," *Sloan Management Review*, Summer 1981, pp. 15–27.

ZENOFF, DAVID, *Management Principles for Finance in the Multinational*, London: Euromoney Publications Limited, 1980, 208 pp.

DISCUSSION QUESTIONS

1. Consonant with the "multiple audiences-of-interest" focus in Chapter 7 is the question of "whose" rate of return to consider when evaluating foreign direct investment opportunities, that is, local ver-

sus parent currency returns. Describe, in a paragraph or two, the internal reporting dimensions of this issue.

2. Enumerate all the parameters you would consider in measuring a multinational company's cost of capital.

3. "Forecasting foreign exchange rates is a futile exercise. You can't outguess the market so you shouldn't try." Do you agree or disagree with this statement? What are the implications of your stance for managerial accountants?

4. Compare and contrast the terms *translation, transaction* and *economic exposure*. Will FAS No. 52 resolve the issue of accounting versus economic exposure?

5. List ten ways of reducing a firm's foreign exchange exposure in a devaluation-prone subsidiary. In each instance, identify the cost-benefit trade-offs that need to be measured and communicated to financial managers attempting to hedge such risks.

6. Briefly distinguish the information systems implications of the ethnocentric organizational philosophies of multinational enterprises.

7. List six arguments supporting a parent company's use of its domestic control systems for its foreign operations. List six arguments against such a practice.

8. At present, the financial vice-president of your company's overseas operations is held responsible for achieving a dollar profit before taxes, but after foreign currency translation and conversion gains and losses. In your capacity as an independent outside director of the company, draft a short discussion memorandum to the chairman of the board evaluating the merits of this policy.

9. Foreign exchange rates enter the budgetary control process when establishing the initial budget and when tracking actual performance. Of the various exchange rate combinations enumerated in this chapter, which do you favor and why? Does your viewpoint remain the same with respect to factoring local inflation into the budgetary control process?

10. The chapter text cites a number of examples of dysfunctional performance evaluation practices by multinational companies. Take two of the examples cited or, alternatively, offer two of your own and, following the caveats suggested for appraising the results of foreign operations, suggest ways of improving the performance evaluation procedures employed.

EXERCISES

1. Review the operating data incorporated in Table 10.1 for the hypothetical U.S. Israeli subsidiary.
    Required: Using Figure 10.1 as a guide, prepare a cash flow report identifying the components of the expected return stream for the Israeli investment for the first two years of its operations from a parent currency perspective. While the U.S. parent company would like the

Israeli project to repatriate all of its local currency earnings, it is only allowed to receive 70 percent of its affiliate's reported net income, after Israeli corporate income taxes, as dividends. The parent company's U.S. tax rate is 45 percent. However, a credit offsetting U.S. taxes payable is granted by the IRS for any foreign income taxes paid.

2.   Table 10.11 is the balance sheet of the Newport Pagnel Company, a U.S. British affiliate, as of year-end 19X4. The exchange rate in effect at the financial statement date is $1.80 = £1.

TABLE 10.11   Newport Pagnel Company Balance Sheet

Cash	£ 50,000	Current liabilities	£ 50,000[a]
Receivables	100,000	Long-term debt	100,000
Inventory (LCM)	80,000		
Fixed assets	120,000	Owners' equity	200,000
Total	£350,000	Total	£350,000

[a] Of the £50,000 current liabilities balance, £9,000 is denominated in U.S. dollars and due to the parent company.

Required:
A.   Assuming there are no offsetting pound exposures elsewhere in the corporate system and that inventories are carried at market under the lower-of-cost-or-market rule, what is Newport Pagnel's contribution to its U.S. parent company's translation exposure if the functional currency is the U.S. dollar? The U.K. pound?
B.   What would the magnitude of the translation adjustment be if the pound were expected to devalue shortly by 20 percent?
C.   What hedging actions might be considered to minimize the potential loss?

3.   Drawing on the information in Exercise 2, assume that the Newport Pagnel Company's income statement for 19X4 is as shown in Table 10.12. Exports account for 50 percent of sales with export prices denominated in pounds. All factors of production are sourced locally.

TABLE 10.12   Newport Pagnel Company Income Statement

Sales (90,000 units at £5 per unit)	£450,000
Variable costs of production (90,000 units at £3 per unit)	270,000
Administrative and other costs	90,000
Depreciation	12,000
Net operating income	78,000
Income tax expense (40%)	31,200
Net income	£ 46,800

As the 20 percent devaluation of the pound does not affect the company's production costs, selling prices are not raised resulting in a doubling of both export and domestic sales. The increased sales

volume will require an initial increase in net working capital of
£50,000 which will be recaptured in five years.
Required: Barring any changes in unit sales, prices and production
costs

A.   Calculate what effect the pound devaluation will have on Newport Pagnel's cash flows for the next five years.

B.   Compare the parent company's economic exposure calculated in (A) with both translation losses calculated in Exercise
3.

C.   On the basis of your comparison, were the hedging options
you identified in the preceding exercise warranted?

4.   Global Enterprises, Inc., uses a number of performance criteria to
evaluate its overseas operations including return on investment.
Compagnie de Calais, its French subsidiary, submits the performance report shown in Table 10.13 for the current fiscal year (translated to U.S. dollar equivalents).

TABLE 10.13   Compagnie de Calais Performance Report

Sales	$ 2,100,000	
Other income	60,000	$ 2,160,000
Costs and expenses		
Cost of sales	$ 1,600,000	
Selling and administrative	165,000	
Depreciation	80,000	
Interest	81,000	
Exchange gains and losses	184,000	2,110,000
Income before taxes		$ 50,000
Income taxes		21,000
Net income		$ 29,000
Purchasing power gains		1,600
Adjusted income		$ 30,600

Included in sales are $250,000 worth of components sold by Com-
pagnie de Calais to its sister subsidiary in Brussels at a transfer
price set by corporate headquarters at 40 percent above an arm's-
length price. Cost of goods sold includes excess labor costs of
$75,000 owing to local labor laws. Administrative expenses in-
clude $25,000 of headquarters expenses which are allocated by
Global Enterprises to its French affiliate. The parent company
holds all of its subsidiaries responsible for their "fair share" of corporate expenses. Local financing decisions are centralized at corporate treasury as are all matters related to tax planning. At the
same time, Global Enterprises feels that all subsidiaries should be
able to cover reasonable financing costs. Moreover, it feels that
foreign managers should be motivated to use local resources as
efficiently as possible. Hence, Compagnie de Calais is assessed a
capital charge based on its net assets and the parent company's
average cost of capital. This figure, which amounts to $60,000, is

included in the $81,000 interest expense figure. One-half of the exchange gains and losses figure is attributed to transactions losses resulting from the French subsidiary's export activities. The balance is due to translating the French accounts to U.S. dollars for consolidation purposes. Exchange risk management is also centralized at corporate treasury.

Required: On the basis of the foregoing information prepare a performance report which isolates:

A.   Those elements that should be included in performance appraisals of the foreign unit.

B.   Those elements that should be included in evaluation of the foreign manager.

5.   To encourage its foreign managers to incorporate expected exchange rate changes into their operating decisions, Global Enterprises requires that all foreign currency budgets be set in dollars using exchange rates projected for the end of the budget period. To further motivate its local managers to react to unexpected rate changes, operating results at period's end are translated to dollars at the actual spot rate prevailing at that time. However, deviations between actual and budgeted exchange rates are discarded when subsequently judging the manager's performance.

At the start of the 19X4 fiscal year, budgeted results for a Mexican affiliate, the Cuernavaca Corporation, were as follows (amounts in thousands):

Sales	P 800,000	$ 6,400
Expenses	640,000	5,120
Income	P 160,000	$ 1,280

Actual results for the year in dollars were: sales, $5,400,000; expenses, $4,200,000; and net income, $1,200,000. Relevant exchange rates for the peso during the year were as follows:

1/1/X4 spot rate:	$.01 = P 1
Global Enterprise's one-year forecast:	$.008 = P 1
12/31/X4 spot rate:	$.006 = P 1

Based on the foregoing information, did the Mexican manager perform well? Support your answer using the variance analysis suggested in the chapter.

CASE

Assessing Foreign Subsidiary
Performance in a World of
Floating Exchange Rates

General Electric Company's worldwide performance evaluation system is based on a policy of decentralization. The policy reflects its conviction that managers will become more responsible and their business will be better managed if they are given the authority and necessary tools to budget and achieve a targeted net income—in dollar terms. Moreover, decentralization permits the company to overcome the difficulty of centrally exercising detailed control over its large and diverse operations. Foreign affiliate managers, like their domestic counterparts, are accountable for dollar income—a practice not followed by many MNCs.

In the words of one financial executive, "Although many U.S. corporations are decentralized in their U.S. operations, they seem to be less so with regard to their foreign operations. One reason may be the concern as to whether foreign managers are sufficiently trained in some aspects of international finance, such as foreign exchange exposure management. We feel this is essential training, and our people get that training."[44]

General Electric does not have any rigid standards for comparing the performances of its affiliates. Strategic and operating plans are agreed upon for each business, including financial targets. Like most other companies, GE generally requires a higher rate of return from investment proposals in riskier countries and has a system of ranking countries according to relative risk. If a proposed investment is in a high-risk area, it will have more difficulty being approved—and a higher return on investment (ROI) will generally be required. But approval depends on both the forecasted ROI and the company's total strategic objectives in each country.

The system of budgeting and forecasting extends five years into the future. The first year of the long-range forecast becomes a preliminary budget for the year ahead. A year later, the budget is reforecast, a comparison is made between it and the original forecast, and changes are accounted for.

Measurement of an affiliated company's performance is related to the objectives of its strategic plan and the annual budgets that are derived from the plan. The primary financial measure is success in achieving the affiliates' committed dollar net income. Other measurements include ROI (calculated as the sum of reported net income plus after-tax interest expense, divided by the sum of net worth plus borrowings), net income to sales ratio, market share, inventory and receivable turnover rates, and currency exposure.

While both the performance of an affiliate and its manager are measured primarily on bottom-line results, the review of the manager himself encompasses other measurements. These include how well he has dealt with government relations, the progress he has made toward achieving certain targets such as increasing market share, and his success in maintaining good employee relationships. These measurements are based on the strategic plan and targets that were established between the manager and his supervisor at the start of a period.

Periodically, GE conducts operating reviews. Each manager is reviewed by the level above. The focus is on planning, results, and most recent estimates.

---

[44] Czechowicz et al., *Assessing Foreign Subsidiary Performance*, p. 104.

This provides corporate management with an opportunity to determine whether short-term actions are being taken at the expense of long-range goals.

To minimize currency exposure, GE finances fixed assets with equity and holds the affiliate responsible for maintaining a balanced position on working capital. The policy is modified as necessary for varying circumstances.

Unlike MNCs that have centralized the financing and exposure management functions at the head office, GE makes exposure management a responsibility of its local managers, with an overview by sector and corporate personnel. In order to avoid the transaction costs of having, say, a French affiliate hedge its position by buying French francs forward, GE has provisions for internal hedging arrangements. Corporate treasury obtains currency exposure data from all affiliates and provides needed information on offsets. Therefore, units can execute a hedging agreement between themselves without going to outside sources.

In setting the budget, the affiliate's manager uses the exchange rate he expects to prevail. General Electric feels that, although predicting rates of exchange is not an exact science, the managers of its foreign businesses have the necessary authority and tools to take those actions that will enable them to achieve their budgeted income. These tools include hedging and pricing decisions. Not only can the manager raise prices, cut costs, lead payments, lag receivables, borrow locally, and remit dividends quickly, but he can also take out forward contracts if they are available.

Since the affiliate manager has the responsibility and authority to protect his business against currency fluctuations, he is accountable for dollar profits regardless of changes in the exchange rate. According to one company spokesperson, "If an unexpected devaluation occurs, the affiliate's performance is still measured in terms of dollar income vis-à-vis budget. GE considers changes in the rate of exchange in the same way as other risks that occur in a country. For example, if an affiliate's sales are less than those budgeted for, because of a recession in that economy, countermeasures are available to the affiliate. If one contends that these things are not controllable, how does one manage a company? We're not saying it's controllable in the sense that it can be prevented from happening, but it is susceptible to the countermeasures—some before and some after the event occurs."[45]

Required

1. Compare GE's approach to performance evaluation with that of ICI mentioned in the chapter.
2. Critically evaluate the strengths and weaknesses of each company's approach to the performance evaluation of its foreign managers as it relates to the problem of fluctuating currency values.
3. Which approach to performance evaluation do you support and why?

[45] Ibid., p. 106.

11

Transfer Pricing and International Taxation

MULTINATIONAL TRANSFER PRICING

The successful conduct of business operations abroad entails coping with a myriad of environmental considerations. Of all the adaptive mechanisms employed by the multinational company, perhaps none have proved as flexible nor as troublesome as the technique of pricing resource, service, and technology transfers between affiliates of the multinational enterprise. The dimensions of the problem become readily apparent when we recognize that transfer pricing (a) is conducted on a relatively larger scale internationally than it is domestically; (b) is affected by a larger number of variables than are found in a strictly domestic setting; (c) varies from company to company, industry to industry, and country to country; (d) lacks any theoretical or operationally optimum solutions; and (e) affects social, economic, and political relationships in entire countries.

In the first half of this chapter, we examine the features that characterize and compound the problem of transfer pricing in an international milieu. Emphasis is placed on creating an awareness of the many issues that exist in this vital yet traditionally secretive area of multinational corporate policy.

Complicating Variables

Transfer pricing, as a corporate stratagem, is of relatively recent origin. Sharav tells us that transfer pricing in the United States developed as a corollary to the decentralization movement that took place in many American business organizations during the first half of the present century.[1] Complex manufacturing and selling organizations began to decentralize their formerly centralized operations into numerous profit centers as a means of spurring productivity. Under conditions of increased local autonomy, the need arose for a system of internal pricing that would (a) assure that resources would be allocated within the corporate system in an optimal fashion, (b) motivate subunit managers to operate their profit centers as efficiently as possible and promote the welfare of the corporate group as a whole, and (c) serve as a monitoring device in the evaluation of subunit performance.

Despite some limited literature on the subject, or perhaps owing to it, the actual creation and implementation of a firm's transfer pricing policy has remained a difficult task. Conceptual approaches that function well under stated assumptions often prove nonoperational when applied to specific business situations. Given its present state, transfer pricing may be characterized as an area where ad hoc solutions generally prevail in the everyday conduct of business affairs.

Once a company expands into the international business sphere, the problem quickly magnifies. To begin with, multinational companies typically transfer greater proportions of their total output between related companies than between strictly domestic counterparts. It is estimated that about 40 percent of all international trade consists of transfers between related business entities. Cross-country transactions also expose the multinational company to a host of environmental influences that both create and negate opportunities for increasing enterprise profits through the medium of internal price adjustments. Variables, such as differential taxes, tariffs, competition, inflation rates, currency values, restrictions on fund transfers, political risks, and the interests of joint-venture partners complicate transfer pricing decisions tremendously. On top of all this, transfer pricing decisions generally give rise to numerous trade-offs, unforeseen and seldom accounted for.

Tax considerations.   Consider the influence of the corporate income tax. Other things being the same, profits accruing to the corporate system as a whole can be increased by setting high transfer prices to siphon profits from subsidiaries domiciled in high tax countries and setting low transfer prices to move profits to subsidiaries located in low tax countries. As an example, Blu Jeans–Hong Kong, a wholly owned manufacturing subsidiary of Global Enterprises (USA), currently ships 500,000 pairs of designer blue jeans to a related U.S. sales affiliate, Blu Jeans–USA (also wholly owned by Global Enterprises), for $6 a pair. Assuming each garment wholesales for $12 in the

---

[1] Itzhak Sharav, "Transfer Pricing—Diversity of Goals and Practices," *Journal of Accountancy,* April 1974, p. 56.

TABLE 11.1   Consolidated Profits from Blu Jeans

	BLU JEANS–HK	BLU JEANS–USA	GLOBAL ENTERPRISES
Sales	$ 3,000,000	$ 6,000,000	$ 6,000,000
Cost of sales	2,100,000[a]	3,000,000[b]	2,100,000
Gross margin	$ 900,000	$ 3,000,000	$ 3,900,000
Operating expenses	500,000	1,500,000	2,000,000
Before-tax income	$ 400,000	$ 1,500,000	$ 1,900,000
Income tax			
(16.5%/46%)	66,000	690,000	756,000
Net income	$ 334,000	$ 810,000	$ 1,144,000

[a] Equal to 70 percent of sales.
[b] Based on a transfer price of $6 per unit.

United States, consolidated profits (after eliminating intercompany sales and costs) and taxes would total $1,144,000 and $756,000, respectively. This is shown in Table 11.1.

Given a U.S. corporate tax rate of 46 percent versus only 16.5 percent in Hong Kong, an increase in the transfer price of blue jeans from $6 to $8.50 a pair would produce systemwide benefits as shown in Table 11.2.[2]

In this example, raising the transfer price charged by the Hong Kong affiliate increases taxable income there and reduces taxable income for the U.S. affiliate by $1,250,000. Owing to the differential tax rate of 29.5 percent between the United States and Hong Kong, corporate income taxes for the system as a whole decreased by $368,750 (1,250,000 × .295), with a corresponding increase in consolidated after-tax earnings.

Such actions, unfortunately, often create problems that are not anticipated when the pricing decisions are first made. Governments faced with potential losses of tax revenues, owing to the tax avoidance policies of corporate taxpayers, often take steps to counteract such measures. In the United States,

TABLE 11.2   Consolidated Profits from Blu Jeans with Transfer Price Increase

	BLU JEANS–HK	BLU JEANS–USA	GLOBAL ENTERPRISES
Sales	$ 4,250,000	$ 6,000,000	$ 6,000,000
Cost of sales	2,100,000	4,250,000	2,100,000
Gross margin	$ 2,150,000	$ 1,750,000	$ 3,900,000
Operating expenses	500,000	1,500,000	2,000,000
Before-tax income	$ 1,650,000	$ 250,000	$ 1,900,000
Income tax			
(16.5%/46%)	272,250	115,000	387,250
Net income	$ 1,377,750	$ 135,000	$ 1,512,750

[2] The foregoing effects would not hold if Blu Jeans–Hong Kong were simply a passive entity that merely takes title to completely manufactured items and sells them to Blu Jeans–USA. Under these circumstances, all earnings of Blu Jeans–HK would be taxed in the United States whether repatriated or not. The transfer pricing maneuver would only have an effect on consolidated results if the Hong Kong dollar were expected to devalue.

such actions are sanctioned by Section 482 of the U.S. Internal Revenue Code which states in part:

> In any case of two or more organizations, trades, or business (whether or not incorporated, whether or not organized in the United States, and whether or not affiliated) owned or controlled directly or indirectly by the same interests, the Secretary or his delegate may distribute, apportion, or allocate gross income, deductions, credits, or allowances between or among such organizations, trades, or businesses, if he determines that such distribution, apportionment, or allocation is necessary in order to prevent evasion of taxes or clearly to reflect the income of any such organizations, trades, or businesses.[3]

This phenomenon is not limited to the United States. The U.K. 1975 Finance Act, for example, empowers British tax authorities to scrutinize closely cross-border pricing and they have done just that. As its first major test case, the U.K. Inland Revenue service took on the giant Swiss pharmaceutical firm, Hoffman-LaRoche. Having recast the income statements of Hoffman-LaRoche's British operations over a seven-year period, the British government was successful in forcing the Swiss conglomerate to acquiesce to a settlement for back taxes of £1.85 billion!

Internally, transfer pricing schemes designed to minimize global taxes often produce aberrations in the multinational control system. When each subsidiary is evaluated as a separate profit center, pricing policies that result in inequitable performance measures generally lead to conflicts between subsidiary and enterprise goals. Returning to our earlier example, Blu Jeans–USA would report a lower profit than its sister affiliate in Hong Kong. Despite this result (due largely to factors beyond its control) the management of the U.S. subsidiary may be far more productive and efficient than the management team in Hong Kong. Under these circumstances, concluding that one subsidiary, on the basis of its accounting statements, is a better or poorer performer than the other would be a gross injustice. What seems called for at this point are accounting reports that allow management to discriminate between performance measures for tax purposes and those for control purposes. Dual sets of accounts are a possibility in this regard. Alternatively, the transfer price adjustments could be programmed in subsidiary budgets, and their performance measured according to these targets even if a loss was intended. And yet, one could cite numerous accounts in which headquarters management overlooks the facts of the case or, if it remembers, often feels constrained from taking corrective steps. One MNC executive, for example, candidly states:

> Our transfer prices are determined by our tax department. They try to minimize our total tax to the extent possible within the tax rules and regulations of the countries in which all operate. The transfer prices are not necessarily the ones we would use if our sale goal was to evaluate the performance of our subsidiaries. We've talked about developing a system that would correct for this, say using dual prices—one for the tax authorities and one for internal control. But the cost

---

[3] Treas. Reg. sec. 1.482-1.

and time needed to set up and administer such a system would be substantial. Furthermore, if the tax authorities find out that we are using a dual pricing system, we might encounter some difficulties. So we probably won't make any modification in our system and will hope that the transfer prices we use will not cause too great a distortion in our performance evaluation process.[4]

Such reservations notwithstanding, unless some provision is made to account for the inequities in the measurement and evaluation of subsidiary performance, subsidiary managers would be motivated to engage in nonoptimal behavior. In the context of our textile example, Blu Jeans–HK would be motivated to increase its reported profits (a dysfunctional decision) or experience a morale problem, the effects of which could outweigh any tax savings achieved.

Tariffs on imported goods are another tax consideration affecting the transfer pricing policies of multinational companies. A company exporting goods to a subsidiary domiciled in a high tariff country, for example, could reduce the tariff assessment by lowering the prices of merchandise sent there. Conversely, it could also be advantageous for the exporting company to transfer goods at high prices to subsidiaries domiciled in low tariff countries.

In addition to the trade-offs identified earlier in this section, the multinational company would also have to consider additional costs and benefits both external and internal. Externally, it would have now two taxing authorities to contend with—the customs officials of the importing country as well as the income tax administrators of both exporting and importing countries. A high tariff paid by the importer would necessarily result in a lower base with respect to income taxes. Internally, the enterprise would have to evaluate the benefits of a lower (higher) income tax in the importing country against a higher (lower) import tariff as well as the potentially higher (lower) income tax paid by the company in the exporting country.

Competitive factors.   To facilitate the establishment of a foreign subsidiary abroad, a parent company could supply the subsidiary with inputs invoiced at very low prices. These price subsidies could gradually be removed as the foreign affiliate strengthened its competitive foothold in the foreign market. In similar fashion, lowered transfer prices could be used to shield an existing operation from the deleterious effects of increased foreign competition. Indirect competitive effects are also possible. To improve a foreign subsidiary's access to local capital markets, its reported earnings and financial position could be bolstered by setting low transfer prices on the subsidiary's inputs and high transfer prices on its outputs. In some instances, transfer prices could be used to weaken a subsidiary's competitors. Strategies of this nature would more likely be employed by companies processing control over raw material supplies in a given industry.

Again, competitive considerations such as those just discussed would

[4] I. James Czechowicz, Frederick D. S. Choi, and Vinod B. Bavishi, *Assessing Foreign Subsidiary Performance: Systems and Practices of Leading Multinational Companies* (New York: Business International Corporation, 1982), p. 61.

have to be balanced against a number of offsetting disadvantages. Externally, transfer prices with competitive designs may call forth antitrust actions by host governments or other retaliatory actions by local competitors. Internally, pricing subsidies do little to instill a competitive mode of thinking in the minds of managers who presumably benefit from such actions. The obvious danger here is that what started out as a temporary management aid may all too easily evolve into a permanent management crutch. Thus, the long-run implications of a competitive transfer pricing policy need to be thoughtfully considered.

Environmental risks. Whereas competitive considerations abroad might warrant the setting of low transfer prices to foreign subsidiaries, the risks of severe price inflation might necessitate just the reverse action. Because inflation erodes the purchasing power of a firm's monetary assets, high transfer prices on goods or services provided to a subsidiary located in an inflationary environment are designed to remove as much cash from the subsidiary as possible.

Balance of payments problems, related in many cases to the inflationary problems just discussed, often prompt foreign governments to devalue their currencies and/or impose a number of restrictions on the repatriation of profits from foreign-owned companies. Again, currency exchange restrictions may be sidestepped and losses from currency devaluations avoided by shifting funds to the parent or related affiliates through inflated transfer prices. If transfer prices can be set high enough, some margin of cash may be returned to the parent company each time a transaction with the foreign subsidiary is made.

As a final example, high transfer prices are also employed as a means of minimizing a firm's exposure to expropriatory actions by host governments. Whereas high transfer prices on subsidiary imports may remove excess cash to safer havens, low transfer prices on subsidiary exports may allow a subsidiary to export physical inventories otherwise subject to confiscation.

What are some of the trade-offs that must be considered under conditions of risk? High transfer prices charged on exports to subsidiaries domiciled in high risk environments naturally produce an increased income tax base in the parent country. A question which, therefore, needs to be addressed is, Do the benefits of the transfer pricing decision more than offset the increased tax burden of the entity as a whole? Another equally vexing question is, What are the costs of strategic transfer pricing policies in terms of the company's relationship with host governments? Drastic changes in transfer prices seldom go unnoticed nowadays. Thus, the firm must increasingly assess the effective costs of compensating strategies, not to mention the costs of deterioration of firm government relationships.

Accounting contributions. Accountants, as measurement and communications specialists, can play a very significant role in quantifying the various trade-offs necessitated by transfer pricing strategy. The challenge to accountants in this regard lies not so much in the measurement process per se as it is in the acquisition and maintenance of a global perspective when mapping out the benefits and costs associated with any given intracorporate pricing decision. The effects of a specific transfer pricing policy on the multinational system as a whole must now take precedence over more orthodox managerial accounting and reporting modes.

This enlarged role of accountants is far from easy, however. Quantifying the numerous trade-offs is rendered difficult by the fact that environmental influences must be considered not individually but in concert. Consider, for example, the dilemma faced by accountants in attempting to measure the trade-offs surrounding transfer pricing policies applicable to a subsidiary located in a country with high income taxes, high import tariffs, government price controls, a thin capital market, a chronic rate of inflation, foreign exchange controls, and an unstable government. Based on our previous analysis, a high transfer price would result in lowering the subsidiary's income taxes and removing excess cash to the parent country. It might also, however, result in higher import duties, impair the subsidiary's competitive position due to higher input prices, exacerbate the rate of inflation, raise the subsidiary's capital costs, and possibly evoke retaliatory actions by the host government to protect its balance of payments position, made worse by the loss of foreign exchange. The problem is compounded by the fact that all the variables hypothesized above are constantly changing.

The complexity of the cost-benefit calculus associated with multinational transfer pricing is thus a challenge of no small proportion. Despite the magnitude of the problem, however, one thing is clear. Naive calculations of the effects of transfer pricing policy on individual units within a multinational system are no longer sufficient nor acceptable.

Transfer Pricing Methodology

The simultaneous effects of environmental influences on transfer prices also raise questions of pricing methodology. How are transfer prices established? Are standard market prices generally preferred to those based on some measure of cost? Or, are negotiated prices the only feasible alternative? Assuming some conclusions can be reached on this score, do multinational enterprises the world over employ similar transfer pricing methodologies or do cultural factors have a bearing here? Can a single transfer pricing methodology serve all purposes equally well? The following sections are intended to shed some light on these troublesome questions.

Cost versus market versus . . . ?   In a world of perfectly competitive markets, the determination of prices for intercompany resource and service transfers would not pose much of a problem. To the extent that transferred production could be purchased or sold in such markets, transfer prices could be based on either incremental cost or market prices and neither system would necessarily conflict with the other. Competitive markets, unfortunately, seldom exist externally for products transferred between related entities. Accordingly, cost- and market-based transfer prices no longer remain neutral with respect to their business effects. Mention should thus be made of some of the major features associated with either pricing method.[5]

The use of market-oriented transfer prices offers several advantages. Since market prices represent an opportunity cost to the transferring entity of not satisfying external demand, their employment will usually encourage efficient use of the firm's scarce resources. Their use is also said to be consistent with decentralized profit center orientation. In providing meaningful criteria for evaluating performance, market prices help differentiate profitable from unprofitable operations.

Market prices are also easier to defend as "arm's-length" prices. The notion of an arm's-length price, defined as a price that would have been paid to an unrelated party for the same or similar goods under identical or similar circumstances, is especially germane to host governments sensitive to anticompetitive practices associated with artificial transfer prices. There appears to be an emerging concensus among host governments that arm's-length pricing is the appropriate norm in arriving at profits for tax purposes. In addition to being endorsed by the U.S. Group of Experts on Tax Treaties between Developed and Developing Countries, the principle of arm's-length prices has been adopted in bilateral taxation conventions between member states of the Organization for Economic Cooperation and Development (OECD) and between OECD members and other states.[6]

The advantages associated with market-based transfer prices must be weighed against a number of shortcomings. One problem with using market prices is the frequent absence of an intermediate market for the product or service in question. This is especially likely to be the case for semifinished goods or specialized components. Even if such markets were available, they would seldom be perfectly competitive or internationally comparable. Adherence to market prices may also lead to neglect in gathering important cost data that would eventually become lost in the shuffle. Finally, market prices do not afford a firm much room for maneuvering prices for competitive or strategic purposes.

Cost-based transfer pricing systems overcome many of the limitations just cited. Moreover, cost-based systems are (a) simple to use, (b) based on data that are readily available, (c) easy to justify before tax authorities, and (d) easily routinized, thus helping to avoid internal frictions that often accompany more arbitrarily determined systems.

As one might suspect, cost-based transfer pricing systems are not flawless

[5] Two excellent references in this regard are Charles T. Horngren, *Cost Accounting, A Managerial Emphasis,* 5th ed. (Englewood Cliffs, N.J.: Prentice-Hall, Inc., 1982); and Gordon Shillinglaw, *Cost Accounting: Analysis and Control* (Homewood, Ill.: Richard D. Irwin, Inc., 1967).

[6] Organization for Economic Cooperation and Development, *Transfer Pricing and Multinational Enterprises* (Paris: OECD, 1979), pp. 8–9.

TABLE 11.3   Subsidiary Y Performance

	BUY FROM X		BUY FROM Z	
Additional revenue		$19		$19
Additional cost				
Transfer price from X	$15			
Price from Z			$13	
Additional costs in Y	5	20	5	18
		($ 1)		$ 1

either. Transferring goods or services at actual cost, for example, is said to provide little incentive for transferring units to control their costs. Production inefficiencies may simply be passed on to the buying unit in the form of inflated prices. Although the substitution of standard or budgeted costs could remedy the situation somewhat, it still would not avoid the more serious problem of suboptimal decision making. For example, assume that subsidiary X supplies certain parts to its sister subsidiary Y at a standard cost of $15 a unit, including a charge of $6 for fixed overhead. Both X and Y are currently operating at less than full capacity. The additional cost incurred by Y to proccess and market the final product is $5 a unit. An external supplier, Z, offers to sell Y the same component part for $13 a unit. Assuming that Y can retail the product for no more than $19 a piece, it would purchase the component from Z rather than X as its performance would be improved at the rate of $2 per unit (Table 11.3). The firm as a whole would benefit, however, if Y purchased from X rather than Z, by a $4 a unit (Table 11.4).

In this example, transfer prices based on costs (actual or budgeted) would lead Y to treat X's fixed costs as variable, thus leading to a dysfunctional decision for the firm as a whole.

In addition to overemphasizing historical costs, which ignore competitive demand and supply relationships, there is the age-old problem of allocating costs to particular products or services in a satisfactory manner. The problem of cost determination is compounded internationally, as cost accounting concepts are not uniform but vary from country to country.

While the pros and cons associated with both cost- and market-based transfer pricing models reveal something of their nature, they do not enable us to say, a priori, which method is optimal. Theoretical work in the area of inter-

TABLE 11.4   Performance of Firm as a Whole

	BUY FROM X		BUY FROM Z	
Additional revenue		$19		$19
Additional cost				
X	$ 9			
Z			$13	
Y	5	14	5	18
		$ 5		$ 1

national transfer pricing is still in its infancy.[7] Applied policy guidelines are also less than definitive. Despite international recognition of the arm's-length principle, its measurement is far from uniform. For example, the OECD identifies several broad methods of ascertaining an arm's-length price. Resembling those specified by Section 482 of the U.S. Internal Revenue Code, they are as follows:

1. *The comparable uncontrolled price method*—a transfer price set by reference to a sale in which at least one party to the transaction is not a member of the affiliated group
2. *The resale price method*—an uncontrolled price that is subsequently reduced by an appropriate markup representing the seller's profit
3. *The cost-plus method*—a transfer price based on the seller's cost plus an appropriate markup

That multinational companies are afforded considerable leeway in determining what constitutes an arm's-length price can be seen in the following OECD quote:

> Clearly the comparable uncontrolled price method is basically preferable to other methods since it uses evidence most closely related to an arm's length price, but there may be cases where the evidence of resale profit mark-ups, production costs or other data may be more complete, more conclusive and more easily obtained than undisputable evidence of open market prices. There should always be the possibility, therefore, of selecting the method which provides the most cogent evidence in a particular case. It has to be recognized that an arm's length price will in many cases not be precisely ascertainable and that in such circumstances it will be necessary to seek a reasonable approximation to it. Frequently, it may be useful to take account of more than one method of reaching a satisfactory approximation to an arm's length price in the light of the evidence available.[8]

Current practices.   In the absence of uniform transfer pricing norms, a survey of existing corporate practices is useful in obtaining a glimpse of the current state of the art. Owing to the sensitiveness of many transfer pricing issues, corporate pricing policies are often considered privy information. Accordingly, empirical evidence on the subject is understandably spotty. Still, the limited information that is available enables us to make a number of observations.

Domestically, transfer pricing practices have not conformed to any single approach, either cost- or market-based, no matter how conceptually superior it may have been professed to be. Rather, company objectives and their related transfer pricing strategies have determined the pricing methodology employed. A study sponsored by the National Industrial Conference Board revealed that two-thirds of the companies queried use some form of cost-based transfer prices. At the same time, over 50 percent of these same firms also use market-

---

[7] Larry J. Merville and J. William Petty II offer an initial attempt at constructing a multiple objective transfer pricing optimization model in their "Transfer Pricing for the Multinational Firm," *Accounting Review*, October 1978, pp. 935–951.

[8] OECD, *Transfer Pricing*, p. 33.

based systems.[9] In a more recent study sponsored by the National Association of Accountants, Benke and Edwards confirm the use of multiple transfer pricing techniques. Whereas large segments within a given company tend to use a single technique for the majority of their internal sales, secondary transfer pricing techniques were employed whenever the primary technique was deemed inappropriate.[10] In vertically integrated operations, transfers from one stage of production to the next have generally been at cost when the transferring unit is a cost center, and at cost plus a profit markup when the transferer is a profit center. Lateral transfers between units engaged in the same stage of production or distribution are usually executed at cost plus handling charges.

Practical compromises seemingly determine just what constitutes cost and market in many instances. Thus, most companies employing cost-based transfer prices prefer to use actual cost data derived from production and cost records. Standard costs, while preferable in many instances to actual cost information, are used but only when standard cost information is available. Interestingly, marginal costs, generally supported in cost accounting literature as the theoretically preferable choice, were used least frequently among firms responding to the NICB study.

Most firms employing a market-based methodology utilize actual market prices obtained from intermediate markets for the transferred item. When direct market quotes are not available, several alternatives are resorted to. For those units enjoying a high degree of local autonomy, competitive bidding and negotiation between subsidiary managers constitute a basis of arriving at "acceptable" market prices. Components or other patented items, which also lack any outside price equivalent, are typically priced on a cost-plus basis. But just what constitutes "cost-plus" is an open question. Should it include selling and administrative expenses? What about research and development costs? Should costs be stated in terms of actual or budgeted amounts? In practice, all of these variations and more were found to be employed as pricing bases.

Due in large measure to the absence of any outside equivalents, transfer prices for services rendered, such as management fees and royalties, are even more difficult to establish. Many companies in these instances reportedly "play it by ear." If tax officials or others with an interest in the transfer price do not complain too severely, the general presumption is that the price established must have been "reasonable."

Some causal variables.   In addition to the various gyrations that characterize transfer pricing methodology, several variables seem to be clearly associated with any given pricing construct. Acknowledging at the outset that much more research of the empirical variety is warranted on this subject, transfer pricing methods, whether market- or cost-oriented, appear related to a

---

[9] National Industrial Conference Board, *Interdivisional Transfer Pricing* (New York: NICB, 1967).

[10] Ralph L. Benke, Jr., and James Don Edwards, "Transfer Pricing: Techniques and Uses," *Management Accounting*, June 1980, p. 45.

firm's organizational philosophy, its size, its degree of international involvement, and its cultural milieu.

Take a firm's organizational pattern. Highly decentralized operations are characterized by subunit managers with maximum autonomy to establish transfer prices and to compare alternatives outside the organization. Moreover, interdependencies among subunits organized as variable profit centers tend to be minimal. Under these circumstances, market-based transfer prices, being the antithesis of centrally administrated price systems, would appear appropriate. In contrast, actual cost systems, or some variant thereof, are appropriate where transfer pricing decisions are "manufactured" higher up the corporate ladder. The reason is that cost-based prices, as opposed to external market prices, tend to be more permeable in nature.

SIZE

Size is another variable that has a bearing here. Despite variations of the two basic transfer pricing themes under consideration, large firms tend to gravitate toward cost-based systems. This is attributed to the fact that large firms tend to operate in more oligopolistic markets. As a result, their pricing policies tend to be shielded from competitive pressures that would otherwise influence the choice of a transfer price orientation. In addition, since larger firms tend to do more income maneuvering, they are much more concerned with transfer price determination and its subsequent effects.[11] Smaller firms, in contrast, are generally not in a position to justify departures from prevailing market prices for their products. Consequently they generally have no choice but to accept market prices as given.

DEGREE OF INTERNATIONAL INVOLVEMENT

Closely allied with the factor of size is the degree of a company's international involvement. Exposed to a broader spectrum of risks and problems than their domestic counterparts, transfer prices of multinational companies tend to be influenced by a greater range of environmental considerations. Burns recently surveyed 62 U.S.-based MNCs to obtain corporate assessments of the perceived importance of 14 environmental variables thought to influence transfer pricing decisions.[12] Ranked in descending order of importance, they appear in Table 11.5. Also included in that table are the results of another corporate survey by Kim and Miller.[13] What distinguishes the latter survey from the former is its concentration on U.S.-based MNCs with affiliates in developing as opposed to highly industrialized countries.

While the results of both studies are conditioned by the variables chosen for study, they are helpful in identifying the numerous influences that impact

[11] Jeffrey S. Arpan, "International Intracorporate Pricing: Non-American Systems and Views," *Journal of International Business Studies,* Spring 1972, p. 17.

[12] Jane O. Burns, "Transfer Pricing Decisions in U.S. Multinational Corporations," *Journal of International Business Studies,* Fall 1980, pp. 23–39.

[13] Seung H. Kim and Stephen W. Miller, "Constituents of the International Transfer Pricing Decision," *Columbia Journal of World Business,* Spring 1979, pp. 69–77.

TABLE 11.5   Environmental Influences on Transfer Prices

BURNS SURVEY		KIM & MILLER SURVEY	
Rank	Variable	Rank	Variable
1	Market conditions in foreign country	1	Profit repatriation restrictions within host country
2	Competition in foreign country	2	Exchange controls
3	Reasonable profit for foreign affiliate	3	Joint-venture constraints within host country
4	U.S. federal income taxes	4	Tariffs/customs duties within host country
5	Economic conditions in foreign country	5	Income tax liability within host country
6	Import restrictions	6	Income tax liability within the U.S.
7	Customs duties	7	Quota restrictions within the U.S.
8	Price controls	8	Credit status of U.S. parent firm
9	Taxation in foreign country	9	Credit status of foreign affiliate
10	Exchange controls		
11	U.S. export incentives		
12	Floating exchange rates		
13	Management of cash flow		
14	Other U.S. federal taxes		

Sources: Jane O. Burns, "Transfer Pricing Decisions in U.S. Multinational Corporations," *Journal of International Business Studies,* Spring 1972, p. 17; and Seung H. Kim and Stephen W. Miller, "Constituents of the International Transfer Pricing Decision," *Columbia Journal of World Business,* Spring 1979, pp. 69–77.

multinational transfer pricing policies. The Kim and Miller study also suggests that environmental influences vary depending on the specific domicile of foreign operations. Thus, whereas earlier studies identified income tax liabilities as highly influential factors in transfer pricing decisions in general, current research suggests that the influence of a given variable will vary with the nature of a particular foreign environment.

CULTURAL INFLUENCES

And what of culture? Does the nationality of a parent company's management have anything to do with the determination of internal pricing practices? Evidence suggests that it does. Whereas U.S., French, British, and Japanese managements seem to prefer cost-oriented systems, Canadians, Italians, and Scandinavians seem to prefer market-oriented systems. No particular orientation or preference was discernible for Belgian, Dutch, West German, or Swiss managers. In all cases, however, the setting of transfer pricing policy is the absolute perogative of parent company executives.[14]

Although non-U.S. companies generally consider the same environmental variables when formulating guidelines for transfer prices (especially among the larger companies), there are distinguishable national differences in the relative importance attached to each of these considerations. Thus, American, Ca-

[14] Arpan, "International Intercorporate Pricing," p. 18.

nadian, French, and Italian companies considered income taxes to be the most important variable affecting transfer pricing policy. British companies considered improvement of the financial appearance of their U.S. subsidiaries as most important. With the exception of Scandinavia, inflation was also identified as a variable receiving attention in transfer pricing policy deliberations.

In a more recent comparative study, Tang, Walter, and Raymond find that Japanese corporations place significantly greater emphasis on environmental influences such as devaluation of and revaluation of foreign currencies, the interests of local joint-venture partners, and foreign inflation than U.S. companies.[15]

In contrast to external influences such as those just mentioned, non-U.S. multinationals reportedly consider only about half as many internal parameters as their American counterparts. With the exception of the British, most firms under consideration view transfer pricing more as a means of controlling subsidiary operations than as a technique for motivating and evaluating subsidiary performance. This is largely explained by the fact that the profit center concept is not very widespread among non-U.S. firms. Aside from control, the other major consideration deemed important by all firms is the acceptability of transfer prices to both host and parent country governments alike.

Transfer Pricing and Government Relations

International differences notwithstanding, a major concern shared by multinational companies the world over is the acceptability of their transfer prices to governments hosting cross-country transfers. This concern has been discussed throughout the chapter and for good reason. Aware of the usefulness of these devices to the multinational enterprise in effecting income shifts and worried by the economic and social consequences of such actions, governments are increasing their scrutiny of multinational operations. As examples:[16]

1. Members of the Tokyo High Prosecutor's Office recently confiscated some 1,500 sets of files from Shell Oil's subsidiary headquarters in Japan to begin an investigation of its oil prices there.
2. In West Germany, members of the Berlin Cartel Office are investigating paper and drug prices that multinationals currently charge their subsidiaries in Germany.
3. The British government (as part of the 1975 Finance Act, mentioned previously) has issued a new set of tax regulations regarding transfer prices being set in connection with the sale of North Sea oil.
4. In the United States, the Federal Energy Administration has started administrative proceedings against Gulf Oil Corporation. Gulf is alleged to have overcharged itself for oil purchased from certain of its foreign subsidiaries to keep profits out of the United States and thus cut its U.S. tax bill.

[15] Roger Y. W. Tang, C. K. Walter, and Robert H. Raymond, "Transfer Pricing—Japanese vs. American Style," *Management Accounting*, January 1979, pp. 15–16.

[16] William M. Carley, "Profit Probes: Investigations Beset Multinational Firms with Stress on Pricing," *Wall Street Journal*, December 19, 1974, p. 1.

5. The developing countries are also getting in on the act. IBM's transfer pricing practices are reportedly under investigation in a number of such nations.

What does all of this portend for the future? Will governments so severely constrain transfer prices as to bring on the demise of such a critical management policy tool? We think not, at least not in the foreseeable future. Granted, both home and host governments are desirous of enforcing "arm's-length" and, therefore, "fair" pricing between related affiliates of multinational companies. The problem here is determining what is arm's-length or fair. Does "fair" refer to market-based or cost-based prices, or both? In addition, which variant of cost or market would be the appropriate one? Add to this puzzle the myriad of products to which such pricing decisions apply, not to mention currency fluctuations, language barriers, and other qualitative considerations, and presto we have a problem of gargantuan proportions! And what of enforcement? Given the limited size of most governmental policing staffs relative to the large number of transfer price "setters," this problem also becomes a nightmare.

Even if these problems could be overcome, however, we feel that governments will sooner or later have to face the question of whether the gains accruing from such policing activities really warrant the effort involved. As it currently stands, increased governmental revenues from transfer pricing "reforms" would probably pale in relation to the benefits that multinational enterprises provide host countries in the form of employment, technology transfers, indirect taxes, exports, and the like. It is doubtful whether host governments would willingly give these benefits up in the quest for a theoretical "arm's-length price." What we do envision is a new set of limits on transfer pricing policy based on practical compromises by both host countries and multinational enterprises. The range of these limits, furthermore, will be functionally related to the macro benefits that the multinational company's presence will contribute to the welfare of its national host. Within these limits, multinational enterprises will still be able to maneuver their transfer prices to enable the firm to adapt to the complex set of taxes, competition, and risks that characterize its ever-changing environment. Transfer pricing, in short, will continue to challenge the ingenuity of accounting and financial managers in the years to come.

INTERNATIONAL TAXATION

A treatise on international accounting would not be complete without some attention to international taxation. Of all the environmental variables considered thus far, none, with the possible exception of foreign exchange, has such a pervasive influence on all aspects of multinational operations as taxation. Where to invest, how to market, what form of business organization to employ, when and where to remit liquid funds, how to finance, and what transfer prices to charge are examples of management actions colored by tax implications.

Despite substantial effects on business decisions, international taxation remains a mystery for many executives because of the enormous complexity involved. To begin with, financial managers must contend with a number of special rules, formulated at home, with respect to the taxation of foreign source income. Then, too, the countries in which a multinational operates possess fundamentally different tax systems. Being an instrument of national economic policy, tax systems worldwide are understandably as diverse as the nations that create them. Finally, international tax agreements, laws, and regulations are constantly changing. This increases the aforementioned complexity since changes in one country's tax provisions often affect relative advantages in a multinational tax network overall. Computer-based tax simulation systems are promising management aids in this regard.

For all its complexity, the potential rewards of international tax planning are enticing in terms of enhancing both corporate cash flows and bottom-line results. For many companies this is where much of the "real action" occurs. Consider a couple of examples. Owing to differences in national tax laws, it may be possible to structure an industrial lease transaction whereby both a U.S. lessee and a U.K. lessor are considered owners of the same underlying property. Accordingly, both would qualify for tax depreciation and investment credit incentives in their respective countries. The use of "link companies," as an intervening holding company between, say, a Canadian parent and its U.S. subsidiaries, is another example of international "double-dipping." Under this arrangement, a link or holding company is incorporated under U.S. law but managed and controlled from Canada. Serving as a financing conduit to purchase one or more U.S. subsidiaries, interest expense incurred by the link company is deductible for both U.S. and Canadian tax purposes.[17]

It is not possible to provide, in a single chapter, a working acquaintance with major tax provisions in all the economically important countries of the world. We therefore limit our scope to a general overview of the major considerations that frequently impact multinational corporate policy decisions. In addition to the references cited at the end of this chapter, a wide range of international tax literature is available, including professional reference services. Pamphlets dealing with general individual country situations are published by the U.S. Department of Commerce, the major international banks, and the major CPA firms. Much literature is readily available in public, college, and university libraries.

Initial Concepts

Rules governing the taxation of foreign corporations and profits earned abroad appear at first glance to consist of a bewildering maze of detailed and complicated provisions characterized by little continuity or logic. Closer examination, however, reveals a few basic concepts that underlie the entire process. The notions of tax *equity* and *neutrality* are two such concepts.

The principle of tax equity emphasizes the fact that taxpayers who are similarly situated should be similarly treated. Thus, foreign taxes paid on in-

---

[17] James E. Power and Emil M. Sunley, "Using the Tax Variable: Tactics for Home and Abroad," *Dun's Business Month*, June 1982, p. 105.

come earned abroad by, say, a U.S. resident should be regarded as equivalent to the payment of U.S. taxes up to the level of taxes that would be levied in the U.S. on a similar amount of U.S.-source income. Under ideal conditions, adherence to the equity principle would render *neutral* the effect of taxes on decisions about whether to carry on profit-seeking operations in the United States or abroad. In practice disagreement exists over the interpretation of tax neutrality. To some the notion of neutrality connotes an equalization of tax burdens for similar activities at home and abroad. For example, under this viewpoint (*domestic neutrality*), a U.S. foreign subsidiary is simply a U.S. concern that happens to be operating abroad. Another viewpoint (*foreign neutrality*) holds that tax burdens of foreign affiliates should be equal to those experienced by local competitors. United States affiliates overseas are looked upon as foreign companies that happen to be owned by U.S. residents. We shall find that actual tax practices internationally waver between these two extremes.

U.S. Taxation of Foreign Operations

Under the principle of national sovereignty, every nation claims the right to tax income originating within its borders. The United States is no exception. What differs internationally are national philosophies regarding the taxation of foreign earnings. Countries such as Argentina, Hong Kong, Panama, Switzerland, and Venezuela, for example, adopt the *territorial* principle of taxation and confine their tax collection efforts to income generated within their borders. The United States, in contrast, adopts the *worldwide* principle and taxes income arising both within and outside its national boundaries.

In taxing foreign-source income, the U.S. Internal Revenue Code considers the organizational form of a foreign operation. Specifically, activities undertaken by a branch or division are considered extensions of the parent. As such, their earnings are fully taxed in the year earned whether remitted to the parent or not. Similarly, operating losses are deductible from other income earned by the parent. Earnings of a foreign subsidiary, however, are not taxed until remitted to the U.S. parent as a dividend. The *deferral* feature is advantageous as deferred taxes on earnings retained abroad operate as an interest-free loan from the U.S. government. From a planning perspective, companies anticipating losses in the early years of a foreign venture are well advised to consider the branch form of organization as losses of a foreign corporation are deductible only upon liquidation. When operations turn profitable, branches may be reorganized as a subsidiary to enjoy the benefits of the deferral privilege.

Foreign tax credit.   A direct consequence of the worldwide principle of taxation is that the foreign earnings of a U.S. MNC are subject to the full tax levies of at least two countries. To prevent this from happening, in keeping with the concept of domestic neutrality, U.S. companies can elect to treat foreign taxes paid as a *credit* against the parent's U.S. tax liability or as a *deduction* from taxable income. Companies generally opt for the former as a foreign tax credit results in a dollar for dollar reduction against U.S. taxes payable whereas the benefits of a deduction are limited to the product of the foreign tax expense and the parent company's marginal tax rate (i.e., a dollar of foreign tax expenses reduces U.S. corporate taxes by only 46 cents).

Limited to income taxes actually paid (indirect levies such as foreign sales taxes are not creditable), foreign tax credits may be categorized as *direct* and *indirect*. Direct taxes are those imposed by a foreign government on a U.S. taxpayer. Included here are income taxes paid on foreign branch earnings and any taxes withheld at the source such as dividends, interest, and royalties remitted to a U.S. investor. Direct foreign tax credits on royalty and foreign branch earnings, permitted by Section 901 of the U.S Internal Revenue Code, are calculated as shown in the first two columns of Table 11.6. Withholding taxes on royalty and divided payments are assumed to be 20 percent in countries A and C; income tax rates in countries B and C are assumed to be 30 percent and 40 percent, respectively. Note that royalty income and branch earnings are "grossed up," that is, included in U.S. income before deducting foreign taxes paid. \

 As the first two columns of Table 11.6 illustrate, the effect of the foreign tax credit is to limit the total foreign income tax paid to the higher of the two countries. If the foreign tax is lower than the U.S. rate, the U.S. government receives tax revenues on the foreign income. If the opposite occurs, no U.S. taxes are paid.[18]

Now, suppose that a U.S. parent corporation owns 10 percent or more of the voting shares of a foreign (investee) corporation from which it receives a dividend. In addition to a direct tax credit for any withholding taxes paid, Section 902 of the U.S. Tax Code allows the U.S. parent to claim an indirect tax for a portion of any foreign income taxes paid by the investee (i.e., the U.S. parent is deemed to have paid them). Reported dividends on a U.S. tax return would thus be grossed up to include the deemed tax paid plus any applicable foreign withholding taxes. It is as if the U.S. parent received a dividend inclusive of the tax due the foreign country and then paid it.

The allowable foreign indirect tax credit is determined as follows

$$\frac{\text{Dividend (including withholding tax)}}{\text{Earnings net of foreign income tax}} \times \text{Foreign income tax}$$

Column 3 of Table 11.6 illustrates the calculation of the indirect foreign tax credit. In that example, deemed taxes paid is 20 ($30/60 \times 40$) giving rise to an excess foreign tax credit (3) which can be used to offset U.S. taxes on other foreign source earnings. Note also the differential tax effects of foreign operations conducted as a branch as opposed to a foreign subsidiary (e.g., total taxes of 46

---

[18] Effective November 1976, the foreign tax credit is denied to a taxpayer who participates in, or cooperates with, an international boycott.

TABLE 11.6 U.S. Taxation of Foreign-Source Income

	ROYALTIES FROM COUNTRY A	BRANCH IN COUNTRY B	SUBSIDIARY IN COUNTRY C[a]	TOTAL FOREIGN-SOURCE INCOME
Branch/subsidiary				
Before-tax earnings		100.00	100	
Foreign income taxes		30.00	40	
After-tax earnings		70.00	60	
Dividend paid			30	
Other foreign income				
Income	20.00			
Foreign withholding taxes	4.00	–0–	6	
U.S. taxpayer				
Income	20.00[b]	100.00[b]	30[b]	150
Dividend gross-up ($^{30}/_{60} \times 40$)			20	20
Taxable income	20.00	100.00	50	170
U.S. tax (gross at 46%)	9.20	46.00	23.00	78.20
Foreign tax credit				
Paid	(4.00)	(30.00)	(6.00)	(40.00)
Deemed paid			(20.00)	(20.00)
Total	(4.00)	(30.00)	(26.00)	(60.00)
U.S. tax (net)	5.20	16.00	(3.00)[c]	18.20
Foreign taxes	4.00	30.00	6.00	40.00
Total taxes of U.S. taxpayer	9.20	46.00	3.00[d]	58.20

[a] Affiliate owned 10 percent or more.
[b] Grossed up to include foreign taxes actually paid.
[c] Excess foreign tax credit absorbed by net U.S. tax on other foreign source income.
[d] Excludes deferred tax on undistributed earnings of affiliate.

for a branch versus taxes of 3 for a subsidiary on before-tax earnings of 100).

The indirect tax credit may also be extended to taxes paid in connection with dividends distributed by second and third tier foreign corporations in a multinational network providing the U.S. parent's indirect ownership in such corporations exceeds 5 percent. Forward planning in the use of such credits can produce worthwhile tax benefits. Assume in this example that a U.S. parent owns 100 percent of the shares of Company X (a first tier foreign corporation). Company X owns 100 percent of the voting stock of Company Y (a second tier foreign corporation). During the period, Company Y pays a dividend of 100 to Company X. Company X, in turn, remits a dividend of 100 to the U.S. parent as follows:

	US PARENT	CO. X (First tier)	CO. Y (Second tier)
1. Pre-tax earnings	100	200	200
2. Foreign income tax		30	80
3. After-tax earnings		170	120
4. Dividends		100	100
5. Deemed foreign taxes paid	57 (100/170 × 97)	67 (100/120 × 80)	
6. Total taxes (2.+5.)		97	

Company X will be deemed to have paid 67 of the foreign income taxes paid by Company Y. In turn, the U.S. parent company will receive an indirect credit against U.S. taxes payable of 57 based on its share of taxes actually paid and deemed to have been paid by Company X (30 + 97). In this illustration, a dividend from Company Y to Company X increases the allowable U.S. foreign tax credit attendant upon a dividend from Company X to the U.S. parent when the income taxes in Company Y's country of domicile exceed that of Company X's and conversely.

To prevent foreign tax credits from offsetting taxes on U.S.-source income, an overall limit is imposed on the amount of foreign taxes creditable in any one year. The limitation is computed on a basis that combines foreign-source income and losses from all countries, thereby reducing foreign income and the total tax credit permitted. An example is shown in Table 11.7.

The overall tax credit limitation is a specific instance where U.S. tax law deviates from the principle of tax neutrality, which is one of the objectives of the tax credit mechanism. For example, when tax rates abroad exceed those in the United States, U.S. taxpayers receive equitable treatment when foreign taxes paid are creditable up to the level of U.S. taxation. Failure to credit foreign taxes when they exceed the U.S. level poses an additional burden on foreign versus purely domestic investments.

The U.S. approach to the issue of tax neutrality contrasts with other national approaches. Countries such as Canada, France, and the Netherlands, for

TABLE 11.7   Foreign Tax Credit Limit

	COUNTRY 1	COUNTRY 2
Taxable income received abroad	$1,000	$1,000
Foreign creditable taxes	500	600
United States tax computation		
Foreign taxable income		
(Countries 1 and 2)		$2,000
U.S. source income		
(assumed)		3,000
Total U.S. taxable income		$5,000
U.S. tax at 46 percent		$2,300
Less foreign tax credit[a]		1,000
U.S. taxes payable		$1,300

[a] Foreign tax credit (overall limitation):

Taxable income (Countries 1 and 2)	$2,000
Total foreign taxes (Countries 1 and 2)	1,100

$$\frac{\text{Total foreign taxable income}}{\text{Total taxable income}} \times \text{U.S. tax} = \frac{\$2,000}{\$5,000} \times \$2,300 = \$920$$

$920 is less foreign taxes paid (i.e. $1,100) so only $920 can be allowed; the excess $180 may be carried back two years and forward five years.

example, generally exempt either partially or in total foreign subsidiary or branch earnings from domestic taxes. While avoiding the phenomenon of double taxation, these policies trade off tax equality for domestic taxpayers as well as domestic tax neutrality with regard to domestic versus foreign investments. These countries favor the benefits of foreign neutrality over factors of equity and domestic neutrality.

Exceptions to General Rules

Previous discussion has established that the United States generally taxes worldwide income of U.S. residents currently as earned or accrued with foreign liabilities creditable against U.S. taxes. Income of U.S. foreign affiliates, however, is not taxed until repatriated. Let us now consider some significant exceptions to these rules.

Controlled foreign corporations.   The tax deferral privilege accorded U.S. foreign affiliates (an exception to the principle of domestic neutrality) was originally granted by the U.S. government to allow U.S. firms to expand abroad and compete on an equal footing with foreign competitors enjoying similar tax breaks. Unfortunately, it often proved all too easy for some firms to circumvent the intent if not the letter of the tax code. Tax avoidance rather than tax deferral was frequently achieved. This was typically accomplished by establishing a foreign holding company, preferably with a tax haven domicile. The major purpose of such a "shell" corporation was to receive tax-free the profits earned by its operating subsidiaries. These holding companies, for example, would be granted exclusive agency to export the products of the parent company. A portion of the profits that would otherwise accrue to the parent company would thus be shifted to the foreign holding company. Similarly, parent company patents would often be assigned to the foreign holding company, thus entitling it to collect royalties from sister subsidiaries that benefited therefrom. These and other devices thus allowed profits earned abroad to be accumulated and later redeployed for financing other foreign investments without ever being repatriated to the United States where they would be taxed.

To remedy this situation, the Revenue Act of 1962 added an amendment (Subpart F) to that part of the Internal Revenue Code governing the taxation of foreign-source income. Under this novel and complex provision (amended again in 1976), shareholders of controlled foreign corporations are taxable on certain undistributed income of that corporation. The intent here is to limit deferral to those activities in which foreign neutrality is truly a factor.

A controlled foreign corporation (CFC) is one in which more than 50 percent of the voting shares are owned by U.S. stockholders. In determining the 50 percent level, only stockholders holding more than a 10 percent interest are counted. The Subpart F provision applies to so-called passive income, including dividends, interest, rents, sales commissions from agency relationships, and fees received for a variety of services performed by the controlled company for its sister subsidiaries.

There are, however, several exceptions to the exception! To begin with, if less than 10 percent of the controlled foreign company's gross income comes from sources such as those listed above, the provisions of Subpart F do not apply. Subpart F income above 70 percent is taxed in full; income greater than 10 percent but less than 70 percent is taxed according to a series of graduated rates. Second, if the combined income tax, both U.S. and foreign, paid on any income distributed by the foreign controlled corporation, approximates the U.S. tax rate, Subpart F provisions again do not apply. Finally, income earned by controlled foreign corporations domiciled in less developed countries is not subject to Subpart F treatment if reinvested in these countries.

Domestic International Sales Corporation (DISC).   Normally, income from export transactions is taxed in the year earned. To encourage U.S. enterprises to engage in export activities and thus stem a worsening U.S. balance of payments position, Congress in 1971 authorized American companies to conduct their overseas sales through domestic as opposed to foreign subsidiaries. Rather than exporting goods and services directly, a U.S. parent company can sell them to its domestic international sales affiliate (DISC), which in turn exports them at an appropriate markup. For an affiliate to qualify as a Domestic International Sales Corporation the following conditions must hold:

1. At least 95 percent of its gross receipts must be attributed to exports of qualified goods and services.
2. At least 95 percent of its assets must be "qualified export assets," that is, monetary and nonmonetary assets used in generating export income.

3. A capitalization of at least $2,500 consisting of one class of stock must be maintained throughout the taxable year.
4. DISC status must be elected specifically (with the Internal Revenue Service).

Instead of being taxed on its profits directly, DISC earnings are taxed to the shareholders (normally the parent company) and, then, only when distributed as a dividend or deemed distributed. Specifically, 57½ percent of the current year's taxable income of a DISC in excess of the sum of certain amounts that are deemed distributed for the year is treated as distributed to the U.S. parent. The deemed distribution, in turn, is determined by the following formula:

$$\frac{67\% \text{ of average base period gross receipts}}{\text{Gross export receipts for current year}} \times \begin{array}{c} \text{Disc taxable income} \\ \text{for current year} \end{array}$$

The foregoing feature, in effect, allows for a deferral of taxable income of the DISC in excess of that attributable to a base period of export receipts. For an existing DISC, the base period for the 1984 taxable year would be the four years 1977–1980; for 1985 the base period would be 1978–1981, and so on. A newly formed DISC would have no base to speak of. Hence, all export income would qualify for DISC benefits.

To illustrate, assume that a DISC, established in 1977, has an adjusted net income in 1984 of $100,000 on $400,000 of export revenues. Gross export receipts for the 1977–1980 base period averaged $300,000. The portion of taxable income deferred would be determined as follows:

Taxable income for current year	$ 100,000
Deemed distribution $\dfrac{.67 \times 300,000}{400,000} \times 100,000$	50,250
Excess	$ 49,750
Incremental distribution (57½% × $49,750)	28,606
Deferred taxable income	$ 21,144

In addition to the deferral feature, normally reserved for U.S. foreign corporations, a DISC may lend some of its deferred income to the parent company (normally the producer of the exported goods). This *producer's loan* means that a parent company is entitled to free use of what would otherwise be a taxable dividend. A DISC is also subject to more permissive transfer pricing rules regarding intracompany transfers. Thus, a DISC can purchase exportable goods from its parent at a lower than arm's-length price as long as the increased DISC income resulting thereby does not exceed the highest of the following three options:

1. Four percent of export receipts from sale of the acquired goods plus 10 percent of related promotion expenses.
2. Fifty percent of the combined taxable income of the DISC and its parent related to the sale plus 10 percent of the DISC's related promotion expenses.
3. Taxable income determined if arm's-length pricing were employed.

Relaxation of the arm's-length pricing requirement of Section 482 (discussed earlier in this chapter) can reportedly reduce the tax rate on export profits from 46 to 35 percent in the case of option 2 above and perhaps as low as 23 percent under option 1.[19]

Possessions corporation.   An exception to the principle of taxing U.S. corporations on their worldwide income applies if the corporation conducts its business in a U.S. possession (e.g., American Samoa, Guam, the Panama Canal Zone, Puerto Rico, Wake Island, and Midway Island).[20] Not counting Guam, the Virgin Islands, and Puerto Rico, a U.S. taxpayer may exclude from U.S. taxation income earned outside the United States unless the income is *received* in the United States. To qualify for this treatment, a domestic U.S. corporation must derive at least 80 percent of its gross income from within the U.S. possession and at least 50 percent from the active conduct of a trade or business in the three years immediately preceeding the close of its taxable year. As a result of the Tax Equity and Fiscal Responsibility Act of 1982, the active trade or business test is increased to 65 percent over a three-year period—55 percent in 1983, 60 percent in 1984, and 65 percent in 1985 and thereafter.[21]

In the case of Puerto Rico, companies meeting the foregoing requirements can also repatriate income to the United States free of U.S. taxes. This is accomplished by computing a U.S. tax on a possessions corporation's worldwide income and granting a 100 percent credit for the U.S. tax imposed upon business or qualified investment income regardless of whether any tax is actually paid to the government of the U.S. possession. However, passive investment income derived from nonpossessions sources are taxed under normal U.S. tax rules.

The possessions corporation can remit dividends to its U.S. parent with the latter claiming a 100 percent dividends received deduction regardless of when the income was earned. Accordingly, retained earnings from previous years can be repatriated with virtually no tax on the remittance. As a result of these attractive provisions, numerous U.S. companies have set up affiliates and now produce in Puerto Rico.

U.S. expatriates.   Internationally, the United States has been unique in imposing taxes on a U.S. expatriate's worldwide income. This philosophy was reinforced in 1976 when Congress reduced to $15,000 the amount of a U.S. expatriate's foreign income that could be excluded from U.S. taxation. Prior to 1976, U.S. foreign residents (i.e., bona fide residents of a foreign country for an entire taxable year or those domiciled abroad for 17 out of 18 months) were permitted to exclude up to $25,000 (depending on length of stay abroad) and could take a foreign tax credit or deduction for any foreign income taxes paid.

---

[19] Paul R. McDaniel and Hugh J. Ault, *Introduction to United States International Taxation* (Deventer: Kluwer, 1981), p. 106.

[20] Payment of income taxes in Guam and the Virgin Islands generally satisfies the U.S. tax liability on such income.

[21] Alexander Grant Company, *1982 Tax Increases* (Chicago, 1982), par. 11.2.

In addition to lowering the exclusion limits, the Tax Reform Act of 1976 stipulated that foreign taxes paid on excluded income could not be claimed as a credit or deduction. In effect, U.S. taxes were levied on income including the $15,000, then reduced by a foreign tax credit on foreign earnings without the $15,000! Moreover, reimbursements received for such things as foreign housing, educational expenses for one's children, and home leave transportation were treated as taxable income to the overseas worker.

To ameliorate the undesirable effects of the 1976 Act on the expatriate compensation and ultimately the competitiveness of U.S. companies operating abroad, Congress passed the Revenue Act of 1978 which provided a new special deduction for "excess" living costs incurred by U.S. citizens working abroad. However, it also eliminated the exclusion for all but a limited category of employees. Recognizing that most industrial democracies do not tax their citizens living and working abroad, the 1981 Economic Recovery Tax Act restores the pre-1978 concept of an exclusion for foreign service earnings and dramatically increases the level of the exclusion. From $75,000 in 1982 this amount is scheduled to rise $5,000 each year until it reaches $95,000 in 1986.

As a result of the new law, expatriate tax planning must now focus on minimizing both U.S. and foreign taxes, depending on an expatriate's particular situation. Given the large exclusion permitted by the new tax rules, planning that effectively lowers taxes paid by a U.S. expatriate to foreign countries may produce overall tax savings.

Intercompany allocations.   In addition to Subpart F, other sections of the U.S. Internal Revenue Code may, to some extent, eliminate deferral of foreign source income of U.S. foreign corporations. Section 482, described in conjunction with our discussion on transfer pricing, authorizes U.S. tax authorities to recompute gross income, deductions, and credits between related corporate taxpayers (a) to prevent the evasion of taxes and/or (b) to properly reflect the income of the related companies. For instance, intercompany loans that bear an interest rate significantly below or above an appropriate market rate would invite the scrutiny of the Internal Revenue Service (IRS). In most instances, the IRS would impute an interest rate usually ranging between 6 to 8 percent. In a similar vein, other related party transactions such as the provision of intercompany services, the transfer of both tangible and intangible assets, as well as the purchase of inventories would have to be based on arm's-length prices as defined earlier in this chapter.

Once Section 482 determinations are made, Sections 861 and 862 are employed to determine whether the income and deductions so allocated constitute U.S.- or foreign-source items. In general, these sections, effective in 1977, tend to allocate a greater portion of deductible expenses, such as interest, R & D, and overhead to foreign-source income thus reducing the available foreign tax credit for U.S. taxation purposes. This effect is illustrated in Table 11.8. In that table a downward adjustment of a foreign affiliate's before-tax earnings of $20 million reduces the U.S. foreign tax credit from $44 million to $39.2 million. If the foreign government recognizes the allocation for purposes

TABLE 11.8   Tax Effects of Intercorporate Allocations

	BEFORE ADJUSTMENT	ADJUSTMENT
Foreign Affiliate		
Before-tax earnings (millions)	100	100[a]
Income taxes (30%)	30	24
After-tax earnings	70	76
Dividends	70	76
Withholding tax	14	15.2
U.S. Parent		
Dividend from affiliate	70	76
Dividend gross-up	30 (70/70 × 30)	24 (76/76 × 24)
Taxable income	100	100
U.S. tax (gross @ 46%)	46	46
Foreign tax credit		
Paid	(14.0)	(15.2)
Deemed paid	(30.0)	(24.0)
Total	(44.0)	(39.2)
U.S. tax (net)	2.0	6.8
Foreign withholding tax	14.0	15.2
Total taxes	16.0	22.0
Total taxes—affiliate & parent	46.0	46.0

[a] Earnings computed under U.S. tax rules; not affected by $20 adjustment of foreign affiliate's taxable income. Assume affiliate distributes all of its post-tax earnings.

of reducing foreign taxes paid, a U.S. corporation would suffer no hardship as total taxes paid by the foreign affiliate and the U.S. parent would remain unchanged (i.e., $46.0 million). However, if the foreign tax authorities refuse to recognize such allocations, taxes paid by the corporate system as a whole would increase (e.g., from $46.0 to $50.8 million in our example).

International Dimensions

Tax planning for multinational operations also requires an acquaintance with the national tax systems of the host countries in which the firm operates. Differences among national tax systems range from assessment and collection philosophies previously described, to tax computations and procedures. The sections that follow describe various dimensions of the international tax environment that should be factored into multinational tax planning systems including (a) types of taxes, (b) tax burdens, (c) tax treaties, and (d) tax havens.

Types of taxes.   A company operating abroad encounters a variety of direct and indirect taxes. Direct taxes typically include income and capital gains taxes. Indirect taxes are more numerous and include, among the major ones, turnover taxes, value-added taxes, border taxes, excise taxes, net worth taxes, and withholding taxes.

CORPORATE INCOME TAXES

Internationally, the income tax is probably more widely used than any other major tax, with the possible exception of customs duties. In the United States this direct tax on both corporate and personal income is the major source of government revenue. Owing to low per capita income in the developing countries, individual income taxes or general sales taxes are not very appropriate. In these countries, the corporate income tax provides a larger share of government revenues than in industrial countries. Most other countries rely heavily on direct taxes.

TURNOVER TAXES

Turnover taxes are indirect taxes assessed on total sales at one or more stages in the production process. In Canada, for example, the turnover tax is assessed when production is complete; in England, when merchandise is wholesaled; in the United States, when merchandise is retailed (sales tax); and in West Germany, at all stages in the cycle. In the last instance, since credit is not received for turnover taxes previously paid, the final sales price usually includes all prior taxes.

VALUE-ADDED TAX

To remedy the compounding effect of turnover taxes, many countries, notably in Central Europe and Scandinavia, have turned to the value-added tax. This tax is levied at each stage of production or distribution, but only on the value added during that particular stage. This is done by applying the given tax rate to total sales less purchases from any intermediate sales unit. Thus, if a Norwegian merchant purchased 500,000 kroner of merchandise from a Norwegian wholesaler and then sold it for 600,000 kroner, the value added would be 100,000 kroner and the tax assessed on this increment.

Value-added tax rates vary not only by country but by types of items (e.g., luxury vs. necessities, etc.). Some rate examples include Brazil, 15 percent; Chile, 20 percent; Denmark, 22 percent; France, 7–33 percent (depending on type of goods); Germany, 6.5–13 percent; Ireland, 0–25 percent; Italy, 2–35 percent; Korea, 10 percent; Malaysia, 10 percent; Mexico, 10 percent; Norway, 20 percent; and the United Kingdom, 15 percent.[22] Owing to its many advantages over other taxes, including ease of understanding and collection, the value-added tax is frequently recommended for adoption in the United States.

BORDER TAXES

Value-added taxes often serve as a basis for border taxes. Like import duties, border taxes generally aim at keeping domestic goods competitive with imports. Accordingly, taxes assessed on imports typically parallel excise and other indirect taxes paid by domestic producers of similar goods.

[22] Coopers & Lybrand, *International Tax Summaries,* New York, 1980, various pp.

NET WORTH AND WITHHOLDING TAXES

Two other taxes, generally met in international business affairs, are net worth and withholding taxes. The former are those taxes assessed on the undistributed earnings of a company. They are designed to encourage firms to source finances for investment projects externally. Development of domestic capital markets is thus fostered. Under these circumstances, net worth taxes are often substantial (e.g., 56% in Germany).

Withholding taxes are those imposed by host governments on dividend and interest payments to foreign investors. Thus, a foreign purchaser of Italian corporate bonds would receive only 85 percent of any interest return expected from his or her investment, given a 15 percent withholding tax in Italy. As the name indicates, these taxes, while legally imposed on the foreign recipient, are typically withheld at the source by the issuing corporation, which, in turn, remits the proceeds to its government. Since withholding taxes often retard the international flow of long-term investment capital, they are usually modified by bilateral tax treaties, which will be described shortly.

Tax burdens.   Differences in overall tax burdens are another feature of the international business scene. Varying statutory rates of income tax are an obvious source of these differences. For example, while the corporate income tax rate is 46 percent in the United States, it may range anywhere from as low as zero in Bermuda and other tax-haven countries to as high as 60 percent in India. Statutory tax rates in countries accounting for over 80 percent of the recent overseas earnings of U.S. companies are listed in Table 11.9.

Differential tax rates, however, tell only part of the story. A number of other considerations weigh just as heavily on relative tax burdens for multinational enterprises. Differences in definitions of taxable income are a major consideration. "What is income?" is likely to elicit as many answers as there are sovereign nations. Even if there were some consensus regarding the concept of income, little agreement would exist as to allocation between countries. The United States, for example, generally has its own views as to what constitutes an appropriate transfer price on transactions between related affiliates of the multinational company (discussed earlier).

Foreign governments also have their own views on the matter and these seldom conform to those of the U.S. tax authorities. Opinions as to what constitutes appropriate charges by a parent company for research and development, promotion, administration, and various technical services also differ internationally, so much so that domestic operations are often charged for such expenditures to avoid debates over the issue with foreign tax authorities.

Investment allowances and credits, special reserves to stabilize employment, the timing of depreciation deductions and other expense recognition, as well as asset valuations also vary from country to country. For example, business firms in England are allowed to write off immediately up to 100 percent of the total acquisition cost of a plant during the year of acquisition. In Australia, the figure is 20 percent; in India, 25 percent.[23] Other countries depreciate an

[23] Ibid.

TABLE 11.9   Statutory Tax Rates in Selected Foreign Countries

COUNTRY	STATUTORY PROFITS TAX RATE	DIVIDEND WITHHOLDING RATE
Australia	46.0	30.0
Austria	55.0	20.0
Belgium	45.0	20.0
Brazil	35.0	15.0
Canada	46.0	25.0
China, People's Republic of	40.0	20.0
Denmark	40.0	30.0
France	50.0	25.0
Germany		
Undistributed	56.0	25.0
Distributed	36.0	
Hong Kong	16.5	0.0
Ireland	50.0	0.0
Italy	30.0	32.4
Japan		
Undistributed	42.0	20.0
Distributed	32.0	
Korea	38.0	10.0
Luxembourg	40.0	15.0
Mexico	42.0	21.0
Netherlands	48.0	25.0
New Zealand	45.0	30.0
Norway		
Undistributed	50.8	25.0
Distributed	23.0	
Sweden	40.0	30.0
Switzerland	3.6–49.8	35.0
United Kingdom	52.0	0.0

Note: The rates listed are for entities incorporated in the foreign jurisdictions and are for the highest levels of income. The dividend withholding data does not reflect U.S. treaties.

Source: Data extracted from Ernst & Whinney, *Foreign and U.S. Corporate Income and Withholding Tax Rates* (New York, December 1982).

asset after its estimated useful life. Rather than granting a tax deduction, some countries allow a direct credit against taxes payable equal to some percentage of an investment's initial cost, such as the 10 percent investment tax credit in the United States. In Sweden, firms are allowed to establish reserves from profits which may subsequently be used for investments in industries or areas which are economically depressed. And, as pointed out in Chapter 5, countries in South America and elsewhere increasingly adjust their assets for changing price levels. These adjustments often significantly affect reported income for tax purposes.

Tax administration systems also affect relative tax burdens internationally. We can identify at least three major systems now in use: (1) the classical system, (2) the split-rate system, and (3) the imputation or tax credit system.

Under the classical system, corporate income taxes are levied at a single rate. Dividends are then taxed as income to shareholders at their personal income tax rates. Examples of countries that use this system include Italy, Luxembourg, the Netherlands, Spain, Sweden, most Commonwealth countries except the United Kingdom (which switched to the tax credit system in 1973), and the United States.

Under the split-rate system, taxes are levied at two different rates depending on whether profits are distributed or retained. In Norway, for example, profit distributions are taxed at a rate of 23.0 percent, whereas retained earnings are taxed at 50.8 percent. Table 11.9 identifies other countries employing the split-rate system.

Under the tax credit or imputation system, a tax is levied on corporate income at a given rate; however, part of the tax paid can be treated as a credit against the personal income tax on dividends. Belgium, the United Kingdom, France, and (most recently) West Germany have adopted this system. The European Economic Community, as a part of its effort to harmonize taxes among its member countries, is seriously proposing the uniform adoption of the imputation system.

The administration systems just identified are not mutually exclusive, nor are their effects on differential tax burdens minimal. For example, West Germany is included under both the split-rate system and the imputation system. While corporate income taxes on distributed earnings are currently 36 percent, German shareholders are permitted to deduct the dividend tax from their personal income tax. Thus shareholders in effect pay no tax on dividends. United States–owned companies in Germany, however, are not allowed to participate in this scheme. For example, while they would have to pay the current tax on corporate earnings in Germany, shareholders—in this case, U.S.-based parent companies—would not benefit from the dividend exclusion. The result is that income taxes on United States and other foreign-owned subsidiaries in Germany are raised by almost 10 percent.[24]

Dufey identifies a final item that accounts for intercountry differences in effective tax burdens.[25] This relates to social overhead in any host country. Many less developed countries charge lower corporate tax rates than developed countries. Designed to attract investment capital, these incentives, however, rarely fulfill their promise. These countries need to finance government and other social services just as any other country. Lower corporate tax rates, therefore, generally result in higher rates of indirect taxation and/or a reduction in the quantity and quality of public services provided. In the first case, one form of tax is simply replaced by another. More importantly, the purchasing power of the marketplace is reduced. This, in a general sense, "taxes" the potential earnings streams of a multinational investor. In the second case, reduced corporate taxes may also mean a higher cost structure, which a deficient social overhead system imposes on multinational operations. Examples would

---

[24] "U.S. Subsidiaries Get Caught By Tax Reform," *Business Week,* June 7, 1976, pp. 42–43.

[25] Gunter Dufey, "Myths About Multinational Corporations," *Michigan Business Review,* May 1974, p. 15.

include poor transportation, inadequate postal services, nonfunctioning tele-phone systems, and power shortages.

These and other variations among countries suggest that effective tax rates seldom equal nominal rates. Intercountry comparisons based on statutory tax rates are therefore insufficient. Tax burdens internationally should always be determined by examining *effective* tax rates.

Tax treaties.   While foreign tax credits shield, to some extent, foreign-source income from double taxation, tax treaties go further than this. Signa-tories to such a treaty generally agree on how taxes will be imposed, shared, or otherwise eliminated on business income earned in one taxing jurisdiction by nationals of another. Thus, most tax treaties between the United States and

TABLE 11.10   Foreign Withholding Rates Under U.S. Income Tax Treaties as of December 1982

COUNTRY	DIVIDENDS (%)	INTEREST (%)	ROYALTIES (%)
Australia	15	N/A	N/A
Austria	10[a]	E	E
Belgium	15	15	E
Canada	10	15	10
Denmark	15[a]	E	E
France	15[a]	10	5
Germany	15	E	E
Ireland	N/A	E[b]	E
Italy	15[a]	N/A	E
Japan	15[a]	10	10
Korea	15[a]	12	5
Luxembourg	7.5[a]	E	E
Netherlands	15[a]	E	E
Netherlands Antilles	15[a]	E[b]	E
New Zealand	N/A	15	15
Norway	15	E	E
Philippines	25[a]	15	25
Sweden	15[a]	E	E
Switzerland	15[a]	5	E
United Kingdom	N/A[c]	E	E

Notes: E = the income is exempt from withholding tax under the treaty;

N/A = the treaty does not limit the tax applicable to this type of income.

[a] The treaty withholding tax rate is reduced to 5 percent (10% in the case of Japan and Korea, and 20% in the Philippines) if among other conditions, the recipient is a corporation owning a specific percentage of the voting power of the distributing corporation.

[b] Exemption does not apply if the recipient corporation controls directly or indirectly more than 50 percent of the voting power of the paying corporation.

[c] Dividends from U.K. corporations are subject to Advance Corporation Tax (ACT), a portion of which is refunded to U.S. shareholders.

Source: Ernst & Whinney, *Foreign and U.S. Corporate Income and Withholding Tax Rates* (New York, 1982), p. 31.

other countries provide that profits earned by a U.S. enterprise in the other country shall not be subject to its taxes unless the U.S. enterprise maintains a permanent establishment there. Tax treaties also affect withholding taxes on dividends, interest, and royalties paid by enterprises of one country to foreign shareholders. They usually grant reciprocal reductions in withholding taxes on dividends and they often exempt royalties and interest from withholding entirely.

Table 11.10 sets forth, in general fashion, various rates of withholding tax when income is paid to a U.S. corporation from a country with which the United States has an income tax treaty. The withholding rates may not apply if the U.S. corporation has a permanent establishment in the treaty country.

Foreign tax incentives. Countries eager to accelerate their economic development have been aware of the positive influences of the multinational company. To attract multinational enterprises, many countries offer a number of tax incentives. These are often nontaxable cash grants applied toward the cost of fixed assets of new industrial undertakings, or relief from paying taxes for certain periods (tax holidays). Other forms of temporary tax relief include reduced income tax rates, tax deferrals, and reduction or elimination of various indirect taxes.

Some countries, particularly those with few natural resources, offer permanent tax inducements. These so-called "tax havens," include the following:[26]

1. The Bahamas, Bermuda, and the Cayman Islands, which have no taxes at all
2. The British Virgin Islands, and Gibraltar, which assess very low tax rates
3. Hong Kong, Liberia, and Panama, which tax locally generated income but exempt income from foreign sources
4. Countries that allow special privileges that are suitable as tax havens for very limited purposes.

COMPARATIVE ILLUSTRATIONS OF SELECTED NATIONAL TAX PROVISIONS

We now turn to some specific countries for tax illustrations. For purposes of comparison, with the United States, we shall examine non–U.S. taxation of unremitted foreign earnings and how other countries afford relief from international double taxation. Countries examined include Belgium, France, West Germany, Italy, Japan, the Netherlands, and the United Kingdom.[27]

---

[26] Jean Doucet and Kenneth J. Good, "What Makes a Good Tax Haven?" *Banker,* May 1973, p. 493.

[27] Based on expert testimony by Arthur Andersen & Company before the U.S. Senate Committee on Finance, April 1976.

Taxation on Unremitted Foreign Earnings

Recall that, in the case of foreign subsidiaries, the United States generally taxes foreign source earnings only when remitted to the United States. Under Subpart F provisions, however, certain undistributed income is taxed even though not remitted. Like the United States, West Germany, Italy, Japan, and the United Kingdom tax dividends from their companies' foreign subsidiaries. They do not, however, tax unremitted earnings. Belgium and France tax foreign subsidiary dividend remissions but only on a limited basis. They, too, do not assess taxes on unremitted earnings. The Netherlands stands alone in taxing either foreign subsidiary dividends or retained earnings of those subsidiaries.

Of the countries that tax foreign dividends, West Germany, Japan, and the United Kingdom allow a foreign tax credit equivalent to that granted by the United States. While Italy does not grant such a credit, it only subjects such dividends to partial taxation and permits a credit for withholding taxes subject to some special limitations.

Existing legislation, as well as government attitudes in many of these countries, encourages the use of tax-haven holding companies (referred to earlier) as a means of minimizing or eliminating the taxation of foreign dividends. The large Japanese trading companies use such vehicles on a regular basis. Attitudes in Italy toward the use of foreign tax shelters are so favorable that government-owned industrial enterprises such as Instituto Ricostruzione Industriale, Ente Nazionale Idrocarburi, and Instituto Mobiliare Italiano use such tax-haven vehicles in their corporate groups. The United Kingdom permits setting up offshore nonresident corporations. Although legal entities of the United Kingdom, they are free from U.K. taxation on their foreign income. United Kingdom multinational enterprises are also able to utilize tax-haven holding companies to own and control foreign subsidiaries.

Foreign branch operations of U.S. multinational companies are taxed just as if they were U.S. operations. This is in keeping with the U.S. philosophy of taxing U.S. company income wherever earned. United States taxes on income earned abroad are reduced by foreign income taxes paid under the foreign tax credit rules described earlier.

Japan, the Netherlands, and the United Kingdom tax branch operations in a manner similar to the United States. The Dutch credit for taxes incurred in the country of operations, however, is determined to be at the rate of the Dutch corporate income tax, regardless of the rate actually paid. In effect, then, no tax is applied by the Dutch government on branch income.

Belgium and West Germany do not tax branches of their corporations in other treaty countries. France, as a matter of tax policy, does not tax foreign branch income at all. Under a new tax system initiated in 1974, Italy does not tax branch income for local income tax purposes providing that the branch has separate management and accounting systems. Italy does tax branch income for national income tax purposes with a foreign tax credit allowed, subject to certain limitations.

Relief from Double Taxation

Foreign tax credit arrangements differ among the United States and the countries under consideration due to basic underlying differences in their taxation systems. To illustrate, since Belgium, West Germany, and France do not tax foreign branch income, they do not allow a foreign tax credit for taxes paid by those branches. The Netherlands, in effect, does not tax branch income at all. Belgium, France, and the Netherlands do not tax foreign subsidiary dividends and therefore do not allow a deemed foreign tax credit.

Recall that the United States generally limits the amount of foreign taxes creditable in any one year. This limitation is computed on an overall basis that combines foreign-source income and losses from all countries. Under this method, the combined foreign-source taxable income is expressed as a percentage of U.S. taxable income to determine the limitations on the credit.

Belgium, France, West Germany, Italy, and the United Kingdom differ in their limits on allowable foreign tax credits. They generally employ a per country limitation. While the United Kingdom has a rather restrictive limitation, U.K. companies are able to minimize the problem. This is accomplished by using foreign holding companies to receive dividends and averaging the foreign tax credits involved so as to achieve an effective overall limitation. Japan and the Netherlands have an overall limitation similar to that of the United States. Japan, however, exempts losses from overseas branches in determining the overall limitation, thus offering Japanese investors a higher limitation on foreign tax credits than their American counterparts.

In the United States, important indirect costs (such as general and administrative expenses of corporate headquarters) are allocated against all foreign income in determining the allowable foreign tax credit. The countries under discussion are generally more liberal in determining the amount of the limitation. Of the seven, only the Netherlands requires an allocation of indirect expenses to all foreign income in determining the allowable credit. Japan requires an allocation of certain indirect expenses but only to income from foreign branches. The other countries have no such allocation requirements.

SELECTED REFERENCES

BARRETT, EDGAR M., "Case of the Tangled Transfer Price," *Harvard Business Review,* May-June, 1977, pp. 20–22, 26, 27, 32, 34, 36, 176, 177.

BENKE, RALPH L., JR., and JAMES DON EDWARDS, *Transfer Pricing: Techniques and Uses,* New York: National Association of Accountants, 1980.

BURNS, JANE O., "Transfer Pricing Decisions in U.S. Multinational Corporations," *Journal of International Business Studies,* Fall 1980, pp. 23–29.

COOPERS & LYBRAND, *International Tax Summaries,* New York, 1980.

ERNST & WHINNEY, *Foreign and U.S. Corporate Income and Withholding Tax Rates,* New York, 1982.

FEINSCHREIBER, ROBERT, "The Foreign Tax Credit under Seige," *Financial Executive*, October 1979, pp. 56–62.

KIM, SEUNG H., and STEPHEN W. MILLER, "Constituents of the International Transfer Pricing Decision," *Columbia Journal of World Business*, Spring 1979, pp. 69–77.

McDANIEL, PAUL R., and HUGH J. AULT, *Introduction to United States International Taxation*, Deventer: Kluwer, 1981.

MERVILLE, LARRY J., and J. WILLIAM PETTY II, "Transfer Pricing for the Multinational Firm," *Accounting Review*, October 1978, pp. 935–951.

NOBES, C. W., "Imputation Systems of Corporate Taxation in the EEC," *Accounting and Business Research*, Spring 1980.

NORDHAUSER, SUSAN L., and JOHN L. KRAMER, "Repeal of the Deferral Privilege for Earnings from Direct Foreign Investments: An Analysis," *Accounting Review*, January 1981, pp. 54–69.

ORGANIZATION FOR ECONOMIC COOPERATION AND DEVELOPMENT, *Transfer Pricing and Multinational Enterprises*, Paris: OECD, 1979.

PLASSCHAERT, S. R. F., "The Multiple Motivations for Transfer Pricing Modulations in Multinational Enterprises: An Attempt at Clarification," *Management International Review*, Vol. 4, 1981, pp. 49–63.

POWER, JAMES E., and EMIL M. SUNLEY, "Using the Tax Variable: Tactics for Home and Abroad," *Dun's Business Month*, June 1982, pp. 99–106.

SALE, J. TIMOTHY, and KAREN B. CARROL, "Tax Planning Tools for the Multinational Corporation," *Management Accounting*, June 1979, pp. 37–41.

SCHWARTZ, B. N., "Partial Income Tax Allocation and Deferred Taxation: An International Accounting Issue," *Management International Review*, Vol. 20, 1980, pp. 74–82.

SHULMAN, J. S., "Transfer Pricing in the Multinational Firm," *European Business*, January 1969, pp. 46–54.

TANG, ROGER Y. W., C. K. WALTER, and ROBERT H. RAYMOND, "Transfer Pricing—Japanese vs. American Style," *Management Accounting*, January 1979, pp. 12–16.

WILLIAMS, THOMAS J., "The Creditability of Foreign Income Taxes: An Overview," *Taxes*, October 1980, pp. 699–709.

WU, FREDERICK H., and DOUGLAS SHARP, "An Empirical Study of Transfer Pricing Practice," *International Journal of Accounting*, Spring 1979, pp. 71–99.

DISCUSSION QUESTIONS

1. Compare and contrast the role of transfer pricing in national versus multinational operations.

2. Multinational transfer pricing is a subject that evokes serious concern among various corporate stakeholders. Identify potential concerns from the viewpoint of (a) Minority owners of a foreign affiliate, (b) Foreign taxing authorities, (c) Home country taxing authorities, (d) Foreign subsidiary managers, and (e) Headquarters' managers.

3. Briefly dimension the role of managerial accountants in the multinational transfer pricing decision.

4. Identify the major bases for pricing intercompany transfers and comment briefly on their relative merits. Which measurement construct seems most optimal from the viewpoint of the multinational executive suite?

5. Explain the significance of Section 482 of the U.S. Internal Revenue Code as it relates to transfer pricing. Does the notion of an arm's-length price specified by Section 482 resolve the measurement issue in pricing intracompany transfers?

6. What is meant by the term *domestic neutrality* and how does it differ from the concept of *foreign neutrality*? Which of the two concepts seems to underlie the U.S. tax treatment of foreign-source income and what are the related implications thereof for multinational operations?

7. What are tax credits and what role do they play in international taxation? What considerations might cause the operation of tax credits to fall short of their intended results?

8. Briefly distinguish, by way of examples, (a) classical, (b) split-rate, and (c) imputation tax systems. Then describe what you feel are the major advantages and disadvantages of each from the perspective of a multinational corporate taxpayer.

9. National differences in statutory tax rates are the most obvious and yet least significant determinants of a company's effective tax burden. Do you agree with this statement? Explain.

10. Carried to its logical extreme, tax planning implies a conscientious policy of tax avoidance. This mode of thinking raises an ethical question for international tax executives. It is well known that deliberate tax evasion is commonplace in many parts of the world. In Italy, for example, tax legislation is generally honored only in the breach. Even then, actual tax settlements are usually subject to negotiation between the individual taxpayer and the tax collector. Under these conditions, should multinational corporations operating in such environments adopt a policy of "when in Rome do as the Romans do" or should they adhere to taxation norms generally subscribed to in their domestic environments?

EXERCISES

1. Global Enterprises has a manufacturing affiliate in Country A which incurs costs of $700,000 for goods that are sold to its sales affiliate in Country B. The sales affiliate resells these goods to final consumers for $1,800,000. Both affiliates incur operating expenses of $100,000 each. Countries A and B levy a corporate income tax of 50 percent on taxable income in their jurisdictions.
   Required:
   A. If Global Enterprises raises the aggregate transfer price such that shipments from its manufacturing to its sales affiliate increase from $1,000,000 to $1,200,000, what effect would this have on consolidated taxes?
   B. What would be the tax effects of the foregoing pricing action if corporate income tax rates were 30 percent in Country A and 50 percent in Country B?

2. Drawing on the background facts in Exercise 1, assume that the total manufacturing cost per unit, based on operations at full capacity, is $70 and that the uncontrolled selling price of the unit in Country A is $120. Costs to transport the goods to the distribution affiliate in Country B is $16 per unit and a reasonable profit margin on such cross-border sales is 20 percent of cost.

    In this exercise, Country B levies a corporate income tax of 40 percent on taxable income (versus 30 percent in Country A) as well as a tariff of 20 percent on the declared value of the imported goods.

    The minimum declared value legally allowed in Country B is $100 per unit with no upper limit. Import duties are deductible for income tax purposes.

    Required:
    A.   On the basis of the foregoing information, formulate a transfer pricing strategy that would minimize Global Enterprise's overall tax burden.
    B.   What issues are raised by your pricing decision?

3. A 100 percent owned Brazilian affiliate of a U.S.-based MNC has foreign earnings before taxes of $200,000. After paying a corporate income tax of 35 percent, the Brazilian affiliate remits a dividend of $50,000 to its U.S. parent.

    Required:
    A.   Given a dividend withholding tax of 15 percent, calculate the applicable U.S. tax.
    B.   What would the tax have been if the Brazilian entity were a branch of the U.S. parent instead?

4. In 1985 Global Manufacturing Enterprises anticipates exporting merchandise costing $3,000,000 to the EEC for $4,000,000. Gross export receipts during the recent past exhibited the following pattern:

1978	$ 500,000
1979	1,100,000
1980	1,600,000
1981	2,000,000
1982	1,800,000
1983	2,500,000
1984	2,700,000

    Required: Assuming a U.S. corporate income tax rate of 46 percent and current export-related expenses of $200,000, what benefits would Global Manufacturing experience by forming a DISC?

5. Assume that a French jewelry manufacturer purchases an ounce of gold from a precious metals dealer for 2,800 francs (FF). The manufacturer fabricates the raw material into an item of jewelry and sells it to a retail jeweler for FF 5,600. The jeweler then sells the finished product to a customer for FF 10,500.
    Required: Compute the value-added tax due from each firm given that France has a value-added tax on luxury items of 33 percent.

CASE

Congress Giveth and Congress Taketh

The tax morality of the multinational corporation has become a popular topic of debate among American and foreign politicians, business people, economists, labor leaders, academicians, and journalists. Opinions range from complete support of the multinational corporation to accusations that it is one of the most exploitative institutions of capitalism ever created. In addition to exporting jobs, adversely affecting a country's balance of payments, and hurting domestic investment, multinationals are accused of not paying their fair share of taxes to either host country or home country governments. Calling the foreign tax credit and foreign income deferral policy "the biggest loopholes in the whole tax law," Congress continues to consider the issue of ending existing international tax provisions for U.S. multinationals. More specifically, proposals have been advanced that would eliminate the deferral of taxes on profits held abroad and eliminate the U.S. tax credit on taxes paid to foreign governments. The latter payments would be treated as expenses or reductions in taxable income rather than reductions in the amount of federal taxes owed.

As an impartial observer of the international business scene, you are commissioned by Congress to evaluate the long-run effects of the foregoing proposal on the international competitive position of U.S. multinationals and the implications of your findings for the U.S. economy.

To help make your point, consider the effects of the proposals on the profitability of identical investments made in Mexico by U.S., West German, and Japanese-owned subsidiaries in that country. In your case analysis, assume that a U.S. company, a West Germany company, and a Japanese company each own 100 percent of the voting shares of a foreign manufacturing corporation in Mexico. The Mexican affiliate of each produces a before-tax income of $500,000 annually and retains all earnings in the business. The income tax rate in Mexico is 42 percent. Recall that both Japan and West Germany, with effective tax rates of 56 and 40 percent, respectively, do not tax unremitted earnings. Book value of the Mexican investment is $3,000,000.

Required

1. Based on the foregoing assumptions, determine in comparative fashion what the effective tax rates and rates of return on equity will be for each investor assuming the United States adopts a policy of taxing unremitted earnings but allows a deemed foreign tax credit for foreign taxes paid.
2. Repeat the analysis called for in (1) but assume instead that Congress allows only a deduction for foreign taxes paid.
3. Discuss the major policy issues stemming from your analysis.

12

International
Standards
and Organizations

Internationalization of accounting standards is an endeavor of conflicts. Since in some countries accounting standards are established politically and in others through private professional mechanisms, there is the question of how international standards should be derived. Also, there is a question about appropriate underlying concepts. For instance, the concept of internationalization utilized by the agencies of the European Economic Community (EEC) is one of "harmonization." This means that different standards might prevail in individual countries, so long as they are "in harmony" with each other—meaning that they should not logically conflict. As we shall explain later, the Fourth Directive of the EEC permits not only historical cost financial accounting measurements but also price level-adjusted historical cost measurements and current cost measurements. So long as the basis of measurement is clearly disclosed and by allowing primary and supplementary disclosure of more than a single measurement basis, the EEC directive "harmonizes" utilization of several different financial accounting measurement approaches.

Standardization, on the other hand, means that a single standard or rule is applied to all situations. For instance, the inflation accounting standard in the United States is that historical cost-based financial statements are to be prepared as primary statements and general purchasing power-adjusted historical cost statements and/or current cost statements are in some cases to be furnished as supplementary schedules to the primary financial statements. Notice that "harmonization" allows, with appropriate disclosures, German firms to employ historical cost valuations and Dutch firms to employ replacement value valuations. "Standardization," as in the United States, means that all firms must prepare historical cost statements, and inflation effects recognition is limited to supplementary schedules.

Further conflicts come about through questions of applicability of internationalized accounting standards. Should all enterprises, large or small, in all industries of a given economy be subject to the same standards? Similarly, should highly developed countries be subject to the same accounting standards as less developed or developing countries? Are government-owned and operated companies in the so-called mixed economies as susceptible to accounting standards internationalization as private companies with wide ownership dispersion in the free or administered market economies? Internationalization of accounting standards is therefore best considered along several dimensions. After exploring the standardization issue further, we turn our attention to the major organizations involved in proposing and/or setting international financial accounting standards. Toward the end of the chapter, international organizations are covered which do not attempt to set standards on their own but encourage and support standardization goals.

Advantages of International Standards

At the Twelfth International Congress of Accountants in Mexico City in October 1982, John N. Turner, former minister of finance, Minister of Justice and Attorney-General of Canada, and first chairman of the Interim Committee of the International Monetary Fund, cited these advantages of "universally applicable standards":

> The greatest benefit that would flow from harmonization would be the comparability of international financial information. Such comparability would eliminate the current misunderstandings about the reliability of "foreign" financial statements and would remove one of the most important impediments to the flow of international investment. . . .
> A second advantage of harmonization would be the time and money saved that is currently spent to consolidate divergent financial information when more than one set of reports is required to comply with different national laws or practice. . . .
> A third improvement from harmonization would be the tendency for accounting standards throughout the world to be raised to the highest possible level and to be consistent with local economic, legal and social conditions.[1]

Supporting and Deterring Forces

To understand how harmonization or standardization in international accounting came about, it is helpful to gain an appreciation of the forces which tend to promote or deter these endeavors. Professor Stephen A. Zeff grappled

---

[1] John N. Turner, "International Harmonization: A Professional Goal," *Journal of Accountancy*, January 1983, pp. 58–59.

with this issue in a major address delivered at the 1981 annual meeting of the European Accounting Association. His catalog of positive or supporting factors follows:

1. The Press—the best example today being "The Financial Times," including its monthly "World Accounting Report" and its annual (critical) studies of the financial reporting practices of major world companies. Domestically, in the U.K. (1967–69), U.S. (1960's), and Australia (1960's), the Press has served as a forum for criticism. What has been the measure of the influence of the Press?

2. Textbooks—American textbooks are widely used in Canada, Australia, and Latin America. To what degree has the international adoption and use of textbooks led to a transfer of accounting technology?

3. The growth of multinationals and the insistence of the U.S. Securities and Exchange Commission that foreign subsidiaries use American "generally accepted accounting principles." Does accounting influence follow economic influence?

4. Amalgamation of public accounting firms, and the consequent growing influence of head-office training in developed and developing countries.

5. Growing importance of international capital markets and the perception by companies of the importance of having a respectable international image for financial reporting candor.

6. Activities of international lending agencies in encouraging the use of internationally "accepted" accounting (and auditing) practices by borrowers in developing countries. What countries' models are, in effect, being exported?

7. Actions by the International Accounting Standards Committee and the Organization for Economic Co-operation and Development. To what degree have these bodies, through their recommendations, furthered "harmonization"? The IASC has had difficulty in obtaining information from member countries about their success in gaining implementation, in accordance with their "best endeavours," of recommendations. Why, for example, has Australia (after at least four exposure drafts since 1968) still not adopted equity-method accounting for long-term investments after the U.K. (1971), the U.S. (1971), Canada (1972), New Zealand (1974), and the IASC (1976) all acted favorably?

8. Actions of regional groups such as the Union Européenne des Experts Comptables, Economiques et Financiers, the Asociación Interamericana de Contabilidad, and the Confederation of Asian and Pacific Accountants.

9. Practices of certain qualifying bodies of examining candidates in other than their home countries (e.g., Association of Certified Accountants, Institute of Cost and Management Accountants, Australian Society of Accountants).

10. Habit of students taking accounting degrees in other than their home countries and thereafter returning to practice or teach in their home countries (Malaysians in Australia, Australians and Canadians obtaining doctorates in the U.S.; Latin Americans in the U.S.).

11. Related to 10, the activities of American business schools in founding or guiding overseas business schools (e.g., London Business School, Manchester Business School, INSEAD, IESE, IMEDE, INCAE, ESAN, Getúlio Vargas School, IESA, IPADE). Also, the Canadian presence in Malaysia and Kenya.[2]

[2] Stephen A. Zeff, "The Forces at Play," paper delivered at the Annual Meeting of the European Accounting Association, 1981.

Deterring or conditioning forces were also identified by Professor Zeff. We interpret them as enumerated below.

1. *National pride.* As Theodore Wilkinson commented in 1969, "No accountant, no matter how eager a proponent of minimizing differences, willingly accepts the idea that someone else's accounting principles are better than his."
2. *Different audiences-of-interest.* Key objects of financial accounting and reporting in North America are investor and creditor groups; in Europe, labor unions, employees, and political officials serve as focal points.
3. *Different purposes of financial reports.* Key purposes may range from investment decision making and managerial control to taxation, social control, and national economic planning (some of these differences are discussed at greater length in Chapter 2).
4. *Differential development of capital markets.* Bayer AG in Germany reports that toward the end of 1981 it has 350,000 shareholders in 119 different countries. Yet Bayer shares are listed on only a handful of stock exchanges, which in turn have a large influence on the company's financial reporting format.
5. *Different legal systems.* The strong impact upon accounting and financial reporting of code law versus common law systems has been demonstrated throughout the book.
6. *Conflicts between parties seeking to have an impact on international standards.* As evidenced by the discussion later on in this chapter, the United Nations wants international accounting standards as a means to foster the interests of Third World countries and control MNC activities. On the other hand, the Financial Accounting Standards Board (FASB) in the United States does not wish to relinquish its national standard-setting jurisdiction and authority to any outside groups.
7. *Economic consequences.* These affect a company's ability to sell financial securities, affect the wealth of international banks and professional accounting service firms, and more generally impinge the allocation of economic resources.[3]

Applicability of International Standards

Internationalized accounting standards are applied either as a result of (a) international or political agreement, or (b) voluntary (or professionally encouraged) compliance. The application of the EEC accounting-related directives is an illustration of the first case. All other international standards efforts in accounting fall into the second category.

When accounting standards are applied through political, legal, or regulatory processes, there are typically statutory rules that govern the process. Interested parties determine what the underlying rules are, what implementation regulations relate to them, and how legal and regulatory cases have fine-tuned the process. This procedure is explained below as far as the ten member countries of the EEC are concerned. We note that the EEC is the only instance to date where a form of internationalization of accounting standards is broadly applicable and legally enforceable.

[3] Ibid.

All other international standards efforts in accounting are voluntary in nature and depend, for their acceptance, upon the goodwill of those using accounting standards. The easiest situation occurs when an international standard simply reiterates a national standard. In such a case there is no conflict, and acceptance and compliance with national standards can then be said to extend to acceptance of and compliance with international standards as well.

When national and international standards differ one from the other, present practices accord "primacy" to national standards. For privately promulgated international standards there exists therefore a hierarchy of priority from national standards to international standards. Where business competition or financial market pressures have pushed multinational enterprises into or toward using international accounting standards, they then do so concurrently with accepting and using national standards requirements. Such multiple acceptance, in most cases, necessarily results in multiple financial reporting—once according to applicable national standards and once more (concurrently) according to established international standards. The multiple approach to financial reporting by MNCs is likely to gain momentum as the internationalization of accounting standards proceeds.

On the applicability of international accounting standards to small and large, uninational and multinational, service and manufacturing firms alike, there is the implied intention of all international standard setters and recommenders that their standards should apply as comprehensively as possible. Thus, type-of-business distinctions are out of place here. The International Accounting Standards Committee (IASC) has deliberately addressed the topic of *Disclosures in Financial Statements of Banks* to make the point that its standards apply more widely than merchandising and industrial enterprises alone.[4]

In fact, though, enterprise size and degree of multinationality are likely variables of discrimination. Small and medium-sized national companies are not very likely to need, or, for that matter, accept, sophisticated international standards. They are best served by their respective national standards, which quite often discriminate even further between publicly and closely held companies. For example, closely held companies in the United States are exempted from several requirements of the FASB.

Multinational enterprises or larger national enterprises tapping international money capital markets are the prime targets for the internationalization of accounting standards. It is with these types of companies in mind that many international accounting standards are set in the first place. Therefore acceptance of international accounting standards, as far as it has come and is likely to continue to come in the near future, is significantly centered in multinationally active companies.

Varied Reactions

As the title of a recent article by P. Graham Corbett expressed it, "Having invented a better mousetrap, how do you persuade the world's ratcatchers to

---

[4] London: IASC, 1980 (Discussion Paper).

use it?"[5] To put a broadened perspective on the international standards issue, published opinions are reproduced below—one each from a standard setter, a member of the practicing profession, and an MNC president.

Addressing the May 1982 meeting of the Council of the American Institute of Certified Public Accountants (AICPA), J. A. Burggraaff, then Chairman of the Board of the IASC, observed:

> In more and more countries, standards are published on a growing number of subjects, going into increasing detail. And more and more, national standards diverge. Some countries require what others prohibit. This state of affairs is of concern to business enterprises and to the accounting profession. Clearly, life would be much easier for business and for auditors if accounting standards were in harmony worldwide.
>
> The IASC has undertaken that harmonization. We are developing accounting standards that are meant to be truly international. That implies that we have no intention of copying the standards of any individual country, even if such country has a long and profound experience in this field.[6]

Forbes magazine mentions a senior West German accountant's "go slow" note:

> According to Reinhard Goerdeler, chairman of Klynveld Main Goerdeler, the Amsterdam-based affiliate of Main Hurdman and one of the five largest accounting firms in the world, one of the basic problems has been a drive for *too much* standardization. After all, corporations must respond to the varying social, political and economic pressures of their individual nations, and cannot be expected to subscribe to an all-purpose accounting system.[7]

Dirk de Bruyne, president of Royal Dutch Petroleum Company and Chairman of the Committee of Managing Directors of the Royal Dutch/Shell Group of Companies, would like to see some agreement on "basics" before international standard-setting proceeds much farther:

> A regular forum of the national bodies that could reach an agreement on the fundamentals of accounting theory, and that would seek to promote adoption and adaptation of national standards for reasonable compliance with that theory, would be highly desirable.[8]

We recognize, of course, that not all commentary about international standards is applicable to each and every one of the numerous standard-setting bodies.

For purposes of our exposition, we start from the premise that all international accounting groups and organizations are either directly engaged in

---

[5] *CA Magazine*, July 1978, pp. 36–39.

[6] J. A. Burggraaff, "IASC Developments: An Update," *Journal of Accountancy*, September 1982, p. 106.

[7] "A Little Harmony," *Forbes*, December 7, 1981, p. 153.

[8] Dirk de Bruyne, "Global Standards: A Tower of Babel?" *Financial Executive*, February 1980, p. 37.

standard-setting activites or actively sponsor and support standardization or harmonization. Four categories of organizations are utilized: (1) political, (2) private professional, (3) regional, and (4) supportive. There is no order of importance or other value judgment in the chosen sequence of presentation.

THE POLITICAL ARENA

From an accounting perspective, political power means control. In turn accounting can be used as a control device. The EEC Council has the objective to control the 10 member countries to the extent that their legal systems and requirements are in harmony with each other. The U.N. General Assembly is eager to provide political power to the smaller among its 153 member nations, especially with respect to controlling the activities of MNCs. The Organization for Economic Cooperation and Development (OECD) with 24 member countries represents the industrialized Western nations to establish, if nothing else, a counterweight (i.e., influence or degree of control) to the United Nations, the International Confederation of Free Trade Unions (ICFTU), the World Bank, and so forth. The African Accounting Council is a 23-member country group seeking to control outside accounting influences targeted for the African continent.

To reiterate an earlier point, only the EEC has full enforcement powers for its directives across the national borders of its ten member nations. Thus, national political sovereignty is subordinated in some important respects to the will of the Community. This is a far-reaching and highly significant first in Western civilization.

All other pronouncements of international accounting standards are not legally enforceable and depend upon voluntary acquiescence or indirect economic or social pressures for their acceptance. Therefore, from an implementation and enforcement point of view, the EEC is uniquely situated.

European Economic Community (EEC)

When the Treaty of Rome established the EEC on March 25, 1957, a specific objective was cited as "the approximation of their respective national laws to the extent required for the Common Market to function in an orderly manner." Since codes of commerce and/or companies or corporation laws were on the books of all member countries, the EEC Commission embarked upon a major program of EEC company law harmonization almost from the start.

The process by which this is done entails various preliminary work leading to the issuance of a so-called "draft directive" (i.e., exposure draft) by the EEC Commission. Hearings and various other evaluation procedures are then conducted and a given draft directive may be reissued several times over. When the Commission finally feels that a draft directive is broadly acceptable, it submits it to the member states for ratification after approval to do so from the EEC Council of Ministers.

A distinction is necessary here between regulations, directives, decisions, recommendations, and opinions. With regard to the implementation of the Treaty of Rome and with specific respect to the EEC Council and the Commission, regulations are of general application and binding in every respect with the direct force of law in every member state. Directives are binding on member states to which they are addressed with respect to the results to be achieved, but mode and means of implementation are left to the discretion of national authorities. Decisions, whether addressed to governments or companies or private individuals, are binding in every respect on the party or parties named. Recommendations and opinions are not binding.

Since EEC directives (or drafts thereof) cover all aspects of companies law, we propose to single out only those that have a direct bearing on accounting.

Fourth Directive.   The EEC's Fourth Directive, issued on July 26, 1978, is the broadest and most comprehensive set of accounting rules existing within the EEC framework. Both public and private companies must comply. As of August 1982, Denmark and the United Kingdom had officially adopted legislation to implement the Directive. Belgium, West Germany, Italy, and the Netherlands had appropriate draft laws pending, and no published information was yet available from France, Greece, Ireland, and Luxembourg.

> Under the Directive, the annual financial statements must include a balance sheet, an income statement, and notes to financial statements. Although there is no requirement for a statement of changes in financial position or for a statement of changes in stockholders' equity, member countries may adopt legislation requiring them.
>
> The overriding requirement is for the financial statements and their footnotes to give a "true and fair view" of a company's financial position and results of its operations. There is a general presumption that if a company complies with the Directive's provisions, it will meet this requirement. However, member countries may require companies to disclose additional information, or they may specify circumstances under which companies must depart from certain provisions. The EEC encourages whatever disclosures are necessary to give a "true and fair view."
>
> The Directive does not say exactly what it means by a "true and fair view." Although the concept has been fundamental to financial statements in the United Kingdom for some thirty years, precisely what it requires has been a matter of individual judgment. Generally, management should provide *all* the information that a financial statement user needs to have the same view of a company's true position as does management. If the Directive's provisions are insufficient, a company must present enough additional information for users to have a true and fair view of its financial position and operating results. In U.S. terminology, auditors' reports refer to financial statements being "fairly presented" in conformity with generally accepted accounting principles. Thus, the U.K. term "true and fair view" is substantially the same in concept as "fairly presented."
>
> The Directive allows member countries to select one or both of the alternative balance sheet formats. A member country may prescribe a horizontal balance sheet format (similar to the format used in the United States, except that items are presented in reverse order of liquidity), a vertical format (a narrative form that arrives at shareholders' equity by deducting each classification of liabilities from its respective classification of assets) or both formats.

For the income statement, member countries may select from four formats. They may choose between horizontal and vertical formats (or both), and between classifying expenses by nature or by function. In the U.S., income statements are generally vertical and expenses are classified by function.

If a member country adopts all the prescribed formats, each company may select the one it considers the most appropriate.

The Directive also requires specific financial statement captions. No matter which format it uses, a company must disclose a required amount of detail under these captions:

> Main headings, representing major financial statement classifications (e.g., current assets).
>
> Subheadings, representing financial statement components (e.g., inventory).
>
> Subsidiary subheadings, representing detailed financial statement captions (e.g., raw materials, work in process, and finished goods).

The Directive requires extensive detail. The prescribed horizontal balance sheet format, for instance, includes 11 main headings, 13 subheadings, and 44 subsidiary subheadings.

The overriding requirement—that companies must give a true and fair view—holds true for footnote disclosures, just as it does for financial statements. Therefore, companies may have to make disclosures beyond those specifically required, which are:

> A description of major accounting policies.
>
> A list of affiliates in which a company holds 20% or more of shares.
>
> Details of changes in shareholders' equity and the number of shares in each class of stock outstanding. (Note that a statement of changes in shareholders' equity is not required.)
>
> Details of long-term and secured debt.
>
> Details of commitments and contingencies, including separate disclosure of pension obligations.
>
> Segment information, including sales by type of product and by geographical area. A company may omit this information if it is "seriously prejudicial" to its activities.
>
> The average number of employees and total personnel cost—for example, wages, social security, and pensions by category of employees.
>
> Directors' compensation, loans, and advances.
>
> Differences between income taxes currently payable and the amount charged to operations, and the extent to which operating results have been affected by special income tax incentives.

Financial statement elements must be stated in accordance with certain fundamental accounting concepts, including historical cost, going concern, prudence, accrual accounting, and consistency. The Directive also requires the following specific practices and alternatives:

> *Property, plant and equipment*— Fixed assets with a limited useful economic life must be depreciated by systematic annual charges to operations. If a member country allows any special tax incentives that result in excessive depreciation charges to income for any period, companies must disclose the nature and amount of the charge.

Intangible assets—Amounts capitalized, such as goodwill, formation and start-up expenses, and research and development costs, should be amortized over a period no longer than five years. If they wish, member countries may authorize a longer period of amortization for research and development costs and for goodwill—but the period may not exceed the asset's economic useful life.

Inventories—Stated amounts must be valued at the lower of cost or market. Member countries may allow actual cost, FIFO, LIFO, weighted average, or a similar cost method. Or they may allow more than one of these methods. If there is a material difference between replacement cost and the stated amount at the balance sheet date, as happens with LIFO, companies must disclose the difference.

Current assets—Individual items should be valued at the lower of cost (purchase price or production cost) or market.

Liabilities—All foreseeable liabilities and potential losses must be provided for, even if they become apparent after year end.

Inflation accounting—Member countries may either permit or require companies to present primary or supplementary inflation-adjusted financial statements. The member country's legislation should specify in detail the methods companies must follow in arriving at reported amounts. The Directive lists the following possible bases for this accounting:

1. Revaluation of tangible fixed assets (i.e., property, plant and equipment) and financial fixed assets, such as investments or loans.
2. Replacement cost for plant, equipment, and inventories.
3. Valuation of all financial statement items by a method designed to recognize the effects of inflation.

By 1985, the Commission must advise the Council to reexamine the historical cost–inflation adjusted issue in light of economic and monetary trends in the EEC.[9]

Directive to publish interim financial reports. The Directive to Publish Interim Financial Reports, issued on February 15, 1982, applies to all companies whose shares are listed on a stock exchange in a Common Market country. No reporting currency is specified in the Directive, which means that any EEC currency should be acceptable for reporting purposes. Reporting language must be acceptable to the respective national authorities. Interim reports published outside the EEC may be acceptable if equivalent information is disclosed.

The Directive becomes effective in the individual countries no later than June 30, 1983, and calls for publication of the six-months statement within four months of the end of the accounting period. Companies must provide an explanatory statement that enables a comparison to be made with the corresponding period of the preceding year. The report need not be audited but it must contain as minimum information:

Net turnover and profit or loss before or after tax

An explanatory statement describing the previous year's results

[9] Reprinted from Ernst & Whinney, *Fourth Directive—European Company Law* (New York: E & W International Series, 1980), pp. 4–6.

Results and trends of the company's activities in the current six months

Any special factors influencing those activities

The explanatory statement should also describe, as far as possible, the company's likely future development in the current year. The report may be prepared on either a consolidated or nonconsolidated basis.

The Directive requiring the six-months report affects both companies in the Common Market and foreign companies whose shares are listed on a Common Market stock exchange. United States companies and others that prepare interim financial statements in the normal course of events may use such statements to comply with the Directive. European companies that ordinarily do not prepare interim financials will have to prepare special statements to meet the requirements.

Proposed Fifth Directive.   Included in the proposed Fifth Directive, issued on September 29, 1972, are proposals dealing with the structure, management, and outside audits of larger corporations. The draft anticipates a two-tier corporate board system based on the German or Dutch models—thereby rejecting the classical management structure prevalent in the United Kingdom. For this and several other reasons raised since the January 1, 1973, admission of Denmark, the Republic of Ireland, and the United Kingdom to EEC membership, the proposed Fifth Directive has been withdrawn for the time being. How the resulting vacuum is to be filled cannot yet be determined. Perhaps the directive will be redrafted and perhaps its auditing provisions will become the subject of a separate draft directive. We are unable at this time to forecast the likely outcome of the present holding action. Discussion of the matter in the European Parliament is the most likely next step.

Seventh Directive.   The Seventh Directive, issued on June 13, 1983, has been controversial since its initial proposal in 1976. It addresses the issue of consolidated financial statements on which we commented earlier in Chapter 6.

As adopted, the Seventh Directive represents a major compromise between the EEC Council of Ministers and the interests of the member states. National implementation of this Directive is obligatory by January 1, 1988, with mandatory application to consolidated financial statements for financial years beginning January 1, 1990. Under the Directive, the member states are given wide latitude for optional details of consolidation requirements in individual national legislation.

Fundamentally, the Seventh Directive requires consolidation where either the parent or subsidiary company is a limited liability company, regardless of the location of its registered office. Legal power of control determines the consolidation requirement. Control exists if the parent company has:

1. Majority of voting rights, or
2. Right to appoint majority of board of directors, or
3. Right to exercise dominant influence pursuant to a control contract, or

4. Control over majority of voting rights pursuant to agreement with other shareholders.

There are specified exemptions for sub-group consolidations within the EEC. Outright grounds for non-consolidation include:

1. Undertaking is of negligible importance.
2. Severe long-term restrictions exist.
3. There is disproportionate expense or undue delay.
4. Share are held for subsequent resale.

Fifty-one articles comprise the Seventh Directive. They cover, aside from the foregoing, items like:

1. Different methods to account for business combinations (see discussion in Chapter 6)
2. Equity method accounting for holdings in associated companies
3. Direct tie-in to the provisions of the Fourth Directive
4. Line-by-line consolidation methodology
5. Treatment of good will (positive and negative)
6. Exemption of banks and insurance companies
7. Listing of applicable accounting principles (e.g., consistency and inter-company eliminations)
8. Extensive disclosure requirements
9. Auditing
10. Periodic reporting

Issuance of the Seventh Directive significantly solidified and extended the financial accounting and reporting goals of the EEC.

Proposed Eighth Directive.   The proposed Eighth Directive was published in May 1978 and amended in December 1979. This proposal addresses the professional qualifications of statutory auditors. It is mainly concerned with educational and professional training as well as examination requirements. There are draft requirements relating to professional independence and the formation of professional companies or associations. Transitional arrangements are proposed for persons entitled now to carry out statutory audits but who do not fulfill the requirements of the proposed directive. Moreover, there is a stipulation that each member state maintain an official list of authorized statutory auditors.

Other proposals.   Beginning in 1981, the EEC Commission began to publish directives aimed at industry-specific financial statements. For example, there now exist unnumbered proposed directives on financial statements of banks, insurance companies, and branches of banks headquartered outside the EEC.

Banks and insurance companies were specifically excluded from the provisions of the Fourth Directive. It is unclear how these latest proposals will be handled by the European Parliament, the Council of Ministers, and the Economic and Social Committee. Some expediting procedures at the various approval levels can probably be expected with regard to these more narrowly focused proposals.

Organization for Economic Cooperation and Development (OECD)

The OECD is an international organization established in 1960 by the governments of 24 of the world's most industrialized countries. The OECD Convention was signed in Paris on December 14, 1960.

In January, 1975 the Council of the OECD established a Committee on International Investment and Multinational Enterprises (CIIME). In June 1976, the OECD issued its Declaration on Investment in Multinational Enterprises. The Annex to this Declaration contains financial reporting guidelines for multinational enterprises. The guidelines on "Disclosure of Information" follow:

> Enterprises should, having due regard to their nature and relative size in the economic context of their operations and to requirements of business confidentiality and to cost, publish in a form suited to improve public understanding a sufficient body of factual information on the structure, activities and policies of the enterprise as a whole, as a supplement, in so far as necessary for this purpose, to information to be disclosed under the national law of the individual countries in which they operate. To this end, they should publish within reasonable time limits, on a regular basis, but at least annually, financial statements and other pertinent information relating to the enterprise as a whole, comprising in particular:
>
> i.   The structure of the enterprise, showing the name and location of the parent company, its main affiliates, its percentage ownership, direct and indirect, in these affiliates, including shareholdings, between them;
>
> ii.   the geographical areas where operations are carried out and the principal activities carried on therein by the parent company and main affiliates;
>
> iii. the operating results and sales by geographical area and the sales in the major lines of business for the enterprise as a whole;
>
> iv.   significant new capital investment by geographical area and, as far as practicable, by major lines of business for the enterprise as a whole;
>
> v.   a statement of the sources and uses of funds by the enterprises as a whole;
>
> vi.   the average number of employees in each geographical area;
>
> vii. research and development expenditure for the enterprise as a whole;
>
> viii. the policies followed in respect of intra-group pricing;
>
> ix.   the accounting policies including those on consolidation, observed in compiling the published information.[10]

In a follow-up step in 1978, CIIME established an Ad Hoc Working Group on Accounting Standards. The Group reviewed private and government efforts underway in member countries and at international organizations

---

[10] Organization for Economic Cooperation and Development, *International Investment and Multinational Enterprises*, pamphlet (Paris: OECD, 1976), pp. 14–15.

to improve the comparability of accounting standards. Acting upon a report of the Ad Hoc Group, CIIME organized a permanent Working Group on Accounting Standards in 1979 with a mandate to

> Support existing efforts (by states, groups of states, and international professional bodies) aimed at increasing accounting standards comparability;
>
> Provide technical clarifications of the accounting terms contained in the *Disclosure of Information* chapter of the *1976 OECD Guidelines;* and
>
> Function as a forum for an exchange of views on U.N. work on accounting and disclosure standards.[11]

During 1980 the Working Group devoted the major portion of its time to the clarification of a number of accounting terms contained in the disclosure of information guidelines listed above. It agreed on clarifications for sales, new capital investment, and average number of employees. These clarifications were formally approved by CIIME in December 1980.

In 1981 the Group continued work on clarification of additional accounting terms. It approved a paper on *Accounting Policies, Sources and Uses of Funds and Research and Development Expenditures.* Working sessions were held on the 1980 OECD survey study entitled *International Investments and Multinational Enterprises—Accounting Practices in OECD Member Countries.* These discussions focused on definitions of operating results and segment disclosures. Agreement was also reached on actions to promote comparability and harmonization of international accounting standards. There is to be a regular exchange of information on national standard setting developments and appropriate contacts with standard setting bodies. Special problem areas are to be addressed in subgroups.

The first harmonization problem area chosen for consideration in a subgroup was the relationship between taxation and financial reporting. The subgroup's mandate was to identify the main differences in approaches to this issue, the consequences of the differences, and solutions to any problems arising. There was considerable disagreement over the extent and manner in which the subgroup's report should refer to the desirability of separation between rules governing reporting for taxes and financial reporting.

The full Group's May 1982 session produced a comprehensive future work program. In regard to its efforts to promote greater comparability of accounting standards, the Group agreed to begin consideration of the issue of consolidation, and to have a subgroup consider foreign currency translation. Initiating a new phase of its work, the application of the disclosure of information guidelines to the service industry, the Group agreed to consider banking questions and insurance issues. The Group also continued discussion of its paper on operating results and segmentation.[12]

---

[11] U.S. Department of State, Office of Investment Affairs, *Current Status Report* (Wash., D.C.: OIA, July 1982), p. 21.

[12] The last two paragraphs describing OECD activities and the following subsection on UN activities are adopted, with permission, from *Current Status Report: Selected Interna-*

United Nations

In 1973, in response to a resolution of the United Nations Economic and Social Council (ECOSOC), the Secretary General appointed a group to study the impact of multinational corporations on development and international relations. In its report, issued in 1974, the group noted a serious lack of both financial and nonfinancial information in usable form about the activities of transnational corporations, as well as the limited comparability of corporate reports. The report recommended that a group of experts be convened under the auspices of the Commission on Transnational Corporations (TNCs), an intergovernmental subsidiary body of the Council, to consider the formation of an international system of standardized accounting and reporting. The recommendation was endorsed by the Commission and the Council and, in 1976, the Secretary General appointed a Group of Experts on International Standards of Accounting and Reporting.

The Group of Experts consisted of 14 members from diverse backgrounds and geographic areas. In 1977, the Group issued a four-part report, *International Standards of Accounting and Reporting for Transnational Corporations,* which was submitted to the Secretary General. The report and the recommendations of the Secretary General were presented at the fourth session of the Commission held in May 1978. However, the report was not adopted, primarily because the members of the Group of Experts were not government representatives of their respective countries.

Instead, the Commission on TNCs recommended that ECOSOC establish a new, intergovernmental group to formulate priorities for further steps in the field of international standards of accounting and reporting. The new group was to be comprised of experts selected by governments. The Commission also recommended that the group focus on accounting and reporting standards as they related to concurrent other U.N. efforts and discussions on a code of conduct relative to TNCs. In the fall of 1979, ECOSOC approved the Commission's recommendation. An Ad Hoc Intergovernmental Working Group of Experts on International Standards of Accounting and Reporting (The Group) was appointed. It consisted of 34 members all of whom are governmental representatives. It allowed observers from the International Accounting Standards Committee, the International Federation of Accountants, the International Confederation of Free Trade Unions, and the International Chamber of Commerce.

Consistent with its ECOSOC mandate, the Group reviewed Paragraph 43 (on public information disclosure) of the proposed U.N. Code of Conduct relating to TNCs. The Group reached basic agreement on a new draft text for Paragraph 43, which it submitted to the Code Intergovernmental Working Group (IGWG) for consideration. The Code group did not accept the Accounting Group's text as a draft Code provision and instead drafted its own

tional Organization Activities Relating to Transnational Enterprises (U.S. Department of State, Office of Investment Affairs, July 1982).

text. The latest (Fall 1982) version of the text in question is reprodu(
Table 7.5.

Aside from its efforts on Paragraph 43 the Group engaged in subst
follow-up discussion of financial and nonfinancial information for disc
by the enterprise as a whole and by individual member enterprises. In A
1981 the Group submitted its interim report.

1981–1982 U.N. recommendations.   The 1981 interim report
Ad Hoc Intergovernmental Working Group reflects wide divergence of
on many matters. The Group tried to come up with its own list of ite1
disclosure, but experienced difficulty in reaching a common position on
points, including in particular such fundamental issues as segmentation
counts, treatment of depreciation, classification, and questions of val(
The Group also could not reach agreement on the fundamental assump1
accounting: whether TNCs should provide "accurate and honest" fin
statements (favored by the less developed countries) or whether they :
present a "true and fair view" (favored by developed countries). There w
widespread disagreement on the nature of information disclosed by indi
member enterprises, and particularly on disclosure of financial items. Ho
there was a somewhat greater degree of consensus on financial items f
closure by the enterprise as a whole.

Significantly, the Group's report endorsed a number of principle
Group (1) agreed that the principle of nondiscrimination between TN(
national enterprises should be observed in the application of general-p
reporting requirements; (2) in defining the scope of disclosure, stress
need to bear in mind materiality; and (3) agreed that the term *enterprise*
be used in preference to the term *company.*

In 1982, the Group prepared its final report. Part of the final repo
ply incorporates material from the interim report. However, in a sectic
viding further review of the 1977 Expert Group's report, the final
stresses that accounting and reporting by TNCs should take into acco(
information needs of both home and host countries; that comparability
formation is an important factor; that costs of providing information
bear a reasonable relationship to the benefits to be derived therefrom; a1
business confidentiality should be taken into account. Minimum lists of
cial and nonfinancial items for disclosure are included as an annex to the
(with disagreements on particular items noted). The Group recommen
the Commission that TNCs should take into account the Group's discuss
financial and nonfinancial information, particularly the agreed items. I1
tion, the Group agreed that ". . . with regard to information disclosu
principle of nondiscrimination between individual enterprises of transn;
corporations and national individual member enterprises should be ob;
in a manner not inconsistent with the relevant provisions of the future C
Conduct."[13] These formulations are significant in that they clearly i1

[13] Ibid., pp. 4–5.

both the voluntary nature of the Group's recommendations and support for the national treatment principle.

The Group was not able to make a unified recommendation on future U.N. activities in the accounting area. Accordingly, the final report indicates that most delegates (i.e., those from the developing countries and the Europeans) recommend to the Commission that a permanent intergovernmental working group of experts on international standards of accounting and reporting be established which would meet annually for two weeks (essentially a continuation of the present Group on a permanent basis). However, other delegations (i.e., the United States and Japan) recommended an ad hoc group be authorized to meet periodically (approximately once every two years) *after* the adoption of the Code of Conduct. Nevertheless, there was a general consensus that any new group should have a relatively limited mandate, and specifically should (1) consider issues of accounting and reporting falling within the TNC Commission's work, (2) take into account the Ad Hoc Group's work, (3) consult with international bodies, (4) and report to the Commission on further steps to be taken in pursuit of the long-term objective of international harmonization.

At its meeting in Manila in September 1982, the Commission on TNCs recommended that an experts group be established to meet no more than once a year to review developments in the field but not set standards. There will be a review after three years of the advisability of continuing the group. ECOSOC needs to endorse this recommendation in order to become effective.

Mixed responses.   The U.N. foray into international accounting standard setting has met with mixed international reactions. The general director of research for the CICA in Canada feels that "accounting standards are best set in the private sector."[14] The International Chamber of Commerce said, "The expressed UN objectives would be better served through outright support of the work of the IASC and national accounting groups."[15] Similar sentiments were expressed by the International Organization of Employees (IOE).

In an official position dated September 2, 1982, the U.S. Financial Executives Institute (FEI) stated:

> FEI reaffirms a previous position that setting international accounting standards should be left to established and functioning bodies in the private sector (i.e., the International Accounting Standards Committee). It states that, before reports are required, the need for information should be established, the information required should be more precisely defined and, if such reports are determined to be necessary, they should be required on a consolidated basis only.[16]

[14] "UN to Set Accounting Standards?" *CA Magazine,* November 1978, p. 12.

[15] "Disclosure Rules for International Firms Proposed by UN Are Arousing Opposition," *Wall Street Journal,* May 4, 1978, p. 8.

[16] Financial Executives Institute, "Official Positions of the Institute," *FEI Bulletin,* No. 309, October 25, 1982, p. 7.

African Accounting Council (AAC)

The AAC is the most recently organized international accounting organization, dating from June 1979. Although there were several years of preliminary discussions and several preparatory conferences, it was not until the aforementioned date that representatives from 27 African countries gathered in Algiers to organize the AAC.

Membership in the AAC is open to countries belonging to the Organization for African Unity and that approve the AAC's Constitution.

The primary objectives of AAC may be summarized as follows:[17]

1. Promote standardization of accounting among African countries
2. Encourage education and training in accountancy
3. Sponsor and undertake research in accounting matters and related disciplines
4. Promote the development of African accounting teaching materials and provide for publication, translation and distribution of works in the field of accounting by African authors
5. Stimulate regular contacts and exchanges between members of the AAC and other African accounting specialists and experts
6. Establish communication links with international organizations and with professional associations in other countries whose works and activities are similar to or of interest to the AAC
7. Promote the use of standardized management accounting methods so as to facilitate the flow of management information between African countries

The effectiveness of the AAC is as yet undetermined. As is apparent from the foregoing list of objectives, the AAC is not only a standard-setting group but also an information facilitator and an administrative liaison agent. Broadly speaking, the AAC has the goal of assisting in the overall economic development of Africa.

The AAC Assembly plans to meet at three-year intervals. Its president, two vice-presidents, an Executive Committee, and a secretary-general will carry out its continuing professional activities. An initial major activity is the conduct of a survey of accounting and accountants in the 27 member countries.

PRIVATE-SECTOR PROFESSIONAL EFFORTS

In sharp contrast to the politically based standard-setting activities just described, there is a more convincing and by most measures more successful endeavor underway within the accounting profession itself. While the private-sector efforts lack the compelling implementation force of law, they enjoy deep-seated and widespread professional sympathy and support. Inter-

---

[17] "Accounting Council Aiming for Far-Ranging Impact," *World Accounting Report,* August 1979, p. 18.

national cooperation or standardization is always a risky business. Yet, in accounting, immense forward progress has been made in this respect since the formation of the IASC in 1973. In a quiet and often frustratingly patient way, the international professional bodies have been able to garner respect for their activities. To be sure, there are many outspoken critics and the actual application of recommended international standards is still quite limited. However, there are a great many more enthusiastic supporters of private professional international standard setting than there are detractors. As far as your authors are aware, there has been no national legislation prohibiting or constraining any standards recommendation of private professional accounting bodies. Also, there have been no legal actions seeking "cease and desist" judgments. While a full battery of problems still plagues the private international accounting standards movement, many notable recent successes must be acknowledged. There can be little doubt that the international standards movement is here to stay.

Four important standard-setting bodies are covered in this section—two worldwide in scope and two regional. By the very nature and scope of its activities, the IASC is the most significant of the four in terms of accounting standards.

International Accounting
Standards Committee (IASC)

In 1973, IASC was founded by agreement between professional accounting organizations in 9 countries. By 1982, about 50 countries were represented among its members. The scope of IASC activities covers:

> The international professional activities of the accountancy bodies were organised under the International Federation of Accountants (IFAC) in 1977. In 1981, IASC and IFAC agreed that IASC has full and complete autonomy in the setting of international accounting standards and in the issue of discussion documents on international accounting issues. . . .
>
> Specifically, the objectives of IASC contained in its Constitution are:
>
> (a) to formulate and publish in the public interest accounting standards to be observed in the presentation of financial statements and to promote their worldwide acceptance and observance;
>
> (b) to work generally for the improvement and harmonisation of regulations, accounting standards and procedures relating to the presentation of financial statements. . . .
>
> The essence of IASC's work is the worldwide harmonisation and improvement of accounting principles used in the preparation of financial statements for the benefit of the public. The achievement of this is not adversely affected by the more detailed requirements of some countries nor the need for adaptation to national circumstances.[18]

---

[18] International Accounting Standards Committee, *Objectives and Procedures* (London: IASC, 1982).

The operating structure of IASC covers a broad spectrum of interested parties. It consists of the following:

The IASC Board. The business of IASC is conducted by the Board assisted by a full-time Secretariat.

The Consultative Group. International organisations representing many of the principal preparers of financial statements participate in the Consultative Group.

Steering Committees. Steering Committees are formed to consider the issues relating to a particular accounting topic.

Liaison with national standard-setting bodies. To be fully aware of the difficulties facing individual national standard-setting bodies IASC believes close liaison is required.[19]

The operating procedures involved in producing an International Accounting Standard (IAS) are comprised of the following steps:

(a) After discussion, the IASC Board selects a topic that is felt to need an International Accounting Standard, and assigns it to a Steering Committee. All IASC member bodies are invited to submit material for consideration.

(b) The Steering Committee, assisted by the IASC Secretariat, considers the issues involved and presents a point outline on the subject to the Board.

(c) The Steering Committee receives the comments of the Board and prepares a preliminary draft of the proposed standard.

(d) Following review by the Board, the draft is circulated to all member bodies for their comments.

(e) The Steering Committee prepares a revised draft, which, after approval by at least two-thirds of the Board, is published as an Exposure Draft. Comments are invited from all interested parties.

(f) At each stage in the consideration of drafts, member bodies refer for guidance to the appropriate accounting research committees in their own organisations.

(g) At the end of the exposure period (usually six months) comments are submitted to IASC and are considered by the Steering Committee responsible for the project.

(h) The Steering Committee then submits a revised draft to the Board for approval as an International Accounting Standard.

(i) The issue of a Standard requires approval by at least three-quarters of the Board, after which the approved text of the Standard is sent to all member bodies for translation and publication.[20]

To carry out this process takes approximately three years.

Through mid-1983, the following final standards have been produced:

IAS-1   Disclosure of Accounting Policies

IAS-2   Valuation and Presentation of Inventories in the Context of the Historical Cost System

IAS-3   Consolidated Financial Statements

[19] Ibid.
[20] Ibid.

IAS-4   Depreciation Accounting

IAS-5   Information to Be Disclosed in Financial Statements

IAS-6   Accounting Responses to Changing Prices

IAS-7   Statement of Changes in Financial Position

IAS-8   Unusual and Prior Period Items and Changes in Accounting Policies

IAS-9   Accounting for Research and Development Activities

IAS-10   Contingencies and Events Occurring after the Balance Sheet Data

IAS-11   Accounting for Construction Contracts

IAS-12   Accounting for Taxes on Income

IAS-13   Presentation of Current Assets and Current Liabilities

IAS-14   Reporting Financial Information by Segment

IAS-15   Information Reflecting the Effects of Changing Prices

IAS-16   Accounting for Property, Plant and Equipment

IAS-17   Accounting for Leases

IAS-18   Revenue Recognition

IAS-19   Accounting for Retirement Benefits in the Financial Statements of Employers

IAS-20   Accounting for Government Grants and Disclosure of Government Assistance

IAS-21   Accounting for the Effects of Changes in Foreign Exchange Rates

Recognition and support for IASC and its standards.   The degree of international awareness of IASC's work is reflected best in the IASC *Objectives and Procedures* brochure:

> Standing alone, neither the IASC nor the accountancy profession has the power to enforce international agreement or to require compliance with International Accounting Standards. The success of IASC's efforts is dependent upon recognition and support for its work from many different interested groups acting within the limits of their own jurisdiction.
>
> Recognition of IASC's work comes from groups such as:
>
> (a)   The international bodies representing financial institutions, financial executives, trade unions, employers, stock exchanges and financial analysts involved in the Consultative Group.
>
> (b)   The United Nations (UN) and the Organization for Economic Co-operation and Development (OECD) which began discussing accounting and disclosure policies in the late 1970s. Both organizations invited IASC to participate at an early stage and IASC has been involved in the discussions ever since.
>
> Support for IASC's work comes from groups such as:
>
> (a)   The International Federation of Accountants (IFAC) representing the professional accountancy bodies, which fully supports the work of IASC and recognises IASC as the sole body having responsibility and authority to issue pronouncements on international accounting standards with full authority in so doing to negotiate and associate with outside bodies, and to promote the worldwide acceptance and observance of those standards.

In the Mutual Commitments of IASC and IFAC the professional accountancy bodies continue the support of the work of IASC by:

   (i)   publishing every International Accounting Standard approved for issue by the Board of IASC; and by

   (ii)   using their best endeavours to persuade Governments, national standard-setting bodies, regulatory bodies and the financial, industrial and business community, that published financial statements should comply in all material respects with International Accounting Standards and should disclose the fact; and by

   (iii)   using their best endeavours to ensure that auditors satisfy themselves that International Accounting Standards are complied with in all material respects.

  (b)   National stock exchanges which have long been supporters of the work of IASC in many important business centres. An increasing number accept from foreign registrants financial statements prepared in accordance in International Accounting Standards.

  (c)   Regional groups of accountants, such as the Groupe d'Etudes, Confederation of Asian and Pacific Accountants, Union Européenes des Experts Comptables, Inter-American Accounting Association.[21]

Many professional accounting groups around the world actively seek compliance with IASC standards. The 1976 Australian policy reads as follows:

> Each future Australian Accounting Standard will be drafted only after a detailed consideration of the relevant International Accounting Standard (if in existence) and the Australian Standard will refer to any unavoidable divergence between the two. Consequently, conformity with Australian Accounting Standards should normally result in conformity also with International Accounting Standards.[22]

The Malaysian Association of CPAs has made it mandatory for its members to comply with IAS Nos. 1 to 10.

In Canada, the Toronto Stock Exchange is an active supporter of IASC's work:

> In 1980, the chief executive officers of the Toronto Stock Exchange 300 Index companies were asked to support the work of the International Accounting Standards Committee (IASC) by making reference to International Accounting Standards in their annual reports. In February 1981, J. P. Bunting, president of the Toronto Stock Exchange, wrote a similar letter to the chief executive officer of the listed companies.
>
> The following enterprises have given their support to this initiative, and have referred to their adherence to International Accounting Standards in their annual reports:

Agnico–Eagle Mines Ltd.	Anglo United Development Corpora-
Alcan Aluminum Limited	tion Limited
Aluminum Company of Canada Ltd.	ATCO Ltd.

---

[21] Ibid.

[22] National Council of The Institute of Chartered Accountants in Australia and General Council of the Australian Society of Accountants, "Conformity with Accounting Standards," *Statements K1 and 300* (Melbourne: ICAA, ASA, 1976), para. 3.

Barbecon Inc.
Bell Canada and Subsidiary Companies
Bow Valley Industries Ltd.
Bramalea Limited
Brascan Ltd.
British Columbia Telephone Company
Canada Tungsten Mining Corporation Limited
Canadian Cablesystems Ltd.
Canadian Corporate Management Company Limited
The Canadian Institute of Chartered Accountants
Canron Inc.
Carling O'Keefe Limited
Celanese Canada Inc.
Consolidated-Bathurst Inc.
Consumers Glass Company Limited
Copperfields Mining Corporation
Costain Limited
Cyprus Anvil Mining Corp.
DRG Limited
Dominion Textile Inc.
Du Pont Canada Inc.
Emco Limited
Fraser Inc.
Federal Industries Ltd.
Hudson's Bay Company
Hudson's Bay Oil and Gas Co. Ltd.
Imperial Oil Limited
Indal Ltd.
La Verendrye Management Corp.

Lawson & Jones Ltd.
MPG Investment Corporation Limited
Magnasonic Canada Inc.
S.B. McLaughlin Associates Limited
Melcor Developments Ltd.
Midland-Doherty Limited
Monarch Investments Limited
Monenco Limited
Northern Telecom Limited
NOVA, An Alberta Corporation
PCL Industries Limited
Polysar Limited
Provigo Inc.
The Reader's Digest Association (Canada) Ltd.
Reichhold Limited
Reitmans (Canada) Ltd.
Rothmans of Pall Mall Canada Limited
RoyNat Inc.
Scottish & York Holdings Limited
Standard Broadcasting Corp. Ltd.
Steinberg Inc.
Teck Corporation
Toromont Industries Ltd.
The Toronto Stock Exchange
Trimac Limited and Subsidiary Companies
Union Oil Co. of Canada Ltd.
Wabasso Inc.
Westmin Resources Ltd.
Yellowknife Bear Resources Inc.[23]

International Federation of Accountants (IFAC)

The IFAC came into being on October 7, 1977, when 63 professional bodies from 49 different countries signed the agreement to establish the organization. By year-end 1981, IFAC membership stood at 80 accountancy bodies from 59 different countries. On the basis of this membership (which is institutional only), the IFAC represents approximately 750,000 professional accountants around the globe.

According to Paragraph 7 of its Constitution, the IFAC's governing bodies consist of (a) an assembly and (b) a council.

The assembly is comprised of one representative designated as such by each member body of the IFAC. The assembly, among other obligations, elects

---

[23] "Support for International Accounting Standards," *CA Magazine* (Toronto: Canadian Institute of Chartered Accountants, January, 1982) p. 68.

members of the IFAC Council, approves financial contributions to be paid by member bodies, and determines the timing and location of International Congresses of Accountants.

The IFAC Council consists of 15 representatives of member bodies from 15 countries. The Council has a long list of duties, including (but not limited to):[24]

1. Appointment of standing committees for such terms as are deemed appropriate.
2. Establishment of rules of procedures consistent with provisions of the IFAC Constitution.
3. Determination of the professional accountancy bodies to be admitted to IFAC as members.
4. Determination of criteria for recognition of regional organizations.
5. Appointment of auditors and determination of their remuneration.
6. Preparation and distribution of an annual report on activities, including audited annual accounts.
7. Resolution of disputes between professional bodies as to who shall represent their country on the IFAC Council by deciding whether that country should be represented and, if so, which professional body should designate the representative.
8. Suspension from membership of a member body for nonpayment of its financial contribution.
9. Initiation of any action that is in the general interest of IFAC and that is not expressly denied to it by its constitution, provided that it does not involve itself in the domestic affairs of a member body.

The IFAC publishes a quarterly newsletter as well as the above-mentioned periodic annual report.

To accomplish its technical agenda, IFAC has established seven standing committees:

1. Education
2. Ethics
3. International Auditing Practices
4. International Congresses
5. Management Accounting
6. Planning
7. Regional Organizations

Each of the foregoing committees has been given special terms of reference and specifically defined authority. For example, the terms of reference for the Planning Committee are "To maintain the relevance of IFAC's continuing objectives and to contribute to their advancement by reviewing strategy, plans and constitutional matters prior to discussion by the Council."[25]

[24] Condensed from International Federation of Accountants, *Constitution* (New York: IFAC, 1977, mimeographed), para. 7 (b).

[25] *IFAC Newsletter*, June 1978.

In terms of international standard setting, only the IFAC International Auditing Practices Committee has the specific authority to issue, on behalf of the IFAC Council, exposure drafts and guidelines relating to generally accepted auditing practices and the form and content of audit reports. Since the International Auditing Practices Committee does not need prior approval of the IFAC Council when it publishes a definitive international auditing guideline, it has the status of a "senior" IFAC Committee.

The nature of the IFAC's International Auditing Guidelines and the authority attaching to them are set forth in Chapter 9.

The IFAC's 1982 *Annual Report* contains a section on "Highlights of the First Five Years." Here are some excerpts therefrom:

> Issued 11 definitive International Auditing Guidelines and exposure drafts of 4 proposed auditing guidelines.
>
> Issued 1 Ethics Guideline, 4 Statements of Guidance and 3 exposure drafts of proposed statements of guidance.
>
> Issued 2 Guidelines on Education.
>
> Issued a discussion paper on the Definition and Scope of Management Accounting. Distributed a summary of responses received on the involvement of management accountants in the activities of the member bodies. Issued a summary of research projects on management accounting topics which have been published or are in progress and a bibliography for management accounts.
>
> Developed contacts with other world and governmental organizations which have resulted in IFAC having a greater role on the world scene, particularly where initiatives developed by other world and governmental organizations have an impact on the accounting profession. In addition, these contacts have resulted in agreements to jointly sponsor conferences or seminars.
>
> Prepared a Statement of Policy to be used by Council in recognizing new regional organizations, and outlines of Constitutions for use by new regional organizations, including guidance on the possible contents of the various sections of the Constitutions. Developed procedures for ensuring there is a regular exchange of information among the regional organizations and between IFAC and the regional organizations and increased involvement of regional organizations in the work program of IFAC. Inaugurated the formation of the Association of Accountancy Bodies in West Africa (ABWA).[26]

Union Européenne des Experts Comptables Economiques et Financiers (UEC)

The discussion of the UEC is divided into three parts—in the present context we simply mention the organization as a private sector professional standard setting body. Since the UEC is recommending standards (i.e. statements on auditing and professional ethics) only in the area of auditing, its relevant pronouncements are covered in Chapter 9. The UEC as a regional organization is discussed in the section immediately following.

In a policy statement adopted by the UEC Assembly of Delegates on De-

---

[26] International Federation of Accountants, "Highlights of the First Five Years," *Annual Report* (New York: IFAC, 1982), p. 5.

cember 1, 1976, in Florence, Italy, the standard-setting activity of the group is well circumscribed:

1. UEC Member Organisations have concluded that there is a need—
   1.1 to raise the standard of auditing in Europe;
   1.2 to harmonize the audit of financial statements;
   1.3 to promote the development of auditing principles and techniques;
   1.4 to improve the mutual understanding of auditors' reports on financial statements of business enterprises.
2. The present programme of UEC auditing statements does not meet the needs set out above because UEC Member Organisations have not been under any obligation to take steps to promote their observance.
3. Member Organisations have now decided to remedy this position. Accordingly UEC Member Organisations undertake, in addition to their obligations under Article II of the Constitution:
   3.1 to support UEC auditing statements by way of—
      3.1.1. bringing to the notice of their members the content of UEC draft statements;
      3.1.2. *either*   bringing to the notice of their members the content of UEC definitive statements
      3.1.2. *or alternatively* incorporating in their national auditing standards the principles on which UEC definitive statements are based;
      3.1.3. using their best endeavors, in those countries where audit procedures are prescribed by law, to get the laws adapted accordingly;
      3.1.4. using their best endeavors to ensure that bodies responsible for the maintenance of professional standards are aware of UEC auditing statements.[27]

The UEC's Auditing Statements and Professional Ethics Statements have received international recognition. Since both the IFAC and the UEC are producing international auditing guidelines (i.e., statements of standards), the two bodies are coordinating their work. This is accomplished as follows:

Following discussions between U.E.C. and IFAC, it has been agreed that IFAC's Auditing Practices Committee should continue its programme of work in order to present a framework of International Auditing Guidelines. In doing so, it will take into account the programme of ASB to avoid duplication. The intention is that if IAPC finds that ASB has already produced a Statement, IAPC will take note of that Statement for IAPC's purposes, rather than start work *ab initio* in the same field.

ASB will continue its current programme for Statements currently in progress which do not duplicate the work programme of IAPC. Thereafter, as appropriate, ASB will initiate Statements that have specific relevance to members of U.E.C., or on matters of topical interest to the members, as well as adapt or expand upon IAPC Guidelines as necessary for U.E.C. purposes.

The Chairmen of ASB and of IAPC are to meet annually to co-ordinate work programmes and exchange information. This will ensure that the programmes meet the objectives outlined above.[28]

[27] UEC Assembly of Delegates, *Policy Statement*, Approved December 1, 1976 in Florence, Italy, p. P/1.

[28] "U.E.C. and IFAC," *U.E.C. Information*, No. 5, February 1982.

ASEAN Federation of Accountants (AFA)

A group within the Association of Southeast Asian Nations (ASEAN), the AFA has only limited standard-setting objectives. Its nature and scope are discussed in the section on regional organizations immediately following in this chapter.

To date, the AFA has issued two exposure drafts:

ED-1   Introduction to ASEAN Accounting Standards
ED-2   Fundamental Accounting Principles

The first is a general introduction to AFA aims and the proposed working procedures of the AFA's Committee on Accounting Principles and Standards. Also, ED No. 1 outlines how support is to be marshalled for ASEAN Accounting Standards (AAS). The second exposure draft is a synthesis of survey replies received on the topic from AFA member organizations. If adopted, ED No. 2 will give authoritative support to accounting principles already pervasive in the ASEAN region.

The full texts of the two AFA Exposure Drafts appear as an appendix to Professor F. D. S. Choi's "ASEAN Federation of Accountants."[29]

FOCUS ON REGIONAL AFFAIRS

The jump from purely domestic or unilateral (i.e., uninational) interests and viewpoints to the global village idea is sizable and complex. Individual professionals and their national institutes often fail to see any direct benefits to them of monies spent to support global interests or international organizations. International work still has an aura of jetsetting—more personal pleasure than hard work. Thus, expense reimbursement beyond national borders is sometimes difficult to justify to local groups, as is a working language other than their own. Why go all the way to Sidney, Australia, to have a subcommittee meeting?

Somewhat as a buffer between strictly national and broadly international interests, five regional associations of professional accountants have established themselves from the Pacific Rim to West Africa. These groups and their objectives and working procedures are fully international, but limited in scope to defined geographic regional areas. The issues and problems perceived for a particular region become the focal points of these organizations. Typically, they work through elaborate committee structures and openly support the cause of accounting internationalism through periodic congresses or conferences. Often they also conduct workshops and seminars and operate a number of educational programs. These regional professional accounting organizations exist in Europe, North and South America, Asia and the Pacific, Scandinavia,

[29] Frederick D. S. Choi, "ASEAN Federation of Accountants: A New International Accounting Force, *International Journal of Accounting*, Fall 1979, pp. 53–75.

and West Africa. A few highly summarized descriptive comments are offered on each of these groups in turn.

Union Européenne des Experts Comptables Economiques et Financiers (UEC)

The UEC was founded in Paris in November 1951 and has as charter members 12 professional associations of independent (or certified) accountants from Austria, Belgium, France, West Germany, Italy, Luxembourg, the Netherlands, Portugal, Spain, and Switzerland. Thirty years later, there were 25 member organizations from 19 nations. Four accountancy bodies from Greece, Israel, and Yugoslavia are correspondent members. Thus, the UEC represents European accounting interests in terms of more nations than the European Economic Community (EEC).

Among the world's regional accounting bodies, the UEC is the most active. It has a permanent secretariat in Munich (formerly in Paris) and engages in a continuous program of professional activity. Essentially, the UEC works through five permanent committees on which membership revolves. These committees prepare reports and present resolutions through the UEC Executive Committee. Aside from the Auditing Statements Board (see Chapter 9), there are committees covering Education, Ethics, Lexicology, and Technical Research.

With respect to publications, the UEC operates an extensive quality program. The mainstay of this program is the quarterly newsletter entitled *U.E.C. Information.* In addition to the Auditing and Ethics Statements, there are Technical and Research Studies, Special Studies (e.g., Preparation and Audit of Consolidated Financial Statements, 1978), and Occasional Papers. The UEC's *Accounting Dictionary* now covers eight languages (Danish, Dutch, English, French, German, Italian, Portuguese, and Spanish) and is in its second edition (1974).

Members of the UEC meet at Congresses organized every three to four years. The First UEC Congress took place in Florence and Rome in 1953; the Second, in Brussels in 1955; the Third, in Nice in 1958; the Fourth, in Zurich in 1961; the Fifth, in Vienna in 1964; the Sixth, in Copenhagen in 1969; the Seventh, in Madrid in 1973; the Eighth, in Dublin in 1978; and the Ninth, in Strasbourg in 1983. The *Proceedings* of these Congresses yield valuable multinational accounting descriptive materials. Earlier *Congress Proceedings* are available in the French and German languages only.

Aside from the more formal membership congresses, the UEC also operates study conferences and cross-national seminars. Examples are the Seminar on "International Professional Collaboration" held in Nice, October 15–16, 1981, and the Franco-British Workshop on "Audit of Small and Medium Sized Companies" held in London April 22–23, 1982.

The UEC is a strong international accounting force. It is recognized by authorities of the European Economic Community and the International Federation of Accountants. If nothing else, it has been an agent in producing significantly higher visibility and social and professional status for independent accountants in Europe.

Asociación Interamericana de Contabilidad (AIC)

The AIC is also known as the InterAmerican Accounting Association. Prior to 1975, it was referred to as InterAmerican Accounting Conference. Papers, proceedings, and other references are likely to be catalogued under any one of these three names.

The AIC has a Western Hemisphere orientation and thus is comprised of North Central and South American accounting bodies. Since most nations in the Western Hemisphere have Spanish as their national language, the proceedings of the AIC are normally published in Spanish, as are many of the papers presented at the periodic conferences of this group.

The First Interamerican Accounting Conference took place in San Juan, Puerto Rico, in 1949; the Second, in Mexico City in 1951; the Third, in São Paulo in 1954; the Fourth, in Santiago, Chile, in 1957; the Sixth, in New York in 1962; the Seventh, in Mar del Plata, Argentina, in 1965; the Eighth, in Caracas in 1967; the Ninth, in Bogota in 1970; the Tenth, in Punta de Este, Uruguay, in 1972; the Eleventh, in San Juan in 1974; the Twelfth, in Vancouver, B.C., Canada, in 1977; the Thirteenth, in Panama in 1979; the Fourteenth, in Santiago in 1981; and the Fifteenth, in Rio de Janeiro in 1983. The Fifth Conference in the sequence was planned for Havana but had to be canceled because of the then-prevailing political situation in Cuba.

The AIC Conferences have a character all their own. They are sincere and fraternal and in keeping with the relative lightheartedness of Latin American people in general. Many of the Conference activities and technical program sessions are devoted to problems of accounting development rather than to descriptions of existing circumstances. The AIC Conferences clearly identify themselves with Western Hemisphere accounting problems, particularly as they apply to the South American countries.

The AIC operates a secretariat located in Lima, Peru and works through a structure of integrative and technical committees. The headquarters location revolves among the member countries. The administrative activity is similar to that of the UEC. Continuing technical committees report at the periodic Conferences, and some committee reports and other technical items are published separately. The AIC also publishes a quarterly newsletter entitled *Boletín Interamericano de Contabilidad* and a monthly *Carta Interamericana*.

Confederation of Asian and Pacific Accountants (CAPA)

The CAPA was initially known as the Asian and Pacific Accounting Convention and later as the Conference of Asian and Pacific Accountants. It is a relative newcomer to the group of international accounting meetings; yet it has established itself quickly and successfully. The first Asian and Pacific Accounting Convention (at that time called the Far East Conference of Accountants) was held in Manila in 1957. The Second Convention followed in Canberra and Melbourne in 1960. The Third took place in Kyoto and Tokyo in 1962 and the Fourth, in New Delhi in 1965. Other conferences in this series are Wellington and Christchurch in 1968; Singapore and Kuala Lumpur in 1970; and Bangkok in 1973. More recently, the Eighth CAPA Conference occurred in Hong Kong in 1976, the Ninth in Manila in 1979, and the Tenth in New Delhi in 1983.

The model of the International Congresses is followed closely by CAPA Conventions and Congresses. A student of the technical papers of the various international accounting meetings will easily recognize the names of certain individuals appearing again and again as formal program participants, contributors to discussions, members of arrangements or executive committees, and so on.

Quite naturally, papers delivered at CAPA Congresses focus on Pacific Rim countries and their particular problems. Since available literature on the Asian and Pacific Region is much more limited than international accounting literature in general, the CAPA papers are a useful source of information. Moreover, these papers are available in the English language, whereas much of the native literature in the Asian and Pacific Region is available only in the respective native languages.

The CAPA has a membership of approximately 30 professional accounting organizations from some twenty countries. Its permanent Secretariat is headquartered in Hong Kong. At intervals, a *CPA Newsletter* is published. The CAPA's aim is to develop a coordinated regional accounting profession. Available evidence indicates that it is doing just that.

Nordic Federation of Accountants (NFA)

All professional accounting organizations from Denmark, Finland, Iceland, Norway, and Sweden are members of the NFA. Together they represent 4,000–5,000 practicing accountants. The NFA governs itself through an Assembly of Delegates which meets periodically at sites throughout Scandinavia. Its 1982 meeting was held in northern Norway.

At its Twelfth Congress held in Helsinki, August 24–27, 1981, the NFA celebrated its fiftieth anniversary. This makes the NFA the oldest regional organization of professional accountants. The main theme of the 1981 Congress was "Society's Expectations of the Accountant." Other topics dealt with continuing education, management consultancy, and quality control of professional services. One interesting sidelight of the Helsinki meeting was the availability of a weekend tour to Leningrad in the Soviet Union.

As needed, the NFA appoints appropriate committees and task forces. For instance, it made major inputs to the accounting and financial reporting provisions of the Nordic Companies Act, which went a long way toward harmonizing accounting requirements throughout Scandinavia. The relationship between the IFAC and the NFA is apparently most satisfactory to both parties.

ASEAN
Federation of Accountants (AFA)

The Association of Southeast Asian Nations (ASEAN) is developing closer economic linkages internally and better relationships with the rest of the world externally for its five member nations—Indonesia, Malaysia, the Philippines, Singapore, and Thailand. It was only a matter of time before ASEAN spawned AFA, which happened officially on March 12, 1977, in Bangkok. The major objectives of AFA are stated as follows in its constitution:

> ... to provide an organization for the ASEAN accountants for the further advancement of the status of the profession in the region with the view to establishing an ASEAN philosophy on the accounting profession, ... to establish a medium for closer relations, regional cooperation, and assistance among ASEAN accountants, and ... to work in cooperation with ASEAN business regional groupings whose economic development efforts may be complemented by ASEAN accountants.[30]

The AFA has a permanent secretariat in Manila. It governs itself by a Council composed of one representative from each ASEAN country. Furthermore, the AFA has been officially recognized by the ASEAN Council of Foreign Ministries.

The four standing committees of the AFA are (1) Accounting Principles and Standards, (2) Auditing Principles and Standards, (3) Education, and (4) Professional Development. The two exposure drafts available from the Accounting Principles and Standards Committee were mentioned earlier in this chapter.

Relationships between the AFA and the IFAC are functioning well. The same can be said with respect to AFA-CAPA relations, where memberships overlap. The link to the IASC is complementary rather than competitive. As Professor F. D. S. Choi put it, "An important function of AFA will be to buffer individual ASEAN countries against the wholesale adoption of international accounting pronouncements that may not be suitable to local circumstances. More importantly, active participation ... would enable AFA to sensitize IASC to the views and concerns of the less industrialized world."[31]

Association of Accountancy
Bodies in West Africa (ABWA)

The ABWA is the latest entry to the group of regional organizations. It was formed in 1981 by the Institute of Chartered Accountants in Nigeria and the Institute of Chartered Accountants (Ghana). Representative professional bodies from an additional 15 countries are eligible for ABWA membership. Further details were unavailable at the time of this writing.

---

[30] Frederick D. S. Choi, "ASEAN Federation of Accountants," p. 61.
[31] Ibid., p. 64.

SUPPORTIVE ACTIVITIES

There are a great many other conferences, institutes, seminars, and organizations that support the cause of international accounting standards in varying degrees. Also, many of the individuals involved in the activities sketched in this section are broadly supportive of the field of international accounting. Space limitations dictate that we mention only a few representative examples. In a sense, this leads us back to Chapter 1 where we portray the recent growth of the international accounting area and refer to the numerous sources of support which have fostered and nourished this growth.

International Congresses
of Accountants

The International Congresses of Accountants are probably the most prestigious and most elaborate of all the international accounting meetings. At present these Congresses are held every five years. Nearly 3,000 persons from 48 countries registered for the 1957 Congress. That number almost doubled for the 1977 Congress. Congress registrants come from as many as 60 different countries. The IFAC together with local IFAC member organizations sponsor these gatherings.

The First International Congress to Accountants was held in St. Louis in 1904, the Second, in Amsterdam in 1926; the Third, in New York in 1929; the Fourth, in London in 1933; the Fifth, in Berlin in 1937; the Sixth, in London, in 1952; the Seventh, in Amsterdam in 1957; the Eighth, in New York in 1962; the Ninth, in Paris in 1967; the Tenth, in Sydney in 1972; the Eleventh, in Munich in 1977; the Twelfth, in Mexico City in 1982; and the Thirteenth will be held in Tokyo in 1987.

The program pattern of these Congresses now is that general interest papers are presented at plenary sessions, and international summary reports on specific technical topics are read at technical sessions. Underlying each technical summary report are a number of national position papers officially submitted through the professional accounting institutes that send formal delegates to these Congresses. Additionally, many small concurrent discussion groups on technical topics have become a feature of the International Congresses of Accountants since the 1962 New York Congress. These small groups are limited to about 25 participants each and typically meet in the boardrooms of major corporations headquartered at the Congress site.

Up to the time of the Sydney Congress in 1972, each International Congress of Accountants was pretty much an individual venture. No permanent technical committees stayed at work; there was no carry-forward in secretariat organizations and no continuing exchange of ideas between Congress organizers and/or participants. The Sydney Congress spawned an International Coordination Committee for the Accountancy Profession (ICCAP), which in turn became the progenitor of the IFAC.

As a final note on the International Congresses of Accountants, we would like to point out that the proceedings of these meetings and the technical papers presented at them are some of the more important multinational accounting raw materials. They have not only historical value but high levels of descriptive accuracy as well as occasional conceptual depth and analytic potential. (The latter two characteristics are outside the usual specifications for these papers.)

International Conferences on Accounting Education

Even though the International Congresses of Accountants welcome independent practitioners, industrial accountants, and academic accountants alike, their focus essentially remains with the first group. For this reason, an International Accounting Education Conference now piggybacks each International Congress. The Education Conferences are organized from the viewpoint of accounting academics and have a focus on education and research. About 300 persons now attend these International Education Conferences held in conjunction with the quintennial International Congresses.

In 1962, the University of Illinois at Champaign-Urbana was about to establish its Center for International Accounting Education and Research when several accounting educators from various countries were preparing to journey to the New York Congress. So the question was asked, Why not have a meeting of interested academics immediately before the New York Congress takes place? Thus, the International Conference on Accounting Education first met in 1962 on the campus of the University of Illinois.

The Second Conference was organized in conjunction with the 1967 Paris Congress by the City of London Polytechnic and met at Guildhall in London. The Third Conference was cosponsored by Sydney University, the University of New South Wales, and Macquarie University, with portions of it taking place on each of the respective three campuses in the Greater Sydney area. For convenience, the Third Conference was scheduled after the 1972 Congress. The Fourth Conference was organized in West Berlin, preceding the 1977 Munich Congress. The Fifth Conference again followed the Mexico City Congress in Monterrey, Mexico. The three sponsoring universities were the Instituto Technológico y de Estudios Superiores de Monterrey, the Universidad Autónoma de Nuevo León, and the Universidad de Monterrey. Proceedings containing copies of papers presented are available for all International Conferences on Accounting Education held thus far.

Academic Associations

Worldwide, there are six major academic associations of accountants—all having education and research as their major concerns. These associations are the American Accounting Association (AAA), the Canadian Association of Academic Accountants (CAAA), the European Accounting Association (EAA), the Japan Accounting Association (JAA) and the Association of University Instructors in Accounting—one each in the United Kingdom and Australia–New Zealand.

The foregoing groups and their individual members and committees have carried a material portion of the research conducted in the international accounting area and teaching and seminar development undertaken. The American, European, and Japan Associations operate senior committees or full sections devoted to international accounting matters. Also, these three associations regularly have major program slots allocated to international topics during their annual meetings.

Since 1962, the AAA has operated international accounting education and research committees. In 1976, the AAA formally established the International Accounting Section within the Association. This section periodically publishes a newsletter and intermittently research monographs, bibliographies, and readings collections.

Among the specific goals of the AAA International Accounting Section are the following:[32]

1. Encouragement of international accounting research and active exchange of research results
2. Sponsorship of technical sessions at regional, national and/or international meetings to provide a forum for the discussion of research results.
3. Establishment of multinational advisory groups for specific research projects, with multilingual communications capacities
4. Facilitation of international faculty and student exchanges
5. Organization of permanent or ad hoc committees or task forces to address important developing international accounting issues
6. Development of resources to support section-sponsored international accounting education and research programs.

As of 1982, the AAA International Accounting Section had some 600 members from all over the globe, 14 active committees, and an outstanding publications record. Its programs and seminars have consistently received high praise. It is the premier academic advocate of international accounting.

Financial Analysts' Federations

As an important user group of published financial statements, Financial Analysts' Federations at national and international levels have structured committees and financial statement evaluation task forces to address international accounting issues. Professional examinations in the financial analysts' field regularly contain international accounting questions and the journals of these federations often run articles concerned with comparative financial reporting and disclosure questions.

Research on international accounting topics related to financial report-

[32] International Accounting Section, American Accounting Association, *Membership Roster* (Sarasota, Fla.: AAA, 1983), p. 81.

ing, disclosure effects, or securities price effects in multilaterally comparative or international settings should not proceed without careful checks of the Financial Analysts' literature. This is especially so where surveys of published financial statements are concerned.

Financial Executives

In the United States, the Financial Executives Institute (FEI) regularly prepares formal responses to international accounting standards proposals. The same Institute, through its Research Foundation, has been an early sponsor of research studies concerned with international dimensions. The well-known study *Financial Control of Multinational Operations* appeared in 1971.[33] *The Effects of Tax Policy on Capital Formation* contains major sections with international content like "Taxation Abroad" (40 pages).[34] Examples of other relevant FEI research studies are:

1981   Coping with Inflation—Experiences of Financial Executives in the UK, West Germany, and Brazil
1981   Criteria for Management Control Systems
1980   Evaluating the Financial Performance of Overseas Operations
1979   Assessing the Economic Impact of FASB No. 8
1977   Accounting for the Multinational Corporation

Similar attention to international accounting matters occurs at the U.S.-based National Accountants Association (NAA). In a research study published in 1960, the NAA was the first to recognize the conceptual appeal of the monetary-nonmonetary foreign exchange translation method.[35] The NAA has active chapters all over the world, including, for example, Zurich and Tokyo. The Canadian Society of Registered Industrial Accountants has a similar international outlook. For the three professional groups mentioned, their international annual meetings always have major program components addressing international accounting topics.

The monthly journals of the three groups are *Financial Executive* (FEI), *Management Accounting* (NAA), and *Cost and Management* (SRIA). All three regularly carry articles, case studies, and reports of international accounting interest.

Professional Institutes

It almost goes without saying that the professional accounting institutes, especially those who are members of the IASC and the IFAC, have strong internal divisions dealing with questions of international practice, responding to

---

[33] Financial Executives Research Foundation, *Financial Control of Multinational Operations* (New York: FERF, 1971), 230 pp.

[34] Financial Executives Research Foundation, *The Effects of Tax Policy on Capital Formation* (New York: FERF, 1977), 220 pp.

[35] National Association of Accountants, *Accounting Problems in Foreign Operations*, Research Report No. 36 (New York: NAA, 1960), 71 pp.

exposure draft recommendations of international bodies, and informing members of international professional developments. On behalf of the American Institute of CPAs, this is accomplished through its significant International Practice Division. The Canadian Institute of Chartered Accountants is no less internationally oriented in its policies and operations, and NIvRA in the Netherlands has probably the longest and strongest international commitment among national professional accounting groups. A concise explanation of NIvRA's international activities and commitments is given by its director, Henk Volten, in a paper entitled "Internationalization: A National Perspective."[36]

It goes almost without saying that the monthly journals of the national professional accounting institutes are a material source of international accounting periodical literature.

Stock Exchanges

The interest of stock exchanges in international accounting development and issues is literally axiomatic. As money capital markets internationalize, so must the financial reporting and other information systems that support these markets.

The World Federation of Stock Exchanges was among the first formal bodies actively encouraging its members to "include in their listing requirements reference to compliance with standards issued by the International Accounting Standards Committee."[37] As a follow-up, among other developments, the London Stock Exchange issued a statement to the effect that such compliance is expected of all listed companies incorporated within the United Kingdom and the Republic of Ireland as well as any incorporated outside the United Kingdom that do not have to conform to U.K. accounting standards. The corresponding and rather assertive effort of the Toronto Stock Exchange was described earlier in this chapter.

Stock exchanges encourage international accounting affairs in other ways as well. International listing and trading statistics are useful, as are filings of financial statements that exceed national accounting requirements in an effort to become internationally visible and accepted. There is a perceptible trend of "internationalization" of listing requirements on major stock exchanges around the world (i.e., data and audit requirements exceeding national minima and thereby reaching for the international financial reporting plateau established by major stock exchanges like London, New York, and Tokyo).

Universities

Accounting programs at universities have done their share to "internationalize." In the United States, at the University of Illinois at Champaign-Urbana, a Center for International Education and Research in Accounting op-

---

[36] In *The Internationalization of the Accountancy Profession*, W. John Brennan, ed. (Toronto: Canadian Institute of Chartered Accountants, 1979).

[37] Quoted in *CA Magazine* (Toronto: Canadian Institute of Chartered Accountants, January 1975), p. 52.

erates under the direction of Professor Vernon K. Zimmerman. The Center boasts an annual International Accounting Seminar, publishes the semiannual *International Journal of Accounting,* and intermittently publishes in several research monograph series.

At the University of Lancaster in the United Kingdom, Professor Edward Stamp is the Director of the International Centre for Research in Accounting. The Centre attracts international scholars and publishes an active research monograph series. Its Occasional Paper No. 17 is one of the few rigorous studies available on the question of the feasibility to implement international financial accounting standards effectively in the near future.[38]

Other international accounting focal points, all located in the United States, are the University of Washington at Seattle, the University of Texas at Dallas, the University of Connecticut, and California State University at Northridge. Seattle emphasizes Ph.D. research in international accounting, Dallas is primarily concerned with economic development questions, Connecticut features a computerized data bank on the international activities of 2,500 U.S.-based firms and another 2,500 non-U.S.-based corporations, and Northridge has produced various international accounting lecture series.

SELECTED REFERENCES

AMERICAN ACCOUNTING ASSOCIATION, *Accounting Education and the Third World* (Report of the Committee on International Accounting Operations and Education, 1976–1978), Sarasota, Fla.: AAA, 1978, 109 pp.

BRENNAN, W. JOHN, ed., *The Internationalization of the Accountancy Profession,* Toronto: Canadian Institute of Chartered Accountants, 1978, 172 pp.

BURGGRAAFF, J. A, "IASC Developments: An Update," *Journal of Accountancy,* September 1982, pp. 104, 106–110.

BURTON, JOHN C., ed., *The International World of Accounting—Challenges and Opportunities* (1980 Proceedings of the Arthur Young Professors' Roundtable), Reston, Va.: Council of Arthur Young Professors, 1981, 218 pp.

CARTY, JAMES, "Accounting Standards and the United Nations," *World Accounting Report,* September 1982, pp. 9–15 (Special Feature).

CHOI, FREDERICK D. S., "ASEAN Federation of Accountants: A New International Accounting Force," *International Journal of Accounting,* Fall 1979, pp. 53–75.

CHOI, FREDERICK D. S., and VINOD B. BAVISHI, "International Accounting Standards: Issues Needing Attention," *Journal of Accountancy,* March 1983, pp. 62–68.

DALEY, LANE A., and GERHARD G. MUELLER, "Accounting in the Arena of World Politics—Crosscurrents of International Standard-Setting Activities," *Journal of Accountancy,* February 1982, pp. 40–46, 48, 50.

DE BRUYNE, D., "Global Standards: A Tower of Babel?" *Financial Executive,* February 1980, pp. 30, 32, 34, 36–37.

DELOITTE HASKINS & SELLS, *International Accounting Standards and Guidelines,* New York, January 1981, 43 pp.

[38] Alister K. Mason, *The Development of International Financial Reporting Standards,* Occasional Paper No. 17 (Lancaster, U.K.: University of Lancaster, International Centre for Research in Accounting, 1978).

DENMAN, JOHN H., "The OECD and International Accounting Standards," *CA Magazine,* February 1980, pp. 56–59.

INTERNATIONAL ACCOUNTING STANDARDS COMMITTEE, *Objectives and Procedures,* London: IASC, October 1982, unpaginated.

INTERNATIONAL FEDERATION OF ACCOUNTANTS, *1982 Annual Report,* New York: IFAC, 1982, 28 pp.

MASON, ALISTER K., *The Development of International Financial Reporting Standards* (ICRA Occasional Paper No. 17), Lancaster, U.K.: International Centre for Research in Accounting, University of Lancaster, 1978, 366 pp.

MUELLER, GERHARD G., "St. Louis to Munich: The Odyssey of the International Congresses of Accountants," *International Journal of Accounting,* Fall 1979, pp. 1–12.

PRICE WATERHOUSE & CO., *EEC Bulletin,* Brussels, various issues (usually 4 or 5 issues published per year).

UNION EUROPÉENNE DES EXPERTES COMPTABLES ECONOMIQUES ET FINANCIERS, *U.E.C. Annual Report 1981,* Munich, Germany: UEC, 1982, unpaginated.

UNITED NATIONS ECONOMIC AND SOCIAL COUNCIL, COMMISSION ON TRANSNATIONAL CORPORATIONS, *Comprehensive Information System: International Standards of Accounting and Reporting (E/C. 10/81),* New York: UN ECOSOC May 27, 1981, 45 pp. plus 2 annexes and 2 appendices.

UNITED STATES DEPARTMENT OF STATE, OFFICE OF INVESTMENT AFFAIRS, *Current Status Report—Selected International Organization Activities Relating to Transnational Enterprises,* Washington, D.C., July 1982, 24 pp.

WASHINGTON, SYCIP, "The Role of CAPA in Achieving Harmonization," *SGV Journal* (Manila: The SGV Group), No. 1, 1982, pp. 2–7.

DISCUSSION QUESTIONS

1. What do you consider to be the key rationale supporting the development and widespread application of international standards of financial accounting and reporting? Make a judgment on the present cost-benefit trade-off involved in international accounting standard-setting activities.

2. What important factors or forces support the development of international accounting standards, and what factor or forces hinder it?

3. Identify three instances in which the provision of EEC directives or proposed directives differs significantly from British-American generally accepted practices.

4. How is the OECD approaching the international accounting standards issue? In what important respects is the OECD approach different from the U.N. approach?

5. What is the nature of the interrelationship between the IASC and the IFAC? Who controls these two organizations and by what means? How are the International Congresses of Accountants related to the IFAC?

6. What distinguishes the EEC from the UEC? Compare the objectives and activities of the UEC and the AICPA to the best of your ability.

7. The CAPA, the AIC and the UEC are major regional professional organizations in accounting. Compare and contrast their respective

forms of organization and scope of activities. Which of the three do you deem the most effective? Why?

8. The chapter identifies six regional private (i.e., nongovernmental) associations of professional accountants. These associations have enjoyed varying degrees of organizational success and professional impact. Develop some pros and cons on the formation of additional regional accounting groups.

9. Suppose the International Conference on Accounting Education were to organize itself as a service organization of accounting educators worldwide. What organizational format might be appropriate for such a purpose? How would such a structure relate to national academic accounting organizations—for example, the American Accounting Association? List five merits and five drawbacks of a possible worldwide organization of accounting academics.

10. The FEI publishes research studies addressing international accounting issues whereas the IASC does not. Does this difference relate to the respective involvement of the two organizations in international standard setting? Should standard setters also be the researchers on critical accounting measurement and reporting issues?

EXERCISES

1. The following quotes are extracted from the report of the 1980–1981 International Accounting and Auditing Standards Committee of the American Accounting Association:

> There appears to be little doubt that IASC and IFAC have been promulgating standards which emanate for the most part from British-American standards. The rationale for this hegemony over world standards is that British-American accounting is the most advanced in the world and therefore all other nations should "rise" to this level of sophistication.
>
> Some British-American accounting standards, however, may not be viewed as being ideologically neutral. They support an economic system—investor-capital-oriented—which is alien or prenatal to the experience or aspirations of many countries of the Third World. For example, while a standard on "Disclosure of Accounting Policies" is probably ideologically neutral, a standard on "Valuation and Presentation of Inventories in the Context of the Historical Cost System" is not. . . .
>
> As soon as international accounting and auditing standards are considered to become linked with the interests of MNC's, purity of purpose is seen to be sacrificed to fears of foreign control and exploitation. Accounting and auditing standards are thus viewed as a facilitator of MNC activities and not as bodies of professional knowledge (such as meteorology) which presumably benefit people everywhere. . . .
>
> The entry of the large multinational accounting service firms into tne developing and non-investor, non-capital-oriented countries has perhaps increased the resistance to international accounting and auditing standards.[39]

[39] American Accounting Association, *Report of the International Accounting and Auditing Standards Committee 1980–81*, Sarasota, Fla.: AAA, mimeographed, pp. 34–36.

Required:
   A. Who benefits most from the existence of international ac-
       counting standards?
   B. Should international accounting standards be set through po-
       litical mechanisms?
   C. Has the present international accounting standard-setting
       procedure and philosophy worked to the advantage of the
       large multinational accounting service firms?
   D. Has there been a transfer of income from host to home coun-
       tries attributable to accounting and auditing services rendered
       abroad?

2. The organizational structure and working procedures of the IASC
    are described in the text.
    Required:
    A. Prepare a flow chart illustrating how an accounting issue
        reaches the IASC agenda and eventually becomes an IAS.
    B. What is the approximate elapsed time between selection of an
        issue by the IASC and issuance of a corresponding IAS?

3. The EEC Fourth Directive is discussed at some length in the chap-
    ter. Certain "generally accepted accounting principles" can be dis-
    tilled from the provisions of this Directive. For example, one GAAP
    might be stated as follows:

    Enterprise financial statements and their footnotes must give a true and fair view.
    Compliance in all material respects with the provisions of the Fourth Directive
    results in a true and fair view.

    Required: Distill seven additional GAAP from the provisions of the
    EEC Fourth Directive as reported in the chapter.

4. Twenty-one IASC standards and their respective titles are identified
    in the chapter.
    Required: For each IAS, identify its closest U.S. authoritative count-
    erpart and indicate whether it is a FAS, an Accounting Principles
    Board (APB) opinion, or an AICP Accounting Research Bulletin
    (ARB). Organize your work into the following format:

IAS	TITLE/SUBJECT	U.S. COUNTERPART
No. 1	Disclosure of Accounting Policies	APB Opinion No. 22
. . . . .	. . . . .	. . . . .
. . . . .	. . . . .	. . . . .

5. Refer to the national representation data furnished with respect to
    ten important world accounting organizations in the case appearing
    below. Divide the world into seven major geographic regions,
    namely, Africa, Asia, Middle East, Europe, North America, Middle
    and South America, and South Pacific.

Required:
A. Prepare a table that lists the seven geographic areas identified horizontally and the ten world accounting bodies vertically.
B. Allocate the total membership of each accounting organization to the appropriate geographic area and calculate the number of total representations per area.
C. Is there any disparity among geographic representations? Is "balanced" geographic representation important to international standard setting and/or international accounting development? Support your responses adequately.

CASE

International Accounting Influence Derby

Table 12.2, reprinted from Daley and Mueller, lists country representation on major international accounting organizations identified in the chapter.

Table 12.1 shows the number of cross representations. The intercept for each organization represents total country membership, that is, 5 nation members for the AFA, 18 for the UEC, and 30 for the U.N. Intergovernmental Working Group of Experts on International Standards of Accounting and Reporting. Membership on accounting-related committees or commissions is typically less than total agency membership. For example, the OECD has 24 nation members of whom 23 participate in accounting-related matters. Of the approximately 150 total members of the United Nations, 34 countries were appointed

TABLE 12.1   Cross-Representation on Major International Accounting Organizations

BODY	AAC	AFA	CAPA	EEC	UEC	AIC	IASC	IFAC	OECD	UN[a]
AAC	23	—	—	—	—	—	1	1	—	3
AFA	—	5	5	—	—	—	3	5	—	1
CAPA	—	5	18	—	—	2	13	16	5	5
EEC	—	—	—	9	9	—	9	9	9	5
UEC	—	—	—	9	18	—	16	16	17	5
AIC	—	—	2	—	—	21	5	11	2	7
IASC	1	3	13	9	16	5	42	39	20	17
IFAC	1	5	16	9	16	11	39	53	22	21
OECD	—	—	5	9	17	2	20	22	23	8
UN[a]	3	1	5	5	5	7	17	21	8	30

Source: Lane A. Daley and Gerhard G. Mueller, "Accounting in the Arena of World Politics—Crosscurrents of International Standard Setting," *Journal of Accountancy*, February 1982, p. 45. Adapted from United Nations Report E/C.10/AC.3/7 of September 9, 1980. Second session of the Ad Hoc Intergovernmental Working Group on International Standards of Accounting and Reporting–Commission on Transnational Corporations–UN Economic and Social Council.

[a] Member of the UN intergovernmental working group.

TABLE 12.2   Representation on Major International Accounting Organizations

COUNTRY*	AAC	AFA	CAPA	EEC	UEC	AIC	IASC	IFAC	OECD	UN**
Canada	—	—	X	—	—	X	X	X	X	X
France	—	—	—	X	X	—	X	X	X	X
Germany	—	—	—	X	X	—	X	X	X	X
Italy	—	—	—	X	X	—	X	X	X	X
Netherlands	—	—	—	X	X	—	X	X	X	X
Great Britain	—	—	—	X	X	—	X	X	X	X
United States	—	—	X	—	—	X	X	X	X	X
Belgium	—	—	—	X	X	—	X	X	X	—
Denmark	—	—	—	X	X	—	X	X	X	—
Ireland	—	—	—	X	X	—	X	X	X	—
Japan	—	—	X	—	—	—	X	X	X	X
Luxembourg	—	—	—	X	X	—	X	X	X	—
Norway	—	—	—	—	X	—	X	X	X	X
Philippines	—	X	X	—	—	—	X	X	—	X
Australia	—	—	X	—	—	—	X	X	X	—
Brazil	—	—	—	—	—	X	X	X	—	X
Finland	—	—	—	—	X	—	X	X	X	—
Greece	—	—	—	—	X	—	X	X	X	—
India	—	X	X	—	—	—	—	X	—	X
Malaysia	—	X	X	—	—	—	X	X	—	—
Mexico	—	—	—	—	—	X	X	X	—	X
New Zealand	—	—	X	—	—	—	X	X	X	—
Nigeria	X	—	—	—	—	—	X	X	—	X
Panama	—	—	—	—	—	X	X	X	—	X
Pakistan	—	—	X	—	—	—	X	X	—	X
Portugal	—	—	—	—	X	—	X	X	X	—
Singapore	—	X	X	—	—	—	X	X	—	—
Spain	—	—	—	—	X	—	X	X	X	—
Sweden	—	—	—	—	X	—	X	X	X	—
Argentina	—	—	—	—	—	X	—	X	—	X
Bangladesh	—	—	X	—	—	—	X	X	—	X
Cyprus	—	—	—	—	—	—	X	X	—	—
Dominican Republic	—	—	—	—	—	X	—	X	—	X
Fiji	—	—	X	—	—	—	X	X	—	—
Iceland	—	—	—	—	X	—	—	X	X	—
Sri Lanka	—	—	X	—	—	—	X	X	—	—
Thailand	—	X	X	—	—	—	—	X	—	—
Representatives	1	5	14	9	16	7	32	37	21	19
Total number of representations in body	23	5	18	9	18	21	42	53	23	30

Source: Lane A. Daley and Gerhard G. Mueller, "Accounting in the Arena of World Politics—Crosscurrents of International Standard Setting," *Journal of Accountancy*, February 1982, p. 43.

* Adapted from United Nations Report E/C.10/AC.3/7 of September 9, 1980. Second session of the Ad Hoc Intergovernmental Working Group on International Standards of Accounting and Reporting–Commission on Transnational Corporations–U.N. Economic and Social Council.

** Member of the UN intergovernmental working group.

to the Intergovernmental Working Group but only 30 participate on a regular basis.

Required

1. Each AFA member country is represented on the IFAC as are 16 out of 18 members for both the CAPA and the UEC. For the U.N. Working Group, only 21 out of 30 are IFAC members, and for the AAC the ratio is 1 out of 23. What may explain this diversity? The IFAC is younger than the IASC, yet the former has more nations represented among its membership. Formulate some explanations of this apparent anomaly.
2. In terms of the information provided in the case, Third World countries appear most completely represented on the IFAC and the IASC. Is this representation effective? Are the accounting interests of Third World countries better served in global organizations like the United Nations or in regional organizations like the AFA? From the viewpoint of the developing countries, what might be an effective approach to stronger representation in the world councils of accounting?
3. For many years Argentina has been a leader of accounting thought and practice in South America. Yet, Argentina is only modestly represented among international accounting organization membership. Would you advise Argentine accounting leaders to seek greater involvement in international accounting organizations? Offer support for the opinion you formulate.
4. Switzerland is one of the countries discussed in Chapter 3. Since it does not appear on the membership list provided in this case, Switzerland must have less than three national representations on international accounting organizations. What might be some reasons for this relative noninvolvement? Finland and Sweden, both strongly neutral countries, have four representations each. Are their respective situations materially different than Switzerland's? Do you have any recommendations for Swiss accounting leaders in this respect?

Index